WHY I AM NOT
a Muslim

Muslims are the first victims of Islam. Many times I have observed in my travels in the Orient, that fanaticism comes from a small number of dangerous men who maintain the others in the practice of religion by terror. To liberate the Muslim from his religion is the best service that one can render him.

—E. Renan

WHY I AM NOT
a Muslim

by IBN WARRAQ

 Prometheus Books

59 John Glenn Drive
Amherst, New York 14228-2197

Published 2003 by Prometheus Books

Inquiries should be addressed to
Prometheus Books
59 John Glenn Drive
Amherst, New York 14228–2197.
VOICE: 716–691–0133, ext. 207; FAX: 716–564–2711
WWW.PROMETHEUSBOOKS.COM

10 09 08 07   7 6 5 4

Library of Congress Cataloging-in-Publication Data

Ibn Warraq.
    Why I am not a Muslim / by Ibn Warraq.
       p.   cm.
    Includes bibliographical references and index.
    ISBN-13: 978–0–87975–984–1 (hardcover : alk. paper)
    ISBN-10: 0–87975–984–4 (hardcover : alk. paper)
    ISBN-13: 978–1–59102–011–0 (pbk. : alk. paper)
    ISBN-10: 1–59102–011–5 (pbk. : alk. paper)
    1. Islam—Controversial literature. I. Title.
BP169.I28   1995
297—dc20   95–6342
                                                        CIP

Printed in the United States of America on acid-free paper

Dedication

To my mother, my wife, my sister, and my daughters, who came through despite religious fascism.

Contents

Foreword

R. Joseph Hoffmann
Westminster College, Oxford

Few books about religion deserve the attribution "courageous." This book, I am
pleased to report, does. It is courageous because it is (as the term originally de-
noted) full of heart (*coeur*) and courageous because it is an act of intellectual honesty and bravery, an act of faith rather than of faithlessness. It will undoubtedly be
a controversial book because it deals personally and forthrightly with a subject
widely misunderstood by theists and nontheists of various stripes. That subject is
the Islamic faith.

New religions depend for their sustenance on the energy of converts. Thus
Christianity in the first century of the common era and Islam in the sixth depended
on the enthusiasm of the newly persuaded. Each had its prophet, each its network
of zealous missionary-evangelists and later organization-minded hierarchs and
caliphs to drive and sustain the structures that faith invented. Christianity and
Islam (like rabbinic Judaism before them) arose as monotheistic reform movements with strong legalistic and dogmatic tendencies. Both idealized, if only the
former idolized, the work, teaching, and revelations of their prophets in the form
of sacred scripture. Both proclaimed the true God, the importance of charity toward the dispossessed, the quality of mercy. Yet both were inclined, as circumstances required and need dictated, to propagate their ideals and to enlarge the
kingdom of God by force when persuasion failed. The *dar-al-Islam* and the
kingdom of Christ, once called Christendom, were in many respects evolutionary
twins for the better part of twelve centuries. The unlikely symbol of this relationship is the fraternal feud over proprietorship of the religious womb of the book religions—the wars known as the Crusades. It is Jacob's legacy that his progeny
would learn to hate each other and fight religious wars in the name of his God.

For all their likeness, the historical course of Christianity has differed remarkably from that of Islam since the late Middle Ages. The cliche that Islam
somehow got intellectually stalled in the European feudal era overlooks too much
that is undeniably rich, new, and momentous about "the Arab mind," as a standard

ix

title describes the culture of Islam. Most Westerners who are not simply islama-phobes are willing to acknowledge where our system of numerical notation comes from; where algebra got started; how Aristotle was saved from puritan schoolmen in the Middle Ages; indeed, where scientific thinking in a number of disciplines originated. The culture of Islam, ranging in its missionary extent from Baghdad to Malaysia, is humanistically rich and potent. And yet. The Middle Eastern culture which spurred humanistic learning and scientific thinking remains a *re-ligious* culture in a way that befuddles liberal Christians and secularists, and in a way that has not existed in the West since the decline and fall of Christendom in the Reformation. At least a part of our befuddlement stems from the fact that the Reformation is often seen by historians, not as a fall or a falling apart but as a rejuvenation of Christian culture. The persistence of misperceptions about what "happened" with the advent of humanistic thinking in the late Middle Ages stems from the view that the Christian reform was a "back to basics" movement—an attempt to restore biblical teaching and practice to the church rather than (as it was at its roots) a radical challenge to systems of religious authority, a challenge that would eventually erode even the biblical pillars of authority upon which the Reformation itself was based. Islam underwent no such change and entertained no such challenge to Koranic teaching; its pillars remained strong while those of Christianity, unknown even to those who advocated the reform of the church "in head and members," were crumbling.

To misunderstand the disjoining of Islam and Christianity as religious twins is, I would argue, the key to Western misunderstanding of the Islamic faith. The Christian reformation in the West (there was nothing remotely like it in the Eastern church, which, not coincidentally, provides a much closer analogy to Islamic conservatism) proceeded on the false assumption that knowlege of Scripture was ultimately compatible with human knowledge—discovery of the original meanings of texts, linguistic and philological study, historical investigation, and so on. Without tracing the way in which this assumption developed, the fragmented churches that exited the process of cultural, geographical, and denominational warfare between the sixteenth and the twentieth centuries proved the assumption false. Europe would never again be Christendom, and the New World would emerge as an archetype of the bifurcations, rivalries, and half-way compromises that the failure of religious authority had made necessary in the Old. By the end of the nineteenth century, liberal Christian scholarship, with its inherent historical skepticism, which did not spare even the divinity of the founder nor the sacredness of sacred scripture, was verdict enough on the marriage between humanistic learning and divine knowledge, as it was promoted energetically by the early Christian reformers. From the end of the eighteenth century to the present day, Christianity was a recipient religion, which found itself either at war with humanistic learning (as among the evangelicals from Paley's day onward) or, to use Berger's term, an accommodationist faith, whose role in the world seemed to be to accept the truths that culture provided and to express them, whenever possible, in a Christian idiom. Islam scarcely represented a "fundamentalist" reaction to contemporary culture, since the humanistic renaissance it sponsored was not implicitly a rejection of the structures of religious authority. Nor was the "accommodationist" option available to Muslims, since what constituted "secular" truth could not be equated with the prophetic truths of sacred scripture. Islam could only look at what Niebuhr once called the "Christ and Culture" debate with astonishment and as a debate that Christianity sooner or later must lose. To Western ears, Islamic talk of "decadence" seems offensive. In fact, it is an expression of the Islamic view that Christianity has lost the moral contest between secular culture and religious truth.

Islam as a religious culture has not confused humanistic learning with the revealed word; accordingly, it has been spared—or in any event has avoided—the historical acids that have eroded biblical faith and Christian "culture" since the sixteenth century. Its methods of exegesis, legal reasoning, and political argumentation look peculiar and retrograde to the Westerner precisely because the Westerner—whether a liberal Anglican or an evangelical Christian—stands on the other shore of a sea that Islam has not chosen to cross. It is small consolation to those who yearn for a restoration of Christian values or biblical religion that Christianity did not *mean* to cross the sea of faith either, or at least had expected, in embarking on its intellectual journey during the Renaissance, to find God on the other side.

And so to the present work. This book is all about a journey: a journey from the certainties of childhood in a Muslim family (but they could be any childhood certainties) through a process of doubt and, finally, negation, as a result of exposure to what some might dismiss as a "Western" way of thinking about revealed religion. There must be many Muslims who have undertaken such a journey—who have, so to speak, crossed the sea of faith and who have in their personal lives traveled through the intellectual equivalent of a protestant reformation, which their religious culture, as a whole, did not travel through. All such odysseys must be very lonely ones. (For that matter, Odysseus himself was lonely.) The religious pilgrim—and I consider the author of this work to be one—is bound to feel isolated. He does not have the benefit of a convert "to" a new religion, that is to say, a made-to-order group to support and sustain him in hours of crisis and doubt, to assuage his fears and prevent his wavering. In writing a book like this, the religious pilgrim reaches out to an unseen audience for hearing and understanding, in the hope that what he says will ring true for some (certainly not for all) who have shared his faith and who may now share his rejection of it.

It is my privilege to recommend this book as one rich in reflection and intelligence. It is a helpful and in some respects a ground-breaking effort to provide a critical perspective on a faith that is too often—and usually for all the wrong reasons—regarded as uncritical, bellicose, and regressive. What we have is surely no more than one former Muslim's view of his "former" life; but we are mistaken to read this as a coming-out saga. It is part-for-whole a late twentieth-century account of the shrinkage of religious culture, the universality of knowledge, and the inescapability of the humanistic culture, which will survive all particular forms of religion in the twenty-first century. Whether that process, inevitable as it seems, will be marked by violence or accepted with enlightened resignation by defenders of old religious orders and regimes will depend, it seems to me, on how books such as this one are read and received.

Preface

I was born into a Muslim family and grew up in a country that now describes itself as an Islamic republic. My close family members identify themselves as Muslim: some more orthodox, others less. My earliest memories are of my circumcision and my first day at Koranic school—psychoanalysts may make what they wish of that. Even before I could read or write the national language I learned to read the Koran in Arabic without understanding a word of it—a common experience for thousands of Muslim children. As soon as I was able to think for myself, I discarded all the religious dogmas that had been foisted on me. I now consider myself a secular humanist who believes that all religions are sick men's dreams, false—demonstrably false —and pernicious.

Such is my background and position, and there the matter would have rested but for the Rushdie affair and the rise of Islam. I, who had never written a book before, was galvanized into writing this one by these events. Many of my postwar generation must have wondered how we would personally have stood in the ideologically charged atmosphere of the 1930s—for Nazism, for Communism, for freedom, for democracy, for king and country, for anti-imperialism? It is rare in one's life that one has an opportunity to show on what side of an important life and death issue one stands—the Rushdie affair and the rise of Islam are two such issues and this book is my stand. For those who regret not being alive in the 1930s to be able to show their commitment to a cause, there is, first the Rushdie affair, and, second, the war that is taking place in Algeria, the Sudan, Iran, Saudi Arabia, and Pakistan, a war whose principal victims are Muslims, Muslim women, Muslim intellectuals, writers, ordinary, decent people. This book is my war effort. Each time I have doubted the wisdom of writing such a book, new murders in the name of God and Islam committed in Algeria or Iran or Turkey or the Sudan have urged me on to complete it.

The most infuriating and nauseating aspect of the Rushdie affair was the spate of articles and books written by Western apologists for Islam—journalists, scholars, fellow travelers, converts (some from communism)—who claimed to be speaking for Muslims. This is surely condescension of the worst kind, and it is untrue: these authors do not speak for all Muslims. Many courageous individuals from the Muslim world supported and continue to support Rushdie. The Egyptian journal, *Rose al-Youssef* even published extracts from the *Satanic Verses* in January 1994. The present work attempts to sow a drop of doubt in an ocean of dogmatic certainty by taking an uncompromising and critical look at almost all the fundamental tenets of Islam. Here, anticipating criticism, I can only cite the words of the great John Stuart Mill, and those of his greatest modern admirer, Von Hayek. First from Mill, *On Liberty*: "Strange it is, that men should admit the validity of the arguments for free discussion, but object to their being 'pushed to an extreme'; not seeing that unless the reasons are good for an extreme case, they are not good for any case."[1] Again from Mill:

> But the peculiar evil of silencing the expression of an opinion is, that it is robbing the human race; posterity as well as the existing generation; those who dissent from the opinion, still more than those who hold it. If the opinion is right, they are deprived of the opportunity of exchanging error for truth: if wrong, they lose, what is almost as great a benefit, the clearer perception and livelier impression of truth, produced by its collision with error. . . . We can never be sure that the opinion we are endeavouring to stifle is a false opinion; and if we were sure, stifling it would be an evil still.[2]

Now Von Hayek:

> In any society freedom of thought will probably be of direct significance only for a small minority. But this does not mean that anyone is competent, or ought to have power, to select those to whom this freedom is to be reserved. . . . To deprecate the value of intellectual freedom because it will never mean for everybody the same possibility of independent thought is completely to miss the reasons which give intellectual freedom its value. What is essential to make it serve its function as the prime mover of intellectual progress is not that everybody may be able to think or write anything, but that any cause or idea may be argued by somebody. So long as dissent is not suppressed, there will always be some who will query the ideas ruling their contemporaries and put new ideas to the test of argument and propaganda.
>
> This interaction of individuals, possessing different knowledge and different views, is what constitutes the life of thought. The growth of reason is a social process based on the existence of such differences.[3]

Acknowledgments

I am not a scholar or a specialist. I certainly do not lay claim to originality; I lean heavily on the works of real scholars. I present to the reader in a more digestible form what I have culled from their works. I have quoted extensively, and where I have not quoted, I have paraphrased, all with the proper acknowledgments in the notes and bibliography. There is hardly an image or thought that I can claim to be my own creation. If some critic were to dub this work "an extended annotated bibliography" I would not be offended.

I have found the first and second edition of the *Encyclopedia of Islam* particularly useful—especially the first edition which manages to retain a certain amount of skepticism lacking in the second edition, where political and religious correctness have blunted the critical faculties. The *Dictionary of Islam* has also proved indispensable and is, like the first edition, healthily skeptical. A glance at the notes and bibliography is alone sufficient to indicate my indebtedness to the works of two modern scholars in particular: Bernard Lewis and Montgomery Watt. Bernard Lewis must surely be one of the great prose writers of English of the last fifty years—elegant, urbane, and subtle—if, at times, frustratingly evasive. Though I have harsh things to say about Professor Watt, he remains a great scholar who also writes clear, unpretentious, if not exactly elegant, English. A series of articles in the *New Humanist* by Ibn al-Rawandi somehow gave me enormous moral encouragement and support. Perhaps unfairly I should also like to single out the following scholars (see bibliography for details):

chap. 1. D. Pipes
chap. 2. W. Tisdall, M. Boyce, S. Zwemer, C. C. Torrey, and A. Geiger
chap. 3. S. Hurgronje, I. Goldziher, J. Schacht, M. Cook, and P. Crone
chap. 4. A. Jeffrey and W. Muir
chap. 5. R. Bell/W. M. Watt, and A. Dashti
chap. 6. G. H. Bousquet and J. Schacht
chap. 7. A. E. Mayer

chap. 8. I. Goldziher

chap. 9. B. Ye'or; the whole of this chapter has been almost entirely constructed out of her three books.

chap. 10. G. Vadja, R. Walzer, and I. Goldziher

chap. 11. M. Plessner, Pines, R. A. Nicholson, and A. J. Arberry

chap. 12. A. J. Arberry

chap. 13. R. A. Nicholson and A. Rihani

chap. 14. G. Ascha; everything of value in this chapter comes from him and Bousquet.

chap. 15. Articles Khamriyya, Ghidha, Liwat in EI2, and F. J. Simoons

chap. 16. W. M. Watt, D. S. Margoliouth, and W. Muir

chap. 17. M. Hiskett

In a conversation with Eckermann, Goethe advised an author accused of plagiarism to say "what is there is mine, and whether I got it from a book or from life is of no consequence. The only point is, whether I have made a right use of it." I doubt whether many Islamic scholars would openly approve of the use I have made of their research and scholarship; thus it is no formality to emphasize that all responsibility for the harsh, final judgments on Islam in this book is mine.

Introduction

It is well to bear in mind while reading this book the distinction between theory and practice; the distinction between what Muslims ought to do and what they in fact do; what they should have believed and done as opposed to what they actually believed and did. We might distinguish three Islams: Islam 1, Islam 2, and Islam 3. Islam 1 is what the Prophet taught, that is, his teachings as contained in the Koran. Islam 2 is the religion as expounded, interpreted, and developed by the theologians through the traditions (Hadith); it includes the sharia and Islamic law Islam 3 is what Muslims actually did do and achieved, that is to say, Islamic civilization.

If any general thesis emerges in this book it is that Islam 3, Islamic civilization, often reached magnificent heights despite Islam 1 and Islam 2, and not because of them. Islamic philosophy, Islamic science, Islamic literature, and Islamic art would not have attained those heights had they rested only on Islam 1 and Islam 2. Take poetry, for example. At least early on, Muhammad despised the poets: "Those who go astray follow the poets" (sura 26.224); and in the collection of traditions known as the Mishkat, Muhammad is made to say: "A belly full of purulent matter is better than a belly full of poetry." Had the poets adhered to Islam 1 and Islam 2, we certainly would not have had the poems of Abu Nuwas singing the praises of wine and the beautiful buttocks of young boys, or any of the other wine poems for which Arabic literature is justly famous.

As for Islamic art, the *Dictionary of Islam* (*DOI*) says,[4] Muhammad cursed the painter or drawer of men and animals (Mishkat, 7, ch. 1, pt. 1), and consequently they are held to be unlawful. As Ettinghausen[5] points out in his Introduction to *Arab Painting,* the Hadith are full of condemnation for "makers of figured pictures," who are called the "worst of men." They are condemned for competing with God, who is the only Creator. "The canonical position gave no scope to the figural painter." Mercifully, contact with older civilizations with rich artistic traditions induced newly converted Muslims to flout the orthodox position, and was responsible for such masterpieces of representational art as the Persian and Moghul miniatures.

1

Thus, the creative impulse underlying Islamic art, Islamic philosophy, Islamic science, and Islamic literature came from outside Islam 1 and Islam 2, from contact with older civilizations with a richer heritage. Artistic, philosophical, and scientific traditions were totally lacking in Arabia. Only poetry emerged from the Arab past, and its continued creativity owed little to specifically Islamic inspiration. Without Byzantine art and Sassanian art there would have been no Islamic art; Islam 1 and Islam 2 were hostile to its development. Similarly, without the influence of Greek philosophy and Greek science there would not have been Islamic philosophy or Islamic science, for Islam 1 and Islam 2 were certainly ill-disposed to these "foreign sciences." For the orthodox, Islamic philosophy was a contradiction in terms, and Islamic science futile.

Some of the greatest representatives in these fields, or those who played a crucial role in their development, were either non-Muslim or actually hostile to some or even all of the tenets of Islam 1 and Islam 2. For instance, Hunain ibn Ishaq (809–873), the most important translator of Greek philosophy into Arabic, was a Christian. Ibn al-Muqaffa (d. 757), a translator from Pahlavi into Arabic and "one of the creators of Arabic prose,"[6] was a Manichaen who wrote an attack on the Koran. Nicholson[7] selected for discussion the following five poets as the most typical of the Abbasid period: Muti ibn Iyas, Abu Nuwas, Abu'l-Atahiya, al-Mutanabbi, and al-Ma'arri. All of them were accused or suspected of heresy or blasphemy and are discussed in chapter 10. Also discussed in chapter 11 is Ar-Razi, the greatest physician (European or Islamic) of the Middle Ages and the greatest representative of Islamic science. Razi was totally hostile to every single tenet of Islam 1 and Islam 2; he even denied the prophethood of Muhammad.

The treatment of women, non-Muslims, unbelievers, heretics, and slaves (male and female) was appalling both in theory and practice. In other words, Islam 1, Islam 2, and Islam 3 all stand condemned. The horrendous behavior toward women, non-Muslims, heretics, and slaves manifested in Islamic civilization was a direct consequence of the principles laid down in the Koran and developed by the Islamic jurists. Islamic law is a totalitarian theoretical construct, intended to control every aspect of an individual's life from birth to death. Happily, the law has not always been applied to the letter—Islamic civilization would scarcely have emerged otherwise. Theoretically Islam 1 and Islam 2, the Koran, and Islamic law condemn wine drinking and homosexuality; in reality, Islamic civilization tolerates both. However, the sharia still does govern the practices in certain areas of human life, for example, the family (marriage, divorce, etc.).

In some areas of human life Islamic practice has been more severe than required by the sharia. Circumcision is not mentioned in the Koran, and most jurists at most only recommend it, but without exception all male Muslim children are circumcised. Female circumcision is also not discussed in the Koran but the practice persists in certain Islamic countries. The Koran expressly talks of the basic equality of all adult male Muslims; unhappily the reality was far different, as Muslims of non-Arab blood discovered throughout the early years of Islam. Here Islam 1 and Islam 2 taught moral principles that were not respected by Islam 3.

1

The Rushdie Affair

Before 14 February 1989

In 1280 C.E. there appeared in Baghdad a remarkable book written in Arabic by a Jewish philosopher and physician Ibn Kammuna. It is usually known by the name of *Examination of the Three Faiths*. It is remarkable because of its scientific objectivity and its critical attitude toward Judaism, Christianity, and above all Islam. "Deism bordering on agnosticism permeates the little volume."[8]

The prophet Muhammad is described as someone unoriginal: "We will not concede that [Muhammad] added to the knowledge of God and to obedience to Him anything more than was found in the earlier religions."[9] Nor is the Prophet perfect: "There is no proof that Muhammad attained perfection and the ability to perfect others as claimed." People generally convert to Islam only "in terror or in quest of power, or to avoid heavy taxation, or to escape humiliation, or if taken prisoner, or because of infatuation with a Muslim woman." A rich non-Muslim well-versed in his own faith and that of Islam will not convert except for some of the preceeding reasons. Finally, Muslims seem unable to provide good arguments—let alone proofs—for the prophethood of Muhammad. How did the Muslims take to this skepticism? The thirteenth century chronicler Fuwati (1244–1323) describes the events occurring four years after the publication of the treatise.

> In this year (1284) it became known in Baghdad that the Jew Ibn Kammuna had written a volume . . . in which he displayed impudence in the discussion of the prophecies. God keep us from repeating what he said. The infuriated mob rioted, and massed to attack his house and to kill him. The amir . . . and a group of high officials rode forth to the Mustansiriya madrasa, and summoned the supreme judge and the [law] teachers to hold a hearing on the affair. They sought Ibn Kammuna but he was in hiding. That day happened to be a Friday.

3

The supreme judge set out for the prayer service but as the mob blocked him, he returned to the Mustansiriya. The amir stepped out to calm the crowds but these showered abuse upon him and accused him of being on the side of Ibn Kammuna, and of defending him. Then, upon the amir's order, it was heralded in Baghdad that, early the following morning outside the city wall, Ibn Kammuna would be burned. The mob subsided, and no further reference to Ibn Kammuna was made.

As for Ibn Kammuna, he was put into a leather-covered box and carried to Hilla where his son was then serving as official. There he stayed for a time until he died.[10]

Fuwati's narrative exemplifies how throughout the history of Islam ordinary Muslims, and not just so-called fundamentalists, have reacted to putative insults to their religion. Two comic examples come from India. The American economist, John Kenneth Galbraith, got into difficulty while American ambassador to India (1961–63), when it became known that he had named his pet cat "Ahmed"— Ahmed also being one of the names by which the prophet Muhammad was known. When the *Deccan Herald* in Bangalore published a short story entitled "Muhammad the Idiot," Muslims burned down the newspaper offices. As it turned out, the story had nothing to do with the Prophet but with a crazed man who bore the same name. More recently, ten Indians were jailed in the Gulf emirate of Sharjah for staging a Malayalam drama called *The Ants That Eat Corpses*, that, according to the authorities, contained remarks against Muhammad.

Muslims who dared to criticize were branded heretics and usually beheaded, crucified, or burned; I discuss the plight of some of them during the Golden Age of Islam in chapter 10. Here I shall confine myself to comparatively recent examples of criticism of Islam by Muslims.

Many of my examples are taken from Daniel Pipes' excellent book, *The Rushdie Affair.* Pipes describes those groups of Muslim writers and thinkers who were punished for their heretical works and those who escaped without retribution for their error. Before describing his tragic fate, I shall look at some of the startling criticisms Dashti leveled at some of the Muslims' most cherished beliefs in his classic *Twenty-Three Years.* Although the book was written in 1937, it was only published in 1974, and probably in Beirut, since between 1971 and 1977 the regime of the Shah of Iran forbade publication of any criticism of religion. After the Iranian Revolution of 1979 Dashti authorized its publication by underground opposition groups. His book, whose title refers to the prophetic career of Muhammad, may well have sold over half a million copies in pirated editions between 1980 and 1986.

First, Dashti defends rational thought in general and criticizes blind faith since "belief can blunt human reason and common sense,"[11] even in learned scholars. Rational thought requires more "impartial study." He vigorously denies any of the miracles ascribed to Muhammad by some later, overeager Muslim commentators. Dashti submits the orthodox view that the Koran is the word of God Himself, that it is miraculous by virtue of its eloquence and subject matter, to a thorough, skeptical examination. He points out that even some early Muslim scholars, "before bigotry and hyperbole prevailed, openly acknowledged that the arrangement and syntax of the Koran are not miraculous and that work of equal or greater value could be produced by other God-fearing persons."[12]

> Furthermore, the Koran contains sentences which are incomplete and not fully intelligible without the aid of commentaries; foreign words, unfamiliar Arabic words, and words used with other than the normal meaning; adjectives and verbs inflected without observance of the concords of gender and number; illogically and ungrammatically applied pronouns which sometimes have no referent; and predicates which in rhymed passages are often remote from the subjects. These and other such aberrations in the language have given scope to critics who deny the Koran's eloquence. . . . To sum up, more than one hundred Koranic aberrations from the normal rules have been noted.[13]

What of the claim that the subject matter is miraculous? Like Ibn Kammuna, Ali Dashti points out, that the Koran

> contains nothing new in the sense of ideas not already expressed by others. All the moral precepts of the Koran are self-evident and generally acknowledged. The stories in it are taken in identical or slightly modified forms from the lore of the Jews and Christians, whose rabbis and monks Muhammad had met and consulted on his journeys to Syria, and from memories conserved by the descendants of the peoples of "Ad and Thamud." . . . In the field of moral teachings, however, the Koran cannot be considered miraculous. Muhammad reiterated principles which mankind had already conceived in earlier centuries and many places. Confucius, Buddha, Zoroaster, Socrates, Moses, and Jesus had said similar things. . . . Many of the duties and rites of Islam are continuations of practices which the pagan Arabs had adopted from the Jews.[14]

Dashti ridicules the superstitious aspects of much ritual, especially that which occurs during the pilgrimage to Mecca. Muhammad himself emerges as a shifty character who stoops to political assassinations, murder, and the elimination of all opponents. Among the Prophet's followers, killings were passed off as "services to Islam." The position of women under Islam is examined and their inferior status is admitted. The Muslim doctrine of God is criticized. The God of the Koran is cruel, angry, and proud—qualities not to be admired. Finally, it is quite clear that the Koran is not the word of God, since it contains many instances that confuse the identities of the two speakers, God and Muhammad.

Dashti died in 1984 after spending three years in Khomeini's prisons, where he was tortured despite his age of eighty-three. He told a friend before he died: "Had the Shah allowed books like this to be published and read by the people, we would never have had an Islamic revolution."[15]

Ali Abd al-Raziq, a sheikh at the famous Islamic University of al-Azhar in Cairo, published *Islam and the principles of Government* in 1925.[16] In this book, al-Raziq argued for a separation of religion and politics since he sincerely believed that this was what Islam really preached. Such a view proved unacceptable, and al-Raziq was tried by a tribunal of other sheikhs who found him guilty of impiety. He was dismissed from the university and forbidden from holding any religious post.

Another graduate of al-Azhar was the Egyptian man of letters Taha Husayn.[17] He was also educated in France where he acquired a skeptical frame of mind. Inevitably on his return to Egypt, he submitted her outworn traditions to severe criticism. Husayn's views also proved unacceptable to the religious establishment and he was forced to resign from public posts. In his *On Pre-Islamic Poetry,* Taha Husayn had written that the fact that Abraham and Ishmael appear in the Koran "is not sufficient to establish their historical existence."

In April 1967,[18] just before the Six-Day War, an issue of the Syrian army magazine *Jayash ash-Sha'b* contained an article attacking not just Islam, but God and religion in general as "mummies which should be transferred to the museums of historical remains." In a scene reminiscent of the Ibn Kammuna case, mobs took to the streets in many of the major cities of Syria, and the disorder led to violence, strikes, and arrests.

When the old ruse of blaming the incident on a Zionist-American conspiracy failed to quell the violence, the article's author, Ibrahim Khalas, and two of his editors on the magazine were court-martialed, found guilty, and sentenced to life imprisonment with hard labor. Happily, they were eventually released.

In 1969, after the disastrous defeat of the Arabs by Israel in 1967, a Syrian Marxist intellectual produced a brilliant critique of religious thought. Sadiq al-Azm[19] was educated at the American University of Beirut, received his doctorate in philosophy from Yale University, and has published a study of the British philosopher, Bishop Berkeley. Al-Azm's devastating criticisms of Islam and religion were not appreciated by the Sunni establishment in Beirut. He was brought to trial on charges of provoking religious troubles but was acquitted, perhaps because of the political connections of his distinguished Syrian political family. Nonetheless, al-Azm thought it prudent to live abroad for a while.

Sadiq al-Azm takes the Arab leaders to task for not developing the critical faculties in their people, and for the leaders' own uncritical attitude to Islam and its outmoded ways of thought. Arab reactionaries used religious thought as an ideological weapon, and yet, no one submitted their thought to

> a critical, scientific analysis to reveal the forgeries they employ to exploit the Arab man. . . . [The leaders] refrained from any criticism of the Arab intellectual and social heritage. . . . Under the cover of protecting the people's traditions, values, art, religion, and morals, the cultural effort of the Arab liberation movement was used to protect the backward institutions and the medieval culture and thought of obscurantist ideology.[20]

Every Muslim will have to face the challenge of the scientific developments of the last hundred and fifty years. Scientific knowledge directly conflicts with Muslim religious beliefs on a number of issues. But the more fundamental difference is a question of methodology—Islam relies on blind faith and the uncritical acceptance of texts on which the religion is based, whereas science depends on critical thought, observation, deduction, and results that are internally coherent and correspond to reality. We can no longer leave religious thought uncriticized: all the sacred texts must be scrutinized in a scientific manner. Only then will we stop gazing back and only then will religion stop being an obscurantist justification for the intellectual and political status quo.

Sadiq al-Azm's book is important and deserves to be better known, but as far as I know it has not been translated from the original Arabic. More recently, Sadiq al-Azm has very courageously defended Rushdie in an article in *Die Welt des Islams* 31 (1991).

Another attempt at reforming Islam from within also ended in tragedy. Sudanese theologian Mahmud Muhammad Taha[21] tried to minimize the role of the Koran as a source of law. Taha felt it was time to devise new laws that would better meet the needs of people in the twentieth century. To propagate his principles, Taha founded the Republican Brethren. Religious authorities in Khartoum did not take kindly to Taha's ideas and in 1968 declared him guilty of apostasy, which under Islamic law, carries normally a punishment of death. His writings were burned, but Taha himself managed to escape execution for seventeen years. He was tried again, and was publicly hanged at seventy-six years of age in Khartoum in January 1985.

Perhaps the most famous contemporary Muslim mentioned by Pipes is the Libyan leader, Mu'ammar al-Qaddafi,[22] whose public statements on Muhammad, the Koran, and Islam amount to a blasphemy far greater than anything discussed so far. Qaddafi confined sharia to private matters; his own ideas were promulgated in the public domain. He changed the Islamic calendar, mocked Meccan pilgrims as "guileless and foolish," criticized the prophet Muhammad, and claimed that his own achievements were greater than those of the Prophet. In general, he showed extreme skepticism about the truth of the Koran and even about the details of the life of the Prophet. Though religious leaders found Qaddafi anti-Islamic and deviant, and condemned his "perjury and lies," there were no calls for his death, nor were any of his writings banned. In fact, if the CIA had their wits about them, they could reprint and freely circulate the Libyan leader's blasphemous thoughts on Islam, and let the fundamentalists do the rest.

Two other skeptics[23] also doubted Islam's ability to provide any solutions to modern-day problems. In 1986, a Cairo lawyer, Nur Farwaj, wrote an article criticizing the sharia, the Islamic law, as "a collection of reactionary tribal rules unsuited to contemporary societies." Also in 1986, Egyptian lawyer and essayist Faraj Fada published a pamphlet under the aggressive title of *NO To Sharia*. The work argued for the separation of religion and state because Islam could not provide the secular constitutional framework necessary for running a modern state. Fada's polemical essay enjoyed great success, rivaling in popularity the writings of the dogmatic Sheikh Kashk. It was translated into Turkish, Persian, Urdu, and other languages of the Islamic world.

One other work published before February 1989 deserves mention. In *L'Islam en Questions* (Grasset, 1986), twenty-four Arab writers reply to the following five questions:

1. Does Islam retain its universal vocation?
2. Could Islam be a system of government for a modern state?
3. Is an Islamic system of government an obligatory step in the evolution of the Islamic and Arab peoples?
4. Is the "return to Islam," the phenomenon that is observable in the last ten years in the majority of Muslim countries, something positive?
5. What is the principal enemy of Islam today?

It is clear from the scholars' replies that a majority of these Arab intellectuals do not see Islam as the answer to the social, economic, and political problems besetting the Islamic world. The majority of the respondents fervently advocate a secular state. Nine writers give an emphatic and categoric no to question 2, "Could Islam be a system of government for a modern state? " Another six are equally emphatical in favor of a secular state. Even those writers who answer yes to question 2, do so very tentatively in responses hedged with qualifications such as, "provided rights are respected," or "as long as we have a modern interpretation of Islam," etc. Almost all of them find the "return to Islam," a negative phenomenon, and consider religious fanaticism as the greatest danger facing all Muslims. One of the writers in the above book is Rachid Boudjedra, novelist, playwright, essayist, communist, and self-confessed atheist. He makes scathing remarks[24] about religion in Algeria and assails the hypocrisy of the majority—eighty percent—of the "believers" is his figure—who only pray or pretend to pray in the month of Ramadan, the holy month of fasting; who go on pilgrimage for the social prestige; who drink and fornicate and still claim to be good Muslims. To the question "could Islam be a system of government for a modern state?" Boudjedra unequivocally replies:

> No, absolutely not. It's impossible; that is not just a personal opinion, it's something objective. We saw that when Nemeiri [head of the Sudan] wanted to apply the Sharia: it didn't work. The experiment ended abruptly after some hands and feet were chopped off. . . . There is a reaction even among the mass of Muslims against this sort of thing—stoning women, for example, is hardly carried out, except in Saudi Arabia, and extremely rarely. . . . Islam is absolutely incompatible with a modern state. . . . No, I don't see how Islam could be a system of government.

It is not generally known that Boudjedra has had a fatwa pronounced against him since 1983, and that despite death threats he remains in Algeria, trying to carry on as normally as possible, moving from place to place in heavy disguise. To compound his "errors," in 1992 Boudjedra wrote a ferocious attack on the FIS, the Islamicist Party, that was set to win the elections in 1992, exposing it as an extremist undemocratic party, and even comparing it to the Nazi party of the thirties. Boudjedra has nothing but contempt for those who remain silent and those who are not only uncritical of the Islamicists, but who also pretend to see something "fertile" in their regression to medieval times. The fatwa of 1983 leads naturally to the fatwa of 1989.

After 14 February 1989

Spring 1989 will always remain as a kind of watershed in intellectual and world history. In February 1989, the Ayatollah Khomeini delivered his infamous fatwa on Salman Rushdie. Immediately following in its wake came short interviews with or articles by Western intellectuals, Arabists, and Islamologists blaming Rushdie for bringing the barbarous sentence onto himself by writing the *Satanic Verses*. John Esposito, an American expert on Islam, claimed he knew "of no Western scholar of Islam who would not have predicted that [Rushdie's] kind of statements would be explosive."[25] That is sheer hypocrisy coming from a man who has published extracts from Sadiq al-Azm's previously quoted book, that had also dared to criticize Islam.

Some writers included condescending asides about understanding the hurt felt by the Muslims, who were urged, in some cases, to beat up Rushdie in some back alley. A respected historian, Professor Trevor-Roper even gave the tacit approval to the brutish call for the murder of a British citizen: "I wonder how Salman Rushdie is faring these days under the benevolent protection of British law and British police, about whom he has been so rude. Not too comfortably I hope. . . . I would not shed a tear if some British Muslims, deploring his manners, should waylay him in a dark street and seek to improve them. If that should cause him thereafter to control his pen, society would benefit and literature would not suffer."[26]

Nowhere in any of these articles is there any criticism of the call to murder. Even worse, a recommendation was made that Rushdie's book be banned or removed from circulation. Astonishingly, there was no defense of one of the fundamental principles of democracy, the principle without which there can be no human progress, namely, the freedom of speech. One would have thought that this was one principle that writers and intellectuals would have been prepared to die for.

Will that "closet hooligan" Trevor-Roper wake up from his complacent slumbers, when those "poor hurt Muslims" begin demanding the withdrawal of those classics of Western literature and intellectual history that offend their Islamic sensibilities but must be dear to Professor Roper's heart?

Will these Muslims start burning Gibbon, who wrote: "[The Koran is an] endless incoherent rhapsody of fable, and precept, and declamation, which seldom excites a sentiment or an idea, which sometimes crawls in the dust, and is sometimes lost in the clouds." Elsewhere Gibbon points out that "the prophet of Medina assumed in his revelations, a fiercer and more sanguinary tone, which proves that his former moderation was the effect of weakness." Muhammad's claim that he was the Apostle of God was "a necessary fiction."

> The use of fraud and perfidy, of cruelty and injustice, were often subservient to the propagation of the faith; and Mohammad commanded or approved the assassination of the Jews and idolaters who had escaped from the field of battle. By the repetition of such acts the character of Mohammed must have been gradually stained. . . . Of his last years ambition was the ruling passion; and a politician will suspect that he secretly smiled (the victorious impostor!) at the enthusiasm of his youth, and the credulity of his proselytes. . . . In his private conduct Mohammad indulged the appetites of a man, and abused the claims of a prophet. A special revelation dispensed him from the laws which he had imposed on his nation; the female sex, without reserve, was abandoned to his desires.[27]

What of Roper's beloved Hume who wrote:[28] "[The Koran is a] wild and absurd performance. Let us attend to his [Muhammad's] narration; and we shall soon find that he bestows praise on such instances of treachery, inhumanity, cruelty, revenge, and bigotry as are utterly incompatible with civilized society. No steady rule of right seems there to be attended to; and every action is blamed or praised, so far only as it is beneficial or hurtful to the true believers." Hume also refers to Muhammad as the "pretended prophet." It should be clear to everyone by now that the notion of the Koran being Muhammad's performance and his narration is totally blasphemous.

What of Hobbes who thought that Muhammad "to set up his new religion, pretended to have conferences with the Holy Ghost in form of a dove."[29]

What of The Divine Comedy, the greatest poem in Western literature. "See how Mahomet is mangled! Before me Ali weeping goes, cleft in the face from chin to forelock; and all the others, whom thou seest here were in their lifetime sowers of scandal and of schism; and therefore are they thus cleft."[30]

In his notes to his translation of The Divine Comedy Mark Musa sums up Dante's reasons for consigning Muhammad to Hell: "[Muhammad's] punishment, to be split open from the crotch to the chin, together with the complementary punishment of Ali, represents Dante's belief that they were initiators of the great schism between the Christian Church and Mohammedanism. Many of Dante's contemporaries thought that Mahomet was originally a Christian and a cardinal who wanted to become pope."[31]

Carlyle and Voltaire also had harsh things to say about the Koran and Muhammad, but in 1989, Western apologists of Islam were busy either attacking

Rushdie, or churning out works of Islamic propaganda and not expressing their criticisms of the faith. By explaining away "Islamic fundamentalism" in terms of economic misery or in terms of notions such as "loss of identity," "feeling threatened by the West," or "white racism," these apologists legitimated barbaric behavior, and inevitably shifted moral responsibility from the Muslims onto the West. "The problem is not Islam," the argument goes, "but the extremists who have hijacked the Koran. Islam is a tolerant religion and the Ayatollah Khomeini is not following the true spirit or principles of Islam. What he has so obscenely applied in Iran is not truly Islamic, it is a grotesque caricature. Islam has always tolerated dissent."

Even more dishonest is the continuing attempt to exonerate Islam itself—especially by using phrases such as "Islamic fundamentalist," "Muslim fanatic," and so on.

The term "Islamic fundamentalist "is in itself inappropriate, for there is a vast difference between Christianity and Islam. Most Christians have moved away from the literal interpretation of the Bible; for most of them, "It ain't necessarily so."[32] Thus we can legitimately distinguish between fundamentalist and nonfundamentalist Christians. But Muslims have not moved away from the literal interpretation of the Koran: all Muslims—not just a group we have called "fundamentalist"—believe that the Koran is literally the word of God.

The preceding examples of mob riots show that ordinary Muslims very easily take offense at what they perceive to be insults to their holy book, their prophet, and their religion. Most ordinary Muslims supported Khomeini's fatwa against Rushdie.

Muslim moderates, along with Western liberals and the woefully misguided Christian clergy, argue in a similar manner, namely, that Islam is not what Khomeini has applied in Iran. But the Muslim moderates and all the others cannot have their cake and eat it too. No amount of mental gymnastics or intellectual dishonesty is going to make the unpalatable, unacceptable, and barbaric aspects of Islam disappear. At least the Islamic "fundamentalist "is being logical and honest, given the premise that the Koran is the Word of God. Khomeini's actions directly reflect the teachings of Islam, whether found in the Koran, in the acts and sayings of the Prophet, or the Islamic law based on them. To justify the call to murder implicit in the fatwa on Rushdie, Iranian spokesmen examined the details of Muhammad's life. There they found numerous precedents for political assassinations, including the murder of writers who had written satirical verses against the Prophet (discussed in chapter 4). Khomeini himself responds to the Western apologists and Muslim moderates:

> Islam makes it incumbent on all adult males, provided they are not disabled and incapacitated, to prepare themselves for the conquest of [other] countries so that the writ of Islam is obeyed in every country in the world.
> But those who study Islamic Holy War will understand why Islam wants to conquer the whole world. . . . Those who know nothing of Islam pretend

that Islam counsels against war. Those [who say this] are witless. Islam says: Kill all the unbelievers just as they would kill you all! Does this mean that Muslims should sit back until they are devoured by [the unbelievers]? Islam says: Kill them [the non-Muslims], put them to the sword and scatter [their armies]. Does this mean sitting back until [non-Muslims] overcome us? Islam says: Kill in the service of Allah those who may want to kill you! Does this mean that we should surrender to the enemy? Islam says: Whatever good there is exists thanks to the sword and in the shadow of the sword! People cannot be made obedient except with the sword! The sword is the key to Paradise, which can be opened only for Holy Warriors! There are hundreds of other [Koranic] psalms and Hadiths [sayings of the Prophet] urging Muslims to value war and to fight. Does all that mean that Islam is a religion that prevents men from waging war? I spit upon those foolish souls who make such a claim.[33]

Khomeini is quoting directly from the Koran and is giving practically a dictionary definition of the Islamic doctrine of Jihad. The celebrated *Dictionary of Islam* defines *jihad* as: "a religious war with those who are unbelievers in the mission of Muhammad. It is an incumbent religious duty, established in the Quran and in the Traditions as a divine institution, enjoined specially for the purpose of advancing Islam and of repelling evil from Muslims."[34]

If the Koran is the word of God, as Khomeini and all Muslims believe, and its mandates are to be obeyed absolutely, then who is being more logical, Khomeini or the Muslim moderates and the Western apologists of Islam? Q.E.D.

A similar dishonesty is discernible in the sad attempts by modernist Muslim intellectuals—male and female—to pretend that the "real Islam treats women well"; that no contradiction exists between democracy and Islam, between human rights and Islam. (See chap. 7 for further discussion of these discrepancies.)

The Islamic Threat: Myth or Reality? inquired John Esposito, an American Islamicist at Holy Cross University, in a book of the same name published in 1991. The book is based on the same dishonesty as soft-core pornography. Despite its apparently daring title, it promises more than it can deliver, and we know in advance what its answer will be without opening the book. We know perfectly well that, since the Rushdie affair, the Oxford University Press would never have accepted a book that dared to criticize Islam, nor would Mr. Esposito have cared to incur the wrath of the entire Muslim world. What Esposito and all Western apologists of Islam are incapable of understanding is that Islam *is* a threat, and it is a threat to thousands of *Muslims*. As Amir Taheri put it, "the vast majority of victims of 'Holy Terror' are Muslims." One writer from a country ruled under Islamic principles recently pleaded, "You must defend Rushdie, because in defending Rushdie you are defending us."[35] In an open letter to Rushdie, the Iranian writer Fahimeh Farsaie points out[36] that in focusing solely on Rushdie, we are forgetting the unhappy lot of hundreds of writers throughout the world. In Iran alone, soon after 14 February 1989, "many people, i.e., authors and journalists, were executed and buried in mass graves together with other political prisoners because they had written a book or an article and expressed their own views. To mention just a few names: Amir Nikaiin, Monouchehr Behzadi, Djavid Misani, Abutorab Bagherzadeh. . . . They followed the bitter fate of their young colleagues who had been kidnapped, tortured, and shot a few months before in a dark night: two poets called Said Soltanpour and Rahman Hatefi."

When we compare the evasive and sycophantic statements of Western apologists such as Edward Mortimer and Esposito, who blamed everything on Rushdie, with the following declaration by Iranians, we realize the cowardliness and dishonesty of the apologists and the courage of the Iranians.

It is now three years since the writer Salman Rushdie began living under the death threat voiced by Khomeini, and yet no collective action has been taken by Iranians to condemn this barbaric decree. As this outrageous and deliberate attack on freedom of speech was issued in Iran, we feel that the Iranian intellectuals should condemn this Fatwa and defend Salman Rushdie more forcefully than any other group on earth.

The signers of this declaration, who have shown in many different ways their support for Salman Rushdie now and in the past, believe that freedom of speech is one of the greatest achievements of mankind, and point out, as Voltaire once did, that this freedom would be meaningless unless human beings had the liberty to blaspheme. No one and no group has the right to hamper or hinder this freedom in the name of this or that sanctity.

We emphasize the fact that Khomeini's death sentence is intolerable, and stress that in judging a creative work of art no considerations are valid other than aesthetic ones. We raise our voices unanimously in the defense of Salman Rushdie, and remind the whole world that Iranian writers, artists, journalists, and thinkers inside Iran are persistently under the merciless pressure of religious censorship, and that the number of those who have been imprisoned or even executed there for "blasphemy" is not negligible.

We are convinced that any tolerance shown toward the systematic violation of human rights in Iran cannot but encourage and embolden the Islamic regime to expand and export its terrorist ideas and methods worldwide.[37]

Signed by about fifty Iranians living in exile.

They, at least, have understood that the Rushdie affair is more than just foreign interference in the life of a British citizen who has not committed any crime under British law, that it is more than just Islamic terrorism. The Rushdie affair involves principles, namely, freedom of thought and expression, principles that are the hallmarks, the defining characteristics of freedom in Western civilization—indeed, in any civilized society.

A considerable number of other writers and intellectuals from the Islamic world very courageously gave their total support to Rushdie. Daniel Pipes has recorded many of their views and statements in his book. In November 1993, in France appeared another book, *Pour Rushdie,* in which a hundred Arab and Muslim intellectuals gave their support to Rushdie and freedom of expression.

Meanwhile, contrary to what many had feared, as a consequence of the fatwa, books and articles criticizing Islam, the Prophet, and the Koran have continued to be published. One book mocks the Prophet;[38] another refers to the Prophet as a child molester[39] (alluding to Muhammad's nine-year-old bride, Aisha). One philosopher thinks of Allah as presented in the Koran as a kind of cosmic Saddam Hussein.[40] Critical thought has not been silenced.

It was perhaps understandable but disappointing that so few academics in the field of Islamic studies supported freedom of expression. However, I think it was also rather hypocritical of them to stay aloof from the fray because a mere glance at the bibliography of any introductory book on Islam reveals that some of the recommended reading is, in many cases, blasphemous. We can find a neutral example in scholar Gibb's *Islam*, a short introduction to the faith of Islam published by Oxford University Press. As the first entry on his list, the late scholar cites R. A. Nicholson's *A Literary History of the Arabs*, which contains this blasphemous sentence, among others: "the Koran is an exceedingly human document."[41] Another book by Nicholson mentioned in the bibliography is *The Mystics of Islam*, which contains this passage: "European readers of the Koran cannot fail to be struck by its author's vacillation and inconsistency in dealing with the greatest problems."[42] I counted seven other books in Gibb's bibliography that would be disapproved of by a Muslim. More recently, Rippin in "Muslims, Their Religious Beliefs and Practices" has listed about thirty-five books "For Further Reading," at least fifteen of which, in my view, would be considered offensive to Muslims. Almost all the great scholars of the past—Noldeke, Hurgronje, Goldziher, Caetani, Lammens, and Schacht—express views that would be unacceptable to Muslims, but we cannot study Islam without referring to the scholarly works. What is encouraging is the fact that most of these works were still available in 1993, and some have been reprinted recently. And perhaps most ironically of all, you can buy them from the Islamic Bookshop in London and be served by a Muslim girl wearing the traditional head scarf beloved by fundamentalists!

Certainly, if academics wish to continue to work unhindered, they will have to defend academic freedom and freedom of expression. They should not inconsistently and hypocritically criticize Rushdie when they themselves are writing or recommending blasphemous works. Rushdie's battle is their battle also.

Trahison des Clercs

This book is first and foremost an assertion of my right to criticize everything and anything in Islam—even to blaspheme, to make errors, to satirize, and mock. Muslims *and* non-Muslims have the right to critically examine the sources, the history, and dogma of Islam. Muslims avail themselves of the right to criticize in their frequent denunciations of Western culture, in terms that would have been deemed racist, neocolonialist, or imperialist had a European directed them against Islam. Without criticism, Islam will remain unassailed in its dogmatic, fanatical, medieval fortress; ossified in its totalitarian, intolerant, paranoid past. It will continue to stifle thought, human rights, individuality, originality, and truth.

Western scholars and Islamicists have totally failed in their duties as intellectuals. They have betrayed their calling by abandoning their critical faculties when it comes to Islam. Some, as I shall show, have even abandoned any attempt to achieve objectivity, to aim at objective truth.

Some Islamicists have themselves noticed the appalling trend among their colleagues. Karl Binswanger[43] has remarked on the "dogmatic Islamophilia" of most Arabists. In 1983 Jacques Ellul[44] complained that "in France it is no longer acceptable to criticize Islam or the Arab countries." Already in 1968 Maxime Rodinson had written, "An historian like Norman Daniel has gone so far as to number among the conceptions permeated with medievalism or imperialism, any criticisms of the Prophet's moral attitudes and to accuse of like tendencies any exposition of Islam and its characteristics by means of the normal mechanisms of human history. Understanding has given way to apologetics pure and simple."[45]

Patricia Crone and Ibn Rawandi have remarked that Western scholarship lost its critical attitude to the sources of the origins of Islam around the time of the First World War. John Wansbrough has noted that "as a document susceptible of analysis by the instruments and techniques of Biblical criticism it [the Koran] is virtually unknown."[46] By 1990, we still have the scandalous situation described by Andrew Rippin:

> I have often encountered individuals who come to the study of Islam with a background in the historical study of the Hebrew Bible or early Christianity, and who express surprise at the lack of critical thought that appears in introductory textbooks on Islam. The notion that "Islam was born in the clear light of history" still seems to be assumed by a great many writers of such texts. While the need to reconcile varying historical traditions is generally recognized, usually this seems to pose no greater problem to the authors than having to determine "what makes sense" in a given situation. To students acquainted with approaches such as source criticism, oral formulaic composition, literary analysis and structuralism, all quite commonly employed in the study of Judaism and Christianity, such naive historical study seems to suggest that Islam is being approached with less than academic candor.[47]

Accompanying an uncritical attitude toward Islam goes a corresponding myth of its superiority: its greater tolerance, its greater rationality, its sense of brotherhood, its greater spirituality, and the myth of Muhammad as a wise and tolerant lawgiver. It is worthwhile examining the reasons for the uncritical attitude to Islam to see how the myths arose. I shall begin with very general reasons and then move on to more specific historical ones.

1. The need and desire to see an alien culture as in some way superior is as great as the need to see it as inferior, to be enchanted as much as to be disgusted. Familiarity with one's own culture does indeed breed contempt for it. Children finding their friends' house so much nicer, and adults in a foreign land finding that "they" do everything better are but examples of the same attitude. A person will always have a natural tendency to turn a blind eye to those

embarrassing aspects of the culture that he or she admires; the stranger in a strange land will see what he or she wants to see for personal, emotional, or theoretical reasons. Margaret Mead found "confirmation" for her theories of human nature in Samoa. What she wrote in *Coming of Age in Samoa,* "was true to our hopes and fears for the future of the world."[48] True to our hopes, maybe, but not true to the facts.

As Russell said, "One of the persistent delusions of mankind is that some sections of the human race are morally better or worse than others. . . . [Some writers] tend to think ill of their neighbors and acquaintances, and therefore to think well of the sections of mankind to which they themselves do not belong."[49]

2. Despite appearances to the contrary, the majority of the people of Western Europe and the United States retain religious beliefs, even if they are vestigial. According to a Gallup poll, only 9 percent of Americans identify themselves as either atheist, agnostic, or of no religion at all. In France, only 12 percent of all those interviewed declared themselves atheist. It is not surprising that

> for the sake of comfort and security there pours out daily, from pulpit and press, a sort of propaganda which, if it were put out for a nonreligious purpose, would be seen by everyone to be cynical and immoral. We are perpetually being urged to adopt the Christian creed not because it is true but because it is beneficial, or to hold that it must be true just because belief in it is beneficial. . . . Religion is gravely infected with intellectual dishonesty. . . . In religion it is particularly easy to escape notice, because of the common assumption that all honesty flows from religion and religion is necessarily honest whatever it does.[50]

On the whole, Western society in general and the media in particular are totally uncritical of religion. To quote Richard Dawkins, there is the widespread belief that

> religious sensitivities are somehow especially deserving of consideration—a consideration not accorded to ordinary prejudice. . . . Even secular activists are incomprehensibly soft when it comes to religion. We join feminists in condemning a work of pornography because it degrades women. But hands off a holy book that advocates stoning adultresses to death (having been convicted in courts where females are decreed unfit to give evidence)! Animal liberationists attack laboratories that scrupulously use anesthetics for all operations. But what about ritual slaughter houses in which animals have to be fully conscious when their throats are cut? . . . The rest of us are expected to defend our prejudices. But ask a religious person to justify his faith and you infringe "religious liberty."[51]

The uncritical attitude to Islam and the genesis of the myth of Islamic tolerance must be seen against the general intellectual background of Europe's first encounter with non-European civilizations especially in the sixteenth century—the Age of Exploration—when the notion of the "noble savage "was first fully developed. Of course, even prior to the discovery of the Americas, the Greeks and the Romans had the corresponding myths of a "golden age" and the virtuousness of the bar-barians. The expulsion of Adam and Eve from the Garden of Eden is but a variation of the idea of a golden age of simplicity and natural virtue putatively enjoyed in an unspoiled, ecologically sound wilderness by our ancestors.

In his *Germania,* written in 98 C.E., Tacitus contrasts the virtues of the Germans with the vices of contemporary Rome, the noble simplicity of the Teutonic culture with the corruption and pretentiousness of Roman civilization. Significantly, as an "ethnological treatise it was singularly incoherent,"[52] but it worked well as a morality tale. Montaigne, Rousseau, and Gibbon all felt its influence.

Perhaps the real founder of the sixteenth-century doctrine of the noble savage was Peter Martyr Anglerius (1459–1525). In his *De Rebus Oceanicis et Orbo Nove* of 1516, Peter Martyr criticized the Spanish conquistadors for their greed, narrow-mindedness, intolerance, and cruelty, contrasting them with the Indians, "who are happier since they are free from money, laws, treacherous judges, deceiving books, and the anxiety of an uncertain future."

But it was left to Montaigne, under the influence of Peter Martyr, to develop the first full-length portrait of the noble savage in his celebrated essay "On Cannibals" (ca. 1580), which is also the source of the idea of cultural relativism. Deriving his rather shaky information from a plain, simple fellow, Montaigne describes some of the more gruesome customs of the Brazilian Indians and concludes:

> I am not so anxious that we should note the horrible savagery of those acts as concerned that, while judging their faults so correctly, we should be so blind to our own. I consider it more barbarous to eat a man alive than to eat him dead; to tear by rack and torture a body still full of feeling, to roast it by degrees, and then give it to be trampled and eaten by dogs and swine—a practice which we have not only read about but seen within recent memory, not between ancient enemies, but between neighbors and fellow-citizens and, what is worse, under the cloak of piety and religion—than to roast and eat a man after he is dead.[53]

Elsewhere in the essay, Montaigne emphasizes the Indians' enviable simplicity, state of purity, and freedom from corruption. Even their "fighting is entirely noble."

Although Montaigne, like Tacitus and Peter Martyr, possesses only rather dubious, secondhand knowledge of these noble savages, his scant information does not prevent him from criticizing and morally condemning his own culture and civilization: "[We] surpass them in every kind of barbarity."

The seventeenth century saw the first truly sympathetic accounts of Islam, but the most influential of these, those of Jurieu and Bayle, served the same purpose as those of Tacitus, Peter Martyr, and Montaigne. Let us hear Mr. Jurieu:

> It may be truly said that there is no comparison between the cruelty of the Saracens against the Christians, and that of Popery against the true believers. In the war against the Vaudois, or in the massacres alone on St. Bartholomew's Day, there was more blood spilt upon account of religion, than was spilt by

the Saracens in all their persecutions of the Christians. It is expedient to cure men of this prejudice; that Mahometanism is a cruel sect, which was propagated by putting men to their choice of death, or the abjuration of Christianity. This is in no wise true; and the conduct of the Saracens was an evangelical meekness in comparison to that of Popery, which exceeded the cruelty of the cannibals.[54]

The whole import of Jurieu's *Lettres Pastorales* (1686–89) only becomes clear when we realize that Jurieu was a Huguenot pastor, the sworn enemy of Bossuet, and he was writing from Holland after the revocation of the Edict of Nantes. Jurieu is using the apparent tolerance of the Muslims to criticize Roman Catholicism; for him the Saracens' "evangelical meekness" is a way of contrasting Catholicism's own barbarity as demonstrated on St. Bartholomew's Day.

Pierre Bayle was much influenced by Jurieu and continued the myth of Islamic tolerance that persists to this day (see chap. 9). He contrasts the tolerance of the Turks to the persecutions of Brahmins carried out by the Portuguese in India, and the barbarities imposed on the Indians by the Spaniards in America. "[The Muslims] have always had more humanity for other religions than the Christians": Bayle was a champion of toleration—was he not himself made a victim of intolerance and forced to flee to Holland?

For Jurieu and Bayle in the seventeenth century, Turk was synonymous with Muslim; thus, Turkish tolerance turned into Muslim tolerance in general. The two writers showed no knowledge whatsoever of Muslim atrocities: the early persecutions of Christians and Jews; the massacres of Hindus and Buddhists in the early conquest of the Indian province of Sind; the intolerance of the Almohads; the persecution of the Zoroastrians, especially in the province of Khurasan. The Frenchmen even seem unaware of the slaughter of Christians in their beloved Turkey at the fall of Constantinople, when the streets literally ran red with blood—there was not much evangelical meekness in evidence then. Nor do the thinkers refer to the inhumane system of the *devshirme* in operation in contemporary Turkey.

Many religious minorities escaping Catholic or orthodox persecution sought and found refuge in Turkey: Jewish refugees from Spain after their expulsion in 1492 and 1496, the Marranos, Calvinists from Hungary, and others from Russia and Silesia. But these emigrants were there on sufferance, tolerated as second-class citizens. I discuss these questions more fully in chapter 10; however, I should like to add that it was quite fraudulent of Jurieu and Bayle to talk of Muslim tolerance in general on the basis of their scanty knowledge of Islamic history, because the religious situation varied enormously from century to century, in country to country, from ruler to ruler. One thing is certain: There never was an interfaith utopia.

Even in the seventeenth-century Turkey so admired by Bayle and Jurieu, the situation was far from rosy. Here is how the English ambassador at Constantinople described the scene in 1662:

The present vizier has in no way diminished the tyranny or the severity of his father, rather he has surpassed him by his natural hatred of Christians and their religion. As to the churches which were burnt down here two years ago at Galata and Constantinople, the site was bought at an exorbitant price from the Great Sultan by the Greeks, Armenians and Romans, but without permission to build anything in the style of churches, nor to practise rites and religious services. But these religions being too zealous, not only have they built edifices in the style of churches, but there celebrated, almost publicly, their holy services. The vizier has taken advantage of this welcome opportunity to demolish and raze to the ground their churches, something he has done with much malice and passion. He condemned the principal culprits to heavy prison sentences, except my chief dragoman.[55]

One scholar summed up the situation in the "tolerant "Turkish empire: "For strategic reasons the Turks forced the populations of the frontier region of Macedonia and the north of Bulgaria to convert, notably in the XVI and XVII centuries. Those who refused were executed or burnt alive."[56]

Letters Written by a Turkish Spy, published at the end of the seventeenth century, inaugurated the eighteenth-century vogue for the pseudoforeign letter, such as Montesquieu's *Lettres Persanes* (1721), Madame de Grafigny's *Lettres d'une Peruvienne* (ca. 1747), D'Argen's *Lettres Chinoises* (1750), Voltaire's "Asiatic" in the *Dictionnaire Philosophique* (1764), Horace Walpole's "Letter from Xo Ho, a Chinese Philosopher at London, to his friend Lien-Chi, at Peking" (1757), and Goldsmith's *Citizen of the World* (1762), in which Lien Chi Altangi pronounces philosophical and satirical comments on the manners of the English.

Thus, by the eighteenth century, the noble savage was simply a device to criticize and comment on the follies of one's own civilization. The noble savage is no longer a simpleton from the jungle but a sophisticated and superior observer of the contemporary scene in Europe. By emphasizing the corruption, vice, and degradation of the Europeans, eighteenth-century writers exaggerated the putative superiority of the alien culture, the wisdom of the Chinese, Persian, or Peruvian moralist and commentator. The European authors were not really interested in other cultures for their own sake; in fact, they had very little knowledge of these civilizations.

Against this intellectual background, we can understand why the eighteenth century so readily adopted the myth of Muhammad as a wise and tolerant ruler and lawgiver, when it was presented as such by Count Henri de Boulainvilliers (1658–1722). Boulainvilliers's apologetic biography of Muhammad appeared posthumously in London in 1730. It is impossible to exaggerate the importance of this book in shaping Europe's view of Islam and its founder, Muhammad; it certainly much influenced Voltaire and Gibbon.

Boulainvilliers had no knowledge of Arabic and had to rely on secondary sources; thus his work is by no means a work of serious scholarship. On the contrary it contains many errors and "much embroidery."[57] Nonetheless, Boulainvilliers was able to use Muhammad and the origins of Islam as "a vehicle of his own theological prejudices," and as a weapon against Christianity in general and the clergy in particular. He found Islam reasonable; it did not require one to believe in impossibilities—no mysteries, no miracles. Muhammad, though not divine, was an incomparable statesman and a greater legislator than anyone produced by ancient Greece.

Jeffery has rightly called this work "a bombastic laudation of Mohammad in the interests of belittling Christianity." Hurgronje calls it "an anti-clerical romance, the material of which was supplied by a superficial knowledge of Islam drawn from secondary sources." A little tar from Boulainvilliers's brush can be detected in Gibbon's *History of the Decline and Fall of the Roman Empire.*[58]

George Sale's translation of the Koran (1734) is the first accurate one in English. Like Boulainvilliers, whose biography of Muhammad he had carefully read, Sale firmly believed that the Arabs "seem to have been raised up on purpose by God, to be a scourge to the Christian church, for not living answerably to that most holy religion which they had received."[59]

The attitude of Voltaire can be seen as typical of the sentiments prevailing throughout the entire century. Voltaire seems to have regretted what he had written of Muhammad in his scurrilous and—to a Muslim—blasphemous play *Mahomet* (1742), which presents the Prophet as an impostor who enslaved men's souls: "Assuredly, I have made him out to be more evil than he was."[60] But, in his *Essai sur les Moeurs* (1756) and various entries in the *Dictionnaire Philosophique,* Voltaire shows himself to be prejudiced in Islam's favor at the expense of Christianity in general, and Catholicism in particular. Like Boulainvilliers and Sale, both of whom he had read, Voltaire uses Islam as a pretext to attack Christianity, which for him remained the "most ridiculous, the most absurd, and bloody religion that has ever infected the world."[61] Like many eighteenth-century intellectuals, Voltaire was a deist, that is, "he believed in the existence of God; while opposing revealed religion—miracles, dogmas, and any kind of priesthood."

In his "The Sermon of the Fifty" (1762), Voltaire attacks Christian mysteries like transubstantiation as absurd, Christian miracles as incredible, and the Bible as "full of contradictions." The God of Christianity was a "cruel and hateful tyrant." The true God, the sermon continues, "surely cannot have been born of a girl, nor died on the gibbet, nor be eaten in a piece of dough." Nor could he have inspired "books filled with contradictions, madness and horror."[62]

By contrast, Voltaire finds the dogmas of Islam simplicity itself: there is but one God, and Muhammad is his Prophet. For all deists, the superficial rationality of Islam was appealing: no priests, no miracles, no mysteries. To this was added other false beliefs such as Islam's absolute tolerance of other religions, in contrast to Christian intolerance.

Gibbon was much influenced by Boulainvilliers in particular, but also by the eighteenth-century Weltanschauung with its myths and preoccupations, in short, what we have been examining throughout this chapter. By the time Gibbon came round to writing his *History* (the first volume of *Decline and Fall* came out in 1776), there was, as Bernard Lewis puts it, "a vacancy for an Oriental myth. Islam was in many ways suitable." But what happened to the previously mentioned

Chinese, who also managed to fascinate Europeans? Here is how Lewis sums up the situation in the latter half of the eighteenth century:

> Europe, it seems, has always needed a myth for purposes of comparison and castigation. . . . The eighteenth-century Enlightenment had two ideal prototypes, the noble savage and the wise and urbane Oriental. There was some competition for the latter role. For a while the Chinese, held up as a model of moral virtue by the Jesuits and of secular tolerance by the philosophers, filled it to perfection in the Western intellectual shadowplay. Then disillusionment set in, and was worsened by the reports of returning travellers whose perceptions of China were shaped by neither Jesuitry nor philosophy, but by experience. By the time Gibbon began to write, there was a vacancy for an Oriental myth. Islam was in many ways suitable.[63]

What Bernard Lewis tells us about Gibbon is applicable to almost all the writers on Islam in the seventeenth and eighteenth centuries: "[Gibbon's] own imperfect knowledge and the defective state of European scholarship at the time hampered his work and sometimes blunted the skepticism which he usually brought to the sources and subjects of his historical inquiries. . . . The Muslim religious myths enshrined in the traditional biographical literature on which all his sources ultimately rest were more difficult for him to detect, and there are failures of perception and analysis excusable in a historian of the time."[64]

Gibbon, like Voltaire, painted Islam in as favorable a light as possible to better contrast it with Christianity. The English historian emphasized Muhammad's humanity as a means of indirectly criticizing the Christian doctrine of the divinity of Christ. Gibbon's anticlericalism led him to underline Islam's supposed freedom from that accursed class, the priesthood. Indeed, the familiar pattern is reemerging— Islam is being used as a weapon against Christianity.

Gibbon's deistic view of Islam as a rational, priest-free religion, with Muhammad as a wise and tolerant lawgiver, enormously influenced the way all Europeans perceived their sister religion for years to come. Indeed, it established myths that are still accepted totally uncritically by scholars and laymen alike.

Both Voltaire and Gibbon subscribed to the myth of Muslim tolerance, which to them meant Turkish tolerance. But eighteenth-century Turkey was far from being an inter-faith utopia. The traveler Carsten Niebuhr recalls that Jews were treated contemptuously. Another British ambassador describes the situation in Constantinople in 1758: "The Great Sultan himself has shown us that he is determined to maintain and enforce his laws, those concerning clothes have often been repeated and with remarkable solemnity. . . . A Jew during his sabbath was the first victim; the Great Sultan, who was walking around incognito, met him, . . . and had him executed, his throat was cut on the spot. The next day, it was the turn of an Armenian, he was sent to the vizier. . . . A universal terror has struck everyone."[65]

Another ambassador in Constantinople in 1770 writes that a law was passed whereby any Greeks, Armenians, and Jews seen outside their homes after nightfall were to be hanged without exception. A third ambassador writing in 1785 describes how any Christian churches that were secretly repaired by the Christians were dismantled by the Turkish authorities because of protests by Muslim mobs.[66]

Carlyle's account of Muhammad in *Heroes and Hero Worship* (1841) is often considered the first truly sympathetic portrait of the Islamic leader by a Western intellectual. According to Professor Watt, Thomas Carlyle "laughed out of court the idea of an impostor being the founder of one of the world's great religions."[67] Laughter is no substitute for argument, and valid arguments are singularly lacking in Carlyle's essay. Instead, we are presented "violent exclamatory rhetoric,"[68] and wild mumblings about "mysteries of nature." What "arguments" there are are fallacious. Muhammad cannot have been an impostor. Why not? It is inconceivable that so many people could have been taken in by a mere trickster and insincere fraud. His genuineness lies in the success of his religion—truth by numbers. Carlyle parades the total number of Muslims, which he takes to be 180 million, in front of our eyes to impress us and imply falsely that Muhammad could not have persuaded so many to embrace a false religion. But Muhammad only persuaded a few thousand people—the rest have simply followed and copied one another. A large number of Muslims blindly follow the religion of their fathers as something given. It is absurd to suggest that the vast majority have examined the arguments for and against the sincerity of Muhammad.

To assess the truth of a doctrine by the number of people who believe it is also totally ridiculous. The number of people who believe in Scientology is increasing yearly. Is its truth also growing year by year? There are more Christians worldwide than Muslims—is Christianity more true than Islam? When a book entitled *100 Authors Against Einstein* was published, Einstein remarked, "If I were wrong, then one would have been enough!" The converse is also true.

"But, at least, an insincere man could not have been so successful, leaving aside the truth of what he preached." Again, an obviously fallacious argument. How do we know Muhammad was sincere? "Because otherwise he would not have been so successful." Why was he so successful? "Because he was sincere"? A patently circular argument! According to an anecdote, L. Ron Hubbard bet Arthur C. Clarke that he could start a new religion; the former therapist then went out and founded the religion of Scientology. It is especially difficult to know how much of their own mumbo jumbo charlatans believe. Televangelists; mediums; gurus; the Reverend Moon; the founders of religions, cults, and movements— there is a bit of the Elmer Gantry in all of them.

Like his predecessors, Carlyle had a superficial knowledge of Islam—we can safely say that as a piece of scholarship, his essay on Muhammad is totally worthless—but, unlike them, he used Islam as a weapon against materialism and Benthamite utilitarianism. Deeply perturbed by the mechanistic world that was emerging because of the Industrial Revolution, he had to resort to the comforting myth of the wisdom of the East. Like Flaubert's Bouvard, Carlyle longed for and expected from the Orient the regeneration that would wake the West from its spiritual paralysis. Carlyle adumbrated certain ideas that were to reappear throughout the nineteenth and twentieth centuries. The historian saw Islam as a confused form of Christianity, a bastard kind of Christianity, shorn of its absurd details. Where Dante and his contemporaries had seen Islam as Christian heresy, and as something inferior, Carlyle saw it more positively: "Mahomet's Creed we called a kind of Christianity; . . . I should say a better kind than that of those miserable Syrian Sects, with their vain janglings about Homoiousion and Homoousion, the head full of worthless noise, the heart empty and dead!"[69]

Carlyle's actual portrait of Muhammad is but a reformulation of the idea of the noble savage but in religious garb: as someone in direct touch with the mysteries of existence, life, and Nature; full of mystical intuition of the real nature of things denied to us in the skeptical, civilized West. "A spontaneous, passionate, yet just, true-meaning man! Full of wild faculty, fire and light: of wild worth, all uncultured; working out his life-task in the depths of the Desert there. . . . The word of such a man is a Voice direct from Nature's own heart." Elsewhere, Carlyle describes Muhammad as "an uncultured semi-barbarous Son of Nature, much of the Bedouin still clinging to him."[70]

The Scottish essayist sees the Arabs in general as active but also meditative, with wild strong feelings, and they possess that supreme quality "religiosity." Their religion is heartily believed. What is most important is sincerity, not truth—it hardly matters what is believed as long as it is believed with a fierceness that goes beyond mere reason. "The very falsehoods of Mahomet are truer than the truths of [an insincere man]."[71]

Russell and others have seen in Carlyle's ideas the intellectual ancestry of fascism. Carlyle's fascism can be seen not only in his uncritical adulation of the strong leader, but also in his sentimental glorification of violence, cruelty, extremism, and irrationalism, in his contempt for reason: "A candid ferocity . . . is in him; he does not mince matters."[72] It is astonishing that anyone took any of Carlyle's drivel seriously. But it is equally sad that Muslims peddle this nonsense as a separate pamphlet, as a kind of seal of approval to show that a European takes their Prophet seriously. It is also surprising, since a careful reading of the chapter shows Muhammad in less than a flattering light—he is not always sincere, his moral precepts are not of the finest, he is by no means the truest of prophets, and so on. Above all, this chapter contains the famous insult to the Koran: "A wearisome confused jumble, crude, incondite; endless iterations, longwindedness, entanglement; most crude incondite—insupportable stupidity, in short! Nothing but a sense of duty could carry any European through the Koran."[73] Or us through Carlyle!

The publication of this chapter as a separate pamphlet has meant that most Muslims have been consciously or unconsciously protected from the extraordinary following chapter on "Hero As Poet," where Carlyle takes back everything positive he ever said about Muhammad. The historian advises us that first, one would have to be at a fairly primitive stage of development to believe in prophets. Second, Muhammad "speaks to great masses of men, in the coarse dialect adapted to such; a dialect filled with inconsistencies, crudities, follies: on the great masses alone can he act, and there with good and with evil strangely blended."[74] Third, Muhammad's impact wanes:

> It was intrinsically an error that notion of Mahomet's, of his supreme Prophethood: and has come down to us inextricably involved in error to this day; dragging along with it such a coil of fables, impurities, intolerances, as makes it a questionable step for me here and now to say, as I have done, that Mahomet was a true Speaker at all, and not rather an ambitious charlatan, perversity and simulacrum; no Speaker, but a Babbler! Even in Arabia, as I compute, Mahomet will have exhausted himself and become obsolete. . . . Alas, poor Mahomet; all that he was conscious of was a mere error; a futility and triviality.[75]

And the fourth and final blasphemy: "His Koran has become a stupid piece of prolix absurdity; we do not believe, like him, that God wrote that!"[76]

Many of the European apologists of Islam of the seventeenth and eighteenth centuries had no proper acquaintance with the Arabic sources; most had only a superficial knowledge of their subject. They used Islam as a weapon against intolerance, cruelty, dogma, the clergy, and Christianity.

Many European apologists of Islam of the nineteenth and twentieth centuries had a far greater knowledge of Islam and were, by contrast, devout Christians—priests, missionaries, curates—who realized that to be consistent they had to accord Islam a large measure of religious equality, to concede religious insight to Muhammad. They recognized that Islam was a sister religion, heavily influenced by Judeo-Christian ideas; and Christianity and Islam stood or fell together. They knew that if they started criticizing the dogmas, doctrines, and absurdities of Islam, their own fantastic structure would start to crumble and would eventually crash around them. They perceived a common danger in certain economic, philosophical, and social developments in the West—the rise of rationalism, skepticism, atheism, secularism; the Industrial Revolution; the Russian Revolution; and the rise of communism and materialism. Sir Hamilton Gibb writes of Islam as a Christian "engaged in a common spiritual enterprise."[77] But let us beware of skepticism: "Both Christianity and Islam suffer under the weight of worldly pressure, and the attack of scientific atheists and their like," laments Norman Daniel.[78]

Hence, Christian scholars tend to be rather uncritical of Islam, a tendency arising from a wish not to offend Muslim friends and Muslim colleagues. A writer might offer explicit apologies for penning something that might be offensive to Muslim eyes, or use various devices to avoid seeming to take sides, or avoid making judgments about the issue under discussion. Professor Watt in his preface to his biography of Muhammad provides an example of this maneuvering: "In order to avoid deciding whether the Quran is or is not the Word of God, I have refrained from using the expressions 'God says' and 'Muhammad says' when referring to the Quran, and have simply said 'the Quran says.' "[79] Bernard Lewis has remarked that such measures have tended to make the discussions of modern orientalists "cautious and sometimes insincere."[80] That is putting the matter kindly. Professor Watt is a devout Christian who does not believe that the Koran is the word of God. Even more shocking is the way in which the work of great Islamicists has been amended so as not to offend Muslim sensibilties, "without changing" the meaning of the text, we are assured. As Richard Robinson said, "Religion is gravely infected with intellectual dishonesty."

The Christian scholar Watt was curate of St. Mary Boltons, London, and Old St Paul's, Edinburgh, and an ordained Episcopalian minister. By common consent, he is the greatest and one of the most influential living Islamic scholars in Britain and, perhaps, the West. Professor Watt and Sir Hamilton Gibb saw skepticism, atheism, and communism as the common enemies of all true religion. They followed Carlyle in hoping for spiritual inspiration from the East. Here Watt assesses the state of religion: "Islam—or perhaps one should rather say, the East—has tended to overemphasize divine sovereignty, whereas in the West too much influence has been attributed to man's will, especially in recent times. Both have strayed from the true path, though in different directions. The West has probably something to learn of that aspect of truth which has been so clearly apprehended in the East."[81] (Notice how the East has the last word. Has the East nothing to learn from the West?)

Throughout his article "Religion and Anti-Religion," Professor Watt can barely disguise his contempt for secularism. "The wave of secularism and materialism is receding," notes Watt[82] with approval. "Most serious minded men in the Middle East realize the gravity of the problems of the present time, and are therefore aware of the need for a religion that will enable them to cope with the situations that arise from the impingement of these problems on their personal lives." Watt then goes on to discuss the work of Manfred Halpern, who

> speaks of the Muslim Brethren in Egypt, Syria and elsewhere, together with movements like Fida'iyan-i Islam in Persia and Khaksars and Jama'at-i Islam in Pakistan, as neo-Islamic totalitarianism, and points out their resemblances to fascism, including the National Socialism of Germany under Adolf Hitler. From a purely political point of view this may be justified, and the resemblances certainly exist. Yet in a wider perspective this characterization is misleading. It is true that these movements sometimes "concentrate on mobilizing passion and violence to enlarge the power of their charismatic leader and the solidarity of the movement," . . . and that "they champion the values and emotions of a heroic past, but repress all free critical analysis of either past roots or present problems." Yet political ineptitude and even failure do not outweigh their positive significance as marking a resurgence of religion. . . . The neo-Islamic mass movements, far from being tantamount to national socialism or fascism, are likely to be an important barrier against such a development.

Watt's wonderful euphemism for fascism is "political ineptitude"; he asks us to overlook this fascism, and asks us instead to admire it for its "positive significance as marking a resurgence of religion." Watt's support for what Amir Taheri calls

"Holy Terrorists" is worth pondering. It must not be forgotten that the Muslim Brethren was a terrorist organization whose founder made no secret of his admiration for Hitler and Mussolini. After the end of the Second World War, Hassan's Muslim Brethren launched a series of attacks on civilian targets; cinemas, hotels, and restaurants were bombed or set on fire, and women dressed incorrectly were assailed with knives. The group also launched a series of assassinations.

Yes—we are asked to overlook this in the name of religious resurgence.

Watt reveals even more disturbing qualities—a mistrust of the intellect and a rejection of the importance of historical objectivity and truth: "This emphasis on historicity, however, has as its complement a neglect of the truth of symbols; and it may be that ultimately 'symbolic truth' is more important than 'historical truth.' "[83] In "Introduction to the Quran," Watt seems to have a very tenuous grasp on the notion of truth; indeed, objective truth is abandoned altogether in favor of total subjectivism:

> The systems of ideas followed by Jews, Christians, Muslims, Buddhists and others are all true insofar as they enable human beings to have a more or less satisfactory "experience of life as a whole." So far as observation can tell, none of the great systems is markedly inferior or superior to the others. Each is therefore true. In particular the Quran is in this sense true. The fact that the Quranic conception of the unity of God appears to contradict the Christian conception of the unity of God does not imply that either system is false, nor even that either conception is false.
>
> Each conception is true in that it is part of a system which is true. Insofar as some conception in a system seems to contradict the accepted teaching of science—or, that of history in so far as it is objective—that contradiction raises problems for the adherents of the system, but does not prove that the system as a whole is inferior to others. That is to say, the Quranic assertion that the Jews did not kill Jesus does not prove that the Quranic system as a whole is inferior to the Christian, even on the assumption that the crucifixion is an objective fact.[84]

In this astonishing passage of intellectual dishonesty, Watt performs all sorts of mental gymnastics in an effort to please everyone, to not offend anyone. Leaving aside the problem of the vagueness of Watt's terminology—terms like "experience of life as a whole," "conception," "Quranic system"—we can now understand why British Islamicists have been so uncritical of Islam. The non-Muslim scholar, continues Watt, "is not concerned with any question of ultimate truth, since that, it has been suggested, cannot be attained by man. He *assumes the truth* [my emphasis], in the relative sense just explained, of the Quranic system of ideas." Under such conditions, the scholar is not likely to be critical of anyone's "belief system" as long as it meets his or her "spiritual needs."

The attitude here exemplified by Watt was brilliantly exposed and attacked by Julien Benda in his classic *Betrayal of the Intellectuals*, whose French title I took as the motto to this section. Benda wrote:

But the modern "clerks" [intellectuals] have held up universal truth to the scorn of mankind, as well as universal morality. Here the "clerks" have positively shown genius in their effort to serve the passions of the laymen. It is obvious that truth is a great impediment to those who wish to set themselves up as distinct; from the very moment when they accept truth, it condemns them to be conscious of themselves in a universal. What a joy for them to learn that this universal is a mere phantom, that there exist only particular truths, Lorrain truths, Provencal truths, Britanny truths, the harmony of which in the course of centuries constitutes what is beneficial, respectable, true in France.[85]

Watt would add a Muslim truth, a Christian truth, and so on; or as he put it in *Islamic Revelation,* "Each [great religion] is valid in a particular cultural region, but not beyond that."

Benda was trying to combat the rise of nationalism in the twenties, as was Russell in his "The Ancestry of Fascism," which brilliantly demonstrated that the abandonment of the idea of objective truth leads to fascism. For Hitler the conception of science as the pursuit of truth, objective truth, was meaningless. Hitler rejected or accepted doctrines on political grounds.

The fever of nationalism which has been increasing ever since 1848 is one form of the cult of unreason. The idea of one universal truth has been abandoned; there is English truth, French truth, German truth, . . . Rationality, in the sense of an appeal to a universal and impersonal standard of truth, is of supreme importance to the well-being of the human species, not only in ages in which it easily prevails, but also, and even more, in those less fortunate times in which it is despised and rejected as the vain dream of men who lack the virility to kill where they cannot agree.[86]

Karl Popper also attacks moral and intellectual relativism as the main philosophical malady of our time, and his comments are pertinent in this context—one even has the impression that Popper is replying directly to Watt. Popper begins by looking at one deceptive argument that is often used in defense of relativism a la Watt. Quoting Xenophanes, Popper agrees that we tend to see our gods, and our world from our own point of view—we tend to be subjective. But it is going too far to conclude that our own particular historical and cultural background is an insurmountable barrier to objectivity:

We can, in stages get rid of some of this bias [or subjectivity], by means of critical thinking and especially of listening to criticism. . . . Secondly it is a fact that people with the most divergent cultural backgrounds can enter into fruitful discussion, provided they are interested in getting nearer to the truth, and are ready to listen to each other, and to learn from each other. . . . [It is also important not to take] this step towards criticism, for a step towards relativism. *If two parties disagree, this may mean that one is wrong, or the other, or both:* this is the view of the criticist. *It does not mean,* as the relativist will have it, *that both may be equally right.* They may be equally wrong, no doubt, though they need not be. *But anybody who says that to be equally wrong means to be equally right is merely playing with words* or with metaphors.

It is a great step forward to learn to be self-critical; to learn to think that the other fellow may be right—more right than we ourselves. But there is a great danger involved in this: we may think that both, the other fellow and we ourselves, may be right. But this attitude, modest and self-critical as it may appear to us, is neither as modest nor as self-critical as we may be inclined to think; *for it is more likely that both . . . are wrong.* Thus self criticism should not be an excuse for laziness and for the adoption of relativism.[87] (my emphases)

Apart from its sentimentality and laziness, such a view as that espoused by Watt has logical consequences that Watt himself would not accept. If there is total incommensurability between "religous beliefs," then it is sheer arrogance to talk of higher and lower religions. As I ask later in chapter 10, why is monotheism seen as something higher than polytheism? Why not allow equal intellectual respectability to the Church of Scientology or the Bahais or the Moonies; the cults of Reverend Jones, the Children of God, or any of those cults discussed in Professor Evans's *Cults of Unreason*? Watt can no longer legitimately use the terms "inferior" or "superior," or even, for that matter, "true."

Furthermore, there is extraordinary condescension implicit in such an attitude. Watt is treating Muslims and Christians as imbecile children whose beliefs in Santa Claus and the Tooth Fairy must not be questioned because they do them no harm, but do bring them comfort. "It is not by delusion, however exalted, that mankind can prosper, but only by unswerving courage in the pursuit of truth," wrote Russell.

Time and again Watt tells us that what is important is "symbolic truth" and not historical truth. But both Muslims and Christians themselves explicitly reject this. J. L. Thompson has pointed out that "many Old Testament scholars have been inclined to believe that not only is history central to the message of Israel, but that an acceptance of the historicity of Israel's early traditions, particularly those about the biblical patriarchs, is essential to Christian faith, even, that belief in the resurrection depends directly on the historical facticity of the promise to the patriarchs." Roland de Vaux has asserted several times that the task of scientifically establishing the historical foundations of these biblical traditions is of the utmost importance, "for if the historical faith of Israel is not founded in history, such faith is erroneous, and therefore, our faith is also." De Vaux maintains that if faith is to survive, the close relationship between religious history and objective history must be maintained. He claims that to reject the historicity of Israel's "religious history" would be to question, in an ultimate way the ground of faith itself."[88]

An example similar to Watt's doublethink comes from another Western apologist of Islam, Norman Daniel, who writes:

It is essential for Christians to see Muhammad as a holy figure; to see him, that is, as Muslims see him. If they do not do so, they must cut themselves off from comprehension of Islam. This does not mean that they must assert that Muhammad was holy, or even perhaps, think that he was so, it is possible not to accept as true the fact alleged by Muslims, that God spoke through Muhammad, but yet to judge the resulting situation as though it were true. If people believe it to be true, that will not make it true, but their actions will be the same as they would have been, if it had been true. . . . But if some such spiritual and mental borrowing does not take place, no further progress is possible."[89]

As Rodinson remarked truly, understanding has given way to apologetics. Daniel also seems unable to grasp the notion of objective truth. Daniel and Watt and, in France, scholars like Louis Massignon have all emphasized the common spiritual struggle in which all monotheistic creeds are engaged. Even the Vatican Ecumenical Council conceded in 1962 that Islam had given mankind important truths about God, Jesus, and the prophets.

In view of the arguments developed earlier, it is not at all surprising that Christian and Jewish religious leaders joined hands and closed ranks to condemn Rushdie without scarcely a murmur against the un-Christian call to murder. The Vatican's semiofficial mouthpiece, *L'Osservatore Romano*, criticized Rushdie more roundly than the ayatollah. Cardinal John O'Connor of New York urged Catholics not to read the book, while Cardinal Albert Decourtray of Lyons called *The Satanic Verses* an insult to religion. Meanwhile in Israel, the chief Ashkenazi rabbi, Avraham Shapira, wanted the book banned: "One day this religion is attacked, and the next day it will be that one."[90] More recently, but in the same vein, the Archbishop of Canterbury, Dr. Carey, expressed his understanding of the hurt feelings of the Muslims, since Rushdie's book "contained an outrageous slur on the Prophet."

What will Dr. Carey make of the outrageous slur on Jesus Christ contained in the Koran? The Koran explicitly denies the crucifixion; in fact, in the words of Rice, "There is not one cardinal fact concerning the life, person, and work of the Lord Jesus Christ which is not either denied, perverted, misrepresented, or at least ignored in Mohammedan theology."[91] As the *Muslim World* put it, "Islam is, in a sense, the only anti-Christian religion."[92] Will Dr. Carey forgo his vicarious pleasure at this punishment of atheists and wake up from his dogmatic slumbers when Muslims begin slashing paintings depicting the Crucifixion in the National Gallery? After all, every crucifixion, in whatever form, is an insult to Muslims and denies the veracity of the Koran, which remains, for all Muslims, "the Word of God Himself."

As the *Economist* said, "Rabbis, priests and mullahs are it seems, uniting to restrain free speech, lest any member of their collective flock should have his feelings hurt. . . . The Rushdie affair is showing not just that some Muslims do not understand the merits of free speech. It shows that many Western clerics do not either."[93]

This unexpected support from Christian and Jewish clerics was gratefully received in Iran: "[They] have understood the conditions and objectives of these colonialist efforts to negate divine values and to insult the divine prophets."[94] Muslims paid Christians back for their support: in Istanbul one had the extraordinary spectacle of Muslims joining hands with Christians to protest against the showing of *The Last Temptation of Christ.*

By the 1920s, left-wing and liberal intellectuals in the West had begun to feel decidedly uneasy about European colonialism and imperialism. As Russell remarked, "A rather curious form of this admiration for groups to which one does not belong is the belief in the superior virtue of the oppressed: subject nations."[95] Any criticism of Islam or Islamic countries was seen as a racist attack, or worse, as a Western-Zionist conspiracy. Just to see the influence of Roman law on Islamic law was now, to quote Patricia Crone,

> considered ethnocentric and offensive to Islam; and though Greco Roman influences are likely to be somewhat less offensive than Jewish ones, it is only in the the field of Islamic art, science and philosophy that the classical Fortleben is nowadays discussed without circumlocution or apology. (All three fields are of course considerably more marginal to the Muslim self-definition than theology and law.) As the old-fashioned Orientalist has given way to the modern historian, Arabist or social scientist with a tender post-colonial conscience and occasionally more substantial interest in maintaining Muslim goodwill, both the inclination and the ability to view the Werden und Wesen of the Islamic world from the point of view of the Fertile Crescent have been lost, and Islamic civilization has come to be taught and studied with almost total disregard for the Near East in which it was born.[96]

By the mid-1960s and early 1970s, there was a growing minority of Muslims in western Europe, and in the interests of multiculturalism, we were taught that each civilization is its own miracle. Multicultural workshops arose in schools and universities, where even the thought of a critical attitude was an anathema. I discuss cultural relativism, multiculturalism, and their disastrous consequences more fully in chapter 17. Suffice it to say here that in such a climate "criticism" was equated with racism, neocolonialism, and fascism.

The wake of the Rushdie affair bears striking parallels to the situation in the '20s, '30s, '40s, and '50s, when left-wing intellectuals were reluctant to criticize either the theory or practice of communism—there was, as Russell pointed out, "a conspiracy of concealment."[97] When Russell's courageous book criticizing Soviet Russia and Communism in general first came out in 1920, it met with hostility from the left. V. S. Naipaul's *Amongst the Believers* got a similar reception from intellectuals and Islamophiles, because the author dared to criticize the Iranian Revolution and, subtly, Islam itself.

George Orwell, Arthur Koestler, and Robert Conquest have all pointed out the lies left-wing intellectuals swallowed about Lenin, Stalin, and Communism so as not to play into the hands of reactionary forces. In modern parlance, truth was less important than political correctness. Such a climate held criticism and debate taboo: "any critical utterance was regarded by the worshipers as blasphemy and crime."[98] There was also, in Koestler's phrase, an unconditional surrender of the critical faculties.[99]

Again, without pushing the analogy too far, one might compare Sartre's attitude to Stalin's forced labor camps to Foucault's stance on Khomeini's atrocities. Sartre[100] thought the evidence for the labor camps should be ignored or suppressed in order not to demoralize the French proletariat. Foucault, writing in October 1978, enthused over the events in Iran, "which recalled something that the West had forgotten since the Renaissance and the great crises of Christianity, namely the possibility of a 'political spirituality.' "[101] An Iranian girl wrote an eloquent letter complaining of Foucault's fatuous admiration for Islam:

> After 25 years of silence and oppression do the Iranian people only have the choice between the Savak [the Shah's secret police] and religious fanaticism? Spirituality? A return to the popular source of Islam? Saudi Arabia is gorging itself at the same source. Lovers' heads and robbers' hands are falling. For the Left in the West. . . . Islam is desirable—but elsewhere. Many Iranians like me are confused and in despair at the idea of an Islamic government. [These Iranians] know what they are talking about. In the countries surrounding Iran, Islam is sheltering feudal or pseudo-revolutionary oppression. Often in countries like Tunisia, Pakistan and Indonesia, and in my own country, Islam, unfortunately, is the only means of expression for a muzzled people. The Liberal Left in the West should realize what a dead weight Islamic Law can be for a society that is desirous of change, and ought not to be seduced by a cure that is worse than the disease.

Foucault wrote an incomprehensible "reply"—incomprehensible in that his reply did not address itself to any of the charges leveled against the Left's romanticizing of Islam. Later, after Khomeini had seized power, and even more heads (in their thousands) were falling, Foucault was unrepentant and unapologetic and refused to criticize Khomeini's "political spirituality."

It is worth noting the recurring theme of hatred of the West in the writings of fellow travelers of Communism and Islam, like Foucault ("something that the West had forgotten"), and the age-old myth of Eastern spirituality, "political spirituality." Indeed, the self-hatred displayed by Western intellectuals deserves a chapter of its own—their self-abasement is truly astonishing. They criticize the West and its values in terms that would be denounced or repressed, condemned as "imperialist," "racist," or "colonialist" if they were applied to Islamic civilization. All the while, these intellectuals earn nice salaries from Western universities.

It would be fitting to end this section with the case of Roger Garaudy. At one moment Comrade Garaudy was the official philosopher of the French Communist party and an important member of the party's political bureau. One English critic has described him as "formerly witchfinder general, now dispenser of extreme unction, in quick succession, champion of Stalin and defender of the Khruschevite faith."[102] After the Communist party expelled Garaudy for factionalism, the classic Stalinist converted to various causes. He first flirted with "Marxist Humanism," then finally converted to Islam—from one form of totalitarianism to another—not such a big step after all. One hopes for him that this is truly his final resting place, for the penalty for apostasy in Islam is death.

Given their uncritical attitude, it is hardly surprising that Islamologists are accused "by reformers and secularists of supporting and encouraging conservative and fundamentalist forces in their resistance to change." Professor Bernard Lewis continues: "I have often heard such charges, with anger from strangers and with anguish from friends, and I must admit that they are not entirely unjustified, since some of the fundamentalists are clearly of the same opinion." Having conceded that much, Lewis takes it all back by claiming, "the coincidence of views between Islamologists and Islamic fundamentalists is apparent, not real, and the reformers' accusations of complicity in reaction arise from a failure to distinguish between descriptive and prescriptive statements."[103]

But it is quite clear for reasons I have already discussed throughout this chapter that scholars like Watt, Daniel, and Esposito are more apologists than objective historians. Watt expressly rejects the possibility of objectivity. Norman Stillman describes Watt's justification of the murder of between 600 and 900 Jews of Qurayzah by the Muslims under Muhammad as "as strong an apologetic defense of Muhammad's conduct on this occasion as might be expected from any devout Muslim."[104] Watt also goes beyond the descriptive when he describes in triumphant words al-Ghazali's encounter with Greek philosophy, an encounter "from which Islamic theology emerged victorious and enriched."[105] It is clear where Watt's allegiances lie. Professor Lewis himself is clearly moving beyond the descriptive to the realms of the prescriptive when he advocates a "Christian remedy" to the problems of the contemporary Middle East, in other words, the separation of the church and state.[106]

Another disturbing development in recent years explains the uncritical attitude of Islamicists toward Islam. A British university dismissed one scholar from his academic post as lecturer in Islamic studies because of pressure from the Saudi Arabian sponsors, who decided that they did not like the way he was teaching Islam.[107]

An Algerian friend, a well-educated Muslim who is not particularly religious, came across Russell's *Why I Am Not a Christian* while looking through my books. He pounced on it with evident glee. As I learned later, he apparently considered Russell's classic to be a great blow to Christianity; at no time was my friend aware that Russell's arguments applied, mutatis mutandis, to Islam. I often wondered if I were to substitute the word "Allah" every time I used the word "God" (Allah simply being Arabic for God), would my friend be startled from his self-protecting cocoon? For example, in this passage from Nietzsche I have simply substituted "Allah" for every occurence of "God." Would my friend find this altered version more shocking than the original? "The concept of *Allah* was until now the greatest objection to existence. We deny *Allah,* we deny the responsibility in *Allah*: only thereby do we redeem the world." And what of Nietzsche's "God is dead"? It becomes *"Allah* is dead."

This is but an absurd fantasy to bring home to Muslims, in any way I can, the fact that they cannot remain oblivious to intellectual, scientific, and social developments in the West; these have implications for everyone. Muslims cannot hide forever from the philosophical implications of the insights of Nietzsche, Freud, Marx, Feuerbach, Hennell, Strauss, Bauer, Wrede, Wells, and Renan. Hume's writings on miracles are equally valid in the Islamic context—even Muslims attest to Jesus' miracles. The Koran contains references to various Old Testament and New Testament figures: Abraham, Ishmael, Isaac, Jacob, Moses, David, Jonah, Enoch, Noah, and Jesus, to name but a few. What of the rise of the critical method in Germany in the nineteenth century, and its application to the study of the Bible and religion in general? When biblical scholars say that Jonah never existed or that Moses did not write the Pentateuch, then, implicitly, the veracity of the Koran is being called into question.

Can the Koran also withstand the onslaught of Western scientific thought? What of Darwin and the theory of evolution that were to deal such a decisive blow to the biblical account of man and creation? Both the Bible and the Koran talk of Adam and Eve. Many Christians have accepted the results of science, adjusted their beliefs accordingly, and are no longer committed to the literal existence of their biblical parents. Muslims have yet to take even this first step.

2

The Origins of Islam

The most important stages in [Islam's] history were characterised by the assimilation of foreign influences. . . . Its founder, Muhammad, did not proclaim new ideas. He did not enrich earlier conceptions of man's relation to the transcendental and infinite. . . . The Arab Prophet's message was an eclectic composite of religious ideas and regulations. The ideas were suggested to him by contacts, which had stirred him deeply, with Jewish, Christian, and other elements.[108]

Ignaz Goldziher

Muhammad was not an original thinker: he did not formulate any new ethical principles, but merely borrowed from the prevailing cultural milieu. The eclectic nature of Islam has been recognized for a long time. Even Muhammad knew Islam was not a new religion, and the revelations contained in the Koran merely confirmed already existing scriptures. The Prophet always claimed Islam's affiliation with the great religions of the Jews, Christians, and others. Muslim commentators such as al-Sharestani have acknowledged that the Prophet transferred to Islam the beliefs and practices of the heathen or pagan Arabs, especially into the ceremonies of the pilgrimage to Mecca. And yet Muslims in general continue to hold that their faith came directly from heaven, that the Koran was brought down by the angel Gabriel from God himself to Muhammad. The Koran is held to be of eternal origin, recorded in heaven, lying as it does there upon the Preserved Table (suras 85.21, 6.19; 97). God is the source of Islam—to find a human origin for any part of it is not only vain but also meaningless and, of course, blasphemous.

Perhaps Muslims have the unconscious fear that if we can trace the teachings of the Koran to a purely human and earthly source, then the entire edifice of Islam will crumble. But as Renan used to say, "Religions are facts; they must be discussed as facts, and subjected to the rules of historical criticism."[109] To paraphrase Renan again,[110] the critical study of the origins of Islam will only yield definitive historical results when it is carried out in a purely secular and

34

profane spirit by people uninfluenced by dogmatic theology. Only then will we recover the historical Muhammad, and only then will his extraordinary life be integrated as a part of human history, with a secular meaning for all of us— Muslims and non-Muslims alike.

The works of Ignaz Goldziher and Henri Corbin on the influence of Zoroastrianism on Islam; the works of Geiger, Torrey, and Katsch on the influence of Judaism; Richard Bell's pioneering work on the influence of Christianity; the work of Wellhausen, Noldeke, Hurgronje, and Robertson Smith on the influence of Sabianism and pre-Islamic Arabia; and the work of Arthur Jeffery on the foreign vocabulary of the Koran, all combine to make us concur with Zwemer's conclusion that Islam "is not an invention, but a concoction; there is nothing novel about it except the genius of Mohammad in mixing old ingredients into a new panacea for human ills and forcing it down by means of the sword."[111]

Arabian Idolatry

It is undoubtedly true that in many passages of the Koran "the Islamic varnish only thinly covers a heathen substratum,"[112] as for example in sura 113: "In the name of the merciful and compassionate God. Say: 'I seek refuge in the Lord of the Daybreak, from the evil of what He has created; and from the evil of the night when it comes on; and from the evil of the witches who blow upon knots, and from the evil of the envious when he envies.' "

Islam owes many of its most superstitious details to old Arabian paganism especially in the rites and rituals of the Pilgrimage to Mecca (see suras 2.153; 22.28–30; 5.1–4; 22.37). We can also find traces of paganism in the names of certain old deities (suras 53.19.20; 71.22.23); in the superstitions connected with *jinns*; and in old folk tales such as those of Ad and Thamud.

Pilgrimage

People come from far corners of the land
to throw pebbles (at the Satan) and to kiss the (black stone).
How strange are the things they say!
Is all mankind becoming blind to truth?[113]

* * *

O fools, awake! The rites ye sacred hold
Are but a cheat contrived by men of old
Who lusted after wealth and gained their lust
And died in baseness—and their law is dust

Al-Ma'ari

I search for the way, but not the way to the Ka'ba and the temple
For I see in the former a troop of idolaters and in the latter a band of
    self-worshipers.

Jalal Uddin Rumi[114]

Had I not seen the Prophet kiss you, I would not kiss you myself.

Caliph 'Umar, addressing the Black Stone at Kaaba[115]

From an ethical standpoint, the Mecca pilgrimage, with its superstitious and
childish ritual, is a blot upon Mohammedan monotheism.

S. Zwemer[116]

The entire ceremony of the pilgrimage has been shamelessly taken over from
pre-Islamic practice: "a fragment of incomprehensible heathenism taken up un-
digested into Islam."[117] The Hajj or the Greater Pilgrimage to Mecca is performed
in the month of Dhu al-Hijjah, or the twelfth month of the Muslim year. It
is the fifth pillar of Islam, and an incumbent religious duty founded upon injunctions
in the Koran. Every Muslim in good health and with sufficient means must perform
the pilgrimage once in his lifetime.

The first seven days constitute the lesser pilgrimage (Umrah) that can be
performed at any time except the eighth, ninth, and tenth days of the month
of Dhu al-Hijjah. These are reserved for the Greater Pilgrimage (Hajj), which
begins on the eighth.

FIRST FIVE DAYS

When the pilgrim first arrives at a point several miles outside Mecca, he prepares
himself so that he is in a state of ritual purity or state of consecration. After
donning simple pilgrim's dress and performing the necessary ablutions and prayers,
the pilgrim enters the sacred precincts of Mecca, where he is expected to abstain
from killing animals, tearing up plants, indulging in violence, and taking part
in sexual intercourse. He makes further ablutions and prayers at the sacred mosque
of Mecca, al-Masjid al-Haram; then he kisses the sacred Black Stone, which is
set within the eastern corner of the Kaaba, the cubelike building in the center
of the roofless courtyard of the Sacred Mosque.

The pilgrim then turns to the right and circumambulates the Kaaba seven
times, three times at a quick pace, and four times at a slow pace. Each time
he passes around the Kaaba he touches the Yamani corner, where another auspicious
stone is encased, and also kisses the sacred Black Stone.

The pilgrim then proceeds to the Maqam Ibrahim (the place of Abraham),
where Abraham is said to have prayed toward the Kaaba. He performs two further
prayers and returns to the Black Stone and kisses it. Nearby is the sacred well
of Zem Zem, where according to Muslim tradition Hagar and Ishmael drank
in the wilderness. The pilgrims move on to an enclosure known as the al-Hijr,

where Muslims believe that Hagar and Ishmael are buried, and where Muhammad himself is said to have slept on the night of his miraculous journey from Mecca to Jerusalem.

SIXTH TO TENTH DAY

The pilgrim leaves the sacred mosque by one of its twenty-four gates. Outside, he climbs the gentle hill known as Mt. As Safa, all the while reciting verses from the Koran. He then runs from the top of As Safa to the summit of al-Marwah seven times, repeating various prayers. This absurd ritual commemorates Hagar's putative search for water in the wilderness.

This is the sixth day of the pilgrimage; the evening is spent at Mecca where he goes around the Kaaba once more. On the seventh day, he listens to an oration in the Great Mosque, and then, on the eighth he proceeds to Mina, where he performs the usual services of the Muslim ritual and remains the night. On the ninth day, after morning prayers, the pilgrim proceeds to Mount Arafat where the rite of "standing" (*wuquf,* in Arabic) is performed. According to Muslim tradition, Adam and Eve met here after their fall from Paradise. Here the pilgrim recites the usual prayers and listens to another oration on the theme of repentance. He then hurries (the Arabic word means "stampede") to Muzdalifah, a place between Mina and Arafat, where he is required to arrive for the sunset prayer.

The next day, the tenth, is the Day of Sacrifice, celebrated throughout the Muslim world as Id 'l-Azha. Early in the morning in Muzdalifah, the worshipers say their prayers and move on to the three pillars in Mina. The pilgrim casts seven stones at each of these pillars, the ceremony being called *ramyu 'r rijam,* the casting of stones. "Holding the pebble between the thumb and forefinger of the right hand, the pilgrim throws it at a distance of not less than fifteen feet, and says, 'In the name of God, the Almighty, I do this, and in hatred of the devil and his shame.' " The remaining pebbles are thrown in the same way. He then returns and performs the sacrifice of a goat or lamb. After the feast, the pilgrims celebrate the rite of deconsecration, when many pilgrims shave their head or simply have a few locks clipped.

Muslims rationalize this particular superstition as symbolizing Abraham's repudiation of the devil, who tried to keep the great patriarch from his divinely commanded duty of sacrificing his greatly cherished son Ishmael. The sacrifice of a lamb or goat simply commemorates the divine substitution of a ram for Abraham's sacrifice.

How did an iconoclastic, uncompromising monotheist like Muhammad ever come to incorporate these pagan superstitions into the very heart of Islam? Most historians agree that had Jews and Christians rejected Moses and Jesus and favorably received Muhammad as a prophet who taught the religion of Abraham at Mecca when Muhammad made Jerusalem the Kiblah (the direction of prayer), then Jerusalem and not Mecca would have been the sacred city, and the ancient rock (Sakrah) and not the Kaaba would have been the object of superstitious reverence.

Frustrated by the intransigence of the Jews, realizing that there was little chance of them accepting him as their new prophet, Muhammad conveniently received a command from God to change the Kiblah (sura 2.138f.) from Jerusalem to the Kaaba in Mecca. He knew that he had a good chance of eventually capturing Mecca with all its historic associations.

In A.H. 6, Muhammad tried to enter Mecca with his followers but failed. The Meccans and Medinans met at Hudaibiyah on the frontier of the sacred territory. After much negotiation, the Muslims agreed to return to Medina, but were given permission to celebrate the feast in Mecca the following year. Muhammad, with many of his followers, came to Mecca in A.H. 7 and performed the circuit of the Kaaba, kissing the Black Stone as a part of the rites.

Mecca was captured by Muhammad the following year, in A.H. 8. At first many Muslims joined the hajj along with the unbelieving Arabs, but without the Prophet himself. Soon, however, a revelation from God declared that all treaties between the Muslims and unbelievers must be revoked, and that nobody who was not a true believer might approach Mecca or the hajj (sura 9.1ff., and 28).

Finally, to quote Zwemer,

In the tenth year A.H. Muhammad made his pilgrimage to Mecca, the old shrine of his forefathers, and every detail of superstitious observance which he fulfilled has become the norm in Islam. As Wellhausen says the result is that "we now have the stations of a Calvary journey without the history of the Passion." Pagan practices are explained away by inventing Moslem legends attributed to Bible characters, and the whole is an incomprehensible jumble of fictitious lore.[118]

Islam is the creation of Central and Western Arabia. Unfortunately, our knowledge of the religion of the heathen Arabs in these regions is scanty. Lacking epigraphical evidence, the scholars have had to rely on Ibn al-Kalbi (d. A.D. 819), the author of *The Book of Idols,* on the so-called theophorous proper names, that is, names that describe the bearer as servant or gift, favor, etc., of this or that deity; on fragments of pre-Islamic poetry; and on certain polemical allusions in the Koran. "Finally," to quote Noldeke,

we have to take into consideration the fact that Muhammad incorporated in his religion a number of heathen practices and beliefs, with little or no modification; and also that various relics of heathenism, which are alien to orthodox Islam, have been retained by the Arabs down to the present day. That the adoption of a new faith does not completely transform popular beliefs, and that the old conceptions, disguised under somewhat different names, frequently persist, with or without the sanction of the religious authorities, is a matter of common observation.[119]

One might add that Muhammad very skillfully concentrated into the Muslim pilgrimage rites several ceremonies that, previously, were accomplished totally independently in different sanctuaries or localities.

Society in pre-Islamic Central Arabia was organized around the tribe, and each tribe had its principal deity, which was worshipped in a fixed sanctuary even by the wandering nomads. The deity resided in a stone and was not necessarily in human form. Sometimes the sacred stone was a statue or sometimes simply a big block of rock whose shape resembled a human. The heathen Arabs evidently imagined that the block of stone that served as a fetish was pervaded by a divine power and, in its turn, exercised a divine influence.

The names of the two hills As Safa and al-Marwa signify a stone, that is, an idol. Pagans ran between the two hills in order to touch and kiss Isaf and Naila, the idols, placed there as a means of acquiring luck and good fortune.

THE SACRED BLACK STONE AND HUBAL

We have evidence that black stones were worshipped in various parts of the Arab world; for example, Clement of Alexandria, writing ca. 190, mentioned that "the Arabs worship stone," alluding to the black stone of Dusares at Petra. Maximus Tyrius writing in the second century says, "The Arabians pay homage to I know not what god, which they represent by a quadrangular stone"; he alludes to the Kaaba that contains the Black Stone. Its great antiquity is also attested by the fact that ancient Persians claim that Mahabad and his successors left the Black Stone in the Kaaba, along with other relics and images, and that the stone was an emblem of Saturn.

In the vicinity of Mecca are various other sacred stones that were originally fetishes, "but have acquired a superficially Muhammadan character by being brought into connection with certain holy persons." [120]

The Black Stone itself is evidently a meteorite and undoubtedly owes its reputation to the fact it fell from the "heavens." It is doubly ironic that Muslims venerate this piece of rock as that given to Ishmael by the angel Gabriel to build the Kaaba, as it is, to quote Margoliouth, "of doubtful genuineness, since the Black Stone was removed by the . . . Qarmatians in the fourth [Muslim] century, and restored by them after many years: it may be doubted whether the stone which they returned was the same as the stone which they removed." [121]

Hubal was worshipped at Mecca, and his idol in red cornelian was erected inside the Kaaba above the dry well into which one threw votive offerings. It is very probable that Hubal had a human form. Hubal's position next to the the Black Stone suggests there is some connection between the two. Wellhausen thinks that Hubal originally was the Black Stone that, as we have already remarked, is more ancient than the idol. Wellhausen also points out that God is called Lord of the Kaaba, and Lord of the territory of Mecca in the Koran. The Prophet railed against the homage rendered at the Kaaba to the goddesses al-Lat, Manat, and al-Uzza, whom the pagan Arabs called the daughters of God, but Muhammad stopped short of attacking the cult of Hubal. From this Wellhausen concludes that Hubal is no other than Allah, the "god" of the Meccans. When the Meccans defeated the Prophet near Medina, their leader is said to have shouted, "Hurrah for Hubal."

Circumambulation of a sanctuary was a very common rite practiced in many localities. The pilgrim during his circuit frequently kissed or caressed the idol. Sir William Muir thinks that the seven circuits of the Kaaba "were probably emblematical of the revolutions of the planetary bodies."[122] While Zwemer goes so far as to suggest that the seven circuits of the Kaaba, three times rapidly and four times slowly were "in imitation of the inner and outer planets."[123]

It is unquestionable that the Arabs "at a comparatively late period worshipped the sun and other heavenly bodies."[124] The constellation of the Pleiades, which was supposed to bestow rain, appears as a deity. There was the cult of the planet Venus which was revered as a great goddess under the name of al-Uzza.

We know from the frequency of theophorous names that the sun (Shams) was worshipped. Shams was the titular goddess of several tribes honored with a sanctuary and an idol. Snouck Hurgronje[125] sees a solar rite in the ceremony of "wukuf" (see above page 37).

The goddess al-Lat is also sometimes identified with the solar divinity. The god Dharrih was probably the rising sun. The Muslim rites of running between Arafat and Muzdalifah, and Muzdalifah and Mina had to be accomplished after sunset and before sunrise. This was a deliberate change introduced by Muhammad to suppress this association with the pagan solar rite, whose significance we shall examine later. The worship of the moon is also attested to by proper names of people such as Hilal, a crescent, Qamar, a moon, and so on.

Houtsma[126] has suggested that the stoning that took place in Mina was originally directed at the sun demon. This view is lent plausibility by the fact that the pagan pilgrimage originally coincided with the autumnal equinox. The sun demon is expelled, and his harsh rule comes to an end with the summer, which is followed by the worship, at Muzdalifah, of the thunder god who brings fertility.

Muzdalifah was a place of fire worship. Muslim historians refer to this hill as the hill of the holy fire. The god of Muzdalifah was Quzah, the thunder god. As Wensinck says: "A fire was kindled on the sacred hill also called Quzah. Here a halt was made and this wukuf has a still greater similarity to that on Sinai, as in both cases the thunder god is revealed in fire. It may further be presumed that the traditional custom of making as much noise as possible and of shouting was originally a sympathetic charm to call forth the thunder."[127]

Frazer in the *Golden Bough* has another explanation for the ceremony of stone throwing:

> Sometimes the motive for throwing the stone is to ward off a dangerous spirit; sometimes it is to cast away an evil, sometimes it is to acquire a good. Yet, perhaps, if we could trace them back to their origin in the mind of primitive man, we might find that they all resolve themselves more or less exactly into the principle of the transference of evil. . . . This notion perhaps explains the rite of stone throwing . . . at Mecca; . . . the original idea may perhaps have been that the pilgrims cleanse themselves by transferring their ceremonial impurity to the stones which they fling on the heap. [128]

According to Juynboll, the hajj originally had a magical character

> Its purpose in early times must have been to get a happy new year with plenty of rain and sunshine, prosperity, and abundance of cattle and corn. Great fires were lit at Arafat and Muzdalifah, probably to induce the sun to shine in the new year. Water was poured on the ground as a charm against drought. Perhaps the throwing of stones at certain places in Mina, a relic of the primitive heathenism, was originally a symbol of throwing away the sins of the past year, and in this way a sort of charm against punishment and misfortune.[129]

Similarly, the hurrying between Arafat and Muzdalifah, and from Muzdalifah to Mina may have had a magical significance. The feasting at the end of all the rituals was probably a symbol of the abundance that was hoped for at the end of the year. The various obligations of abstinence imposed on the pilgrim was originally to bring the pilgrim into a state of magical power.

The Kaaba

The idol was generally placed in a sacred precinct delimited by stones. This sacred enclosure was an area of asylum for all living things. One often found a well within this sacred precinct. We do not know when the Kaaba was first constructed, but the selection of the spot undoubtedly owes something to the presence of the well Zam Zam, which provided precious water to the caravans that passed through Mecca to Yemen and Syria.

The believers rendered homage with offerings and sacrifices. Inside the Kaaba was a dry well in which offerings were placed. The pilgrim coming to pay homage to the idol often shaved his head within the sacred precinct or the sanctuary. One notices that all these rituals are present in one form or another in the Muslim hajj.

According to Muslim writers, the Kaaba was first built in heaven, where a model of it still remains, two thousand years before the creation of the world. Adam erected the Kaaba on earth but this was destroyed during the Flood. Abraham was instructed to rebuild it; Abraham was assisted by Ishmael. While looking for a stone to mark the corner of the building, Ishmael met the angel Gabriel, who gave him the Black Stone, which was then whiter than milk; it was only later that it became black from the sins of those who touched it. The above is, of course, an adaptation of the Jewish legend of the heavenly and earthly Jerusalem.

While Muir and Torrey are convinced that the Abrahamic origin of the Kaaba was a popular belief long before the time of Muhammad, Snouck Hurgronje and Aloys Sprenger agree that the association of Abraham with the Kaaba was Muhammad's personal invention, and it served as a means to liberate Islam from Judaism. Sprenger's conclusion is harsh: "By this lie, . . . Mohammed gave to Islam all that man needs and which differentiates religion from philosophy: a nationality, ceremonies, historical memories, mysteries, an assurance of entering heaven, all the while deceiving his own conscience and those of others."[130]

Allah

Islam also owes the term "Allah" to the heathen Arabs. We have evidence that it entered into numerous personal names in Northern Arabia and among the Nabatians. It occurs among the Arabs of later times, in theophorous names and on its own. Wellhausen also cites pre-Islamic literature where Allah is mentioned as a great deity. We also have the testimony of the Koran itself where He is recognized as a giver of rain, a creator, and so on; the Meccans only crime was to worship other gods beside Him. Eventually Allah was only applied to the Supreme Deity. "In any case it is an extremely important fact that Muhammad did not find it necessary to introduce an altogether novel deity, but contented himself with ridding the heathen Allah of his companions subjecting him to a kind of dogmatic purification. . . . Had he not been accustomed from his youth to the idea of Allah as the Supreme God, in particular of Mecca, it may well be doubted whether he would ever have come forward as the preacher of Monotheism."[131]

Islam also took over—or rather, retained—the following customs from the pagan Arabs: polygamy, slavery, easy divorce, and social laws generally, circumcision, and ceremonial cleanliness. Wensinck, Noldeke, and Goldziher have all contributed to the study of the animistic elements in the rituals connected with Muslim prayer.[132] In the preparations for the five daily prayers, especially in the process of ablution, the object is to free the worshipper from the presence or the influence of evil spirits and has nothing to do with bodily purity as such. It is clear from countless traditions that Muhammad himself perpetuated innumerable superstitions on the subject of demonic pollution, which he had acquired from the prevailing paganism of his youth. According to one tradition, Muhammad said, "If any of you wakens up from sleep let him blow his nose three times. For the devil spends the night in a man's nostrils." On another occasion when Muhammad saw that a certain man had left a dry spot on his foot after his ablutions, he told him to go back and wash better and then gave this homily: "If a Muslim servant of God performs the ablution, when he washes his face every sin is taken away by it with the water or with the last drop of water. And when he washes his hands, the sins of his hands are taken away with the water. And when he washes his feet all the sins which his feet have committed are taken away with water or with the last drop of water until he becomes pure from sin altogether." This bears out what Goldziher has shown: that according to semitic conception water drives away demons. The Prophet used to "wash" his feet when he wore sandals by simply passing his hands over the outside of his sandals.

Traditionally, a Muslim is required to cover his head, especially the back part of his skull. Wensinck thinks this is to prevent evil spirits from entering the body. Many other gestures, movements, the cry of the muezzin, the raising of the hands, etc., have been shown to be animistic in origin and often employed with the intention of warding off evil spirits.

Zoroastrianism

The thesis of the influence of Zoroastrianism—sometimes called Parsism—on the world's religions has been disputed by some scholars and vigorously defended by others. Widengren unhesitatingly states:

> The historical importance of the Iranian religions lies in the great role they played in Iranian developments and in the significant influence Iranian types of religion exercised in the West, especially on postexilic Jewish religion; on Hellenistic mystery religions such as Mithraism; on Gnosticism; and on Islam, in which Iranian ideas are found both in Shi'ah, the most important medieval sect, and in popular eschatology [doctrines dealing with the last times].[133]

Widengren showed the influence of Zoroastrianism on the Old Testament during the Babylonian exile of the Jews in *Die Religionen Irans* (1965). Morton Smith was perhaps the first to point out the striking similarities between Isaiah 40–48 and the Zoroastrian hymns known as Gatha, especially Gatha 44:3–5: the notion that God created light and darkness appears in both. John Hinnels has written of "Zoroastrian Savior Imagery and Its Influence on the New Testament," with this influence stemming from the contacts between the Jews and the Parthians in the second century B.C. and the middle of the first century B.C.[134]

Islam was directly influenced by the Iranian religion, but the indirect influence on Islam of Judaism and Christianity, has never been doubted. For this reason, it is worth pursuing the parallels between Judaism and Zoroastrianism.

> Ahura Mazda, the supreme lord of Iran, omniscient, omnipresent, and eternal, endowed with creative power, which he exercises especially through the medium of his Spenta Mainyu—Holy Spirit—and governing the universe through the instrumentality of angels and archangels, presents the nearest parallel to YHWH that is found in antiquity. But Ormuzd's power is hampered by his adversary, Ahriman, whose dominion, however, like Satan's shall be destroyed at the end of the world. . . . There are striking parallels . . . in their eschatological teachings—the doctrine of a regenerate world, a perfect kingdom, the coming of a Messiah, the resurrection of the dead, and the life everlasting. Both . . . are revealed religions: in the one Ahura Mazda imparts his revelation and pronounces his commandments to [Zoroaster] on the mountain of the two holy communing ones; in the other YHWH holds a similar communion with Moses on Sinai. The [Zoroastrian] laws of purification, morover, more particularly those practised to remove pollution incurred through contact with dead or unclean matter, are given in the Avestan Vendidad quite as elaborately as in the Levitical code. . . . The six days of creation in Genesis find a parallel in the six periods of Creation described in the Zoroastrian scriptures. Mankind according to each religion is descended from a single couple and Mashya (man) and Mashyana are the Iranian Adam (man) and Eve. In the Bible a deluge destroys all people except a single righteous individual and his family; in the Avesta a winter depopulates the earth except in the Vara (enclosure) of the blessed Yima. In

each case the earth is peopled anew with the best two of every kind, and is afterward divided into three realms. The three sons of Yima's successor Thraetaona, Airya, Sairima and Tura are the inheritors in the Persian account; Shem, Ham and Japheth in the semitic story. [Judaism] was strongly influenced by Zoroastrianism in views relating to angelology and demonology, and probably also in the doctrine of the resurrection.[135]

The first Islamicist of repute to take seriously the idea of the direct influence of Zoroastrianism on Islam was probably Goldziher, on whose article I rely heavily in this section.[136]

The Muslim victory, over the Sassanian Persian army at the Battle of Qadisiya in 636 A.D., marks the beginning of the first direct contact of the two peoples. This contact with a superior culture had a profound influence on the Arabs and Islam. Recently converted Persians were to bring a new sense of the religious life into Islam.

When the Umayyad dynasty was overthrown, the Abbasids founded a theocratic state under the influence of Persian religio-political ideas; indeed, the revolution of Abu Muslim, which brought the Abbasids to power, was originally a Persian movement. The Abbasids were to adopt many of the traditions of the Sassanians: they took the title of king of Persia, being perfectly aware of the relation between the institution of the khalifah and the conception of Persian kingship; their kingdom was an ecclesiastical state and they were its religious heads; like the Sassanians they considered themselves divine. There was an intimate relation between government and religion, an interdependence, nay, a perfect union with it. Government and religion were identical, and therefore religion was the government of the people.

The concept of acquiring religious merit by reciting various parts of the Koran is an echo of the Persian belief in the merit of reciting the Avestan Vendidad. In both creeds, the recital of the sacred Book relieves man of any demerits acquired on earth; it is essential, even, for the salvation of the soul. Both Muslims and Zoroastrians read the Holy Book for several days after the death of a member of family. Both communities condemn expressions of mourning for the dead.

The Muslim eschatological doctrine of the "mizan" or balance, that is, the scales on which the actions of all men shall be weighed, is borrowed from the Persians (Koran, sura 21.47). Under their influence of the scales, the Muslims calculate the value of the good deeds and bad deeds as so many units in weight. For example, the Prophet is reputed to have said: "Whoever says a prayer over the bier of the dead earns a kirat but whoso is present at the ceremony till the body is interred merits two kirats of which one is as heavy as the Mount Chod." The prayer in congregation has a value twenty-five times higher than individual prayer.

According to Muslim commentators, on Judgment Day, the angel Gabriel will hold the scales on which the good and bad deeds will be weighed, one side hanging over paradise and the other over hell. Similarly, in Parsism, on Judgment

Day, two angels will stand on the bridge between heaven and hell, examining every person as he passes. One angel, representing divine mercy, will hold a balance in his hand to weigh the actions of all men; if good deeds preponderate the persons will be permitted to pass into heaven; otherwise the second angel, representing God's justice, will throw them into hell. Other elements in the Islamic ideas of the balance come from heretical Christian sects and are part of our further discussion.

The Muslim institution of five daily prayers also has a Persian origin. Muhammad himself, at first, instituted only two daily prayers. Then, as recounted in the Koran, a third was added, giving the morning prayer, the evening prayer, and the middle prayer, which corresponded to the Jewish shakharith, minkah, and arbith. But on encountering the religious fervor of the Zoroastrians, Muslims, not wishing to be outdone in devotion, simply adopted their custom; henceforth, Muslims paid homage to their God five times a day, in imitation of the five gahs (prayers) of the Persians.

Over and above the influence of Persian ideas through Judaism and Christianity, how did Persian notions enter pre-Islamic Arabia? The merchants of Mecca constantly came in contact with Persian culture; while several Arabic poets are known to have traveled to the Arab Kingdom at al-Hira on the Euphrates, which had long been under Persian influence and as Jeffery says, "was a prime center for the diffusion of Iranian culture among the Arabs,"[137] poets, such as al-Asha, wrote poems that are full of Persian words. A large number of Persian words from Avestan and Middle Persian (that is, Pahlavi) and other expressions appear in Arabic. There is even evidence of some pagan Arabs in those regions becoming Zoroastrians. Persian influence was also felt in South Arabia, where Persian officials exercised authority in the name of the Sassanians. Above all we have the testimony of the Koran itself, which refers to the Zoroastrians as Madjus and puts them on the same level as the Jews, Sabians, and Christians, as those who believe (sura 22.17). Ibn Hisham, the biographer of the Prophet, tells us that there was one an-Nadr ibn al-Harith who used to recount to the Meccans the stories of great Rustem and of Isfandiyar and the kings of Persia, always boasting that the tales of Muhammad were not better than his own. As Torrey says, "the prophet saw his audience vanish, and was left to cherish the revenge which he took after the battle of Badr. For the too entertaining adversary, taken captive in the battle, paid for the stories with his life."[138] We also learn from Ibn Hisham that among the companions of the Prophet there was one Persian called Salman, who may well have taught Muhammad something of the religion of his ancestors.

Muhammad may well have been influenced by the Zoroastrians in his attitude to the sabbath and his hostility to the preposterous idea that God needed to take a rest after creating the world in six days. The Parsi theologians took a similar position against the Jewish sabbath. For Muhammad and all Muslims, Friday is not the sabbath, the day of repose, but a day of assemblage for the weekly celebration of the cult.

According to tradition, Muhammad journeyed to heaven where he met the angel Gabriel, Moses, and Abraham et al., on an animal called the Buraq, a white, two-winged animal of a size between that of an ass and a mule. Buraq is said to resemble the Assyrian gryphon, but it has been shown by Blochet that the Muslim conception owes everything to Persian ideas. The details of the actual ascent to heaven are also borrowed from Zoroastrian literature.The Muslim account goes something like this (Muhammad is the speaker):[139]

> Gabriel mounted me upon Buraq, and having carried me upwards to the lowest heaven called out to open the gate. "Who is this?" one cried. "It is Gabriel." "Who is with thee?" "It is Muhammad." "Was he summoned?" "O yes!" was Gabriel's answer. "Then welcome him; how good it is that he has come." And so he opened the gate. Entering, Gabriel said, Here is your father Adam, make the salutation to him. So I made to him my salaam, and he returned it to me; on which he said, Welcome to an excellent Prophet. Then Gabriel took me up to the second heaven, and lo there were John (the Baptist) and Jesus. In the third heaven there was Joseph; in the Fourth Idris (Enoch); in the Fifth Aaron; and in the Sixth Moses. As he returned the salutation, Moses wept and on being asked the reason said: "I mourn because more of the people of him that was sent after me do enter Paradise than of mine." Then we ascended the seventh heaven; "This is your father Abraham," said Gabriel, and salutation was made as before. At the last we made the final ascent, where there were beautiful fruits and leaves like the ears of an elephant. "This," said Gabriel, "is the last heaven; and lo! four rivers, two within, and two without." "What are these, O Gabriel?" I asked. Those within, he said, are the rivers of Paradise; and those without, are the Nile and the Euphrates.

This ascent to heaven (or Miraj in Arabic) can be compared to the account in the Pahlavi text called Arta (or Artay) Viraf written several hundred years before the Muslim era.[140] The Zoroastrian priests felt their faith fading away and so sent Arta Viraf to heaven to find out what was taking place there. Arta ascended from one heaven to another and finally came back to earth to tell his people what he had seen:

> Our first advance upwards was to the lower heaven; . . . and there we saw the Angel of those Holy Ones giving forth a flaming light, brilliant and lofty. And I asked Sarosh the holy and Azar the angel: "What place is this, and these, who are they? "[We are then told that Arta similarly ascended to the second and third heavens.] "Rising from a gold-covered throne, Bahman the Archangel led me on, till he and I met Ormazd with a company of angels and heavenly leaders, all adorned so brightly that I had never seen the like before. My leader said: This is Ormazd. I sought to salaam to him, and he said he was glad to welcome me from the passing world to that bright and undefiled place. . . . At the last, says Arta, my guide and the fire angel, having shown me Paradise, took me down to hell; and from that dark and dreadful place, carried me upward to a beautiful spot where were Ormazd and his company of Angels. I desired to salute him, on which he graciously said: Arta Viraf, go to the material world,

you have seen and now know Ormazd, for I am he; whosoever is true and righteous, him I know.

In Muslim traditions, we also find the notion of the "road," Sirat. Sometimes, the right way of religion is meant, but more often this term is used to refer to the bridge across the infernal fire. The bridge is described as being "finer than a hair and sharper than a sword, and is beset on each side with briars and hooked thorns. The righteous will pass over it with the swiftness of the lightning, but the wicked will soon miss their footing and will fall into the fire of hell."

This idea has obviously been adopted from the Zoroastrian system. After death, the soul of man must pass over the Bridge of the Requiter, Chinvat Peretu, which is sharp as a razor to the unrighteous and therefore impossible to pass.

The Indian and Iranian religions share a common cultural heritage, since the ancestors of the Indians and the Iranians once formed one people—the Indo-Iranians, who in turn were a branch of an even greater family of nations, the Indo-Europeans. Thus, it is not surprising to find the idea of a bridge (Chinvat Peretu) in ancient Hindu texts (e.g., Yajur Veda). The Muslim vision of paradise thus closely resembles both Indian and Iranian accounts. The Zoroastrian text, *Hadhoxt Nask,* describes the fate of a soul after death. The soul of the righteous spends three nights near the corpse, and at the end of the third night, the soul sees its own religion (daena) in the form of a beautiful damsel, a lovely fifteen-year-old virgin; thanks to good actions she has grown beautiful; they then ascend heaven together. This vision resembles the Hindu stories of the Apsarasas, described as "seductive celestial nymphs who dwell in Indra's paradise,"[141] and often are dancers of the gods, but who also welcome the soul into paradise. "They are the rewards in Indra's paradise held out to heroes who fall in battle."[142]

Thus, the Hindu account in many ways resembles the Muslim view of paradise, with its vivid and voluptuous scenes of houris and virgins that so scandalized early Christian commentators. These maidens are also offered in heaven to Muslim warriors who die in the Muslim cause. Some of the words used in the Koran to describe paradise are clearly of Persian origin: "ibriq," water jug; "araik," couches. Here is what Jeffery has to say on this subject: "It does seem certain that the word 'hour' in its sense of whiteness, and used of fairskinned damsels, came into use among the Northern Arabs as a borrowing from the Christian communities, and then Muhammad, under the influence of [an Iranian word] used it of maidens of Paradise."[143]

A Pahlavi text describing paradise talks of every place resembling a garden in spring, in which are all kinds of flowers and trees. This reminds us very much of the Muslim vision of Gardens of Delight (sura 56.12–39; 76.12–22; 10.10; 55.50): "But for those that fear the Lord there are two gardens . . . planted with shady trees. . . . Each is watered by a flowing spring. . . . Each bears every kind of fruit in pairs."

There are striking similarities between the Zoroastrian concept of the archetypal religious man and the specially Sufi Muslim concept of the Perfect Man. Both creeds require an intention to worship in order for it to be acceptable. Both hold certain numbers in superstitious awe: e.g., the figure 33 plays an important part in Parsi ritual, and in Islam: 33 angels carry the praise of man to heaven; whenever sacred litanies are referred to we find the mention of 33 tasbih, 33 tahmid, 33 Takbir, and so on.

Jinns, Demons, and Other Shadowy Beings

Given all the gross superstitious elements in Islam, already described, one wonders how eighteenth-century philosophers ever came to regard it as a rational religion. Had they delved a little deeper into Muslim ideas of jinn, demons, and evil spirits, they would have been even more embarrassed at their own naiveté.

The belief in angels and demons is said to have been acquired from the Persians (the Koranic word "ifrit" meaning "demon" is of Pahlavi origin). If this is the case then it was acquired long ago, for the pagan Arabs before Islam already had a confused notion of a class of shadowy beings "everywhere present yet nowhere distinctly perceived," the jinn or djinn. The word *jinn* probably means covert or darkness. Jinns are the personifications of what is uncanny in nature, or perhaps the hostile and unsubdued aspects of it. In heathen Arabia, they were seen mainly as objects of fear; it was only with the advent of Islam that they began to be seen, on occasions, as benevolent as well.

For the heathen Arabs, the jinn were invisible but were capable of taking various forms, such as those of snakes, lizards, and scorpions. If a jinn entered a man, it rendered him mad or possessed. Muhammad, brought up in crass superstition, maintained a belief in these spirits: "in fact the Prophet went so far as to recognize the existence of the heathen gods, classing them among the demons (see sura 37.158). Hence these primitive superstitions not only held their ground in [Muslim] Arabia but were further developed, spread over the rest of the [Muslim] world, and often combined with similar, in some cases much more elaborate conceptions which prevailed among foreign peoples."

Professor Macdonald recounts how the poet and close friend of Muhammad, Hassan ibn Thabit, first came to write poetry under the influence of a female jinn.

> She met him in one of the streets of Medina, leapt upon him, pressed him down and compelled him to utter three verses of poetry. Thereafter he was a poet, and his verses came to him . . . from the direct inspiration of the Jinn [Djinn]. He refers himself to his "brothers of the Jinn" who weave for him artistic words, and tells how weighty lines have been sent down to him from heaven. . . . The curious thing is that the expressions he uses are exactly those used of the sending down, that is revelation of the Quran.[144]

Macdonald further points to the extraordinary parallel between the terms used in the story of Hassan ibn Thabit's inspiration and the account of Muhammad's first revelation:

> Just as Hassan was thrown down by the female spirit and had verses pressed out of him, so the first utterances of prophecy were pressed from Mohammad by the angel Gabriel. And the resemblances go still farther. The angel Gabriel is spoken of as the companion of Mohammad, just as though he were the Jinni accompanying a poet, and the same word, nafatha, blow upon, is used of an enchanter, of a Jinni inspiring a poet and of Gabriel revealing to Mohammad.

Muhammad's own beliefs in jinns are to be found in the Koran, which contains numerous allusions and references to them: sura 72 (entitled "The Jinn"); 6.100, where the Meccans are reproached for making them companions of Allah; 6.128, where the Meccans are said to have offered sacrifices to them; 37.158, where the Meccans assert the existence of a kinship between them and Allah; 55.14, where God is said to have created them from smokeless fire. There is a vast literature on the beliefs surrounding jinns. For our purposes, it is sufficient to realize that this superstition is sanctioned by the Koran, and jinns are in Islam officially fully recognized, and as Macdonald says, the full consequences of their existence has been worked out. "Their legal status [in Islamic law] in all respects was discussed and fixed, and the possible relations between them and mankind, especially in questions of marriage and property, were examined."[145] Ibn Sina was perhaps the first Islamic philosopher forthrightly to reject the very possibility of their existence.

The Koran also sanctions another widespread superstition in the entire Muslim world, the evil eye, which is considered a very frequent cause of misfortune (sura 113). Muhammad himself is said to have believed in its baneful influence: Asma bint Umais relates that she said, "O Prophet, the family of Jafar are affected by the baneful influences of an evil eye; may I use spells for them or not?" The Prophet said, "Yes, for if there were anything in the world which would overcome fate, it would be an evil eye."

The Muslim Debt to Judaism

> Islam is nothing more nor less than Judaism plus the apostle-ship of Moham-mad.
>
> —S. M. Zwemer[146]

We have the testimony of the Muslim historians themselves that the Jews played an important part in the social and commercial life of Medina. We know of the Jewish tribes of Banu Qaynuqa, Banu Qurayza, and Banu Nadir, that were wealthy enough to own land and plantations. There were also many skilled craftsmen, artisans, and tradesmen working in the city. The Jews had sizable communities in other cities in North Arabia, such as Khaibar, Taima, and Fadak. Torrey seems to think there were Jews in Taima as early as the sixth century B.C. Certainly by the beginning of the Christian era, there were Jewish settlements in that area; further migrations took place after the destruction of Jerusalem in A.D. 70. In South Arabia, we also have evidence of Jewish communities founded by traders. They also exercised considerable influence, as indicated by the presence of Jewish religious ideas on South Arabian religious inscriptions. A famous tradition holds that a Himyarite king, Dhu Nuwas, converted to Judaism.

"Unquestionably, the first impression gained by a reader of the Koran is that Mohammad had received the material of his faith and practice mainly from the Jews of the Hijaz. On almost every page are encountered either episodes of Hebrew history, or familiar Jewish legends, or details of rabbinical law or usage, or arguments which say in effect that Islam is the faith of Abraham and Moses." [Torrey, p. 2]

Some scholars, such as Noldeke and Wellhausen, agree with the Muslim tradition that Muhammad was illiterate; while Torrey and Sprenger are convinced that he was literate. It seems unlikely, considering Muhammad's social background, that he did not receive any education. He came from a respected family, and it is unthinkable that a rich widow would have asked him to take care of her business affairs if he had been unable to read or write. It is true Muhammad did not want to be seen as a man of book learning, for that would have undermined his assertion that his revelations came directly from heaven, from God.

Where and how did the Prophet acquire his knowlege of Jewish history, law, and lore? Two important passages in the Koran indicate that he may well have had a Jewish teacher, probably a rabbi. In sura 25.5f., the unbelievers accuse him of listening to old stories, dictated to him by someone else. Muhammad does not deny the human teacher, but insists his inspiration is divine. In sura 16.105, the angel of revelation tells us, "We know very well that they say: it is only a mortal man who has taught him. But the language of him to whom they refer is foreign, while this language is clear Arabic!" Torrey has argued this instructor must have been a Babylonian Jew from Southern Mesopotamia.

Besides learning from particular individuals, by visiting the Jewish quarter, Muhammad learned from direct observation the rites and rituals of Jewish practice. In any case, the Arabs who came into contact with the Jewish communities had already acquired a knowledge of Jewish customs, stories, legends, and practice; much of this material is to be found in pre-Islamic poetry.

It is evident from the early suras of the Koran that Muhammad was much impressed with the Jews and their religion. He did his utmost to please them by adopting their practices (choosing Jerusalem as the direction for prayer, for example) and tried to convince them that he was only carrying on the traditions of the old prophets.

Zwemer, basing himself on Geiger's *Judaism and Islam*, has very conveniently tabulated the influence of Judaism on Islam in the following way:

A. Ideas and Doctrines

    1. Rabbinical Hebrew Words in the Koran
    2. Doctrinal Views
    3. Moral and Ceremonial Laws
    4. Views of Life

B. Stories and Legends

1. Rabbinical Hebrew Words in the Koran

Geiger lists fourteen words from the Hebrew that represent Jewish ideas not found in pagan Arabia or among the heathen Arabs:

    a. Tabut—ark; the *-ut* termination shows the rabbinical Hebrew origin, since no pure Arabic word ends in this way.
    b. Torah (Taurat)—Jewish revelation.
    c. Jannatu Adn—paradise, Garden of Eden.
    d. Jahannam (Gehinnom)—Hell (from the Vale of Hinnom where idol worship was rife, thus the word later came to mean hell).
    e. Ahbar—teacher
    f. Darasa—to reach the deep meaning of the scripture by exact and careful research.
    g. Rabbani—teacher
    h. Sabt—day of rest (Sabbath).
    i. Sakinat—the Presence of God.
    j. Taghut—error.
    k. Furqan—deliverance, redemption.
    l. Maun—refuge.
    m. Masani—repetition.
    n. Malakut—government; God's rule.

Evidently Muhammad was unable to express certain concepts in his native Arabic, since the Koran also contains a great many Aramaic and Syriac words indicating extensive borrowing of ideas—words such as Sawt (scourge), Madina, Masjid (a place of worship), Sultan, Sullam (a ladder), Nabi (a prophet).

Key Islamic doctrinal views were also borrowed from Judaism, among which the following are the most important:

UNITY OF GOD

As we have already noticed, the oneness of God is not something new in pagan Arabia; nonetheless, it was the uncompromising monotheism of Judaism that profoundly impressed Muhammad and led him to preach a strict monotheism also.

THE WRITTEN REVELATION

The idea that Allah guided and helped mankind through revelations written down by inspired men was of central importance to Muhammad's development. He had been profoundly moved in the way that the learned Jews had shown such deep knowledge of their scriptures: "They know the Book as they know their own children!" (2.141; 6.20). He was determined to have an Arabian book that his followers would also learn in the same spirit and manner. Eventually the Koran itself is said to be a copy, the original of which is written in a table kept in heaven (85.22). This idea finds an echo in Pirke Aboth, v. 6, which also talks of the heavenly tables of the law.

CREATION

Muhammad's account of the creation is clearly based on that found in Exodus 20.11: "We did create the heavens and the earth and what is between the two in six days, and no weariness touched us" (sura 1.37). Elsewhere, the Koran speaks of the earth being created in two days (41.8–11).

SEVEN HEAVENS, SEVEN HELLS

The Koran often refers to the seven heavens (17.46; 23.88; 41.11; 65.12), a notion also found in Chegiga 9.2. In the Koran, hell is said to have seven divisions or portals (15.44); in Zohar 2.150, we find the same description. These notions go back to old Indo-Iranian sources, because in both Hindu and Zoroastrian scriptures we find the seven creations and seven heavens. In sura 11.9 we are told of God's throne being above the waters; compare this to the Jewish Rashi, commenting on Genesis 1.2: "The glorious throne stood in the heavens and moved over the face of the waters." In sura 43.76, we find reference to Malik as the keeper of hell who presides over the tortures of the damned; similarly the Jews talk of the Prince of Hell. Malik is obviously a corruption of the Fire God of the Ammonites, Molech, mentioned in Leviticus, I Kings, and Jeremiah.

In sura 7.44 there is a mention of a wall or partition called Aaraf which separates paradise and hell: "And between the two there is a veil and on al-Aaraf are men who know each other by marks; and they shall cry out to the fellows of Paradise, 'Peace be upon you!' they cannot enter it although they so desire." In the Jewish Midrash on Ecclesiastes 7.14 we have: "How much room is there between? Rabbi Jochanan says a wall, Rabbi Acha says a span; their teachers however hold that they are so close together that people can see from one into the other." Again we find similar passages in Zoroastrian writings: "The distance is but as that between light and darkness."

In certain passages of the Koran (suras 15.17; 37.7; 67.5) we are told of Satan listening stealthily and being driven away with stones; similarly we find in Jewish writings that the Genii "listened behind the curtain "in order to gain knowledge of things to come."

In sura 1.29 we read: "On the day we shall say unto hell, art thou full? and it shall reply, Is there yet any more?" In the rabbinical book Othioth Derabbi Akiba 8.1, we find: "The Prince of Hell shall say, day by day, Give food that I may be full."

In suras 11.42 and 23.27, it is said of the Flood: "the oven boiled over." In a Jewish work we are told that the People of the Flood were punished with boiling water. When talking of the difficulty of attaining paradise, the rabbis talk of the elephant entering the eye of the needle whereas the Koran (sura 7.38) mentions the camel passing through the eye of a needle.

According to the Talmud, a man's limbs themselves shall give testimony against him (Chegiga 16, Taanith 11). One passage reads, "The very members of a man bear witness against him, for it is said 'Ye yourselves are my witness saith the Lord.' " Compare this to sura 24.24: "the day when their tongues and hands and feet shall bear witness against them of what they did" (Cf. 36.65; 41.19).

Compare sura 22.46, "A day with the Lord is as a thousand years of what ye number," with Psalms 90.4, "For a thousand years in thy [the Lord's] sight are but as yesterday." (Cf. sura 32.4 and Sanhedrin 96.2.)

THE MOUNT CAF

The traditions recount that one day "Abdallah asked the Prophet what formed the highest point on the earth. 'Mount Caf,' he said. . . . [It is made] of green emeralds." This story is a garbled and misunderstood version of a passage in the Hagigah where we meet this comment on the word "thohu" in Genesis 1.2: "Thohu is a green line (Cav or Caf) which surrounds the whole world, and hence comes darkness."

MORAL AND LEGAL LAWS

These are some of the moral precepts borrowed from the Talmud by Muhammad. Children are not to obey their parents when the latter demand that which is evil—Jebhamoth 6; sura 29.7. Concerning eating and drinking during the fast of Ramzan, sura 2.187 tells us: "Eat and drink until ye can distnguish a white thread from a black thread by the day-break, then fulfil the fast." In the Mishnah Berachoth, 1.2. we learn that the Shema prayer is to be performed "at the moment when one can but distinguish a blue thread from a white thread." At sura 4.46 we are told that believers ought not to pray when drunk, polluted, or when they had touched women. All these restrictions are found in Berachoth 31.2 and 111.4, and Erubin 64. Prayer may be performed standing, walking, or even riding—Berachoth 10; suras 2.230, 3.188, 10.13. Devotions may be shortened in urgent cases, without committing sin—Mishnah Berachoth 4.4; sura 4.102. The washing rituals prescribed in sura 5.8 are comparable to those demanded in Berachoth

46. According to sura 4.46 and 5.8, when lacking water, purification with sand is acceptable. The Talmud tells that he who "cleanses himself with sand has then done enough" (Berachoth 46). Prayers must not be too loud (sura 17.110); Berachoth 31.2 makes the same point.

The Koran (sura 2.28) stipulates a waiting period of three months before divorced women can remarry. Again Mishna Jabhamoth 4.10 lays down the same law. The degrees of affinity within which marriages are lawful is adopted in the Koran (sura 2.33) evidently from Talmud Kethuboth 40.1. Both religions insist that a woman is to suckle her child for two years—compare sura 31.13 and sura 2.223 with Kethuboth 60.1.

Torrey sums up some of the other doctrines Muhammad borrowed from Judaism:

> The resurrection of all men, both the just and the unjust; an idea familiar at least since Daniel 12.2f.; and always powerfully influential. The Judgment Day, yom dina rabba, when the "books" are opened, and every man is brought to his reckoning. The reward of heaven, the garden, and the punishment of hell, with the everlasting fire of Gehinnam; ideas which Mohammad of course enriched mightily from his own imagination. The doctrine of angels and evil spirits; in particular the activities of Iblis, and of Gabriel, the angel of revelation. Mohammad must have been profoundly impressed by the first chapter of Genesis, judging from the amount of space given in the Koran to the creation of heaven and earth, of man, and of all the objects of nature.[147]

STORIES AND LEGENDS

As Emanuel Deutsch said, "It seems as if he [Muhammad] had breathed from his childhood almost the air of contemporary Judaism, such Judaism as is found by us crystallized in the Talmud, the Targum, and the Midrash."

These Old Testament characters are mentioned in the Koran:

Aaron—Harun; Abel—Habil; Abraham—Ibrahim; Adam—Adam; Cain—Qabil; David—Daud; Elias—Ilyas; Elijah—Alyasa; Enoch—Idris; Ezra—Uzair; Gabriel—Jibril; Gog—Yajuj; Goliath—Jalut; Isaac—Ishaq; Ishmael—Ismail; Jacob—Yacub; Job—Aiyub; Jonah—Yunus; Joshua—Yusha'; Joseph—Yusuf; Korah—Qarun; Lot—Lut; Magog—Majuj; Michael—Mikail; Moses—Musa; Noah—Nuh; Pharaoh—Firaun; Saul—Talut; Solomon—Sulaiman; Terah—Azar.

These incidents and tales are taken from the Old Testament, but as the *Dictionary of Islam* puts it, "with a strange want of accuracy and a large admixture of Talmudic fable":

Aaron makes a calf: 20.90
Cain and Abel: 5.30
Abraham visited by angels: 11.72; 15.51
Abraham ready to sacrifice his son: 37.101
The fall of Adam: 7.18; 2.84

Korah and his company: 28.76; 29.38; 40.25
Creation of the World: 16.3; 13.3; 35.1,12
David's praise of God: 34.10
Deluge: 54.9; 69.11; 11.42
Jacob goes to Egypt: 12.100
Jonah and the fish: 6.86; 10.98; 37.139; 68.48
Joseph's history: 6.84; 12.1; 40.86
Manna and quails: 7.160; 20.82
Moses strikes the rock: 7.160
Noah's ark: 11.40
Pharoah: 2.46; 10.76; 43.45; 40.38
Solomon's judgment: 21.78
Queen of Sheba: 27.72

Muhammad evidently wished to establish "a clear and firm connection with the previous religions of the Book, and especially with the Hebrew scriptures."[148] Despite all the incidents and characters Muhammad borrowed from the Old Testament, most scholars agree that he cannot possibly have had a firsthand acquaintance with it. As Obermann says,

> Not only the Hebrew original, but any sort of translation would surely have precluded the gross discrepancies, inaccuracies and delusions he exhibits, almost invariably, when his revelation involves data from the Old Testament; or for that matter from the New Testament. The decisive thing, however, is that in a great many instances where a biblical element appears misrepresented or distorted in the revelation of Mohammad, the very same misrepresentation and distortion can be shown to recur in postbiblical sources as homiletical or expository embellishments characteristic of the treatment of Scripture both in the Jewish Synagogue and in the Christian church.[149]

But in taking over elements from the Talmud and other Jewish sources, Muhammad showed little creativity. As Torrey puts it,

> His characters are all alike, and they utter the same platitudes. He is fond of dramatic dialogue, but has very little sense of dramatic scene or action. The logical connection between successive episodes is often loose, sometimes wanting; and points of importance, necessary for the clear understanding of the story, are likely to be left out. There is also the inveterate habit of repetition, and a very defective sense of humor. . . . In sura 11.27–51 is given a lengthy account of Noah's experiences. . . . It contains very little incident, but consists chiefly of the same religious harangues which are repeated scores of time throughout the Koran, uninspired and uniformly wearisome. We have the feeling that one of Noah's contemporaries who was confronted with the prospect of forty days and forty nights in the ark would prefer to take his chances with the deluge.[150]

Furthermore, Muhammad had only the fuzziest notions of Hebrew chronology. He knew that Saul, David, and Solomon were subsequent to the Patriarchs, but not the order of the other prophets nor the time at which they lived. Muhammad had bizarre notions about Ezra, and was unable to place him.

> Elijah, and Elisha, Job, Jonah, and Idris are left by him floating about, with no secure resting place. He had heard nothing whatever as to the geneology of Jesus (the claimed descent from David), nor of his contemporaries (excepting the family of John the Baptist), nor of any Christian history. He associated Moses with Jesus, evidently believing that very soon after the revelation to the Hebrew lawgiver there had followed the similar revelation which had produced the Christians and their sacred book. This appears in his identification of Mary the mother of Jesus with Miriam the sister of Moses and Aaron.

Muhammad transfers to the time of Solomon one event that rabbis placed at the time of Noah. Other confusions include Muhammad's making Noah live 950 years up to the time of the Flood (sura 29.13), whereas this is really the whole term of his life (Gen. 9.29). Muhammad is also confused about Ham's evil conduct, which, according to Genesis (9.22), took place after the Deluge. It is not clear why Noah's wife is classified as an unbeliever. In the Koran there is also an obvious confusion between Saul and Gideon (cf. sura 2.250 and Judg. 7.5).

THE CREATION OF ADAM

In Sura 2.28–33 we read:

> When thy Lord said to the angels, "Verily I am going to place a substitute on earth," they said, "Wilt thou place there one who will do evil therein and shed blood? but we celebrate Thy praise and sanctify thee." God answered: "Verily I know that you know not." He taught Adam the names of all things, and then proposed them to the angels, and said, "Tell Me the names of these things if what you say be true." They replied, "Praise be unto You, we have no knowledge but what You have taught us. For You are wise and all-knowing." God said, "O Adam, tell them their names." And when he had told them their names, God said, "Did I not tell you that I know the secrets of heaven and earth, and know that which you reveal and that which you hide."

Let us trace the sources of this fable.

> When God intended to create man, He advised with the angels and said unto them, We will make man in our own image" (Gen. 1.26) Then said they, What is man, that Thou rememberest him (Ps. 8.5), what shall be his peculiarity? He answered, His wisdom is superior to yours. Then brought He before them cattle, animals, and birds, and asked for their names, but they knew it not. After man was created, He caused them to pass before Him, and asked for their names and he answered, This is an ox, that an ass, this a horse, and that a camel. But what is thy name? To me it becomes to be called earthly, for from earth

I am created (Midrash Rabbah on Leviticus, Parashah 19, and Genesis, Parashah 8; and Sanhedrin 38).

Various suras also recount that God commanded the angels to worship Adam (7.10–26; 15.29–44; 18.48; 20.115; 37.71–86). They obeyed with the exception of Satan. This agrees with the account in Midrash of Rabbi Moses.

CAIN AND ABEL

Geiger gives the story of Cain and Abel as an example of what Torrey criticized in Muhammad's narrative style—important points of the story are left out. Geiger points out that as it stands in the Koran (sura 5.35) it is not entirely coherent, and we only arrive at a clearer understanding when we look at a passage from the Mishna Sanhedrin 4.5. The murder of Abel in the Koran is borrowed from the Bible, but the conversation of Cain with Abel before Cain kills him is taken from the Targum of Jerusalem, generally known as pseudo-Jonathan. In the Koran, after the murder God sent a raven that scratched the earth to show Cain how to bury Abel:

> And God sent a raven which scratched the earth to show him how he should hide his brother's body. He said, "Woe is me! I am not able to be like this raven"; and he became one of those that repent. *For this cause we wrote unto the children of Israel that we who slayeth a soul—without having slain a soul or committed wickedness in the earth—shall be as if he had slain all mankind; and whosoever saveth a soul alive shall be as if he had saved all mankind.* (sura 5.30–35)

The lines in italics have no connection with what has gone before. They only become clear if we look at Mishna Sanhedrin 4.5:

> We find it said in the case of Cain who murdered his brother: The voice of thy brother's bloods crieth. It is not said here blood in the singular but bloods in the plural i.e. his own blood and the blood of his seed. Man was created single in order to show that to him who kills a single individual, it shall be reckoned that he has slain the whole race; but to him who preserves the life of a single individual it is counted that he hath preserved the whole race.

The part omitted served as the connecting link between the two passages in the Koran, without which they are unintelligible.

NOAH

A part of the story of Noah in the Koran obviously comes from Genesis, but an account of Noah's character is drawn from rabbinical sources (suras 7.57; 10.72; 22.43, etc.). The conversations Noah has with the people while he is building the ark are the same as those found in Sanhedrin 108; and both the Koran and the rabbinical scriptures declare that the generation of the Flood was punished with boiling water (Rosh Hashanah 16.2 and Sanhedrin 108; suras 11.42, 33.27).

ABRAHAM SAVED FROM NIMROD'S FIRE

The story of Abraham (Ibrahim) is found scattered throughout the Koran—suras 2.260; 6.74-84; 21.52-72; 19.42-50; 26.69-79; 29.15,16; 37.81-95; 43.25-27; 60.4; etc. The Muslim traditions also dwell much on the patriarch's life. It has been shown by Geiger and also by Tisdall that the source of the Koranic and traditional accounts lies in the Jewish Midrash Rabbah. Both the Midrashic and the Muslim sources are at variance with the biblical account. In Genesis we simply learn that Nimrod is the grandson of Ham, and that he founded a great empire. In the Muslim and Midrashic story, Abraham is punished for having destroyed the idols worshipped by the people of Nimrod. He is thrown into a fire but emerges unscathed. According to Tisdall,[151] the whole story is based on a misunderstanding of Gen. 15.7: "I am the Lord that brought thee out of Ur of the Chaldees." "Ur" in Babylonian means city, and the Chaldaean Ur was Abraham's hometown. But "Ur" in speech closely resembles another word, "Or," meaning light or fire. Years later, a Jewish commentator, Jonathan ben Uzziel, translated the same verse from Genesis as "I am the Lord that delivered thee out of the Chaldean fiery oven." The commentator compounded his error by insisting that all this happened "at the time when Nimrod cast Abraham into the oven of fire, because he would not worship the idols." Of course, even if Nimrod ever existed, he certainly was not Abraham's contemporary if we accept the account in Genesis.

JOSEPH

Although the story of the great patriarch is taken in the main from the Bible, Torrey[152] shows that there is an incoherence in the Koranic account of the life of Joseph in sura 12, where the entire sura is devoted to the patriarch; and that only if we fill in the missing links by passages from the Midrash does the story make any sense (Midrash Yalqut 146).

Potiphar's wife tries to seduce Joseph, who at first refuses but at last becomes ready to yield when he sees a vision that deters him. Typically, the Koran leaves us in the dark as to the nature of the vision. However, from Sotah 36.2, from which the Koranic account is taken, we know that: "Rabbi Jochanan saith, 'Both intended to commit sin; seizing him by the garment, she said, "Lie with me." . . . Then appeared to him the form of his father at the window who called to him, "Joseph! Joseph! the names of thy brothers shall be engraven upon the stones of Ephod, also thine own; wilt thou that it shall be erased?" ' "

The sequel to the story in the Koran is not entirely intelligible without consulting the source, in this case the Midrash Yalkut 146. The story continues with Potiphar's wife inviting all the women who had laughed at her infatuation to a feast where they see Joseph's handsomeness for themselves, and in their excitement cut themselves with knives. In the Koran, it is not at all clear why they had knives; in the Midrash Yalkut, however, we learn that it is to eat fruit.

In the Koran we learn that Jacob tells his sons to enter at different gates; similarly, in Midrash Rabbah on Genesis, Parashah 91, Jacob "said to them, enter not through one and the same gate." Torrey takes up the story.

> When the cup is found in Benjamin's sack, and he is proclaimed a thief, his brethren say, "If he has stolen, a brother of his stole before him." The commentators are at their wit's end to explain how Joseph could have been accused of stealing. The explanation is furnished by the Midrash which remarks at this point that Benjamin's mother before him had stolen; referring of course to the time when Rachel carried off her father's household gods (Genesis xxxi.19–35).
>
> Again, the Koran tells us that Jacob knew by revelation that his son Joseph was still alive (sura xii.86) but it is in the Midrash Yalkut cxliii, that we learn whence he obtained the information: "An unbeliever asked our master, Do the dead continue to live? Your parents do not believe it, and will ye receive it? Of Jacob it is said, he refused to be comforted: had he believed that the dead still lived, would he not have been comforted? But he answered, Fool, he knew by the Holy Ghost that he still really lived, and about a living person people need no comfort."

HUD, MOSES, AND OTHERS

The details of the patriarch Hud, who is usually identified with the biblical Eber, are also taken from rabbinical writings (compare sura 11.63 and Mishnah Sanhedrin 10.3). Similar borrowings abound in the Koranic account of Moses and Pharaoh. To take some random samples: In Rashi on Exod. 15.27, the Jewish commentators add that twelve fountains were found near Elim and that each of the tribes had a well. Muhammad transposes the statement and declares that twelve fountains sprang from the rock that Moses had struck at Rephidim. In Aboda Sarah 2.2, we have the fabulous tale of God covering the Israelites with Mount Sinai, on the occasion of the lawgiving. The Koran gives the following version (sura 7.170): "We shook the mountain over them, as though it had been a covering, and they imagined that it was falling upon them; and We said, 'Receive the law which we have brought unto you with reverence.' "

SOLOMON AND SHEBA

The Koran makes much of the story of Solomon, especially his encounter with the Queen of Sheba. The Koran refers to Solomon's wisdom by alluding to his ability to converse with birds; the Jewish commentators held the same opinion. In various suras we learn that winds or spirits obeyed him, and demons, birds, and beasts formed part of his standing army (suras 21.81, 27.15, 34.11, 38.35). In the second Targum of the Book of Esther, we read, "demons of various kinds, and evil spirits were subject to him." Muhammad tells the fable of how the demons helped in the building of the Temple, and being deceived, continued it after his death (sura 34). This is borrowed directly from the Jews (Gittin 68).

ALEXANDER THE GREAT

Sura 18 of the Koran is unusual in containing all sorts of legendary material that is not from the usual sources, namely, the Old Testament, rabbinical literature, or Arabian lore. Before tracing the sources, we begin with the story of Moses and his servant in search of the confluence of two rivers (Madjma' al-Bahrain), recounted in verses 59 to 81.

> When they reach this place, they find that as a result of the influence of Satan they have forgotten the fish which they were taking with them. The fish had found its way into the water and had swum away. While looking for the fish [they] meet a servant of God. Moses (Musa) says that he will follow him if he will teach him the right path. They come to an arrangement but the servant of God tells Moses (Musa) at the beginning that he will not understand his doings, that he must not ask for explanations, and as a result will not be able to bear with him. They set out on the journey, however, during which the servant of God does a number of apparently outrageous things, which causes Moses (Musa) to lose patience so that he cannot refrain from asking for an explanation, whereupon the servant of God replies: "Did I not tell you that you would be lacking in patience with me?" He finally leaves Moses (Musa) and on departing gives him the explanation of his actions, which had their good reasons.

Noldeke and others have traced the sources of this story to (1) the epic of Gilgamesh; (2) the Alexander romance; (3) the Jewish legend of Elijah and Rabbi Joshua ben Levi.

1. The Epic of Gilgamesh. This Babylonian poem dating from the eighteenth century B.C.E. recounts the heroic tale of two friends, Enkidu and Gilgamesh. When eventually Enkidu dies, Gilgamesh, dreading death himself, goes in search of immortality. He begins by searching for his ancestor Utnapishtim, who lives at the mouth of two rivers, for Gilgamesh is aware that Utnapishtim is the only mortal who has acquired immortality. His ancestor tells him of a plant that has the property of rejuvenating the old, but that it can only be found at the bottom of the sea. At the last moment, Gilgamesh is robbed of his plant by a serpent.

2. The Alexander Romance. The immediate source of the Alexander romance was to be found in Syriac literature, in the Lay of Alexander, whose ultimate source was the Alexander Romance of pseudo-Callisthenes, perhaps reaching as far back as 100 B.C. The Syriac version recounts how Alexander and his cook Andreas go in search of the Spring of Life. At one stage Andreas is washing a salted fish at a spring; the contact with the water makes the fish live again and it swims away. Andreas jumps in after the fish and thereby acquires immortality. When Alexander later learns of the story, he realizes that he has just

missed discovering the very spring he had been looking for. Unfortunately they fail to find the spring again.

3. Elijah and Rabbi Joshua ben Levi. The Jewish legend tells how Rabbi Joshua ben Levi goes on a journey with Elijah. Like the servant of God in the Koran, Elijah lays down a number of similar conditions. Again, Elijah does a number of apparently outrageous things that affects the rabbi in the same way that Moses was affected.

Wensinck sums up the result of comparing all the sources. "The figure of Joshua ben Levi, with which Muhammad first became acquainted through the Jews and which does not again appear in Muslim legend, was identified . . . with Joshua b. Nun. This identification may have resulted in a confusion of his master Elijah with Joshua b. Nun's master, Moses. Musa [Moses] thus represents Gilgamesh and Alexander in the first part of the Koranic story and Elijah in the second."[153]

Finally, Alexander himself puts in an appearance in verses 82 to 96, as Dhu'l-Karnain, "He of the Two Horns." We know from the Syriac version of the legend that Alexander was called Two-Horned because God "caused horns to grow upon my head, so that I may crush the kingdoms of the world with them." The Koranic account then goes on to mix in the story of Gog and Magog with that of Alexander (cf., Gen. 10.2, Ezek. 38).

OTHER BORROWINGS

Muhammad often refers to God as *rabb,* "lord," sometimes as *rabb al-al-'alamin,* "lord of the worlds" (sura 56.79, 82.29, 83.6).[154] In Jewish liturgy as well as the Aggadah we find *ribbon ha-olamin.* Muhammad also speaks of God as *ar-rahman,* the Merciful (55.1; 78.3.) At the head of each sura, but elsewhere in the Koran it occurs over fifty times, almost as a personal name of God. This term seems to have been used in Arabia before Islam; it has been found in South Arabian inscriptions. Bell doubts that Muhammad was directly dependent on Judaism for its adoption. However Obermann points out that *ha-rahman* is also used frequently in Jewish liturgy. Jeffery sums up his opinion thus: "The fact that the word occurs in old poetry and is known to have been in use in connection with the work of Muhammad's rival Prophets, Musailama of Yamama and al-Aswad of Yemen, would seem to point to a Christian rather than a Jewish origin, though the matter is uncertain."[155]

CHRISTIANITY

He had very little idea of Christian teaching, or of what the Christian Church was. In fact, he never did acquire very intimate knowledge of these things. As Noldeke pointed out long ago, the man who made such a stupid story of the chief Christian sacrament, as that in sura v.111ff., one of the latest parts of the Quran, could not have known much about the Christian Church.

—Richard Bell[156]

Christianity was widely diffused throughout Arabia at the time of the birth of Muhammad, but it was probably of the Syrian kind, whether Jacobite or Nestorian. In al-Hira many important Christian families, were Monophysite. We know that the language Syriac is the "most copious source of Quranic borrowings." Undoubtedly, the major part of the Syriac influence on Arabic came from the Syriac used by the Christians of al-Hira. A Christian community also arose in South Arabia at Najran; many inhabitants were Nestorians, but a considerable number were Monophysites related to the Monophysite Church of Abyssinia. According to the Muslim traditions, Muhammad himself had had personal contact with the Christians of the Syrian Church. We know from Muslim sources that as a young man, Muhammad went on trading journeys to Syria; and there is an account of how on one occasion he listened to a sermon by Quss, Bishop of Najran, at the festival of Ukaz near Mecca.

For a long time there had also been close contact with Abyssinia in the form of trade; and, of course, South Arabia had been under Abyssinian rule for some time before the birth of Muhammad. We have the well-known story of a group of Meccans who converted to Islam and fled to Abyssinia to avoid any persecution. Torrey dates the new interest in Christianity that was awakened in Muhammad from this time.

Yet, despite this effort, Muhammad never even understood the doctrine of the Trinity. What is in the Koran about Christianity derives from heretical sects.

THE SEVEN SLEEPERS

The legend of the Seven Sleepers of Ephesus arose around the end of the fifth century and soon spread all over western Asia and Europe. Perhaps the first mention of this legend appeared in the Syriac of James of Sarug, a Syrian bishop (452–521), and it was then translated into Latin by Gregory of Tours (ca. 540–90), "De Gloria Martyrum" (1. i.c; 95). As Gibbon puts it, "this popular tale, which Mahomet might learn when he drove his camels to the fairs of Syria, is introduced, as a divine revelation into the Koran" (sura 18.8–26). The Koranic account begins thus: "Hast thou reflected that the companions of the cave and of al-Raqim were one of our wondrous signs." According to the fable, certain Christian youths escaped to a cave in the mountains to escape persecution under the Emperor Decius. Their pursuers found their hiding place and sealed them up. The youths miraculously survived and re-emerged nearly two hundred years later. Commentators have disputed over the meaning of the term "al Raqim" for years. Torrey[157] has suggested that this curious name is simply a misreading of the name Decius written in the Aramaic script.

MISUNDERSTANDING OF THE STORY OF MARY
AND THE DOCTRINE OF THE TRINITY

In sura 19.28, 29, we read that after the birth of Jesus, the people came to Mary and said, "O Mary, now you have done an extraordinary thing! O sister of Aaron! Your father was not a bad man, nor was your mother a whore!" Elsewhere, Mary is named "the daughter of Imran" (sura 66.12; 3.31); and again, "We gave unto Moses the Book and appointed him his brother Aaron as vizier." It is pretty obvious that Muhammad has confused Miriam the sister of Moses, with Mary the mother of Jesus. The commentators have verily taxed their brains to explain this "marvelous confusion of space and time."

In sura 19, we read that Mary the Mother of Jesus, receives a visit from an angel who tells her that she will give birth to a child, even though she is a virgin, as this is God's wish. The sura continues (verse 20ff.):

> So she conceived him, and she retired with him into a remote place. And the labor pains came upon her at the trunk of a palm tree, and she said, "O that I had died before this, and been forgotten out of mind" and he called to her from beneath her, "Grieve not, for the Lord has placed a stream beneath thy feet; and shake towards thee the trunk of the palm tree, it will drop upon thee fresh dates fit to gather; so eat, and drink and cheer thine eyes, and if thou shouldst see any mortal say, 'Verily, I have vowed to the Merciful one a fast, and I will not speak today with a human being.' "

We can immediately see the source of this story in the apocryphal book called the History of the Nativity of Mary and the Saviour's Infancy, where the infant Jesus asks the palm tree, "Send down thy branches here below, that my mother may eat fresh fruit of thee. Forthwith it bent itself at Mary's feet, and so all ate of its fruit. . . . [Then Jesus tells the tree to] open the fountain beneath thee. . . . At once the tree became erect, and began to pour from its roots water beautifully clear and sweet before them."

Other parts of the story in the Koran are taken from the Protevangelium of James the Less, written in Hellenic Greek, and also from the Coptic History of the Virgin.

JESUS

At sura 4.155, 156, the Crucifixion of Jesus is denied: "Yet they slew him not, and they crucified him not, but they had only his likeness." Some have conjectured that this was Muhammad's invention, but we know that several heretical sects denied the Crucifixion, sects such as the Basilidians, who claimed that Simon the Cyrenean was crucified in Christ's place.

There are also various tales of Jesus speaking in the cradle, breathing life into birds of clay (sura 5.121), etc., which are taken from the Coptic work, The

Gospel of St. Thomas. In sura 5, we also have the story of the Descent of the Table from heaven, whose origin undoubtedly lies in the supper that Jesus partook of with his disciples the night before his death.

THE TRINITY

The Christian doctrine of the Trinity is mentioned in three suras.

> Believe therefore in God and His Apostles, and say not, "Three." (sura 4.169)

> They misbelieve who say, "Verily God is the third of three." . . The Messiah, the son of Mary, is only a prophet,. . . . and his mother was a confessor, they both ate food. (sura 5.77)

> And when God shall say, "O Jesus son of Mary hast thou said unto mankind, 'Take me and my mother as two Gods besides God?' " (sura 5.116)

The highly revered Muslim commentator al-Baidawi remarks that the Christians made the Trinity consist of God, Christ, and Mary; and it seems clear that that was Muhammad's own view.

THE BALANCE

As we saw earlier, from Persia came an element of the Islamic idea of the balance, that is, the scales on which the actions of men shall be weighed on Judgment Day. But other elements are clearly borrowed from a heretical work, "The Testament of Abraham," perhaps dating from the second century. Ultimately this work probably got most of its ideas from the Egyptian Book of the Dead.

We have already seen how the Prophet's Ascent is largely based on the Pahlavi text. But again, large elements were taken from the "Testament of Abraham." In the apocryphal work, the Patriarch is taken to heaven by the Archangel Michael and is shown a vision of the two roads leading to heaven and hell:

> [Abraham] beheld also two gates, one wide like its road, and another narrow like the other road. Outside the two gates they beheld a Man [Adam] sitting on a golden throne, his aspect terrible like unto the Lord. They saw a multitude of souls driven by the angels through the wide gate, but few souls led by the angels through the narrow one. And when the great Man . . . saw but a few passing through the narrow gate, and so many through the wide gate, he grasped the hair of his head . . . , and cast himself weeping and groaning from his throne upon the ground. But when he saw many souls entering in by the narrow gate, he arose from the ground, and with joy and rejoicing seated himself again upon the throne.

According to the Muslim work *Mishkat'l Masabih,* we learn that on his visit to heaven Muhammad saw Adam: "Lo! a man seated, on his right hand were dark figures, and on his left dark figures. When he looked to his right he laughed; when to the left, he wept. And he said, Welcome to the righteous prophet, and to the excellent Son. It is Adam . . . the people on his right are the inhabitants of Paradise, and the dark figures on his left are those of the Fire; when he looks to his right he smiles; and when he looks to his left, he weeps."

THE EYE OF A NEEDLE

In sura 7.38, we learn, "They that charge our signs with falsehood and proudly reject them, the gates of heaven shall not be opened to them, nor shall they enter Paradise until a camel pass through the eye of a needle"—a remarkable echo of the Matt. 19.24, "It is easier for a camel to go through the eye of a needle, than for a rich man to enter into the kingdom of God." (See also Mark 10.25 and Luke 18.25)

THE SABIANS

Many scholars, such as Muir, for instance, have conjectured that Muhammad and his contemporaries in seventh-century Central Arabia must have been influenced by the Sabians. The situation is rather confused, since this term refers to two distinct sects. According to Carra de Vaux, in the *Encyclopedia of Islam*, 1st edition, the Koranic reference to the Sabians as the "People of the Book" along with the Jews and the Christians, suggests that the Mandaeans are meant. The Mandaeans were a Judeo-Christian sect that practiced baptism, and perhaps originated east of the Jordan in the first or second century. However, other scholars such as Bell and Torrey think it highly unlikely that Muhammad meant to indicate the Mandaeans by the term "sabi'in."

The second group intended by this term was the pagan sect of Sabians of Harran, who worshipped the stars and admitted the existence of astral spirits. Among these spirits are to be found administrators of the seven planets that are like their temples. According to al-Sharastani, one group of Sabians worship the stars, called temples, directly; and the other group worships handmade idols representing the stars in temples made by man. Insofar as the Sabians may have influenced Muhammad, we may note the prevalence of oaths by the stars and planets in the Koran (sura 56.75: "I swear by the falling of the stars . . ."; sura 53, entitled "The Star," verse 1: "By the star when it plunges . . ."). The Sabians may well have influenced the rites and ceremonies of the pagan Meccans—we know, for instance, that the Meccans kept 360 idols in the Kaaba; and the ceremony of circling the Kaaba seven times, as Muir suggested, is perhaps symbolic of the motion of the seven planets.

3

The Problem of Sources

In our sceptical times there is very little that is above criticism, and one day or other we may expect to hear that Muhammad never existed.
—Snouck Hurgronje[158]

The traditional Muslim account of the life of Muhammad and the story of the origin and rise of Islam are based exclusively on Muslim sources, namely, (1) the Koran (2); the Muslim biographies of Muhammad; and (3) the Hadith, that is, the Muslim traditions.

1. The Koran. Not only do Muslims make extraordinary claims for the Koran, but there also are traditional Muslim accounts of the history of the formation of the Koran texts. As we shall see, all the claims are false, and the traditional accounts are "a mass of confusion, contradiction and inconsistencies."[159] Serious scholars have called into question the authenticity of the Koran itself, and we shall look at their powerful arguments. Here we shall simply note the names of the most revered Muslim commentators on the Koran, as we shall need to refer to their work later in the chapter:

Muhammad ibn-Jarir al-Tabari (d. A.D. 923)
Al-Baghawi (d. 1117 or 1122)
Al-Zamakhshari (d. 1143)
Al-Baydawi (d. 1286 or 1291)
Fakhr-al-Din al-Razi (d. 1210)
Jalal-al-Din al-Mahalli (d. 1459)
Jalal-al-Din al-Suyuti (d.1505)

2. Muslim Biographies. The Prophet Muhammad died in A.D. 632. The earliest material on his life that we possess was written by Ibn Ishaq in A.D. 750, in other words, a hundred twenty years after Muhammad's death. The question of authenticity becomes even more critical, because the original form of Ibn Ishaq's work is lost and is only available in parts in a later recension by Ibn Hisham

who died in A.D. 834, two hundred years after the death of the Prophet. Other sources include the *Annals* of Al-Tabari who also quotes from Ibn Ishaq. These are the principal sources of information on Muhammad's life:

a. Ibn Ishaq (d. 768). Apart from the biography of Muhammad, he also wrote a history of the caliphs that is cited by al-Tabari.

b. Ibn Hisham (d. 834) wrote the *Sirah* or *Life of Muhammad,* or perhaps, to speak more accurately, edited Ibn Ishaq's work.

c. Sayf b. 'Umar (d. ca. 796) was al-Tabari's principal source for the early years of Islam.

d. Al-Waqidi (d. 823) also wrote a biography of the Prophet and his campaigns; extensively used by al-Tabari and al-Baladhuri (d. 829)

e. Muhammad ibn Sa'd (d. 843) was the chief editor of al-Waqidi and the compiler of a biographical dictionary.

f. Al-Tabari (d. 923) was a polymath who wrote on many subjects (including a commentary on the Koran), but is perhaps most famous for his *History of the World,* which extends to July 915.

g. Ali b. Muhammad al-Madaini (d. 840)—important for the Arab conquests of Persia

3. The Hadith. The Hadith or the Books of tradition are a collection of sayings and doings attributed to the Prophet and traced back to him through a series of putatively trustworthy witnesses (any particular chain of transmitters is called an "isnad," while the text or the real substance of the report is called matn"). Apart from what Muhammad did and enjoined, these traditions include what was done in his presence that he did not forbid, and even the authoritative sayings and doings of the companions of the Prophet. Another term used in this context is "sunna," which means custom, use, and wont. Thus the Prophet's sunna comprises his deeds, utterances, and tacit approval. As Wensinck said, "Observance of the Sunna might be in a way called 'Imitatio Muhammadis.' " The two terms should be kept carefully distinct from one another. The hadith is an oral communication derived from the Prophet, whereas the sunna is the traditional norm in the rites and laws that govern the practical conduct of life; the sunna refers to a religious or legal point without there necessarily being an oral tradition for it. In other words, something can be taken to be sunna without there being a hadith relating to it.

Perhaps nonspecialists and non-Muslims do not sufficiently appreciate how greatly the hadith is revered in the Islamic world. "The Hadith is held in great reverence next to the Koran throughout the whole [Islamic] world. . . . In some cases it is even believed that the actual word of God is to be found in the Hadith as well as in the Koran." These books of tradition serve as the theoretical basis for Islamic law and hence Islam itself.

There are said to be six correct or authentic collections of traditions accepted by Sunni Muslims, namely, the compilations of (a) al-Bukhari (d. 870), (b) Muslim ibn al-Hajjaj (d. 875), (c) Ibn Maja (d. 887), (d) Abu Dawud (d. 889), (e) al-Tirmidhi (d. 892), and (f) al-Nisai (d. 915).

One usually adds to this list the name of Ahmed ibn Hanbal (d. 855), whose great encyclopedia of traditions called Musnad contains nearly 29,000 traditions and has "been the subject of pious reading."

Skepticism and Doubts

The historical and biographical tradition concerning Muhammad and the early years of Islam were submitted to a thorough examination at the end of the nineteenth century. Up to then, scholars were well aware of the legendary and theological elements in these traditions, and that there were traditions that originated from party motive and that intended "to give an appearance of historical foundation to the particular interests of certain persons or families; but it was thought that after some sifting there yet remained enough to enable us to form a much clearer sketch of Muhammad's life than that of any other of the founders of a universal religion."[160] This illusion was shattered by Wellhausen, Caetani, and Lammens who called "one after another of the data of Muslim tradition into question."

Wellhausen[161] divided the old historical tradition as found in the ninth- and tenth-century compilations into two: first, an authentic primitive tradition, definitively recorded in the late eighth century, and second, a parallel version that was deliberately forged to rebut this. The second version was full of tendentious fiction and was to be found in the work of historians such as Sayf b. Umar. Prince Caetani and Father Lammens even cast doubt on data hitherto accepted as "objective." The biographers of Muhammad were too far removed from his time to have true data or notions; far from being objective the data rested on tendentious fiction. Furthermore, the biographers'·aim was not to know things as they really happened, but to construct an ideal vision of the past, as it ought to have been. "Upon the bare canvas of verses of the Koran that need explanation, the traditionists have embroidered with great boldness scenes suitable to the desires or ideals of their particular group: or to use a favorite metaphor of Lammens, they fill the empty spaces by a process of stereotyping which permits the critical observer to recognize the origin of each picture."[162] As Lewis puts it, "Lammens went so far as to reject the entire biography as no more than a conjectural and tendentious exegesis of a few passages of biographical content in the Quran, devised and elaborated by later generations of believers. [Lewis (4), p. 94] "Even scholars who rejected the extreme skepticism of Caetani and Lammens were forced to recognize that "of Muhammad's life before his appearance as the messenger of God, we know extremely little; compared to the legendary biography as treasured by the faithful, practically nothing."[163]

The ideas of the positivist Caetani and the Jesuit Lammens were never forgotten; indeed, they were taken up by a group of Soviet Islamologists and pushed to their extreme but logical conclusions. The ideas of the Soviet scholars were in turn taken up in the 1970s and pose a serious challenge to the orthodox, whether the true believers or the conservative infidel researchers. N. A. Morozov propounded a theory that Islam was indistinguishable from Judaism until the Crusades and that only then did Islam receive its independent character, while Muhammad and the first caliphs were mythical figures. Morozov's arguments, which were put forward in his book *Christ* in 1930, are summarized by Smirnov:

> In the Middle Ages Islam was merely an off-shoot of Arianism evoked by a meteorological event in the Red Sea area near Mecca; it was akin to Byzantine iconoclasm. The Koran bears traces of late composition, up to the eleventh century. The Arabian peninsula is incapable of giving birth to any religion— it is too far from the normal areas of civilization. The Arian Islamites, who passed in the Middle Ages as Agars, Ishmaelites, and Saracens, were indistinguishable from the Jews until the impact of the Crusades made them assume a separate identity. All the lives of Muhammad and his immediate successors are as apocryphal as the accounts of Christ and the Apostles.[164]

As we shall discuss later, Morozov's ideas have a remarkable similarity to some devastating views put forward by a group of Cambridge Islamicists in the 1970s. Under the influence of Morozov, Klimovich published an article called "Did Muhammad Exist?" (1930), in which he makes the valid point that all the sources of our information on the life of Muhammad are late. Muhammad was a necessary fiction since it is always assumed that every religion must have a founder. Tolstov compares the myth of Muhammad to the "deified shamans" of the Yakuts, the Buryats, and the Altays: "The social purpose of this myth was to check the disintegration of the political block of traders, nomads, and peasants, which had brought to power the new, feudal aristocracy." Vinnikov also compares the myth of Muhammad to "shamanism," pointing to the primitive magic aspects of such rituals as Muhammad having water poured on him.[165]

What Caetani and Lammens did for historical biography, Ignaz Goldziher did for the study of hadith. Goldziher has had an enormous influence in the field of Islamic studies, and it is no exaggeration to say that he is, along with Hurgronje and Noldeke, one of the founding fathers of the modern study of Islam. Practically everything he wrote between roughly 1870 and 1920 is still studied assiduously in universities throughout the world. In his classic paper, "On the Development of the Hadith," Goldziher "demonstrated that a vast number of hadith accepted even in the most rigorously critical Muslim collections were outright forgeries from the late 8th and 9th centuries—and as a consequence, that the meticulous isnads [chains of transmitters] which supported them were utterly fictitious."[166]

Faced with Goldziher's impeccably documented arguments, historians began to panic and devised spurious ways of keeping skepticism at bay, by, for instance, postulating ad hoc distinctions between legal and historical traditions. But as Humphreys says,[167] in their formal structure, the hadith and historical traditions were very similar; furthermore, many eighth- and ninth-century Muslim scholars had worked on both kinds of texts. "Altogether, if hadith isnads were suspect, so then should be the isnads attached to historical reports."

As Goldziher puts it himself,[168] "closer acquaintance with the vast stock of hadiths induces skeptical caution"; and he considers by far the greater part of the hadith "as the result of the religious, historical and social development of Islam during the first two centuries." The hadith is useless as a basis for any scientific history and can only serve as a "reflection of the tendencies" of the early Muslim community.

Here I need to interpose a historical digression, if we are to have a proper understanding of Goldziher's arguments. After the death of the Prophet, four of his companions succeeded him as leaders of the Muslim community; the last of the four was Ali, the Prophet's cousin and son-in-law. Ali was unable to impose his authority in Syria where the governor Muawiya adopted the the war cry of "Vengeance for Uthman" against Ali. (Muawiya and Uthman were related and both belonged to the Meccan clan of Umayya.) The forces of the two met in an indecisive battle at Siffin. After Ali's murder in 661, Muawiya became the first caliph of the dynasty we know as the Umayyad, which endured until A.D. 750. The Umayyads were deposed by the Abbasids, who lasted in Iraq and Baghdad until the thirteenth century.

During the early years of the Umayyad dynasty, many Muslims were totally ignorant in regard to ritual and doctrine. The rulers themselves had little enthusiasm for religion and generally despised the pious and the ascetic. The result was that there arose a group of pious men who shamelessly fabricated traditions for the good of the community and traced them back to the authority of the Prophet. They opposed the godless Umayyads but dared not say so openly, so they invented further traditions dedicated to praising the Prophet's family, hence indirectly giving their allegiance to the party of Ali supporters. As Goldziher puts it,[169] "the ruling power itself was not idle. If it wished an opinion to be generally recognized and the opposition of pious circles silenced, it too had to know how to discover a hadith to suit its purpose. They had to do what their opponents did: invent and have invented, hadiths in their turn. And that is in effect what they did." "Official influence," continues Goldziher,

> on the invention, dissemination and suppression of traditions started early. An instruction given to his obedient governor al-Mughira by Muawiya is in the spirit of the Umayyads: "Do not tire of abusing and insulting Ali and calling for God's mercifulness for Uthman, defaming the companions of Ali, removing them and omitting to listen to them (i.e., to what they tell and propagate as hadiths); praising in contrast, the clan of Uthman, drawing them near to you and listening to them." This is an official encouragement to foster the rise and spread of hadiths directed against Ali and to hold back and suppress hadiths favoring Ali. . . . The Umayyads and their political followers had no scruples in promoting tendentious lies in a sacred religious form, and they were only concerned to find pious authorities who would be prepared to cover such falsifications with their undoubted authority. There was never any lack of these.[170]

Hadiths were liable to be fabricated for even the most trivial ritualistic details. Tendentiousness included the suppression of existing utterances friendly to the rival party or dynasty. Under the Abbasids, the fabrications of hadiths greatly multiplied, with the express purpose of proving the legitimacy of their own clan against the Alids. For example, the Prophet was made to say that Abu Talib, father of Ali, was sitting deep in hell: "Perhaps my intercession will be of use to him on the day of resurrection so that he may be transferred into a pool of fire which reaches only up to the ankles but which is still hot enough to burn the brain." Naturally enough this was countered by the theologians of the Alids by devising numerous traditions concerning the glorification of Abu Talib, all sayings of the Prophet. In fact, as Goldziher shows, among the opposing factions "the mischievous use of tendentious traditions was even more common than with the official party."[171]

Eventually storytellers made a good living inventing entertaining hadiths, which the credulous masses lapped up eagerly. To draw the crowds the storytellers shrank from nothing. "The handing down of hadiths sank to the level of a business very early. . . . Journeys [in search of hadiths] favored the greed of those who succeeded in pretending to be a source of the hadith, and with increasing demand sprang up an ever increasing desire to be paid in cash for the hadiths supplied."[172]

Of course many Muslims were aware that forgeries abounded. But even the so-called six authentic collections of hadiths compiled by al-Bukhari and others were not as rigorous as might have been hoped. The six had varying criteria for including a hadith as genuine or not: some were rather liberal in their choices, others rather arbitrary. Then there was the problem of the authenticity of the texts of these compilers. For example, at one point there were a dozen different Bukhari texts, and apart from these variants, there were deliberate interpolations. As Goldziher warns us, "it would be wrong to think that the canonical authority of the two [collections of Bukhari and Muslim ibn al-Hajjaj] is due to the undisputed correctness of their contents and is the result of scholarly investigations."[173] Even a tenth-century critic pointed out the weaknesses of two hundred traditions incorporated in the works of Hajjaj and Bukhari.

Goldziher's arguments were followed up, nearly sixty years later, by those of another great Islamicist, Joseph Schacht, whose works on Islamic law are considered classics in the field of Islamic studies. Schacht's conclusions were even more radical and perturbing, and the full implications of these conclusions have not yet sunk in.

Humphreys[174] sums up Schacht's theses as: (1) that isnads [the chain of transmitters] going all the way back to the Prophet only began to be widely used around the time of the Abbasid Revolution—i.e., the mid-eighth century; (2) that ironically, the more elaborate and formally correct an isnad appeared to be, the more likely it was to be spurious. In general he concluded, *no* existing hadith could be reliably ascribed to the Prophet, though some of them might ultimately be rooted in his teaching. And though [Schacht] devoted only a few pages to historical reports about the early caliphate, he explicitly asserted that the "same strictures should apply to them." Schacht's arguments, backed up by a formidable list of references, could not be easily dismissed.

Schacht himself[175] sums up his own thesis thus:

> It is generally conceded that the criticism of traditions as practiced by the Muhammadan scholars is inadequate and that, however many forgeries may have been eliminated by it, even the classical corpus contains a great many traditions which cannot possibly be authentic. All efforts to extract from this often self-contradictory mass an authentic core by "historic intuition" . . . have failed. Goldziher, in another of his fundamental works, has not only voiced his "sceptical reserve" with regard to the traditions contained even in the classical collections [i.e., the collections of Bukhari, Hajjaj, et al.], but shown positively that the great majority of traditions from the Prophet are documents not of the time to which they claim to belong, but of the successive stages of development of doctrines during the first centuries of Islam. This brilliant discovery became the corner-stone of all serious investigation.
>
> This book [i.e., Schacht's own book] will be found to confirm Goldziher's results, and go beyond them in the following respects: a great many traditions in the classical and other collections were put into circulation only after Shafi'i's time [Shafi'i was the founder of the very important school of law that bears his name; he died in A.D. 820]; the first considerable body of legal traditions from the Prophet originated towards the middle of the second [Muslim] century [i.e., eighth century], in opposition to slightly earlier traditions from Companions and other authorities, and to the living tradition of the ancient schools of law; traditions from Companions and other authorites underwent the same process of growth, and are to be considered in the same light, as traditions from the Prophet; the isnads show a tendency to grow backwards and to claim higher and higher authority until they arrive at the Prophet; the evidence of legal traditions carries us back to about the year 100 A.H. [A.D. 718] only.

Schacht proves that a tradition did not exist at a particular time, for example, by showing that it was not used as a legal argument in a discussion that would have made reference to it imperative, if it had existed. For Schacht every legal tradition from the Prophet must be taken as inauthentic and the fictitious expression of a legal doctrine formulated at a later date: "We shall not meet any legal tradition from the Prophet which can positively be considered authentic."[176]

Traditions were formulated polemically to rebut a contrary doctrine or practice; Schacht calls these traditions "counter traditions." Doctrines in this polemical atmosphere were frequently projected back to higher authorities: "traditions from Successors [to the Prophet] become traditions from Companions [of the Prophet], and traditions from Companions become traditions from the Prophet." Details from the life of the Prophet were invented to support legal doctrines.

Schacht then criticizes isnads that "were often put together very carelessly. Any typical representative of the group whose doctrine was to be projected back on to an ancient authority, could be chosen at random and put into the isnad. We find therefore a number of alternative names in otherwise identical isnads."

Schacht "showed that the beginnings of Islamic law cannot be traced further back in the Islamic tradition, than to about a century after the Prophet's death."[177] Islamic law did not directly derive from the Koran but developed out of popular and administrative practice under the Ummayads, and this "practice often diverged from the intentions and even the explicit wording of the Koran." Norms derived from the Koran were introduced into Islamic law at a secondary stage.

A group of scholars was convinced of the essential soundness of Schacht's analysis and proceeded to work out in full detail the implications of Schacht's arguments. The first of these scholars was John Wansbrough, who in two important, though formidably difficult books, *Quranic Studies: Sources and Methods of Scriptural Interpretation* (1977) and *The Sectarian Milieu: Content and Composition of Islamic Salvation History* (1978), showed that the Koran and the hadith grew out of sectarian controversies over a long period—perhaps as long as two centuries—and then were projected back onto an invented Arabian point of origin.[178] He further argued that Islam emerged only when it came into contact with and under the influence of rabbinic Judaism, "that Islamic doctrine generally, and even the figure of Muhammad, were molded on Rabbinic Jewish prototypes." "Proceeding from these conclusions, The Sectarian Milieu analyses early Islamic historiography—or rather the interpretive myths underlying this historiography— as a late manifestation of Old Testament 'salvation history.' "

Once again, to appreciate Wansbrough's arguments, we need to look at the traditional account of the collection of the Koran. The problem is that there is no one tradition but several incompatible ones. According to one tradition, during Abu Bakr's brief caliphate (632–634), Umar, who himself was to succeed to the caliphate in 634, became worried at the fact that so many Muslims who had known the Koran by heart were killed during the battle of Yamama, in Central Arabia. There was a real danger that parts of the Koran would be irretrievably lost unless a collection of the Koran was made before more of those who knew the Koran by heart were killed. Abu Bakr eventually gave his consent to such a project, and asked Zayd ibn Thabit, the former secretary of the Prophet, to undertake the task. So Zayd proceeded to collect the Koran "from pieces of papyrus, flat stones, palm leaves, shoulder blades and ribs of animals, pieces of leather and wooden boards, as well as from the hearts of men." Once complete, the Koran was handed over to Abu Bakr, and on his death passed to Umar, and upon his death passed to Umar's daughter, Hafsa. However, there are different versions of this tradition—in some it is Umar who gets the credit for first collecting the Koran, in others it is Ali, the fourth caliph. Further, there is no conclusive evidence that those who died did know the Koran by heart. It is also unlikely that in so short a time (two years) such an important task could have been completed. One would also expect such a collection to have some sort of authority, but we find no such authority attributed to Abu Bakr's Koran. Indeed, in the different provinces, other collections of the Koran were considered authoritative. It seems unlikely that an official Koran would have been given to Umar's daughter for safekeeping. It is highly probable that the story of the collection of the Koran under Abu Bakr was fabricated and circulated by the enemies of the third caliph, Uthman, to take away from him some of the glory attendant on being credited with having made the first collection.

According to tradition, the next step was taken under Uthman (644–656). One of Uthman's generals asked the caliph to make such a collection because serious disputes had broken out among his troops from different provinces in regard to the correct readings of the Koran. Uthman chose Zayd ibn Thabit to prepare the official text. Zayd carefully revised the Koran, comparing his version with the "leaves" in the possession of Umar's daughter; and as instructed, in case of difficulty as to the reading, Zayd followed the dialect of the Quraysh, the Prophet's tribe. The copies of the new version, which must have been completed between 650 and Uthman's death in 656, were sent to Kufa, Basra, Damascus, and perhaps Mecca; and of course one was kept in Medina. All other versions were ordered to be destroyed. This version of events is also open to criticism. We are not sure of the nature of the "leaves" that Hafsa, Umar's daughter, possessed. The number of persons working on this project also varies; the Arabic found in the Koran is not a dialect; and so on.

Nonetheless, this last tradition has prevailed, but as Michael Cook has put it, "the choice is a somewhat arbitrary one; the truth may lie anywhere within the limits of the discordant traditions, or *altogether outside them*" [my emphasis].[179]

For orthodox Muslims of today, the Koran we have is the one that was established under Uthman in the seventh century. "Muslim orthodoxy holds further that Uthman's Quran contains all of the revelation delivered to the community faithfully preserved without change or variation of any kind and that the acceptance of the Uthmanic Quran was all but universal from the day of its distribution. The orthodox position is motivated by dogmatic factors; it cannot be supported by the historical evidence."[180]

This brings us to Wansbrough's dismissal of the previous traditions. Wansbrough shows that far from being fixed in the seventh century, the definitive text of the Koran had still not been achieved as late as the ninth century. An Arabian origin for Islam is highly unlikely; the Arabs gradually formulated their creed as they came into contact with rabbinic Judaism *outside* the Hijaz (Central Arabia, containing the cities of Mecca and Medina).

> Quranic allusion presupposes familiarity with the narrative material of Judaeo-Christian scripture, which was not so much reformulated as merely referred to. . . . Taken together, the quantity of reference, the mechanically repetitious employment of rhetorical convention, and the stridently polemical style, all suggest a strongly sectarian atmosphere in which a corpus of familiar scripture was being pressed into the service of as yet unfamiliar doctrine.[181]

Elsewhere Wansbrough says, "[The] challenge to produce an identical or superior scripture (or portion thereof), expressed five times in the Quranic text can be explained only within a context of Jewish polemic."[182]

Earlier scholars such as Torrey, recognizing the genuine borrowings in the Koran from rabbinic literature, had jumped to conclusions about the Jewish population in the Hijaz (i.e., Central Arabia). But as Wansbrough puts it, "References in Rabbinic literature to Arabia are of remarkably little worth for purposes of historical reconstruction, and especially for the Hijaz in the sixth and seventh centuries."[183]

Much influenced by the rabbinic accounts, the early Muslim community took Moses as an exemplar, and then a portrait of Muhammad emerged—but only gradually and in response to the needs of a religious community. It was anxious to establish Muhammad's credentials as a prophet on the Mosaic model; this evidently meant there had to be a Holy Scripture, which would be seen as testimony to his prophethood. Another gradual development was the emergence of the idea of the Arabian origins of Islam. To this end, there was elaborated the concept of a sacred language, *lingua sacra,* Arabic. The Koran was said to be handed down by God in pure Arabic. It is significant that the ninth century also saw the first collections of the ancient poetry of the Arabs: "The manner in which this material was manipulated by its collectors to support almost any argument appears never to have been very successfully concealed."[184] Thus Muslim philologists were able to give an early date, for instance, to a poem ascribed to Nabigha Jadi, a pre-Islamic poet, in order to "provide a pre-Islamic proof text for a common Quranic construction." The aim in appealing to the authority of pre-Islamic poetry was twofold: first, to give *ancient* authority to their own Holy Scripture, to push this sacred text back into an earlier period, and thus, give their text greater authenticity, a text that in reality had been fabricated, along with all the supporting traditions, in the later ninth century. Second, it gave a specifically Arabian flavor, an Arabian setting to their religion, making it something distinct from Judaism and Christianity. Exegetical traditions were equally fictitious and had but one aim, to demonstrate the Hijazi origins of Islam. Wansbrough gives some negative evidence to show that the Koran had not achieved any definitive form before the ninth century:

> Schacht's studies of the early development of legal doctrine within the community demonstrate that with very few exceptions, Muslim jurisprudence was not derived from the contents of the Quran. It may be added that those few exceptions are themselves hardly evidence for the existence of the canon, and further observed that even where doctrine was alleged to draw upon scripture, such is not necessarily proof of the earlier existence of the scriptural source. Derivation of law from scripture . . . was a phenomenon of the ninth century. . . . A similar kind of negative evidence is absence of any reference to the Quran in the Fiqh Akbar I.[185]

The latter is a document, dated to the middle of the eighth century, which was a kind of statement of the Muslim creed in face of sects. Thus the *Fiqh Akbar I* represents the views of the orthodoxy on the then-prominent dogmatic questions.

It seems unthinkable that had the Koran existed no reference would have been made to it.

Wansbrough submits the Koran to a highly technical analysis with the aim of showing that it cannot have been deliberately edited by a few men, but "rather the product of an organic development from originally independent traditions during a long period of transmission."

Wansbrough was to throw cold water on the idea that the Koran was the only hope for genuine historical information regarding the Prophet, an idea summed up by Jeffery:[186] "The dominant note in this advanced criticism is 'back to the Koran.' As a basis for critical biography the Traditions are practically worthless; in the Koran alone can we be said to have firm ground under our feet."

But as Wansbrough was to show: "The role of the Quran in the delineation of an Arabian prophet was peripheral: evidence of a divine communication but not a report of its circumstances. . . . The very notion of biographical data in the Quran depends upon exegetical principles derived from material external to the canon."[187]

A group of scholars influenced by Wansbrough took an even more radical approach; they rejected wholesale the entire Islamic version of early Islamic history. Michael Cook, Patricia Crone, and Martin Hinds, writing between 1977 and 1987,

> regard the whole established version of Islamic history down at least to the time of Abd al-Malik (685–705) as a later fabrication, and reconstruct the Arab Conquests and the formation of the Caliphate as a movement of peninsular Arabs who had been inspired by Jewish messianism to try to reclaim the Promised Land. In this interpretation, Islam emerged as an autonomous religion and culture only within the process of a long struggle for identity among the disparate peoples yoked together by the Conquests: Jacobite Syrians, Nestorian Aramaeans in Iraq, Copts, Jews, and (finally) Peninsular Arabs.[188]

Before looking at their arguments in detail, we once again need to have the traditional account of the life of Muhammad and the rise of Islam, before we can assess its plausibility. Muhammad was born, probably in A.D. 570, in Mecca to a family that once had been powerful and much respected, but that had fallen on hard times: the Hashim, who belonged to the Arab tribe of Quraysh. Muhammad grew up an orphan and was brought up by his uncle, Abu Talib, with whom Muhammad is said to have gone on trading journeys to Syria. He began working as the commercial agent for a rich widow, Khadija. The enterprise prospered and he eventually married her.

While sojourning on Mount Hira, as was his wont, Muhammad experienced visions, as a result of which he eventually became convinced that God had specially commissioned him to be his messenger. In A.D. 610, he told his relatives and close friends of his experiences and three years later was commanded by God to speak more publicly. The pagan Meccans tolerated him until he began attacking their gods. Mecca at that time was a thriving commercial center, having won control of many trade routes. Thus, opposition to Muhammad came from prosperous merchants who feared his success and resented his criticism of their way of life. Muhammad seems to have even compromised his monotheism, at first, to make peace with the Meccans. This is the incident retold in *The Satanic Verses,* and since the story comes from impeccable Muslim sources (al-Tabari, Ibn Sa'd), Muslims are not justified in blaming infidels for its fabrication. While Muhammad was still hoping to compromise with the Meccan merchants, he received a revelation that the favorite deities of the Meccans—al-Lat, al-Uzza, and Manat—might be regarded as divine beings whose intercession was effectual with God. But Muhammad soon recognized these verses as interpolations of Satan and received further revelations abrogating the Satanic verses, but retaining the names of the goddesses, and adding that it was unfair that God should have daughters while humans had sons (sura 53.19–23). During this period the powerful merchants may have been boycotted by Muhammad and his entire family. After the death of his uncle, Abu Talib, and his wife Khadija, Muhammad's position become more and more unsupportable, and he sought to establish himself in Taif without success.

The Hijra or Emigration to Medina, A.D. 622

Muhammad met a group of people from the oasis of Yathrib (or Medina, as it later came to be known), who realized that Muhammad might help them with their domestic political problems. They absorbed Islam from Muhammad and returned to Medina to preach the new religion. In 622, a larger group of Medinese pledged their support and agreed to grant him protection. Muhammad urged his Meccan supporters to emigrate to Medina, while he himself became the last to leave the town. This migration (the Hijra) of the Prophet was later taken as the starting point of Muslim chronology. (According to tradition, the Hijra took place in September 622; however, the Muslim era starts at the beginning of the Arab year in which the Hijra took place, i.e., 16 July 622.)

Medina at the time of Muhammad's arrival was inhabited by eight large clans of Arabs and three major clans of Jews. For years there had been feuding between the clans, culminating in a great battle in 618, in which many were slaughtered. With the aim of creating political stability, Muhammad established a community or people (umma) made up of his followers from Mecca and the people of Medina. All important problems were to be laid before him and God. All the new arrangements are contained in a document called the Constitution of Medina, and as Cook puts it, "[one of the major interests] of the parties of the document is the waging of war."

After six months in Medina, Muhammad began sending out raiding parties to attack and capture Meccan caravans on their way to Syria. Unsuccessful at first, Muhammad's men finally managed to capture a Meccan caravan by attacking during the pagan sacred month. Muhammad took a fifth of the booty. Initially, the Medinans were shocked at the profanation of the sacred month, but eventually one of their leading men gave him support to the extent of taking part in the raids.

At about this time, Muhammad's relations with the Jews became more and more strained. At first, he had hoped to be accepted as a prophet, because he had always emphasized that the message that he was preaching was no different from that preached by Moses; besides, he had adopted many of the Jews' practices. But as the Jews refused to recognize him as a true prophet, Muhammad began developing the idea of the religion of Abraham and broke free from Judaism and Christianity. Islam was an independent religion far superior to both these monotheistic creeds. In the end, the Jews were either banished from Medina or exterminated.

Muhammad learned that a rich Meccan caravan was to pass nearby and decided to attack it at Badr. The Meccans had learned of Muhammad's plans and accordingly gathered a vastly superior army to teach the Muslims a lesson. Although the Muslims were obviously surprised to find themselves confronting an immense army instead of a mere caravan, they were inspired by Allah and their Prophet and won a resounding battle in 624. Several prisoners were taken, two were executed on Muhammad's order—one of the two was none other than al-Nadr, he who had pinched the Prophet's audience in Mecca by telling more entertaining stories. The following year, the Meccans, led by Abu Sufyan, had their revenge when they inflicted a heavy defeat on the Muslims at the battle of Uhud. Muhammad continued his raids for two years, while the Meccans prepared for an all-out attack. In 627, the Meccans besieged the Muslims for a fortnight but withdrew, unable to penetrate the barrier of a trench dug by the Muslims on the suggestion of Salman the Persian. When the Meccans withdrew, Muhammad decided to attack the remaining Jewish group, the Qurayza, who eventually surrendered. The men of this clan were all executed, and the women and children sold.

The following year, 628, Muhammad signed a treaty at al-Hudaybiya, by which the Muslims were to be allowed to make a pilgrimage to Mecca the following year. By now Muhammad was powerful enough to try and take Mecca itself, which he did in 630, with very little bloodshed. He consolidated his power in Central Arabia, and eventually most of the Arab tribes threw in their lot with him.

It is clear from the traditional accounts that just before his death in 632, Muhammad had visions of extending his power and influence beyond Arabia. In 631, he is said to have gathered an enormous army (thirty thousand men, ten thousand horses) to attack the Romans at Tabuk, a city between Medina and Damascus, but nothing came of this expedition. A portion of this force was sent to Dumah, where the Muslim commander Khalid received the submission of Jewish and Christian tribes. Muhammad had also planned to send his army into Roman territory in Palestine, but the plan was never realized because of his death in 632.

Throughout the twenty-three years of his prophetic mission Muhammad received revelations directly from God, whereby "the basic rituals and duties of Islam were established or further refined: washing, prayer, alms-giving, fasting, pilgrimage." The revelations also concerned practical matters, religious law, inheritance, marriage, divorce, and so on.

Such is the tradition that is no longer accepted by Cook, Crone, and Hinds. In the short but pithy monograph on Muhammad in the Oxford Past Masters series, Cook gives his reasons for rejecting the biographical traditions:

> False ascription was rife among the eighth-century scholars, and that in any case Ibn Ishaq and his contemporaries were drawing on oral tradition. Neither of these propositions is as arbitrary as it sounds. We have reason to believe that numerous traditions on questions of dogma and law were provided with spurious chains of authorities by those who put them into circulation; and at the same time we have much evidence of controversy in the eighth century as to whether it was permissible to reduce oral tradition to writing. The implications of this view for the reliability of our sources are clearly rather negative. If we cannot trust the chains of authorities, we can no longer claim to know that we have before us the separately transmitted acounts of independent witnesses; and if knowledge of the life of Muhammad was transmitted orally for a century before it was reduced to writing, then the chances are that the material will have undergone considerable alteration in the process.[189]

Cook then looks at the non-Muslim sources: Greek, Syriac, and Armenian. Here a totally unexpected picture emerges. Although there is no doubt that someone called Muhammad existed, that he was a merchant, that something significant happened in 622, and that Abraham was central to his teaching, there is no indication that Muhammad's career unfolded in inner Arabia, there is no mention of Mecca, and the Koran makes no appearance until the last years of the seventh century. Further, it emerges from this evidence that the Muslims prayed in a direction much further north than Mecca; hence their sanctuary cannot have been in Mecca. "Equally, when the first Koranic quotations appear on coins and inscriptions towards the end of the seventh century, they show divergences from the canonical text. These are trivial from the point of view of content, but the fact that they appear in such formal contexts as these goes badly with the notion that the text had already been frozen."[190] The earliest Greek source speaks of Muhammad being alive in 634, two years after his death according to Muslim tradition. Where the Muslim accounts talk of Muhammad's break with the Jews,

> the Armenian chronicler of the 660s describes Muhammad as establishing a community which comprised both Ishmaelites (i.e., Arabs) and Jews, with Abrahamic descent as their common platform; these allies then set off to conquer Palestine. The oldest Greek source makes the sensational statement that the prophet who had appeared among the Saracens (i.e., Arabs) was proclaiming the coming of the (Jewish) messiah, and speaks of the Jews who mix with

the Saracens', and of the danger to life and limb of falling into the hands of these Jews and Saracens. We cannot easily dismiss this evidence as the product of Christian prejudice, since it finds confirmation in the Hebrew apocalypse. [An eighth-century document in which is embedded an earlier apocalypse that seems to be contemporary with the conquests.] The break with the Jews is then placed by the Armenian chronicler immediately after the Arab conquest of Jerusalem.[191]

Although Palestine does play some sort of role in Muslim traditions, it is already demoted in favor of Mecca in the second year of the Hijra, when Muhammad changed the direction of prayer for Muslims from Jerusalem to Mecca. Thereafter it is Mecca that holds center stage for his activities. But in the non-Muslim sources, Palestine is the focus of his movement and provides the religious motive for its conquest. The Armenian chronicler gives a further rationale for this attachment: Muhammad told the Arabs that, as descendants of Abraham through Ishmael, they too had a claim to the land that God had promised to Abraham and his seed. The religion of Abraham is in fact as central in the Armenian account of Muhammad's preaching as it is in the Muslim sources, but it is given a quite different geographical twist.

> If the external sources are in any significant degree right on such points, it would follow that tradition is seriously misleading on important aspects of the life of Muhammad, and that even the integrity of the Koran as his message is in some doubt. In view of what was said above about the nature of the Muslim sources, such a conclusion would seem to me legitimate; but is only fair to add that it is not usually drawn. [192]

Cook points out the similarity of certain Muslim beliefs and practices to those of the Samaritans (discussed below). He also points out that the fundamental idea Muhammad developed of the religion of Abraham was already present in the Jewish apocryphal work (dated to ca. 140–100 B.C.) called the Book of Jubilees and may well have influenced the formation of Islamic ideas. We also have the evidence of Sozomenus, a Christian writer of the fifth century, who "reconstructs a primitive Ishmaelite monotheism identical with that possessed by the Hebrews up to the time of Moses"; and he goes on to argue from present conditions that Ishmael's laws must have been "corrupted by the passage of time and the influence of pagan neighbours."

Sozomenus goes on to describe how certain Arab tribes that learned of their Ishmaelite origins from Jews adopted Jewish observances. Again, there may have been some influence on the Muslim community from this source. Cook also points out the similarity of the story of Moses (exodus, etc.) and the Muslim hijra (or exodus from Mecca). In Jewish messianism,

> the career of the messiah was seen as a re-enactment of that of Moses; a key event in the drama was an exodus, or flight, from oppression into the desert,

whence the messiah was to lead a holy war to reconquer Palestine. Given the early evidence connecting Muhammad with Jews and Jewish messianism at the time when the conquest of Palestine was initiated, it is natural to see in Jewish apocalyptic thought a point of departure for his political ideas.

Cook and Patricia Crone had developed these ideas in their intellectually exhilarating work, *Hagarism: The Making of the Islamic World* (1977). Unfortunately, they adopted the rather difficult style of their "master" Wansbrough, which may well put off all but the most dedicated readers; as Humphreys says, "their argument is conveyed through a dizzying and unrelenting array of allusions, metaphors, and analogies."[193] The summary already given of Cook's conclusions in "Muhammad" will help nonspecialists to have a better grasp of Cook and Crone's (CC, henceforth) arguments in "Hagarism." We might further tabulate the steps in their arguments thus:

1. Skepticism of Historicity of Islamic Tradition
2. The Use of Non-Muslim Sources
3. Judeo-Arab Solidarity and Hostility toward Christians
4. Early Muslim Conquests
5. Shedding of Judaism
6. Softening of Attitude toward Christians
7. Doctrinal Literacy: the Influence of Samaritans
8. Creation of Arab Prophet on the Model of Moses
9. Creation of Holy Sanctuary
10. Creation of Holy Capital

It would be appropriate to begin with an explanation of CC's frequent use of the terms "Hagar," "Hagarism," and "Hagarene." Since a part of their thesis is that Islam only emerged later than hitherto thought, after the first contacts with the older civilizations in Palestine, the Near East, and the Middle East, it would have been inappropriate to use the traditional terms "Muslim," "Islamic," and "Islam" for the early Arabs and their creed. It seems probable that the early Arab community did not call itself "Muslim" while it was developing its own religious identity. On the other hand, Greek and Syriac documents refer to this community as "Magaritai," and "Mahgre" (or "Mahgraye"), respectively. The Mahgraye are the descendants of Abraham by Hagar, hence the term "Hagarism." But there is another dimension to this term; for the corresponding Arabic term is "muhajirun"—the muhajirun are those who take part in a hijra, an exodus. "The 'Mahgraye' may thus be seen as Hagarene participants in a hijra to the Promised Land; in this pun lies the earliest identity of the faith which was in the fullness of time to become Islam."[194]

Relying on hitherto neglected non-Muslim sources, CC give a new account of the rise of Islam, an account, on their admission, unacceptable to any Muslim. The Muslim sources are too late, unreliable; and there are no cogent external grounds for accepting the Islamic tradition. CC begin with a Greek text (dated ca. 634–636), in which the core of the Prophet's message appears as Judaic messianism. There is evidence that the Jews themselves, far from being the enemies of Muslims as traditionally recounted, welcomed and interpreted the Arab conquest in messianic terms. The evidence "of Judeo-Arab intimacy is complemented by indications of a marked hostility towards Christianity." An Armenian chronicle written in the 660s also contradicts the traditional Muslim insistence that Mecca was the religious metropolis of the Arabs at the time of the conquest; in contrast, it points out the Palestinian orientation of the movement. The same chronicle helps us understand how the Prophet "provided a rationale for Arab involvement in the enactment of Judaic messianism. This rationale consists in a dual invocation of the Abrahamic descent of the Arabs as Ishmaelites: on the one hand to endow them with a birthright to the Holy Land, and on the other to provide them with a monotheist genealogy."[195] Similarly, we can see the Muslim hijra, not as an exodus from Mecca to Medina (for no early source attests to the historicity of this event), but as an emigration of the Ishmaelites (Arabs) from Arabia to the Promised Land.

The Arabs soon quarreled with the Jews, and their attitude to Christians softened—the Christians posed less of a political threat. There still remained a need to develop a positive religious identity, which they proceeded to do by elaborating a full-scale religion of Abraham, incorporating many pagan practices but under a new Abrahamic aegis. But they still lacked the basic religious structures to be able to stand on their two feet as an independent religious community. Here they were enormously influenced by the Samaritans.

The origins of the Samaritans are rather obscure. They are Israelites of Central Palestine, generally considered the descendents of those who were planted in Samaria by the Assyrian kings in about 722 B.C. The faith of the Samaritans was Jewish monotheism, but they had shaken off the influence of Judaism by developing their own religious identity, rather in the way the Arabs were to do later on. The Samaritan canon included only the Pentateuch, which was considered the sole source and standard for faith and conduct.

The formula "There is no God but the One" is an ever-recurring refrain in Samaritan liturgies. A constant theme in their literature is the unity of God and His absolute holiness and righteousness. We can immediately notice the similarity of the Muslim proclamation of faith, "There is no God but Allah." And of course, the unity of God is a fundamental principle in Islam. The Muslim formula "In the name of God" (Bismillah) is found in Samaritan scripture as "beshem." The opening chapter of the Koran is known as the Fatiha, opening or gate, often considered as a succinct confession of faith. A Samaritan prayer that can also be considered a confession of faith begins with the words: *Amadti kamekha al-fatah rahmekha,* "I stand before Thee at the gate of Thy mercy." Fatah is the Fatiha, the opening or gate.[196]

The sacred book of the Samaritans, the Pentateuch, embodied the supreme revelation of the divine will and was accordingly highly venerated. Muhammad also seems to know only the Pentateuch and Psalms and shows no knowledge of the prophetic or historical writings.

The Samaritans held Moses in high regard, Moses being the prophet through whom the law was revealed. For the Samaritans, Mt. Gerizim was the righful center for the worship of Jahweh; and it was further associated with Adam, Seth, and Noah, and Abraham's sacrifice of Isaac. The expectation of a coming Messiah was also an article of faith—the name given to their Messiah was the Restorer. Here we can also notice the similarity of the Muslim notion of the Mahdi.

MOSES, EXODUS, PENTATEUCH, MT. SINAI/MT. GERIZIM, AND SHECHEM

Muhammad, Hijra, Koran, Mt. Hira, and Mecca

Under the influence of the Samaritans, the Arabs proceeded to cast Muhammad in the role of Moses as the leader of an exodus (hijra), as the bearer of a new revelation (Koran) received on an appropriate (Arabian) sacred mountain, Mt. Hira. It remained for them to compose a sacred book. CC point to the tradition that the Koran had been many books, of which Uthman (the third caliph after Muhammad) had left only one. We have the further testimony of a Christian monk who distinguishes between the Koran and the Surat al-baqara as source of law. In other documents, we are told that Ḥajjaj (661–714), the governor of Iraq, had collected and destroyed all the writings of the early Muslims. Then, following Wansbrough, CC conclude that the Koran "is strikingly lacking in overall structure, frequently obscure and inconsequential in both language and content, perfunctory in its linking of disparate materials and given to the repetition of whole passages in variant versions. On this basis it can be plausibly argued that the book [Koran] is the product of the belated and imperfect editing of materials from a plurality of traditions."[197]

The Samaritans had rejected the sanctity of Jerusalem and had replaced it with the older Israelite sanctuary of Shechem. When the early Muslims disengaged from Jerusalem, Shechem provided an appropriate model for the creation of a sanctuary of their own.

> The parallelism is striking. Each presents the same binary structure of a sacred city closely associated with a nearby holy mountain, and in each case the fundamental rite is a pilgrimage from the city to the mountain. In each case the sanctuary is an Abrahamic foundation, the pillar on which Abraham sacrificed in Shechem finding its equivalent in the rukn [the Yamani corner of the Kaaba, see this volume, page 41] of the Meccan sanctuary. Finally, the urban sanctuary is in each case closely associated with the grave of the appropriate patriarch: Joseph (as opposed to Judah) in the Samaritan case, Ishmael (as opposed to Isaac) in the Meccan.[198]

CC go on to argue that the town we now know as Mecca in Central Arabia (Hijaz) could not have been the theater of the momentous events so beloved of Muslim tradition. Apart from the lack of any early non-Muslim references to Mecca, we do have the startling fact that the direction in which the early Muslims prayed (the qiblah) was northwest Arabia. The evidence comes from the alignment of certain early mosques and the literary evidence of Christian sources. In other words, Mecca was only chosen as the Muslim sanctuary much later by the Muslims, in order to relocate their early history within Arabia, to complete their break with Judaism, and finally to establish their separate religious identity.

In the rest of their fascinating book, CC go on to show how Islam assimilated all the foreign influences that came under it in consequence of their rapid conquests; how Islam acquired its particular identity on encountering the older civilizations of antiquity, through its contacts with rabbinic Judaism, Christianity (Jacobite and Nestorian), Hellenism, and Persian ideas (rabbinic law, Greek philosophy, neoplatonism, Roman law, and Byzantine art and architecture). But they also point out that all this was achieved at great cultural cost. "The Arab conquests rapidly destroyed one empire, and permanently detached large territories of another. This was, for the states in question, an appalling catastrophe."[199]

In *Slaves on Horses: The Evolution of the Islamic Polity* (1980), Patricia Crone dismisses the Muslim traditions concerning the early caliphate (down to the 680s) as useless fictions. In *Meccan Trade and the Rise of Islam* (1987), she argues that many so-called historical reports are "fanciful elaborations on difficult Koranic passages."[200] In *Meccan Trade,* Crone convincingly shows how the Koran "generated masses of spurious information." The numerous historical events that are supposed to have been the the causes of certain revelations (for example, the battle of Badr, see p. 93)," are likely to owe at least some of their features, occasionally their very existence, to the Quran." Clearly storytellers were the first to invent historical contexts for particular verses of the Koran. But much of their information is contradictory (for example, we are told that when Muhammad arrived in Medina for the first time, the city was torn by feuds, and yet at the same time we are asked to believe that the people of Medina were united under their undisputed leader Ibn Ubayy); and there was a tendency "for apparently independent accounts to collapse into variations on a common theme" (for example, the large number of stories around the theme of "Muhammad's encounter with the representatives of non-Islamic religions who recognise him as a future prophet"). Finally, there was a tendency for the information to grow the farther away one went from the events described; for example, if one storyteller should happen to mention a raid, the next one would tell you the exact date of this raid, and the third one would furnish you with even more details. Waqidi (d. 823) who wrote several decades after Ibn Ishaq (d. 768), "will always give precise dates, locations, names, where Ibn Ishaq has none, accounts of what triggered the expedition, miscellaneous information to lend colour to the event, as well as reasons why, as was usually the case, no fighting took place. No wonder that scholars are fond of Waqidi: where else does one find such wonderfully precise information about everything one wishes to know? But given that this information was all unknown to Ibn Ishaq, its value is doubtful in the extreme. And if spurious information accumulated at this rate in the two generations between Ibn Ishaq and Waqidi, it is hard to avoid the conclusion that even more must have accumulated in the three generations between the Prophet and Ibn Ishaq." It is obvious that these early Muslim historians drew on a common pool of material fabricated by the storytellers. Crone takes to task certain conservative modern historians, such as Watt, for being unjustifiably optimistic about the historical worth of the Muslim sources on the rise of Islam. And we shall end this chapter on the sources with Crone's conclusions regarding all these Muslim sources:

> [Watt's methodology rests] on a misjudgement of these sources. The problem is the very mode of origin of the tradition, not some minor distortions subsequently introduced. Allowing for distortions arising from various allegiances within Islam such as those to a particular area, tribe, sect, or school does nothing to correct the tendentiousness arising from allegiance to Islam itself. The entire tradition is tendentious, its aim being the elaboration of an Arabian Heilgeschichte, and this tendentiousness has shaped the facts as we have them, not merely added "some partisan statements we can deduct."[201]

4

Muhammad and His Message

It is worthy of note . . . that the scholars who are most familiar with Arabic sources and have got closest to an understanding of the life of the period, scholars such as Margoliouth, Hurgronje, Lammens, Caetani, are the most decisive against the prophetic claims of Mohammed; and one must confess that the further one goes in one's own study of the sources the more difficult it becomes in one's own thinking to escape the conclusions of these scholars.

Arthur Jeffery (1926)[202]

One fact must be familiar to all those who have any experience of human nature— a sincerely religious man is often an exceedingly bad man.

Winwood Reade (1872)[203]

Either we conclude with Cook, Crone, Wansbrough, and others that we do not know a great deal about the man we call Muhammad, or we make do with the traditional sources. Muslims would perhaps be better off accepting the former alternative, since the picture that emerges of the Prophet in these traditional accounts is not at all flattering. Furthermore, Muslims cannot complain that this is a portrait drawn by an enemy.

Probably the first work in the West to apply the historicocritical method to the problem of the life of Muhammad was Gustav Weil's *Mohammad der Prophet, sein Leben und sein Lehre* (1843), in which is put forward the idea that Muhammad suffered from epilepsy. This was followed by, among others, the works of Sprenger, Noldeke, and Muir. We shall examine Sprenger's views in a moment. Noldeke's great work on the Koran, *Geschichte des Qorans* (1860) will also be discussed in the next chapter on the Koran.

Muir's *Life of Mahomet* appeared between 1856–61, in four volumes, based on the original Muslim sources, the very sources whose reliability was questioned in the last chapter, but which Muir accepted as worthy of attention. Muir was

86

to pass a judgment on Muhammad's character that was to be repeated over and over again by subsequent scholars. The scholar[204] divided Muhammad's life into two periods, the Meccan period and the Medinan period; during the first period, in Mecca, Muhammad was a religiously motivated, sincere seeker after truth; but in the second period, Muhammad the man shows his feet of clay, and is corrupted by power and worldly ambitions:

> In the Meccan period of his life there certainly can be traced no personal ends or unworthy motives. . . . Mahomet then was nothing more than he professed to be, "a simple Preacher and a Warner"; he was the despised and rejected prophet of a gainsaying people, having no ulterior object but their reformation. He may have mistaken the right means for effecting this end, but there is no sufficient reason for doubting that he used those means in good faith and with an honest purpose.
>
> But the scene changes at Medina. There temporal power, aggrandisement, and self-gratification mingled rapidly with the grand object of the Prophet's life; and they were sought and attained by just the same instrumentality. Messages from heaven were freely brought down to justify political conduct, in precisely the same manner as to inculcate religious precept. Battles were fought, executions ordered, and territories annexed, under cover of the Almighty's sanction. Nay, even personal indulgences were not only excused but encouraged by the divine approval or command. A special license was produced, allowing the Prophet many wives; the affair with Mary the Coptic bond-maid was justified in a separate Sura; and the passion for the wife of his own adopted son and bosom friend was the subject of an inspired message in which the Prophet's scruples were rebuked by God, a divorce permitted, and marriage with the object of his unhallowed desires enjoined. If we say that such "revelations" were believed by Mahomet sincerely to bear the divine sanction, it can only be in a modified and peculiar sense. He surely must be held responsible for that belief; and, in arriving at it, have done violence to his judgement and the better principles of his nature.
>
> As the natural result, we trace from the period of Mahomet's arrival at Medina a marked and rapid declension in the system he inculcated. Intolerance quickly took the place of freedom; force, of persuasion. The spiritual weapons designed at first for higher objects were no sooner devoted to the purposes of temporal authority, than temporal authority was employed to give weight and temper to those spiritual weapons. The name of the Almighty imparted a terrible strength to the sword of the State; and the sword of the State yielded a willing return by destroying "the enemies of God" and sacrificing them at the shrine of the new religion. "Slay the unbelievers wheresoever ye find them," was now the watchword of Islam. "Fight in the ways of God until opposition be crushed and the Religion become the Lord's alone." The warm and simple devotion breathed by the Prophet and his followers at Mecca, when mingled with worldly motives, soon became dull and vapid; while faith degenerated into a fierce fanaticism, or evaporated in a lifeless round of formal ceremonies.

Muir went on to say that so long as the Koran remained the standard of belief, certains evils would continue to flow: "Polygamy, Divorce, and Slavery strike at the root of public morals, poison domestic life, and disorganize society; while the Veil removes the female sex from its just position and influence in the world. . . . Freedom of thought and private judgment are crushed and annihilated. Toleration is unknown, and the possibility of free and liberal institutions foreclosed."

Muir points out the inconsistencies in Muhammad's character:

Simultaneously with the anxious desire to extinguish idolatry and promote religion and virtue in the world, there arose . . . a tendency to self-indulgence; till in the end, assuming to be the favorite of Heaven, he justified himself by "revelations," releasing himself in some cases from social proprieties, and the commonest obligations of self restraint.

Muir's final judgment is "The sword of Mahomet, and the Coran [Koran], are the most stubborn enemies of Civilization, Liberty, and Truth, which the world has yet known."[205]

Caetani, writing at the beginning of the century, came to a similar conclusion. In Medina, Muhammad is far more sure of himself, is conscious of his superiority.

It is thus the person of Mohammed that stands out above all in the front rank, till to God is given a secondary position in His capacity as the auxiliary of the Prophet. He is no longer the Supreme Being, for whose service everything should be sacrificed, but rather the all-powerful Being who aids the Prophet in his political mission, who facilitates his victories, consoles him in defeat, assists him in unravelling all the mundane and worldly complications of a great Empire over men, and helps him smooth over the difficulties which rise up every day as he works out these new phases of his prophetic and political career. This "deus ex machina" becomes supremely useful to him in a society of rude, violent, sanguinary men, quickly angered, immoveable in hatred and their passion for revenge, indifferent towards human blood, greedy of plunder, changeable as the wind in their sympathies. . . . It is from [Muhammad's] mouth and not from God that [Muhammad's men] await replies to questions, the verdict which is to decide their destinies, and for the most part it is no longer God that counts but only the Prophet. Mohammed is a fact more visible and tangible every day; God becomes ever more a useful theory, a supreme principle, who from above the heavens follows with affectionate solicitude the capricious movements and the neither few nor small weaknesses of his favorite prophet, assisting him with legions of angels in brigand expeditions, meeting with revealed verses every troublesome question, smoothing over errors, legalising faults, encouraging fierce instincts with all the immoral brutality of the tyrannical God of the Semites.

If Mohammed deviated from the path of his early years, that should cause no surprise; he was a man as much as, and in like manner as, his contemporaries, he was a member of a still half-savage society, deprived of any true culture, and guided solely by instincts and natural gifts which were decked out by badly understood and half-digested religious doctrines of Judaism and Christianity. Mohammed became thus the more easily corruptible when fortune in the end smiled upon him. . . . [In Medina], he offered very little resistance to the corrupting action of the new social position, more particularly in view of the fact that the first steps were accompanied by bewildering triumphs and by fatal sweetness of practically unlimited political power. . . . The deterioration of his moral character was a phenomenon supremely human, of which history provides not one but a thousand examples. It is easier to die holy on the cross or at the stake than on a throne after a titanic struggle against pitiless and obstinate enemies. The figure of Mohammed loses in beauty, but gains in power.

Later I shall examine Muir's and Caetani's arguments to see whether they are justified or not in their assessments of the character of the Prophet. Here I want to look at Sprenger's work on the life of Muhammad. The Muslim sources are full of references to the strange fits to which the Prophet was subject, particularly at the time of the revelations he periodically received. Here is how Margoliouth describes them:

The notion . . . that he was subject to epilepsy finds curious confirmation in the notices recorded of his experiences during the process of revelation—the importance of which is not lessened by the probability that the symptoms were often artificially produced. The process was attended by a fit of unconsciousness, accompanied (or preceded) at times by the sound of bells in the ears or the belief that someone was present: by a sense of fright, such as to make the patient burst out into perspiration: by the turning of the head to one side: by foaming at the mouth: by the reddening or whitening of the face: by a sense of headache.[206]

Sprenger decided that these apparent fits of epilepsy were a key to Muhammad's character. Most scholars dismissed his speculations as too fanciful, except the eminent Danish scholar, Franz Buhl, who put forward a modified form of the same theory. Buhl[207] thought that, in his Medinan phase, Muhammad reveals the unattractive side of his character: cruelty, slyness, dishonesty, untrustworthiness; someone whose leading principle was "the end justifies the means"; a despot who demanded absolute obedience, his sensuality inordinately increased, so that:

even his revelations were made the means of sanctioning his erotic tendencies or of restoring order to his harem. . . . The supposition is forced upon us that the earlier forms of revelation may now have been artificial means for keeping alive his reputation, and that in reality he may often consciously have been guilty of pious fraud.

Not only do his peculiar attacks . . . point to a pathological condition, but in many other ways he betrays an hysterical nature with decided anomalies. A characteristic which constantly runs through such natures is the complete inability to distinguish falsehood from truth; being governed entirely by compelling ideas, it is impossible for them to view matters in their true relation, and they are so thoroughly convinced of their own right, that not even the most compelling reasoning can persuade them to the contrary.

But Buhl denies that there was a complete transformation of Muhammad's character—we can find traces of his earlier idealism in his Medinan period.

Dr. Macdonald in his *Aspects of Islam* puts forward a psychoanalytic theory, whereby the Prophet is seen as a pathological case, and that "how he passed over at last into that turpitude is a problem again for those who have made a study of how the most honest trance mediums may at any time begin to cheat."[208]

In *Mohammed and the Rise of Islam* (London, 1905), Margoliouth[209] develops the idea of Islam as a secret society and compares Muhammad to modern mediums and Joseph Smith the founder of the Mormons. Margoliouth describes the subterfuges and chicanery of the mediums and shows that Muhammad uses similar techniques to establish and extend his power over the minds of the early Meccans who became the first converts. Two quotes from Margoliouth's book will make clear its tone and substance:

In an empty room he [Muhammad] professed to be unable to find sitting-place,—all the seats being occupied by angels. He turned his face away modestly from a corpse, out of regard for two Houris who had come from heaven to tend their husband. There is even reason for supposing that he, at times, let confederates act the part of Gabriel, or let his followers identify some interlocutor of his with that angel. The revelations which he produced find a close parallel in those of modern mediums, which can be studied in the history of Spiritualism by Mr. F. Podmore, whose researches cast great doubt on the proposition that an honourable man would not mystify his fellows; and also make it appear that the conviction produced by the performances of a medium is often not shaken by the clearest exposure. Of one of the mediums whose career he describes, this author observes that he possessed the friendship and perfect trust of his sitters, was aided by the religious emotions inspired by his trance utterances, and could appeal to an unstained character and a life of honourable activity. The possession of these advantages greatly helped this medium in producing belief in his sincerity, but the historian of Spiritualism, though uncertain how to account for all the phenomena, and acknowledging the difficulties which attend his explanation, is inclined to attribute all that is wonderful in the medium's performances to trickery. What is clear is that Mohammed possessed the same advantages as Podmore enumerates, and thereby won adherents; that nevertheless the process of revelation was so suspicious that one of the scribes employed to take down the effusions became convinced that it was imposture and discarded Islam in consequence. But to those who are studying merely the political effectiveness of supernatural revelations the sincerity of the medium is a question of little consequence.

A fair amount of the Koran must have been in existence when Abu Bakr started his mission; at least he must have been able to assure the proselytes that his Prophet was in receipt of divine communications, such as he could allege in proof of his personal acquaintance with the real God; and it is probable that with the gradual increase in the numbers of the believers, the Koran transformed itself from the "mediumistic" communications with which it began to the powerful sermons with which its second period is occupied. For a very small audience the processes undergone by the medium are exceedingly effective. The necessity of excluding strangers keeps those present in a state of alarm; the approach of the "superior condition" shown by the medium collapsing, requiring to be wrapped up, and then revealing himself in a violent state of perspiration, is highly sensational; the marvellous processes which the spectators have witnessed make them attach extraordinary value to the utterances which the medium produces, as the result of his trance. If any unbelievers are present the medium (in many cases) cannot act: and the words of the biographers imply that in the case of these early converts they signified their belief before they were brought into Mohammed's presence. As the Prophet more and more identified himself with his part he endeavoured to live up to it. It is said that he habitually wore a veil, and this practice may have begun at the time of these mysterious trances, of which it served to enhance the solemnity. In course of time he acquired a benign and pastoral manner; when he shook hands he would not withdraw his hand first; when he looked at a man he would wait for the other to turn away his face. Scrupulous care was bestowed by him on his person: every night he painted his eyes, and his body was at all times fragrant with perfumes. His hair was suffered to grow long till it reached his shoulders; and when it began to display signs of grey, these were concealed with dyes. He possessed the art of speaking a word in season to the neophytes— saying something which gratified the special inclinations of each, or which manifested acquaintance with his antecedents. How many of the stories which illustrate the latter talent are true it is hard to say; but there is little doubt that he was acquainted with the devices known to modern mediums by which private information can either be obtained, or the appearance of possessing it displayed. Moreover, in the early period none were admitted to see the Prophet in character of whom the missionary was not sure, and who had not been prepared to venerate.

We can now look at the incidents in Muhammad's life that elicited the severe judgment from Muir and Caetani. It should be made clear from the start that these incidents are recounted in the Muslim sources (Ibn Ishaq, al-Tabari, and others).

Political Assassinations; The Massacre of the Jews

Medina in 622 was inhabited by several Jewish tribes; the most important of these were the Banu 'l-Nadir, the Banu Qurayza, and the Banu Qaynuqa. There were also pagan Arab inhabitants who were divided into two clans, the Aws and the Khazraj. The Jews were divided in their loyalties, with the Nadir and the Qurayza siding with the Aws, and the Qaynuqa with the Khazraj. Years of bitter and bloody rivalry had left the parties concerned and exhausted. Muhammad arrived on this scene in September 622. Soon after his arrival, Muhammad is said to have established an agreement that was a kind of federation between the various groups in Medina and the new arrivals from Mecca. This document, known as the Constitution of Medina, is described thus, by Ibn Ishaq:

> The Messenger of God wrote a document between the Emigrants [i.e., the Muslim followers of Muhammad from Mecca] and the Ansar [i.e., the new converts among the Medinans], and in it he made a treaty and covenant with the Jews, establishing them in their religion and possessions, and assigning to them rights and duties.

According to several eminent[210] scholars, this constitution showed that right from the start Muhammad meant to move against the Jews. For Wellhausen, it revealed "a certain mistrust of the Jews"; while Wensinck believed that "Muhammad drafted the Constitution merely to neutralize the politically influential Jewish clans; he was stalling for time until he could find an opportunity to subdue them." Moshe Gil believes that:

> Through his alliance with the Arab tribes of Medina the Prophet gained enough strength to achieve a gradual anti-Jewish policy, despite the reluctance of his Medinese allies. . . . In fact, this inter-tribal law [i.e., the Constitution of Medina] had in view the expulsion of the Jews even at the moment of its writing.
>   The document, therefore, was not a covenant with the Jews. On the contrary, it was a formal statement of intent to disengage the Arab clans of Medina from the Jewish neighbors they had been with up to that time.[211]

At first, Muhammad had to proceed cautiously since not all the Medinese had welcomed him, and his financial position was weak. He was further chagrined to learn that the Jews rejected his claims to prophethood. Muhammad began sending out raiding parties; in effect, he was no more than the head of a robber community, unwilling to earn an honest living. Muhammad himself led three expeditions that were unsuccessful attacks on Meccan caravans on the way to, or from, Syria. Their first success came at Nakhla, when the Muslims—this time without Muhammad himself being present—attacked the Meccans during the sacred month, when bloodshed was forbidden. A Meccan was killed, two were taken prisoner, and much booty was carried back to Medina. But, much to Muhammad's surprise, many Medinese were shocked at the profanation of the sacred month. Nonetheless, Muhammad accepted a fifth of the ill-gotten gains and, to salve his guilty conscience conveniently "received" a revelation "justifying warfare even in the sacred months as a lesser evil than hostility to Islam." Sura 2.217: "They will ask you concerning the Sacred months, whether they may war therein. Say: Warring therein is grievous; but to obstruct the way of God and to deny Him, to hinder men from the holy temple, and to expel His people thence, that is more grievous than slaughter." Muhammad readily accepted a ransom of forty ounces of silver for each prisoner.

At about this time, the head of the Aws, Sa'd b. Mu'adh, took the decision to support Muhammad and even took part in raiding parties. Thus some Medinese were slowly beginning to accept Muhammad, but the Jews continued to reject his claims to prophethood and began criticizing him, saying that some passages of his revelations contradicted their own scriptures. His acceptance of certain Jewish practices was of no avail, and he realized that the Jews posed a real danger to his slowly increasing power in Medina.

The turning point in Muhammad's fortunes is, without doubt, the battle of Badr, in which with the help of Allah and a thousand angels, forty-nine Meccans were killed, as many taken prisoner, and much booty gathered. As the severed head of Muhammad's enemy was cast at The Prophet's feet, Muhammad cried out, "It is more acceptable to me than the choicest camel in all Arabia."

Then began a series of assassinations as Muhammad, feeling more confident, moved against his enemies, settled old scores, and ruthlessly established his power. First he ordered the execution of al-Nader—he who had scoffed at Muhammad during his days at Mecca and had told better stories than the Prophet himself. Here is how Muir describes the murder of another prisoner, Ocba:

> Two days afterwards . . . Ocba was ordered out for execution. He ventured to expostulate, and demand why he should be treated more rigorously than the other captives. "Because of thine enmity to God and his Prophet," replied Mahomet. "And my little girl!" cried Ocba, in the bitterness of his soul—"who will take care of her?" "Hell-fire!" exclaimed the Prophet; and on the instant the victim was hewn to the ground. "Wretch that thou wast!" he continued, "and persecutor! unbeliever in God, in his Prophet, and in his Book! I give thanks unto the Lord that hath slain thee, and comforted mine eyes thereby."

Again, these assassinations are sanctioned by a revelation in sura 8.68: "It has not been for any prophet to take captives until he has slaughtered in the land."

From now on Muhammad proceeded to rid himself of opposition dangerous to him. "Even secret conversations were reported to the Prophet, and on such information he countenanced proceedings that were sometimes both cruel and unscrupulous."

The next person that Muhammad moved against was the poetess Asma bint Marwan, who belonged to the Aws tribe. She had never concealed her dislike of Islam, and had composed couplets on the folly of trusting a stranger who fought his own people:

> Fucked men of Malik and of Nabit
> And of Aws, fucked men of Khazraj
> You obey a stranger who does not belong among you
> Who is not of Murad, nor of Madh'hij
> Do you, when your own chiefs have been murdered, put your hope in him
> Like men greedy for meal soup when it is cooking?
> Is there no man of honour who will take advantage of an unguarded moment
> And cut off the gulls' hopes?[212]

On hearing these lines Muhammad said, "Will no one rid me of this daughter of Marwan?" One zealous Muslim, Umayr ibn Adi, decided to execute the Prophet's wishes, and that very night crept into the writer's home while she lay sleeping, surrounded by her young children. There was even one at her breast. Umayr removed the suckling babe and then plunged his sword into the poetess. "Next morning, in the mosque at prayer, Mahomet [Muhammad], who was aware of the bloody design, said to Omeir [Umayr]: 'Hast thou slain the daughter of Merwan?' 'Yes,' he answered; 'but tell me now, is there cause for apprehension?' 'None,' said Mahomet; 'a couple of goats will hardly knock their heads together for it.' " Muhammad then praised him in front of the Muslims gathered in the mosque for his services to God and his Prophet. As Sprenger says, the rest of the family was forced to accept Islam since a blood feud was out of the question for them.

Soon afterwards, Muhammad decided to rid himself of another whose verses had dared to criticize The Prophet. Abu Afak, said to be more than a hundred years old, belonged to a Khazrajite clan. He was murdered while he slept.

In the meantime, Muhammad was only waiting for a suitable excuse to attack the Jews. A silly quarrel in the marketplace led to the Jewish tribe's, the Banu Qaynuqa, being besieged in their fortified settlement. As Muir justly notes, though bound by a friendly treaty, Muhammad did nothing to sort out the minor incident that was the initial cause of the feud. "And had there not been relentless enmity and predetermination to root out the Israelites, the differences might easily have been composed." Eventually the Jews surrendered, and preparations were made for execution. But the head of the Khazrajites, Abd Allah b. Ubayy, pleaded on their behalf, and Muhammad, not feeling confident enough to reject such a request, had to agree. The Banu Qaynuqa were banished from Medina and eventually settled in Syria. Their belongings were divided among the the army, after Muhammad had received his royal fifth. On this occasion Muhammad received the verses that form part of sura 3.12–13: "Say to those who disbelieve—You will be defeated and gathered into Hell, and what an evil resting place is that!"

There followed various other, not always very successful raids on Meccan caravans, and a few months of calm. But the assassinations continued—"another of those dastardly acts of cruelty which darken the pages of the Prophet's life." Kab ibn al-Ashraf was the son of a Jewess of the Banu Nadir. He had gone to Mecca after the battle of Badr and had composed poems in praise of the dead, trying to stir up the Meccans to avenge their heroes of Badr. Rather foolishly he returned to Medina, where Muhammad prayed aloud, "O Lord, deliver me from the son of Ashraf, in whatsoever way it seems good to you, because of his open sedition and his verses." But the Banu Nadir were powerful enough to protect Kab, and the Muslims who volunteered to murder him explained to the Prophet that only by cunning could they hope to accomplish their task. The conspirators met in Muhammad's house, and as they emerged at night, the Prophet gave them his full blessings. Pretending to be Kab's friends, the Muslims lured him out into the night and, in a suitable spot near a waterfall, murdered him. They threw Kab's head at the Prophet's feet. Muhammad praised their good work in the cause of God. As one of the conspirators recalled: "The Jews were terrified by our attack upon Allah's enemy. And there was not a Jew there who did not fear for his life."

On the morning after the murder of Kab, the Prophet declared: " 'Kill any Jew who falls into your power.' So Muhayyisa b. Masud fell upon Ibn Sunayna, one of the Jewish merchants with whom his family had social and commercial relations and killed him." When his brother remonstrated with him, Muhayyisa replied that had Muhammad commanded him to murder his brother, he would have done so. Whereupon his brother Huwayyisa, who was not yet a Muslim, converted to Islam saying, "any religion that can bring you to this is indeed wonderful!" These assassinations faithfully illustrate "the ruthless fanaticism into which the teaching of the Prophet was fast drifting."[213]

As we saw earlier the battle of Uhud was a serious defeat for the Muslims and threatened to undermine the Prophet's authority and prestige. In the aftermath of the war, we may record two further executions ordered by Muhammad: those of Abu Uzza, a prisoner left over from the battle of Badr, and Uthman ibn Moghira.

Needing a victory, Muhammad decided to attack the Jewish tribe of Nadir, who are said to have expressed joy at the defeat of the Muslims. On the pretext that he had received a divine warning of their intention to assassinate him, Muhammad ordered them to leave Medina within ten days on pain of death. After a siege of several weeks, the Jews surrendered and were allowed to leave; they left and joined the Jews of Khaybar, only to be massacred there two years later. This victory over the Jews is referred to at length in sura 59. The Prophet had been well aware of the wealth of the departing Nadir, whose land was divided between the Muslims; Muhammad's share made him financially independent.

In 627 the Meccans and their allies began their attack on Medina. The siege lasted only two weeks and was later known as the Battle of the Trench. The last Jewish tribe in Medina, the Banu Qurayza, contributed to the city's defense, but on the whole remained neutral. However, their loyalty was questioned and inevitably, after the siege, Muhammad moved against them. Realizing that they had no chance of surviving, the Banu Qurayza agreed to surrender on condition that they quit Medina empty-handed. Muhammad refused and wanted nothing less than unconditional surrender. The Jews then appealed to their ancient friendship with the Banu Aws and asked that Abu Lubaba, an ally belonging to that tribe, be allowed to visit them. He was asked what Muhammad's intentions were; by way of reply Abu Lubaba drew his hand across his throat, indicating that they must fight to the end, as death was all that they could hope for. At last, after several weeks, the Jews surrendered on condition that their fate should be decided by their allies, the Banu Aws. The latter were inclined to show mercy, but Muhammad decided that the fate of the Jews was to be decided by one of the Banu Aws. Muhammad nominated Sa'd ibn Muadh to be the judge. Sa'd was still suffering from a wound sustained at the Trench. He pronounced, "My judgment is that the men shall be put to death, the women and children sold into slavery, and the spoil divided among the army." Muhammad adopted the verdict as his own: "Truly the judgment of Sad is the judgment of God pronounced on high from beyond the seventh heaven."

> During the night trenches sufficient to contain the dead bodies of the men were dug across the market place of the city. In the morning, Mahomet, himself a spectator of the tragedy, commanded the male captives to be brought forth in companies of five or six at a time. Each company as it came up was made to sit down in a row on the brink of the trench destined for its grave, there beheaded, and the bodies cast therein. . . . The butchery, begun in the morning, lasted all day, and continued by torchlight till the evening. Having thus drenched the market place with the blood of seven or eight hundred victims, and having given command for the earth to be smoothed over their remains, Mahomet returned from the horrid spectacle to solace himself with the charms of Rihana, whose husband and all her male relatives had just perished in the massacre.[214]

The booty was divided, slave girls given as presents, women sold, and property auctioned. And yes, a revelation came down from heaven justifying the stern punishment meted out to the Jews: sura 33.25—"And He has caused to descend from their strongholds the Jews that assisted them. And he struck terror into their hearts. Some you slaughtered and some you took prisoner."

In face of such manifest cruelty, barbarity, and inhumanity modern historians have adopted many different positions.

1. Those still left with a robust sense of right and wrong, historians such as Tor Andrae, H. Z. Hirschberg, Salo Baron, and William Muir (as we shall see) have condemned the savage treatment. Tor Andrae, whose biography of Muhammad is considered one of the two most important in the last sixty years, unhesitatingly reproaches the Prophet for this "inhuman verdict" and adds, "On this occasion he again revealed that lack of honesty and moral courage which was an unattractive trait in his character." However, Andrae does try to see "Mohammed's cruelty toward the Jews against the background of the fact that their scorn and rejection was the greatest disappointment of his life."[215]

2. The apologists such as Watt (astonishingly) totally exonerate the Prophet; on reading their sophistical apologies, one is reminded of Lord Acton's dictum, "Every villain is followed by a sophist with a sponge." But as Rodinson rightly says, it is "difficult to accept the Prophet's innocence." Nothing in his previous or subsequent behavior shows any mercy for the Jews. As Moshe Gil showed, right from the start Muhammad had at least the expulsion of the Jews in mind. Further he had expressly ordered the murder of various Jews and had given out the general command to kill any Jew that came into Muslim hands. And given Abu Lubaba's gesture, it is obvious that the fate of the Banu Qurayza had already been decided. The choice of Sa'd was no accident either; a man wounded (he was to die soon afterwards) during the siege against the Qurayza; a devout Muslim; and, as Andrae puts it, "one of Muhammad's most fanatical

followers" (someone who had been one of the first to give Muhammad allegiance). Finally Muhammad's wholehearted endorsement of Sa'd's verdict speaks for itself.

3. Then there are the relativists—moral and cultural—who argue, "Neither blame nor vindication are in order here. We cannot judge the treatment of the Qurayza by present-day moral standards. Their fate was a bitter one, but not unusual according to the harsh rules of war during that period."[216] . I have already referred to relativism as a malady of modern times, and I shall have occasion to discuss it again in my last chapter. But here I shall make the following comments, addressing some logical points first.

• One of the objections to the above proposition is "that this proposition itself cannot be asserted as objective. Relativism can't be stated, because the proposition that expounds relativism cannot itself be relative. You claim absolute truth for it."[217] In other words, there is something inherently illogical in relativism.

• If there is total incommensurability between our times and some remote time in the past then, logically, not only can we not decline to pass adverse moral judgments, but we cannot pass favorable judgments either. We cannot praise a past society, or an individual from it, from our twentieth-century perspective. And yet, inconsistently, relativists constantly use value-laden adjectives to describe Muhammad, as for example, "compassionate" (Rodinson, p. 313). In the preceding quote from Norman Stillman, the fate of the Qurayza is described as "bitter." From which perspective is it bitter? The twentieth-century or seventh-century? Further, Stillman talks of the "harsh" rules of war—"harsh" from which perspective?

It is practically impossible to write history in perfectly neutral terms, even if it were desirable to do so. Stillman's own book, *The Jews of Arab Lands,* is full of morally evaluative expressions such as "tolerance." And no relativist can legitimately praise Muhammad in such absolutist terms as "one of the greatest of the sons of Adam" (Watt).

• If relativism is true, then as a consequence we cannot compare Jesus Christ or Socrates or Solon with Hitler. We cannot truly say that Jesus was morally superior to Hitler, which is absurd. If morals were entirely relative, then "American citizens and British subjects might disapprove of slavery and of persecuting Jews, but they could not argue that these things were wrong in any absolute sense or that it was their business to try to stop them."[218]

• Buried in Stillman's proposition quoted earlier is another quite separate thesis, namely, the idea that we cannot blame a man or woman for being "someone of his times." Such a thesis shifts the moral blame from the individual to the "period" in which the person under discussion lived. But this will not do as a defense of Muhammad. If Muhammad lived in barbaric times, then he was a barbarian: no worse than any other member of his society; but no better either. (And, of course, the relativist cannot merely blame the "times.")

Now some empirical observations.

1. It simply is not true that seventh-century Arabia is so morally remote

from us. Stillman's remark is condescending in the extreme. As Muir[219] says, in reference to the murder of the Jew Ibn Sunayna, "There can be little doubt that some Moslems were at times scandalised by crimes like this; though it is not in the nature of tradition to preserve the record of what they said. The present is one of the few occasions on which such murmurs have come to light. When Merwan was governor of Medina, he one day asked Benjamin, a convert from Kab's tribe, in what manner Kab met his death. 'By guile and perfidy,' said Benjamin." Rodinson[220] makes the same point, "The care taken by the texts to exculpate Muhammad shows that it must have aroused some feeling. Details emerge even from these very texts which make it difficult to accept the Prophet's innocence."

It is absurd to postulate that mercy, compassion, and generosity were totally unknown to the Arabs of seventh-century Arabia. As Isaiah Berlin[221] has remarked, "The differences among peoples and societies can be exaggerated. No culture that we know lacks the notions of good and bad; true and false. Courage, for example, has so far as we can tell, been admired in every society known to us. There are universal values. This is an empirical fact about mankind." Barbarity remains barbarity in whichever epoch one finds it.

Muhammad himself, ironically, taught that true nobility lay in forgiveness, that in Islam those who restrain their anger and pardon men shall receive Paradise as well-doers (sura 3.128; 24.22). Yet, he singularly failed to do that in his treatment of the Banu Qurayza.

2. Eminent historians have not hesitated to pass moral judgments on historical personages. Sir Steven Runciman in his classic *History of the Crusades* describes the Sultan Baibars as "cruel, disloyal, and treacherous, rough in his manners and harsh in his speech. . . . As a man he was evil."[222]

After the extermination of the Jews of Banu Qurayza, Muhammad continued his banditry and the assassinations. A group of the banished Banu'l-Nadir had settled at Khaybar, a nearby oasis, and were suspected of encouraging the Bedouin tribes to attack the Muslims. Muhammad ordered the murder of the chief of the Jews, Abi 'l Huqayq. The Prophet's henchmen assassinated Huqayq in his bed. Realizing that this latest assassination had not solved his problems, Muhammad devised a new plan; he sent out a delegation to Khaybar to persuade their new leader, Usayr b. Zarim, to come to Medina to discuss the possibility of his being made ruler of Khaybar. Solemn guarantees of his safety were given. Usayr set out, unarmed, with thirty of his men. On the way, on the flimsiest of pretexts, the Muslims turned on their invited, unarmed guests and killed all but one of them who escaped. On their return, the Muslims were greeted by Muhammad who, on learning the fate of the Jews, gave thanks and said, "Verily, the Lord hath delivered you from an unrighteous people." On another occason, Muhammad gave his philosophy of war: "War is deception."

Muhammad and his men attacked the forts that studded the vale of Khaybar one by one, all the while crying, "O you who have been given victory, kill! kill!" One by one the forts fell, until the Muslims arrived at the fort of Khamus, which also eventually succumbed. The chief of the Jews, Kinana b. al-Rabi, and his cousin were led out and accused by Muhammad of concealing the treasure of the Banu'l-Nadir. The Jews protested that they no longer had anything left. Then [here I am quoting from the much revered biography of the Prophet by Ibn Hisham] "Muhammad gave Kinana over to al-Zubayr, one of Muhammad's own men, saying, 'Torture him until you extract it from him.' Al-Zubayr struck a fire with flint on his chest until he expired. Then the Apostle [Muhammad] gave him over to Muhammad b. Maslama who cut off his head as part of his revenge for his brother Mahmud b. Maslama."[223]

The Jews of the other forts of Khaybar were eventually attacked and forced to surrender on terms, "except that is for the Nadir, who were given no quarter."

Assassinations, murder, cruelty, and torture must all be taken into consideration in any judgment on the moral character of Muhammad. But, unfortunately this sorry catalogue of misdeeds is incomplete. We need to examine his conduct on several other occasions, as always basing our account on the Muslim sources.

The Zaynab Affair

One day the Prophet set out to visit his adopted son Zaid. Zaid had been one of the earliest converts to Islam—the third, in fact—and he was very loyal to his foster father, who in return held him in high regard. Zaid was married to Zaynab bint Jahsh, a cousin of the Prophet. By all accounts—and this point is very important for our story—she was very beautiful.

On the day concerned, Zaid was not at home, but Zaynab, rather lightly clad, and hence revealing a great many of her charms, opened the door to the Prophet, and asked him in. As she hastily prepared to receive him, Muhammad was smitten by her beauty: "Gracious Lord! Good Heavens! How you do turn the hearts of men!" exclaimed the Prophet. He declined to enter and went away in some confusion. However, Zaynab had heard his words and repeated them to Zaid, when he returned home. Zaid went straight to the Prophet and dutifully offered to divorce his wife for him. Muhammad declined, adding, "Keep your wife and fear God." Zaynab now seemed quite taken with the idea of marrying the Prophet, and Zaid, seeing that Muhammad still yearned for her, divorced her. Still, fear of public opinion made Muhammad hesitate: after all, an adopted son was in every respect equal to a natural son; therefore, such a union would have been seen as incestuous by the Arabs of his time. As always, a revelation came to him in time, enabling him to "cast his scruples to the wind." While Muhammad was sitting next to his wife Aisha, he suddenly went into one of his prophetic swoons. When he had recovered, he said, "Who will go and congratulate Zaynab and say that the Lord has joined her to me in marriage?" Thus we find in sura 33.2–33.7:

God has not given to a man two hearts within him. . . . neither has He made your adopted sons to be as your own sons. . . . Let your adopted sons go by their own father's name. This is more just with God.

And it is not for a believer, man or woman, to have any choice in their affairs, when God and His Apostle have decreed a matter. . . . And remember, when you said to the person whom God has shown favor, and to whom you also have shown favor, "Keep your wife to yourself, and fear God" and you did conceal in your soul what God was about to reveal and you did fear [the opinion] of men when you should have feared God. And when Zaid had settled concerning her to divorce her, we married her to you, that it might not be a crime in the faithful to marry the wives of their adopted sons, when they have settled the affair concerning them. God's bidding must be performed. Muhammad is not the father of any man among you, but he is the Apostle of God, and the seal of the Prophets.

The most natural and immediate reaction to the preceding account must surely be that of the Prophet's own wife, Aisha, who is said to have remarked wittily on this occasion, "Truly your God seems to have been very quick in fulfilling your prayers."

How do the apologists defend the indefensible? Watt and others have tried to argue that the marriage was contracted for political reasons; there was nothing sexually improper about Muhammad's conduct. They point to the fact that Zaynab was thirty-five at the time and hence could not have been very desirable. But this is nonsense. The Muslim sources themselves give the entire story a sexual interpretation: Zaynab's beauty, her state of undress, her charms revealed by a gust of wind, Muhammad's remarks and signs of confusion. Clearly, some of Muhammad's followers were disquieted, but what perturbed them was not the Prophet's amorousness. "What struck them as odd was that the rule [revealed in the above sura] should have been so exactly calculated to satisfy desires which were for once in conflict with social taboos." Rodinson continues,

> As for thinking with that most learned Muslim apologist Muhammad Hamidullah, that Muhammad's exclamations at the beauty of Zaynab merely signified his astonishment that Zayd [Zaid] should not have managed to get on with such a lovely woman, this is out of the question since it is in flat contradiction to the obvious meaning of the text. Even the passage from the Koran, brief though it is, implies that the Prophet certainly wanted to do what the revelation did not command him to do until later, and that only fear of public opinion prevented him. Hamidullah's theory only shows once again the over subtleties which can result from the desire to prove theories the truth of which has already been proclaimed by dogma.[224]

Another sexual scandal threatened to disturb the domestic bliss of the Prophet's harem. To prevent jealousy among his wives, Muhammad used to divide his time equally among them, spending one night with each of them in turn. On a day when it was his wife Hafsa's turn, she was out visiting her father. Returning unexpectedly, she surprised Muhammad in her bed with Mary the Coptic maid, his legal concubine. Hafsa was furious and reproached him bitterly; what is more, she threatened to expose him to others in the harem. Muhammad begged her to keep quiet and promised to stay clear of the hated Mary. Hafsa was unable to keep the news to herself and told Aisha, who also hated Mary. The scandal spread throughout the harem, and soon Muhammad found himself ostracized by his own wives. As in the Zaynab affair, a divine revelation interposed to sort out his domestic problems. The heavenly message disallowed the earlier promise to keep away from the seductive maid and reprimanded the wives for their insubordination; it even hinted that the Prophet would divorce all the wives in the whole harem and replace them with more submissive ones. Then, Muhammad retired with Mary and stayed aloof from his wives for a month. Eventually, on the intercession of Umar and Abu Bakr, Muhammad made peace and forgave the wives. Harmony returned again to the harem. The sura concerned is 66.15:

> O Prophet! Why have you forbidden yourself that which God has made lawful unto you [i.e., Mary], out of desire to please your wives, for God is forgiving and merciful? Verily God has sanctioned the revocation of your oaths; . . . The Prophet had entrusted a secret to one of his wives but she repeated it and God revealed it to him. . . . If he divorces you, God will give him in your stead wives more submissive unto God, believers, pious, repentant, devout, fasting; both Women married previously, and virgins.

As Muir says, "there is surely no grotesquer utterance than this in the 'Sacred Books of the East'; and yet it has been gravely read all these ages, and is still read, by the Moslem, both in public and private, as part of the eternal Coran."[225]

The Satanic Verses

Again, we have from impeccable Muslim sources (al-Tabari; Waqidi), the damaging story of the Satanic Verses (an expression coined by Muir in the late 1850s, and now well known). During his days in Mecca, before the flight to Medina, Muhammad was sitting with some eminent men of Mecca next to the Kaaba, when he began to recite sura 53, which describes Gabriel's first visit to Muhammad and then goes on to the second visit:

> He also saw him [Gabriel] another time
> By the Lote tree at the furthest boundary
> Near to which is the Paradise of rest,
> When the Lote tree covered that which it covered,
> His sight turned not aside, neither did it wander
> And verily he beheld some of the greatest Signs of his Lord
> What do you think of Lat and Uzza
> And Manat the third beside?

At this point, we are told that Satan put into his mouth words of reconciliation and compromise:

> These are exalted Females
> Whose intercession verily is to be sought after.

Of course, the Meccans were delighted at this recognition of their deities and are said to have prayed with the Muslims. But Muhammad himself was visited by Gabriel who reprimanded him and told him that the true ending to the verse should have been:

> What! shall there be male progeny unto you, and female unto Him?
> That were indeed an unjust partition!
> They are naught but names, which ye and your fathers have invented.

Muslims have always been uncomfortable with this story, unwilling to believe that the Prophet could have made such a concession to idolatry. But if we accept the authenticity of the Muslim sources in general, there is no reason to reject the story. It seems unthinkable that such a story could have been invented by a devout Muslim such as al-Tabari, or that he could have accepted it from a dubious source.[226] Besides, it explains the fact why those Muslims who had fled to Abyssinia returned: they had heard that the Meccans had converted. It seems apparent that this was no sudden lapse on the part of Muhammad, but had been carefully calculated to win the support of the Meccans. It also casts serious doubts on Muhammad's sincerity: Even if Satan had really put the words in his mouth, what faith can we put in a man so easily led astray by Satan? Why did God let it happen? How do we know there are no other passages where Muhammad has not been led astray?

The Peace if Hudaibiya

Muhammad was also criticized by his followers on another occasion, when he was thought to have compromised his principles once again. Muhammad, feeling very confident after the consolidation of his position in Medina, decided that the moment had come to take Mecca. But realizing that the time was not right, he changed his mind at the last moment and entered into negotiations with the Meccans. By the treaty of Hudaibiya, Muhammad was to be permitted to perform the pilgrimage the following year, but in return he was to refrain from calling himself "prophet," and to refrain from using the formulae of Islam. Later Muhammad was to break the truce with the Meccans.

With these elements we are in a better position to understand Dr. Margoliouth's references[227] in his summary of the picture that emerges of Muhammad in the biography by Ibn Ishaq:

The character attributed to Mohammed in the biography of Ibn Ishaq is exceedingly unfavorable. In order to gain his ends he recoils from no expedient, and he approves of similar unscrupulousness on the part of his adherents, when exercised in his interest. He profits to the utmost from the chivalry of the Meccans, but rarely requites it with the like. He organises assassinations and wholesale massacres. His career as tyrant of Medina is that of a robber chief, whose political economy consists in securing and dividing plunder, the distribution of the latter being at times carried out on principles which fail to satisfy his follower's ideas of justice. He is himself an unbridled libertine and encourages the same passion in his followers. For whatever he does he is prepared to plead the express authorization of the deity. It is, however, impossible to find any doctrine which he is not prepared to abandon in order to secure a political end. At different points in his career he abandons the unity of God and his claim to the title of Prophet. This is a disagreeable picture for the founder of a religion, and it cannot be pleaded that it is a picture drawn by an enemy: and even though Ibn Ishaq's name was for some reason held in low esteem by the classical traditionalists of the third Islamic century, they make no attempt to discredit those portions of the biography which bear hardest on the character of their Prophet.

A final assessment of Muhammad's achievement must wait until we have looked at the Koran and its doctrines, in the next chapter.

5

The Koran

Timeo hominem unius libri.

—St. Thomas Aquinas

The truth is that the pretension to infallibility, by whomsoever made, has done endless mischief; with impartial malignity it has proved a curse, alike to those who have made it and those who have accepted it; and its most baneful shape is book infallibility. For sacerdotal corporations and schools of philosophy are able, under due compulsion of opinion, to retreat from positions that have become untenable; while the dead hand of a book sets and stiffens, amidst texts and formulae, until it becomes a mere petrifaction, fit only for that function of stumbling block, which it so admirably performs. Wherever bibliolatry has prevailed, bigotry and cruelty have accompanied it. It lies at the root of the deep-seated, sometimes disguised, but never absent, antagonism of all the varieties of ecclesiasticism to the freedom of thought and to the spirit of scientific investigation. For those who look upon ignorance as one of the chief sources of evil; and hold veracity, not merely in act, but in thought, to be the one condition of true progress, whether moral or intellectual, it is clear that the biblical idol must go the way of all other idols. Of infallibility, in all shapes, lay or clerical, it is needful to iterate with more than Catonic pertinacity, Delenda est.[228]

—T. H. Huxley, *Science and Hebrew Tradition*

May any Muslims who happen to read these lines forgive my plain speaking. For them the Koran is the book of Allah and I respect their faith. But I do not share it and I do not wish to fall back, as many orientalists have done, on equivocal phrases to disguise my real meaning. This may perhaps be of assistance in remaining on good terms with individuals and governments professing Islam; but I have no wish to deceive anyone. Muslims have every right not to read the book or to acquaint themselves with the ideas of a non-Muslim, but if they do so, they must expect to find things put forward there which are blasphemous to them. It is evident that I do not believe that the Koran is the book of Allah.

—Maxime Rodinson[229]

The Koran is written in Arabic and divided into chapters (suras or surahs) and verses (ayah; plural, ayat). There are said to be approximately 80,000 words, and between 6,200 and 6,240 verses, and 114 suras in the Koran. Each sura, except the ninth and the Fatihah (the first sura), begins with the words "In the name of the Merciful, the Compassionate." Whoever was responsible for the compilation of the Koran put the longer suras first, regardless of their chronology, that is to say, regardless of the order in which they were putatively revealed to Muhammad.

For the average, unphilosophical Muslim of today, the Koran remains the infallible word of God, the immediate word of God sent down, through the intermediary of a "spirit" or "holy spirit" or Gabriel, to Muhammad in perfect, pure Arabic; and every thing contained therein is eternal and uncreated. The original text is in heaven (the mother of the book, 43.3; a concealed book, 55.77; a well-guarded tablet, 85.22). The angel dictated the revelation to the Prophet, who repeated it after him, and then revealed it to the world. Modern Muslims also claim that these revelations have been preserved exactly as revealed to Muhammad, without any change, addition, or loss whatsoever. The Koran is used as a charm on the occasions of birth, death, or marriage. In the words of Guillaume, "It is the holy of holies. It must never rest beneath other books, but always on top of them; one must never drink or smoke when it is being read aloud, and it must be listened to in silence. It is a talisman against disease and disaster." Shaykh Nefzawi, in his erotic classic *The Perfumed Garden,* even recommends the Koran as an aphrodisiac: "It is said that reading the Koran also predisposes for copulation."

Both Hurgronje and Guillaume point to the mindless way children are forced to learn either parts of or the entire Koran (some 6,200 odd verses) by heart at the expense of teaching children critical thought: "[The children] accomplish this prodigious feat at the expense of their reasoning faculty, for often their minds are so stretched by the effort of memory that they are little good for serious thought."[230]

Hurgronje observed:

This book, once a world reforming power, now serves but to be chanted by teachers and laymen according to definite rules. The rules are not difficult but not a thought is ever given to the meaning of the words; the Quran is chanted simply because its recital is believed to be a meritorious work. This disregard of the sense of the words rises to such a pitch that even pundits who have studied the commentaries—not to speak of laymen—fail to notice when the verses they recite condemn as sinful things which both they and the listeners do every day, nay even during the very common ceremony itself.

The inspired code of the universal conquerors of thirteen centuries ago has grown to be no more than a mere text-book of sacred music, in the practice of which a valuable portion of the youth of well-educated Muslims is wasted.[231]

The Word of God?

Suyuti, the great Muslim philologist and commentator on the Koran, was able to point to five passages whose attribution to God was disputable. Some of the words in these passages were obviously spoken by Muhammad himself and some by Gabriel. Ali Dashti[232] also points to several passages where the speaker cannot have been God.

For example, the opening sura called the Fatihah:

> In the name of the Merciful and Compassionate God. Praise belongs to God, the Lord of the Worlds, the merciful, the compassionate, the ruler of the day of judgment! Thee we serve and Thee we ask for aid. Guide us in the right path, the path of those Thou art gracious to; not of those Thou art wroth with, nor of those who err.

These words are clearly addressed *to* God, in the form of a prayer. They are Muhammad's words of praise to God, asking God's help and guidance. As many have pointed out, one only needs to add the imperative "say" at the beginning of the sura to remove the difficulty. This imperative form of the word "say" occurs some 350 times in the Koran, and it is obvious that this word has, in fact, been inserted by later compilers of the Koran, to remove countless similarly embarrassing difficulties. Ibn Masud, one of the companions of the Prophet and an authority on the Koran, rejected the Fatihah and suras 113 and 114 that contain the words "I take refuge with the Lord," as not part of the Koran. Again at sura 6.104, the speaker of the line "I am not your keeper" is clearly Muhammad:

"Now proofs from your Lord have come to you. He who recognises them will gain much, but he who is blind to them, the loss will be his. I am not your keeper." Dawood in his translation adds as a footnote that the "I" refers to Muhammad.

In the same sura at verse 114, Muhammad speaks the words, "Should I [Muhammad] seek other judge than God, when it is He who has sent down to you the distinguishing book [Koran]?" Yusuf Ali in his translation adds at the beginning of the sentence the word "say," which is not there in the original Arabic, and he does so without comment or footnote. Ali Dashti also considers sura 111 as the words of Muhammad on the grounds that these words are unworthy of God: "It ill becomes the Sustainer of the Universe to curse an ignorant Arab and call his wife a firewood carrier." The short sura refers to Abu Lahab, the Prophet's uncle, who was one of Muhammad's bitterest opponents: "The hands of Abu Lahab shall perish, and he shall perish. His riches shall not profit him, neither that which he has gained. He shall go down to be burned into flaming fire, and his wife also, bearing wood having on her neck a cord of twisted fibres of a palm tree." Either these are Muhammad's words or God is fond of rather feeble puns, since "Abu Lahab" means "father of flames." But surely these words are not worthy of a prophet either.

As Goldziher[233] points out, "Devout Mu'tazilites voiced similar opinions [as the Kharijites who impugned the reliability of the text of the Quran] about those parts of the Quran in which the Prophet utters curses against his enemies (such as Abu Lahab). God could not have called such passages " 'a noble Quran on a well-guarded tablet.' " As we shall see, if we were to apply the same reasoning to all parts of the Koran, there would not be much left as the word of God, since very little of it is worthy of a Merciful and Compassionate, All-Wise God.

Ali Dashti[234] also gives the example of sura 17.1 as an instance of confusion between two speakers, God and Muhammad: "Gloried be He Who carried His servant by night from the Inviolable Place of worship [mosque at Mecca] to the Far Distant Place of Worship [mosque at Jerusalem], the neighborhood whereof We have blessed, that We might show him of our tokens! Lo! He is the Hearer, the Seer."

Dashti comments:

> The praise of Him who carried His servant from Mecca to Palestine cannot be God's utterance, because God does not praise Himself, and must be Mohammad's thanksgiving to God for this favor. The next part of the sentence, describing the Furthest Mosque [whose precincts "We have blessed"], is spoken by God, and so too is the following clause ["so that We might show him of our tokens"]. The closing words ["He is the Hearer, the Seer"] seem most likely to be Mohammad's.

Again, in the interest of dogma, translators are led to dishonesty when confronted by sura 27.91, where the speaker is clearly Muhammad: "I have been commanded to serve the Lord of this city." Dawood and Pickthall both interpolate "say" at the beginning of the sentence which is lacking in the Arabic. At sura 81.15-29, one presumes it is Muhammad who is swearing: "I swear by the turning planets, and by the stars that rise and set and the close of night, and the breath of morning." Muhammad, unable to disguise his pagan heritage, swears again at sura 84.16-19, "I swear by the afterglow of sunset, and by the night and all that it enshrouds, and by the moon when she is at the full." There are other instances where it is possible that it is Muhammad who is speaking, e.g., 112.14-21 and 111.1-10.

Even Bell and Watt[235], who can hardly be accused of being hostile to Islam, admit that

> The assumption that God is himself the speaker in every passage, however leads to difficulties. Frequently God is referred to in the third person. It is no doubt allowable for a speaker to refer to himself in the third person occasionally, but the extent to which we find the Prophet apparently being addressed and told about God as a third person, is unusual. It has, in fact, been made a matter of ridicule that in the Quran God is made to swear by himself. That he uses oaths in some of the passages beginning, "I swear (not) . . ." can hardly be denied [e.g., 75.1, 2; 90.1]. . . . "By thy Lord," however, is difficult in the

mouth of God. . . . Now there is one passage which everyone acknowledges to be spoken by angels, namely 19.64: "We come not down but by command of thy Lord; to him belongs what is before us and what is behind us and what is between that; nor is thy Lord forgetful, Lord of the heavens and the earth and what is between them; so serve him, and endure patiently in his service; knowest thou to him a namesake?"

In 37.161–166 it is almost equally clear that angels are the speakers. This, once admitted, may be extended to passages in which it is not so clear. In fact, difficulties in many passages are removed by interpreting the "we" of angels rather than of God himself speaking in the plural of majesty. It is not always easy to distinguish between the two, and nice questions sometimes arise in places where there is a sudden change from God being spoken of in the third person to "we" claiming to do things usually ascribed to God, e.g., 6.99; 25.45.

THE FOREIGN VOCABULARY OF THE KORAN

Although many Muslim philologists recognized that there were numerous words of foreign origin in the Koran, orthodoxy silenced them for a while. One tradition tells us that "anyone who pretends that there is in the Koran anything other than the Arabic tongue has made a serious charge against God: 'Verily, we have made it an Arabic Koran' " (sura 12.1). Fortunately, philologists like al-Suyuti managed to come up with ingenious arguments to get around the orthodox objections. Al-Tha'alibi argued that there were foreign words in the Koran but "the Arabs made use of them and Arabicized them, so from this point of view they are Arabic." Although al-Suyuti enumerates 107 foreign words, Arthur Jeffery in his classic work finds about 275 words in the Koran that can be considered foreign: words from Aramaic, Hebrew, Syriac, Ethiopic, Persian, and Greek. The word "Koran" itself comes from the Syriac, and Muhammad evidently got it from Christian sources.

VARIANT VERSIONS, VARIANT READINGS

We need to retrace the history of the Koran text to understand the problem of variant versions and variant readings, whose very existence makes nonsense of Muslim dogma about the Koran. As we shall see, there is no such thing as *the* Koran; there never has been a definitive text of this holy book. When a Muslim dogmatically asserts that the Koran is the word of God, we need only ask "Which Koran?" to undermine his certainty.

After Muhammad's death in A.D. 632, there was no collection of his revelations. Consequently, many of his followers tried to gather all the known revelations and write them down in codex form. Soon we had the codices of several scholars such as Ibn Mas'ud, Ubai b. Kab, Ali', Abu Bakr, al-Ash'ari, al-Aswad, and others. As Islam spread, we eventually had what became known as the Metropolitan Codices in the centers of Mecca, Medina, Damascus, Kufa, and Basra. As we saw earlier, Uthman tried to bring order to this chaotic situation by canonizing the Medinan Codex, copies of which were sent to all the metropolitan centers, with orders to destroy all the other codices.

Uthman's codex was supposed to standardize the consonantal text; yet we find that many of the variant traditions of this consonantal text survived well into the fourth Islamic century. The problem was aggravated by the fact the consonantal text was unpointed, that is to say, the dots that distinguish, for example, a "b" from a "t," or a "th" were missing. Several other letters (f and q; j, h, and kh; s and d; r and z; s and sh; d and dh; t and z) were indistinguishable. As a result, a great many variant readings were possible according to the way the text was pointed (had dots added). The vowels presented an even worse problem. Originally, the Arabs had no signs for the short vowels—these were only introduced at a later date. The Arabic script is consonantal. Although the short vowels are sometimes omitted, they can be represented by orthographical signs placed above or below the letters—three signs in all, taking the form of a slightly slanting dash or a comma.

After having settled the consonants, Muslims still had to decide what vowels to employ: using different vowels, of course, rendered different readings.

This difficulty inevitably led to the growth of different centers with their own variant traditions of how the texts should be pointed and vowelized. Despite Uthman's order to destroy all texts other than his own, it is evident that the older codices survived. As Charles Adams[236] says, "It must be emphasized that far from there being a single text passed down inviolate from the time of Uthman's commission, literally thousands of variant readings of particular verses were known. . . . These variants affected even the Uthmanic codex, making it difficult to know what its true original form may have been." Some Muslims preferred codices other than the Uthmanic, for example, those of Ibn Masud, Ubayy ibn Kab, and Abu Musa. Eventually under the influence of the great Koranic scholar Ibn Mujahid (d. A.D. 935), there was a definite canonization of one system of consonants and a limit placed on the variations of vowels used in the text that resulted in acceptance of the systems of the seven:

1. Nafi of Medina (d. A.D. 785)
2. Ibn Kathir of Mecca (d. A.D. 737)
3. Ibn Amir of Damascus (d. A.D. 736)
4. Abu Amr of Basra (d. A.D. 770)
5. Asim of Kufa (d. A.D. 744)
6. Hamza of Kufa (d. A.D. 772)
7. Al-Kisai of Kufa (d. A.D. 804)

But other scholars accepted ten readings, and still others accepted fourteen readings. Even Ibn Mujahid's seven provided fourteen possibilities, since each of the seven was traced through two different transmitters, viz.,

1. Nafi of Medina according to Warsh and Qalun
2. Ibn Kathir of Mecca according to al-Bazzi and Qunbul

3. Ibn Amir of Damascus according to Hisham and Ibn Dhakwan
4. Abu Amr of Basra according to al-Duri and al-Susi
5. Asim of Kufa according to Hafs and Abu Bakr
6. Hamza of Kufa according to Khalaf and Khallad
7. Al-Kisai of Kufa according to al-Duri and Abul Harith

In the end three systems prevailed, for some reason—to quote Jeffery[237]—"which has not yet been fully elucidated," those of Warsh (d. 812) from Nafi of Medina, Hafs (d. 805) from Asim of Kufa, and al-Duri (d. 860) from Abu Amr of Basra. At present in modern Islam, two versions seem to be in use: that of Asim of Kufa through Hafs, which was given a kind of official seal of approval by being adopted in the Egyptian edition of the Koran in 1924; and that of Nafi through Warsh, which is used in parts of Africa other than Egypt.
To quote Charles Adams:

> It is of some importance to call attention to a possible source of misunderstanding with regard to the variant readings of the Quran. The seven [versions] refer to actual differences in the written and oral text, to distinct versions of Quranic verses, whose differences, though they may not be great, are nonetheless real and substantial. Since the very existence of variant readings and versions of the Quran goes against the doctrinal position toward the holy Book held by many modern Muslims, it is not uncommon in an apologetic context to hear the seven [versions] explained as modes of recitation; in fact the manner and technique of recitation are an entirely different matter.[238]

Guillaume also refers to the variants as "not always trifling in significance."[239]
Any variant version or reading poses serious problems for orthodox Muslims. Thus it is not surprising that they should conceal any codices that seem to differ from the Uthman text. Arthur Jeffery describes just such an attempt at concealment:

> [The late Professor Bergstrasser] was engaged in taking photographs for the Archive and had photographed a number of the early Kufic Codices in the Egyptian Library when I drew his attention to one in the Azhar Library that possessed certain curious features. He sought permission to photograph that also, but permission was refused and the Codex withdrawn from access, as it was not consistent with orthodoxy to allow a Westen scholar to have knowledge of such a text. . . . With regard to such variants as did survive there were definite efforts at suppression in the interests of orthodoxy.[240]

PERFECT ARABIC?

The great scholar Noldeke[241] pointed out the stylistic weaknesses of the Koran long ago:

On the whole, while many parts of the Koran undoubtedly have considerable rhetorical power, even over an unbelieving reader, the book aesthetically considered, is by no means a first rate performance. . . . Let us look at some of the more extended narratives. It has already been noticed how vehement and abrupt they are where they ought to be characterised by epic repose. Indispensable links, both in expression and in the sequence of events, are often omitted, so that to understand these histories is sometimes far easier for us than for those who heard them first, because we know most of them from better sources. Along with this, there is a good deal of superfluous verbiage; and nowhere do we find a steady advance in the narration. Contrast in these respects the history of Joseph (xii) and its glaring improprieties with the admirably conceived and admirably executed story in Genesis. Similar faults are found in the non narrative portions of the Koran. The connexion of ideas is extremely loose, and even the syntax betrays great awkwardness. Anacolutha [want of syntactical sequence; when the latter part of a sentence does not grammatically fit the earlier] are of frequent occurrence, and cannot be explained as conscious literary devices. Many sentences begin with a "when" or "on the day when" which seems to hover in the air, so that commentators are driven to supply a "think of this" or some such ellipsis. Again, there is no great literary skill evinced in the frequent and needless harping on the same words and phrases; in xviii, for example "till that" occurs no fewer than eight times. Mahomet in short, is not in any sense a master of style.

We have already quoted Ali Dashti's criticisms of the Prophet's style (chap. 1). Here, I shall quote some of Ali Dashti's[242] examples of the grammatical errors contained in the Koran. In verse 162 of sura 4, which begins, "But those among them who are well-grounded in knowledge, the believers, . . . and the performers of the prayer, and the payers of the alms-tax," the word for "performers" is in the accusative case; whereas it ought to be in the nominative case, like the words for "well-grounded," "believers," and "payers."

In verse 9 of sura 49, "If two parties of believers have started to fight each other, make peace between them," the verb meaning "have started to fight" is in the plural, whereas it ought to be in the dual like its subject "two parties." (In Arabic, as in other languages, verbs can be conjugated not only in the singular and plural, but also in the dual, when the subject is numbered at two).

In verse 63 of sura 20, where Pharaoh's people say of Moses and his brother Aaron, "These two are magicians," the word for "these two" (*hadhane*) is in the nominative case; whereas it ought to be in the accusative case (*hadhayne*) because it comes after an introductory particle of emphasis.

Ali Dashti concludes this example by saying,

Othman and Aesha are reported to have read the word as 'hadhayne. The comment of a Moslem scholar illustrates the fanaticism and intellectual ossification of later times: "Since in the unanimous opinion of the Moslems the pages bound in this volume and called the Quran are God's word, and since there can be no error in God's word, the report that Othman and Aesha read hadhayne instead of hadhane is wicked and false."

Ali Dashti estimates that there are more than one hundred Koranic aberrations from the normal rules and structure of Arabic.

VERSES MISSING, VERSES ADDED

There is a tradition from Aisha, the Prophet's wife, that there once existed a "verse of stoning," where stoning was prescribed as punishment for fornication, a verse that formed a part of the Koran but that is now lost. The early caliphs carried out such a punishment for adulterers, despite the fact that the Koran, as we know it today, only prescribes a hundred lashes. It remains a puzzle— if the story is not true—why Islamic law to this day decrees stoning when the Koran only demands flogging. According to this tradition, over a hundred verses are missing. Shiites, of course, claim that Uthman left out a great many verses favorable to Ali for political reasons.

The Prophet himself may have forgotten some verses, the companions' memory may have equally failed them, and the copyists may also have mislaid some verses. We also have the case of the Satanic Verses, which clearly show that Muhammad himself suppressed some verses.

The authenticity of many verses has also been called into question not only by modern Western scholars, but even by Muslims themselves. Many Kharijites, who were followers of Ali in the early history of Islam, found the sura recounting the story of Joseph offensive, an erotic tale that did not belong in the Koran. Even before Wansbrough there were a number of Western scholars such as de Sacy, Weil, Hirschfeld, and Casanova who had doubted the authenticity of this or that sura or verse. It is fair to say that so far their arguments have not been generally accepted. Wansbrough's arguments, however, are finding support among a younger generation of scholars not inhibited in the way their older colleagues were, as described in chapter 1 ("Trahison des Clercs").

On the other hand, most scholars do believe that there are interpolations in the Koran; these interpolations can be seen as interpretative glosses on certain rare words in need of explanation. More serious are the interpolations of a dogmatic or political character, such as 42.36–38, which seems to have been added to justify the elevation of Uthman as caliph to the detriment of Ali. Then there are other verses that have been added in the interest of rhyme, or to join together two short passages that on their own lack any connection.

Bell and Watt[243] carefully go through many of the alterations and revisions and point to the unevenness of the Koranic style as evidence for great many alterations in the Koran:

> There are indeed many roughnesses of this kind, and these, it is here claimed, are fundamental evidence for revision. Besides the points already noticed—hidden rhymes, and rhyme-phrases not woven into the texture of the passage—there are the following: abrupt changes of rhyme; repetition of the same rhyme word or rhyme phrase in adjoining verses; the intrusion of an extraneous subject into

a passage otherwise homogeneous; a differing treatment of the same subject in neighbouring verses, often with repetition of words and phrases; breaks in grammatical construction which raise difficulties in exegesis; abrupt changes in the length of verses; sudden changes of the dramatic situation, with changes of pronoun from singular to plural, from second to third person, and so on; the juxtaposition of apparently contrary statements; the juxtaposition of passages of different date, with the intrusion of late phrases into early verses.

In many cases a passage has alternative continuations which follow one another in the present text. The second of the alternatives is marked by a break in sense and by a break in grammatical construction, since the connection is not with what immediately precedes, but with what stands some distance back.

The Christian al-Kindi,[244] writing around A.D. 830, criticized the Koran in similar terms: "The result of all this [process by which the Quran came into being] is patent to you who have read the scriptures and see how, in your book, histories are all jumbled together and intermingled; an evidence that many different hands have been at work therein, and caused discrepancies, adding or cutting out whatever they liked or disliked. Are such, now, the conditions of a revelation sent down from heaven?"

Here, it might be appropriate to give some examples. Verse 15 of sura 20 is totally out of place; the rhyme is different from the rest of the sura. Verses 1–5 of sura 78 have obviously been added on artificially, because both the rhyme and the tone of the rest of the sura changes; in the same sura verses 33 and 34 have been inserted between verses 32 and 35, thus breaking the obvious connection between 32 and 35. In sura 74, verse 31 is again an obvious insertion since it is in a totally different style and of a different length than the rest of the verses in the sura. In sura 50, verses 24–32 have again been artificially fitted into a context in which they do not belong.

To explain certain rare or unusual words or phrases, the formula "What has let you know what . . . is?" (or "What will teach you what . . . is?") is added on to a passage, after which a short explanatory description follows. It is clear that these explanatory glosses—twelve in all—have been added on at a later time, since in many instances the "definitions" do not correspond to the original meaning of the word or phrase. Bell and Watt[245] give the example of sura 101.9–11, which should read: "his mother shall be 'hawiya.' And what shall teach you what it is? A blazing fire." "Hawiya" originally meant "childless" owing to the death or misfortune of her son, but the explanatory note defines it as "Hell." Thus most translators now render the above sentence as, "shall plunge in the womb of the Pit. And what shall teach you what is the Pit? A blazing fire!" (See also 90.12–16.)

Of course any interpolation, however trivial, is fatal to the Muslim dogma that the Koran is literally the word of God as given to Muhammad at Mecca or Medina. As Regis Blachere in his classic *Introduction to the Koran* said, on this point, there is no possible way of reconciling the findings of Western philologists and historians with the official dogma of Islam.

We also have the story of Abd Allah b. Sa'd Abi Sarh[246]:

The last named had for some time been one of the scribes employed at Medina
to write down the revelations. On a number of occasions he had, with the Prophet's
consent, changed the closing words of verses. When the Prophet had said "And
God is mighty and wise," Abd Allah suggested writing down "knowing and
wise" and the Prophet answered that there was no objection. Having observed
a succession of changes of this type, Abd Allah renounced Islam on the ground
that the revelations, if from God, could not be changed at the prompting of
a scribe such as himself. After his apostasy he went to Mecca and joined the
Qorayshites.

Needless to say, the Prophet had no qualms about ordering his asssassination once
Mecca was captured, but Uthman obtained Muhammad's pardon with difficulty.

ABROGATION OF PASSAGES IN THE KORAN

William Henry Burr, the author of *Self-Contradictions of the Bible,* would have
a field day with the Koran, for the Koran abounds in contradictions. But Burr's
euphoria would be short-lived; for Muslim theologians have a rather convenient
doctrine, which, as Hughes[247] puts it, "fell in with that law of expediency which
appears to be the salient feature in Muhammad's prophetical career." According
to this doctrine, certain passages of the Koran are abrogated by verses with a
different or contrary meaning revealed afterwards. This was taught by Muhammad
at sura 2.105: "Whatever verses we [i.e., God] cancel or cause you to forget,
we bring a better or its like." According to al-Suyuti, the number of abrogated
verses has been estimated at from five to five hundred. As Margoliouth[248] remarked,

> To do this, withdraw a revelation and substitute another for it, was, [Muhammad]
> asserted, well within the power of God. Doubtless it was, but so obviously
> within the power of man that it is to us astonishing how so compromising
> a procedure can have been permitted to be introduced into the system by friends
> and foes.

Al-Suyuti gives the example of sura 2.240 as a verse abrogated (superseded)
by verse 234, which is the abrogating verse. How can an earlier verse abrogate
a later verse? The answer lies in the fact that the traditional Muslim order of
the suras and verses is not chronological, the compilers simply having placed
the longer chapters at the beginning. The commentators have to decide the
chronological order for doctrinal reasons; Western scholars have also worked out
a chronological scheme. Though there are many differences of detail, there seems
to be broad agreement about which suras belong to the Meccan (i.e., early) period
of Muhammad's life and which belong to the Medinan (i.e., later) period. It is
worth noting how time-bound the "eternal" word of God is.

Muslims have gotten themselves out of one jam only to find themselves in
another. Is it fitting that an All-Powerful, Omniscient, and Omnipotent God should
revise His commands so many times? Does He need to issue commands that

need revising so often? Why can He not get it right the first time, after all He is all-wise? Why does He not reveal the better verse first? In the words of Dashti,[249]

It seems that there were hecklers in those days too, and that they were persistent. A reply was given to them in verses 103 and 104 of sura 16: "When We have replaced a verse with another verse—and God knows well what He sends down—they say, 'You are a mere fabricator.' But most of them have no knowledge. Say (to them), 'The Holy Ghost brought it down from your Lord, truly so, in order to confirm the believers.' "

On the assumption that the Quran is God's word, there ought to be no trace of human intellectual imperfection in anything that God says. Yet in these two verses the incongruity is obvious. Of course God knows what He sends down. For that very reason the replacement of one verse by another made the protesters suspicious. Evidently even the simple, uneducated Hejazi Arabs could understand that Almighty God, being aware of what is best for His servants, would prescribe the best in the first place and would not have changes of mind in the same way as His imperfect creatures.

The doctrine of abrogation also makes a mockery of the Muslim dogma that the Koran is a faithful and unalterable reproduction of the original scriptures that are preserved in heaven. If God's words are eternal, uncreated, and of universal significance, then how can we talk of God's words being superseded or becoming obsolete? Are some words of God to be preferred to other words of God? Apparently yes. According to Muir, some 200 verses have been canceled by later ones. Thus we have the strange situation where the entire Koran is recited as the word of God, and yet there are passages that can be considered not "true"; in other words, 3 percent of the Koran is acknowledged as falsehood.

Let us take an example. Everyone knows that Muslims are not allowed to drink wine in virtue of the prohibition found in the Koran sura 2.219; yet many would no doubt be surprised to read in the Koran at sura 16.67, "And among fruits you have the palm and the vine, from which you get wine and healthful nutriment: in this, truly, are signs for those who reflect" (Rodwell). Dawood has "intoxicants" and Pickthall, "strong drink," and Sale, with eighteenth-century charm, has "inebriating liquor" in place of "wine." Yusuf Ali pretends that the Arabic word concerned, "sakar," means "wholesome drink," and in a footnote insists that nonalcoholic drinks are being referred to; but then, at the last moment, he concedes that *if* "sakar must be taken in the sense of fermented wine, it refers to the time before intoxicants were prohibited: this is a Meccan sura and the prohibition came in Medina."

Now we can see how useful and convenient the doctrine of abrogation is in bailing scholars out of difficulties. Of course, it does pose problems for apologists of Islam, since all the passages preaching tolerance are found in Meccan, i.e., early suras, and all the passages recommending killing, decapitating, and maiming are Medinan, i.e., later: "tolerance" has been abrogated by "intolerance." For example, the famous verse at sura 9.5, "Slay the idolaters wherever you find them," is said to have canceled 124 verses that dictate toleration and patience.

The Doctrines of the Koran

There is no deity but God ("la ilaha illa llahu"). Islam is uncompromisingly monotheistic—it is one of the greatest sins to ascribe partners to God. Polytheism, idolatry, paganism, and ascribing plurality to the deity are all understood under the Arabic term "shirk." Theological apologists and perhaps nineteenth-century cultural evolutionists have all uncritically assumed that monotheism is somehow a "higher" form of belief than "polytheism." It seems to me that philosophers have paid little attention to polytheism until very recently. Is it so obvious that monotheism is philosophically or metaphysically "superior" to polytheism? In what way is it superior? If there is a natural evolution from polytheism to monotheism, then is there not a natural development from monotheism to atheism? Is monotheism doomed to be superseded by a higher form of belief, that is, atheism—via agnosticism, perhaps? In this section I wish to argue at:

1. Monotheism is not necessarily philosophically or metaphysically superior to polytheism, given that no proof for the existence of one and only one God is valid.

2. Historically speaking, monotheistic creeds often secretly harbor at the popular level a de facto polytheism, despite the official dogma.

3. Superstitions are not reduced in monotheism but concentrated into the one god or his apostle.

4. Historically speaking, monotheism has often shown itself to be ferociously intolerant, in contrast to polytheism on behalf of which religious wars have never been waged. This intolerance follows logically from monotheistic ideology. Monotheism has a lot to answer for. As Gore Vidal[250] says

> The great unmentionable evil at the centre of our culture is monotheism. From a barbaric Bronze Age text known as the Old Testament, three anti-human religions have evolved—Judaism, Christianity and Islam. These are sky-god religions. They are patriarchal—God is the omnipotent father—hence the loathing of women for 2,000 years in those countries afflicted by the sky-god and his male delegates. The sky-god is jealous. He requires total obedience. Those who would reject him must be converted or killed. Totalitarianism is the only politics that can truly serve the sky-god's purpose. Any movement of a liberal nature endangers his authority. One God, one King, one Pope, one master in the factory, one father-leader in the family.

5. Islam did not replace Arabian polytheism because it better met the spiritual needs of the Arabs, but because it offered them material rewards in the here and now. The unjustified assumption of the superiority of monotheism has colored the views of historians in regard to the causes of the adoption of Islam in Arabia.

6. Far from raising the moral standard of the Arabs, Islam seems to have sanctioned all sorts of immoral behavior.

Monotheism does seem to bring some kind of superficial intellectual order into the welter of "primitive" gods, apparently reducing superstition. But this is only apparent, not real. First, as Zwi Werblowsky[251] observed, "When polytheism is superseded by monotheism, the host of deities is either abolished (theoretically) or bedevilled (i.e., turned into demons), or downgraded to the rank of angels and ministering spirits. This means that an officially monotheistic system can harbor a functional de facto polytheism."

Hume[252] made the same observation:

It is remarkable, that the principles of religion have a kind of flux and reflux in the human mind, and that men have a natural tendency to rise from idolatry to theism and to sink from theism into idolatry. . . . But the same anxious concern for happiness, which engenders the idea of these invisible, intelligent powers, allows not mankind to remain long in the first simple conception of them; as powerful but limited beings; masters of human fate, but slaves to destiny and the course of nature. Men's exaggerated praises and compliments still swell their idea upon them; and elevating their deities to the utmost bounds of perfection, at last beget the attributes of unity and infinity, simplicity and spirituality. Such refined ideas, being somewhat disproportioned to vulgar comprehension, remain not long in their original purity; but require to be supported by the notion of inferior mediators or subordinate agents, which interpose betwixt mankind and their supreme deity. These demi-gods or middle beings, partaking more of human nature, and being more familiar to us, become the chief objects of devotion, and gradually recall that idolatry, which had been formerly banished by the ardent prayers and panegyrics of timorous and indigent mortals.

This is nowhere more real than in Islam where a belief in angels and jinn is officially recognized by the Koran.[253] Edward Lane divides this species of spiritual beings in Islam into five orders: Jann, Jinn, Shaitans, Ifrits, and Marids. "The last . . . are the most powerful, and the Jann are transformed Jinn, like as certain apes and swine were transformed men. . . . The terms Jinn and Jann are generally used indiscriminately as names of the whole species, whether good or bad. . . . Shaitan is commonly used to signify any evil genius. An Ifrit is a powerful evil genius; a Marid, an evil genius of the most powerful class." Many evil jinn are killed by shooting stars," hurled at them from heaven." Jinn can propagate their species in conjunction with human beings, in which case the offspring partakes of the nature of both parents. "Among the evil Jinn are distinguished the five sons of their chief, Iblis; namely Tir who brings about calamities, losses, and injuries; al-Awar, who encourages debauchery; Sut, who suggests lies; Dasim, who causes hatred between man and wife; and Zalambur, who presides over places of traffic. . . . The Jinn are of three kind: one have wings and fly; another are snakes and dogs; and the third move about from place to place like men."

Enough has been said to show that such a system is as rich and superstitious as any Greek, Roman, or Norse polytheistic mythology.

The veneration of saints in Islam serves the very purpose that Hume so perceptively ascribed to mediators between man and God. Here is how Goldziher[254] puts the point:

> Within Islam . . . the believers sought to create through the concept of saints, mediators between themselves and omnipotent Godhead in order to satisfy the need which was served by the gods and masters of their old traditions now defeated by Islam. Here too applies what Karl Hase says of the cult of saints in general: that it "satisfies within a monotheistic religion a polytheistic need to fill the enormous gap between men and their god, and that it originated on the soil of the old pantheon."

The Muslim doctrine of the Devil also comes close at times to ditheism, i.e., the positing of two powerful Beings. The Devil is said to have been named Azazil and was created of fire. When God created Adam from clay, the Devil refused to prostrate before Adam as commanded by God, whereupon he was expelled from Eden. Eventually he will be destroyed by God, since it is only God who is all-powerful. But given the prevalence of evil in the world—wars, famines, disease, the Holocaust—one wonders if the Devil is not more powerful. Why he has not been destroyed already is a puzzle. Also it seems rather inconsistent of God to ask Satan, before his fall, to *worship* Adam, when God forbids man to worship anyone but God Himself.

Nowhere does the Koran give a real philosophical argument for the existence of God; it merely assumes it. The closest one gets to an argument is perhaps in the Koranic notion of "signs," whereby various natural phenomena are seen as signs of God's power and bounty.

> The phenomena most frequently cited [in the Koran] are: the creation of the heavens and the earth, the creation or generation of man, the various uses and benefits man derives from the animals, the alternation of night and day, the shining of sun, moon and stars, the changing winds, the sending of rain from the sky, the revival of parched ground and the appearance of herbage, crops and fruits, the movement of the ship on the sea and the stability of the mountains. Less frequently cited are: shadows, thunder, lightning, iron, fire, hearing, sight, understanding and wisdom.[255]

In philosophy such an argument is known as the argument from design or the teleological argument, and like all arguments for the existence of God it is found wanting by most philosophers. All the phenomena adduced by Muhammad in the Koran can be explained without assuming the existence of a God or cosmic designer. But in any case, to return to monotheism, why should there be only one cosmic architect or planner? As Hume[256] asks,

> And what shadow of an argument, continued Philo, can you produce, from your Hypothesis, to prove the Unity of the Deity? A great number of men join in building a house or ship, in rearing a city, in framing a Commonwealth:

Why may not several deities combine in contriving and framing a world? This is only so much greater similarity to human affairs. By sharing the work among several, we may so much farther limit the attributes of each, and get rid of that extensive power and knowledge, which must be suppos'd in one deity, and which, according to you, can only serve to weaken the proof of his existence. And if such foolish, such vicious creatures as man can yet often unite in framing and executing one plan, how much more those deities or demons, whom we may suppose several degrees more perfect?

To multiply causes without necessity is indeed contrary to true philosophy: but this principle applies not to the present case. Were one deity antecedently prov'd by your theory, who were possessed of every attribute, requisite to the production of the universe; it wou'd be needless, I own (*tho' not absurd*) [my emphasis] to suppose any other deity existent. But while it is still a question, whether all these attributes are united in one subject, or dispersed among several independent beings: by what phenomena in nature can we pretend to decide the controversy? Where we see a body rais'd in a scale, we are sure that there is in the opposite scale, however, concealed from sight, some counterpoising weight equal to it: But it is still allow'd to doubt, whether that weight be an aggregate of several distinct bodies, or one uniform united Mass. And if the weight requisite very much exceeds any thing which we have ever seen conjoin'd in any single body, the former supposition becomes still more probable and natural. An intelligent being of such vast power and capacity, as is necessary to produce the universe, or to speak in the language of ancient philosophy, so prodigious an animal, exceeds all analogy and even comprehension.

One of the great achievements of Muhammad, we are told, was ridding Arabia of polytheism. But this, I have tried to argue, is monotheistic arrogance. There are no compelling arguments in favor of monotheism, as opposed to polytheism. Indeed, as Hume showed, there is nothing inherently absurd in polytheism. And as to the Koranic hint at the argument from design, Hume[257] showed that all hypotheses regarding the origins of the universe were equally absurd. There is no justification for believing any of the forms of the argument from design: "We have no data to establish any system of cosmogony. Our experience, so imperfect in itself, and so limited both in extent and duration, can afford us no probable conjecture concerning the whole of things. But if we must needs fix on some hypothesis, by what rule, pray, ought we to determine our choice?"

Monotheism has also been recognized as inherently intolerant. We know from the Koran itself the hatred preached at all kinds of belief labeled "idolatry" or "polytheism." As the *Dictionary of Islam* says, Muslim writers are "unanimous in asserting that no religious toleration was extended to the idolaters of Arabia in the time of the Prophet. The only choice given them was death or the reception of Islam." Implicit in all kinds of monotheism is the dogmatic certainty that it alone has access to the true God, it alone has access to truth. Everyone else is not only woefully misguided but doomed to perdition and everlasting hell-fire. In the words of Lewis, "Traditional Christianity and Islam differed from Judaism and agreed with each other in that both claimed to possess not only universal but exclusive truths. Each claimed to be the sole custodian of God's final revelation to mankind. Neither admitted salvation outside its own creed."[258]

Schopenhauer[259] asks us to reflect on the "cruelties to which religions, especially the Christian and Mohammedan, have given rise" and "the misery they have brought on the world." Think of the fanaticism, the endless persecutions, then the religious wars, that bloody madness of which the ancients had no conception. Think of the crusades which were a quite inexcusable butchery and lasted for two hundred years, their battle cry being: "It is the will of God." Christianity is no more spared than Islam in Schopenhauer's indictment. The object of the Crusades was

> to capture the grave of him who preached love, tolerance, and indulgence. Think of the cruel expulsion and extermination of the Moors and Jews from Spain; of the blood baths, inquisitions, and other courts for heretics; and also of the bloody and terrible conquests of the Mohammedans in three continents. . . . In particular, let us not forget India . . . where first Mohammedans and then Christians furiously and most cruelly attacked the followers of mankind's sacred and original faith. The ever-deplorable, wanton, and ruthless destruction and disfigurement of ancient temples and images reveal to us even to this day traces of the *monotheistic fury* [my emphasis] of the Mohammedans which was pursued from Mahmud of Ghazni of accursed memory down to Aurangzeb the fratricide.

Schopenhauer contrasts the peaceable historical record of the Hindus and the Buddhists with the wickedness and cruelty of the monotheists, and then concludes:

> Indeed, intolerance is essential only to monotheism; an only God is by nature a jealous God who will not allow another to live. On the other hand, polytheistic gods are naturally tolerant; they live and let live. In the first place, they gladly tolerate their colleagues, the gods of the same religion, and this tolerance is afterwards extended even to foreign gods who are accordingly, hospitably received and later admitted, in some cases, even to an equality of rights. An instance of this is seen in the Romans who willingly admitted and respected Phrygian, Egyptian and other foreign gods. Thus it is only the monotheistic religions that furnish us with the spectacle of religious wars, religious persecutions, courts for trying heretics, and also with that of iconoclasm, the destruction of the images of foreign gods, the demolition of Indian temples and Egyptian colossi that had looked at the sun for three thousand years; all this because their jealous God had said: "Thou shalt make no graven image" and so on.

Nearly a hundred years earlier than Schopenhauer, Hume[260] with his customary genius saw the same advantages of polytheism:

> Idolatry is attended with this evident advantage, that, by limiting the powers and functions of its deities, it naturally admits the gods of other sects and nations to a share of divinity, and renders all the various deities, as well as rites, ceremonies, or traditions, compatible with each other. . . . While one sole object of devotion is acknowledged [by monotheists], the worship of other deities is regarded as

absurd and impious. Nay, this unity of object seems naturally to require the unity of faith and ceremonies, and furnishes designing men with a pretext for representing their adversaries as prophane [profane], and the subjects of divine as well as human vengeance. For as each sect is positive that its own faith and worship are entirely acceptable to the deity, and as no one can conceive that the same being should be pleased with different and opposite rites and principles; the several sects fall naturally into animosity, and mutually discharge on each other, that sacred zeal and rancor, the most furious and implacable of all human passions.

The tolerating spirit of idolaters both in ancient and modern times, is very obvious to any one, who is the least conversant in the writings of historians or travelers. . . . The intolerance of almost all religions, which have maintained the unity of god, is as remarkable as the contrary principle in polytheists. The implacable, narrow spirit of the Jews is well-known. Mahometanism set out with still more bloody principles, and even to this day, deals out damnation, tho' not fire and faggot, to all other sects.

Professor Watt, in his enormously influential and important two-volume biography of Muhammad, has presented an interpretation of the rise of Muhammad and his message that is still accepted by many despite skepticism of scholars such as Bousquet and, more recently, Crone. Watt's entire account is permeated, unsurprisingly, with the assumption that the monotheism preached by Muhammad is superior to the polytheism prevalent in Central Arabia. Watt contends that the very success of Muhammad's message lies in the fact that this message responded to the deep spiritual needs of the people. Mecca, at the time, argues Watt, was beset with a social malaise—nay, even a spiritual crisis that found no answers in the local cults and gods. The Meccans were sunk in moral degradation and idolatry until Muhammad came along and lifted them up onto a higher moral and spiritual level. Such is Watt's argument. But as Crone and Bousquet pointed out there is very little evidence for a social malaise in Mecca. As Crone[261] argues:

The fact is that the tradition knows of no malaise in Mecca, be it religious, social, political or moral. On the contrary, the Meccans are described as eminently successful; and Watt's impression that their success led to cynicism arises from his otherwise commendable attempt to see Islamic history through Muslim eyes. The reason why the Meccans come across as morally bankrupt in the [Muslim] sources is not that their traditional way of life had broken down, but that it functioned too well: the Meccans preferred their traditional way of life to Islam. It is for this reason that they are penalized in the sources; and the more committed a man was to this way of life, the more cynical, amoral, or hypocritical he will sound to us: Abu Sufyan [a leader of the aristocratic party in Mecca hostile to Muhammad] cannot swear by a pagan deity without the reader feeling an instinctive aversion to him, because the reader knows with his sources that somebody who swears by a false deity is somebody who believes in nothing at all.

As for the spiritual crisis, there does not appear to have been any such thing in sixth century Arabia.

But how do we explain the mass conversion of Arabia to Islam? As we saw in chapter 2, society was organized around the tribe, and each society had its principal deity, which was worshipped in the expectation that it would help the tribe in some practical way, especially with bringing rain, providing fertility, eliminating disease, generally protecting them from the elements. The tribal gods did not embody "ultimate truths regarding the nature and meaning of life," neither were they "deeply entrenched in everyday life." Hence it was easy to renounce one god for another since it did not require any change in outlook or behavior. Furthermore, the Muslim god "endorsed and ennobled such fundamental tribal characteristics as militance and ethnic pride." The Muslim God offered something more than their own idols: He offered "a program of Arab state formation and conquest: the creation of an umma [a people or a nation], the initiation of jihad [holy war against the unbelievers]." "Muhammad's success evidently had something to do with the fact that he preached both state formation and conquest: without conquest, first in Arabia and next in the Fertile Crescent, the unification of Arabia would not have been achieved." Of course, as Muhammad proved more and more successful in Medina, his followers increased, realizing that Allah is indeed great, and certainly greater than any of their own deities: the true God is the successful God, the false, the unsuccessful. Scholars such as Becker had argued that the Arabs had been impelled to their conquests by the gradual drying up of Arabia, but as Crone maintains:

> We do not need to postulate any deterioration in the material environment of Arabia to explain why they found a policy of conquest to their taste. Having begun to conquer in their tribal homeland, both they and their leaders were unlikely to stop on reaching the fertile lands: this was, after all, where they could find the resources which they needed to keep going and of which they had availed themselves before. Muhammad's God endorsed a policy of conquest, instructing his believers to fight against unbelievers wherever they might be found. . . . In short, Muhammad had to conquer, his followers liked to conquer, and his deity told him to conquer: do we need any more?
>
> But holy war was not a cover for material interests; on the contrary, it was an open proclamation of them. "God says . . . 'my righteous servants shall inherit the earth'; now this is your inheritance and what your Lord has promised you. . . ." Arab soldiers were told on the eve of the battle of Qadisiyya, with reference to Iraq: "if you hold out . . . then their property, their women, their children, and their country will be yours." God could scarcely have been more explicit. He told the Arabs that they had a right to despoil others of their women, children, and land, or indeed that they had a duty to do so: holy war consisted in obeying. Muhammad's God thus elevated tribal militance and rapaciouness into supreme religious virtues.

To summarize, far from answering the spiritual doubts and questions of the tribes (there were no such doubts or spiritual crises), Muhammad created a people and offered the Arabs what they had been accustomed to: namely, military conquests with all the attendant material advantages, loot, women, and land. Allah was preferable to the old gods simply because He had not failed them, He had delivered the goods here and now. Allah was certainly not preferable to the gods for some deep metaphysical reason; the Arabs had not suddenly learned the use of Occam's Razor. "Indeed," as Crone points out, "in behavioral terms the better part of Arabia was still pagan in the nineteenth century."

As early as 1909, Dr. Margoliouth[262] had anticipated Watt's thesis and had found it wanting. What is also important in Margoliouth's work is that he denies that Islam somehow lifted the newly converted to a higher moral level: "There is no evidence that the Moslems were either in personal or altruistic morality better than the pagans." In fact the contrary seems to have been the case:

> When [Muhammad] was at the head of a robber community it is probable that the demoralising influence began to be felt, it was then that men who had never broken an oath learned that they might evade their obligations, and that men to whom the blood of the clansmen had been as their own began to shed it with immunity in the cause of God; and that lying and treachery in the cause of Islam received divine approval, hesitation to perjure oneself in that cause being reprehended as a weakness. It was then, too, that Moslems became distinguished by the obscenity of their language. It was then, too, that the coveting of goods and wives (possessed by the Unbelievers) was avowed without discouragement from the Prophet.

This is not all. Monotheism has been criticized for suppressing human freedom. Many scholars have argued that it inevitably leads to totalitarianism; whereas more and more modern philosophers see polytheism as a possible source of pluralism, creativity, and human freedom. Feminists have also criticized the monotheistic God as a male chauvinist who is unwilling to change, and is insensitive to "femininity."

THE MUSLIM CONCEPT OF GOD

The omnipotence of God is asserted everywhere in the Koran; man's will is totally subordinate to God's will to the extent that man cannot be said to have a will of his own. Even those who disbelieve in Him, disbelieve because it is God who wills them to disbelieve. This leads to the Muslim doctrine of predestination that prevails over the doctrine of man's free will, also to be found in the Koran. As Macdonald[263] says, "The contradictory statements of the Kuran on free-will and predestination show that Muhammad was an opportunist preacher and politician and not a systematic theologian."

"Taqdir, or the absolute decree of good and evil, is the sixth article of the Muhammadan creed, and the orthodox believe that whatever has, or shall come to pass in this world, whether it be good or bad, proceeds entirely from the Divine Will, and has been irrevocably fixed and recorded on a preserved tablet by the pen of fate." Some quotes from the Koran illustrate this doctrine:

54.49. All things have been created after fixed decree.

3.139. No one can die except by God's permission according to the book that fixes the term of life.

87.2. The Lord has created and balanced all things and has fixed their destinies and guided them.

8.17. God killed them, and those shafts were God's, not yours.

9.51. By no means can anything befall us but what God has destined for us.

13.30. All sovereignty is in the hands of God.

14.4. God misleads whom He will and whom He will He guides.

18.101. The infidels whose eyes were veiled from my warning and had no power to hear.

32.32. If We had so willed, We could have given every soul its guidance, but now My Word is realized—"I shall fill Hell with jinn and men together."

45.26. Say unto them, O Muhammad: Allah gives life to you, then causes you to die, then gathers you unto the day of resurrection.

57.22. No disaster occurs on earth or accident in yourselves which was not already recorded in the Book before we created them.

But there are inevitably some passages from the Koran that seem to give man some kind of free-will:

41.16. As to Thamud, We vouchsafed them also guidance, but to guidance did they prefer blindness.

18.28. The truth is from your Lord: let him then who will, believe; and let him who will, be an unbeliever.

But as Wensinck,[264] in his classic *The Muslim Creed*, said, in Islam it is predestination that ultimately predominates. There is not a single tradition that advocates free will, and we have the further evidence of John of Damascus, who "flourished in the middle of the eighth century A.D., and who was well acquainted with Islam. According to him the difference regarding predestination and free-will is one of the chief points of divergence between Christianity and Islam."

It is evident that, toward the end of his life, Muhammad's predestinarian position hardened; and "the earliest conscious Muslim attitude on the subject seems to have been of an uncompromising fatalism."

Before commenting on the doctrine of predestination, I should like to consider the Koranic hell. Several words are used in the Koran to evoke the place of torment that God seems to take a particular delight in contemplating. The word "Jahannum" occurs at least thirty times and describes the purgatorial hell for all Muslims. According to the Koran, all Muslims will pass through hell: (sura 19.72) "There is not one of you who will not go down to it [hell], that is settled and decided by the Lord." The word "al-nar" meaning the fire appears several times. Other terms for hell or hellfire are

Laza (the blaze): "For Laza dragging by the scalp, shall claim him who turned his back and went away, and amassed and hoarded." (sura 97.5)

Al-Hutamah (the crusher): "It is God's kindled fire, which shall mount above the hearts of the damned." (sura 104.4)

Sair (the blaze): "Those who devour the property of orphans unjustly, only devour into their bellies fire, and they broil in sair." (sura 4.11)

Saqar: "The sinners are in error and excitement. On the day when they shall be dragged into the fire on their faces. Taste the touch of saqar." (sura 54.47)

Al-Jahim (the Hot Place) and Hawiyah also occur in sura 2 and 101, respectively. Muhammad really let his otherwise limited imagination go wild when describing, in revolting detail, the torments of hell: boiling water, running sores, peeling skin, burning flesh, dissolving bowels, and crushing of skulls with iron maces. And verse after verse, sura after sura, we are told about the fire, always the scorching fire, the everlasting fire. From sura 9.69 it is clear that unbelievers will roast forever.

What are we to make of such a system of values? As Mill[265] said, there is something truly disgusting and wicked in the thought that God purposefully creates beings to fill hell with, beings who cannot in any way be held responsible for their actions since God Himself chooses to lead them astray: "The recognition, for example, of the object of highest worship in a being who could make a Hell; and who could create countless generations of human beings with the certain foreknowledge that he was creating them for this fate. . . . Any other of the outrages to the most ordinary justice and humanity involved in the common Christian conception of the moral character of God sinks into insignificance beside this dreadful idealization of wickedness." Of course, Mill's words apply, mutatis mutandis, to the Muslim conception also, or to any god of predestination.

We cannot properly call such a system an ethical system at all. Central to any valid system of ethics is the notion of moral responsibility, of a moral person who can legitimately be held responsible for his actions: a person who is capable of rational thought, who is capable of deliberation, who displays intentionality, who is capable of choosing and is, in some way, free to choose. Under the Koranic system of predestination, "men" are no more than automata created by a capricious deity who amuses himself by watching his creations burning in hell. We cannot properly assign blame or approbation in the Koranic system; man is not responsible for his acts, thus it seems doubly absurd to punish him in the sadistic manner described in the various suras quoted earlier.

Bousquet[266] begins his classic work on Islamic views on sex with the blunt sentence: "There is no ethics in Islam." The Muslim is simply commanded to obey the inscrutable will of Allah; "good" and "bad" are defined as what the Koran, and later, Islamic law considers permissible or forbidden. The question posed by Socrates in the *Euthyphro,* "Whether the pious or holy is beloved by the gods because it is holy, or holy because it is beloved of the gods?" receives a very definitive answer from an orthodox Muslim: something is good if God wills it, and bad if God forbids it; there is nothing "rationally" or independently good or bad. But as Plato pointed out this is not a satisfactory answer. As Mackie[267] puts it (n.d., p. 256): "If moral values were constituted wholly by divine commands, so that goodness consisted in conformity to God's will, we could make no sense of the theist's own claims that God is good and that he seeks the good of his creation." In an earlier work (1977, p. 230), Mackie[268] observes that the Muslim view has the consequence:

> that the description of God himself as good would reduce to the rather trivial statement that God loves himself, or likes himself the way he is. It would also seem to entail that obedience to moral rules is merely prudent but slavish conformity to the arbitrary demands of a capricious tyrant. Realizing this, many religious thinkers have opted for the first alternative [i.e., "the pious or holy is beloved by the gods because it is holy"]. But this seems to have the almost equally surprising consequence that moral distinctions do not depend on God, . . . hence ethics is autonomous and can be studied and discussed without reference to religious beliefs, that we can simply close the theological frontier of ethics.

It is worth emphasizing the logical independence of moral values from any theistic system. Russell[269] formulates this insight in this manner:

> if you are quite sure there is a difference between right and wrong, you are then in this situation: is that difference due to God's fiat or is it not? If it is due to God's fiat, then for God Himself there is no difference between right and wrong, and it is no longer a significant statement to say that God is good. If you are going to say, as theologians do, that God is good, you must then say that right and wrong have some meaning which is independent of God's fiat, because God's fiats are good and not bad independently of the mere fact that He made them. If you are going to say that, you will then have to say that it is not only through God that right and wrong came into being but that they are in their essence logically anterior to God. (n.d., p. 19)

We cannot escape our moral responsibility that our independent moral understanding gives us.

Nor can we regard the concept of hell as ethically admirable. All but two suras (i.e., the fatihah and sura 9) tell us that God is merciful and compassionate, but can a truly merciful God consign somebody to hell or everlasting torment for not believing in Him? As Russell put it, "I really do not think that a person with a proper degree of kindliness in his nature would have put fears and terrors of that sort into the world." As Antony Flew[270] remarked there is an inordinate disparity between finite offenses and infinite punishment. The Koranic doctrine of hell is simply cruelty and barbaric torture and divinely sanctioned sadism. More than that, it means Islam is based on fear, which corrupts true morality. ("There is no God but I, so fear Me" [sura 16.2]). As Gibb said, "Man must live in constant fear and awe of [God], and always be on his guard against Him— such is the idiomatic meaning of the term for 'fearing God' which runs through the Koran from cover to cover" (1953, p. 38).[271] Instead of acting out of a sense of duty to our fellow human beings, or out of spontaneous generosity or sympathetic feelings, under Islam we act out of fear to avoid divine punishments and, selfishly, to gain rewards from God in this life and the life to come. Mackie[272] (p. 256) argues correctly that

> This divine command view can also lead people to accept, as moral, requirements that have no discoverable connection—indeed, no connection at all—with human purposes or well-being, or with the well-being of any sentient creatures. That is, it can foster a tyrannical, irrational morality. Of course, if there were not only a benevolent god but also a reliable revelation of his will, then we might be able to get from it expert moral advice about difficult issues, where we could not discover what are the best policies. But there is no such reliable revelation. Even a theist must see that the purported revelations, such as the Bible and the Koran, condemn themselves by enshrining rules that we must reject as narrow, outdated, or barbarous. As Hans Küng says, "We are responsible for our morality." More generally, tying morality to religious belief is liable to devalue it, not only by undermining it temporarily if the belief decays, but also by subordinating it to other concerns while the belief persists.

GOD'S WEAKNESSES

We are told that God is omnipotent, omniscient, and benevolent; yet He behaves like a petulant tyrant, unable to control his recalcitrant subjects. He is angry, He is proud, He is jealous: all moral deficiencies surprising in a perfect Being. If He is self-sufficient, why does He need mankind? If He is All-powerful, why does He ask the help of humans? Above all, why does He pick an obscure Arabian merchant in some cultural backwater to be His last messenger on earth? Is it consistent with a supremely moral being that He should demand praise and absolute worship from creatures He Himself has created? What can we say of the rather curious psychology of a Being who creates humans—or rather automata—some of whom are preprogrammed to grovel in the dirt five times a day in homage to Himself? This obsessive desire for praise is hardly a moral virtue and is certainly not worthy of a morally supreme Being. Palgrave [DOI, p. 147] gave this[273] vivid but just description of the Koranic God:

> Thus immeasurably and eternally exalted above, and dissimilar from, all creatures, which lie leveled before Him on one common plane of instrumentality and inertness, God is One in the totality of omnipotent and omnipresent action, which acknowledges no rule, standard, or limit, save His own sole and absolute will. He communicates nothing to His creatures, for their seeming power and act ever remain His alone, and in return He receives nothing from them; for whatever they may be, that they are in Him, by Him and from Him only. [sura 8.17.] And secondly, no superiority, no distinction, no pre-eminence, can be lawfully claimed by one creature over its fellow, in the utter equalisation of their unexceptional servitude and abasement; all are alike tools of the one solitary Force which employs them to crush or to benefit, to truth or to error, to honour or shame, to happiness or misery, quite independently of their individual fitness, deserts, or advantage, and simply because "He wills it," and "as He wills it."
>
> One might at first sight think that this tremendous Autocrat, this uncontrolled and unsympathizing Power, would be far above anything like passions, desires, or inclinations. Yet such is not the case, for He has, with respect to His creatures, one main feeling and source of action, namely, jealousy of them, lest they should perchance attribute to themselves something of what is His alone and thus encroach on His all-engrossing kingdom. Hence He is ever more prone to punish than to reward, to inflict pain than to bestow pleasure, to ruin than to build. It is His singular satisfaction to let created beings continually feel that they are nothing else than His slaves, His tools—and contemptible tools too—that they may thus the better acknowledge His superiority, and know His power to be above their power, His cunning above their cunning, His will above their will, His pride above their pride; or rather, that there is no power, cunning, will, or pride, save His own. (For pride, see sura 59; God as schemer, 3.47; 8.30.)
>
> "But He Himself, sterile in His inaccessible height, neither loving nor enjoying aught save His own and self-measured decree, without son, companion, or counsellor, is no less barren of Himself than for His creatures, and His own barrenness and lone egoism in Himself is the cause and rule of His indifferent and unregarding despotism around." The first note is the key of the whole tune, and the primal idea of God runs through and modifies the whole system and creed that centers in Him.
>
> That the notion here given of the Deity, monstrous and blasphemous as it may appear, is exactly and literally that which the Coran conveys or intends to convey, I at present take for granted. But that it indeed is so, no one who has attentively perused and thought over the Arabic text . . . can hesitate to allow. In fact, every phrase of the preceding sentences, every touch in this odious portrait, has

been taken, to the best of my ability, word for word, or at least meaning for meaning, from the "Book," the truest mirror of the mind and scope of its writer.

And that such was in reality Mahomet's mind and idea, is fully confirmed by the witness-tongue of contemporary tradition. Of this we have many authentic samples. . . . I will subjoin a specimen . . . a repetition of which I have endured times out of number from admiring and approving Wahhabis in Nejd.

"Accordingly, when God . . . resolved to create the human race, He took into His hands a mass of earth, the same whence all mankind were to be formed, and in which they after a manner pre-existed; and having then divided the clod into two equal portions, He threw the one half into hell, saying, 'These to eternal fire, and I care not'; and projected the other half into heaven adding, 'and these to Paradise, I care not' " [Mishkatu 'l-Masabih Babu 'l Qadr].

But in this we have before us the adequate idea of predestination, or, to give it a truer name, pre-damnation, held and taught in the school of the Coran. Paradise and hell are at once totally independent of love or hatred on the part of the Deity, and of merits or demerits, of good or evil conduct, on the part of the creature; and in the corresponding theory, rightly so, since the very actions which we call good or ill-deserving, right or wrong, wicked or virtuous, are in their essence all one and of one, and accordingly merit neither praise nor blame, punishment nor recompense, except and simply after the arbitrary value which the all-regulating will of the great despot may choose to assign or impute to them. In a word, He burns one individual through all eternity amid red-hot chains and seas of molten fire, and seats another in the plenary enjoyment of an everlasting brothel between forty celestial concubines, just and equally for His own good pleasure, and because He wills it.

Men are thus all on one common level, here and hereafter, in their physical, social, and moral light—the level of slaves to one sole Master, of tools to one universal Agent.

AND MUHAMMAD IS HIS APOSTLE

Every national church or religion has established itself by pretending some special mission from God, communicated to certain individuals. The Jews have their Moses; the Christians their Jesus Christ, their apostles and saints; and the Turks their Mahomet, as if the way to God was not open to every man alike. Each of those churches show certain books, which they call revelation, or the Word of God. The Jews say that their Word of God was given by God to Moses, face to face; the Christians that their Word of God came by divine inspiration; and the Turks say that their Word of God (the Koran) was brought by an angel from heaven. Each of those churches accuses the other of unbelief; and for my own part, I disbelieve them all.

—Thomas Paine, *The Age of Reason*[274]

Allah or God chose Muhammad to be a messenger to all mankind. Though Muslim and sympathetic Western commentators deny it, it is clear that Muhammad himself thought that he had seen God Himself in person, as in sura 53.2–18. At other times, Muhammad talked to the angel Gabriel, who periodically revealed

God's message. How did Muhammad himself know that he had seen God or an angel? How did he know that the particular experiences he had were manifestations of God? Even if we grant Muhammad's sincerity, could he not have been sincerely mistaken? Most people claiming that they had direct access to God would now be seen as mentally ill. How do we know that in Muhammad's case it really was God or an angel that delivered God's message? As Paine[275] said (n.d., P. 52),

> But admitting for the sake of a case, that something has been revealed to a certain person, and not revealed to any other person, it is revelation to that person only. When he tells it to a second person, a second to a third, a third to a fourth, and so on, it ceases to be revelation to all those persons. It is revelation to the first person only, and *hearsay* to every other, and consequently they are not obliged to believe it.
>
> It is a contradiction in terms and ideas, to call anything a revelation that comes to us at second-hand, either verbally or in writing. Revelation is necessarily limited to the first communication—after this it is only an account of something which that person says was a revelation made to him; and though he may find himself obliged to believe it, it cannot be incumbent on me to believe it in the same manner; for it was not a revelation made to *me*, and I have only his word for it that it was made to him. When Moses told the children of Israel that he received the two tables of the commandments from the hands of God, they were not obliged to believe him, because they had no other authority for it than his telling them so; and I have no other authority for it than some historian telling me so. The commandments carry no internal evidence of divinity with them; they contain some good moral precepts, such as any man qualified to be a lawgiver, or legislator, could produce himself, without having recourse to supernatural intervention.
>
> When I am told that the Koran was written in heaven and brought to Mahomet by an angel, the account comes too near the same kind of hearsay evidence and second-hand authority as the former. I did not see the angel myself and, therefore, I have a right not to believe it.

Given the theory of Wansbrough, Crone, and Cook (that Islam emerged later than hitherto thought, under the influence of rabbinic Judaism, and taking Moses as an example of a prophet with a revelation, invented Muhammad as an Arabian prophet with a similar revelation), Paine's choice and juxtapositioning of the two examples of Moses and Muhammad is rather appropriate.

Moreover, as Paine says, very importantly, the revelations, as later recorded in the Bible or the Koran, do not carry any internal evidence of divinity with them. On the contrary, the Koran contains much—far too much—that is totally unworthy of a deity. In addition, the Bible and the Koran often contradict each other. On which basis should we decide between them? Both sides claim divine authority for their scriptures. In the end, we can only say that no specific revelation has reliable credentials.[276]

It is very odd that when God decides to manifest Himself, He does so to only one individual. Why can He not reveal Himself to the masses in a football stadium during the final of the World Cup, when literally millions of people around the world are watching? But as Patricia Crone said, "It is a peculiar habit of God's that when he wishes to reveal himself to mankind, he will communicate only with a single person. The rest of mankind must learn the truth from that person and thus purchase their knowledge of the divine at the cost of subordination to another human being, who is eventually replaced by a human institution, so that the divine remains under other people's control." [TLS, January 21, 1994, p. 12]

ABRAHAM, ISHMAEL, MOSES, NOAH, AND OTHER PROPHETS

We are told that [Abraham] was born in Chaldea, and that he was the son of a poor potter who earned his living by making little clay idols. It is scarcely credible that the son of this potter went to Mecca, 300 leagues away in the tropics, by way of impassable deserts. If he was a conqueror he no doubt aimed at the fine country of Assyria; and if he was only a poor man, as he is depicted, he founded no kingdoms in foreign parts.

—Voltaire[277]

For the historian, the Arabs are no more the descendents of Ishmael, son of Abraham, than the French are of Francus, son of Hector.

—Maxime Rodinson[278]

It is virtually certain that Abraham never reached Mecca.

—Montgomery Watt[279]

The essential point . . . is that, where objective fact has been established by sound historical methods, it must be accepted.

—Montgomery Watt[280]

According to Muslim tradition, Abraham and Ishmael built the Kaaba, the cube-like structure in the Sacred Mosque in Mecca. But outside these traditions there is absolutely no evidence for this claim—whether epigraphic, archaeological, or documentary. Indeed Snouck Hurgronje has shown that Muhammad invented the story to give his religion an Arabian origin and setting; with this brilliant improvisation Muhammad established the independence of his religion, at the same time incorporating into Islam the Kaaba with all its historical and religious associations for the Arabs.

Given the quantity of material in the Koran that comes from the Pentateuch—Moses: 502 verses in 36 suras; Abraham: 245 verses in 25 suras; Noah: 131 verses in 28 suras—it is surprising that higher biblical criticism has had no impact on Koranic studies. The Muslims as much as the Jews and the Christians are committed to the Pentateuch being authored by Moses. In the Koran, the Pentateuch is referred to as the Taurat (word derived from the Hebrew Torah).

Scholars have been casting doubt on the historical veracity of one biblical story after another, and Islam cannot escape the consequences of their discoveries and conclusions. As long ago as the seventeenth century, La Peyrere, Spinoza, and Hobbes were arguing that the Pentateuch could not have been written by Moses: "From what has been said, it is thus clearer than the sun at noonday that the Pentateuch was not written by Moses, but by someone who lived long after Moses," concludes Spinoza in *A Theologico-Political Treatise*.[281]

Then, in the nineteenth century, higher critics such as Graf and Wellhausen showed that the Pentateuch (that is, the books of Genesis, Exodus, Leviticus, Numbers, and Deuteronomy) was a composite work, in which one could discern the hand of four different "writers," usually referred to by the four letters J, E, D, and P.

Robin Lane Fox[282] takes up our story:

> In the Bible the four earlier sources were combined by a fifth person, an unknown author who must have worked on them at some point between c. 520 and 400 B.C., in my view, nearer to 400 B.C. As he interwove these sources, he tried to save their contents and have the best of several worlds (and Creations). He was a natural sub-editor . . . he was not, in my view, a historian, but I think he would be amazed if somebody told him that nothing in his amalgamated work was true. . . . Its chances of being historically true were minimal because none of those sources was written from primary evidence or within centuries, perhaps a millennium of what they tried to describe. How could an oral tradition have preserved true details across such a gap? . . . As for the "giants on earth," the Tower of Babel or the exploits of Jacob or Abraham, there is no good reason to believe any of them: the most detailed story in Genesis is the story of Joseph, a marvelous tale, woven from two separate sources, neither of which needs to rest on any historical truth.

The Torah was not written by, nor "given" to, Moses, and there is no good reason to believe any of the exploits of Abraham and others to be true. Certainly no historian would dream of going to the Muslim sources for the historical verification of any biblical material; the Muslim accounts of Abraham, Moses, and others are, as we saw earlier, taken from rabbinical Jewish scriptures or are nothing more than legends (the building of the Kaaba, etc.) invented several thousand years after the events they purport to describe.

Historians have gone even farther. There seems to be a distinct possibility that Abraham never existed: "The J tradition about the wandering of Abraham is largely unhistorical in character. By means of the theological leitmotif of the wandering obedient servant of Yahweh, it gives a structure to the many independent stories at J's disposal. It is an editorial device used to unite the many disparate Abraham and Lot traditions" (Thompson 1974). Thompson goes on to say (p. 328):

> not only has "archaeology" not proven a single event of the patriarchal traditions to be historical, it has not shown any of the traditions to be likely. On the

basis of what we know of Palestinian history of the Second Millennium B.C., and of what we understand about the formation of the literary traditions of Genesis, it must be concluded that any such historicity as is commonly spoken of in both scholarly and popular works about the patriarchs of Genesis is hardly possible and totally improbable.

Finally, "the quest for the historical Abraham is a basically fruitless occupation both for the historian and the student of the Bible."[283]

And Lane Fox observes: "Historians no longer believe the stories of Abraham as if they are history: like Aeneas or Heracles, Abraham is a figure of legend."[284]

Noah and the Flood

The building of the ark by Noah, the saving of all the animals, the universal deluge are all taken over into the Koran from Genesis. As the manifest absurdities of the tale were pointed out, Christians were no longer prone to take the fable literally; except, of course, the literal minded fundamentalists, many of whom still set out every year to look for the remnants of the lost ark. Muslims, on the other hand, seem immune to rational thought, and refuse to look the evidence in the face. I shall set out the arguments to show the absurdities in the legend, even though it may seem I am belaboring the obvious. I wish more people would belabor the obvious, and more often.

Noah was asked to take into the ark a pair from every species (sura 11.36–41). Some zoologists[285] estimate that there are perhaps ten million living species of insects; would they all fit into the ark? It is true they do not take up much room, so let us concentrate on the larger animals: reptiles, 5,000 species; birds, 9,000 species; and 4,500 species of class Mammalia (p. 239). In all, in the phylum Chordata, there are 45,000 species (p. 236). What sized ark would hold nearly 45,000 species of animals? A pair from each species makes nearly 90,000 individual animals, from snakes to elephants, from birds to horses, from hippopotamuses to rhinoceroses. How did Noah get them all together so quickly? How long did he wait for the sloth to make his slothful way from the Amazon? How did the kangaroo get out of Australia, which is an island? How did the polar bear know where to find Noah? As Robert Ingersoll asks,[286] "Can absurdities go farther than this?" Either we conclude that this fantastic tale is not to be taken literally, or we have recourse to some rather feeble answer, such as, for God all is possible. Why, in that case, did God go through all this rather complicated, time-consuming (at least for Noah) procedure? Why not save Noah and other righteous people with a rapid miracle rather than a protracted one?

No geological evidence indicates a universal flood. There is indeed evidence of local floods but not one that covered the entire world, not even the entire Middle East. We now know that the biblical accounts of the Flood, on which the Koranic account is based, are derived from Mesopotamian legends: "There is no reason to trace the Mesopotamian and Hebrew stories back to any one flood in particular; the Hebrew fiction is most likely to have developed from the Mesopotamians' legends. The stories are fictions, not history."[287]

David and the Psalms

The Koran also commits Muslims to the belief that David "received" the Psalms in the way Moses received the Torah (sura 4.163-65). But once again biblical scholars doubt that David wrote many, if any, of them. David probably lived around 1000 B.C., but we know that the Psalms were put together much later in the post-exilic period, that is, after 539 B.C.:

> The Book of Psalms consists of five collections of hymns, mostly written for use in the second temple (the temple of Zerubbabel). Though very old poems may have been adapted in several instances, these collections appear to be wholly, or almost wholly, post-exilian. Probably none of the psalms should be ascribed to David. Several of them, praising some highly idealised monarch, would seem to have been written in honour of one or other of the Hasmonean kings [142-63 B.C.].[288]

Adam and Evolution, Creation and Modern Cosmology

> Many Muslims have not yet come to terms with the fact of evolution . . . the story of Adam and Eve . . . has no place in a scientific account of the origins of the human race.
>
> —Watt[289]

The Koran gives a contradictory account of the creation, posing great problems for the commentators:

> Of old we created the heavens and the earth and all that is between them in six days, and no weariness touched us. (sura 50.37)

> Do you indeed disbelieve in Him who in two days created the earth? Do you assign Him equals? The Lord of the World is He. And He has placed on the earth the firm mountains which tower above it, and He has blessed it and distributed its nourishments throughout it (for the craving of all alike) in four days. Then He applied Himself to the heaven which was but smoke; and to it and to the earth He said, "Do you come in obedience or against your will?" And they both said, "We come obedient." And He completed them as seven heavens in two days, and He assigned to each heaven its duty and command; and He furnished the lower heavens with lights and guardian angels. This is the disposition of the Almighty, the All-Knowing One." (sura 41.9)

Two days for the earth, four days for the nourishment, and two days for the seven heavens make eight days (sura 41), whereas in sura 50 we are told the creation took six days. It is not beyond the commentators to apply some kind of hocus-pocus to resolve this contradiction.

The heavens and the earth and the living creatures that are in them are proof of God and His power (Levy 1957, p. 2, 4]; they and man in particular were not created frivolously (sura 21.16). Men and jinn have been assigned the special duty of worshipping God, and though the privilege of obedience to God's law was first offered to the heavens and the earth and the mountains, it was man who received it after their refusal (sura 33.72) (Levy 1957, p. 2, 4).

What are we to make of this strange doctrine? The heavens, the earth, and the mountains are seen as persons, and furthermore as persons who had the temerity to disobey God! An omnipotent God creates the cosmos, and then asks it if it would accept the "trust" or the "faith," and His own creation declines to accept this burden.

Creation was by the word of Allah, "Be," for all things are by His fiat. Before Creation His throne floated above the primeval waters and the heavens and the earth were of one mass (of water). Allah split it asunder, the heavens being built up and spread forth as a well-protected (supported) roof, without flaws, which He raised above the earth and holds there without pillars, whilst the earth was stretched out and the mountains were cast down upon its surface as firm anchors to prevent its moving with the living creatures upon it, for the world is composed of seven earths. Also the two seas were let loose alongside one another, the one sweet and the other salt, but with a barrier set between them so that they should not mingle. (Levy 1957, p. 2, 5)

Earth was created first, then the heavens. The moon was given its own light (sura 10.5), and for it, stations were "decreed so that it changes like an old and curved palm-branch, for man to know the number of the years and the reckoning" (Levy 1957, p. 2, 5).

As for Adam, "We have created man from an extract of clay; then we made him a clot in a sure depository; then we created the clot congealed blood, and we created the congealed blood a morsel; then we created the morsel bone, and we clothed the bone with flesh; then we produced it another creation; and blessed be God, the best of creators!" (sura 23.12).

Another account tells us that man was created from sperm (an unworthy fluid) (sura 77.22), and yet another version has it that all living things were created out of the same primeval water as the rest of the universe (sura 21.31, 25.56, 24.44). Animals have been created especially for the sake of mankind; men are the masters of these animals: "We have created for them the beasts of which they are masters. We have subjected these to them, that they may ride on some and eat the flesh of others; they drink their milk and put them to other uses" (sura 36.71).

The jinn were created out of fire, before the creation of man out of clay. They live on earth with men.

While Muslim commentators have no problems in reconciling the apparent contradictions, a modern, scientifically literate reader will not even bother to look for scientific truths in the above vague and confused accounts of creation. Indeed, it is that very vagueness that enables one to find whatever one wants to find in these myths, legends, and superstitions. So, many Muslims believe that the whole of knowledge is contained in the Koran or the traditions. As Ibn Hazm said, "Any fact whatsoever which can be proved by reasoning is in the Koran or in the words of the Prophet, clearly set out." Every time there is a new scientific discovery in, say, physics, chemistry or biology, the Muslim apologists rush to the Koran to prove that the discovery in question was anticipated there; everything from electricity to the theory of relativity (Ascha 1989, p. 14). These Muslims point to the Koranic notion of the aquatic origin of living things (sura 21.31), and the current idea in biology that life began, to quote Darwin, in "a warm little pond." Other putative scientific discoveries anticipated in the Koran include the fertilization of plants by wind (sura 15.22) and the mode of life of bees (sura 16.69). No doubt when they hear of the Glasgow chemist A. G. Cairns-Smith's suggestion that the answer to the riddle of the origins of life may lie in ordinary clay, these Muslim apologists will leap up and down with triumph and point to the Koranic doctrine that Adam was created from clay (Dawkins, pp. 148–65).

Since Muslims still take the Koranic account literally, I am duty bound to point out how it does not accord with modern scientific opinion on the origins of the universe and life on earth. Even on its own terms the Koranic account is inconsistent and full of absurdities. We have already noted the contradictions in the number of days for the creation. Allah merely has to say "Be," and His will is accomplished, and yet it takes the Almighty six days to create the heavens. Also, how could there have been "days" before the creation of the earth and the sun, since a "day" is merely the time the earth takes to make a revolution on its axis? We are also told that *before* the creation God's throne floated above the "waters." Where did this "water" come from before the creation? The whole notion of God having a throne is hopelessly anthropomorphic but is taken literally by the orthodox. Then we have several accounts of the creation of Adam. According to the Koran, Allah created the moon and its phases for man to know the number of the years (sura 10.5). Again, a rather primitive Arabian notion, since all the advanced civilizations of the Babylonians, Egyptians, Persians, Chinese, and Greeks, used the solar year for the purpose of time reckoning.

Let us turn to the modern account of the origins of the universe.

In 1929, Edwin Hubble published his discovery that remote galaxies are rushing away from the earth with speeds proportional to their distances from the earth. The Hubble law states that the recessional velocity, v, of a galaxy is related to its distance, r, from the earth by the equation $v = H_o r$, where H_o is the Hubble constant. In other words, the Hubble law is telling us that the universe is expanding. As Kaufmann says:[290] "The universe has been expanding for billions of years, so there must have been a time in the ancient past when all the matter in the universe was concentrated in a state of infinite density. Presumably, some sort of colossal explosion must have occurred to start the expansion of the universe. This explosion, commonly called the Big Bang, marks the creation of the universe." The age of the universe has been calculated to be between fifteen and twenty billion years.

Before what is called the Planck time (approximately ten seconds after the projected time of the Big Bang), the universe was so dense that the known laws of physics are inadequate to describe the behavior of space, time, and matter. During the first million years, matter and energy formed an opaque plasma (called the primordial fireball), consisting of high-energy photons colliding with protons and electrons. About one million years after the Big Bang, protons and electrons could combine to form hydrogen atoms. We had to wait ten billion years before our solar system came into existence. "Our solar system is formed of matter created in stars that disappeared billions of years ago. The Sun is a fairly young star, only five billion years old. All of the elements other than hydrogen and helium in our solar system were created and cast off by ancient stars during the first ten billion years of our galaxy's existence. We are literally made of star dust." (Kaufmann, p. 110) The solar system formed from a cloud of gas and dust, called the solar nebula, which can be described as a "rotating disk of snowflakes and ice-coated dust particles." The inner planets, Mercury, Venus, Earth, and Mars, formed through the accretion of dust particles into planetesimals and then into larger protoplanets. The outer planets, Jupiter, Saturn, Uranus, Neptune, and Pluto, formed through the break up of the outer nebula into rings of gas and ice-coated dust that coalesced into huge protoplanets. The Sun was formed by accretion at the center of the nebula. After about 100 million years, temperatures at the protosun's center were high enough to ignite thermonuclear reactions. (Kaufmann, p. 116)

The preceding account is hopelessly at variance with the account given in the Koran. The earth was not, as the Koran claims (sura 41.12), created before the heavens; we have already noted that the sun and the solar system formed millions of years after the Big Bang, millions of other stars had already formed before our sun. Furthermore, the term "heavens" is hopelessly vague; does it mean our solar system? Our galaxy? The universe? No amount of juggling will make sense of the Koranic or biblical story of the creation of the "heavens" in six, eight, or two days. The light of the moon is, of course, not its own light (pace, sura 10.5) but the reflected light of the sun. The earth orbits the sun, not vice versa.

Those who are tempted to see in the Koran various anticipations of the Big Bang should realize that modern cosmology and physics in general is based on mathematics. Without the developments in mathematics, especially those in the seventeenth century (the calculus, for example), progress and understanding would not have been possible. In contrast to the vagueness of the Koran, the Big Bang in its modern cosmological formulation is stated with precision using advanced mathematics; indeed it is not possible to state these ideas in ordinary language without the loss of precision.

The Origins of Life and the Theory of Evolution

The earth was formed about 4.5 billion years ago, and perhaps less than one billion years later, life appeared on it for the first time after a period of chemical evolution. The Russian biochemist, Oparin, argued in *The Origin of Life* (1938) that the primitive earth contained chemical elements that reacted to the radiation from outer space as well as terrestrial sources of energy. "As a result of prolonged photochemical activity, these inorganic mixtures give rise to organic compounds [including amino acids that are the building blocks from which the protein molecules are constructed]. Through time and chemical selection, these . . . organic systems increased in complexity and stability, becoming the immediate precursors of living things"[291] (Birx, n.d., pp. 417–18). Since Oparin's time, many scientists (Miller, Fox, Ponnamperuma) have succeeded in producing organic compounds from inorganic ones in the laboratory.

> Controversy still surrounds the biochemical explanation for the origin of life on earth, particularly as to whether something analogous to the DNA or RNA molecule arose first or, instead, basic amino acids necessary for protein synthesis. Living things emerged when organic systems became capable of metabolism and reproduction; the development of inorganic syntheses in chemical evolution paved the way for biological evolution and subsequently the adaptive radiation of more and more complex and diversified forms. (n.d., p. 419)

In 1859, Darwin published his *On the Origin of Species by Means of Natural Selection, or the Preservation of Favoured Races in the Struggle for Life*. In the Introduction of his great work, Darwin[292] wrote:

> In considering the Origin of Species, it is quite conceivable that a naturalist, reflecting on the mutual affinities of organic beings, on their embryological relations, their geographical distribution, geological succession, and other such facts, might come to the conclusion that each species had not been independently created, but had descended, like varieties, from other species. Nevertheless, such a conclusion, even if well founded, would be unsatisfactory, until it could be shown how the innumerable species inhabiting this world have been modified, so as to acquire that perfection of structure and coadaptation which most justly excites our admiration.

Darwin's answer to his own question of "the How of Evolution" is, of course, Natural Selection. Species were a result of the long process of natural selection acting on "constantly appearing, random, heritable variations."[293] Darwin put the matter himself in this way:

> As many more individuals of each species are born than can possibly survive; and as, consequently, there is a frequently recurring struggle for existence, it follows that any being, if it vary however slightly in any manner profitable

to itself, under the complex and sometimes varying conditions of life, will have a better chance of surviving, and thus be naturally selected. From the strong principle of inheritance, any selected variety will tend to propagate its new and modified form.[294]

The implications of the theory of evolution for man's place in nature were obvious. Darwin himself noted that "the conclusion that man is the co-descendant with other species of some ancient, lower, and extinct form is not in any degree new. Lamarck long ago came to this conclusion, which has lately been maintained by several eminent naturalists and philosophers; for instance, by Wallace, Huxley, Lyell, Vogt, Lubbock, Buchner, Rolle, &c., and especially Haeckel."

In the eighteenth century, de Lamettrie had classified man as an animal in *L'Homme Machine* (1748). Linnaeus (1707–78) had classified man with the manlike apes as Anthropomorpha. T. H. Huxley in his famous "Man's Relations to Lower Animals,"[295] begins his account by looking at the development of a dog's egg, and then concludes that

the history of the development of any other vertebrate animal, Lizard, Snake, Frog, or Fish, tells the same story. There is always, to begin with, an egg having the same essential structure as that of the Dog:—the yolk of that egg always undergoes division, or "segmentation"; . . . the ultimate products of that segmentation constitute the building materials for the body of the young animal; and this is built up round a primitive groove, in the floor of which a notochord is developed. Furthermore, there is a period in which the young of all these animals resemble one another, not merely in outward form, but in all essentials of structure, so closely, that the differences between them are inconsiderable, while, in their subsequent course, they diverge more and more widely from one another.

Thus the study of development affords a clear test of closeness of structural affinity, and one turns with impatience to inquire what results are yielded by the study of the development of Man. Is he something apart? Does he originate in a totally different way from Dog, Bird, Frog, and Fish, thus justifying those who assert him to have no place in nature and no real affinity with the lower world of animal life? Or does he originate in a similar germ, pass through the same slow and gradually progressive modifications—depend on the same contrivances for protection and nutrition, and finally enter the world by the help of the same mechanism? The reply is not doubtful for a moment, and has not been doubtful any time these thirty years. Without question, the mode of origin and the early stages of the development of man are identical with those of the animals immediately below him in the scale:—without a doubt, in these respects, he is far nearer the Apes, than the Apes are to the Dog.

There is every reason to conclude that the changes [the human ovum] undergoes are identical with those exhibited by the ova of other vertebrated animals; for the formative materials of which the rudimentary human body is composed, in the earliest conditions in which it has been observed, are the same as those of other animals.

But, exactly in those respects in which the developing Man differs from the Dog, he resembles the ape, which, like man, has a spheroidal yolk-sac and a discoidal—sometimes partially lobed—placenta.

So that it is only quite in the later stages of development that the young human being presents marked differences from the young ape, while the latter departs as much from the dog in its development, as the man does.

Startling as the last assertion may appear to be, it is demonstrably true, and it alone appears to me sufficient to place beyond all doubt the structural unity of man with the rest of the animal world, and more particularly and closely with the apes.

The evidence for evolution comes from an impressive range of scientific disciplines: systematics, geopaleontology, biogeography, comparative studies in biochemistry, serology, immunology, genetics, embryology, parasitology, morphology (anatomy and physiology), psychology, and ethology.

This evidence points in the same direction, namely, that man, like all living things, is the result of evolution, and was descended from some apelike ancestor, and certainly was not the product of special creation. In this context, to talk of Adam and Eve as both the Bible and Koran do is meaningless. Man is, at present, classified under the order Primates, along with tree shrews, lemurs, lorises, monkeys, and apes. Thus, not only apes and monkeys, but lemurs and tree shrews must be considered our distant cousins. As J. Z. Young states, "it is harder still to realize that our ancestry goes on back in a direct and continuous father-and-son line to a shrew, and from there to some sort of newt, to a fish, and perhaps to a kind of sea-lily."[296]

God the Creator

Has the famous story that stands at the beginning of the Bible really been understood? the story of God's hellish fear of science? . . . Man himself had turned out to be [God's] greatest mistake; he had created a rival for himself; science makes godlike—it is all over with priests and gods when man becomes scientific. . . . Knowledge, the emancipation from the priest, continues to grow.
—Nietzsche, *The Antichrist*[297]

Nowhere in the foregoing account of the origins of the universe and the origin of life and the theory of evolution did I have recourse to "divine intervention" as an explanation. Indeed, to explain everything in terms of God is precisely not to explain anything—it is to cut all inquiry dead, to stifle any intellectual curiosity, to kill any scientific progress. To explain the wonderful and awesome variety and complexity of living organisms as "miracles" is not to give a very helpful, least of all a scientific, explanation. To quote Dawkins, "To explain the origin of the DNA/protein machine by invoking a supernatural Designer is to explain precisely nothing, for it leaves unexplained the origin of the Designer. You have to say something like 'God was always there,' and if you allow yourself that kind of lazy way out, you might as well just say 'DNA was always there,' or 'Life was always there,' and be done with it."[298]

Darwin made the same point about his own theory in a letter to Sir Charles Lyell, the famous geologist: "If I were convinced that I required such additions to the theory of natural selection, I would reject it as rubbish. . . . I would give nothing for the theory of natural selection, if it requires miraculous additions at any one stage of descent." Quoting the above letter, Dawkins comments: "This is no petty matter. In Darwin's view, the whole point of the theory of evolution by natural selection was that it provided a non-miraculous account of the existence of complex adaptations. For what it is worth, it is also the whole point of this book [*The Blind Watchmaker*]. For Darwin, any evolution that had to be helped over the jumps by God was not evolution at all. It made a nonsense of the central point of evolution."

As for the Big Bang and modern cosmology, Stephen Hawking[299] makes the same point. Trying to make amends for their treatment of Galileo, the Vatican organized a conference to which eminent cosmologists were invited.

> At the end of the conference the participants were granted an audience with the pope. He told us that it was all right to study the evolution of the universe after the big bang, but we should not inquire into the big bang itself because that was the moment of Creation and therefore the work of God. I was glad then that he did not know the subject of the talk I had just given at the conference— the possibility that space-time was finite but had no boundary, which means that it had no beginning, no moment of Creation. (Hawking, p. 122)

Elsewhere in his best-selling book, *A Brief History of Time,* Hawking observes that

> the quantum theory of gravity has opened up a new possibility, in which there would be no boundary to space-time and so there would be no need to specify the behaviour at the boundary. There would be no singularities at which the laws of science broke down and no edge of space-time at which one would have to appeal to God or some new law to set the boundary conditions for space-time. One could say: "The boundary condition of the universe is that it has no boundary." The universe would be completely self-contained and not affected by anything outside itself. It would neither be created nor destroyed. It would just *be*.

A little later, Hawking asks, "What place, then, for a creator?"

Einstein observed that "the man who is thoroughly convinced of the universal operation of the law of causation cannot for a moment entertain the idea of a being who interferes in the course of events. . . . He has no use for the religion of fear."[300]

Similarly, more recently, Peter Atkins argues "that the universe can come into existence without intervention, and that there is no need to invoke the idea of a Supreme Being in one of its numerous manifestations."[301]

Theories that explain the Big Bang by reference to God answer no scientific questions. They push questions of ultimate origin back one step, prompting questions about God's origins. As Feuerbach[302] said, "The world is nothing to religion—the world, which is in truth the sum of all reality, is revealed in its glory only by theory. The joys of theory are the sweetest intellectual pleasures of life; but religion knows nothing of the joys of the thinker, of the investigator of Nature, of the artist. The idea of the universe is wanting to it, the consciousness of the really infinite, the consciousness of the species."

It is only the scientist with a sense of wonder who feels that life's awesome complexity needs explaining, who will propose refutable and testable scientific hypotheses, who will try to unravel the so-called mysteries of the universe. The religious man will content himself with the uninteresting and untestable remark that "it" was all created by God.

Flood, Famine, and Drought

It is rather unfortunate that the Koran gives the example of the elements as signs of God's munificence since they are as much a cause of misery as happiness. Rain, we are told in sura 7.56, is a harbinger of God's mercy. Yet floods claim the lives of thousands of people in, ironically, a Muslim country, namely, Bangladesh. The cyclone of 1991, with winds of 200 kilometers per hour, resulted in floods that left 100,000 dead and 10,000,000 without shelter. Despite the omnipresence of water, Bangladesh goes through a period of drought from October to April. Thus, the wretched population, among the poorest in the world, is submitted to both periodic floods and drought. All the work of God, as sura 57.22 tells us: "No disaster occurs on earth or accident in yourselves which was not already recorded in the Book before we created them."

Indeed, all natural catastrophes from earthquakes to tornadoes seem hard to reconcile with a benevolent God, especially as they seem to be visited on particularly poor, and often Muslim, countries. During the Lisbon earthquake of 1755 literally thousands of people died, many in churches as they prayed, and these deaths had a profound effect on the eighteenth century, particularly on writers like Voltaire. Why were so many innocent people killed? Why were the brothels spared, while pious churchgoers were punished?

Miracles

Eighteenth-century deists, as we saw earlier, exaggerated Islam's rationality, pointing to the fact that Muhammad did not perform any miracles. It is true: throughout the Koran Muhammad says he is a mere mortal unable to perform miracles, he is only God's messenger (suras 29.49, 13.27–30, 17.92–97). Despite these disclaimers, there are at least four places in the Koran that Muslims believe refer to miracles.

1. The clefting of the moon: "The hour has approached, and the moon has been cleft. But if the unbelievers see a sign, they turn aside and say, 'Magic! that shall pass away!' " (sura 54.1, 2).

2. The assistance given to the Muslims at the battle of Badr: "When you said to the faithful: 'Is it not enough for you that your Lord helps you with three thousand angels sent down from high?' No: if you are steadfast and fear God, and the enemy come upon you in hot pursuit, your Lord will help you with five thousand angels with their distinguishing marks" (3.120, 121).

3. The night journey: "We declare the glory of Him who transports his servant by night from Masjidu 'l-Haram to the Masjidu'l-Aqsa [i.e., Mecca to Jerusalem]" (sura 17.1).

4. The Koran itself, for Muslims, remains the great miracle of Islam (sura 29.48).

The traditions are full of Muhammad's miracles, curing the ill, feeding a thousand people on one kid, etc.

As our knowledge of nature has increased, there has been a corresponding decline in the belief in miracles. We are no longer prone to think that God intervenes arbitrarily in human affairs by suspending or altering the normal workings of the laws of nature. As our confidence in our discoveries of the laws of nature has increased, our belief in miracles has receded.

David Hume argued in the following manner:[303]

> A miracle is a violation of the laws of nature; and as a firm and unalterable experience has established these laws, the proof against a miracle, from the very nature of the fact, is as entire as any argument from experience can possibly be imagined. Why is it more than probable, that all men must die; that lead cannot, of itself, remain suspended in the air; . . . unless it be, that these events are found agreeable to the laws of nature, and there is required a violation of these laws, or in other words a miracle to prevent them? Nothing is esteemed a miracle, if it ever happens in the common course of nature. . . . But it is a miracle, that a dead man should come to life; because that has never been observed in any age or country. There must, therefore, be a uniform experience against every miraculous event, otherwise the event would not merit that appellation. And as a uniform experience amounts to a proof, there is here a direct and full proof, from the nature of the fact, against the existence of any miracle; . . .
>
> The plain consequence is . . . "That no testimony is sufficient to establish a miracle, unless the testimony be of such a kind, that its falsehood would be more miraculous, than the fact, which it endeavours to establish."

And in every putative miracle, it is more reasonable and in accordance with our experience to deny that the "miracle" ever happened. People are duped and deluded, are apt to exaggerate, and have this strong need to believe; or as Feuerbach put it, a miracle is "the sorcery of the imagination, which satisfies without contradiction all the wishes of the heart." Koranic miracles occurred a long time ago, and we are no longer in a position to verify them.

Perhaps one of the most important arguments against miracles, an argument often overlooked, is that, to quote Hospers:

> We believe that most of the alleged miracles are in some way unworthy of an omnipotent being. If God wanted people to believe in him, why perform a few miracles in a remote area where few people could witness them? . . . Instead of healing a few people of their disease, why not all sufferers? Instead of performing a miracle in Fatima [a Portuguese village where three illiterate children saw visions of "Our Lady of the Rosary"] in 1917, why not put an end to the enormous slaughter of World War 1, which was occurring at the same time, or keep it from starting.[304]

Jesus in the Koran

THE ANNUNCIATION AND THE VIRGIN BIRTH

The Koran tells us that Jesus was miraculously born of the Virgin Mary. The Annunciation of the Virgin is recounted at sura 19.16–21 and sura 3.45–48:

> Behold! the angels said: "O Mary! God gives you glad tidings of a Word from Him: his name will be Jesus Christ, the son of Mary, held in honour in this world and the hereafter and of those nearest to God; he shall speak to the people in childhood and in maturity. And he shall be of the righteous." "How, O my Lord, shall I have a son, when no man has touched me?" asked Mary. He said, "Thus: God creates whatever He wants, when He decrees a thing He only has to say, 'Be,' and it is. And God will teach him the Book and Wisdom, the Torah and the Gospel."

Although it remains a tenet of orthodox Christian theology, liberal Christian theologians and many Christians now, and even the Bishop of Durham (England), no longer accept the story as literally true, preferring to interpret "virgin" as "pure" or morally without reproach, in other words, symbolically. Martin Luther (1483–1546), writing in the sixteenth century, conceded that "We Christians seem fools to the world for believing that Mary was the true mother of this child, and nevertheless a pure virgin. For this is not only against all reason, but also against the creation of God, who said to Adam and Eve, 'Be fruitful and multiply.' "[305]

The treatment of the Virgin Birth by Christian biblical scholars is a good example of how Muslims cannot hide from their conclusions, for these conclusions have a direct bearing on the veracity or at least the literal truth of the Koran. Charles Guignebert (1867–1939)[306] has made a detailed examination of the legend of the Virgin birth. Guignebert points out the striking parallels to the Virgin birth legend in the Greco-Roman world:

It is here that we find the legend of Perseus, born of Danae, a virgin who was impregnated by a shower of gold, [and] the story of Attis whose mother Nana, became pregnant as a result of eating a pomegranate. It was here especially that the birth of notable men—Pythagoras, Plato, Augustus himself—tended to be explained by some kind of parthenogenesis, or by the mysterious intervention of a god. It is quite conceivable that, in a community in which so many stories of this kind were current, the Christians, desirous of adducing conclusive vindication of their faith in the divinity of Jesus, naturally turned to the sign by which men bearing the divine stamp were commonly identified. There was no question, of course, of a conscious imitation of any particular story, but simply of the influence of a certain atmosphere of belief.

Some scholars, such as Adolf Harnack (1851-1930), believe the Virgin birth legend arose from the interpretation of a prophetic passage in the Old Testament, namely, Isa. 7.14, according to the Greek text of the Septuagint, a translation made in 132 B.C. On this occasion, Ahaz, King of Judah, fears a new attack by the allied kings of Syria and Israel, who have just failed to take Jerusalem. The prophet reassures Ahaz and says:

> Therefore the Lord shall give a sign. Behold the Virgin shall conceive and give birth to a son, and thou shalt call him Emmanuel. Butter and honey shall he eat, that he may know how to refuse the evil and choose the good. But before this child shall know how to recognize good and evil and choose the good, the land whose two kings thou abhorrest shall be forsaken.

The Christians, while searching for all the prophetic sayings concerning the Messiah, discovered this passage from Isaiah and, taking it out of context, gave it a messianic meaning. Most important of all, the Hebrew original does not contain the word "virgin" ("bethulah") but the word "young woman" ("haalmah"); in Greek, "parthenos" and "neanis," respectively. As Guignebert says,

> the orthodox theologians have made every effort to prove that "haalmah" might mean virgin, but without success. The prophet had no thought of predicting a miracle, and the Jews, as soon as they began to attack the Christians, did not miss the opportunity of pointing out that the term to which their opponents appealed was nothing but a blunder.
>
> The Christians, convinced that Christ was born of the Spirit of God, as the accounts of the Baptism must testify must eagerly have seized upon the word parthenos as a means of effectuating this divine relationship.

Guignebert himself does not accept this theory of the origin of the Virgin birth legend put forward by Harnack. Instead, Guignebert offers his own hypothesis [p. 247]:

> It will be observed that in Paul, John, and Mark, none of whom believes in the Virgin Birth, Jesus is characterised as the Son of God. This description

of him is, accordingly, prior to the establishment of the belief in the miracle related by Matthew and Luke, and does not arise out of it. As soon as they were convinced that, not only had Jesus been raised up by God, as a man full of the Holy Spirit, to accomplish his plans, but that his birth into this life for God had been divinely predestined, and glorified by the Holy Ghost, they must have attempted to signalise and to express this special relationship between Jesus and God. They said that he was his "son," because that was the only term in human language by which they could intelligibly, if not completely and adequately, express this relation. Since the idea of the direct generation of a man by God could only appear to the Jewish mind as a monstrous absurdity, the expression was, in reality, to the Palestinians, only a manner of speaking, only a metaphor.

[It is clear] that Jesus never applied it to himself and that, moreover, it had not hitherto, in Israel, any Messianic significance. That is to say, the Jews did not beforehand bestow this title of Son of God upon the expected Messiah. The Messiah must have been for them not the Son, but the Servant, of God (Ebed Yahweh), for such was the designation of the "men of Yahweh." But on Greek soil the Christological belief found an environment very different from that of Palestine. There, the idea of the procreation of a human being by a god was current, and the relation of real sonship between Christ and God the Father could shock no one. . . . On the contrary, the term Son of God was more likely to arouse sympathy in that quarter than the too peculiarly Jewish, too nationalistic, name of Messiah. Hence it was, in all probability, in the first Christian communities among the Gentiles, that the expression arose. Possibly it did so, at first, as a simple translation of the Palestinian Ebed Yahweh, for the Greek word pais means both servant and child, and it would be easy transition from child to son. But it soon took on the colouring of an original Christological idea, the idea which met the needs of the environment which called it forth, the idea expressed in the Epistles of Paul. It found its Pauline and Johannine justification in the doctrine of divine preexistence and of the incarnation of the Lord. The legend of the Virgin Birth is another of its justifications, sprung from a quite different intellectual environment, but analogous to the one just cited, and finding its scriptural confirmation, when the need arose to defend it in controversy, in Isaiah 7:14. Matthew and Luke represent two concrete embodiments, different in form, but similar in spirit and meaning, of the belief: "He is the Son of God. He is born of the Holy Spirit."

THE BIRTH OF JESUS

The account of the birth of Jesus in sura 19.22–34 shows remarkable similarity not only to, as was pointed out by Sale, the story of Leto, but also to something which I have not seen remarked on anywhere, the birth of the historical Buddha. Let us look at the Koran first, sura 19.22f.:

And she conceived him, and retired with him to a far-off place. And the throes came upon her by the trunk of a palm tree. She said: "Oh, would that I had died before this! would that I had been a thing forgotten and out of sight!"

But a voice cried to her from beneath her, "grieve not! for thy Lord has provided a rivulet at your feet; and shake the trunk of the palm tree towards you, it will drop fresh ripe dates upon you. Eat then and drink, and cheer your eye; and if you see anyone, say, "Verily, I have vowed abstinence to the God of mercy. I will not speak with anyone today."

Then she brought it to her people, carrying it. They said, "Oh Mary! you have done a strange thing! O sister of Aaron! your father was not a bad man, nor was your mother a whore!" And she made a sign to them, pointing towards the babe. They said, "How shall we speak with him who is in the cradle, an infant?" [The babe] said, "Verily, I am the servant of God, He has given me a book, and He has made me a prophet, and He has made me blessed wherever I be; and He has required of me prayer and almsgiving so long as I live, and piety towards my mother, and has not made me a miserable tyrant; and peace upon me the day I was born, and the day I die, and the day I shall be raised up alive."

Leto—or in Latin, Latona—was a Titaness, a daughter of Coeus and Phoebe. According to the Homeric hymn to the Delian Apollo, Leto gave birth to Apollo while grasping the sacred palm tree. Apollo is also said to have spoken from Leto's womb. Callimachus (ca. 305–240 B.C.) in his "Hymn in Delum" recounts a similar story.

According to the legends of the birth of the Buddha, Queen Maya Devi dreamed that a white elephant entered her right side. Many Brahmins reassured the king and the queen that their child would one day be a great monarch or a Buddha. The miraculous pregnancy lasted ten months. On her way to her own parents towards the end of her pregnancy, Maya Devi entered the Lumbini garden where, as she grasped the branch of the Shala tree, the child emerged from her right side. As soon as he was born, the future Buddha stood up and took seven steps toward the north, and then toward the other cardinal points of the earth to announce his possession of the universe, and proclaimed that this was his last birth. We have already remarked on the probable direct source of the Koranic story of the birth of Jesus, viz., the apocryphal book called "The History of the Nativity of Mary and the Saviour's Infancy."

Did Jesus Exist?

It may come as a surprise to Muslims that there were, and are still, scholars who doubt the historicity of Jesus, to whose existence Muslims are totally committed. Bruno Bauer (1809–1882), J. M. Robertson (1856–1933), Arthur Drews (1865–1935), van den Bergh van Eysinga, Albert Kalthoff, and in recent years, Guy Fau (*Le Fable de Jesus Christ,* Paris, 1967), Prosper Alfaric (*Origines Sociales du Christianisme,* Paris, 1959), W. B. Smith (*The Birth of the Gospel,* New York, 1957), and Professor G. A. Wells of Birkbeck College, University of London, have all developed the "Christ-Myth" theory.[307] Professor Joseph Hoffmann sums up the situation in this manner:

Scholarly opinion still holds (albeit not tenaciously) to the postulate of an historical figure whose life story was very soon displaced by the mythmaking activity of a cult. [Other scholars hold] the view that the postulation of an historical figure is unnecessary to explain the apparently "biographical" features of the Gospels. A candid appraisal of the evidence would seem to favour the latter view, but we cannot easily dismiss the possibility that an historical figure lies behind the Jesus legend of the New Testament.[308]

I intend to discuss the not-so-negligible evidence for the view that Jesus did not exist for several reasons:

1. First, very generally, the debates, discussions, and arguments on the Jesus-myth are as much the concern of Muslims as Christians; or rather, they should be. I suspect that no book written on Islam has ever discussed the views of Bauer or those of the Radical Dutch school on the historicity of Jesus. It should be the deep concern of all educated people who are interested in our intellectual and spiritual heritage and origins. The early history of Christianity is one of the most important chapters in the history of civilization. For Muslims, Jesus was one of God's prophets and a historical figure who performed various miracles, and who would come again at the last day and kill the Antichrist. If it can be shown that Jesus did not exist, it will have obvious consequences for all Muslims, for such a revelation will automatically throw the veracity of the Koran into question.

However, it is not simply a question of the historicity of Jesus, but what we do and can know about him. Again these questions should be of the utmost importance for all, including Muslims. Muslims believe Jesus existed, therefore, what nearly two hundred years of dedicated and selfless research by some of the greatest historians and intellectuals has revealed about this man should be of passionate interest. Muslims as much as Christians should be concerned with the truth of the matter. Even the Christian theologians who accept Jesus' existence concede a number of problems concerning his life have not been resolved. Most of the stories in the New Testament concerning his life are now accepted, even by conservative Christian theologians, to be legends with no basis in history. The New Testament scholar Ernst Kasemann concluded: "Over few subjects has there been such a bitter battle among the New Testament scholars of the last two centuries as over the miracle-stories of the Gospels. . . . We may say that today the battle is over, not perhaps as yet in the arena of church life, but certainly in the field of theological science. It has ended in the defeat of the concept of miracle which has been tradition in the church."[309]

Where does this leave the Koran? None of the stories of Jesus in the Koran is accepted as true; most of them contain gross superstitions and "miracles" that only the most credulous would deem worthy of attention. It is worth remarking that if the Koran is absolutely true and the literal word of God, why is it that no Christian theologian adduces it as proof of Jesus' existence? No historian has ever looked at the Koran for historical enlightenment, for the simple reason that no historian will look at a document, which he will presume to be of human origin, written some six hundred years after the events it purports to describe when there are documents written some fifty or sixty years after the same events. We also know the source of the Koran stories, namely, heretical Gnostic gospels such as the Gospel of St. Thomas, which in turn have been dismissed as unhistorical.

Even if we do not accept the thesis that Jesus never existed, the conclusions of the New Testament historians throw a very illuminating light on the growth of religions and religious mythology; furthermore, they point to the striking similarities to the recent theories put forward by Islamicist scholars on the rise of Islam and the Muhammad legend of the Muslim traditions.

2. Many of the criticisms of Christianity to be found in the works to be discussed apply, *mutatis mutandis,* to all religions, including Islam.

3. The discussions of the historicity of Jesus have been conducted in Europe and the United States for over a hundred and fifty years now, without any of the scholars who denied Jesus' historicity being threatened by assassination. It is true Bauer was dismissed from his university post in theology at Bonn in 1842, but he continued to publish until the end of his life. Professor Wells is alive (1994) and well and taught at the University of London until 1971, while still vigorously denying that Jesus ever existed. In all this, there is surely a lesson for the Islamic world.

4. Blind dogmatism has shut Muslims off from the intellectually challenging and exhilarating research, debate, and discussion of the last century and a half. In the words of Joseph Hoffmann: "It is through such discussion, however, that we avoid the dogmatism of the past and learn to respect uncertainty as a mark of enlightenment."[310]

5. There is also a deeper methodological moral to be learned from the following discussions. The virtue of disinterested historical inquiry is undermined if we bring into it the Muslim or Christian faith. Historical research only leads to an approximation of the objective truth, after a process of conjectures and refutations, critical thought, rational arguments, presentation of evidence, and so on. However, if we bring subjective religious faith, with its dogmatic certainties, into the "historical approximation process, it inevitably undermines what R. G. Collingwood argued was the fundamental attribute of the critical historian, skepticism regarding testimony about the past."[311]

THE ARGUMENTS

Strauss

In his *Life of Jesus Critically Examined* (1835), David Strauss pointed out that we could not take the gospels as historical biographies; that was not their primary function. The early Christians wanted to win converts to their cause "through the propagation of a synthetic religious myth."[312]

Strauss's main thesis is that the stories in the New Testament were the result of the messianic expectations of the Jewish people.

> The evangelists made Jesus say and do what they expected—from their knowledge of the Old Testament—that the Messiah would say and do; and many passages that in fact make no reference to the Messiah were nevertheless taken as messianic prophecies. Thus, "then shall the eyes of the blind be opened" (Isa. 35) expresses the joy of Jewish exiles in Babylon at the prospect of release from captivity, but was understood by the evangelists as prophesying that the Messiah would cure blindness, which they accordingly make Jesus do.[313]

Bauer

Bauer went a step further and contended that the early Christians fashioned Jesus Christ from the portraits of the prophets found in the Old Testament. Jesus never existed, and Christianity arose in the middle of the first century from a fusion of Judaic and Greco-Roman ideas. Bauer argues, for example, that the Christian use of the Greek term "Logos" ultimately derives from Philo, the Stoics, and Heraclitus. For Philo, the Logos was the creative power that orders the world and the intermediary through whom men knew God. Of course, in St. John's Gospel, the Logos is equated with God, who becomes incarnate in Jesus Christ.

As for other classical influences on Christianity, as early as the fourth century, anti-Christian writers were pointing out the striking resemblances of the life of Jesus to the life of Apollonius of Tyana, a neo-Pythagorean teacher who was born just before the Christian era. He led a wandering and ascetic life, claimed miraculous powers, and was in constant danger of his life during the reigns of Roman emperors Nero and Domitian. His followers referred to him as the son of God; they also claimed he was resurrected before their very eyes and that he ascended into heaven.

The mystery cult of Mithras was first established in the Roman world in the first half of the first century B.C. This cult developed secret rites and rituals and stages of initiation through which the god's devotees had to pass. Mithraic mysteries also showed striking similarities to the Christian Baptism and the Eucharist.

The early Christians attribute words and sayings to Jesus that in reality only reflect the experience, convictions, and hopes of the Christian community. For example, Mark 1.14–15: "Now after that John was put in prison, Jesus came into Galilee, preaching the gospel of the kingdom of God. And saying, 'The time is fulfilled, and the kingdom of God is at hand: repent ye, and believe the gospel.' " Christ never spoke these words—they

> were merely an expression of the earliest Christian community's conviction that the time was ripe for the appearance of Christianity and the diffusion of its beliefs about spiritual salvation. But in time, attempts were made to find historical indications—from the ancient days recorded in the Old Testament to imperial times—that progressive preparations for the age of salvation were apparent. Each new generation has regarded its own time as the time when the ancient promises will be fulfilled. The first Christians believed, from their knowledge of the Old Testament, that before the Savior came Elijah would return to earth. Once they had come to see the historical John the Baptist as Elijah returned, they would naturally believe that the Savior had followed soon after; and eventually a story would be constructed in which this "savior" is made to call John by the name "Elijah." (Mark 9.13)[314]

Wrede

Acknowledging his debt to Bauer, Wilhelm Wrede, writing at the beginning of the twentieth century, showed that Mark's gospel "was saturated with the theological beliefs of the early Christian community. Rather than a biography, the gospel was a reading back into Jesus' life, the faith and hope of the early Church that Jesus was the Messiah and Son of God."[315]

Kalthoff

Albert Kalthoff, also writing at the beginning of this century, argued that we could explain the origins of Christianity without having to posit a historical founder. Christianity arose by spontaneous combustion when "the inflammable materials, religious and social, that had collected together in the Roman empire, came into contact with Jewish messianic expectations."[316] "From the socio-religious standpoint the figure of the Christ was the sublimated religious expression for the sum of the social and ethical forces that were at work in a certain period."

Non-Christian Evidence

Despite the fact that there were approximately sixty historians active during the first century in the Roman world, there is remarkably little corroboration of the Christian story of Jesus outside the Christian traditions. What there is, is very inconclusive and unhelpful—Josephus, Tacitus, Suetonius, the Younger Pliny.[317]

The Gospels

It is now recognized that the Gospels (Matthew, Mark, Luke, and John) were not written by the disciples of Jesus. They are not eyewitness accounts, and they were written by unknown authors some forty to eighty years after the supposed crucifixion of Christ. Matthew, Mark, and Luke are usually called the synoptic Gospels because of the common subject matter and similarity of phrasing to be found in them. Mark is considered the earliest of the three and was probably used by the other two as their source. It now seems highly unlikely that any of the sayings attributed to Jesus in the Gospels were ever spoken by a historical figure. As Hoffmann concludes,

> it is difficult even to speak of an "historical" Jesus, given the proportions and immediacy of the myth-making process that characterises the earliest days of the Jesus-cult. Whether or not there was an historical founder (and such is not needed, as the mystery religions testify, for the success of a cult and a coherent story about its "founder"), scholars now count it a certainty that the Gospels are compilations of "traditions" cherished by the early Christians rather than historical annals.[318]

The Sanhedrin trial, the trial before Pilate, and the main factors in the Passion story all pose serious problems, and we cannot take them as historical events; rather they were "created" by the early Christians' own theological convictions. As Nineham says, much of what we find in Mark may well be "deduction from Old Testament prophecy about what 'must have' happened when the Messiah came."[319]

The Epistles of Paul

The letters of Paul were written before Mark's Gospel, and yet rather surprisingly they do not mention many of the details of Jesus' life that we find in the Gospels: no allusions to Jesus' parents, or to the Virgin Birth, or to Jesus' place of birth; there is no mention of John the Baptist, Judas, nor of Peter's denial of his master. As G. A. Wells[320] points out, "they give no indication of the time or place of Jesus' earthly existence. They never refer to his trial before a Roman official nor to Jerusalem as the place of his execution. They mention none of the miracles he is supposed to have worked." Even when certain doctrines attributed to Jesus in the Gospels would have been of obvious use to Paul in his doctrinal disputes, there is no mention of them.

The early post-Pauline letters, written before A.D. 90, also fail to give any convincing historical details. It is only with the later post-Pauline letters, written between A.D. 90 and 110, do we get those details from the Gospels with which we are familiar. Consequently, Wells[321] concludes:

Since, then, these later epistles do give biographical references to Jesus, it cannot be argued that epistles writers generally were disinterested in his biography, and it becomes necessary to explain why only the earlier ones (and not only Paul) give the historical Jesus such short shrift. The change in the manner of referring to him after A.D. 90 becomes intelligible if we accept that his earthly life in 1st-century Palestine was invented late in the 1st century. But it remains very puzzling if we take his existence then for historical fact.

The Date of Mark's Gospel

When and why did the biography of Jesus with which we are familiar first develop? The details of Jesus' life first appear in Mark, which is considered the earliest gospel and most New Testament scholars date it ca. A.D. 70. But G. A. Wells insists that it was written ca. A.D. 90, when "Palestinian Christianity had been overwhelmed by the Jewish War with Rome, and the gentile Christians who then first linked Jesus with Pilate, and first gave his life altogether a real historical setting, could have had only very imperfect knowledge of what had really happened in Palestine c. A.D. 30."[322] The Christian apologists invented the historical setting and details of the life of Jesus in order to meet the challenge of Docetism that denied the humanity of Jesus, to serve as an antidote to the proliferation of myths in Christian circles, to establish the reality of the resurrection, and generally to answer the questions raised by the early contacts of the Christians with a hostile, skeptical world.

The Rise of Islam and the Origins of Christianity

In chapter 3 we saw the theories on the rise of Islam of a new generation of Islamic scholars. We are now in position to appreciate the resemblance of these theories to the theories presented above on the origins of Christianity. We noted earlier how Goldziher dismissed a vast amount of the hadith or traditions about the life of the Prophet as spurious. Goldziher considered by far the greater part of the hadith as the result of the religious, historical, and social development of Islam during the first two centuries. The hadith was useless as a basis for any scientific history and could only serve as a reflection of the tendencies of the early Muslim community. In the foregoing sections, we noted how the early Christians attributed words and sayings to Jesus that in reality only reflected the experience, convictions, and hopes of the Christian community.

Just as we find that the early Christians fabricated details of the life of Jesus in order to answer doctrinal points, so we find that Arab storytellers invented biographical material about Muhammad in order to explain difficult passages in the Koran.

Let us compare Schacht's[323] comments on the traditions in the legal context and what we said of Wrede's judgment on Mark's Gospel. Traditions were formulated polemically in order to rebut a contrary doctrine or practice; doctrines in this polemical atmosphere were frequently projected back to higher authorities: "Traditions from Successors [to the Prophet] become traditions from Companions [of the Prophet], and Traditions from Companions become Traditions from the Prophet." Details from the life of the Prophet were invented to support legal doctrines.

As discussed earlier, Wrede showed that Mark's Gospel was full of the early Christian community's beliefs and hopes rather than being the actual story of Jesus.[324]

Both religions in their early days, as they came into contact and conflict with a hostile community with a religious tradition of its own, developed and defended their doctrinal positions by inventing biographical details of their founders that they then projected back onto an invented Arabian or Palestinian point of origin. Where Christianity arose from a fusion of Judaic and Greco-Roman ideas, Islam arose from Talmudic Judaic, Syriac Christian, and indirectly, Greco-Roman ideas.

As Morton Smith[325] put it "the first-century [Christian] churches had no fixed body of gospels, let alone a New Testament." Similarly, it is now clear that the definitive text of the Koran still had not been achieved as late as the ninth century.

JUDGMENT DAY

Central to the Islamic creed is the doctrine of the Last Day. Several terms are used in the Koran to indicate this most awesome of days: Day of Standing Up, Day of Separation, Day of Reckoning, Day of Awakening, Day of Judgment, The Encompassing Day, or simply and ominously, The Hour. The ultimate source of Muhammad's notions of the Last Day was Syriac Christianity. These accounts obviously gripped his imagination, for the Koran is full of graphic descriptions of this day: this event will be marked by the sounding of the trumpet, the splitting asunder of the heavens, the reduction of the mountains to dust, the darkening of the sky, the boiling over of the seas, the opening of the graves when men and jinn will be called to account. These beings will then have their deeds weighed in the Balance, will be judged by God, and then either assigned to everlasting bliss in Paradise, or consigned to everlasting torment and torture in Hell. The terrors of the Last Day are emphasized over and over again, especially in the later Meccan passages. Men and women will be restored to life, that is, there will be an actual resurrection of the physical body.

We know that this notion of the resurrection of the body was alien to Arabian thought, for many Meccan pagans scoffed at this manifestly absurd idea. The pagan philosophers in their polemics against the Christians also asked pertinent questions: "How are the dead raised up? And with what body do they come? What was rotten cannot become fresh again, nor scattered limbs be reunited, nor what was consumed be restored. . . . Men swallowed by the sea, men torn and devoured by wild beasts, cannot be given back by the earth."[326]

All doctrines of personal survival, personal immortality, and personal resurrection confront the obvious observation that all men and women die, are buried or cremated, and even if buried their bodies eventually decompose—what is rotten cannot become fresh again.

The Muslim doctrine is committed to the physical survival of the body: "That is their reward for that they disbelieved in our signs, and said, 'What! when we are bones and rubbish, shall we then be raised up a new creation?' Could they not see that God who created the heavens and the earth is able to create the like of them, and to set for them an appointed time; there is no doubt therein, yet the wrong-doers refuse to accept it, save ungratefully!" (sura 17.100).

But there is one objection to such an account that Antony Flew[327] has formulated:

> Certainly Allah the omnipotent must have "power to create their like." But in making Allah talk in these precise terms of what He might indeed choose to do, the Prophet was speaking truer than he himself appreciated. For thus to produce even the most indistinguishably similar object after the first one has been totally destroyed and disappeared is to produce not the same object again, but a replica. To punish or to reward a replica, reconstituted on Judgment Day, for the sins or virtues of the old Antony Flew dead and cremated in 1984 is as inept and as unfair as it would be to reward or to punish one identical twin for what was in fact done by the other.

The Muslim account is further dogged by contradictions. We are told all mankind will have to face their Maker (and Remaker) on the Judgment Day, and yet sura 2.159 and sura 3.169 tell us that those holy warriors who died fighting in God's cause are alive and in His presence now. God has evidently raised them from the dead before the Last Day. Similarly, without waiting for the Last Day, God will send the enemies of Islam straight to hell. Interesting questions arise in this age of organ transplants. If a holy warrior dies fighting for the propagation of Islam, and at the very moment of his death has one of his organs, let us say his heart, transplanted into someone else lying in a hospital waiting for the surgical operation and the organ to save his life, how will the holy warrior be reconstituted. In this case, the same body will not have been refashioned; indeed, it will only be a replica with a different heart.

To answer "all is possible for God" is simply to admit the essential irrationality of the doctrine of reconstitution. In general, despite centuries of seances, table rapping, mediums, magicians, and all kinds of mumbo jumbo, no one has ever come up with a convincing proof of an afterlife. Apart from personal vanity, it is clearly fear of death that causes the persistent belief in a future life, despite all indications to the contrary.

MORAL OBJECTIONS TO THE DOCTRINE OF THE LAST JUDGMENT

What was the one thing that Mohammed later borrowed from Christianity? Paul's invention, his means to priestly tyranny, to herd formation: the faith in immortality—that is, the doctrine of the "judgment."

—Nietzsche, *The Anti Christ*[328]

Apart from the empirical and logical objections to the doctrine of resurrection of the body, there are some powerful moral objections to the whole Islamic notion of the afterlife. Nietzsche has argued in the *Twilight of the Idols* and the *Anti-Christ* that to talk of an afterlife is to do dirt on, to denigrate and besmirch *this* life. Far from making this life meaningful, the doctrine of an afterlife makes this life meaningless.

> To invent fables about a world "other" than this one has no meaning at all, unless an instinct of slander, detraction, and suspicion against life has gained the upper hand in us: in that case, we avenge ourselves against life with a phantasmagoria of "another," a "better" life.[329]

> The "Last judgment" is the sweet comfort of revenge. . . . The "beyond"—why a beyond, if not as a means for besmirching this world?[330]

Furthermore, the beyond is a way for the self-proclaimed prophets and priests to retain control, to terrorize the people with the tortures of hell, and equally to seduce them with the licentious pleasures of paradise. "The concepts 'beyond,' 'Last Judgment,' 'immortality of the soul,' and 'soul' itself are instruments of torture, systems of cruelties by virtue of which the priest became master, remained master.[331]

Muhammad was able to develop one of the worst legacies of the teachings of the Koran, the notion of a Holy War (discussed in chapter 10), with the help of the idea of rewards in paradise for the holy martyrs who died fighting for Islam. As Russell put it, "at a certain stage of development, as the Mohammedans first proved, belief in Paradise has considerable military value as reinforcing natural pugnacity."[332]

Those prepared to die for the faith have been used frighteningly throughout Islamic history, "martyrs" were used for political assassinations long before the Assassins of the eleventh and twelfth century. Modern Middle Eastern terrorists or Mujahheddin are considered martyrs and have been manipulated for political reasons, with considerable effect. Most of them have been immunized against fear, to quote Dawkins, "since many of them honestly believe that a martyr's death will send them straight to heaven. What a weapon! Religious faith deserves a chapter to itself in the annals of war technology, on an even footing with the longbow, the warhorse, the tank and the neutron bomb."[333]

The contingency of this life should make man aware of its beauty and preciousness. The harsh truth that this is the only life we have should make us try and improve it for as many people as possible.

When one places life's center of gravity not in life but in the "beyond"—in nothingness—one deprives life of its center of gravity altogether. The great lie of personal immortality destroys all reason, everything natural in the instincts— whatever in the instincts is beneficent and life-promoting or guarantees a future now arouses mistrust. To live so, that there is no longer any sense in living, *that* now becomes the "sense" of life. Why communal sense, why any further gratitude for descent and ancestors, why cooperate, trust, promote, and envisage any common welfare?[334]

THE ETHICS OF FEAR

Religion is based, I think, primarily and mainly upon fear. It is partly the terror of the unknown, and partly . . . the wish to feel that you have a kind of elder brother who will stand by you in all your troubles and disputes. Fear is the basis of the whole thing—fear of the mysterious, fear of defeat, fear of death. Fear is the parent of cruelty, and therefore it is no wonder if cruelty and religion have gone hand-in-hand.

—Bertrand Russell, *Why I Am Not A Christian*[335]

We have already referred to the fact that the Koranic ethical system is based entirely on fear. Muhammad uses God's wrath-to-come as a weapon with which to threaten his opponents, and to terrorize his own followers into pious acts and total obedience to himself. As Sir Hamilton Gibb put it, "That God is the omnipotent master and man His creature who is ever in danger of incurring His wrath— this is the basis of all Muslim theology and ethics."[336]

The notion of everlasting punishment is also incompatible with and unworthy of a benevolent, merciful God; and even more incomprehensible when we conjoin it with the Koranic doctrine of predestination. God especially creates creatures to consign to hell.

Finally, fear corrupts all true morality—under its yoke humans act out of prudent self-interest, to avoid the tortures of hell, which are no less real to the believers than the delights of the cosmic bordello that goes by the name of paradise.

DIVINE PUNISHMENT

The Koran decrees punishments that can only be described as barbaric. The relativist who defends the inhuman customs prescribed in the Koran by claiming that these were normal practices at the time finds himself stumped by the gruesome revival of most of them in the putatively more enlightened twentieth century. The Koran is the word of God—true for always.

Amputation

Sura 5.38 sets the tone: "As to the thief, male or female, cut off his or her hands: a punishment by way of example from God, for their crime: and God is exalted in power." According to Muslim law, "the right hand of the thief is to be cut off at the joint of the wrist and the stump afterwards cauterized, and for the second theft the left foot, and for any theft beyond that he must suffer imprisonment."[337]

Crucifixion

The same sura (5.33) tells us: "The punishment of those who wage war against God and His Apostle, and strive with might and main for mischief through the land is: execution, or crucifixion, or the cutting off of hands and feet from opposite sides, or exile from the land: that is their disgrace in this world, and a heavy punishment is theirs in the hereafter."

Women to be Immured

As for the offence of "zina," an Arabic term that includes both adultery and fornication, the Koran says nothing about lapidation as a punishment for adultery. Originally, women found guilty of adultery and fornication were punished by being literally immured: sura 4.15: "If any of your women are guilty of lewdness, take the evidence of four witnesses from amongst you, and if these bear witness, then keep the women in houses until death release them, or God shall make for them a way."

Flogging

However, sura 24.2–4 prescribes one hundred lashes for fornication: "The woman and man guilty of fornication, flog each of them with a hundred stripes; let not pity move you in their case."

Lapidation was instituted at a later stage. As noted earlier a lapidation verse may have formed a part of the Koran, but this is disputed by some scholars.

Apologists of Islam often argue the compatibility of Islamic law and human rights. Article 5 of the 1948 Universal Declaration of Human Rights states, "no one shall be subjected to torture or to cruel, inhuman or degrading treatment or punishment." Are amputating a limb, flogging, and lapidation inhuman or not?

Historical Errors in the Koran

At sura 40.38; the Koran mistakenly identifies Haman, who in reality was the minister of the Persian King Ahasuerus (mentioned in the book of Esther), as the minister of the Pharoah at the time of Moses.

We have already noted the confusion of Mary, the mother of Jesus, with the Mary who was the sister of Moses and Aaron. At sura 2.249, 250 there is obviously a confusion between the story of Saul as told therein, and the account of Gideon in Judg. 7.5.

The account of Alexander the Great in the Koran (18.82) is hopelessly confused historically; we are certain it was based on the Romance of Alexander. At any rate, the Macedonian was not a Muslim and did not live to an old age, nor was he a contemporary of Abraham, as Muslims contend.

Regulations for the Muslim Community

The Koran contains a host of other rules and regulations for the proper functioning of the new community. We shall be looking at the position of women, marriage, and divorce in chapter 14, the institution of slavery and the doctrine of the Holy War in chapters 8 and 9, and the taboos concerning food and drink in chapter 15. Other social prescriptions concern legal alms or the poor tax, usury, inheritance, prayers, pilgrimage, and fasts. Some of these are treated in a perfunctory and confused manner. The Koran also enjoins many moral precepts with which, though hardly original or profound, no one would disagree: kindness and respect toward elders and parents, generosity towards the poor, forgiveness instead of revenge. It also contains passages of beauty and grandeur. But on balance, the effects of the teachings of the Koran have been a disaster for human reason and social, intellectual, and moral progress. Far from being the word of God, it contains many barbaric principles unworthy of a merciful God. Enough evidence has been provided to show that the Koran bears the fingerprints of Muhammad, whose moral values were imbued with the seventh-century world view, a view that can no longer be accepted as valid.

Of Religion in General, and Islam in Particular

> One is often told that it is a very wrong thing to attack religion because religion makes men virtuous. So I am told; I have not noticed it.
> —Bertrand Russell, *Why I Am Not a Christian*[338]

There is not sufficient reason to believe that any religion is true. Indeed, most of them make claims that can be shown to be false or highly improbable. Nonetheless, some eminent philosophers argue that, though false, these religions are necessary for moral guidance, moral restraint, and social stability. The philosopher Quine said, "There remains a burning question of the social value of the restraints and ideals imposed by some religions, however false to facts those religions be. If this value is as great as I suspect it may be, it poses a melancholy dilemma between promoting scientific enlightenment and promoting wholesome delusion."[339]

Such a view is both empirically false and morally repulsive. Let us look at the evidence, first, as Russell[340] argued,

> You find this curious fact, that the more intense has been the religion of any period and more profound has been the dogmatic belief, the greater has been

the cruelty and worse has been the state of affairs. In the so called ages of faith, when men really did believe the Christian religion in all its completeness, there was the Inquisition, with its tortures; there were millions of unfortunate women burnt as witches; and there was every kind of cruelty practiced upon all sorts of people in the name of religion.

We are all familiar with the wars perpetrated by Christianity, but less familiar are the ones waged by Muslims. I discuss the intolerance and cruelty of Islam in chapter 9. I shall only point to some of the atrocities committed in the name of Allah in the twentieth century. For the past few years, the self-righteous and sanctimonious leaders of various Islamic groups in Afghanistan have been waging a bitter civil war to gain total power. In between their five prayers to the most compassionate and merciful God, they have managed to kill hundreds of innocent civilians. Many thousands of these civilians have fled to neighboring Pakistan, where they have expressed a distinct nostalgia for the halcyon days of the godless Communists. According to a report in the *International Herald Tribune* (26 April 1994), the civil war, now entering its third year, has claimed more than ten thousand lives. In Kabul alone, fifteen hundred people were killed between January and April 1994.

SUDAN

At the moment of writing (June 1994), genocide is in progress in Sudan where Islamic law was imposed by the then-dictator General Numeiri in 1983, even though almost one-third of the population is not Muslim, but Christian or Animist. The Islamic North of Sudan has been waging a pitiless war on the Christians and Animists of the South. Since 1983, more than half a million people have been killed. An equal number of people have been forcibly displaced from the Sudanese capital, Khartoum, to campsites in the desert where the temperatures can reach 120° F., and where there are no health facilities, water, food, or sanitation. As an article in the *Economist* (9 April 1994) pointedly titled "The Blessings of Religion" said, "Financed by Iran, the Government has equipped its troops with modern Chinese-made weapons. In recent months the war has taken on a still cruder air of jihad, as the ranks of the army have been swelled by large numbers of young Sudanese mujahideen, ready to die for Islam."

INDONESIA

The details of the massacre of somewhere between 250,000 and 600,000 Indonesians in 1965 are only now beginning to emerge. After a failed *coup d'état* in 1965, the Indonesian army (with at least tacit approval from the United States) took its revenge on the Communists. The army encouraged nationalist and Muslim youth to settle old scores; gangs of Muslim youths massacred Chinese peasants in the most horrific manner. " 'No-one went out after 6 pm, recalls a Chinese whose family fled East Java. 'They cut off women's breasts; they threw so many bodies in the sea that people were afraid to eat fish. My brother still had to serve in the shop. In the morning young Muslims would come in swaggering, with necklaces of human ears' " (*Guardian Weekly* [23 September 1990]). In Indonesia's 1975 invasion of East Timor, at least two hundred thousand civilians were killed.

I emphasize these atrocities as a counter to the sentimental nonsense about the "spiritual East," which, we are constantly told, is so much superior to the decadent and atheistic West; and as counterexamples to the belief that religion somehow makes men more virtuous. Europeans and Asians, Christians and Muslims have all been guilty of the most appalling cruelty; whereas there have been thousands of atheists who have not only led blameless lives but have worked selflessly for the good of their fellow humans.

MORAL OBJECTIONS TO THE UTILITY ARGUMENT

> The pragmatic suggestion, that we had better teach the Christian religion whether it is true or not, because people will be much less criminal if they believe it, is disgusting and degrading; . . . and it is a natural consequence of the fundamental religious attitude that comfort and security must always prevail over rational inquiry.
>
> —Robinson[341]

The argument that though religion might be false we must keep it for moral guidance, is also morally reprehensible, since it perverts man's reason and encourages hypocrisy, but above all, it leads to the abandonment of the ideal of truth. As Russell pointed out,

> As soon as it is held that any belief, no matter what, is important for some other reason than that it is true, a whole host of evils is ready to spring up. Discouragement of inquiry, . . . is the first of these, but others are pretty sure to follow. Positions of authority will be open to the orthodox. Historical records must be falsified if they throw doubt on received opinion. Sooner or later unorthodoxy will come to be considered a crime to be dealt with by the stake, the purge, or the concentration camp. I can respect the men who argue that religion is true and therefore ought to be believed, but I can only feel profound moral reprobation for those who say that religion ought to be believed because it is useful, and that to ask whether it is true is a waste of time.[342]

There are even true believers who argue in such fashion. Professor Watt, time and again, argues that the historical truth is less important than the "symbolic" truth or "iconic" truth. But this is intellectual dishonesty. In the words of Paul: "Now if Christ be preached that he rose from the dead, how say some among you that there is no resurrection of the dead? But if there be no resurrection of the dead, then is Christ not risen: And if Christ be not risen, then is our preaching vain, and your faith is also vain" (1 Cor. 15.12–14).

Muslims fervently believe that Abraham built the Kaaba; however, the whole Meccan pilgrimage becomes totally meaningless—"your faith is also vain"—when the historical truth is apprehended, namely, Abraham never set foot in Arabia, and perhaps did not even exist. It is also an astonishing argument coming from a man who believes in God. Surely, God would approve of man's quest for truth. Would God have recourse to lies and subterfuge in order to get man to worship Him?

There is a variation of the utility argument that does seem to me more difficult to dismiss. I am thinking of the case of the person who has suffered horribly, is still suffering; or the person who has no way of bettering his or her life on earth—someone who has lost out in life's cruel lottery. Would we have the right to tell him that his belief in God and the afterlife, when every injustice suffered will be righted, is all a sick man's dream? His belief is the only thing that makes his life endurable for him. I have no answer to this question. But, of course, this question should not be a means of easing our own consciences, an excuse for not doing anything to ameliorate man's lot whenever possible—through education, and political and social action.

6

The Totalitarian Nature of Islam

Bolshevism combines the characteristics of the French Revolution with those of the rise of Islam.

Marx has taught that Communism is fatally predestined to come about; this produces a state of mind not unlike that of the early successors of Mahommet.

Among religions, Bolshevism is to be reckoned with Mohammedanism rather than with Christianity and Buddhism. Christianity and Buddhism are primarily personal religions, with mystical doctrines and a love of contemplation. Mohammedanism and Bolshevism are practical, social, unspiritual, concerned to win the empire of this world.

Bertrand Russell[343]

Perhaps it was Charles Watson who, in 1937, first described Islam as totalitarian and proceeded to show how[344] "By a million roots, penetrating every phase of life, all of them with religious significance, it is able to maintain its hold upon the life of Moslem peoples." Bousquet, one of the foremost authorities on Islamic law, distinguishes two aspects of Islam that he considers totalitarian: Islamic law, and the Islamic notion of jihad that has for its ultimate aim the conquest of the entire world, in order to submit it to one single authority. We shall consider jihad in the next few chapters; here we shall confine ourselves to Islamic law.

Islamic law has certainly aimed at "controlling the religious, social and political life of mankind in all its aspects, the life of its followers without qualification, and the life of those who follow tolerated religions to a degree that prevents their activities from hampering Islam in any way."[345] The all-embracing nature of Islamic law can be seen from the fact that it does not distinguish among ritual, law (in the European sense of the word), ethics, and good manners. In principle this legislation controls the entire life of the believer and the Islamic community. It intrudes into every nook and cranny: everything—to give a random sample—

163

from the pilgrim tax, agricultural contracts, the board and lodging of slaves, the invitation to a wedding, the use of toothpicks, the ritual fashion in which one's natural needs are to be accomplished, the prohibition for men to wear gold or silver rings, to the proper treatment of animals is covered.

Islamic law is a doctrine of duties—external duties—that is to say, those duties "which are susceptible to control by a human authority instituted by God. However, these duties are, without exception, duties toward God, and are founded on the inscrutable will of God Himself. All duties that men can envisage being carried out are dealt with; we find treated therein all the duties of man in any circumstance whatsoever, and in their connections with anyone whatsoever."[346]

Before looking at Islamic law in detail, we need to know why it developed the way it did.

No Separation of State and Church[347]

Jesus Christ himself laid down a principle that was fundamental to later Christian thought: "Render unto Caesar the things which are Caesar's and unto God the things which are God's" (Matt. 22.17). These two authorities, God and Caesar, dealt with different matters and ruled different realms; each had its own laws and its own institutions. This separation of church and state is nonexistent in Islam—indeed, there are no words in classical Arabic for the distinctions between lay and ecclesiastical, sacred and profane, spiritual and temporal. Once again, we must look to the founder of Islam to understand why there was never any separation of state and church. Muhammad was not only a prophet but also a statesman; he founded not only a community but also a state and a society. He was a military leader, making war and peace, and a lawgiver, dispensing justice. Right from the beginning, the Muslims formed a community that was at once political and religious, with the Prophet himself as head of state. The spectacular victories of the early Muslims proved to them that God was on their side. Thus right from the start in Islam, there was no question of a separation between sacred history and secular history, between political power and faith, unlike Christianity, which had to undergo three centuries of persecution before being adopted by "Caesar."

Islamic Law

The sharia or Islamic law is based on four principles or roots (in Arabic, "usul," plural of "asl"): the Koran; the sunna of the Prophet, which is incorporated in the recognized traditions; the consensus ("ijma") of the scholars of the orthodox community; and the method of reasoning by analogy ("qiyas "or "kiyas").

THE KORAN

The Koran, as we saw earlier, is for Muslims the very word of God Himself. Though it contains rules and regulations for the early community on such matters as marriage, divorce, and inheritance, the Koran does not lay down general principles. Many matters are dealt with in a confusing and perfunctory manner, and a far greater number of vital questions are not treated at all.

THE SUNNA

The sunna (literally, a path or way; a manner of life) expresses the custom or manner of life of Muslims based on the deeds and words of the Prophet, and that which was done or said in his presence, and even that which was not forbidden by him. The sunna was recorded in the traditions, the hadith, but these, as we saw earlier, are largely later forgeries. Nonetheless, for Muslims the sunna complements the Koran and is essential for understanding it properly, for clarifying the Koranic vaguenesses and filling in the Koranic silences. Without the sunna Muslims would be at a loss for those details necessary in their daily lives.

The Koran and the sunna are the expressions of God's command, the definitive and inscrutable will of Allah that must be obeyed absolutely, without doubts, without questions, and without qualifications.

But with all their attendant obscurities, we still need some kind of interpretation of the sunna and the Koran, and this is the task of the science of sharia (fiqh). The specialists on law were called "faqih." They founded many "schools" of interpretation, four of which have survived to the present day and share among the whole population of orthodox (sunni) Islam. Oddly, all four are considered equally valid.

1. Malik ibn Abbas (d. 795) developed his ideas in Medina, where he is said to have known one of the last survivors of the companions of the Prophet. His doctrine is recorded in the work, Muwatta, which has been adopted by most Muslims in Africa with the exception of Lower Egypt, Zanzibar, and South Africa.

2. Abu Hanifa (d. 767), the founder of the Hanifi school, was born in Iraq. His school is said to have given more scope to reason and logic than the other schools. The Muslims of India and Turkey follow this school.

3. Al-Shafi'i (d. 820), who was considered a moderate in most of his positions, taught in Iraq and then in Egypt. The adherents of his school are to be found in Indonesia, Lower Egypt, Malaysia, and Yemen. He placed great stress on the sunna of the Prophet, as embodied in the hadith, as a source of the sharia.

4. Ahmad ibn Hanbal (d. 855) was born in Baghdad. He attended the lectures of al-Shafi'i, who also instucted him in the traditions. Despite persecution, ibn Hanbal stuck to the doctrine that the Koran was uncreated. The modern Wahhabis of Saudi Arabia are supposed to follow the teachings of ibn Hanbal.

When the various schools came under criticism for introducing innovations without justification, for adapting religious law to suit worldly interests, and for tolerating abuses, the learned doctors of the law developed the doctrine of the infallibility of the consensus (ijma), which forms the third foundation of Islamic law or sharia.

IJMA

The saying "My community will never agree on an error "was ascribed to the Prophet and, in effect, was to make an infallible church of the recognized doctors of the community as a whole. As Hurgronje says, "this is the Muslim counterpart of the Christian Catholic doctrine of ecclesiastical tradition: 'quod semper, quod ubique, quod ab omnibus creditum est.' " The notion of consensus has nothing democratic about it; the masses are expressly excluded. It is the consensus of suitably qualified and learned authorities.

However, there were still disputes as to whose ijma was to be accepted: some only accepted the ijma of the companions of the Prophet, while others accepted only the ijma of the descendants of the Prophet, and so on.

The doctrine of the infallibility of the consensus of the scholars, far from allowing some liberty of reasoning as one might have expected, worked "in favor of a progressive narrowing and hardening of doctrine; and, a little later, the doctrine which denied the further possibility of 'independent reasoning' sanctioned officially a state of things which had come to prevail in fact."[348]

By the beginning of A.D. 900, Islamic law became rigidly and inflexibly fixed because, to quote Schacht:

> the point had been reached when the scholars of all schools felt that all essential questions had been thoroughly discussed and finally settled, and a consensus gradually established itself to the effect that from.that time onwards no one might be deemed to have the necessary qualifications for independent reasoning in law, and that all future activity would have to be confined to the explanation, application, and, at most, interpretation of the doctrine as it had been laid down once and for all.[349]

This closing of the gate of independent reasoning, in effect, meant the unquestioning acceptance of the doctrines of established schools and authorities. Islamic law until then had been adaptable and growing, but henceforth, it

> became increasingly rigid and set in its final mould. This essential rigidity of Islamic law helped it to maintain its stability over the centuries which saw the decay of the political institutions of Islam. It was not altogether immutable, but the changes which did take place were concerned more with legal theory and the systematic superstructure than with positive law. Taken as a whole, Islamic law reflects and fits the social and economic conditions of the early Abbasid period, but has grown more and more out of touch with later developments of state and society.[350]

KIYAS

Kiyas or analogical reasoning is considered by many learned doctors to be subordinate to, and hence less important than, the other three foundations of Islamic law. Its inclusion may well have been a compromise between unrestricted liberty of opinion and the rejection of all human reasoning in religious law.

THE NATURE OF ISLAMIC LAW

1. All human acts and relationships are assessed from the point of view of the concepts obligatory, recommended, indifferent, reprehensible, and forbidden. Islamic law is part of a system of religious duties, blended with nonlegal elements.[351]

2. The irrational side of Islamic law comes from two of its official bases, the Koran and the sunna, which are expressions of God's commands. It follows from the irrational side of Islamic law that its rules are valid by virtue of their mere existence and not because of their rationality. The irrational side of Islamic law also calls for the observance of the letter rather than of the spirit: this fact has historically facilitated the vast development and acceptance of legal devices such as legal fictions. For example, the Koran explicitly prohibits the taking of interest, and, to quote Schacht:

> this religious prohibition was strong enough to make popular opinion unwilling to transgress it openly and directly, while at the same time there was an imperative demand for the giving and taking of interest in commercial life. In order to satisfy this need, and at the same time to observe the letter of the religious prohibition, a number of devices were developed. One consisted of giving real property as a security for the debt and allowing the creditor to use it, so that its use represented the interest. . . . Another . . . device consisted of a double sale. . . . For instance, the (prospective) debtor sells to the (prospective) creditor a slave for cash, and immediately buys the slave back from him for a greater amount payable at a future date; this amounts to a loan with the slave as security, and the difference between the two prices represents the interest.[352]

How can we characterize the above practices? "Legal fictions" is too kind an expression. Moral evasiveness? Moral hypocrisy? Moral dishonesty?

3.

> Although Islamic law is a sacred law, it is by no means essentially irrational; it was created not by an irrational process of continuous revelation . . . but by a rational method of interpretation, in this way it acquired its intellectualist and scholastic exterior. But whereas Islamic law presents itself as a rational system on the basis of material considerations, its formal juridical character is little developed. Its aim is to provide concrete and material standards, and not to impose formal rules on the play of contending interests [which is the

aim of secular laws]. This leads to the result that considerations of good faith, fairness, justice, truth, and so on play only a subordinate part in the system.[353]

4. Unlike Roman law, Islamic law brings legal subject matter into a system by the analogical method, by parataxis and association. Closely linked to this method is the casuistical way of thinking, which is one of the striking aspects of traditional Islamic law. "Islamic law concentrates not so much on disengaging the legally relevant elements of each case and subsuming it under general rules— as on establishing graded series of cases."[354] For example, on the question of succession, we find discussions of the case of an individual who leaves as sole inheritors his thirty-two great-great-grandparents; the rights of succession of hermaphrodites (since the two sexes do not have the same rights); the inheritance of an individual who has been changed into an animal; and, in particular, the inheritance of that same individual when only half has been transformed, either horizontally or vertically.

Thus, a soul-destroying pedantry, a spirit of casuistry took over. As Goldziher[355] says:

> The task of interpreting God's word and of regulating life in conformity to God's word became lost in absurd sophistry and dreary exegetical trifling: in thinking up contingencies that will never arise and debating riddling questions in which extreme sophistry and hair-splitting are joined with the boldest and most reckless flights of fancy. People debate far-fetched legal cases, casuistic constructs quite independent of the real world. . . . Popular superstition, too, furnishes the jurists with material for such exercises. Since . . . demons frequently assume human shape, the jurists assess the consequences of such transformations for religious law; serious arguments and counterarguments are urged, for example, whether such beings can be numbered among the participants necessary for the Friday service. Another problematic case that the divine law must clarify: how is one to deal with progeny from a marriage between a human being and a demon in human form. . . . What are the consequences in family law of such marriages? Indeed, the problem of (marriages with the jinn) is treated in such circles with the same seriousness as any important point of the religious law.

5. In what we would call penal law, Islamic law distinguishes between the rights of God and the rights of humans.

> Only the rights of god have the character of a penal law proper, of a law which imposes penal sanctions on the guilty. Even here, in the center of penal law, the idea of a claim on the part of God predominates, just as if it were a claim on the part of a human plaintiff. This real penal law is derived exclusively from the Koran and the traditions [hadith], the alleged reports of the acts and sayings of the Prophet and of his Companions. The second great division of what we should call penal law belongs to the category of "redress of torts," a category straddling civil and penal law which Islamic law has retained from the law of pre-Islamic Arabia where it was an archaic but by no means unique

phenomenon. Whatever liability is incurred here, be it retaliation or blood-money or damages, is subject of a private claim, pertaining to the rights of humans. In this field, the idea of criminal guilt is practically nonexistent, and where it exists it has been introduced by considerations of religious responsibility. So there is no fixed penalty for any infringement of the rights of a human to the inviolability of his person and property, only exact reparation of the damage caused. This leads to retaliation for homicide and wounds on one hand, and to the absence of fines on the other.[356]

In sum, sharia is the total collection of theoretical laws that apply in an ideal Muslim community that has surrendered to the will of God. It is based on divine authority that must be accepted without criticism. Islamic law is thus not a product of human intelligence, and in no way reflects a constantly changing or evolving social reality (as does European law). It is immutable, and the fiqh or the science of the sharia constitutes the infallible and definitive interpretation of the Sacred Texts. It is infallible because the group of Doctors of law have been granted the power to deduce authoritative solutions from the Koran and the traditions; and definitive because after three centuries, all the solutions have been given. While European law is human and changing, the sharia is divine and immutable. It depends on the inscrutable will of Allah, which cannot be grasped by human intelligence—it must be accepted without doubts and questions. The work of the learned doctors of the sharia is but a simple application of the words of Allah or His Prophet: it is only in certain narrowly defined limits, fixed by God Himself, that one can use a kind of reasoning known as qiyas, reasoning by analogy. The decisions of the learned, having the force of law, rest on the infallibility of the community, an infallibility that God Himself conferred through Muhammed on his community [Bousquet, Hurgronje, Schacht].

CRITICISMS OF ISLAMIC LAW

1. Two of the roots of Islam are the Koran and the sunna as recorded in the hadith. First, we have already given reasons why the Koran cannot be considered of divine origin—it was composed sometime between the seventh and the ninth centuries, full of borrowings from talmudic Judaism, apocryphal Christianity, the Samaritans, Zoroastrianism, and pre-Islamic Arabia. It contains historical anachronisms and errors, scientific mistakes, contradictions, grammatical errors, etc. Second, the doctrines contained therein are incoherent and contradictory and not worthy of a compassionate deity. Nowhere is there any proof for the existence of any deity. On the other hand, the Koran also contains praiseworthy, even if not particularly original moral principles—the need for generosity, respect for parents, and so on. But these are outweighed by unworthy principles: intolerance of pagans, the call to violence and murder, the lack of equality for women and non-Muslims, the acceptance of slavery, barbaric punishments, and the contempt for human reason.

2. Goldziher, Schacht, and others have convincingly shown that most—and perhaps all—of the traditions (hadith) were forgeries put into circulation in the first few Muslim centuries. If this fact is allowed, then the entire foundation of Islamic law is seen to be very shaky indeed. The whole of Islamic law is but a fantastic creation founded on forgeries and pious fictions. And since Islamic law is seen by many as "the epitome of Islamic thought, the most typical manifestation of the Islamic way of life, the core and kernel of Islam itself," the consequences of Goldziher's and Schacht's conclusions are, to say the least, shattering.

3. Priestly Power:

> That there is a will of God, once and for all, as to what man is to do and what he is not to do; that the value of a people, of an individual, is to be measured according to how much or how little the will of God is obeyed; that the will of God manifests itself in the destinies of a people, of an individual, as the ruling factor, that is to say, as punishing and rewarding according to the degree of obedience. . . . One step further: the "will of God" (that is, the conditions for the preservation of priestly power) must be known: to this end a "revelation" is required. In plain language: a great literary forgery becomes necessary, a "holy scripture" is discovered; it is made public with full hieratic pomp. . . . With severity and pedantry, the priest formulates once and for all, . . . what he wants to have, "what the will of God is." From now on all things in life are so ordered that the priest is indispensable.[357]

Muslim apologists and Muslims themselves have always claimed that there were no clergy in Islam; but in reality, there was something like a clerical class, which eventually acquired precisely the same kind of social and religious authority as the Christian clergy. This is the class I have been referring to throughout this chapter as "the learned doctors" or the "doctors of law," otherwise known as the "ulama." Given the importance attached to the Koran and the sunna (and hadith), there grew a need to have a professional class of people competent enough to interpret the Sacred texts. As their authority grew among the community, they grew more confident and claimed absolute authority in all matters relating to faith and law. The doctrine of "ijma" merely consolidated their absolute power. As Gibb says, "It was . . . only after the general recognition of ijma as a source of law and doctrine that a definite legal test of heresy was possible and applied. Any attempt to raise the question of the import of a text in such a way as to deny the validity of the solution already given and accepted by consensus became a 'bid'a,' an act of 'innovation,' that is to say, heresy."[358]

The continuing influence of the ulama is the major factor why there has been so little intellectual progress in Muslim societies, why critical thought has not developed. Throughout Islamic history, but especially in recent times, the ulama have actively hindered attempts to introduce the idea of human rights, freedom, individualism, and liberal democracy. For example, the ulama reacted violently to Iran's 1906–07 constitution, regarding it as "un-Islamic"; they were totally opposed to the idea of freedom contained within it. The ulama have been involved in the process of Islamization in modern times in three countries in particular, Iran, the Sudan, and Pakistan. In each of these countries, "Islamization" has effectively meant the elimination of human rights or their restrictions by reference to "Islamic criteria."

4. Is the sharia still valid?

We may well ask how a law whose elements were first laid down over a thousands years ago, and whose substance has not evolved with the times can possibly be relevant in the twentieth century. The sharia only reflects the social and economic conditions of the time of the early Abbasids and has simply grown out of touch with all the later developments—social, economic, and moral. It seems improbable but we have progressed morally: we no longer regard women as chattel that we can dispose of as we will: we no longer believe that those who do not share our religious beliefs are not worthy of equal respect; we even accord children and animals rights. But as long as we continue to regard the Koran as eternally true, with an answer for all the problems of the modern world, we will have no progress. The principles enshrined in the Koran are inimical to moral progress.

7

Is Islam Compatible with Democracy and Human Rights?

Islam has never favoured democratic tendencies.

Hurgronje[359]

The Democratic system that is predominant in the world is not a suitable system for the peoples of our region. . . . The system of free elections is not suitable to our country.

King Fahd of Saudi Arabia[360]

At least King Fahd has had the honesty to admit the incompatibility of Islam and democracy. Meanwhile, Western Islamic apologists and modernizing Muslims continue to look for democratic principles in Islam and Islamic history.

Human Rights and Islam

Let us look at the Universal Declaration of Human Rights of 1948[361] and compare it with Islamic law and doctrine.

Article 1: "All human beings are born free and equal in dignity and rights. They are endowed with reason and conscience and should act toward one another in a spirit of brotherhood."

Article 2: "Everyone is entitled to all rights and freedoms set forth in this Declaration, without distinction of any kind, such as race, color, sex, language, religion, political or other opinion, national or social origin, property, birth or other status."

Article 3: "Everyone has the right to life, liberty and security of person."

Article 4: "No one shall be held in slavery or servitude; slavery and the slave trade shall be prohibited in all their forms."

172

Comments. 1. Women are inferior under Islamic law; their testimony in a court of law is worth half that of a man; their movement is strictly restricted; they cannot marry non-Muslims.

2. Non-Muslims living in Muslim countries have inferior status under Islamic law; they may not testify against a Muslim. In Saudi Arabia, following a tradition of Muhammad who said, "Two religions cannot exist in the country of Arabia," non-Muslims are forbidden to practice their religion, build churches, possess Bibles, etc.

3. Nonbelievers—atheists (surely the most neglected minority in history)— do not have "the right to life" in Muslim countries. They are to be killed. Muslim doctors of law generally divide sins into great sins and little sins. Of the seventeen great sins, unbelief is the greatest, more heinous than murder, theft, adultery, etc.

4. Slavery is recognized in the Koran. Muslims are allowed to cohabit with any of their female slaves (sura 4.3); they are allowed to take possession of married women if they are slaves (sura 4.28). The helpless position of the slave in regard to his or her master illustrates the helpless position of the false gods of Arabia in the presence of their Creator (sura 16.77).

Article 5. "No one shall be subjected to torture or to cruel, inhuman or degrading treatment or punishment."

Comment. We have seen what punishments are in store for transgressors of the Holy law: amputations, crucifixion, stoning to death, and floggings. I suppose a Muslim could argue that these were not unusual for a Muslim country, but what of their inhumanity? Again, a Muslim could contend that these punishments are of divine origin and must not be judged by human criteria. By human standards, they *are* inhuman.

Article 6: "Everyone has the right to recognition everywhere as a person before the law."

The whole notion of a person who can make choices and can be held morally responsible is lacking in Islam, as is the entire notion of human rights.

Articles 7, 8, 9, 10, and 11 deal with the rights of an accused person to a fair trial.

Comments. 1. As Schacht has shown, under the sharia considerations of good faith, fairness, justice, truth, and so on play only a subordinate role. The idea of criminal guilt is lacking.

2. Revenge for a killing is officially sanctioned, though a monetary recompense is also possible.

3. The legal procedure under Islam can hardly be called impartial or fair, for in the matter of witnesses all sorts of injustices emerge. A non-Muslim may not testify against a Muslim. For example, a Muslim may rob a non-Muslim in his home with impunity if there are no witnesses except the non-Muslim himself. Evidence given by Muslim women is admitted only very exceptionally and then only if it comes from twice as many women as the required number of men.

Article 16 deals with the rights of marriage of men and women.

Comment. As we shall see in our chapter on women, under Islamic law women do not have equal rights: they are not free to marry whom they wish, the rights of divorce are not equal.

Article 18: "Everyone has the right to freedom of thought, conscience and religion; this right includes freedom to change his religion or belief, and freedom, either alone or in community with others and in public or private, to manifest his religion or belief in teaching, practice, worship and observance."

Comments. 1. Quite clearly under Islamic law, one does not have the right to change one's religion, if one is born into a Muslim family. Applying double standards, Muslims are quite happy to accept converts to their religion, but a Muslim may not convert to another religion—this would be apostasy and punishable by death. Here is how the great commentator Baydawi (ca. 1291) sees the matter: "Whosoever turns back from his belief, openly or secretly, take him and kill him wheresoever you find him, like any other infidel. Separate yourself from him altogether. Do not accept intercession in his regard."

2. Statistics on conversions from Islam to Christianity, and therefore apostasy, are hard to establish for obvious reasons. There is, however, a myth that Muslims are impossible to convert. On the contrary, we do have enough evidence of literally thousands of Muslims abandoning Islam for Christianity from the Middle Ages to modern times, the most spectacular cases being, among others, those of Moroccan and Tunisian princes in the seventeenth century and of the monk Constantin the African. Count Rudt-Collenberg has found evidence at the Casa dei Catecumeni at Rome of 1,087 conversions between 1614 and 1798. According to A. T. Willis and others, between two or three million Muslims converted to Christianity after the massacres of the communists in Indonesia in 1965, described in chapter 5. In France alone, in the 1990s, two or three hundred people convert to Christianity from Islam *each year*. According to Ann E. Mayer,[362] in Egypt conversions have been "occurring with enough frequency to anger Muslim clerics and to mobilize conservative Muslim opinion behind proposals to enact a law imposing the death penalty for apostasy. Ms. Mayer points out that, in the past, many women have been to tempted to convert from Islam to ameliorate their lot.

3. Those who convert to Christianity and choose to stay in a Muslim country do so at great personal danger. The convert has most of his rights denied him; identity papers are often refused him, so that he has difficulties leaving his country; his marriage is declared null and void; his children are taken away from him to be brought up by Muslims; and he forfeits his rights of inheritance. Often the family will take matters into its own hands and simply assassinate the apostate; the family members are, of course, not punished.[363]

Article 19: "Everyone has the right to freedom of opinion and expression; this right includes freedom to hold opinion without interference and to seek, receive and impart information and ideas through any media and regardless of frontiers."

Comments. 1. The rights enshrined in articles 18 and 19 have been consistently violated in Iran, Pakistan, and Saudi Arabia. In all three countries, the rights of their Bahai, Ahmadi, and Shia minorities, respectively, have been denied. All three countries justify their actions by reference to sharia. Christians in these countries are frequently arrested on charges of blasphemy and their rights denied. Amnesty International describes the scene in Saudi Arabia:

> Hundreds of Christians, including women and children have been arrested and detained over the past three years, most without charge or trial, solely for the peaceful expression of their religious beliefs. Scores have been tortured, some by flogging, while in detention. . . . The possession of non-Islamic religious objects—including Bibles, rosary beads, crosses and pictures of Jesus Christ—is prohibited and such items may be confiscated. (AINO 62 July/August 1993)

Similarly scores of Shia Muslims have been harassed, arrested, tortured, and in some cases, beheaded. For example, on September 3, 1992, Sadiq Abdul Karim Malallah was publicly beheaded in al-Qatif after being convicted of apostasy and blasphemy. Sadiq, a Shia Muslim, was arrested in 1988 and charged with throwing stones at a police station, then of smuggling a Bible into the country. He was kept in solitary confinement, where he was tortured.

The situation of Ahmadis in Pakistan is somewhat similar. The Ahmadiyya movement was founded by Mirza Ghulam Ahmed (d. 1908), who is regarded as a prophet by his followers. Amnesty International [ASA/33/15/91] summed up their situation in this manner:

> Ahmadis consider themselves to be Muslims but they are regarded by orthodox Muslims as heretical because they call the founder of the movement al-Masih [the Messiah]: this is taken to imply that Mohammad is not the final seal of the prophets as orthodox Islam holds, i.e., the prophet who carried the final message from God to humanity. According to Ahmadis their faith does not involve the denial of the Prophet Mohammad's status because Mirza Ghulam Ahmed did not claim to bring a new revelation of divine law which could add to, replace or supersede the Koran. Mirza Ghulam Ahmed considered himself a mahdi, a reappearance of the Prophet Mohammad, and thought it his task to revive Islam. As a result of these divergences, Ahmadis have been subjected to discrimination and persecution in some Islamic countries. In the mid-1970s, the Saudi Arabia–based World Muslim League called on Muslim governments worldwide to take action against Ahmadis. Ahmadis are since then banned in Saudi Arabia.

Throughout Pakistan's history, the Ahmadis have been subjected to harassment, which has, on occasion, led to serious bloodshed. Things got worse for them when President Zia-ul Haq came to power in 1977 after a military coup. He introduced a policy of Islamization and imposed severe restrictions on the Ahmadis. In 1984, further legislation was introduced aimed explicitly at these so-called heretics. Henceforth, the Ahmadis could no longer call themselves Muslims. Since then, scores of Ahmadis have been charged and sentenced severely under sections of the Pakistan Penal Code. Thus, Ahmadis can be imprisoned and even sentenced to death solely for the exercise of their right to freedom of religion, including the right to express their religion. Again, it is important to realize that such attitudes to "heretics" is a logical consequence of the orthodox Muslim position that Muhammad is the seal of the Prophets, that Islam is the most perfect and final expression of God's purpose for all mankind, and that salvation outside Islam is not possible.

2. Blasphemy towards God and the Prophet is punishable by death under Islamic law. In modern times, blasphemy has simply become a tool for Muslim governments to silence opposition, or for individuals to settle personal scores, or, as we saw earlier, to seek out and punish "heresy." A report in the *Economist* points out the manipulation of "blasphemy" in Pakistan:

> A judgment by the High Court in Lahore is worrying Pakistan's Christians. The court decided recently that Pakistan's blasphemy laws are applicable to all the prophets of Islam. Jesus is a prophet in Islamic teaching. By worshipping Jesus as the son of God, Christians are, it could be argued, committing a blasphemy. . . . There are about 1.2 [million] Christians in Pakistan, out of a population of 120 [million]. Many of them are of low caste, doing menial jobs. Some have suffered for their beliefs. Tahir Iqbal, a mechanic in the air force who converted to Christianity and was charged with blasphemy, mysteriously died in prison while awaiting trial. Manzoor Masih was accused of blasphemy, given bail and shot dead in the street. . . . Human-rights watchers say there is often sectarian and political rivalry, a dispute over property or competition for jobs. (7 May 1994)

Article 23: Everyone has the right to work, to free choice of employment, to just and favorable conditions of work and to protection against unemployment.

Comments. 1. Women are not free to choose their work under Islamic law. Certain jobs are forbidden to them, even in so-called liberal Muslim countries. Orthodox Islam forbids women from working outside the home (see chap. 14).

2. Non-Muslims are not free to choose their work in Muslim countries or, rather, certain posts are not permitted them. A recent example from Saudi Arabia makes the point. A group of Muslims working in a company owned by a Muslim were shocked when the Muslim owner appointed a new manager, who was Christian. The Muslims demanded a religious ruling asking whether it was permissible in Islam to have a Christian in authority over them. Sheikh Mannaa K. al-Qubtan at the Islamic Law College of Riyadh declared that it was intolerable under Islamic law that a non-Muslim should wield authority over Muslims. He pointed to two verses from the Koran to back up his argument: "Allah will not give the disbelievers triumph over the believers" (sura 4.141).

"Force and power belong to God, and to His Prophet, and to believers" (sura 63.8).

Article 26 deals with the right of education.

Comment. Again, certain fields of learning are denied to women (see chap. 14) It is clear that Islamic militants are quite aware of the incompatibility of

Islam and the 1948 Declaration of Human Rights, for these militants met in Paris in 1981 to draw up an Islamic Declaration of Human Rights that left out all freedoms that contradicted Islamic law. Even more worrisome is the fact that under pressure from Muslim countries in November 1981, the United Nations Declaration on the elimination of religious discrimination was revised, and references to the right "to adopt" (Article 18, preceding) and therefore, to "change" one's religion were deleted, and only the right "to have" a religion was retained [FI, Spring 1984, p. 22].

Democracy and Islam

> Western ideas of individualism, liberalism, constitutionalism, human rights, equality, liberty, the rule of law, democracy, free markets, the separation of church and state often have little resonance in Islamic, Confucian, Japanese, Hindu, Buddhist or Orthodox cultures.
> Samuel P. Huntington, *The Clash of Civilizations?*[364]

The values and principles of democracy are defined and enshrined in the American Constitution, and both the British (1688) and American Bill of Rights (proposed: 1789; ratified: 1791).

SEPARATION OF CHURCH AND STATE

One of the fundamental principles of democracy is the separation of church and state (Amendment 1 to the American Constitution: "Congress shall make no law respecting an establishment of religion, or prohibiting the free exercise thereof."). We have seen that in Islam there is no such separation, instead, we have what Thomas Paine calls the adulterous connection of church and state. Why is this separation of church and state so essential? If Muslims are sincere in espousing the cause of democracy in their own countries, then they must learn the profound reasons underlying the adoption of this separation. They must then decide whether these underlying principles are at all compatible with Islam, or whether they entail too many compromises with the orthodox tenets of their creed. This is not the time for moral, intellectual, and doctrinal evasiveness.

1. The idea of a separation of church and state has been formulated by many Western philosophers: Locke, Spinoza, and the "philosophers" of the Enlightenment. In his *A Letter concerning Toleration,* Locke gives three reasons for adopting this principle:[365]

> First, because the care of souls is not committed to the civil magistrate [i.e., the state], any more than to other men. It is not committed unto him, I say, by God; because it appears not that God has ever given any such authority to one man over another as to compel any one to his religion. Nor can any

such power be vested in the magistrate [state] by the consent of the people, because no man can so far abandon the care of his own salvation as blindly to leave to the choice of any other, whether prince or subject, to prescribe to him what faith or worship he shall embrace. For no man can, if he would, conform his faith to the dictates of another. All the life and power of true religion consists in the inward and full persuasion of the mind; and faith is not faith without believing. . . .

In the second place, the care of souls cannot belong to the civil magistrate, because his power consists only in outward force: but true and saving religion consists in the inward persuasion of the mind, without which nothing can be acceptable to God. And such is the nature of the understanding, that it cannot be compelled to the belief of anything by outward force. . . . It may indeed be alleged that the magistrate may make use of arguments. . . . But it is one thing to persuade, another to command; one thing to press with arguments, another with penalties. . . . The magistrate's power extends not to the establishing of any articles of faith, or forms of worship, by the force of his laws.

Third . . . there being but one truth, one way to heaven, what hope is there that more men would be led into it, if they had no rule but the religion of the court and were put under the necessity to quit the light of their own reason, to oppose the dictates of their own consciences, and blindly to resign themselves up to the will of their governors and to the religion which either ignorance, ambition, or superstition had chanced to establish in the countries where they were born? In the variety and contradiction of opinions in religion, wherein the princes of the world are as much divided as in their secular interests, the narrow way would be much straightened; one country alone would be in the right, and all the rest of the world put under an obligation of following their princes in the ways that lead to destruction.

In other words, it is not the business of the state to interfere with the freedom of conscience and thought of its citizens. The state cannot make people religious by force; at best, it may enforce outward observance, but at the cost of sincerity of belief. Locke's third point—a point also made by Kant—is that by mandating belief in one religion, one is cutting oneself and an entire age or generation off from further enlightenment and progress. As Kant[366] put it: "To unite in a permanent religious institution which is not to be subject to doubt before the public—that is absolutely forbidden." That is to abdicate reason, renounce enlightenment, and trample on the rights of mankind. Locke further argues that we must get away from the notion that we are "born Muslims" or "born Christians" and that we cannot do anything about it. We should be free to enter or leave any particular creed, otherwise there would be no progress, freedom, or reform.

Once the principle of the separation of church and state is admitted, a free discussion of religion should follow without fear of torture. However, this is precisely what theocratic governments or religious autocrats fear—freethought. As Paine[367] put it,

The adulterous connection of church and state, wherever it has taken place, whether Jewish, Christian or Turkish [Muslim], has so effectually prohibited by pains and penalties every discussion upon established creeds, and upon first principles of religion, that until the system of government should be changed, those subjects could not be brought fairly and openly before the world; but that whenever this should be done, a revolution in the system of religion would follow. Human inventions and priestcraft would be detected; and man would return to the pure, unmixed and unadulterated belief of one God, and no more.

Following the example set by Locke, the Founding Fathers of the American Constitutional Convention, especially Madison, defended religious freedom by adopting the Bill of Rights, which, of course, includes the separation of state and church. It has played an important role in safeguarding the rights of religious minorities, dissenters, and heretics who hitherto had suffered persecution, intolerance, disenfranchisement, and discrimination.

In his "Memorial and Remonstrance Against Religious Assessments" of 1785, Madison[368] wrote:

The Religion . . . of every man must be left to the conviction and conscience of every man; and it is the right of every man to exercise it as these may dictate. The same authority which can establish Christianity, in exclusion of all other religions, may establish with the same ease any particular sect of Christians in exclusion of all other Sects. Whilst we assert for ourselves a freedom to embrace, to profess and to observe the Religion which we believe to be of divine origin, we cannot deny an equal freedom to those whose minds have not yet yielded to the evidence which has convinced us.

Madison's greatness can be seen in his generous attitude toward nonbelievers— even the great Locke was intolerant of atheists. Madison's words written at the occasion of the Virginia Ratification Convention of 1788 are even more relevant in this age of multifaith and multi-ethnic societies:

Is a bill of rights security for religion. . . . If there were a majority of one sect, a bill of rights would be a poor protection for liberty. Happily for the states, they enjoy the utmost freedom of religion. This freedom arises from the multiplicity of sects, which pervades America, and which is the best and only security for religious liberty in any society. For where there is such a variety of sects, there cannot be a majority of any one sect to oppress and persecute the rest. . . . There is not a shadow of right in the general government to intermeddle with religion. Its least interference with it would be a most flagrant usurpation. I can appeal to my uniform conduct on this subject, that I have warmly supported religious freedom.[369]

What the separation of church and state means in modern terms was clearly explained by Court Justice Hugo Black in the 1947 *Everson* ruling:

The "establishment of religion" clause of the First Amendment means at least this: Neither a state nor the Federal Government can set up a church. Neither can pass laws which aid one religion, aid all religions, or prefer one religion over another. Neither can force nor influence a person to go to or remain away from church against his will or force him to profess a belief or disbelief in any religion. No person can be punished for entertaining or professing religious beliefs or disbeliefs, for church attendance or non-attendance. No tax in any amount, large or small, can be levied to support any religious activities or institutions, whatever they may be called, or whatever form they may adopt to teach or practice religion. Neither a state nor the Federal Government can, openly or secretly, participate in the affairs of any religious organizations or groups and vice versa. In the words of Jefferson, the clause against establishment of religion by law was intended to erect "a wall of separation between Church and State."[370]

AUTHORITARIANISM, DEMOCRACY, AND ISLAM

As soon as you have an established religious institution that is beyond doubt, then, as Kant and Paine (quoted earlier) showed, you have tyranny, thought police, and an absence of the critical sense that hinders intellectual and moral progress. In the Islamic theocracy, God is the absolute ruler whose words must be obeyed absolutely, without discussion, without doubt, without questions; we cannot plea bargain with God, nor can we override God's veto. The Islamic God is not a democrat; we cannot get rid of Him as we can a human representative elected by the people in a representative democracy. If power corrupts, then absolute power corrupts absolutely.

While one historian of religion,[371] writing in 1942, finds disturbing the fact that the career of Muhammad the Prophet presents "certain analogies to that of a nationalist leader nearer to our own day," so many others in the West find this very absoluteness, self-confidence, and authoritarianism of Islam appealing. For example, in a remarkable passage from a book written in about 1910, J. M. Kennedy[372] first deplores the quietism of the Buddhists and the theosophists, castigates the Jews for being too soft, and then accuses Christianity of "inoculating as much of the world as it can reach with the degenerate principles of humanitarianism, let us be thankful that there are many millions of Moslems to show us a religion which is not afraid to acknowledge the manly virtues of war, courage, strength, and daring—a religion which does not seek new followers by means of cunning dialectics, but which boldly makes converts with the sword."

In recent years, Western apologists of Islam have also argued for "principled autocracy," as exemplified by Franco in Spain. In terms similar to Kennedy's, Martin Lings shows his essential contempt for democracy and his advocacy for a kind of Islamic theocracy in such works as *The Eleventh Hour: the Spiritual Crisis of the Modern World in the Light of Tradition and Prophecy* (1987). [See *New Humanist*, vol. 109, no. 2, pp. 10–12.]

Indeed autocracy and Islam are far more natural bedfellows than Islam and democracy. Democracy depends on freedom of thought and free discussion, whereas Islamic law explicitly forbids the discussions of decisions arrived at by the infallible consensus of the ulama. The whole notion of infallibility, whether of a "book" or a group of people, is profoundly undemocratic and unscientific. Democracy functions by critical discussion, by rational thought, by listening to another point of view, by compromise, by changing one's mind, by tentative proposals that are submitted to criticism, and by the testing of theories by trying to refute them. Islamic law is not legislated but divinely revealed and infallible, and, as T. H. Huxley noted (see motto to chapter 5), the notion of infallibility in all shapes, lay or clerical, has done endless mischief and has been responsible for bigotry, cruelty, and superstition.

Why Islam Is Incompatible with Democracy and Human Rights

1. Islamic law tries to legislate every single aspect of an individual's life. The individual is not at liberty to think or decide for himself; he has but to accept God's rulings as infallibly interpreted by the doctors of law. The fact is we do not have, nor can we have, such a complete ethical code existing in a liberal democracy; we do not and cannot have an all-embracing, all-inclusive scale of values.

2. The measure of any culture's level of democracy is the rights and position it accords to its women and its minorities. Islamic law denies the rights of women and non-Muslim religious minorities. Pagans or nonbelievers are shown no tolerance: for them it is death or conversion. Jews and Christians are treated as second-class citizens. Because Islamic doctrine holds that Muhammad is the last of the true prophets and Islam is the final and most complete word of God, Muslim "sects" such as the Ahmadis are persecuted, harassed, and physically attacked.

Muslims have yet to appreciate that democracy is not merely "majority rule": the tyranny of the majority must be guarded against, and every democratic society must be wary of imposing "its own ideas and practices as rules of conduct on those who dissent from them."

As I discuss elsewhere both the cases of women and non-Muslims under Islam, I shall only summarize their legal status here.

Women are considered inferior to men, and they have fewer rights and duties from the religious point of view. In regard to blood money, evidence, and inheritance, a woman is counted as half a man; in marriage and divorce her position is less advantageous than that of the man; her husband may even beat her, in certain cases.[373]

Here is Schacht's summary of the legal position of non-Muslims:

> The basis of the Islamic attitude toward unbelievers is the law of war; they must be either converted or subjugated or killed (excepting women, children, and slaves); the third alternative, in general, occurs only if the first two are refused. As an exception, the Arab pagans are given the choice only between

conversion to Islam or death. Apart from this, prisoners of war are either made slaves or killed or left alive as free dhimmis or exchanged for Muslim prisoners of war.

Under a treaty of surrender, the non-Muslim is given protection and called a dhimmi.

> This treaty necessarily provides for the surrender of the non-Muslims with all duties deriving from it, in particular the payment of tribute, i.e. the fixed poll-tax (jizya) and the land tax (kharaj). . . . The non-Muslims must wear distinctive clothing and must mark their houses, which must not be built higher than those of the Muslims, by distinctive signs; they must not ride horses or bear arms, and they must yield the way to Muslims; they must not scandalize the Muslims by openly performing their worship or their distinctive customs, such as drinking wine; they must not build new churches, synagogues, and hermitages; they must pay the poll-tax under humiliating conditions. It goes without saying that they are excluded from the specifically Muslim privileges.

The dhimmi cannot be a witness against a Muslim, he cannot be the guardian of his child who is a Muslim.[374]

In the U.S. Constitution, the Fourteenth Amendment says: "no State shall . . . deny to any person within its jurisdiction the equal protection of the laws." Originally intended to end discrimination against black Americans, it was later extended to provide protection against discrimination on criteria other than race, and many minorities felt protected for the first time.

3. Islam continually manifests hostility towards human reason, rationality, and critical discussion without which democracy and scientific and moral progress are not possible.

> Like Judaism and Christianity, Islam condemns the rationalistic attitude. There are many traditions according to which Muhammad emphasized his refusal to be questioned by pointing to earlier examples of communities destroyed in consequence of their disputations. Here tradition has several things in view. Theological speculations are especially referred to in the following hadith: "People will not cease scrutinizing, till they shall say: Here is Allah, the creator of all things, but who has created Him." [Wensinck (1) p. 53–54]

4. The notion of an individual—a moral person who is capable of making rational decisions and accepting moral responsibility for his free acts—is lacking in Islam. Ethics is reduced to obeying orders. Of course, there is the notion of an individual who has legal obligations, but not in the sense of an individual who may freely set the goals and content of his life, of the individual who may decide what meaning he wants to give to his life. Under Islam, God and the Holy law set limits on the possible agenda of your life.

It is worth emphasizing that the American Bill of Rights is essential for safeguarding the civil and political rights of an individual against the government. As Jefferson put it: "A bill of rights is what the people are entitled to against every government on earth, general or particular, and what no just government should refuse, or rest on inference." Individuals have rights that no mythical or mystical collective goal or will can justifiably deny. To quote Von Hayek:[375] "Individual freedom cannot be reconciled with the supremacy of one single purpose to which the whole society must be entirely and permanently subordinated." The First Ten Amendments and the Fourteenth Amendment of the U.S. Constitution limit the power of the governments: they protect individuals from unfair actions by the government; they protect individuals' rights of freedom of religion, speech, press, petition, and peaceful assembly, and the rights of persons accused of crimes against state abuses. They prevent a state from depriving anyone of civil liberties.

Liberal democracy extends the sphere of individual freedom and attaches all possible value to each man or woman. Individualism is not a recognizable feature of Islam; instead, the collective will of the Muslim people is constantly emphasized. There is certainly no notion of individual rights, which only developed in the West, especially during the eighteenth century. The constant injunction to obey the Caliph, who is God's Shadow on Earth, is hardly inducive to creating a rights-based individualist philosophy. The hostility to individual rights is manifest in this excerpt from a recent Muslim thinker A. K. Brohi,[376] a former Minister of Law and Religious Affairs in Pakistan who has written on human rights from an Islamic perspective.

> Human duties and rights have been vigorously defined and their orderly enforcement is the duty of the whole of organized communities and the task is specifically entrusted to the law enforcement organs of the state. The individual if necessary has to be sacrificed in order that the life of the organism be saved. Collectivity has a special sanctity attached to it in Islam.
>
> [In Islam] there are no "human rights" or "freedoms" admissible to man in the sense in which modern man's thought, belief and practice understand them: in essence, the believer owes obligation or duties to God if only because he is called upon to obey the Divine Law and such Human rights as he is made to acknowledge seem to stem from his primary duty to obey God.

The totalitarian nature of this philosophy is evident and further underlined by the line, "By accepting to live in Bondage to this Divine Law, man learns to be free," which reminds one frighteningly of Orwell's "Freedom is Slavery." Another Muslim thinker wrote in 1979[377]:

> The Western liberal emphasis upon freedom from restraint is alien to Islam. . . . Personal freedom [in Islam] lies in surrendering to the Divine Will. . . . It cannot be realized through liberation from external sources of restraint . . . individual freedom ends where the freedom of the community begins. . . . Human rights exist only in relation to human obligations. . . . Those individuals who do not accept these obligations have no rights. . . . Much of Muslim theology tends toward a totalitarian voluntarism.

Here, at least, the author admits the totalitarian nature of Islam.

5. The notion of the infallibility of a group and a "book" is an impediment to moral, political, and scientific progress.

6. A Muslim does not have the right to change his religion. Apostasy is punishable by death.

7. Freedom of thought in various forms and guises is discouraged; any innovation is likely to be branded "blasphemy," which is punishable by death. Perhaps one of the greatest obstacles in Islam to progress toward a liberal democracy is its emphasis that it is the final word of God, the ultimate code of conduct: *Islam never allows the possibility of alternatives.* By contrast, in a liberal democracy, what is meant by the freedom of thought, speech, and press is the right to argue, the freedom to present another side of an argument, anyone may present an alternative philosophy, the majority does not have the right to prevent a minority from expressing its dissent, criticism, or difference.

Human Rights

The idea that there is good reason for ascribing rights to human beings simply because they are human beings is something that developed in Western civilization. Some would trace the idea back to Plato and Aristotle, others to, at least, the Stoics, who maintained that there was a natural law—distinct from the laws of Athens or Rome—a law binding upon all men in such a manner that "whoever is disobedient is fleeing from himself and denying his human nature" (quoted in Melden 1970, p. 1). Some philosophers have tried to ground these rights in human nature or the nature of man; while others, not happy with talk of human nature, since what we sometimes take to be human nature turns out to be a particularity of one specific culture or civilization, prefer to talk of human rights in consequentialist terms. However, modern discussions of human rights by Western philosophers nowhere appeal to God or Divine Will, but only to human reason, rational arguments, and critical thought.

Most philosophers would agree that the notion of human rights involves the accompanying ideas of self-respect, moral dignity, free agency, moral choice, personhood, and the right to equal concern and respect. Since Locke's further development of the idea of human rights in the seventeenth century, modern advocates claim at least three things:

(1) that these rights are fundamental in the sense that without them there could not be any of the specific rights that are grounded in the specific social circumstances in which individuals live, (2) that just these rights cannot be relinquished, transferred, or forfeited (i.e., they cannot be alienated from them by anything that they or anyone else may do), since (3) they are rights that human beings have simply because they are human beings, and quite independently of their varying social circumstances and degrees of merit.[378]

In other words, they are universal, and not culturally bound or relative.

Under Islam, nothing like these ideas has ever developed. Human beings have duties, duties toward God; only God has rights. Under Islam, there is no such thing as "the equal right of all men to be free." Nowhere in modern Muslim discussions is there a clear account of how "human rights" can be derived from "human duties" as described in the sharia.

LEWIS ON "ISLAM AND LIBERAL DEMOCRACY"

In an important article, "Islam and Liberal Democracy,"[379] Bernard Lewis explains very well why liberal democracy never developed in Islam. Like many scholars of Islam, Lewis deplores the use of the term "Islamic Fundamentalist" as being inappropriate. I agree. I have already pointed out that, unlike Protestants, who have moved away from the literal interpretation of the Bible, Muslims—all Muslims—still take the Koran literally. Hence, in my view, there *is no difference between Islam and Islamic fundamentalism.* Islam is deeply embedded in every Muslim society, and "fundamentalism" is simply the excess of this culture.

Lewis himself tells us that the Islamic fundamentalists intend "to govern by Islamic rules if they gain power." The Islamic fundamentalists will apply Islam—the Islam of Islamic law, and all that it entails. Lewis also tells us that "their creed and political program are not compatible with liberal democracy." I also agree. But now we see immediately why Lewis and Islamic apologists, in fact, find this term, "Islamic fundamentalist," so convenient, while at the same time deploring it. It is an extremely useful and face-saving device for those unable to confront the fact that Islam itself, and not just something we call "Islamic fundamentalism," is incompatible with democracy. To repeat, Lewis himself says the Islamic fundamentalists will apply "Islamic rules." Now if their creed is incompatible with democracy, then these "Islamic rules" themselves must be incompatible with democracy. Thus, the term "Islamic fundamentalist" enables apologists to set up a specious distinction, a distinction without any justification.

The curious fact is that Lewis himself shows in his article why, by its very nature, Islam is incompatible with liberal democracy. The West developed certain characteristic institutions that were essential for the emergence of democracy. One such institution was the council or representative assembly, whose effective functioning was made possible by the principle embodied in Roman law, that of the legal person—a corporate entity that for legal purposes is treated as an individual, able to buy and sell, enter into contracts, appear as a defendant, etc. There was no Islamic equivalent of the Roman senate or assembly or parliament. Islam simply lacked the legal recognition of corporate persons. As Schacht put it, "Islam does not recognize juristic persons; not even the public treasury is construed as an institution."[380]

One of the major functions of these Western assemblies was legislative activity, but there was no legislative function in the Islamic state, and thus no need for legislative institutions. The Islamic state was a theocracy, in the literal sense of a polity ruled by God. For pious Muslims, legitimate authority comes from God alone, and the ruler derives his power from God and the holy law, and not from the people. Rulers were merely applying or interpreting God's law as revealed to Muhammad. Lacking legislative bodies, Islam did not develop any principle of representation, any procedure for choosing representatives, any definition of the franchise, or any electoral system. Therefore it is not surprising, concludes Lewis, if the history of the Islamic states is "one of almost unrelieved autocracy. The Muslim subject owed obedience to a legitimate Muslim ruler as a religious duty. That is to say, disobedience was a sin as well as a crime."

Having clearly shown that Islam is incompatible with liberal democracy, Lewis then tries to show that there might, after all, be elements in the Islamic tradition that are not hostile to democracy. He leans particularly heavily on the the elective and contractual element in the Islamic institution of the caliphate. Lewis himself admits that the Islamic caliphate was an "autocracy," but he also insists that it was not "despotism."

Lewis waxes lyrical about the caliph, insisting that the relationship between the caliph and his subjects is contractual: "The bay'a [denoting the ceremony at the inauguration of a new caliph] was thus conceived as a contract by which the subjects undertook to obey and the Caliph in return undertook to perform certain duties specified by the jurists. If a Caliph failed in those duties—and Islamic history shows that this was by no means a purely theoretical point—he could, subject to certain conditions, be removed from office."

First, an autocracy is not a democracy. The distinction between autocracy and despotism is a dangerous and bogus one, often used in the past to legitimize undemocratic rule; indeed T. W. Arnold calls the power of the caliph "despotic" (see next paragraph). Second, as it was originally elaborated, the orthodox doctrine emphasized two essential characteristics of the caliph: that he must be of the tribe of the Kuraish, and that he must receive unhesitating obedience, for anyone who rebels against the caliph rebels against God. This duty of obedience to the established authorities is constantly emphasized in the Koran, e.g., sura 4.59: "O you who believe! Obey God, and obey the messenger and those of you who are in authority." (See also sura 4.83.)

As T. W. Arnold[381] says, "This claim on obedience to the *despotic* [my emphasis] power of the Khalifa as a religious duty was impressed upon the faithful by the designations that were applied to him from an early date—Khalifa of God, and Shadow of God upon earth." Neither of these "essential characteristics is democratic." Third, "the elective" characteristic of the institution was purely "theoretical," for the office, in fact, became hereditary in the families of the Ummayad and the Abbasid. From the reign of Mu'awiya (661–680) almost every caliph had nominated his successor. As Arnold says, "the *fiction* of election was preserved in the practice of bai'a (or bay'a)." Finally the functions of the caliph clearly emphasize the undemocratic nature of the office. Al-Mawardi (d. 1058) and Ibn Khaldun define these functions thus: the defense of the religion and the application of the divinely inspired law or sharia, the sorting out of legal disputes, appointment of officials, various administrative duties, the waging of holy war or jihad against those who refuse to accept Islam or submit to Muslim rule. According to Ibn Khaldun, the caliph must belong to the tribe of Kuraish and be of the male sex: again, not democratic principles. Much has also been made of the Islamic principle of "consultation." But Lewis dismisses this fairly briskly: "This principle has never been institutionalized, nor even formulated in the treatises of the holy law, though naturally rulers have from time to time consulted with their senior officials, more particularly in Ottoman times."

Lewis lays a great store in Islamic pluralism and tolerance. But as I show in the next chapter, there never was an "inter-faith utopia" (to use Lewis's own phrase). Lewis also says: "Sectarian strife and religious persecution are not unknown in Islamic history, but they are rare and atypical." And yet earlier in the same article, Lewis himself tells us: "But Islamic fundamentalism is just one stream among many. In the fourteen centuries that have passed since the mission of the Prophet, there have been several such movements—fanatical, intolerant, aggressive, and violent." If Lewis is not formally contradicting himself, he is certainly seen to be wanting it both ways—"several such movements" as opposed to "rare and atypical."

Conclusion

The truth of the matter is that Islam will never achieve democracy and human rights if it insists on the application of the sharia and as long as there is no separation of church and state. But as Muir put it: "A reformed faith that should question the divine authority on which they [the institutions of Islam] rest, or attempt by rationalistic selection or abatement to effect a change, would be Islam no longer."

Many Islamic reformers wanting to adopt Western institutions have pretended to find Islamic antecedents for them in order to make these foreign institutions palatable to their own people. But this strategy has led to much intellectual dishonesty and has left the problem where it was—"the real Islam treats women as equals," "the real Islam is democratic," etc. The real problem—whether the sharia is any longer acceptable—has been left untouched.

Nor is it necessary to invent Islamic antecedents to accept the principles of democracy, human rights, the separation of church and state. India adopted democracy in 1947, and it has lasted to this day; and as far as I am aware, no one wasted time looking through the copious holy literature to justify the decision to adopt a parliamentary system upon independence. The only country in the Islamic world that can be said to be a democracy is Turkey; and, significantly, it is the only Muslim country that has formally adopted the separation of religion and state as law. Islam has been removed from the Turkish constitution, and the sharia is no longer a part of the law of the country.

I propose to examine Ann Elizabeth Mayer—*Islam and Human Rights*. This is a very important book on Islam, and even though I have one fundamental reservation about her book—to which I shall refer later—I find her analysis excellent and very persuasive. Ms. Mayer shows with the utmost clarity how in various Islamic human rights schemes, "distinctive *Islamic* [my emphasis] criteria" have been used to cut back on the freedoms guaranteed in international law, how for many Muslims the international guarantees exceed the limits of rights and freedoms permitted in Islam.

Ms. Mayer also shows how the official Islamization programs in, especially, the Sudan, Pakistan, and Iran, have led to serious violations of the human rights of women, non-Muslims, the Bahai, the Ahmadis, and other religious minorities. In these countries Islamization "did much to eliminate due process, to erode the independence of the judiciary, to place legal proceedings under the control of political leaders, and to convert courts into instruments of repression and intimidation. Thus, in all three countries Islamization became associated with a decline in the quality of the administration of justice."[382]

Ms. Mayer is refreshingly free of inhibitions when attacking the various Islamic human rights schemes from the perspective of international human rights, which she takes to be universally valid: "The way governments of countries treat those they govern should not be ruled off-limits to critical scholarly inquiry, and judging Islamic schemes of human rights by the standards of the international human rights norms that they seek to replace is entirely appropriate."[383]

Rejecting cultural relativism (without giving any philosophical arguments), Ms. Mayer points out that, as a matter of empirical fact, there are many Muslims throughout the world who have and are risking their lives to "stand up for the same human rights principles that cultural relativists would maintain are not suited for application in the Muslim world because of its dissimilar culture. Cultural relativists may fail to perceive how rapid urbanization, industrialization, and factors like the growing power of the state are creating awareness of the need for human rights guarantees in non-Western cultures." (While writing this chapter, I heard the news of the murder of Youcef Fathallah, president of the Algerian League for Human Rights, by Islamicists [*Le Monde,* 21 June 1994].)

Ms. Mayer compares the Universal Declaration of Human Rights (UDHR) of 1948 with the 1981 Universal Islamic Declaration of Human Rights (UIDHR). The latter was prepared by several Muslim countries under the auspices of the Islamic Council, a private, London-based organization affiliated with the Muslim World League, an international, nongovernmental organization "that tends to represent the interests and views of conservative Muslims."

Other Islamic human rights schemes examined are the Azhar Draft Constitution, prepared by the Islamic Research Academy of Cairo, which is affiliated with Al-Azhar University, "the most internationally prestigious institution of higher education in Sunni Islam, and a center of conservative Islamic thought," the 1979 Iranian Constitution, and the works of Muslim thinkers such as Mawdudi and Tabandeh (Mayer 1991, p. 27). Her conclusion is that "Islam is viewed in these schemes as a device for restricting individual freedoms and keeping the individual in a subordinate place vis-a-vis the government and society."[384]

Ms. Mayer shows how, using the sharia as their justification, Muslim conservatives have refused to recognize women as full, equal human beings who deserve the same rights and freedoms as men. Women under these Islamic schemes are expected to marry, obey their husbands, bring up their children, stay at home, and stay out of public life altogether. They are not permitted to develop as individuals, acquire an education, or get jobs. These Islamic schemes provide no real protection for the rights of religious minorities. "In fact, to the extent that they deal with the question of the rights of religious minorities, they seem to endorse premodern sharia rules that call for non-Muslims to be relegated to an inferior status if they qualify as members of the ahl al-kitab [the People of the Book] and for them to be treated as nonpersons if they do not qualify for such inclusion."[385].

These Islamic schemes afford no real protections for freedom of religion:

> The failure of a single one of these Islamic human rights schemes to take a position against the application of the sharia death penalty for apostasy means that the authors of these schemes have neglected to confront and resolve the main issues involved in harmonizing international human rights and sharia standards. . . . The authors' unwillingness to repudiate the rule that a person should be executed over a question of religious belief reveals the enormous gap that exists between their mentalities and the modern philosophy of human rights.[386]

ONE FUNDAMENTAL OBJECTION TO MS. MAYER'S ANALYSIS

Like practically every single book and article published since February 1989, especially for the nonspecialist reader, Ms. Mayer's book is at pains to point out (1) that "Islam" is not monolithic, that there is no such thing as *the* Islamic tradition, or just "one correct Islam," or one correct interpretation; (2) that, in the Islamic human rights schemes examined and found wanting in terms of International norms, it is not Islam that is at fault, it is, at most, one particular interpretation of it by traditionalists or Muslim conservatives; (3) that there is no such thing as *the* sharia, i.e., Islamic law did not freeze at some arbitrary point in the past; and (4) that, deep down, Islam may not be hostile to rights and democracy, after all.

The above four points are not really argued for—that is not the purpose of her book. She explicitly states that the "core doctrines of Islam" are not being subjected to critical assessment.

However, a close reading of Ms. Mayer's book reveals that after all she is only paying lip service, for ecumenical harmony, to the notion that there is no such thing as "Islam" about which we can make valid generalizations. In reality, Ms. Mayer is as prone to sweeping negative statements and huge unflattering generalizations about "Islam" as any writer who does believe that there are clearly identifiable *Islamic doctrines,* which are independent of any capricious or dubious interpretations of the Koran or the hadith, and, furthermore, that these recognizable doctrines are inimical to human rights and their development.

Here are some such generalizations—all of them true, in my view—about Islam, Islamic civilization, Islamic tradition, Islamic orthodoxy, and Islamic law that contradict Ms. Mayer's pious hopes set forth in the preceding points.

Quote 1. "As we have seen, the individualism characteristic of Western civilisation was a fundamental ingredient in the development of human rights concepts. Individualism, however, is not an established feature of Muslim societies or of Islamic culture, nor can one find a historical example of an Islamic school of thought that celebrated individualism as a virtue. Islamic civilisation did not create an intellectual climate that was conducive to according priority to the protection of individual rights and freedoms."[387]

We might point out that although Ms. Mayer accuses many Westerners of taking Islam as a monolithic system, she herself is quite happy to generalize in such a manner both about Islam *and* the West. Is there such a thing as "the West"?

Quote 2. "Orthodox theologians in Sunni Islam were generally suspicious of human reason, fearing that it would lead Muslims to stray from the truth of Revelation. The prevailing view in the Sunni world . . . has been that because of their divine inspiration, sharia laws supercede reason. . . . Given the dominance of this mainstream Islamic view, it naturally became difficult to realize an Islamic version of the Age of Reason."[388]

Quote 3. "The analysis will show how Islamic rights schemes express and confirm the premodern values and priorities that have predominated in orthodox Islamic thought for more than a millennium."[389]

Quote 4. "In such a scheme any challenges that might be made to Islamic law on the grounds that it denies basic rights guaranteed under constitutions or international law are ruled out ab initio; human reason is deemed inadequate to criticise what are treated as divine edicts. This affirms the traditional orthodox view, that the tenets of the sharia are perfect and just, because they represent the will of the Creator, being derived from divinely inspired sources."[390]

Quote 5. "One notes that Brohi is sometimes speaking of subordination to God and Islamic law, which is clearly required in the Islamic tradition."[391]

Quote 6. "Since there was no human rights tradition in Islamic civilisation. . . ."[392]

Quote 7. "Although in Islamic law one can discern elements that in some ways anticipate modern notions of equality, one does not find any counterpart of the principle of equal protection under the law."[393]

Quote 8. "But Islamic clerics and Islamic institutions have by and large manifested strong opposition to allowing women to escape from their cloistered, subordinate, domestic roles."[394]

Occasionally, Ms. Mayer's desperate attempts to exonerate Islam lead her to bad arguments and contradictions. In her Preface, she writes: "Even without studying the question of how Islam relates to human rights issues, my experience in work on behalf of the cause of human rights would have sufficed to convince me that Islam is not the cause of the human rights problems endemic to the Middle East. Human rights abuses are every bit as prevalent and just as severe in countries where Islamic law is in abeyance or consciously violated as in countries where it is, at least officially, the legal norm."

Her whole book shows that "distinctive Islamic criteria have been used to cut back on the freedoms guaranteed in international law" (p. 2); she herself shows that, at certain stages of Islamic history, one Islamic doctrine prevailed that hindered the development of human rights (quotes 2 and 4, preceding).

To argue in the above way is as illogical as arguing that because human rights were violated in pre-1989 Soviet Russia, where Communism was the state philosophy, and are equally violated in today's—1994—Ukraine, where Communism is no longer the state philosophy, then the human rights violations in the former Soviet Union had nothing to do with the philosophy of Soviet Communism.

She rejects the view that "Islamic culture froze in its premodern formulation" (p. 12), and yet she herself tells us (see earlier quote 3) that certain premodern values have predominated for more than a millennium. I have already quoted Schacht and Hurgronje on the way Islamic law did become fixed and immutable. I shall quote Bousquet to the same effect:

> On the one hand, it is certain that the system of Fiqh [i.e., Science of Islamic Law] is no longer susceptible to adaptation; it has been frozen for a long time, for centuries, the same handbooks have served to teach the principles of the Will of God, such as was established by the Doctors of the sacred books; this interpretation is definitive and immutable."[395]

There are recognizable sharia laws, not dependent on perverse or illegitimate readings of the Koran and the sunna, concerning women, non-Muslims, and religious freedom, which no amount of interpretation or re-interpretation is going to make palatable to someone committed to the principles of international human rights. On women, for example, we may quote a writer referred to by Ms. Mayer in a footnote, Ghassan Ascha: "Islam is not the sole factor in the repression of the Muslim woman, but it constitutes without any doubt a fundamental cause, and remains a major obstacle to the evolution of this situation." Here there is no equivocation, no evasive attempts to exonerate Islam.

Even, if we concede that Muslim conservatives have interpreted the sharia in their own way, what gives us the right to say that their interpretation is the inauthentic one and that of the liberal Muslims, authentic? Who is going to decide what is authentic Islam? For many scholars, the sharia remains the epitome of Islamic civilization. Finally, the sharia may be open to interpretation, but it is not infinitely elastic either.[396]

Happily, Ms. Mayer's commendable efforts not to offend Muslim sensibilities, though leading her into contradictory statements, have not prevented her from showing, in thorough detail, how Islamic schemes of human rights are woefully inadequate for the protection of international human rights.

Conclusion

The major obstacle in Islam to any move toward international human rights is God, or to put it more precisely, in the words of Hurgronje,[397] it is the reverence for the sources, the Koran and the Sunna. In the Universal Islamic Declaration of Human Rights (UIDHR), we are told that it is Divine Revelation that has given "the legal and moral framework within which to establish and regulate human institutions and relationships." The authors of the UIDHR belittle human reason, which is deemed to be an inadequate guide in the affairs of mankind, and they insist that the "teachings of Islam represent the quintessence of Divine guidance in its final and perfect form."

Therefore, as Ms. Mayer points out, it is not surprising that any challenges to Islamic law are ruled out a priori by the authors of the UIDHR. Hence the sharia remains impregnable.

To look for Islamic antecedents for the international human rights principles may seem necessary to make the latter acceptable to a deeply conservative civilization and tradition, but it is ultimately a waste of time, an exercise in mental gymnastics. In my view, *it is a fundamental mistake to look for Islamic antecedents* for the international human rights principles, not simply because there are no such antecedents, but because to argue in such a way is to play into the hands of the ulama, the obscurantist religious class. It is to fight on their own terrain. For every text adduced by the friends of democracy to show that there is compatibility between Islam and human rights, the ulama will produce half a dozen others showing the contrary. If the compatibilitists do not find any antecedents, will they then abandon these principles? The principles of human rights are autonomous, universal, and do not depend on any appeal to divine authority. These principles are rational and can be argued for without recourse to supernatural knowledge. In fact, the compatibilitists accepted the validity of the principles prior to their search for their spurious antecedents.

Progress toward liberal democracy with respect for international human rights in the Muslim world will depend on the radical and critical reappraisal of the dogmatic foundations of Islam, rigorous self-criticism that eschews comforting delusions of a glorious past, of a Golden Age of total Muslim victory in all spheres; the separation of religion and state, and the adoption of secularism. But secularism will never be adopted as long as it is seen as a Western "disease." The Muslim world has to lay aside its unjustified, irrational, and ultimately destructive fear and loathing of the West and come to a just recognition of the West's true values and to a deep understanding of the philosophical foundations of liberalism and democracy; and what the West has already taught it, and what it can still teach it.

Irrational Fear and Loathing of the West

It is paradoxical that Muslims often wish to point out the influence of Islam in the making of modern Europe, to the Muslim contribution toward the very civilization they profess to despise. The Americans would not have walked on the moon, we are told, if it had not been for the "Arab contributions to the exact sciences." At the same time, the West is denounced as being shallow, materialistic, decadent, irreligious, and scientific. This scientific materialism is contrasted with the Muslim's own putative superior spirituality and profundity. (How blind obedience to a book constitutes spirituality is not clear.) Even to talk of the influence of Islam on the West is to betray an inferiority complex, as though only those aspects of Islam that went into the making of the West were worthy of note. And, of course, it reveals the Muslims' sense of present failure and inadequacy.

As Pryce-Jones put it, "If the Arabs had high scientific achievements to their credit, why did they leave the Europeans exclusively to benefit from them? What kind of a scientific tradition could it have been that apparently stopped dead in its tracks? Do such apologetic sentiments have purposes of self-deception in the face of distressing truth? Is it really the dreadful fate of Arabs not to be the men their fathers were?"[398]

Muslims will continue to despise "scientific research and discovery" if they persist in seeing "science" as "unspiritual." But as Popper[399] and others have pointed out, science should not be confounded with technology; science, indeed, is a spiritual activity: "For science is not merely a collection of facts about electricity, etc.; it is one of the most important spiritual movements of our day." Lewis Wolpert makes the same observation: "Science is one of humankind's greatest and most beautiful achievements."[400]

It is unfortunate that many Muslim intellectuals have swallowed whole the shallow criticisms of "Orientalism." Far from being the tool of imperialism, Western scholars gave back to Muslims their culture, that is to say, Western scholarship in its disinterested pursuit of truth and knowledge, revealed to the Muslims themselves aspects of their culture and history that would have been otherwise lost, gave them a deeper understanding of Islamic civilization. It was intellectual inquiry and curiosity that motivated years of study and research—indeed a whole lifetime—among a group of scholars now despised as "Orientalists."

The story of the apparent burning of the Alexandrian library by the Muslims is a perfect example of why mistrust of Western scholarship is totally misplaced. According to the traditional account, after the conquest of Alexandria in 641, the caliph Umar ordered the great library to be destroyed: "If these writings of the Greeks agree with the book of God, they are useless and need not be preserved; if they disagree, they are pernicious and ought to be destroyed." The books were then used to heat the furnaces of the numerous bathhouses of the city. Far from being a Western fabrication to blacken Islam's reputation, this story was a late-twelfth-century Muslim invention, to justify the burning of heretical Ismalian books.

In the words of Lewis, "the original sources of the story are Muslim. . . . Not the creation, but the demolition of the myth was the achievement of European scholarship, which from the eighteenth century to the present day has rejected the story as false and absurd, and thus exonerated the Caliph Umar and the early Muslims from this libel" (*New York Review of Books*, 2 September 1990).

Polemical denunciation of Western "materialism" also blinds Muslims to the spiritual achievements of the West and denies Muslims access to the rich heritage of Europe that should be the patrimony and cause of pride to all mankind, as much as the rich architectural heritage of Islam, for example, is the cause of human pride and wonder. The music of Mozart and Beethoven, the art of the Renaissance should be as much the object of study in Islamic seats of learning as Islamic philosophy. Secularism should open up the intellectual horizons of Muslims, who, at present, are fed a daily diet of misrepresentation of what Western culture stands for. Far from being a culture of "nihilism" or selfishness, the West is full of humanitarian impulses, from the creation of the Red Cross to Doctors without Borders.

The unwillingness to acknowledge any intellectual debts to the West, and the unwillingness that leads to vain searches for Islamic antecedents for human rights, for example, are absurd in the extreme in view of the different elements that have gone into the making of Islam. I have already cited the influence of talmudic Judaism, Syriac Christianity, and Zoroastrianism. The influence of Greek philosophy and science is also well known. The crescent, the emblem of Islam, was originally the symbol of sovereignty in the city of Byzantium. Arabic script, which was developed at a late date, may well have been invented by Christian missionaries and ultimately derived from the Phoenician alphabet, via Nabatean and Aramaic.

Islamic art and architecture owes an enormous debt to the rich and ancient traditions of the Near East with which the Arabs came into contact after the rapid conquests of the seventh century. As the recognized scholar of Islamic architecture, K. A. C. Creswell[401] put it rather bluntly, "Arabia, at the rise of Islam, does not appear to have possessed anything worthy of the name of architecture." Grabar and Ettinghausen also point out that "the conquering Arabs, with few artistic traditions of their own and a limited doctrine on art, penetrated a world which was not only immensely rich in artistic themes and forms yet universal in its vocabulary, but also, at this particular juncture of its history, had charged its forms with unusual intensity."[402]

The famous Dome of the Rock (A.D. 691) in Jerusalem, one of the earliest Islamic monuments, is obviously influenced by the centrally planned buildings known as "martyria," and bears a close relationship to the Christian sanctuaries of the Ascension and the Anastasis. The interior owes a great deal equally to the Christian art of Syria and Palestine, and Byzantine. As for the minaret, Creswell has shown that it was derived architecturally from Syrian church towers.[403]

Ettinghausen, in a chapter pointedly entitled "Byzantine Art In Islamic Garb," in his classic work on Arab painting, writes: "during the Umayyad period the two major elements of Arab painting were classical and Iranian; these elements existed side by side and, apart from a deliberate choice of subject matter, showed no Islamic slant. In the subsequent Abbasid period the Iranian [i.e., non-Islamic or pre-Islamic Iran] element became prevalent. (At the end of the 12th century), the classical element again predominates, this time by way of Byzantine inspiration."[404]

As for Islamic law itself, here is Schacht on the influences that created it: "Elements originating from Roman and Byzantine law, from the canon law of the Eastern Churches, from talmudic and rabbinic law, and from Sasanian law, infiltrated into the nascent religious law of Islam during its period of incubation, to appear in the doctrines of the [A.D.] second [Muslim]/eighth century."[405]

As the Arab philosopher al-Kindi said: "We ought not to be ashamed of applauding the truth, nor appropriating the truth *from whatever source it may come, even if it be from remote races and nations alien to us.* There is nothing that beseems the seeker after truth better than truth itself."[406]

The great Averroes made the same point:

> So if someone else has already enquired into this matter, it is clear that we ought to look at what our predecessor has said to help us in our own undertaking, alike whether that previous investigator was of the same religion as ourselves or not. For in regard to the instrument by which our reasoning is precisely refined it is immaterial to consider, touching its property of refining, whether that instrument was invented by a co-religionist of ours or by one who did not share our faith; the only proviso is that it fulfils the condition of being sound and efficacious.

No civilization is pure; there are no more pure civilizations than there are pure races. Nabokov once said we are all a salad of racial genes; this is even more true of civilizations: civilizations are a salad of cultural genes, different interpenetrating, interinfluencing strands. Most civilizations have not developed in isolation; there has always been an exchange of material goods *and* ideas. Nor have civilizations remained absolutely static and unchanging in all their aspects. Traditions change and evolve—they do not emerge ready-made, fully formed, out of nowhere. Foreign influences are absorbed and assimilated and transmuted. What we take to be ancient traditions deeply rooted in a national past often turn out to be foreign imports of recent origins—this is particularly true of "national culinary dishes." Most spices have originated in the East and have traveled westward, though occasionally the other way also; for example, contrary to what many believe, red chilis, now thought to be an essential ingredient in any Indian dish, are not native to India but were introduced there by the Portuguese in the sixteenth century. (The "traditional" British Christmas is not more than a hundred years old.) Conversely what we take to be "alien" turns out to be homegrown. What emerges is still something unique to the absorbing culture. The various strands that went into the making of Islamic civilization, nonetheless, produced an original, distinct culture that had not existed before. As Braudel said, a great civilization can be recognized not only by its refusal to borrow but also by its ability to receive and borrow. Despite the apparent stagnation of the Islamic world and its conservative nature, modern Western ideas have been penetrating Islamic culture in more ways than one cares to admit. The influence of Western literature on Arabic literature, especially since the nineteenth century, is an obvious example—the Nobel Prize winner Naguib Mahfouz is known, after all, as the "Arab Balzac."

Unfortunately, these ideas have failed to reach the majority of the people in Muslim countries. Here intellectuals and national leaders have failed to educate the people in the principles of liberalism and democracy.

At this stage in world history, in this age of globalism, to cut oneself off from cultural influences, even if it were possible, *simply* because they are seen to be from the West, is childish in the extreme. The works of Beethoven are as much a legacy for the whole of mankind as the works of Ibn Khaldun or the architecture of the Alhambra.

In the past, a simple increase in knowledge has led to a change in culture. In the last century and a half there has been an enormous increase in knowledge, objective knowledge that is of universal validity. This scientific knowledge cannot but have an impact on every single culture on earth. Traditions are not necessarily "good" simply because they are ancient or well-established. As Von Hayek put it, "Follies and abuses are no better for having long been established principles of policy."[407] The British intervened in the affairs of an alien culture and abolished the ancient tradition of suttee, whereby a widow had to throw herself on the funeral pyre of her husband. This must be considered a step forward in the lot of women and the moral progress of mankind.

The preceding section is but a preparation for a plea in favor of secularism, whose Western provenance is not a rational justification for its rejection. As al-Masudi said, "Whatever is good should be recognized, whether it is found in friend or foe."

IN DEFENSE OF SECULARISM

In the last hundred years more defenses of liberalism have been made in the Muslim world than most people realize. Muhammad Ali (1769–1849), the founder of modern Egypt, is often considered the first secularist in the Arab world. In Turkey there was Prince Sabaheddin (d. 1948), who advocated individualism, federalism, and decentralization. In Egypt, there was the disciple of Mill, Ahmad Lutfi al-Sayyid (1872–1963), who defended the rights of individuals and argued for the separation of powers, safeguards against the encroachment of the state in the lives of individuals, and the freedom of the press.

However, the most recent impassioned plea for secularism comes from Fouad Zakariya,[408] writing in 1989, after the Rushdie affair. Zakariya, an Egyptian philosopher teaching at the University of Kuwait, laments the fact that the principles of Islamic religious dogma have never been critically examined, that there is no single periodical devoted entirely to secular thought in Arabic. Zakariya believes that the values embodied in secularism—rationalism, critical spirit, scientific rigor, intellectual independence—are of universal validity. He believes that there were Muslims in the past who fought for the same values, citing the Mu'tazilites, al-Farabi, Averroes, and Ibn al-Haytham.

Secularism is absolutely necessary, concludes Zakariya, especially for those societies threatened by any kind of authoritarian and medieval way of thinking. Since the Muslim world is still plunged in the Dark Ages, secularism is needed more than ever.

8

Arab Imperialism, Islamic Colonialism

> I have to stress that I was traveling in the non-Arab Muslim world. Islam began
> as an Arab religion; it spread as an Arab empire. In Iran, Pakistan, Malaysia,
> Indonesia—the countries of my itinerary—I was traveling, therefore, among
> people who had been converted to what was an alien faith. I was traveling
> among people who had to make a double adjustment—an adjustment to the
> European empires of the nineteenth and twentieth centuries; and an earlier ad-
> justment to the Arab faith. You might almost say that I was among people who
> had been doubly colonized, doubly removed from themselves.
>   V. S. Naipaul, *New York Review of Books* (January 31, 1991)

Open any modern introductory book on Islam and the chances are you will find
that it begins by singing the praises of a people who conquered, in an incredibly
short period, half the civilized world—of a people who established an empire that
stretched from the banks of the Indus in the east to the shores of the Atlantic in
the west. The volume will recount in positively glowing terms a time when Muslims ruled over a vast population of diverse peoples and cultures. One can hardly
imagine a contemporary British historian being able to get away with similar eulogies on the British Empire, of a time when a large part of the world was colored
red in English atlases to indicate the British Empire and possessions. While European colonialism and imperialism (both being general terms of abuse by now)
are blamed for every ill on earth, and something of which all Europeans are made
to feel ashamed, Arab imperialism is held up as something of which Muslims can
be proud, something to be lauded and admired.

Although Europeans are constantly castigated for having imposed their in-
sidious and decadent values, culture, and language on the Third World, no one
cares to point out that Islam colonized lands that were the homes of advanced and
ancient civilizations, and that in doing so, Islamic colonialism trampled under foot
and permanently destroyed many cultures. In the words of Michael Cook,[409]

198

"The Arab conquests rapidly destroyed one empire, and permanently detached large territories of another. This was, for the states in question, an appalling catastrophe"; or, as Cook and Crone put it, the conquests were achieved at "extraordinary cultural costs."[410]

Cook and Crone describe this process of Islamization in their book already discussed earlier. Speros Vryonis in his *The Decline Of Medieval Hellenism in Asia Minor and the Process of Islamization from the Eleventh through the Fifteenth Century* describes how the essentially Hellenic and Christian way of life, with its bishoprics and magnificent monasteries, were destroyed by the Turkish invasions of the 1060s and 1070s—many people fled, were captured, massacred, or enslaved. Vryonis describes a similar decline in the subsequent centuries with the eventual destruction of the Byzantine Empire.[411]

It is sad and ironic that in Algeria, for instance, all teaching in the French language was discontinued because the French language was considered a symbol of French colonialism, an illegitimate imperial presence. It is sad since it cuts a whole generation off from the rich cultural heritage of another civilization, but also ironic since Arabic is itself an imposed language. Arab imperialism not only imposed a new language on a people whose mother tongue was Berber, not Arabic, but even convinced the same people that they were ethnically Arabs—which they were not—and brainwashed them into accepting a religion that was alien to their own religious traditions. Bowing toward Arabia five times a day must surely be the ultimate symbol of this cultural imperialism.

Muslims despise co-religionists who accept what they see as alien Western values, and yet fail to see that they themselves could justifiably be seen as "traitors" to the culture of their ancestors. In India, for example, present-day Muslims are the descendants of Hindu converts, in Iran, of Zoroastrians, in Syria, of Christians. A vast number of Muslims throughout the world have been persuaded to accept a religion that originated thousands of miles away, to read a book in a language that they do not understand, which they learn to read and write before they know their mother tongue or the national language. These Muslims learn more of the history of a people remote from them geographically and ethnically than the past of their own countries *before* the advent of Islam.

Another one of the unfortunate consequences of the triumph of Islam is that it has cut millions of people off from their own rich, *non-Muslim* heritage. As V. S. Naipaul reflected during his travels in Pakistan,

The time before Islam is a time of blackness: that is part of Muslim theology. History has to serve theology. The excavated city of Mohenjodaro in the Indus Valley—overrun by the Aryans in 1500 B.C.—is one of the archaelogical glories of Pakistan and the world. The excavations are now being damaged by waterlogging and salinity, and appeals for money have been made to world organizations. A featured letter in *Dawn* [a daily Pakistani newspaper] offered its own ideas for the site. Verses from the Koran, the writer said, should be engraved and set up in Mohenjodaro in "appropriate places": "Say (unto them,

O Mohammed): Travel in the land and see the nature of the sequel for the guilty. . . . Say (O Mohammad, to the disbelievers): Travel in the land and see the nature of the consequence for those who were before you. Most of them were idolaters."

Naipaul goes on to quote Sir Mohammed Iqbal (1875–1938), the Indian Muslim poet who is often considered the spiritual founder of Pakistan, and a kind of posthumous "national poet." Naipaul writes:

> It was the poet Iqbal's hope that an Indian Muslim state might rid Islam of "the stamp that Arab imperialism was forced to give it." It turns out now that the Arabs were the most successful imperialists of all time; since to be conquered by them (and then to be like them) is still, in the minds of the faithful, to be saved.
>
> History, in the Pakistan school books I looked at, begins with Arabia and Islam. In the simpler texts, surveys of the Prophet and the first four caliphs and perhaps the Prophet's daughter are followed, with hardly a break, by lives of the poet Iqbal, Mr Jinnah, the political founder of Pakistan, and two or three "martyrs," soldiers or airmen who died in the holy wars against India in 1965 and 1971.

This contempt for the pagan past remains to limit the historical imaginations of most Muslims, to narrow the intellectual horizons. Certainly at the beginning, the sciences of Egyptology, Assyriology, and Iranology were the exclusive concerns of European and American scholars. It was left to the dedicated Western archaeologists to recover and give back to mankind a part of its glorious past.

Resistance to Arab Imperialism and Islam

The Arabs of the time just prior to Islam had no time for religion:[412] "Religion of whatever kind it may have been generally had little place in the life of the Arabs, who were engrossed in worldly interests like fighting, wine, games and love." Watt characterizes their way of life as "tribal humanism." Thus it is not surprising that in the early "believers" or "converts" there are some who outwardly confess their belief but have no inclination in their heart toward Islamic morals and dogma and show no understanding of what Muhammad meant by and taught about "giving oneself to God."[413] The desert dwellers, that is, the Bedouin Arabs, were even less inclined to accept the new creed. Some of them, for example, from the tribes Ukl and Urayna, accepted Islam but, feeling uneasy living in a city, asked Muhammad if they could return to their former habitat. Muhammad gave them a herd and a herder and let them leave Medina; but on leaving Medina they killed their herder and reverted to unbelief. The Prophet exacted "a cruel revenge."

Most Bedouins were not at all attracted by Islam, and in return they were despised by the city Arabs who had accepted it. As Goldziher pointed out, "there are countless stories, unmistakably taken from true life, which describe the indifference of the desert Arabs to prayer, their ignorance of the elements of Muslim rites, and even their indifference towards the sacred book of God itself and their ignorance of its most important parts. The Arabs always preferred to hear the songs of the heroes of paganism rather than holy utterances of the Koran."[414]

But the Arabs themselves found the asceticism of Islam in respect to food and wine irksome in the extreme. Many refused to give up wine despite punishments. Goldziher describes the situation in this manner:

> Traditions from the earliest days of Islam show us that amongst the representatives of the true Arab character there were people who valued freedom, to whom the new system, with its condemnation and punishment of free enjoyment, was so repulsive that they preferred to leave that society altogether, when it intended to impose upon them the din [religion, i.e., Islam] in earnest, rather than to lose their freedom. Such a man was Rabi'a b. Umayya b. Khalaf, a much respected man, famous for his generosity. He did not want to relinquish wine-drinking under Islam and even drank during the month of Ramadan. For this [the Caliph] Umar banned him from Medina, thereby making him so bitter against Islam that he did not wish to return to the capital even after Umar's death, though he had reason to believe that Uthman [the third Caliph] would have been more lenient. He preferred to emigrate to the Christian empire and to become a Christian.[415]

Arab Racism

> The myth of Islamic racial innocence was a Western creation and served a Western purpose. Not for the first time, a mythologized and idealized Islam provided a stick with which to chastise Western failings.[416]

ARAB VERSUS ARAB

One of the fundamental reasons for the periodic revolts in the history of Islam has been what Goldziher[417] calls "the increasing arrogance and racial presumption" of the Arabs. Islam unequivocally teaches the equality of all believers, all Muslims (of course, non-Muslims are another matter altogether) before God. The Prophet himself was at pains to instill into the minds of the Arab tribes that from now on Islam, rather than tribal affiliation, was to be the unifying principle of society. However, tribal rivalries continued well into Abbasid times, feuds and competitions lingered long after Islam had condemned them. Tribes were unable to settle their differences and had to be grouped separately in war too, separate quarters, separate mosques.

Perhaps the most destructive and bloody rivalry was the one that existed between the northern and southern Arabs. After the Arab conquest of Andalusia, "these tribal groups had to be settled in different parts of the country in an attempt to prevent civil wars, which occurred nonetheless." Mustafa b. Kamal al-Din al-Siddiqi writes in the year 1137 A.H.: "The fanatical hatred between the Qaysite [northern Arab] and Yemenite [southern Arab] factions continues to this day amongst some ignorant Arabs, and even now wars between them have not ceased, though it is well known that such actions belong to those of the Jahiliyya and are forbidden by the Prophet."[418]

Even within tribes belonging to the same group, some tribes considered themselves far superior to another, to the extent of refusing intermarriage.

Traditions attributed to the Prophet were fabricated and "misused for racial rivalry."As the Arabs conquered more and more territories, the appointments to the most important offices did not satisfy the two rival tribes and were the cause of bloody civil wars. As Goldziher says, the racial rivalry of the first two centuries of Islam shows the lack of success of the Muslim teachings of equality among the Arabs.

ARAB VERSUS NON-ARAB

We come now to another sphere where the Muslim teaching of the equality of all men in Islam remained a dead letter for a long time, never realised in the consciousness of Arabs, and roundly denied in their day to day behaviour. [Goldziher p. 98]

After their spectacular conquests, the Arabs were unwilling to concede equality to the non-Arab converts to Islam, despite Islamic doctrine that expressly forbade discrimination. But for the Arabs there were the conquered and the conquerers, and there was no question of the Arabs giving up their privileges. "Non-Arab Muslims were regarded as inferior and subjected to a whole series of fiscal, social, political, military, and other disabilities."[419] The Arabs ruled as a "sort of conquistador tribal aristocracy," to which only "true Arabs" could belong, a true Arab being one who was of free Arab ancestry on both his father's and mother's side. The Arabs took concubines from the conquered peoples, but their children by these slave women were heavily discriminated against and were not considered full Arabs.

The Arabs practiced a kind of apartheid toward the non-Arab Muslims: "The Arabs looked upon [the non-Arab Muslims] as aliens and, regardless of what class they belonged to, treated them with scorn and contempt. They led them into battle on foot. They deprived them of a share of the booty. They would not walk on the same side of the street with them, nor sit at the same repast. In nearly every place separate encampments and mosques were constructed for their use. Marriage between them and Arabs was considered a social crime."[420]

SLAVERY

> To the Muslims—as to the people of every other civilisation known to history—the civilised world meant themselves. They alone possessed enlightenment and the true faith; the outside world was inhabited by infidels and barbarians. Some of these were recognized as possessing some form of religion and a tincture of civilisation. The remainder—polytheists and idolaters—were seen primarily as sources of slaves.[421]

The Koran accepts the institution of slavery and recognizes the essential inequality of master and slave (suras 16.77; 30.28). Concubinage is permitted (suras 4.3; 23.6; 33.50-52; 70.30). The Koran also enjoins kindness towards slaves, and the liberation of a slave is considered a pious act. The Prophet himself took many prisoners during his wars against the Arab tribes; those that were not ransomed were reduced to slavery.

Under Islam, slaves have no legal rights whatsoever, they are considered as mere "things," the property of their master, who may dispose of them in any way he chooses—sale, gift, etc. Slaves cannot be guardians or testamentary executors, and what they earn belongs to their owner. A slave cannot give evidence in a court of law. Even conversion to Islam by a non-Muslim slave does not mean that he is automatically liberated. There is no obligation on the part of the owner to free him.

In the early years of the Arab conquests, vast numbers of slaves were acquired by capture; "the use of this labor enabled the Arabs to live on the conquered land as a rentier class and to exploit some of the economic potential of the rich Fertile Crescent."[422] But as the conquered peoples began to be given protected status, this source of slaves began to dry up, and Arabs looked farther afield for their supply of slaves. Certain vassal states were annually forced to supply hundreds of male and female slaves as part of a tribute.

Arabs were deeply involved in the vast network of slavetrading—they scoured the slave markets of China, India, and Southeast Asia. There were Turkish slaves from Central Asia, slaves from the Byzantine Empire, white slaves from Central and East Europe, and black slaves from West Africa and East Africa. Every city in the Islamic world had its slave market.

From the moment of their capture to the time of their sale, hundreds of slaves were forced to put up with degrading and inhuman conditions, and hundreds died of exhaustion and disease. The "lucky" ones became domestic servants, while the unlucky ones were exploited to the maximum working in the salt mines, draining the marshes, working in the cotton and sugar plantations.

Though the practice was expressly forbidden by Islam, the female slaves were hired out as prostitutes. Otherwise, of course, they were at the entire sexual disposal of their master. In the words of Stanley Lane-Pool:[423]

The condition of the female slave in the East is indeed deplorable. She is at the entire mercy of her master, who can do what he pleases with her and her companions; for the Muslim is not restricted in the number of his concubines. . . . The female white slave is kept solely for the master's sensual gratification, and is sold when he is tired of her, and so she passes from master to master, a very wreck of womanhood. Her condition is a little improved if she bear a son to her tyrant; but even then he is at liberty to refuse to acknowledge the child as his own, though it must be owned he seldom does this. Kind as the Prophet was himself toward bondswomen, one cannot forget the unutterable brutalities which he suffered his followers to inflict upon conquered nations in the taking of slaves. The Muslim soldier was allowed to do as he pleased with any "infidel" woman he might meet with on his victorious march. When one thinks of the thousands of women, mothers and daughters, who must have suffered untold shame and dishonour by this license, he cannot find words to express his horror And this cruel indulgence has left its mark on the Muslim character, nay, on the whole character of Eastern life.

In discussions of the lot of women under Islam, there is a tendency to forget almost entirely the fate, treatment, conditions, and the very limited rights of the female slave.

ANTI-BLACK PREJUDICE

I wonder what Russians would make of the fact—if they are at all aware of it—that their greatest writer, Pushkin, had black Ethiopian ancestry. Similarly, what do Arabs make of their black, normally Ethiopian, poets, known as the "crows of the Arabs"? There were several Arabic poets during the pre-Islamic and early Islamic periods who were either pure Africans or of mixed Arab and African parentage. It is clear from their poetry that they suffered racial prejudice and even, to a certain extent, developed a kind of self-hatred and self-pity: laments and apologies of the kind, "I am black but my soul is white," "Women would love me if I were white" are frequent in their poetry. We might mention the names of Suhaym (d. 660), Nusayb ibn Rabah (d. 726), a contemporary of Nusayb, al-Hayqutan, and Abu Dulama (d. ca. 776) as the most eminent of these "crows." Black slaves had even lower status in early Muslim society. In the words of Lewis, "In ancient Arabia, as elsewhere in antiquity, racism—in the modern sense of the word—was unknown. The Islamic dispensation, far from encouraging it, condemns even the universal tendency to ethnic and social arrogance and proclaims the equality of all Muslims before God. Yet, from the literature, it is clear that a new and sometimes vicious pattern of racial hostility and discrimination had emerged within the Islamic world."[424]

ABOLITION

Slavery in the Islamic world continued, astonishingly enough, well into the twentieth century. According to Brunschvig,[425] "black slaves of both sexes continued to be imported into Morocco until well into the twentieth century, with some pretence at secrecy since the open traffic from Timbuktu and public sale had become impossible."

There is enough evidence to show that slavery persisted in Saudi Arabia and the Yemen up to the 1950s. Slavery was so deeply rooted in these countries that abolition was a very slow process. It was due to foreign influence that the process began at all. Islam, as Brunschvig points out, has never preached the *abolition* of slavery as a doctrine; and the "fact, brought out in the Kuran, that slavery is in principle lawful, satisfies religious scruples. Total abolition might even seem a reprehensible innovation, contrary to the letter of the holy Book and the exemplary practice of the first Muslims."

In more recent times, workers from Southeast Asia employed in domestic service, in the Arab Middle East, or Saudi Arabia have been treated as slaves—with their passports taken away, often forbidden to leave the house (even locked in their rooms). According to a report in the French magazine, *L Vie* (no. 2562, 6 Oct. 1994) 45,000 young black Africans a year are still kidnapped and reduced to slavery—as servants in the Gulf States and the Middle East.

Anti-Arab Reaction

THE SHU'UBIYA

Taking their name from verse 13 of sura 49, which teaches the equality of all Muslims, the Shu'ubiya was a party that objected to Arab arrogance and even exalted the non-Arab over the Arab whom they thoroughly despised as barbarians from the deserts of Arabia. This party reached its greatest influence during the second and the third Muslim century. Under the Abbasid caliphs, certain Persian families sought the restoration of Zoroastrian customs—a clear indication that Islam meant very little to educated, upper-class Persian circles. For example, the general of the Abbasid caliph al-Mutasim (833), Khaydhar b. Kawus, also known as Afshin, was very active and militarily successful in the religious wars against Christians and "heretics" like Babak—in short, he was an early Islamic hero. And yet it is clear that he:

> was so little a Muslim that he cruelly maltreated two propagandists of Islam who wished to transform a pagan temple into a mosque; he ridiculed Islamic laws and . . . ate meat of strangled animals (a horror to Muslims), and also induced others to do so by saying that such meat was fresher than that of animals killed according to the Islamic rite. . . . He ridiculed circumcision and

other Muslim customs, and paid no attention to them. . . . He dreamed of the restoration of the Persian empire and the "white religion," and mocked Arabs, Maghribines, and Muslim Turks.[426]

As Goldziher says, Afshin is but a typical example of how many non-Arabs joined the Muslim cause for material advantages, all the while hating the Arabs for having destroyed their national Persian independence and ancestral traditions, and dreaming of repaying the rebuffs they had suffered for centuries.[427]

There were many ways of countering the contempt in which the Arabs held various non-Arab groups. These defensive tactics are of intrinsic historical interest, but they are also very important in that many contemporary thinkers, particularly, as we shall see later, Berber intellectuals, see them as a way of escaping Arab imperialism, and even Islam itself, forever.

Every despised group pointed to its own glorious pre-Islamic past to counter Arab contempt. The Persians obviously did not have to exaggerate or invent a past to show the antiquity and sophistication of their civilization. The Nabataeans tried to do the same. The Nabataeans were an ancient Arab people mentioned as early as the seventh century B.C. A Nabataean alchemist, Ibn Wahshiyya,[428] "moved by grim hatred of the Arabs and full of bitterness about their contempt of his compatriots, decided to translate and make accessible the remnants of ancient Babylonian literature preserved by them in order to show that the ancestors of his people, so despised by the Arabs, had had a great civilization and had excelled in knowledge many peoples of antiquity." The so-called translation, "Nabataean Agriculture," is now thought to be Ibn Wahshiyya's forgery. Similarly, the Copts of Egypt wrote books "which described the deeds of the ancient Egyptians with a bias against the Arabs."

In general the achievements of the non-Arabs in all fields are constantly emphasized: "The Shu'ubites do not fail to mention arts and sciences which were given to mankind by non-Arabs: philosophy, astronomy and silk embroidery, which were practised by non-Arabs whilst the Arabs were still in a state of deepest barbarism, while everything that Arabs can be proud of is centred in poetry; but here too they are outdone by others, notably by the Greeks." The games that were invented by non-Arabs, chess and nard, are also mentioned. What have the Arabs to set against such refinements of civilization in order to make good their claim to glory? "In the face of this they are but howling wolves and prowling beasts, devouring one another and engaged in eternal mutual fighting."[429]

THE KHURRAMI AND THE REVOLT OF BABAK[430]

Perhaps the rebellion of the Khurramis gave the Abbasid rulers more cause for concern than any other. The Khurramis represented a social and religious movement that was derived from Mazdakism and came into prominence in the eighth century. Whatever the nature of this movement in the eighth century, when Babak Khurrami (or Korrami) took over its leadership in the early ninth century, he turned it into an anti-Arab, anti-caliphal, and to a certain extent an anti-Muslim revolt. Popular dislike of Arab rule increased the number of his followers in Azerbaijan, but there were Khurramis in many other cities and regions such as Tabarestan, Khorasan, Balk, Isfahan, Qom, and Armenia. Babak successfully resisted the Abbasid forces for nearly twenty years, emerging victorious time and again from battles conducted in narrow mountain passes. Finally the Caliph al-Mutasim appointed al-Afshin (see previous section) as commander, and within two years Babak had been captured. In 838, Babak was publically humiliated and then executed in an extremely cruel fashion on the orders of al-Mutasim.

The Khurrami movement seems to have continued into the ninth century, and there is evidence of a cult of Babak as late as the eleventh century.

Pre-Islamic Glories

It was not until the nineteenth century once again that a Muslim country took an interest in her pre-Islamic past. In 1868, Sheikh Rifa al-Tahtawi, the Egyptian man of letters, poet, and historian, published a history of Egypt, giving full attention to her pharaonic past. Up to then, of course, histories of Egypt had begun with the Arab conquests. Al-Tahtawi sought to define Egyptian identity in national and patriotic terms—not in terms of Islam, or Pan-Arabism. Perhaps for the first time in Islamic history, someone tried to see his country as having a "living, continuing identity through several changes of language, religion, and civilization."[431]

The reason Sheikh Rifa's achievement is so important is that for the first time since the early days of the Shu'ubiyya, someone dared to challenge the official Muslim dogma that pre-Islamic times were times of barbarism and ignorance and unworthy of consideration. He dared sing the praise of pagan Egypt; he dared give voice to the thought that there were, after all, alternatives to Islamic civilization, that civilizations can and did take different forms. If this process of historical education were to continue in other Muslim countries—after all, Iraq and Iran can also boast of a magnificent pre-Islamic past—it would lead to a much-needed broadening of the intellectual life, a deeper tolerance for other ways of life, a simple expansion of historical knowledge that has remained so limited and narrow. Greater knowledge of the pre-Islamic past can only lead to the lessening of fanaticism. If pharaonic and later Christian Egypt were seen to be equal sources of pride, then would not the Copts be accepted as fellow Egyptians, instead of being the persecuted minority in their own ancestral land that they actually are? Would we not get a truer Algerian identity, asks Slimane Zeghidour, if we acknowledged our common and varied past—Berber, Roman, Arab, French? (*Telerama* 1, July 1992) The ideas of *change* and continuity will also have to become a part of the Muslim's consciousness if Muslim societies are to move forward—this will only occur with the recognition of the pre-Islamic past, and a just appraisal of the period of European colonialism.

The deliberate ignoring of the pre-Islamic past has had a subtler corrupting influence on the peoples of the Muslim world. As Naipaul put it, "the faith abolished the past. And when the past was abolished like this, more than an idea of history suffered. Human behavior, and ideals of good behavior, could suffer." Everything is seen through the distorting perspective of the "only true faith." Human behavior is judged according to whether it has contributed to the establishment of this one "truth"—truth, courage, and heroism, by definition, can only belong to "our side." The period before the coming of the faith was to be judged in one way," and what lay outside it was to be judged in another. The faith altered values, ideas of good behavior, human judgments" (*New York Review of Books,* 31 Jan. 1991). The fact that this "true faith" was established with much greed and cruelty is overlooked or excused—cruelty in the service of the faith is even commendable and divinely sanctioned.

This perverted division of the world into the faithful and the infidel has had a disastrous effect on the perception of even nominally secular-minded Arab intellectuals, who, as we shall see, transfer all responsibility for the lamentable state of the Middle East onto the West.

European Imperialism

It is true that the French invaded Algeria, but so did the Arabs and Turks before them. It is true that they colonized the country and appropriated large tracts of land, but so did the Arabs and Turks before them. The French were no doubt guilty of great misdeeds, but were theirs greater than those of their predecessors? In the time of the French there were undoubtedly oppression and poverty, but was the Algeria of the corsairs, or the one which came into being in 1962, an exemplar of freedom, prosperity and justice? How many Algerians, one wonders, are now sighing for the days of the French, such as they were.

Kedourie, *Times Literary Supplement,* 10 July 1992

That Algeria before the French arrived in the 1830s was "uncivilised" by any reasonable definition is certain.

Hugh Thomas[432]

No Indian with any education and some regard for historical truth, ever denied that, with all its shortcomings, British rule had, in the balance, promoted both the welfare and the happiness of the Indian people.

Nirad Chaudhuri[433]

One only hopes that a deeper historical understanding will extend to the period of European imperialism. Let us look at the example of India. After the first heady days of independence in 1947, Indian historians poured out "nationalist" histories that found no redeeming features in the British Empire. Later, every ill, every failure, every shortcoming of the new country in the 1960s and 1970s was ultimately traced back to the satanic period of the British presence, to past

British exploitation. Almost fifty years later, more mature judgments give a more balanced picture of the *benefits* that the British conferred on India. Here is how radical humanist, Tarkunde[434] sums up the British contribution:

> It is one of the myths created by the imagination of Indian nationalists that prior to the establishment of British rule India was a culturally and economically advanced country and that its material and moral degradation was caused by foreign domination. Even a cursory look at Indian history would show the baselessness of this supposition. If India were indeed an advanced country, it could not have been conquered so easily by a handful of traders coming over a distance of nearly 6000 miles in wind-driven wooden vessels. India was then a country of despotism, injustice and near anarchy, and the bulk of the people welcomed the law and order established by British rule. Although British rule in India ceased to have any progressive potentiality by about the beginning of the present century, its initial impact on the country was highly beneficial. Due to the exhilirating contact with the spirit of freedom, rationalism and human dignity represented by British liberal thought, a belated Renaissance began to develop in India. It took the shape of a movement against religious superstition and in favor of such social causes as abolition of Sati, legalisation of widow remarriage, promotion of women's education, prevention of child marriages and opposition to the custom of untouchability.

Parliamentary democracy, the rule of law, and nature of that law are some of the legacies of the British. The Arabs showed very little interest in the history and culture of the conquered peoples. The British in India, by contrast, gave back to all Indians—Muslim, Hindu, Sikh, Jain, Buddhist—their own culture in a series of works of monumental intellectual dedication, works that are a moving testimony to disinterested intellectual inquiry, scientific curiosity, works that in many cases have not been surpassed by modern research. Imperialists like Lord Curzon saved many of India's architectural monuments, including the Taj Mahal, from ruin.

I have taken India as an example, but as Kedourie and others have shown, European imperial rule, in general, with all its shortcomings, ultimately benefited the ruled as much as the rulers. Despite certain infamous incidents, the European powers conducted themselves, on the whole, very humanely.

Of course, many of the the European conquests were achieved at the expense of Islam. The nature of Muslim dogma ill-prepared the Muslims for defeat:

> Political success vindicated Islam, and the course of world history proved the truth of the religion. Muslims fought to extend the bounds of Islam and humble the unbelievers; the fight was holy, and the reward of those who fell was eternal bliss. Such a belief, which the history of Islam itself seemed to establish beyond doubt, inspired in Muslims self-confidence and powerful feelings of superiority. Hence, the long series of defeats at the hands of Christian Europe could not but undermine the self-respect of the Muslims, and result in a far-reaching moral and intellectual crisis. For military defeat was defeat not only in a worldly sense; it also brought into doubt the truth of the Muslim revelation itself.[435]

In this context, it is not surprising that Muslim intellectuals, with one or two exceptions, have been inculcating in the Muslim masses a hatred of the West that can only, in the long term, lead to a retardation of the acceptance for the need for reform, for change, for the adoption of human rights, for the rule of law—in short, for all those ideas that originated in the West, and that are considered the defining characteristics of Western civilization.

It is a depressing fact that during the Gulf War almost every single Muslim and Arab intellectual sympathized with Saddam Hussein, because, we are told, "he stood up to the West." In this explanation is summed up all the sense of Islamic failure, and feelings of inferiority vis-à-vis the West. The Muslim world must indeed be in a dire way if it sees hope in a tyrant who has murdered literally thousands of his own countrymen—Arabs, Kurds, Sunnis, Shiites, Muslims, and Jews. These same intellectuals seem incapable of self-criticism, and still the old battles are being fought—"them" and "us," the Crusades all over again. Every ill, every failure in the Muslim world is still blamed on the West, Israel, or some Zionist conspiracy. As Kanan Makiya[436] so courageously pointed out,

> Old habits die hard. They die hardest of all among people who have made it their duty to awaken pride in self and a sense of collective identity by blaming all ills on some "other"—a foreign agency or "alien" culture outside the community one is trying to extol, and often more powerful and dynamic. The painful thing to observe is the unrelenting stridency of the Arab intelligentsia's attempt to blame every ill on the West or Israel. The language gets more unreal, hysterical, and self-flagellating, the less the Arab world is actually able to achieve politically and culturally in modern times.

The modern Arab intellectual is influencing Arabs to define themselves negatively: "he is who he is because of who he hates, not because of who he loves or is in solidarity with." Inevitably, the same Arab intellectual and his impressionable audience glorify some mythical past, some Golden Age when "one Muslim could singlehandedly defeat one hundred infidels." "His people would be glorious, his state would be all-powerful, but for the machinations of the imperialists (or the Great Satan, which amounts to the same thing)." As Kanan Makiya says, how about trying some self-criticism for a change, a point also made by Fuad Zakariya: "our cultural task at this stage is to take the bull of backwardness by the horns and criticize ourselves before we criticize the image, even if it is deliberately distorted, that others make of us."[437]

Berber Nationalism

The Berber-speaking peoples have been living in North Africa since prehistoric times. "Proto-berbers" have been settled in North Africa since 7000 B.C. The Berbers had some contact with Carthage, but on the whole led independent lives, divided into rival tribes. Occasionally a leader of genius succeeded in uniting these tribes into an impressive empire. Masinissa (238 B.C.–148 B.C.), son of Gaia, king of the eastern Numidian Massyles, was brought up at Carthage, and fought on the side of the Carthaginians against the Romans. But he joined the Romans, and his cavalry played a decisive part in the famous victory of the Romans at Zama (202 B.C.) Masinissa was now able to create a kingdom comprising the whole of Numidia, uniting all the Berber tribes.

My purpose is not to give a history of the Berbers, but merely to adumbrate the existence of a complex and rich civilization, that had its own languages, script, and history before the arrival of the Arabs. This sketch will prepare the background for the views of modern Berber intellectuals who reject Arab imperialism and Islam.

After Masinissa, the successive empires of the Romans, Vandals, and the Byzantines were equally unable to tame the independence of the Berbers. Nor did the first arrival of the Arabs in any way affect the independence of the Berbers. Okba b. Nafi, the Muslim general, tried without success to subdue these wild tribes. In fact, one of their leaders, Kusaila, was able to surprise and kill Okba and three hundred of his men at Tahuda in 683. As with many of the early Arab tribes, the Berbers slowly converted to Islam, not from deep religious conviction but rather from material self-interest, in the hope of winning booty. With the help of the Berbers, some of whom, ironically are glorified as "Arab heroes"—Berbers like Tariq ibn Zaid, who began the conquest of Spain—the Arab generals completed the conquest of North Africa.

But, just as with the non-Arab Muslims in Persia and Syria, the Berbers were offended at being treated as inferiors by the Arabs, and complained that they were not getting a fair share of the booty. Inevitably, they rose in revolt against the Arabs, who suffered a series of spectacular defeats. The eleventh and twelfth centuries saw the establishment of two Berber dynasties, the Almoravids (1056–1147) and the Almohads (1130–1269), and even the later Marinids were also descendants of Berber tribes.

Berber belongs to the Afro-Asiatic (or the Semito-Hamitic) family of languages. At present, some two or three hundred Berber dialects are spoken by a total of approximately 12 million peoples in Egypt, Libya, Tunisia, Algeria, Morocco, Chad, Burkina Faso Niger, Mali, and Mauretania. The main dialects in Algeria are Kabyle and Shawia; Shluh, Tamazight, and Riff in Morocco; Tamahaq (Tamashek) or Tuareg in various Saharan countries. The oldest inscriptions in a Berber language date back perhaps to 200 B.C., and are written in Tifinag, which is still used by the Tamahaq speakers.

MODERN BERBER REJECTION OF ARAB IMPERIALISM

Kateb Yacine (1929–1989), the Algerian writer, was the most famous intellectual to reject the cultural imperialism of Islam and Arabic, and to defend staunchly the language of his ancestors, Berber. He developed religious skepticism early:

"I first went to Koranic school, but I didn't like religion, in fact, I took a dislike to it," recalls Yacine, "especially when they used to smack the soles of our feet with a ruler to make us learn, without understanding anything of it, the Koran. At French school, our teacher was like a second mother to us, I had one who was extraordinary, someone who knew how to interest us, she made us want to go to school" (*Le Monde*, 31 Oct. 1989). In a by-now famous interview on Radio Beur (a station specially for French of Algerian descent), Yacine scandalized everyone by declaring that he was neither Muslim nor Arab, but Algerian. Then in 1987, in an interview for the journal *Awal*, Yacine vented his deep aversion to Islam: "The Algeria Arabo-Islamic is an Algeria against herself, an Algeria alien to herself. It is an Algeria imposed by arms, for Islam does not develop with sweets and roses, it develops with tears and blood. It grows by crushing, by violence, by contempt, by hatred, by the worst humiliation a people can support. We can see the result" [*Le Monde*, 20 May 1994, p. 5]. He expressed the hope that one day "Algeria" ("a touristic term") would be called by its true name, Tamezgha, the country where Berber (Tamazight) is spoken.

Yacine had nothing but harsh words for the three monotheistic religions that, in his view, had caused nothing but unhappiness in the world: "These religions are profoundly evil ('nefastes') and the unhappiness of our people comes from there. The unhappiness of Algeria started there. We have talked of the Romans and the Christians. Now let us talk of the Arabo-Islamic connection: the longest, the hardest, and the most difficult to combat."

Just before his death in 1989, Yacine wrote a passionate preface to a book of songs by Berber singer Ait Menguelet. Yacine begins his preface with a reference to the 1980 banning in Algeria of a conference on ancient Kabyle poetry, a banning that resulted in riots as Berbers defended their ancestral language. Kateb Yacine went on to complain that just as they were once forced to learn French in the hope of creating a French Algeria, the Algerians are being forced to learn Arabic and forbidden to speak their mother tongue, Tamazight or Berber: "Algeria is a country subjugated by the myth of the Arab nation, for it is in the name of Arabization that Tamazight is repressed. In Algeria and throughout the world, there is a belief that Arabic is the language of the Algerians." But it is Tamazight that is the country's first language, and that has lasted despite centuries of foreign domination.

Our armed struggle ended the destructive myth of French Algeria, but we have succumbed to the power of the even more destructive myth of Arab-Islamic Algeria. French Algeria lasted 104 years. Arab-Islamic Algeria has lasted thirteen centuries! The deepest form of alienation is no longer the belief that we are French, but the belief that we are Arabs. There is no Arab race and no Arab nation. There is a sacred language, that of the Koran, used by the rulers to prevent the people from discovering their own identity.

Many Algerians believe themselves to be Arabs, deny their origins, and consider their greatest poet Ait Menguellet, who writes in Berber, a foreigner (*Le Monde,* 3 Nov. 1989).

Berber Identity in Algeria, 1994

In April 1994, a series of marches commemorated the "Berber Spring" of 1980 when the Berbers rioted in favor of their language. They were organized by a number of Berber cultural groups who insist on their Berber identity: "We want," said one of the founders of *Rassemblement pour la culture et la democratie* (RCD), "the recognition of a second national language [i.e., Berber], and a different identity to that of an Arabo-Islamist one, that is a demand for pluralism. It's the Berber Cultural Movement that is the origin of the first Human Rights League in Algeria, and of democracy."

These reform-minded Berbers see no compatibility between the ideas of the Islamists and democracy and human rights. The Berbers believe it is their "duty to oppose the installation of fascism," not wishing to see their country sinking into "barbarism" (*Infomation,* 20 April 1994).

9

The Arab Conquests and the Position of Non-Muslim Subjects

Apologists of Islam still insist on perpetuating the myth of an Islam that accorded equality to her non-Muslim subjects; they talk of a time when all the various religious communities lived in perfect harmony in the Islamic lands. The same apologists minimize, or even excuse, the persecution, the discrimination, the forced conversions, the massacres, and the destruction of the churches, synagogues, fire temples, and other places of worship. This rosy but totally false picture of Islam is also built up by (1) ignoring the destruction and the massacres during the actual process of the Arab conquests; (2) by concentrating almost exclusively on the fate of Jews and Christians, and consequently dismissing the fate of idolaters (are they not human?), Zoroastrians, Hindus, and Buddhists (3) by relying on Muslim sources, as though they are bound to be less biased; (4) by ignoring, or excusing, the appalling behavior of the Prophet toward the Jews; and (5) by ignoring the intolerant, hostile, anti-Jewish, anti-Christian, and above all, anti-pagan sentiments expressed in the Koran, which were the source of much intolerant, fanatical, and violent behavior toward all non-Muslims throughout the history of Islam.

Early Attitudes: Muhammad and the Koran

The Koran has been divided into early and late suras, the Meccan and Medinan suras respectively. Most of the tolerant sentiments of Muhammad are to be found in the early, Meccan suras:

109: "Recite: O Unbelievers, I worship not what you worship, and you do not worship what I worship. I shall never worship what you worship. Neither will you worship what I worship. To you your religion, to me my religion."

214

50.45: "We well know what the infidels say: but you are not to compel them." 43.88, 89: "And [Muhammad] says, 'O Lord, these are people who do not believe.' Bear with them and wish them 'Peace.' In the end they shall know their folly."

The exceptions are to be found in sura 2 which is usually considered Medinan, i.e., late.

2.256: "There is no compulsion in religion."

2.62: "Those who believe [i.e., Muslims] and those who follow the Jewish scriptures, and the Christians and the Sabians, and who believe in God and the Last Day and work righteousness, shall have their reward with their Lord, on them shall be no fear, nor shall they grieve." [But in keeping with other Medinan chapters, it also contains much that is intolerant, and which I quote below.]

Unfortunately, as he gained in confidence and increased his political and military power, Muhammad turned from being a "persuader to being a legislator and warrior, dictating obedience." The Medinan chapters such as suras 2, 4, 5, 8, 9, 22, and 47 reveal Muhammad at his most belligerent, dogmatic, and intolerant.

Muslim theologians are unanimous in declaring that no religious toleration was extended to the idolaters of Arabia at the time of Muhammad. The only choice given them was death or the acceptance of Islam. This total intolerance never seems to be taken into consideration by the apologists of Islam when they lay claim to Islamic tolerance. Unbelievers in general are shown no mercy in the Koran, which is full of lurid descriptions of the punishments awaiting such pagans.

22.9: "As for the unbelievers for them garments of fire shall be cut and there shall be poured over their heads boiling water whereby whatever is in their bowels and skins shall be dissolved and they will be punished with hooked iron-rods."

The Koran also enjoins all Muslims to fight and kill nonbelievers.

47.4: "When you meet the unbelievers, strike off their heads; then when you have made wide slaughter among them, carefully tie up the remaining captives."

Christians and Jews in the Koran

Christians are marginally better regarded than the Jews, but the Koran still accuses them of falsifying the scriptures.

5.75: "They surely are infidels who say, 'God is the third of three'; for there is but one God; and if they do not refrain from what they say, a severe punishment shall light on those who are unbelievers."

They are also accused of worshipping Jesus as the son of God, and like the Jews, as they have been led astray, so they must be brought back to the true religion, that is, Islam.

According to the Koran, Jews have an intense hatred of all true Muslims, and as a punishment for their sins, some of the Jews had, in the past, been changed into apes and swine (sura 5.63), and others will have their hands tied to their necks and be cast into the fire on Judgment Day. The attitude enjoined upon the Muslims toward the Jews can only be described as anti-Semitic, and it certainly was not conducive to a better understanding, tolerance, or co-existence.

5.51: "Believers, do not take Jews or Christians as friends They are but one another's friends. If anyone of you takes them for his friends, then he is surely one of them. God will not guide evil-doers."

5.56–64: "O Believers, do not take as your friends the infidels or those who received the Scriptures before you [Jews and Christians] and who scoff and jest at your religion, but fear God if you are believers. Nor those who when you call them to prayer, make it an object of mirth and derision. This is only because they are a people who do not understand. Say: 'People of the Book: isn't it true that you hate us simply because we believe in God, and in what He has sent down to us, and in what He has revealed to others before; and because most of you are evil-doers?'

"Why don't their rabbis and doctors of law forbid them from uttering sinful words and eating unlawful food? Evil indeed are their works.

" 'The hand of God is chained up,' claim the Jews. Their own hands shall be chained up—and they shall be cursed for saying such a thing."

Jews are often accused, in the Koran, of perverting the scriptures and holding doctrines they never held.

9.29, 30: "Declare war upon those to whom the Scriptures were revealed but believe neither in God nor the Last Day, and who do not forbid that which God and His Apostle have forbidden, and who refuse to acknowledge the true religion [Islam] until they pay the poll-tax without reservation and are totally subjugated.

"The Jews claim that Ezra is a son of God, and the Christians say, 'the Messiah is a son of God.' Those are their claims which do indeed resemble the sayings of the Infidels of Old. May God do battle with them! How they are deluded!"

And they fully deserve any punishment they get.

2.61: "Wretchedness and baseness were stamped upon them [that is, the Jews] and they drew on themselves the wrath of God. This was because they disbelieved the signs of God and slew the Prophets unjustly, and because they rebelled and transgressed."

4.160, 161: Because of the wickedness of certain Jews, and because they turn many from the way of God, We have forbidden them good and wholesome foods which were formerly allowed them; and because they have taken to usury, though they were forbidden it; and have cheated others of their possessions, We have prepared a grievous punishment for the Infidels amongst them."

Such are some of the sentiments expressed in the Koran, which remains for all Muslims, and not just "fundamentalists," the uncreated word of God Himself. It is valid for all times and places; its ideas are, according to all Muslims, absolutely true and beyond any criticism.

I have already described the treatment of the Jews by Muhammad, whose behavior is certainly not above reproach. The cold-blooded extermination of the

Banu Qurayza (between six and nine hundred men) and the expulsion of the Nadir and their later massacre (something often overlooked in the history books) are not signs of magnanimity or compassion. Muhammad's treatment of the Jews of the oasis of Khaybar served "as a model for the treaties granted by the Arab conquerors to the conquered peoples in territories beyond Arabia." Muhammad attacked the oasis in 628, had one of the leaders tortured to find the hidden treasures of the tribe, and then when the Jews surrendered, agreed to let them continue cultivating their oasis only if they gave him half their produce. Muhammad also reserved the right to cancel the treaty and expel the Jews whenever he liked. This treaty or agreement was called a "dhimma," and those who accepted it were known as "dhimmis." All non-Muslims who accepted Muslim supremacy and agreed to pay a tribute in return for "Muslim protection" will henceforth be referred to as dhimmis.

The second caliph, Umar, later expelled the Jews and the Christians from the Hijaz (containing the holy cities of Mecca and Medina) in 640, referring to the dhimma of Khaybar. He is said to have quoted the Prophet on the right to cancel any pact he wished, and the Prophet's famous saying: "Two religions shall not remain together in the peninsula of the Arabs." To this day, the establishment of any other religion in Saudi Arabia is forbidden.

Jihad[438]

The totalitarian nature of Islam is nowhere more apparent than in the concept of jihad, the holy war, whose ultimate aim is to conquer the entire world and submit it to the one true faith, to the law of Allah. To Islam alone has been granted the truth: there is no possibility of salvation outside it. It is the sacred duty—an incumbent religious duty established in the Koran and the traditions—of all Muslims to bring Islam to all humanity. Jihad is a divine institution, enjoined specially for the purpose of advancing Islam. Muslims must strive, fight, and kill in the name of God.

9.5-6: "Kill those who join other gods with God wherever you may find them."

4.76: "Those who believe fight in the cause of God."

8.12: "I will instill terror into the hearts of the Infidels, strike off their heads then, and strike off from them every fingertip."

8.39-42: "Say to the Infidels: If they desist from their unbelief, what is now past shall be forgiven them; but if they return to it, they have already before them the doom of the ancients! Fight then against them till strife be at an end, and the religion be all of it God's."

2.256: "But they who believe, and who fly their country, and fight in the cause of God may hope for God's mercy: and God is Gracious, Merciful."

It is a grave sin for a Muslim to shirk the battle against the unbelievers—those who do will roast in hell.

8.15, 16: "Believers, when you meet the unbelievers preparing for battle do not turn your backs to them. [Anyone who does] shall incur the wrath of God and hell shall be his home: an evil dwelling indeed."

9.39: "If you do not fight, He will punish you severely, and put others in your place."

Those who die fighting for the only true religion, Islam, will be amply rewarded in the life to come.

4.74: "Let those fight in the cause of God who barter the life of this world for that which is to come; for whoever fights on God's path, whether he is killed or triumphs, We will give him a handsome reward."

It is abundantly clear from many of the above verses that the Koran is not talking of metaphorical battles or of moral crusades: it is talking of the battlefield. To read such blood thirsty injunctions in a holy book is shocking.

Mankind is divided into two groups, Muslims and non-Muslims. The Muslims are members of the Islamic community, the umma, who possess territories in the Dar al-Islam, the Land of Islam, where the edicts of Islam are fully promulgated. The non-Muslims are the Harbi, people of the Dar al-Harb, the Land of Warfare, any country belonging to the infidels that has not been subdued by Islam but that, nonetheless, is destined to pass into Islamic jurisdiction, either by conversion or by war (Harb). All acts of war are permitted in the Dar al-Harb.

Once the Dar al-Harb has been subjugated, the Harbi become prisoners of war. The imam* can do what he likes to them according to the circumstances. Woe betide the city that resists and is then taken by the Islamic army by storm. In this case, the inhabitants have no rights whatsoever, and as Sir Steven Runciman says in his *The Fall of Constantinople, 1453.*

> The conquering army is allowed three days of unrestricted pillage; and the former places of worship, with every other building, become the property of the conquering leader; he may dispose of them as he pleases. Sultan Mehmet [after the fall of Constantinople in 1453 allowed] his soldiers the three days of pillage to which they were entitled. They poured into the city. . . . They slew everyone that they met in the streets, men, women and children without discrimination. The blood ran in rivers down the steep streets. . . . But soon the lust for slaughter was assuaged. The soldiers realized that captives and precious objects would bring them greater profits.[439]

In other cases, those conquered in war are sold into slavery, exiled, or treated as dhimmis, who are tolerated as second-class subjects as long as they pay a regular tribute.

---

*A Muslim priest who performs the regular service of the mosque.

The Islamic Conquests

We have already alluded to Patricia Crone's analysis of the causes of the Arab conquests. Here, I shall refer to the thesis put forward by the economist Joseph Schumpeter[440] (1883–1950), a thesis that Bousquet found convincing and important enough to translate into French. My summary is based on Bousquet's French version.

According to Schumpeter (1950), the Arabs had always been a race of warriors who lived by pillage and the exploitation of settled populations. Islam was a war machine that did not stop at anything once it had been set going. War is a normal activity in such a military theocracy. The Arabs did not even search for a motive to conduct their wars; their social organization needed war, and without victories it would have collapsed. Here we have expansionism denuded of any concrete objective, brutal, and born of a necessity in its past. The Arab conquests would have existed without Islam. Certain particular details of Arab imperialism can be explained by the words of the Prophet but its force lay elsewhere. Muhammad would not have succeeded had he preached humility and submission. For the Arab warriors, "true" meant successful, and "false" meant unsuccessful. Thus religion was not the prime cause for the conquests, but rather an ancient warrior instinct.

It is ironic that the early heroes of Islam were, in fact, not at all interested in religion: Khalid, the general successful against the Byzantines has been described as someone who "cared for nothing but war and did not want to learn anything else." The same goes for Amr b. al-As, the conqueror of Egypt, and Othman b. Talha, who amassed a fortune from the conquests. As Wensinck[441] realistically put it, "The more clear-sighted inhabitants of Mekka already foresaw shortly after the unsuccessful siege of Medina that this fact was the turning point in [the Prophet] Muhammed's career. It is not strange therefore that men like Khalid b. al-Walid, Othman b. Talha and Amr b. al-As went over to Islam even before the capture of Mekka. Not much importance is to be attached to the story of their conversion" (1932).

EARLY CONQUESTS

The patriarch Sophronius of Jerusalem (634–638) saw the invaders as "godless barbarians" who burnt churches, destroyed monasteries, profaned crosses, and horribly blasphemed against Christ and the church." In 639, thousands died as a result of the famine and the plague consequent to the destruction and pillage.

After the death of the Prophet, the caliph Abu Bakr organized the invasion of Syria. During the campaign of 634, the entire region between Gaza and Caesarea was devastated; four thousand peasants—Christians, Jews, and Samaritans who were simply defending their land—were massacred. During the campaigns in Mesopotamia between 635 and 642, monasteries were sacked, the monks were killed, and Monophysite Arabs executed or forced to convert. In Elam the population was put to the sword, at Susa all the dignitaries suffered the same fate.

We are better informed of the conquest of Egypt by Amr b. al-As, thanks to the "Chronicle of John," Bishop of Nikiu, written between 693 and 700. For John, the Muslim yoke was "heavier than the yoke which had been laid on Israel by Pharaoh." As Amr advanced into Egypt, he captured the town of Behnesa, near the Fayum, and exterminated the inhabitants: "whoever gave himself up to them [the Muslims] was massacred, they spared neither the old, nor the women or children."[442] Fayum and Aboit suffered the same fate. At Nikiu, the entire population was put to the sword. The Arabs took the inhabitants of Cilicia into captivity. In Armenia, the entire population of Euchaita was wiped out. Seventh-century Armenian chronicles recount how the Arabs decimated the populations of Assyria and forced a number of inhabitants to accept Islam, and then wrought havoc in the district of Daron, southwest of Lake Van. In 642, it was the town of Dvin's turn to suffer. In 643, the Arabs came back, bringing "extermination, ruin, and slavery." Michael the Syrian tells us how Mu'awiya sacked and pillaged Cyprus and then established his domination by a "great massacre."

It was the same ghastly spectacle in North Africa: Tripoli was pillaged in 643; Carthage was razed to the ground and most of its inhabitants killed.

Anatolia, Mesopotamia, Syria, Iraq, and Iran presented a similar spectacle.

INDIA

On the evidence of Baladhuri's account of the conquest of Sind, there were certainly massacres in the towns of Sind when the Arabs first arrived.

C. E. Bosworth[443]

The Muslim conquest of Sind was masterminded by Hajjaj, the governor of Iraq, and effected by his commander Muhammad b. Qasim in A.D. 712. Qasim's instructions were to "bring destruction on the unbelievers . . . [and] to invite and induce the infidels to accept the true creed, and belief in the unity of God . . . and whoever does not submit to Islam, treat him harshly and cause injury to him till he submits."[444]

After the capture of the port of Debal, the Muslim army took three days to slaughter the inhabitants; thereafter Qasim became more tolerant, allowing many to continue their professions and practice their religion. This was not acceptable to Hajjaj, who, on receiving Qasim's report of his victory, wrote back:

My dear cousin, I have received your life-augmenting letter. On its receipt my gladness and joy knew no bounds. It increased my pride and glory to the highest degree. It appears from your letter that all the rules made by you for the comfort and convenience of your men are strictly in accordance with religious law. But the way of granting pardon prescribed by the law is different from the one adopted by you, for you go on giving pardon to everybody, high or low, without any discretion between a friend and a foe. The great God says in the Koran [47.4]: "O True believers, when you encounter the unbelievers, strike off their heads." The above command of the Great God is a great command and must be respected and followed. You should not be so fond of showing mercy, as to nullify the virtue of the act. Henceforth grant pardon to no one of the enemy and spare none of them, or else all will consider you a weakminded man. Concluded with compliments. Written by Nafia in the year ninety-three.

Later, Hajjaj returns to the same theme: "My distinct orders are that all those who are fighting men should be assassinated, and their sons and daughters imprisoned and retained as hostages." Obedient to a fault, Qasim, on his arrival at the town of Brahminabad, "ordered all the men belonging to the military classes to be beheaded with swords. It is said that about 6000 fighting men were massacred on this occasion, some say 16000. The rest were pardoned."

Mahmud of Ghazni (971–1030)

The real conquest of India by the Muslims dates from the beginning of the eleventh century. In A.D. 1000, the head of a Turco-Afghan dynasty, Mahmud of Ghazni, first passed through India like a whirlwind, destroying, pillaging, and massacring. He justified his actions by constant references to the Koranic injunctions to kill idolaters, whom he had vowed to chastise every year of his life. As Vincent Smith put it, "Mahmud was a zealous Muslim of the ferocious type then prevalent, who felt it to be a duty as well as pleasure to slay idolaters. He was also greedy of treasure and took good care to derive a handsome profit from his holy wars." In the course of seventeen invasions, in the words of Alberuni, the scholar brought by Mahmud to India: "Mahmud utterly ruined the prosperity of the country, and performed there wonderful exploits, by which the Hindus became like atoms of dust scattered in all directions, and like a tale of old in the mouth of the people. Their scattered remains cherish, of course, the most inveterate aversion toward all Muslims."[445]

Mahmud began by capturing King Jaipal in the Punjab, then invaded Multan in 1004. On conquering the district of Ghur, he forcibly converted the inhabitants to Islam. Mahmud accumulated vast amounts of plunder from the Hindu temples he desecrated, such as that of Kangra.

Mathura, the holy city of Krishna, was the next victim. "In the middle of the city there was a temple larger and finer than the rest, which can neither be described nor painted." The Sultan [Mahmud] was of the opinion that 200 years would have been required to build it. The idols included "five of red gold, each five yards high," with eyes formed of priceless jewels.

"The Sultan gave orders that all the temples should be burnt with naphtha and fire, and levelled with the ground." Thus perished works of art which must have been among the noblest monuments of ancient India.[446]

At the battle of Somnath, the site of another celebrated Hindu temple, 50,000 were killed as Mahmud assuaged his lust for booty.

Mahmud was equally ferocious with those whom he considered heretics, such as Dawud of Multan. In 1010, Mahmud invaded Dawud's kingdom and slaughtered a great number of his heretical subjects.

Although Muslim historians see him as one of the glories of Islam, in reality, Mahmud was little more than an avaricious bandit undeserving of admiration.

Firuz Shah

In 1351, Firuz Shah ascended the throne and became ruler of the North of India. Though in many ways an enlightened man, when it came to religion he was a bigot of the first order. He is said to have made "the laws of the Prophet his guide." He indulged in wholesale slave-raiding, and is said to have had 180,000 slaves in his city, all of whom "became Muslims." But, as Vincent Smith[447] says, he could be most savage when his religious zeal was aroused. He seized a number of Shias: some he executed, others he lectured, and their books he burned. He caused the ulama to kill a man who claimed to be the Mahdi, "and for this good action," he wrote, "I hope to receive future reward." He went to visit a village where a Hindu religious fair was being held, which was even attended by some "graceless Musalmans." Firuz Shah wrote: "I ordered that the leaders of these people and the promoters of this abomination should be put to death. I forbade the infliction of any severe punishment on the Hindus in general, but I destroyed their idol temples and instead thereof raised mosques."

Later a Brahman who had practiced his rites in public was burned alive.

Firuz Shah was simply carrying on the tradition of the early Muslim invaders, and he sincerely believed "that he served God by treating as a capital crime the public practice of their religion by the vast majority of his subjects [i.e., Hindus]."

Firuz Shah also bribed a vast number of Hindus into embracing Islam, by exempting those who converted from the jizya or poll-tax, which was otherwise rigorously enforced, even on the Brahmans.

Vincent Smith (1985) sums up Firuz Shah in this way:

> Firuz Shah, when due allowance is made for his surroundings and education, could not have escaped from the theory and practice of religious intolerance. It was not possible for him to rise, as Akbar did, to the conception that the ruler of Hindustan should cherish all his subjects alike, whether Muslim or Hindu, and allow every man absolute freedom, not only of conscience but of public worship. The Muslims of the fourteenth century were still dominated by the ideas current in the early days of Islam, and were convinced that the tolerance of idolatry was a sin.

Akbar the Great (1542–1605)

It is significant and ironic that the most tolerant of all the Muslim rulers in the history of India was also the one who moved farthest away from orthodox Islam and, in the end, rejected it for an eclectic religion of his own devising.

Akbar abolished the taxes on Hindu pilgrims at Muttra and remitted the jizya or poll-tax on non-Muslims.

Akbar had shown an early interest in religions other than the rigid Islam he had grown up in. Under the influence of freethinkers at his court like Abul Fazl and Muslim and Hindu mysticism, Akbar developed his interest in comparative religion to the extent of building a special "house of worship" in which to hold religious discussions. At first, the discussions were restricted to Muslim divines, who thoroughly disgraced themselves by their childish behavior. Akbar was profoundly disgusted, for their comportment seemed to cast doubt on Islam itself. Now Akbar decided to include Hindus, Jains, Zoroastrians, Jews, and eventually three Jesuit fathers from the Portuguese colony of Goa. The Jesuit fathers were treated with the utmost respect; Akbar even kissed the Bible and other Christian holy images—something totally revolting to an orthodox Muslim. One of the Jesuits became a tutor to Akbar's son.

There were further acts that alarmed and angered the Muslims. First, Akbar proclaimed the Infallibility Decree, which authorized the emperor to decide with binding authority any question concerning the Muslim religion, provided the ruling should be in accordance with some verse of the Koran. Second, Akbar again scandalized the Muslims by displacing the regular preacher at the mosque and mounting the pulpit himself, reciting verses composed by Faizi, the brother of the freethinking Abul Fazl.

The Muslim chiefs in the Bengal now considered Akbar an apostate and rose up in revolt against him. When he had crushed the rebellion, Akbar felt totally free to do what he wanted. And, in the words of V. Smith,[448] "He promptly took advantage of his freedom by publically showing his contempt and dislike for the Muslim religion, and by formally promulgating a new political creed of his own, adherence to which involved the solemn renunciation of Islam." Akbar rejected the Muslim chronology, establishing a new one that started from his accession. He further outraged the Muslims by issuing coins with the ambiguous phrase "Allahu Akbar," a frequent religious invocation known as the Takbir, which normally means "God is Great" (akbar = great). However, since Akbar was also the emperor's name, "Allahu Akbar "could also mean "Akbar is God."

Throughout his reign Akbar aimed at abating hostility toward Hindus, and his own vague religion was "a conscious effort to seem to represent all his people." He adopted Hindu and Parsee (Zoroastrian) festivals and practices. Thus it is not surprising that "his conduct at different times justified Christians, Hindus, Jains, and Parsis [Parsees] in severally claiming him as one of themselves." Akbar's driving principle was universal toleration, and all the Hindus, Christians, Jains, and Parsees enjoyed full liberty of conscience and of public worship. He married Hindu princesses, abolished pilgrim dues, and employed Hindus in high office. The Hindu princesses were even allowed to practice their own religious rites inside the palace. "No pressure was put on the princes of Amber, Marwar, or Bikaner to adopt Islam, and they were freely entrusted with the highest military commands and the most responsible administrative offices. That was an entirely new departure, due to Akbar himself."

Aurangzeb (1618–1707)

Akbar's great-grandson, Aurangzeb, was, in total contrast, a Muslim puritan, who wished to turn his empire into a land of orthodox Sunni Islam. Aurangzeb ruled in accordance with the principles laid down by the early caliphs. Once again, we enter the world of Islamic intolerance: temples are destroyed (during the campaigns of 1679–80, at Udaipur 123 were destroyed, at Chitor 63, at Jaipur 66), and non-Muslims become second-class citizens in their own country. The imperial bigot—to use Smith's phrase[449]—reimposed the "hated jizya,or polltax on non-Muslims, which Akbar had wisely abolished early in his reign." Aurangzeb's aim was to curb the infidels and demonstrate the "distinction between a land of Islam and a land of unbelievers."

"To most Hindus Akbar is one of the greatest of the Muslim emperors of India and Aurangzeb one of the worst; to many Muslims the opposite is the case. To an outsider there can be little doubt that Akbar's way was the right one. . . . Akbar disrupted the Muslim community by recognizing that India is not an Islamic country: Aurangzeb disrupted India by behaving as though it were."[450]

Buddhism and Buddhists

Between 1000 and 1200 Buddhism disappeared from India, through the combined effects of its own weaknesses, a revived Hinduism and Mohammedan persecution.
                                                                    Edward Conze[451]

[Buddhism in India] declined after Moslem conquest of Sindh, A.D. 712, and finally suppressed by Moslem persecution A.D. 1200.
                                                                    Christmas Humphreys[452]

It is partly, no doubt, because of the furor islamicus that post-Gupta remains are surprisingly few in Bihar.
                                                                    J. C. Harle[453]

Qutb ud din Aibak, described as "merciless and fanatical," sent his general, Muhammad Khilji, to the northern state of Bihar to continue the Muslim conquests that began in the late twelfth century. Buddhism was the main religion of Bihar. In 1193, the Muslim general, considering all Buddhist monks idolaters, put most of them to the sword, and destroyed a great library.

The ashes of the Buddhist sanctuaries at Sarnath near Benares still bear witness to the rage of the image-breakers. Many noble monuments of the ancient civilisation of India were irretrievably wrecked in the course of the early Muslim invasions. Those invasions were fatal to the existence of Buddhism as an organized religion in northern India, where its strength resided chiefly in Bihar and certain adjoining territories. The monks who escaped massacre fled, and were scattered over Nepal, Tibet, and the south.[454]

The Muslim conquests of Central Asia also put an end to its Buddhist art. As early as the eighth century, the monasteries of Kizil were destroyed by the Muslim ruler of Kashgar, and as Benjamin Rowland[455] says, "by the tenth century only the easternmost reaches of Turkestan had escaped the rising tide of Mohammedan conquest." The full tragedy of these devastations is brought out by the words of Rowland: "The ravages of the Mongols, and the mortifying hand of Islam that has caused so many cultures to wither forever, aided by the process of nature, completely stopped the life of what must for a period of centuries have been one of the regions of the earth most gifted in art and religion."

Scholars, Historians, and the Dhimmis

Bat Ye'or is an independent scholar who has been working on the question of dhimmis for the last twenty years, starting with the history of Jews in Egypt in 1971. This was followed by *Le Dhimmi: Profil de l'opprimé en Orient et en Afrique du Nord depuis la conquete arabe* in 1980, with an enlarged English edition in 1985, under the title *The Dhimmi, Jews and Christians under Islam*. In 1991 and 1994 appeared, respectively, *Les Chretientés d' Orient entre Jihad et Dhimmitude* and *Juifs et Chretiens sous l'Islam, les dhimmis face au defi intégriste*.

Jacques Ellul,[456] in his preface to Bat Ye'or's *The Dhimmi, Jews and Christians under Islam*, tells an interesting story. Ellul reviewed the book when it first came out for the famous French newspaper *Le Monde*.

> In reponse to that review I received a very strong letter from a colleague, a well-known orientalist, informing me that the book was purely polemical and could not be regarded seriously. His criticisms, however, betrayed the fact that he had not read the book, and the interesting thing about his arguments (based on what I had written) was that they demonstrated, on the contrary, the serious nature of this work. First of all, he began with an appeal to authority, referring me to certain works whose scholarship he regarded as unquestionable (those of Professors S. D. Goitein, B. Lewis and N. Stillman), that in his opinion adopt a positive attitude toward Islam and its tolerance toward non-Muslims.

It is not surprising that the colleague of Jacques Ellul was disturbed, since the works of Bat Ye'or show with ample documentation the massacres of the early conquests; the subsequent humiliations of the dhimmis; the oppressive fiscal system; the looting and pillaging of homes, churches, and synagogues; and the whole punctuated with forced conversions, which made the lives of the non-Muslims such an ordeal.

However, apologists of Islam will be disappointed if they consult the works of the scholars mentioned by Ellul, hoping to find some sort of exoneration of Islam. Norman Stillman's book *The Jews of Arab Lands: A History and Source Book* (1979) is a general historical survey from the seventh to the nineteenth century, and a source book of translations of the relevant documents. Reviewing Stillman, C. E. Bosworth said: "This is a splendid book, even though the subject is in many ways a *monument to human intolerance and fanaticism*" [my emphasis]. Stillman, on the whole, lets the facts speak for themselves, and the picture that emerges is not at all flattering to Islam:

> The invasion of the Middle East [by the Arabs] was not by any means a joyous, liberating experience. There was a great deal of death and destruction. The inhabitants of towns taken by storm were either killed or led into captivity, and their property was forfeited.[457]

> The jizya and kharaj [taxes] were a crushing burden for the non-Muslim peasantry who eked out a bare living in a subsistence economy.[458]

> Muslim authorities were concerned above all that taxes be paid and that dhimmi subjects acknowledge in a variety of ways, some more and some less humiliating, the dominion of Islam. As long as the non-Muslims complied, they were accorded a good measure of internal self-rule. However, even in the conduct of their own communal affairs, they were not entirely free of government supervision and, at times, downright interference.[459]

> Furthermore, there was a tenuousness in the cordiality of interfaith relationships. The non-Muslim could never entirely disembarrass himself of his dhimmi status.[460]

> The position of a Jewish community could also become precarious in times of civil strife, famine, or other catastrophe. Times of crises brought popular religious frenzy to its height. The Jews were a small, defenseless minority whose status as infidels and humble tribute bearers was defined by Islamic law.

But what of the so-called Golden Age of mutual respect?

> Anti-Semitism, that is, 'the hatred of Jews qua Jews,' did exist in the medieval Arab world *even in the period of greatest tolerance*. . . . Outright persecution . . . was rare but there was always that uncertain possibility. At the whim of the ruler, the harshest interpretations of the sumptuary laws could be strictly enforced. . . . Even in the best of times, dhimmis in all walks of life and at every level of society could suddenly and rudely be reminded of their true status.[461]

Stillman does make one claim refuted by Bat Ye'or. According to Stillman,[462] there were no more than half a dozen forced conversions of Jews over a period of thirteen centuries. Even Stillman concedes that under the Almohad caliphs al-Mumin (d. 1165), Abu Yaqub (d. 1184), and al-Mansur (d. 1199), there were indeed forced conversions. Even if we assume there was only one conversion per reign, that still makes three. In Yemen the Jews were forced to choose between death and conversion to Islam in 1165 and 1678, and in Aden in 1198. Bat Ye'or[463] continues: "There are Muslims in Tripolitania and elsewhere who are descendants of Jews forcibly converted at different periods. The Jews of Tabriz were obliged to convert in 1291 and 1318, and those of Baghdad in 1333 and 1344. Throughout Persia, forced conversions from the sixteenth century to the beginning of the twentieth century decimated the Christian and, even more, the Jewish communities."

Elsewhere, Bat Ye'or[464] writes: "In 1617 and in 1622, Persian Jews, denounced as apostates, suffered a wave of forced conversions and persecution. . . . During the reign of Shah Abbas II (1642–1666) all the Jews of Persia were forced to convert, between 1653 and 1666." There were also forced conversions in Meshed in 1839 (and in the 1840s, according to Lewis) (p. 153).

That makes more than half a dozen! We are, of course, talking of Jews only; the forced conversion of Christians, Hindus, Zoroastrians, and others is another, even more grave, matter.

Bernard Lewis has written a great deal on dhimmis and, more specifically, on Jews under Islam. In his *The Jews of Islam* (1984), Lewis points[465] out that there was never a question of "equality" between Muslims and non-Muslims.

> Traditional Islamic societies neither accorded such equality nor pretended that they were so doing. Indeed, in the old order, this would have been regarded not as a merit but as a dereliction of duty. How could one accord the same treatment to those who follow the true faith and those who willfully reject it? This would be a theological as well as a logical absurdity.
>
> Discrimination was always there, permanent and indeed necessary, inherent in the system and institutionalized in law and practice.
>
> The rank of a full member of society was restricted to free male Muslims. Those who lacked any of these three essential qualifications—that is, the slave, the woman or the unbeliever—were not equal. The three basic inequalities of master and slave, man and woman, believer and unbeliever—were not merely admitted; they were established and regulated by holy law.

"Tolerance" in this context has a negative connotation—the Jews and Christians were there on sufferance. Bat Ye'or points out the difference between "tolerance" and "rights"—while "tolerance" is revocable, rights are inalienable. Bernard Lewis makes more or less the same point. He contrasts the notion of tolerance with that of genuine coexistence: "Tolerance means that a dominant group whether defined by faith or race or other criteria, allows members of other groups some—but rarely if ever all—of the rights and privileges enjoyed by its own members. Coexistence means equality between the different groups composing a political society as an inherent natural right of all of them—to grant it is no merit, to withhold it or limit it is an offense."[466]

It is true Lewis does write, early on, in *The Jews of Islam*: "persecution, that is to say, violent and active repression was rare and atypical."[467] But a little later, Lewis contradicts himself: "Under the Safavid shahs they [the Jews, Christians, and Zoroastrians] were subject to frequent vexations and persecutions, and at times to forced conversion."[468] (Perhaps the adjective "frequent" does not qualify "persecutions.") And toward the end of the book, Lewis tells us that "the Alliance [an international Jewish organization] records include *numerous* stories of ill-treatment, humiliation, and persecution [of Jews]" (my emphasis).[469]

Lewis also tends to play down the violence suffered by the non-Muslims. Confining ourselves to Jews, we can only remind Lewis of the massacre of more than 6,000 Jews in Fez (Morocco) in 1033; of the hundreds of Jews killed between 1010 and 1013 near Cordoba and other parts of Muslim Spain; of the massacre of the entire Jewish community of roughly 4,000 in Granada during the Muslim riots of 1066. Referring to the latter massacre, Robert Wistrich writes: "This was a disaster, as serious as that which overtook the Rhineland Jews thirty years later during the First Crusade, yet it has rarely received much scholarly attention." Wistrich, who takes Bat Ye'or's research seriously, continues:

> In Kairouan (Tunisia) the Jews were persecuted and forced to leave in 1016, returning later only to be expelled again. In Tunis in 1145 they were forced to convert or to leave, and during the following decade there were fierce anti-Jewish persecutions throughout the country. A similar pattern of events occurred in Morocco after the massacre of Jews in Marrakesh in 1232. Indeed, in the Islamic world from Spain to the Arabian peninsula the looting and killing of Jews, along with punitive taxation, confinement to ghettos, the enforced wearing of distinguishing marks on clothes (an innovation in which Islam preceded medieval Christendom), and other humiliations were rife.[470]

Discriminatory Taxes

KHARAJ

The kharaj was a kind of land tax that had both a fiscal and symbolic role. Under kharaj, the peasant no longer owned the land but worked it as a tenant. The kharaj also symbolized the the God-conferred rights of the conquerors over the land of the conquered and the infidels. The peasants were theoretically protected, but, in periods of instability, they suffered the most

JIZYA

The jizya was a poll-tax that, in accordance with the Koran 9.29 ("until they pay the jizya from their hand, being brought low"), had to be paid individually at a humiliating public ceremony to remind the dhimmis that they were inferior to the believers, that is, the Muslims. The Muslim commentator on the Koran, al-Zamakhshari (1075–1144), interpreted sura 9.29 to mean "the jizya shall be taken from them with belittlement and humiliation. [The dhimmi] shall come in person, walking not riding. When he pays, he shall stand, while the tax collector sits. The collector shall seize him by the scruff of the neck, shake him, and say: 'Pay the jizya!' and when he pays it he shall be slapped on the nape of his neck."

OTHER TAXES

Apart from paying higher commercial and travel taxes than Muslims, the dhimmis were subject to other forms of fiscal oppression. In periods of economic hardship, the Muslim rulers often had recourse to arbitrary taxes on dhimmis. Church leaders were imprisoned and tortured until ransoms were paid for them.

These taxes proved such a crushing burden that many villages were abandoned as the villagers fled to the hills or tried to lose themselves in the anonymity of large towns to escape the tax collector. In Lower Egypt, for example, the Copts, utterly ruined by the taxes, revolted in 832. The Arab governor ruthlessly suppressed the insurrection—burning their villages, their vineyards, gardens, and churches. Those not massacred were deported.

Public Office

Various hadith forbid a dhimmi to exercise any authority over a Muslim. Various Koranic verses such as 3.28 were used to bar dhimmis from public office. Despite this, we find that dhimmis held high office. However, in the Middle Ages, any appointment of a dhimmi to a high post often resulted in public outcries, fanaticism, and violence, as for example, in Granada in 1066, Fez in 1275 and 1465, Iraq in 1291, and frequently in Egypt between 1250 and 1517. Many dhimmis accepted conversion to Islam in order to keep their posts.

Inequality before the Law

In all litigation between a Muslim and a dhimmi, the validity of the oath or testimony of the dhimmi was not recognized. In other words, since a dhimmi was not allowed to give evidence against a Muslim, his Muslim opponent always got off scot-free. The dhimmi was forced to bribe his way out of the accusations. Muslims were convinced of their own superiority over all non-Muslims, and this was enshrined in law. For example, any fine imposed on a Muslim for a crime was automatically halved if the victim was a dhimmi. No Muslim could be executed for having committed any crime against a dhimmi. Accusations of blasphemy against dhimmis were quite frequent and the penalty was capital punishment. Since his testimony was not accepted in court, the dhimmi was forced to convert to save his life. Conversely, "in practice if not in law, a dhimmi would often be sentenced to death if he dared raise his hand against a Muslim, even in legitimate self-defence."[471] Even the accidental killing of a Muslim could condemn the whole non-Muslim community to death or exile.

Though a Muslim man may marry a Christian or Jewish woman, a non-Muslim may not marry a Muslim woman. The penalty for such a marriage, or any such sexual relationship, was death.

THE PACT OF UMAR

Some of the disabilities of the dhimmis are summarized in the "Pact of Umar," which was probably drawn up in the eighth century under Umar b. Abd al-Aziz (ruled 717–20):

> We shall not build in our cities or in their vicinity any new monasteries, churches, hermitages, or monks' cells. We shall not restore, by night or by day, any of them that have fallen into ruin or which are located in the Muslims' quarters.
>
> We shall keep our gates wide open for the passerby and travelers. We shall provide three days' food and lodging to any Muslims who pass our way.
>
> We shall not shelter any spy in our churches or in our homes, nor shall we hide him from the Muslims.
>
> We shall not teach our children the Koran.
>
> We shall not hold public religious ceremonies. We shall not seek to proselytise anyone. We shall not prevent any of our kin from embracing Islam if they so desire.
>
> We shall show deference to the Muslims and shall rise from our seats when they wish to seat down.
>
> We shall not attempt to resemble the Muslims in any way. . . .
>
> We shall not ride on saddles.
>
> We shall not wear swords or bear weapons of any kind, or ever carry them with us.
>
> We shall not sell wines.
>
> We shall clip the forelocks of our head.
>
> We shall not display our crosses or our books anywhere in the Muslims' thoroughfares or in their marketplaces. We shall only beat our clappers in our churches very quietly. We shall not raise our voices when reciting the service in our churches, nor when in the presence of Muslims. Neither shall we raise our voices in our funeral processions.
>
> We shall not build our homes higher than theirs.

To which was added, "anyone who deliberately strikes a Muslim will forfeit the protection of this pact."

Even in their religious affairs, dihimmis were not entirely free. Muslims often blocked the appointment of religious leaders.

Nothing could be further from the truth than to imagine that the dhimmis enjoyed a secure and stable status permanently and definitively acquired—that they were forever protected and lived happily ever after. Contrary to this picture perpetrated by Islamic apologists, the status of dhimmis was very fragile indeed and was constantly under threat. The dhimmis were in constant danger of being enslaved. For example, when Amr conquered Tripoli in 643, he forced the Jews and Christians to hand over their women and children as slaves to the Arab army, and they were told to deduct this "handover" from the poll-tax, the dreaded "jizya." Between 652 and 1276, Nubia was forced to send an annual contingent of slaves to Cairo. The treaties concluded under the Umayyads and the Abbasids with the towns of Transoxiana, Sijistan, Armenia, and Fezzan (modern northwest Africa) all stipulated an annual tribute of slaves of both sexes. The principal source of the reservoir of slaves was the constant raids on the villages in the "dar al-harb," and the more disciplined military expeditions that more thoroughly mopped up the cities of the unbelievers. All the captives were deported en masse. In 781, at the sack of Ephesus, 7,000 Greeks were deported in captivity. After the capture of Amorium in 838, there were so many captives that the Caliph al-Mutasim ordered them to be auctioned in batches of five and ten. At the sack of Thessalonica in 903, 22,000 Christians were divided among the Arab chieftains or sold into slavery. In 1064, the Seljuk Sultan, Alp Arslan, devastated Georgia and Armenia. Those he did not take as prisoners, he executed.

The literary sources for Palestine, Egypt, Mesopotamia, Armenia, and later Anatolia and Safavid Persia reveal that those families who could not pay the crushing jizya or poll-tax were obliged to hand over their children and to "deduct" it from the jizya.

For at least three hundred years, Christians suffered one other humiliation not often discussed, a process known as "devshirme." It was introduced by the Ottoman Sultan Orkhan (1326–1359) and consisted of the periodic taking of a fifth of all Christian children in the conquered territories. Converted to Islam, these children, between the ages of fourteen and twenty, were trained to be janissaries or infantry men. These periodic abductions eventually became annual. The Christian children were taken from among the Greek aristocracy and from the Serbs, Bulgarians, Armenians, and Albanians, and often from among the children of the priests.

On a fixed date, all the fathers were ordered to appear with their children in the public square. The recruiting agents chose the most sturdy and handsome children in the presence of a Muslim judge. Any father who shirked his duty to provide children was severely punished.

This system was open to all kinds of abuse. The recruiting agents often took more than the prescribed number of children and sold the "surplus" children back to their parents. Those unable to buy back their children had to accept their being sold into slavery. This institution was abolished in 1656; however, a parallel system, in which young children, between the ages of six and ten, were taken to be trained in the seraglio of the sultan, continued until the eighteenth century.

The number of children taken each year seems to have varied. Some scholars place it as high as 12,000 a year, others at 8,000, but there was probably an average of at least 1,000 a year. The devshirme is an obvious infringement of the rights of the dhimmis—a reminder that their rights were far from secure, once and for all.

Religious Matters

PLACES OF WORSHIP

In the late nineteenth century, al-Sharani[472] summed up the views of the four main Sunni schools on the question of the building of new churches and synagogues:

> All schools agree that it is not allowed to build new churches or synagogues in towns or cities of Islam. They differ whether this is permitted in the neighbourhood of towns. Malik, Shafe'i, and Ahmad do not permit it; Abu Hanifa says that if the place is a mile or less from a town, it is not permitted; if the distance is greater, it is. Another question is, whether it is allowed to restore ruinous or rebuild ruined churches or synagogues in Islamic countries. Abu Hanifa, Malik, and Shafe'i permit it. Abu Hanifa adds the condition that the church is in a place that surrendered peaceably; if it was conquered by force, it is not allowed. Ahmad . . . says that the restoration of the ruinous and the rebuilding of the ruined is never permitted.

The fate of churches and synagogues, as that of Christians and Jews, varied from country to country and ruler to ruler. Some Muslim rulers were very tolerant, others extremely intolerant. In A.D. 722, for example, Usama b. Zaid, the surveyor of taxes in Egypt, attacked convents and destroyed churches. But the caliph Hisham told him to leave the Christians in peace. Some caliphs not only respected the rights of non-Muslims, but very generously paid for the repairs of any churches destroyed by mob violence. Tritton also gives the example of Spain: "During the conquest of Spain the Muslims were much less tolerant. On one of his expeditions Musa destroyed every church and broke every bell. When Marida surrendered the Muslims took the property of those killed in the ambush, of those who fled to Galicia, of the churches, and the church jewels."[473]

Similarly, the caliph Marwan (ruled 744–750) looted and destroyed many monasteries in Egypt while fleeing the Abbasid army. He destroyed all the churches in Tana except one, and he asked three thousand dinars as the price for sparing that.

In A.D. 853 the caliph Mutawakkil ordered all new churches to be destroyed. As Tritton says, from an early date churches were liable to be razed to the ground for some caprice of the ruler. Often the Muslim mob took matters into its own hands. Tritton gives the following examples of riots in which religious buildings were destroyed. In 884 the convent of Kalilshu in Baghdad was destroyed, the gold and silver vessels stolen, and all wood in the building sold. In 924 the church and convent of Mary in Damascus were burned and plundered, and other churches wrecked. Further destruction occurred in Ramleh, Ascalon, Tinnis, and in Egypt during the invasion by Asad ud Din Shirkuh.

Al-Hakim biamr illah gave orders that the churches in his dominions should be destroyed. Their contents were seized and the vessels of gold and silver sold in the markets.... The church lands were confiscated and every one who asked for some got it. A Muslim historian reports that over thirty thousand churches which had been built by the Greeks were destroyed in Egypt, Syria and elsewhere. Bar Hebraeus is more modest, he only says thousands.[474]

The riot of 1321 in Cairo in which several churches were destroyed led in turn to the destruction of churches throughout Egypt—in all more than fifty churches suffered.

On the whole, Muslims disliked the public display of other forms of worship. Umar II and Mutawakkil tried, in vain, to suppress the commonest manifestations of Christianity. "The ringing of bells, the sounding of the ram's horn, and the public exhibition of crosses, icons, banners, and other religious objects were all prohibited."

FORCED CONVERSIONS AND PERSECUTIONS

We have already mentioned the forced conversions of Jews. Islamic history is also full of references to the forced conversion of Christians, Zoroastrians, and pagans. For instance, under al-Ma'mun in the ninth century the pagans of Harran had to choose between Islam and death. Tavernier, the seventeenth-century French traveler describes how in Anatolia, "Everyday there are numerous Greeks who are forced to become Turks."

Armenian Christians seemed to have suffered from particularly severe Muslim persecution. In 704-705, the caliph Walid I gathered together the nobles of Armenia in the church of St. Gregory in Naxcawan and the church of Xram on the Araxis and burned them to death. The rest were crucified and decapitated, while their women and children were taken as slaves. The Armenians suffered even more between 852 and 855.

Given the constant humiliation, degradation, and fiscal and social oppression, it is not surprising that many dhimmis sought a way out of their impossible situation by converting. But though technically not "forced" on pain of death or at the point of a sword, we can still consider these conversions as having been forced on the dhimmis. Surely, there is no moral difference between the two kinds of "forced conversions."

Each century has its own, full account of the horrors. In the eighth century we had the massacres in the Sind. In the ninth century, there were the massacres of Spanish Christians in and around Seville.

In the tenth, the persecutions of non-Muslims under the caliph al-Hakim are well known.

In the eleventh, the Jews of Grenada and Fez met the fate we have already alluded to; we might add that Mahmud destroyed the Hindus and their temples during the same period.

In the twelfth, the Almohads of North Africa spread terror wherever they went.

In the thirteenth, the Christians of Damascus were killed or sold into slavery, and their churches burned to the ground. The Sultan Baibars, whom Sir Steven Runciman calls "evil," not respecting his own guarantees of safety to the garrison of Safed if they surrendered to the Muslims, had all the population decapitated when they did surrender.

> From Toron he sent a troop to destroy the Christian village of Qara, between Homs and Damascus, which he suspected of being in touch with the Franks. The adult inhabitants were massacred and the children enslaved. When the Christians from Acre sent a deputation to ask to be allowed to bury the dead, he roughly refused, saying that if they wished for martyrs' corpses they would find them at home. To carry out his threat he marched down to the coast and slaughtered every Christian that fell into his hands.[475]

As for Baibar's and the Muslims' capture of Antioch in 1268, Runciman's says, "Even the Moslem chroniclers were shocked by the carnage that followed."

In the fourteenth and early fifteenth centuries, we have the terror spread by the infamous Timur the Lame, otherwise known as Tamerlane or the "bloody and insatiate Tamburlaine" of Marlowe's play. Tamerlane constantly referred to the Koran and tried to turn every one of his battles into a holy war, even though in many instances he was fighting fellow Muslims. At least in Georgia, he was able to give his campaign the color of a jihad. In 1400 Tamerlane devastated the country in and around Tifflis. In 1403, he returned to ravage the country again and destroyed seven hundred large villages and minor towns, massacring the inhabitants and razing to the ground all the Christian churches of Tifflis. Rene Grousset[476] summed up Tamerlane's peculiar character by saying that whereas the Mongols of the thirteenth century had killed simply because for centuries this had been the instinctive behavior of nomad herdsmen toward sedentary farmers, Tamerlane killed out of Koranic piety. To the ferocity of the cruel Mongols, Tamerlane added a taste for religious murder. Tamerlane "represents a synthesis, historically lacking up to now, of Mongol barbarity and Muslim fanaticism, and symbolizes that advanced form of primitive slaughter which is murder committed for the sake of an abstract ideology, as a duty and sacred mission."

In terms of non-Muslims, we note that he destroyed the town of Tana, at the mouth of the Don. All the Christians were enslaved and their shops and churches destroyed.

According to the "Zafer Nameh," our main source of information for Tamerlane's campaigns, written at the beginning of the fifteenth century, Tamerlane set forth to conquer India solely to make war on the enemies of the Muslim faith. He considered the Muslim rulers of northern India far too lenient toward pagans, that is to say, the Hindus. The "Zafer Nameh" tells us that "The Koran emphasizes that the highest dignity to which man may attain is to wage war in person upon the enemies of the Faith. This is why the great Tamerlane was always concerned to exterminate the infidels, as much to acquire merit as from love of glory."

Under the pretext that the hundred thousand Hindu prisoners at Delhi presented a grave risk to his army, Tamerlane ordered their execution in cold blood. He killed thousands, and had victory pillars built from the severed heads. On his way out of India, he sacked Miraj, pulled down the monuments, and flayed the Hindu inhabitants alive, "an act by which he fulfilled his vow to wage the Holy War." This strange champion of Islam, as Grousset calls him, plundered and massacred "through blindness or closemindedness to a certain set of cultural values."

Tamerlane systematically destroyed the Christians, and as a result the Nestorians and Jacobites of Mesopotamia have never recovered. At Sivas, 4,000 Christians were buried alive; at Tus there were 10,000 victims. Historians estimate the number of dead at Saray to be 100,000; at Baghdad 90,000; at Isfahan 70,000.

Zoroastrians

According to the "Tarikh-i Bukhara," a history of Bukhara written in about A.D. 944, Islam had to be enforced on the reluctant inhabitants of Bukhara. The Bukharans reverted to their original beliefs no less than four times: "The residents of Bukhara became Muslims. But they renounced [Islam] each time the Arabs turned back. Qutayba b. Muslim made them Muslim three times, [but] they renounced [Islam] again and became nonbelievers. The fourth time, Qutayba waged war, seized the city, and established Islam after considerable strife. . . . They espoused Islam overtly but practiced idolatry in secret."[477]

Many Zoroastrians were induced to convert by bribes, and later, out of economic necessity. Many of these "economic converts" were later executed for having adopted Islam to avoid paying the poll-tax and land tax.

In Khurasan and Bukhara, the Muslims destroyed Zoroastrian fire temples and constructed mosques on these sites. The "Tarikh-i Bukhara" records that there was considerable outrage at these acts of sacrilege, and a concerted resistance to the spread of Islam. One scholar sums up the situation thus: "Indeed, coexistence between Muslims and Zoroastrians was rarely peaceful, cooperation was fleeting, and conflict remained the prime form of intercommunal contact from the initial Arab conquest of Transoxiana until the late thirteenth century A.D." A similar situation existed in Khurasan: "The violent military conflicts between the forces of the Arab commander Abd Allah b. Amir and the local Iranian lords, combined later with the destruction of Zoroastrian religious institutions, produced lasting enmity between Muslims and Zoroastrians in Khurasan."

The early conquests of Zoroastrian Iran were punctuated with the usual massacres, as in Raiy.[478] If the town put up brave resistance to the Muslims, then very few men were spared. For example, at Sarakh, only a hundred men were granted amnesty, and the women were taken into captivity; the children taken into captivity were brought up as Muslims. At Sus a similar situation emerged—about a hundred men were pardoned, the rest killed. At Manadhir, all the men were put to the sword, and the women and children enslaved. At the conquest of Istakhr, more than 40,000 Iranians were slaughtered. The Zoroastrians suffered sporadic persecution, when their fire temples and priests were destroyed, for example, at Kariyan, Kumm, and at Idhaj. In a deliberate act of provocation the caliph al-Mutawakkil had cut down a tree putatively planted by Zoroaster himself. Sometimes the fire temples were converted into mosques.

The fiscal oppression of the Zoroastrians led to a series of uprisings against the Muslims in the eighth century. We might cite the revolts led by Bihafarid between 746 and 748 and the rising of Sinbadh in 755.

Forced conversions were also frequent, and the pressures for conversion often led to conflict and riots, as in Shiraz in 979. To escape persecution and the forced conversions many Zoroastrians emigrated to India, where, to this day, they form a much respected minority known as Parsis. Conditions for the Zoroastrians became even worse from the seventeenth century onwards. In the eighteenth century, their numbers, to quote the *Encyclopaedia of Islam* (2d ed.), "declined disastrously due to the combined effects of massacre, forced conversion and emigration."[479] By the nineteenth century they were living in total insecurity and poverty and suffered increasing discrimination. Zoroastrian merchants were liable for extra taxes; houses were frequently looted; they had to wear distinctive clothing; and were forbidden to build new houses or repair old ones.

The Golden Age?

All scholars agree, and even apologists of Islam cannot deny, that the situation of the dhimmis got progressively worse. Many scholars believe that as the Muslim world became weaker, the position of dhimmis deteriorated correspondingly. The same scholars would put the beginning of the decline at the time of the Crusades. This perception has had the unfortunate consequence of reinforcing the myth of the Golden Age, when supposedly total harmony reigned between the different faiths, especially in Muslim Spain. It is a lovely image, but, as Fletcher[480] put it, this won't do. "The witness of those who lived through the horrors of the Berber conquest, of the Almoravid invasion . . . must give it the lie. The simple and verifiable historical truth is that Moorish Spain was more often a land of turmoil than it was a land of tranquillity." Was there ever tolerance? "Ask the Jews of Grenada who were massacred in 1066, or the Christians who were deported by the Almoravids to Morocco in 1126 (like the Moriscos five centuries later)." I have already alluded to the general causes of the rise of this myth of Islamic tolerance. More specifically, the notion of the Golden Age of Moorish Spain was perpetrated in the nineteenth century by "newly and still imperfectly emancipated" Western European Jews as a means to chastise Western failings. Inevitably, there was a tendency to idealize Islam, to better contrast the situation of the

Jews in Europe and "to serve at once as a reproach and an encouragement to their somewhat dilatory Christian emancipators."[481]
Richard Fletcher has his own analysis.

> So the nostalgia of Maghribi writers was reinforced by the romantic vision of the nineteenth century. This could be flavoured with a dash of Protestant prejudice from the Anglo-Saxon world: it can be detected in Lane-Poole's reference to the Inquisition. . . . In the second half of the twentieth century a new agent of obfuscation makes its appearance: the guilt of the liberal conscience, which sees the evils of colonialism—assumed rather than demonstrated—foreshadowed in the Christian conquest of al-Andalus and the persecution of the Moriscos (but not, oddly, in the Moorish conquest and colonization). Stir the mix well together and issue it free to credulous academics and media persons throughout the western world. Then pour it generously over the truth. . . . *But Moorish Spain was not a tolerant and enlightened society even in its most cultivated epoch.* (my emphasis)[482]

Eighteenth, Nineteenth, and Twentieth Centuries

In general, as a logical consequence of centuries of contempt, humiliation, and persecution, the position of non-Muslims in the eighteenth, nineteenth, and twentieth centuries was very precarious indeed. As Lewis, talking of Jews, says,

> From the late eighteenth century through the nineteenth century, expulsion, outbreaks of mob violence, and even massacres became increasingly frequent. Between 1770 and and 1786 Jews were expelled from Jedda, most of them fleeing to the Yemen. In 1790 Jews were massacred in Tetuan, in Morocco; in 1828, in Baghdad. In 1834 a cycle of violence and pillage began in Safed. In 1839 a massacre of Jews took place in Meshed in Iran followed by the forced conversion of the survivors, and a massacre of Jews occurred in Barfurush in 1867. In 1840 the Jews of Damascus were subject to the first of a long series of blood libels in many cities. Other outbreaks followed in Morocco, Algeria, Tunisia, Libya, and the Arab countries of the Middle East.[483]

Coming to the twentieth century, we may mention the virulent anti-Jewish literature that has been produced in the last forty years in the Islamic world. Much of this hate-filled literature is in the form of translations from European languages of such works as Hitler's *Mein Kampf,* and "The Protocols of the Elders of Zion." But as Wistrich says, Muslim writers, "even when they exploit Western antisemitic images and concepts, usually manage to link these imported notions in a natural, even an organic manner, with ideas from within their own cultural tradition."[484]

MASSACRE OF THE ARMENIANS

Armenian Christians have been subject to persecution by the Muslims for centuries. Here I want to allude to the massacres of 1894, 1895, and 1896. Against a background of hostilities between Russia and Turkey, Armenians looked to Russia for protection. But this did not prevent the massacre of more than 250,000 Armenians in Sasun, Trapezunt, Edessa, Biredjik, Kharput, Niksar, and Wan. Many villages were burned down, and hundreds of churches plundered. Further massacres followed in 1904, and in 1909 when thirty thousand Armenians lost their lives at Adana. According to an article that appeared in *Revue Encyclopédique* in 1896, the massacres of 1894–1896 were deliberately planned and executed—it was no less than a methodical extermination of the Armenians.

Unable to support the idea of another nationality on Turkish soil, the Turks began the liquidation of Armenians, which ended in the infamous mass murders of 1915. These murders of 1915 have been described as the first case of genocide in the twentieth century. Much polemic surrounds the events of 1915, with historians like Bernard Lewis denying that it was "genocide" or "planned." Indeed, Lewis is standing trial in France for his position. Other historians and many Armenians insist that more than a million Armenians were systematically exterminated in cold blood—thousands were shot, drowned (including children), and thrown over cliffs; those who survived were deported or reduced to slavery. This is surely nothing less than genocide, a genocide that seems to have deeply impressed Hitler, and that may well have served as a model for the genocide of the Jews carried out by him.

This Armenian genocide was but the natural culmination of a divinely sanctioned policy toward non-Muslims. It was nothing less than a jihad, perpetrated by Muslims, who alone benefited from the booty: the possessions and houses of the victims, the land, and the enslavement of the women and children. It was not an isolated incident, but a deliberate policy to eliminate any nationalism among the dhimmis and to keep the conquered territory under Islamic jurisdiction. As Bat Ye'or says, "the inner logic of the jihad could not tolerate religious emancipation. Permanent war, the wickedness of the Dar al-Harb, and the inferiority of the conquered harbis constituted the three interdependent and inseparable principles underlying the expansion and political domination of the umma [the Muslim community]."[485]

Three Conclusions

We are now in a position to appreciate the conclusions of the three scholars we quoted here.

A. S. Tritton in his *The Caliphs and their Non-Muslim Subjects* concludes:[486]

[The caliph] Mutasim bought the monastery at Samarra that stood where he wanted to to build his palace. Other caliphs destroyed churches to obtain materials for their buildings, and the mob was always ready to pillage churches and monasteries. Though dhimmis might enjoy great prosperity, yet always they lived on sufferance, exposed to the caprices of the ruler and the passions of the mob.The episode of al-Hakim [an absolute religious fanatic] must be regarded as the freak of a mad man, not typical of Islam. But in later times the position of the dhimmis did change for the worse. They were much more liable to suffer from the violence of the crowd, and the popular fanaticism was accompanied by an increasing strictness among the educated. The spiritual isolation of Islam was accomplished. The world was divided into two classes, Muslims and others, and only Islam counted. There were brilliant exceptions, but the general statement is true. If a Muslim gave any help to the religion of a dhimmi, he was to be summoned thrice to repentance, and then, if obdurate, he was to be put to death. Indeed, the general feeling was that the leavings of the Muslims were good enough for the dhimmis.

C. E. Bosworth,[487] writing some fifty years later, summed up the status of the dhimmi:

Although protected by the contract of dhimma, the dhimmis were never anything but second-class citizens in the Islamic social system, tolerated in large measure because they had special skills such as those of physicians, secretaries, financial experts, etc., or because they fulfilled functions which were necessary but obnoxious to Muslims, such as money-changing, tanning, wine-making, castrating slaves, etc. A Muslim might marry a dhimmi wife but not vice versa, for this would put a believing woman into the power of an unbeliever; for the same reason, a Muslim could own a dhimmi slave but not a dhimmi a Muslim one. The legal testimony of a dhimmi was not admissible in a judicial suit where a Muslim was one of the parties, because it was felt that infidelity, the obstinate failure to recognize the true light of Islam, was proof of defective morality and a consequent incapability of bearing legal witness. In the words of the Hanafi jurist Sarakhsi (d. 483/1090), "the word of a dishonest Muslim is more valuable than that of an honest dhimmi." On the other hand, the deposition of a Muslim against a dhimmi was perfectly valid in law. It was further held by almost all schools of Islamic law (with the exception of the Hanafi one) that the diya or blood money payable on the killing of a dhimmi was only two-thirds or a half of that of a free Muslim.

It is surprising that, in the face of legal and financial disabilities such as these outlined above, and of a relentless social and cultural Muslim pressure, if not of sustained persecution, that the dhimmi communities survived as well as they did in mediaeval Islam.

The third scholar is Bat Ye'or:[488]

These examples are intended to indicate the general character of a system of oppression, sanctioned by contempt and justified by the principle of the inequality between Muslims and dhimmis. . . . Singled out as objects of hatred and contempt by visible signs of discrimination, they were progressively decimated during periods of massacres, forced conversions, and banishments. Sometimes it was the prosperity they achieved through their labor or ability that aroused jealousy; oppressed and stripped of all their goods, the dhimmis often emigrated.

10

Heretics and Heterodoxy, Atheism and Freethought, Reason and Revelation

Throughout the history of Islam there have been a number of, what Robertson calls, "rationalizing heresies." While Islam has shown a remarkable tolerance for these divergent unorthodox opinions—as Goldziher says, "Mutual tolerance coined the hadith formula, traced back to the Prophet: 'Difference of opinion within my community is a (sign of divine) mercy'; thus all four schools of jurisprudence in Sunni Islam are considered equally valid and orthodox"—it has nonetheless also shown itself to be totally intolerant of unbelief, the penalty for which is death, and of all those it considers extremists among the Shi'ites, Kharijites, Murji'ites, Mu'tazilites, and even the Sunnis, those, that is, who deny some of the fundamental tenets of orthodox doctrine such as prophecy, and indulge in outrageous fantasies of reincarnation and metempsychosis. In particular anyone who denied the unity of God and cast doubt on the prophethood of Muhammad and the divine origin of the Koran was considered beyond the Muslim pale.

As we shall see, persecutions of heresies and heretics are more common than the modern apologists of Islam are willing to allow.

Under the influence of Greek philosophy, rationalism—the trust and respect for human reason as a means for arriving at truth and as a guide to the way of living—flourished in certain groups and certain courageous individuals. Philosophers and theologians of a rationalistic tendency, and individual skeptics such as al-Ma'arri, often challenged some of the basic assumptions of the orthodox, but in the end orthodox Islam emerged victorious from the encounter with Greek philosophy. Islam rejected the idea that one could attain truth with unaided human reason and settled for the unreflective comforts of the putatively superior truth of divine revelation. Wherever one decides to place the date of this victory of orthodox Islam (perhaps in the ninth century with the conversion of al-Ashari, or in the eleventh century with the works of al-Ghazali), it has been, I believe, an unmitigated disaster for all Muslims, indeed all mankind, a disaster whose full consequences we are now witnessing in the barbarism of "resurgent Islam" in Algeria, Iran, the Sudan, Pakistan, Saudi Arabia, and Egypt. The consequences of this disaster are also evident in the fact that Islam, in particular political Islam, has totally failed to cope with the modern world and all its attendant problems—social, economic, and philosophical.

Early Years

We know from the Koran itself that there were Arab skeptics in Mecca who did not accept the "fables" recounted by Muhammad—they scoffed at the notion of the resurrection of the body, they doubted the divine origins of his "revelation" and even accused him of plagiarizing the pagan Arab poets. Even now certain verses of the Koran are attributed to the pre-Islamic poet, al-Qays. As Robertson suggests, it is thanks to these Meccan freethinkers that we have so few miracles attributed to Muhammad in the early days of Islam; for these opponents of Muhammad disbelieved in a future life and miracles, and they put to Muhammad challenges that "showed they rationally disbelieved his claim to inspiration. Hence, clearly, the scarcity of miracles in [Muhammad's] early legend, on the Arab side." But, as Robertson concludes, "On a people thus partly 'refined, skeptical, incredulous,' whose poetry showed no trace of religion, the triumph of Islam gradually imposed a tyrannous dogma, entailing abundance of primitive superstition under the aegis of monotheistic doctrine."

Pagan Arabs lacked any deep religious sense; they were not inclined to thank superior powers for their worldly successes. Thus it is not surprising that these pagan attitudes prevailed in the early years of Islam. Arabs converted out of cupidity and hope of booty and success in this world. Thus many outwardly confessed their belief but in fact had no inclination toward Islam and its dogma and ritual. Sprenger estimates that at the death of Muhammad the number who really converted to Muhammad's doctrine did not exceed a thousand. If things went wrong, the Bedouins were ready to drop Islam as quickly as they had adopted it. The fact that Islam restricted wine drinking and sexual intercourse, "the two delicious things," did not endear Muhammad to them, either.

The Arabs also resisted the institution of Muslim prayers and ridiculed the movements of the body connected with them. As Goldziher says,[489]

> there are countless stories, unmistakably taken from true life, which describe the indifference of the desert Arabs to prayer, their ignorance of the elements of Muslim rites and even their indifference toward the sacred book of God itself and their ignorance of its most important parts. The Arabs always preferred to hear the songs of the heroes of paganism rather than holy utterances of

the Koran. It is related that Ubayda b. Hilal, one of the chiefs of the Khawarij, used to ask his men, while they were resting from battle, to come to his tent. Once two warriors came. "What would you prefer," he asked them, "that I should read to you from the Koran, or that I should recite poems to you?" They replied: "We know the Koran as well as we know you; let us hear poems." "You godless men," said Ubayda, "I knew that you would prefer poems to the Koran."

We have already noted the lack of interest in religion manifested by the early "heroes of Islam," such as Khalid b. al-Walid, Othman b. Talha and Amr b. al-As. We might here quote a Muslim leader of the early days who is reputed to have said: "If there were a God, I would swear by his name that I did not believe in him."

The Umayyads (661-750)

The Umayyads have always been considered "godless" by their opponents. The ignorance of Islamic doctrine and ritual continued well into the first Islamic century; indeed, Islam cannot properly be said to have existed in the sense of a fixed set of dogmas until later. We can get a glimpse of the kind of atmosphere that the caliph al-Walid II (ruled 743) grew up in by the verses that he addressed to the Koran, referring to the threats made by the Koran against the stubborn opponents (sura 14.8, 9): "You hurl threats against the stubborn opponent, well then, I am a stubborn opponent myself. When you appear before God at the day of resurrection just say: My Lord, al-Walid has torn me up."[490]

Walid II is said to have stuck the Koran onto a lance and shot it to pieces with arrows while repeating the preceding verses. Walid II certainly did not abide by the interdictions of the Koran. An intensively cultivated man, he surrounded himself with poets, dancing girls, and musicians and lived a merry life of the libertine, with no interest in religion. The Umayyads were not holy minded or given to piety, yet they still believed that they were serving Islam. But their form of government failed to satisfy the pious who dreamed of a theocratic state.

The Abbasids (In Iraq and Baghdad, 749-1258)

The Abbasids overthrew the Umayyads, "because of their godlessness and opposition to religion." The conquerers were more rigorous in applying the principles of Islam, but, in doing so, were far more intolerant toward the practice of other religions, and this, as Goldziher remarks, "marks a morally retrogressive step in comparison with the Umayyads."[491] The Abbasids set about establishing a theocratic state with an ecclesiastical policy, that is, they claimed that ultimate sovereignty belonged to God, but that they were God's representatives on earth or, as they put it, "God's shadow on earth," administering God's law. In the eyes of the pious, the Abbasids already had legitimacy since they were descended from the Prophet's uncle al-Abbas.

The Kharijites

The Kharijites may be considered the earliest of the religious sects of Islam and are important for their development of the theory of the caliphate, and their view that works were an integral element in the definition of faith. They are often called the puritans of Islam, as they demanded purity of conscience as an indispensable complement to purity of body for the validity of acts of worship. They were certainly extremists who were ready to brand everyone who did not accept their point of view as unbelievers and outside the law. Their extreme fanaticism became evident as they carried out terrorist actions, murdering even women and children. The Kharijites denied the claims of Ali to the caliphate on the murder of the third Caliph, Uthman in 655; they equally condemned Uthman's behavior before his murder, which they had no intention of avenging.

Slowly but surely, various fanatical elements rallied to their cause, and Ali was forced to take steps against them. Ali was able to inflict a heavy defeat on the Kharijites at the battle of Nahrawan in 658, when many of the Kharijites were killed. A series of local risings broke out during the following two years, and three years after the battle of Nahrawan, Ali himself was assassinated by a Kharijite (661). Under Mu'awiya, the next caliph and the first of the Umayyad dynasty, there were still a number of Kharijite risings, but they were ruthlessly suppressed, and many of the rebels died. These risings continued into the beginning of the eighth century.

A ferocious subsect of the Kharijites was known as the Azraqites, who held all followers of other doctrines to be infidels and rejected all institutions not laid down in the Koran. They also insisted that all who had committed a grave sin were destined for hell, as this was stated in the Koran. These grave sinners were considered apostates who had to be killed along with their wives and children; for this reason the Azraqites were responsible for numerous appalling massacres. Here we have, as Della Vida says, the principle of religious murder.[492]

In contrast to their intolerance of other Muslims, the Kharijites were very tolerant of non-Muslims, sometimes even recognizing them as equals to Muslims.

As Goldziher points out, before their beliefs took the form of a fixed, positive system the Kharijite theologians showed rationalist tendencies, and in this they influenced the later rationalist Mu'tazilites. One of their groups even impugned the reliability of the Koranic text: they held that sura 12, sura Joseph, did not belong in the Koran as its "contents were worldly and frivolous," an erotic tale with nothing sacred about it, and hence unworthy to be the word of God.

Another Kharijite theologian, Yazid b. Abi Anisa, put forward another idea that was certainly unorthodox. He said that God would reveal a new Koran to a prophet among the Persians and that he would found a new religion for them, a religion divine in the same sense as Judaism, Christianity, and Islam. This clearly goes against the orthodox doctrine of Islam being the final revelation, and Muhammad being the seal of the Prophets.

Thus Kharijites played an important part in the development of Muslim theology by making the Muslims reflect on their faith in a rational manner.

The Qadarites

According to the scholar Hubert Grimme, the prophet Muhammad's predestinarian position hardened toward the end of his life, and the "earliest conscious Muslim attitude on the subject seems to have been of an uncompromising fatalism."[493] This tyrannical view of man's helplessness began to be questioned toward the end of the seventh century, not by freethinkers, but by pious Muslims, influenced by the Christian theological environment. The upholders of the doctrine of free will came to be known as the Qadarites, since they restricted the fixing of fate, qadar; and their opponents as the Jabriya, the people of blind compulsion (jabr).

As Goldziher says,[494] the Qadarite movement is important for the history of Islam as it was "the first step toward liberation from the dominance of traditional notions." There are a vast number of hadiths (traditions) denigrating the Qadarites, thus showing that their views met with little sympathy. The Umayyads, in particular, had political reasons for fearing the disruptive effects of the Qadarite doctrine. The Umayyads, as we saw earlier, were considered godless and illegitimate rulers. The belief in predestination was exactly suited to curb the masses who might riot against their rule. It was God's eternal decree that the Umayyads must rule; all that they do is preordained by God and hence inevitable. The rule of the Umayyads was nothing other than the will of God.

As noted, the Qadarites are important for having taken the first step toward the undermining of simple Islamic orthodoxy.

The Mu'tazilites and Rationalism

There was a great deal of excitement in nineteenth-century liberal circles in Europe when, in 1865, Heinrich Steiner of Zurich in a study devoted to their ideas of the Mu'tazilites spoke of them as the "freethinkers of Islam." Robertson, writing in 1906, still speaks of them as "freethinkers." However it is clear now that the Mu'tazilites were first and foremost Muslims, living in the circle of Islamic ideas, and were motivated by religious concerns. There was no sign of absolute liberated thinking, or a desire, as Goldziher puts it, "to throw off chafing shackles, to the detriment of the rigorously orthodox view of life."

Furthermore, far from being "liberal," they turned out to be exceedingly intolerant, and were involved in the Mihna, the Muslim Inquisition under the Abbasids.

However, the Mu'tazilites are important for having introduced Greek philosophical ideas into the discussion of Islamic dogmas. This, in turn, brought with it skepticism, rationalism, and liberating doubt, which could only lead to opposition to current orthodoxy. They were, as Goldziher reminds us,[495] "the first to expand the sources of religious cognition in Islam so as to include a valuable but previously—in such connection—rigorously avoided element: reason ('aql)." Some of them even said "the first, necessary condition of knowledge is doubt," and others "fifty doubts are better than one certainty." For them, there was a sixth sense besides the usual five, namely, aql, reason.

They raised reason to a touchstone in matters of belief. One of their early representatives, Bishr ibn al-Mu'tamir of Baghdad, wrote a veritable paean to reason, as part of a didactic poem of natural history:

"How excellent is reason as a pilot and companion in good fortune and evil,
As a judge who can pass judgment over the invisible as if he saw it with his own eyes.
. . . one of its actions is that it distinguishes good and evil,
Through a possessor of powers whom God has singled out with utter sanctification and purity."

The Mu'tazilites ruthlessly criticized popular superstitions, especially the mythological elements of eschatology, which they no longer considered a part of Muslim belief. They gave an allegorical explanation of the bridge Sirat (see page 47 for a description of the bridge) that one had to cross to get to the next world. They excised the balance or scales in which the acts of man are weighed and eliminated many other childish fantasies.

The main speculative concerns of the Mu'tazilites were divine justice and unity, but their philosophy is usually summed up in five principles. The first principle entailed the strictest monotheism and the denial of all resemblance between God and his creatures. The divine attributes are recognized but are seen as being identical with the divine being rather than something added to it. Although the Koran talks of the hand and eyes, etc., of God, these anthropomorphisms are interpreted in an allegorical way. In addition, the first principle involves the denial of the Beatific Vision, the affirmation of a personal God and creator, and the affirmation of the revelation of the Prophet.

The second principle was that God is just. He is not responsible for man's evil deeds, because all human actions result from man's free will.

The third principle concerns "practical theology" and discusses problems of belief and unbelief. Sins are divided into grave and petty classes. Belief consists in avoiding grave sins, that is, acts regarding which God has laid down a threat, etc.

The fourth principle concerns the problems of theocracy and the question of whether a Muslim who had committed a grave sin could still be regarded as a Muslim. Wasil, one of the traditional founders of the Mu'tazilites, replied that the grave sinner must be placed in an intermediary position between infidelity and faith.

The fifth principle involves the injunction of right and the prohibition of wrong, or as Nyberg puts it, "the faith must be spread by the tongue, the hand, and the sword."[496]

It is precisely in the discussions of the righteousness or justice of God that the Mu'tazilites' rationalism comes to the fore.

> They are not explicitly regarding Reason as a source of religious truth, but they are assuming the complete validity of their human, rational ideas of justice when applied to God and the complete ability of their finite minds to apprehend eternal Being. When they held that no evil or injustice might be ascribed to God they were thinking of Him as a superior kind of magistrate or administrator. The punishment of evildoers is certainly just, but only where the wrong is the man's own doing. Thus ideas of sublunary justice led them to deny God's supreme control of human affairs.

Thus the doctrine of man's self-determination leads to the rejection of the notion of God's arbitrary rule; divine omnipotence is limited by the requirements of justice. Particularly in the works of al-Nazzam, one of the more rationalist Mu'tazilites, we find that reason reigns supreme in the universe: "He attributed to his rational ideas of value such absoluteness that God Himself must bow before them. God must do what is best for men; God must not assign men to Paradise or Hell except in accordance with just principles."[497]

One of al-Nazzam's pupils, Ahmed b. Habit, went way beyond his master's teachings practically into unbelief, as far as the orthodox were concerned. Ibn Habit taught metempsychosis, the divine nature of the Messiah, criticized the prophet Muhammad for his many wives, and found others more virtuous than Muhammad.

The notion that God "must" do something is close enough to blasphemy for most of the orthodox. The Mu'tazilite insistence on freewill leads to their humanist belief that man's ultimate destiny depends on himself.

The Mu'tazilites further limited the arbitrary power of God by their "law of compensation," whereby those, including animals, who have unjustly suffered on earth must be compensated in the next world. As Goldziher says, the Mu'tazilites, in the end, "set a free man over against a relatively unfree God."[498]

What is good and evil? The orthodox had replied: good is what God commands, and evil what He forbids. But the Mu'tazilites believe in the autonomy of ethics and, in arguments reminiscent of Socrates, hold the view that there "is absolute good and absolute evil, and reason is the instrument for ethical value judgments. Reason is the primus, not the divine will. A thing is good not because God has commanded it, but God has commanded it because it is good." But is this not, asks Goldziher, "tantamount to saying . . . that God, in decreeing His laws, is bound by the categorical imperative?"[499]

Other aspects of their rationalism may be seen in the way the Mu'tazilites looked critically at the Koran. Devoutness and the inability to silence the inner voice of reason made many of them doubt the authenticity of certain verses where the Prophet utters curses against his enemies such as Abu Lahab. They also believed, and this was but a logical outcome of their denying eternal qualities to God, that the Koran was created and not eternal, while the traditionists clung to its uncreatedness and eternity. How, asked the Mu'tazilites, could the words that God had used to address Moses have been eternal and uncreated when Moses was but a creature of time? For the orthodox the Mu'tazilite view spelled disaster:

> If the Koran were allowed to be created, the danger was great that it might next be alleged by those steeped in Neoplatonist thought that God's Word as revealed to Mohammed through the mediation of the archangel Gabriel shared with all created things the imperfection arising from their association with matter. The "incomparable miracle" of the Koran must be maintained at all costs, if Revelation was not to capitulate to Reason in its very stronghold.[500]

Their critical rationalism led the Mu'tazilites to doubt the inimitability of the literary style of the Koran. They asserted "that there is nothing miraculous in that book [the Koran] in respect to style or composition, . . . and that had God left men to their natural liberty, and not restrained them in that particular, the Arabians could have composed something not only equal, but superior to the Koran in eloquence, method, and purity of language."[501]

They also questioned the authenticity of the hadith, where so many of the popular beliefs they were fighting were to be found. They fiercely battled against all forms of anthropomorphism. Finally, to the question, "What is the basis for man's obligation to know God?" the Mu'tazilites answered, "Reason."

THE MIHNA OR THE MUSLIM INQUISITION (A.D. 827–)

The Abbasid Caliph al-Ma'mun took up the Mu'tazilite cause and proclaimed the thesis of the creation of the Koran official state dogma throughout the empire. Chief officials in every province had to publicly profess the dogma that the Koran was created. The caliph himself "tested" the leading theological authorities of Baghdad. The governor of Baghdad was enjoined to test all the religious judges under his jurisdiction, who in turn had to test all witnesses and assistants in the matters of law.

One of the most famous officials who refused to assent to the createdness of the Koran was Ahmad b. Hanbal, who was imprisoned for two years, during which period he seems to have been scourged. Hanbal was released because he was popular, and officials feared an uprising.

Al-Ma'mun's brother and successor al-Mutasim does not seem to have pursued the Mihna with much conviction or rigor. However his son al-Wathik continued the policy of al-Ma'mun. Al-Wathik personally tried to behead one theologian who refused to follow the official doctrine. The caliph did not succeed and eventually had to have professional aid to finish the job. Several other prominent men died in prison, many were tortured and harrassed. Under al-Mutawakkil (reigned 847–

861) the Mihna was stopped, and the caliph even forbade the profession of the creation of the Koran on pain of death. Under al-Mutawakkil, who was also an "unappealing bigot," the persecuted became the persecutors. The Mihna obviously caused irreparable damage to the cause of the Mu'tazilites.

THE INTOLERANCE OF THE MU'TAZILITES

Goldziher was the first to point out the intolerance of the Mu'tazilites and would have nothing of the fantasies of those scholars who hypothesized that the success of the Mu'tazilites would have been salutary to the evolution of Islam. As Goldziher shows many of the Mu'tazilites were ready to assassinate those who rejected their doctrines and advocated the jihad in all regions in which their dogma did not have the ascendancy. Indeed concludes, Goldziher, "It was truly a piece of good fortune for Islam that state patronage of this mentality was limited to the time of those three caliphs. How far would the Mu'tazilites have gone if the instruments and power of the state had been longer at the disposal of their intellectual faith!"[502]

However, pace Goldziher, I am convinced that had the place they had given to *reason* in their theology been respected by subsequent theologians, then surely Islam would have developed in a different and more salutary direction. It is significant that Gibb, who has a horror of atheism and human reason when it is placed above the word of God, felt that

> it was probably to the good of Islam that Mu'tazilite *rationalism* [my emphasis] having done its work but not known where to stop, was defeated. Had it been successful, it is doubtful whether the popular movement out of which . . . the regeneration of Islam was to come, could possibly have been tolerated, much less accommodated, within the framework of orthodoxy. Sooner or later the unity of Islamic culture would have suffered violent disruption and Islam itself might have succumbed under the blows of its enemies.[503]

The modern scholars Kraus and Gabrieli have pointed out that the "European Enlightenment" style of rationalism of the great Ibn al-Rawandi (to be discussed later) was but "the development taken to their logical conclusion, of certain Mu'tazilite positions (e.g., on the miracles of the Prophet and the related tradition), and above all the place they had made for reason and rationality in their theology and theodicy."[504]

Eighteenth-century rationalism is something that Islam badly needs, and it is significant that those modern Arab philosophers who are keen to inaugurate an enlightenment in Islam (e.g., Fouad Zakariya) often refer to the Mu'tazilites with affection, and wonder what they have missed. Gibb abhors the idea of a rationalist victory because of its consequences; I welcome it for the same reasons.

THE DEFEAT OF THE MU'TAZILITES

It would be a gross simplification to say that with the defeat of the rationalizing Mu'tazilites, reason was abandoned, and total irrationality reigned. On the contrary, al-Ashari (d. 935), who is traditionally seen as the theologian who gave the death blow to Mu'tazilism, was, in the words of Wensinck, "infected by its essence," i.e., rationalism. His position may justifiably be described as the support of revelation by reason, but this does imply a subordination of reason. Al-Ashari taught that there had to be a return to the Koran and sunna, which must be understood in their literal sense, without asking questions. He has nothing but contempt for the rationalists who "seek figurative explanations for the concrete terms of the holy scriptures." Some of the disastrous consequences of al-Ashari's victory were noted by Goldziher: "By his far reaching concessions to popular belief, al-Ashari caused the loss to the Muslims of important Mu'tazilite achievements. His position left intact the belief in magic and witchcraft, not to speak of the miracles of saints. The Mu'tazilites had done away with all these."[505]

In contrast to al-Ashari himself, the Asharite school "followed in several particulars the Mu'tazilite road." For example, the Asharite school believed—and this belief was to greatly perturb the conservative theologians—that knowledge supported only by traditional sources was uncertain, only rational proof gave certain knowledge. The Asharites fell between two schools and were despised by the Mu'tazilites and philosophers, on the one hand, and the traditionists on the other. The traditionists had no time for scholastic theology, which, for them, was no different from Aristotelian philosophy—both led to unbelief. The traditionist view ultimately prevailed in Islam, and it consisted in refusing to bend to reason. For the traditionists, reason was not required for religious understanding. Religious truth lay in the Koran and the sunna, both of which had to be accepted without question and doubts. Such an attitude can only lead to a rigid conservatism, and the disastrous consequence has been the inability of the ulama to adapt jurisprudence and theology to the needs of the second half of the twentieth century. In the words of R. A. Nicholson, "About the middle of the tenth century the reactionary spirit assumed a dogmatic shape in the system of Abu 'l-Hasan al-Ashari, the father of Muhammadan Scholasticism, which is essentially opposed to intellectual freedom and has maintained its petrifying influence almost unimpaired down to the present time."[506]

Manes (or Mani) (A.D. 216–276) and Manichaeism

Since we shall be constantly referring to Manichaeism throughout the remainder of this chapter, in our dicussion of heresy, a brief look at its tenets and history would seem to be appropriate.

Mani, the founder of the religion, was born in Southern Babylonia in about A.D. 216. He was said to be of Persian descent and related to the royal house of Parthia. Mani began teaching in about A.D. 240, but was forced to leave for India by the opposition of the Zoroastrian priests. On his return, two years later, he began teaching again. He was welcomed by Shapur I, for whom Mani wrote a book. The royal patronage lasted for thirty years, but eventually the Zoroastrian priests had him impeached and condemned, and Mani was put to death by being flayed alive.

The main characteristic of Mani's system, which was an offshoot of the Gnostic traditions of Persia, was a dualism which rejected "any possibility of tracing the origins of good and evil to one and the same source."[507] There existed a primeval battle between God and matter, light and darkness, truth and error. The world, including man, was a mixture of good and evil, and the purpose of religion was to separate the two principles and render evil harmless.

To achieve this separation, severe asceticism was practiced, including vegetarianism. "Within the sect there was hierarchy of grades professing different standards of austerity: the Elect were supported by the 'Hearers' in their determined missionary endeavors and in an otherworldly state of perfection."[508]

Mani derived his system from a variety of sources, Christian, Buddhist, and Zoroastrian. Manichaeism spread rapidly, and for a time seriously rivaled Christianity. In North Africa, St. Augustine was briefly one of its adherents.

Zindiqs and Zandaqa—From Dualism to Atheism

In Islam, the term "zindiq" was at first applied to those who secretly held dualist doctrines derived from Iranian religions, such as Manichaeism, while publicly professing Islam. Thus a zindiq was a heretic, guilty of zandaqa, heresy. The term was later extended to mean anyone holding unorthodox or suspect beliefs likely to perturb the social order. Finally, zindiq came to be applied to all kinds of freethinkers, atheists, and materialists. Goldziher admirably sums up the different elements that make up what we call the zindiqs:

> Firstly, there are the old Persian families incorporated in Islam who, following the same path as the Shu'ubites, have a national interest in the revival of Persian religious ideas and traditions, and from this point of view react against the Arabian character of the Muhammadan system. Then, on the other hand, there are freethinkers, who oppose in particular the stubborn dogma of Islam, reject positive religion, and acknowledge only the moral law. Amongst the latter there is developed a monkish asceticism extraneous to Islam and ultimately traceable to Buddhistic influences."[509]

DJAD IBN DIRHAM (executed ca. 742)

The first person to be executed on a charge of heresy, zandaqa, was Djad Ibn Dirham, on the orders of the Umayyad caliph Hisham, in 742 or 743. There is no indication that Djad was a dualist; rather he was probably put to death for holding views that were later associated with the Mu'tazilites, of the createdness of the Koran and of free will. He is also said to have denied the divine attributes and, as a consequence, held that "God did not speak to Moses, nor take Abraham as His friend." He is said to have been a materialist, and his followers are said to have accused the prophet Muhammad of lying and to have denied the resurrection.

IBN AL-MUQAFFA (executed A.D. 760)

Serious persecutions of the zindiqs began under the Abbasid caliph al-Mansur (reigned 754–775). Many zindiqs were put to death under his reign, the most famous being Ibn al-Muqaffa. Ibn al-Muqaffa was asked by the caliph Mansur to draw up an amnesty for Mansur's uncle, but the caliph was not at all pleased at the language used by Ibn al-Muqaffa in the finished document. It is generally held that for this reason Mansur had Ibn al-Muqaffa executed in a most horrific manner— his limbs were cut off one by one and fed into a blazing fire. But it is also very probable that Ibn al-Muqaffa's unorthodox religious views played an important role in his condemnation.

Gabrielli, Kraus, and others have shown that an anti-Muslim work of a pronounced rationalist tendency was correctly attributed to Ibn al-Muqaffa.The latter, according to Kraus, was the intellectual heir to the rationalist tradition that flourished at the time of the Sassanid king, Chosroes Anusharwan, who is said to have fostered a "veritable hellenistic Aufklarung." At any rate, from the perspective of the Manichaen faith, Ibn al-Muqaffa attacked Islam, its prophet, its theology and theodicy, and its concept of God. How do we reconcile Ibn al-Muqaffa's rational skepticism and his adherence to Manichaean dualism? Gabrieli[510] points out that intellectuals like Ibn al-Muqaffa had already given an allegorical interpretation to the Manichaen mythology and interpreted the universe and man's place in it in Gnostic terms, rational and hellenistic.

Ibn al-Muqaffa is also renowned for his translations from Pehlevi or Middle Persian literature into Arabic. His translation of the Book of Kalila and Dimna, ultimately derived from the Sanskrit Fables of Bidpai, is considered a model of elegant style.

THE GRAND INQUISITOR

Under Mansur's successors, al-Mahdi (775–785) and al-Hadi (785–786), repression, persecution, and executions were applied with even greater ferocity. Special magistrates were appointed to pursue the heretics, and the whole inquisition was masterminded by the Grand Inquisitor, called the Sahih al-Zanadiqa. It was enough for a simple rumor to be aired for the inquisitor to take immediate steps to incriminate the suspect. Often the zindiqs were arrested in mass, imprisoned, and finally brought before the inquisitor or the ruler, who then questioned them on their beliefs. If the suspects abjured their heretical religion they were released; if they refused, they were beheaded, and their heads displayed on a gibbet. Some were crucified. Al-Hadi seems to have had some strangled also. Their heretical books were cut up with knives.

We have a glimpse of the whole procedure from this comic anecdote about Abu Nuwas, the great lyric poet, (b. 762, d. ca. 806–814), whose twin passions were beautiful boys and wine. One day he entered a mosque drunk as ever, and when the imam recited verse 1 from sura 109: "Say: O! You unbelievers . . . ," Abu Nuwas cried out, "Here I am!" Whereupon the faithful whisked him off to the chief of police, declaring that Abu Nuwas was an infidel, on his own admission. The chief of police then took Abu Nuwas to the inquisitor. However, the latter refused to believe that the poet was a zindiq and refused to proceed any further. But the crowd insisted, and to calm a potentially dangerous situation, he brought a portrait of the prophet of the dualists, Mani, and asked Abu Nuwas to spit on it. Abu Nuwas did even better than that. He pushed a finger down his throat and vomited on the picture, whereupon the inquisitor set him free. We know that on another occasion Abu Nuwas was in prison on the charge of zandaqa. Heresy seems to have penetrated even the Hashimite family, the family to which the Prophet had belonged. Several members of the family were executed or died in prison.[511]

IBN ABI-L-AWJA (executed 772)

Ibn Abi-l-Awja was one of the more interesting zindiqs. Apparently he believed that light had created good, while darkness had created evil. He also taught metempsychosis and the freedom of the will. Before his death, he confessed that he had fabricated more than 4,000 traditions (hadith), in which he forbade Muslims what was in fact permitted, and vice versa, and he made Muslims break the fast when they should have been fasting, and vice versa. He is supposed to have posed the problem of human suffering: "Why," he asked, "are there catastrophes, epidemics, if God is good?" According to al-Biruni, Ibn Abi-l-Awja was wont to shake the faith of simple people with captious questions about divine justice.

Ibn Abi-l-Awja is said to have had a discussion with the imam, Jafar al-Sadiq, which is recorded and reveals the full extent of his unorthodoxy (if, that is, we can accept the historicity of the dialogue): He believes in the eternity of the world; he denies the existence of a Creator. One day he asked Jafar to justify the institution of pilgrimage and refused to accept the answer that it was ordered by God, since this reply merely pushed the question farther back to someone who was not present. He also cast doubt on the justice of some of the punishments described in the Koran. Ibn Abi-l-Awja also accuses some of the prophets mentioned in the Koran of lying, especially Abraham and Joseph. And like so many zindiqs of the period, he doubts the official dogma of the inimitability of the Koran. Even if we cannot specifically link the above dialogue with the historical figure of Ibn Abi-l-Awja, it gives a true picture of the current zindiq beliefs. He was taken prisoner, and put to death in 772.[512]

BASHSHAR IBN BURD (ca.714/715–killed 784/785)

One of the poets who was eventually seized, charged with zandaqa, beaten, and finally thrown in a swamp was Bashshar b. Burd, who was the descendant of a noble Persian family, though his father was a slave, who became a bricklayer upon being freed. Bashshar had strong national sentiments and did not miss an opportunity to glorify the memories of ancient Iran. He did not have a high opinion of the Arabs. He was born blind and was considered very ugly physically, which may go toward explaining, in part, his celebrated misanthrophy. Bashshar b. Burd excelled as a writer of panegyric, elegy, and satire.

His religious views are difficult to establish with certainty since—opportunist that he was—he often concealed his true opinion. According to Vadja, he belonged to the Shiite sect of the Kamiliyya, and anathematized the entire Muslim community. His charge of zandaqa, stemmed from an allegation that Bashshar did not pray in an orthodox manner. What's more, he is said to have mocked the call to prayer by parodying it when drunk.

He is also accused of being unrespectful toward the institution of pilgrimage. On one occasion, he left for the pilgrimage, solely to deflect any suspicion that he was a zindiq, but stopped at Zorara, where he spent his time drinking. As the pilgrims were returning he joined them and pretended on his arrival home to have completed the entire pilgrimage.

One of the charges often leveled at the zindiqs, and Bashshar b. Burd, was their continual undermining of the orthodox view of the miraculous nature of the Koran, which the orthodox considered inimitable. No one, in the orthodox view, was capable of reaching the perfection of the Koran. Goldziher gives this example of the zindiqs' irreverence:

> It is reported that at Basra a group of free thinkers, Muslim and non-Muslim heretics used to congregate and that Bashshar b. Burd did not forego characterising the poems submitted to this assembly in these words: "Your poem is better than this or the other verse of the Koran, this line again is better than some other verse of the Koran, etc." Bashshar did in fact praise one of his own poetic products when he heard it recited by a singing girl in Baghdad as being better than the surat al-Hashr. The way of expression of the Koran was criticised and the similes found wanting. Al-Mubarrad tells of a heretic who ridiculed the parable in sura XXXVII.63 where the fruits of the tree Zakkum in hell are likened to the heads of devils. The critics say: "He compares the visible with the unknown here. We have never seen the heads of devils; what kind of a simile is this?"[513]

Bashshar seems to have denied the resurrection and the last judgment in some of his verses. He may well have believed in metempsychosis, i.e., the transmigration of souls. In some celebrated verses, Bashshar defends Iblis (the devil), being made of fire, for refusing to prostrate himself before Adam, being made of ordinary clay. In another one of his verses, he prayed to the prophet Muhammad to join with him in an attack upon the Deity. He also seems to have held Manichaean beliefs laced with Zoroastrianism.

But, in the words of Blachere, "along with these beliefs there would seem always to have been a profound skepticism mingled with a fatalistic outlook leading Bashshar to pessimism and hedonism."[514] But out of prudence he was obliged to pay lip service to orthodoxy. This view of Bashshar being a skeptic is endorsed by Vadja who argues that it seems totally out of character for someone as dissolute as he to adhere to a religion as ascetic as Manichaeism.

SALIH B. ABD AL-QUDDUS (executed 783)

Salih was also accused of Manichaeism and executed in 783. However his extant poetry is irreproachable, containing nothing heretical. Salih, according to Nicholson, being of a speculative turn of mind, probably fell victim to the Muslim prejudice that connects "the philosophic mind" with positive unbelief.[515]

HAMMAD AJRAD (executed)

Hammad Ajrad belonged to a circle of freethinkers based at Basra. Their reunions, already previously alluded to, were attended by such unorthodox poets as Bashshar, Salih b. Abd al-Quddus, Ibn Sinan of Harran, Ibn Nazir, et al. Hammad was accused of not praying in an orthodox fashion and of preferring some of his verses to those of the Koran. He was accused of the dualist heresy and of composing verses that the zindiqs recited in their prayers. Even if he was not high up in the religious hierarchy of the Manichaeans, Hammad was certainly a sympathizer, to the extent that his religious poetry found its way into the liturgy of the Manichaeans. He was put to death by the governor of Basra.

ABAN B. ABD AL HUMAYD B. LAHIQ AL RAQQASI

Aban was described as another one of the freethinkers of Basra and figures in a satire by Abu Nuwas, partly as a Manichaean dualist, but also as a rationalist:

> I sat one day with Aban (plague on him!), when the time for the first prayer came, and the call was duly uttered by a correct and clear-voiced speaker.
> We all repeated the call to prayer to the end. Then said Aban: "How could you testify to that [i.e. the Muslim formula of faith] without ocular demonstration? So long as I live I shall never attest anything but what I see with my eyes." Then I said: "Glory to God"; he said: "Glory to Manes." Then I said: "Jesus was an Apostle"; he said: "Of Satan." I continued: "Moses was the interlocutor of the Gracious and Faithful One"; he said: "Then your God must have a tongue and an eye. And did He create Himself, or who created Him?" So I held my tongue before this obstinate blasphemer.[516]

It is difficult to know what Aban's real religious views were since we cannot take Abu Nuwas's satire at face value. Aban certainly rendered service to posterity by his versification of many Persian and Hindu works.

OTHER FREETHINKERS OF BASRA

In our sources for this group, certain names keep cropping up, but, unfortunately, often we do not have any other details about their views or works. Thus we are told that Qays b. Zubayr was a notorious atheist, that al-Baqili denied the resurrection, that Ibrahim b. Sayyaba was a zindiq and claimed that pederasty was the first law of zandaqa, and so on.

We do know a little more about Muti b. Iyas, who gives every sign of being a zindiq. But the details we have of his life point rather to someone with a skeptical turn of mind with no real profound interest in any religion.

> He began his career under the Umayyads, and was devoted to the Caliph Walid b. Yazid, who found in him a fellow after his own heart, "accomplished, dissolute, an agreeable companion and excellent wit, reckless in his effrontery and suspected in his religion." When the Abbasids came to power Muti attached himself to the Caliph Mansur. Many stories are told of the debauched life which he led in the company of zindiqs, or freethinkers. . . . His songs of love and wine are distinguished by their lightness and elegance.[517]

ABU 'L ATAHIYA

We are told in one of our sources that Abu 'l Atahiya, fearing arrest by the Grand Inquisitor, passed himself off as a seller of cupping glasses and disappeared in the crowds of the city. Unfortunately we are not told why the inquisitor might have wanted to interview our poet. Nonetheless, Abu 'l Atahiya was often accused of zandaqa by his contemporaries. He may have secretly held Manichaean views, but there is nothing in his poetry that could offend most orthodox Muslims. However Goldziher does profess to see a reference to the Buddha in the following two lines:

> If thou wouldst see the noblest of mankind,
> Behold a monarch in a beggar's garb.

Abu 'l Atahiya seems to have believed "in One God who formed the universe out of two opposite elements which He created from nothing; and held, further, that everything would be reduced to these same elements before the final destruction of all phenomena. Knowledge, he thought, was acquired naturally (i.e., without Divine Revelation) by means of reflection, deduction, and research."

It is not obvious that the above views count as heresy, but Nicholson thinks that Atahiya may have fallen out of favor for being too philosophical rather than religious in his poetry. And, concludes Nicholson, "this was enough to convict him of infidelity and atheism in the eyes of devout theologians who looked askance on moral teaching, however pure, that was not cast in the dogmatic mould."[518]

Atahiya was also accused of claiming that some of his verses were superior to those of the Koran. Others reproached him, unjustly, of denying the resurrection.

Nonetheless, there are some poems that contain much orthodox Muslim belief. What finally emerges is a "profound melancholy and hopeless pessimism" and the vanity of worldly pleasures.

ABU ISA MUHAMMAD B. HARUN WARRAK, OR AL-WARRAQ

Al-Warraq was accused of zandaqa, and is important for, among other reasons, being the teacher of the Great Infidel himself, al-Rawandi. Unfortunately, none of Warraq's literary work survives, and we have tantalizing glimpses of it in the quotations by other Arab scholars. Some of his works are also known from refutations. Al-Warraq started as a Mu'tazilite theologian but seems to have been excommunicated for holding heterodoxic opinions.

He wrote a remarkable history of religions, where his objectivity, rationalism, and skepticism were given free rein. His critical examination of the three branches of Christianity of his time again reveals his dispassionate tone and rationalism, where there is no question of a dependence on revelation.

Al-Warraq may well have had Shiite sympathies, but it is uncertain whether he was really a Manichaen. However, he does seem to have believed in the two principles, and very certainly in the eternity of the world. Massignon correctly sums him up as an independent thinker and skeptic rather than someone who believed in any fixed system of thought. A victim of the Abbasid persecution, al-Warraq died in exile in 909 in Ahwaz.

ABU TAMMAM (d. 846)

Abu Tamman was born near Damascus in 796 or 804, and is famous as a poet and anthologist. He met with much success at the court of the caliph al-Mutasim, where he wrote many eulogies. But as Margoliouth notes,[519] "Various anecdotes are told of his visits to his provincial patrons: when staying with Ibn Radja in Fars, he gave his patron reason to suspect that he neglected the Muslim religious observances, and when questioned on this matter, expressed doubts as to the effectiveness of those observances, a confession which nearly led to his execution." Unfortunately, none of his religious doubts is to be found in his poetical works.

AL-MUTANABBI (915-965)

Al-Mutanabbi is considered by many Arabs as the greatest poet in the Arabic language. Born in Kufa and educated in Damascus, al-Mutanabbi modeled himself on the poetry of Abu Tammam and consciously set out to make a name for himself. According to Blachere, al-Mutanabbi was influenced in his religious and philosophical development by a certain Abu 'l Fadl of Kufa who was a "complete agnostic," and an early patron of his works. Under Abu 'l Fadl's influence, al-Mutanabbi "cast off religious dogmas which he regarded as spiritual instruments of oppression. He then adopted a stoic and pessimistic philosophy. . . . The world is made up of seductions which death destroys; stupidity and evil alone triumph there."[520]

Not achieving the fame he dreamed of, and felt he merited, al-Mutanabbi was now determined to dominate by violent means. He began revolutionary propaganda, and then led a rebellion of a politico-religious character, in which he claimed to be a prophet with a new Koran (hence his name "Mutannabi," in Arabic, "one who pretends to be a prophet"). He was defeated, captured, and imprisoned for two years in Hims. He was obviously extremely fortunate to be spared his life, since to claim to be a prophet is extreme heresy and, equally, to claim to have a new Koran is against all orthodox belief.

After his release, al-Mutanabbi was lucky enough to find patronage at the court of Saif al-Daula at Aleppo. For nine years, al-Mutanabbi sang the praises of this prince, and the odes he composed for him are considered the "greatest masterpieces of Arabic literature."

Al-Mutanabbi seems to have quarreled with Saif al-Daula and was obliged to slip away from Aleppo to Egypt where he found patronage with the Ikhshidid ruler, Kafur. He was to quarrel with the latter, as well, and obliged to flee. He was eventually killed by bandits when returning to Baghdad.

Al-Mutanabbi wrote a vast number of odes sometimes praising second rate patrons and, at other times, the great Saif al-Daula. Some of the odes are full of bombast, and some are sublime, but underneath them all we can discern a skepticism, a certain disillusionment with a world kept in chains by ignorance, stupidity, and superstition, from which only death can liberate us. But, as Margoliouth[521] points out, for many Muslims, al-Mutanabbi's odes are "defaced by utterances which imply disrespect for the prophets and revealed religion." His most offensive line for Muslims is one "in which he tells his patron, an Alid, 'the greatest miracle of the man of Tihamah (i.e., Muhammad, the Prophet) is that he is thy father'; in another he tells a patron that if his sword had hit the head of Lazarus on the battlefield, Jesus would not have been able to restore him to life; and that if the Red Sea had been like his hand, Moses could never have crossed it."

ABU HAYYAN AL-TAUHIDI (d. ca. 1023)

According to literary tradition, the writers al-Rawandi, al-Ma'ari, and al-Tauhidi were the three great Zanadiqa (or zindiqs) of Islam. Al-Rawandi and al-Ma'ari will be examined in detail in a moment; this leaves us with the third great zindiq, al-Tauhidi. According to Margoliouth, al-Tauhidi's works were considered more dangerous than those of the others because, whereas the others proclaimed their unbelief, he expressed his in innuendoes. And yet, those of his works that are extant do not seem particularly heretical. In his "Kitab al-Itma," we find a pessimism reminiscent of al-Mutanabbi, but nothing overtly unorthodox. It is possible that al-Tauhidi's interest in and knowledge of Greek philosophy and science rendered him suspect in the eyes of the orthodox—any such interest was supposed to lead to atheism.

IBN AL-RAWANDI (al-Rawendi) (born ca. 820–830)

Al-Rawandi started as a Mu'tazilite but was expelled from their company for heresy. He then began a series of ferocious attacks on the Mu'tazalites, and thanks to a refutation of his work by al-Khayyat, al-Rawandi's book against his former colleagues is known in part—the work is known as the *Fadihat al-Mu'tazila,* or the *Ignominy of the Mu'tazilites.* Al-Rawandi never hesitated in broaching subjects long considered both taboo and dangerous, and it is not surprising that before long he was branded an infidel and a zindiq, both in the narrow sense of someone believing in dualism, and in the wider sense of a freethinker. He was publically accused by the Mu'tazilites and, eventually, because of government persecution had to leave Baghdad. In his attacks on his former friends, al-Rawandi showed up their inconsistencies and even deduced heretical conclusions from their principles.

As Nyberg[522] has shown, al-Rawandi was condemned and expelled by the Mu'tazilites for his aristotelian tendencies that destroyed the central orthodox dogma of the creation ex nihilo and of the Creator. We know that al-Rawandi wrote a book on the eternity of the world; however, this work has not survived.

It is significant that it was often philosophers and doctors who took him seriously, and some even came to his defense. Al-Haitham, for example, showed that the putative refutations of al-Rawandi were plain wrong.

Al-Rawandi undoubtedly taught dualism in one of his books and, for a time, turned toward a Shiism of a moderate kind. He finally cut all intellectual links with the Muslim community and ended his life as an atheist.

The Mu'tazilites also accused al-Rawandi of attacking the Prophet, the Koran, the hadith, revelation in general—in sum, the whole of the sharia—in such works as the *Kitab al-Damigh, Kitab al-Farid,* and *Kitab al-Zumurrudh.* But as Nyberg and others have pointed out, al-Rawandi was only drawing the logical conclusions of the principles held by the Mu'tazilites themselves.

> The unbelief of ibn al-Rawandi could, in effect, be seen as the inexorable consequence of the effort made by Mu'tazilites to accommodate human reason in the acceptance of revelation. . . . [In so doing] they had placed their trust in a demanding guide that is not always easy to discard half way.[523]

The extracts that we possess of al-Rawandi's *Kitab al-Zumurrudh,* show exactly why he was seen as a radical and dangerous heretic. They contain a trenchant criticism of prophecy in general, and of the prophecy of Muhammad in particular. Al-Rawandi maintains that reason is superior to revelation. Either what the so-called prophets say is in accordance with reason, in which case prophets are otiose and not needed, since ordinary human beings are equally endowed with reason, or it does not conform to reason, in which case it must be rejected. For al-Rawandi all religious dogmas are contrary to reason and therefore are to be rejected; "the miracles attributed to the prophets, persons who may reasonably be compared to sorcerers and magicians, are pure invention" (a thesis that reminds one of Morton White's, that Jesus was a magician). As for the Koran, far from being a miracle and inimitable, it is an inferior work from the literary point of view, since it is neither clear nor comprehensible nor of any practical value, and it is certainly not a revealed book. Besides its putative literary miraculousness "is hardly relevant, as probative evidence, in regard to foreigners to whom Arabic is an alien tongue."524

Al-Rawandi attacks all religious ritual as futile, and any knowledge acquired by the so-called prophets can be explained in natural and human terms without having to attribute its origin to revelation. According to at least one authority, al-Rawandi rejected the very possibility "of a satisfactory rational answer to the question of God's existence and the rationality of His ways."

Al-Rawandi's other views seem to include the eternity of the world, the superiority of dualism over monotheism, and the vanity of divine wisdom.

Al-Ma'arri, in his *Risalatu'l Ghufran*, attributes the following lines to al-Rawandi, addressed to God: "Thou didst apportion the means of livelihood to Thy creatures like a drunkard who shows himself churlish. Had a man made such a division, we should have said to him, 'You have swindled. Let this teach you a lesson.' " No wonder al-Ma'arri exclaimed in-horror, "If these two couplets stood erect, they would be taller in sin than the Egyptian pyramids in size."525

11

Greek Philosophy and Science and Their Influence on Islam

The scholar F. R. Rosenthal[526] has pointed out that the process of assimilation of the heritage of classical antiquity into Islam between the eighth and tenth centuries can justly be called the renaissance of Islam. It is unthinkable how Islamic civilization could have developed without the classical heritage. Rosenthal puts it in a forthright manner:

> Islamic rational scholarship, which we have mainly in mind when we speak of the greatness of Muslim civilisation, depends in its entirety on classical antiquity, down to such fundamental factors as the elementary principles of scholarly and scientific research. More than that, the intellectual life of Islam in its most intimate expressions bowed to the Greek spirit. . . . However, in Islam as in every civilisation, what is really important is not the individual elements but the synthesis that combines them into a living organism of its own. . . . The indisputable fact remains, though, that Islamic civilisation as we know it would simply not have existed without the Greek heritage.

Islamic Philosophy

For many Western scholars and, more importantly, many Muslims, the very idea of an "Islamic philosophy" is a contradiction in terms: "Strictly orthodox sunni Islam has never welcomed philosophic thought." Traditionists have always been hostile to philosophy, a "foreign science," which led, they claimed, to heresy, doubt, and total unbelief. In this, the traditionists fears were well-founded, for many of the philosophers developed views that were far from orthodox, and others, "especially those hostile to the nascent Sunnism, committed themselves entirely to the guidance of reason as that was understood in Greek philosophy, and gave

261

no more than lip service to Islamic religion." Thus the story of Islamic philosophy is, in part, the story of the tension between reason and revelation.

Translations

Although translation of Greek scientific works may well have started under the Umayyads, it was the Abbasid caliph al-Mamun (ruled 813–833) who encouraged and sponsored the translation of Greek philosophy and science. Al-Mamun even established an institution, the House of Wisdom, as a center for research and translation.

The initial impulse for the translations was practical—the need for medical and astronomical knowledge. But prestige and, later, genuine intellectual curiosity also played a part in this feverish activity. Even before the efforts of the translators under al-Mamun, there had been Muslims who had realized the importance of philosophy and logic for the needs of polemics and apologetics.

Most of the translators were Christians. The one famous exception was Thabit b. Qurra, a freethinking pagan whose liberal philosophical opinions brought him into conflict with the pagan community of Harran. Mathematician, physician, and philosopher, Thabit b.Qurra was a highly important figure in this renaissance.

The Greek philosophers translated included Aristotle and his commentators such as Themistius, Simplicius, and Alexander of Aphrodisias; Plato, particularly the *Timaeus, Republic,* and *Laws*; Plotinus and Neoplatonists such as Proclus and Porphyry; pre-Socratics; Galen, Hippocrates, Archimedes, Euclid, and Ptolemy.

The First Period of Islamic Philosophy: Al-Kindi, Al-Farabi, Ibn Sina (Avicenna)

The first period of Islamic philosophy took shape in the East between the ninth and eleventh centuries with al-Kindi, al-Farabi, and Ibn Sina (Avicenna). It is, as Arnaldez says, "a synthesis of Neoplatonic metaphysics, natural science and mysticism: Plotinus enriched by Galen and Proclus."[527]

Al-Kindi was o ttally convinced that there was no fundamental disagreement between the findings of Greek philosophy and the revelations of the Koran, and he worked hard to reconcile the two. On the whole he seems to have believed in and actively defended most of the fundamental tenets of Islam and, thus, is less interesting for us, for, in this chapter, we have concentrated on those writers and thinkers who have challenged the very same tenets—the rationalists, heretics, agnostics, atheists, and freethinkers. However, this is not to deny his importance in the history of Islamic philosophy as an educator of Muslims in the Greek sciences, as an introducer of Neoplatonic ideas into Islam, and as a defender of reason.

AL-SARAKHSI (executed 899)

The spirit of philosophical inquiry did eventually however lead to a questioning of the fundamental tenets of Islamic belief, something which led people like al-Kindi's pupil, Ahmad b. al-Tayyib al-Sarakhsi, into deep trouble. Al-Sarakhsi took an interest in Greek philosophy and was the tutor of the caliph al-Mutadid. Sarakhsi incurred the wrath of the caliph for discussing heretical ideas rather openly such that the caliph was obliged to order his execution. According to al-Biruni, al-Sarakhsi wrote numerous treatises in which he attacked the prophets as charlatans. Al-Sarakhsi was led into his religious skepticism by the rationalism of the Mu'tazilites, with whom he sympathized, and his philosophical inquiries.

AL-FARABI

With al-Farabi (870–950), we do meet with ideas that seem incompatible with orthodox Islam. As Arberry[528] points out, al-Farabi's "conception of life after death appears to leave no room for the resurrection of the body." But al-Farabi is far from consistent on this subject, and as Pines has suggested some of al-Farabi's inconsistencies might be due to considerations of prudence: "But this is not certain, though al-Farabi was certainly not unaware of the necessity of being cautious. In fact, the seemingly deliberate abstractness, which occasionally calls to mind Spinoza's way of expressing himself, may have meant to mask his intentions and the content of his reflections, many of which must have been unacceptable to even a very tolerant religious and political orthodoxy."

Al-Farabi, following Aristotle, assigns immortality only to the intellectual part of the soul. But only those virtuous souls that have attained a certain degree of intellectual apprehension and perfection will find happiness. These virtuous souls lose their individuality after death and become part of the "active intellect" of the kingdom of heaven. Other souls will go through a cycle of rebirth or perish with the body.

Al-Farabi's account of the active intellect, derived from late Neoplatonic speculation, also poses serious problems for the adherents of a rigid monotheism. Al-Farabi sees the active intellect "as a separate metaphysical entity, a kind of intermediary between the spiritual world above the moon and the human mind, through which both the human mind and the human imagination are linked with the divine." Al-Farabi's defense of reason and subordination of prophecy to philosophy also rendered him suspect in the eyes of the orthodox. For al-Farabi, only the perfection of the faculty of reason will lead to human happiness; "as the divine mind rules the universe, so reason should govern and control the life of man. No human faculty higher than reason can be conceived."[529] Unlike al-Kindi, al-Farabi was not content to relegate philosophy to a secondary role as the handmaiden of theology. In any conflict in his philosophical system, it is reason that is the ultimate arbitrator, not revelation. "If the times were propitious, one universal world-state might come into existence; if not, several religions might exist side by side, and, if this also were impracticable, Islam at least might be reshaped according to the demands of the royal power of philosophy, which was the highest perfection of which man was capable."[530]

IBN SINA (980-1037)

Ibn Sina (Avicenna), much influenced by al-Farabi, tried to reconcile philosophy and religion through allegorical interpretation. It is to be doubted whether his account of the afterlife would be found acceptable by the orthodox. Avicenna certainly rejects the idea of the resurrection of the body alone—what of the man eaten by a cannibal?—and of the resurrection of body and soul together. The personality of a man consists in his soul, not in his body, and it is through the soul that the individual personality survives death. A. J. Arberry is convinced that the whole history of Islam would have been different had Avicenna's doctrine, a mixture of Aristotle and Neoplatonism, prevailed: "It is possible that Greek philosophy would have continued upon its vitalising course, and Islam might never have known a Dark Age."[531]

The orthodox theologians did not accept Avicenna's attempt at allegorization, which was fraught with danger. Nor were they reassured when these philosophers started talking about the necessity of having one truth for the masses, and another for the philosophically sophisticated. The orthodox guessed exactly where this kind of double talk would eventually lead. Thus, the only safe course was to return to the truth of the Koran.

AL-GHAZALI AND *THE INCOHERENCE OF THE PHILOSOPHERS*

Al-Ghazali is sometimes referred to as the greatest Muslim after Muhammad. His historical importance can hardly be exaggerated. His positive achievements include: providing Islamic theology with a philosophical foundation (he was much impressed with Aristotelian logic, and he was able to defend the central Sunnite dogmas by Neoplatonic methods and concepts); and bringing Sufism within the fold of orthodoxy.

But, as Arnaldez[532] says, some see al-Ghazali as a reactionary who brought to an end Islam's love affair with Greek philosophy and rationalism and "made supreme a theology which was itself the slave of dogma." His famous work, *The Incoherence of the Philosophers,* attacked the philosophers whose doctrines were found to be incompatible with Islam. However, it is doubtful whether he was solely responsible for the disappearance of philosophy in Islam, since philosophy had already been in decline in the East from other causes before al-Ghazali wrote in 1095; whereas in the Islamic West philosophy in the Greek tradition continued until at least 1200. Nonetheless, Arberry is right in seeing al-Ghazali's condemnation of philosophical speculation as a turning point in the intellectual history of Islam. As Arberry puts it, "the battle was over in the East. Thenceforward, the future belonged to revelation."

Against the philosophers, al-Ghazali wrote, "The source of their infidelity was their hearing terrible names such as Socrates and Hippocrates, Plato and Aristotle." The latter's followers delight to "relate of them how, with all the gravity of their intellects and the exuberance of their erudition, they denied the sacred laws and creeds and rejected the details of the religions and faiths, believing them to be fabricated ordinances and bedizened trickeries." Al-Ghazali finds the arguments of the philosophers heretical on seventeen points, and on three others he regards the philosophers as infidels. He does not hesitate to demand the death penalty for anyone holding these opinions derived from the philosophers: "They are absolutely to be condemned as infidels on three counts. The first of these is the question of the eternity of the world, and their statement that all substances are eternal [the philosophers denied the creation ex nihilo]; the second is their assertion that God does not encompass in His knowledge particular events occurring to individuals; the third is their denial of the resurrection of the body."

Such is al-Ghazali's prestige that none dare criticize him. But even al-Ghazali is not above criticism—I believe that historically his negative influence prevailed and far outweighs his positive contributions. First, he led Muslims back to an unquestioning faith in the Koran that was to be accepted literally—thus all the gains made by the rationalist Mu'tazilites were squandered as Muslims were enjoined to bend their knees in total and abject submission to revelation. All the crass anthropomorphic passages of the Koran, and all the Koranic descriptions of heaven with its voluptuous houris and hell with its pathological imagery of torments were to be accepted as literally true. Worst of all, al-Ghazali reintroduced the element of fear into Islam; in his preaching, he emphasized the "wrath to come" and the punishments of hell.

Though al-Ghazali thought mathematics, logic, and physics were in some ways neutral, he was, nonetheless, apprehensive that their methods would be generalized "rashly," and exceed their proper limits. He was thus opposed to the spirit of free inquiry, intellectual curiosity for its own sake. In section 7, chapter 2 of his *Ihya ulum al-din,* for instance, al-Ghazali tells us that certain of the natural sciences are contrary to the law and religion, and in chapter 3 he tells us to abstain from free thought and accept the conclusions of the prophets.

As to the metaphysics of the Greeks, it is the origin of "innovations and impieties since in this field logical reasoning is not infallibly applied." Again and again, al-Ghazali emphasizes that unaided reason cannot attain truth, and only revelation provides certainty. It is a paradox that al-Ghazali should use reason and all the methods of the philosophers to attack unbridled reason and the speculations of the philosophers, in the name of revelation. Finally, should we applaud his tolerance in not branding as infidels those who held certain heretical propositions (seventeen in all), or rather condemn his intolerance for demanding "the execution of any man who made a public declaration that the body did not share with the soul in immortality"?

ABU BAKR MUHAMMAD B. ZAKARIYA AL-RAZI (865-925)

Perhaps the greatest freethinker in the whole of Islam was al-Razi, the Rhazes of Medieval Europe (or Razis of Chaucer), where his prestige and authority remained unchallenged until the seventeenth century. Meyerhof also calls him the "greatest physician of the Islamic world and one of the great physicians of all time"; while for Gabrieli, he remains the greatest rationalist "agnostic" of the Middle Ages, European and Oriental. Al-Razi was a native of Rayy (near Tehran), where he studied mathematics, philosophy, astronomy, literature, and perhaps, alchemy. It is possible that al-Razi studied under that shadowy figure, the freethinker Eranshahri, who, according to al-Biruni, "did not believe in any of the then existing religions, but was the sole believer in a religion invented by himself, which he tried to propagate."[533] Eranshahri may thus have influenced al-Razi's rather similar dismissal, as we shall see later, of all religions. At Baghdad al-Razi learned his medicine. Baghdad at that time was a great center of learning, and al-Razi had access to libraries and well-equipped hospitals, one of which he later directed.

Al-Razi is credited with at least two hundred works on a wide variety of subjects, with the exception of mathematics. His greatest medical work was an enormous encyclopedia, *al-Hawi,* on which he worked for fifteen years, and which was translated into Latin in 1279. Al-Razi was a thorough empiricist, and not at all dogmatic. This is evident from his extant clinical notebook, in which he carefully recorded the progress of his patients, their maladies, and the results of the treatment. He wrote what was perhaps the earliest treatise on infectious diseases—smallpox and measles. It is based on his own painstaking empirical observations, not neglecting any aspect of those diseases that might help in their treatment—heart, breathing, and so on. He wrote on a vast number of medical topics: skin diseases, diet, diseases of the joints, fevers, poison, etc.

Al-Razi was equally empirical in his approach to chemistry. He shunned all the occultist mumbo jumbo attached to this subject and instead confined himself to "the classification of the substances and processes as well as to the exact description of his experiments." He was perhaps the first true chemist as opposed to an alchemist. Al-Razi's general philosophical attitude was that no authority was beyond criticism; he challenged tradition and authority in every field to which he turned his attention. Though he had great respect and admiration for the great Greek figures of the past, Socrates, Plato and Aristotle, Hippocrates and Galen, he was not at all overawed by them:

> He does not hesitate either to modify their philosophical conclusions if he believes that he knows better, or to add to the store of accumulated medical knowledge what he has found out by his own research and observation. Whenever, for instance, he treats a particular disease he first summarizes everything he can find in Greek and Indian sources, . . . and in the works of earlier Arabic doctors. He never fails to add his own opinion and his own judgment; he never adheres to authority as such.[534]

Like a true humanist, al-Razi has boundless faith in human reason. As al-Razi himself wrote in his book of ethics, the *Spiritual Physick,*[535]

> The Creator (Exalted be His Name) gave and bestowed upon us Reason to the end that we might thereby attain and achieve every advantage, that lies within the nature of such as us to attain and achieve, in this world and the next. It is God's greatest blessing to us, and there is nothing that surpasses it in procuring our advantage and profit. By Reason we are preferred above the irrational beasts, . . . By Reason we reach all that raises us up, and sweetens and beautifies our life, and through it we obtain our purpose and desire. For by Reason we have comprehended the manufacture and use of ships, so that we have reached unto distant lands divided from us by the seas; by it we have achieved medicine with its many uses to the body, and all the other arts that yield us profit, . . . by it we have learned the shape of the earth and the sky, the dimension of the sun, moon and other stars, their distances and motions.

Al-Razi denies the Islamic dogma of creation ex nihilo. For him, the world was created at a finite moment in time, but not out of nothing. Al-Razi believed in the existence of the five eternal principles: Creator, Soul, Matter, Time, and Space. "The ignorant Soul having desired Matter, God, in order to ease her misery, created the world conjoining her with matter, but also sent to her the Intellect to teach her that she would be finally delivered from her sufferings only by putting an end to her union with Matter. When the Soul grasps this, the world will be dissolved."[536] Al-Razi seems to be even impugning the Muslim unity of God, "which could not bear to be associated with any eternal soul, matter, space or time."

In his ethics, the *Spiritual Physick,* al-Razi is absolutely unique in not once referring to the Koran and the sayings of the Prophet—a practice common in such works—or to any specific Muslim doctrine. Arberry describes his attitude as "tolerant agnosticism" and "intellectual hedonism," and "though its origins in classical philosophy are obvious, it reflects very characteristically the outlook of the cultured Persian gentleman, constantly down the ages informing Iranian thought and life."[537] He advocates moderation, disapproves of asceticism, enjoins control of one's passions by reason, and under the influence of Plato's Philebus, develops his theory of pleasure and pain: "pleasure is not something positive but the simple result of a return to normal conditions, the disturbance of which has caused pain."

On life after death he reserves judgment and tries to allay the fear of death by reason, in a manner reminiscent of Epicurus. His attitude to death is summed up in a poem he wrote in old age:

> Truly I know not—and decay
> Hath laid his hand upon my heart,
> And whispered to me that the day
> Approaches, when I must depart—
> I know not whither I shall roam,

Or where the spirit, having sped
From this its wasted fleshly home,
Will after dwell, when I am dead.[538]

This is like a breath of fresh air after the dogmatic certainties of al-Ghazali and his beloved, pathological imagery of the torments of hell.

At last, we come to those views of al-Razi that earned him from Muslims universal condemnation for blasphemy. Ibn Hazm, Nasir-i Khusrau, al-Kirmani, and even al-Biruni joined in the chorus of reproach. Unlike al-Kindi, al-Razi sees no possibility of a reconciliation between philosophy and religion. In two heretical works, one of which may well have influenced the European freethought classic *De Tribus Impostoribus,* al-Razi gave vent to his hostility to the revealed religions. Al-Razi's heretical book *On Prophecy* has not survived, but we know that it maintained the thesis that reason is superior to revelation, and salvation is only possible through philosophy.

The second of al-Razi's heretical works has partly survived in a refutation by an Ismaili author. Its audacity will be apparent as soon as we examine, with the help of Kraus,[539] Pines, and Gabrieli, its principal theses.

All men are by nature equal and equally endowed with the faculty of reason that must not be disparaged in favor of blind faith; reason further enables men to perceive scientific truths in an immediate way. The prophets—these billy goats with long beards, as al-Razi disdainfully describes them—cannot claim any intellectual or spiritual superiority. These billy goats pretend to come with a message from God, all the while exhausting themselves in spouting their lies, and imposing on the masses blind obedience to the "words of the master." The miracles of the prophets are impostures, based on trickery, or the stories regarding them are lies. The falseness of what all the prophets say is evident in the fact that they contradict one another—one affirms what the other denies, and yet each claims to be the sole depository of the truth; thus the New Testament contradicts the Torah, the Koran the New Testament. As for the Koran, it is but an assorted mixture of "absurd and inconsistent fables," which has ridiculously been judged inimitable, when, in fact, its language, style, and its much vaunted "eloquence" are far from being faultless. Custom, tradition, and intellectual laziness lead men to follow their religious leaders blindly. Religions have been the sole cause of the bloody wars that have ravaged mankind. Religions have also been resolutely hostile to philosophical speculation and to scientific research. The so-called holy scriptures are worthless and have done more harm than good, whereas the "writings of the ancients like Plato, Aristotle, Euclid and Hippocrates have rendered much greater service to humanity."

The people who gather round the religious leaders are either feeble-minded, or they are women and adolescents. Religion stifles truth and fosters enmity. If a book in itself can constitute a demonstration that it is true revelation, the treatises of geometry, astronomy, medicine and logic can justify such a claim much better than the Quran, the transcendent literary beauty of which, denied by Razi, was thought by orthodox Muslims to prove the truth of Muhammad's mission.[540]

In his political philosophy, al-Razi believed one could live in an orderly society without being terrorized by religious law or coerced by the prophets. Certainly the precepts of Muslim law, such as the prohibition of wine, did not trouble him in the least. It was, as noted already, through philosophy and human reason that human life could be improved, not through religion. Finally, al-Razi believed in scientific and philosophical progress—the sciences progressed from generation to generation. One had to keep an open mind and not reject empirical observations simply because they did not fit into one's preconceived scheme of things. Despite his own contributions to the sciences, he believed that one day they would be superseded by even greater minds than his. It is clear from the preceding account that al-Razi's criticisms of religion are the most violent that appeared in the entire Middle Ages, whether European or Islamic. His heretical writings, significantly, have not survived and were not widely read; nonetheless, they are a witness to a remarkably tolerant culture and society—a tolerance lacking in other periods and places.

The Second Period of Islamic Philosophy

On the whole, the most important philosophers of the second period are to be found in the Islamic West—namely, Avempace (Ibn Bajja), Ibn Tufayl, and Averroes (Ibn Rushd).

IBN BAJJA (d. 1138)

Ibn Bajja was the least religious of the three philosophers, philosophy being but a vehicle for his moral criticism of the materialistic tendencies of his times. The philosopher should isolate himself from the masses and devote himself to the purely intellectual contemplation of the intelligible with a view to ultimate union with the active intellect. Bajja denies the resurrection of the body or the survival of the individual soul and believes only the intellect survives. But the intellect lacks any individual quality. Hardly any of this philosophy is likely to be of much comfort to the average Muslim—indeed, he may even find it heretical. Ibn Bajja's enemies labeled him an atheist who had rejected the Koran and all the Muslim dogmas and these enemies may have poisoned him.

IBN TUFAYL (d. 1185)

Ibn Tufayl is famous for his philosophical tale "Hayy ibn Yaqzan." The eponymous hero of the tale grows up alone on a desert island and gradually acquires skills to survive. He finally attains philosophical knowledge through unaided reason. Eventually someone called Asal, arrives from a neighboring island. Asal, who has been brought up by traditional religion, but is attracted to allegorical and esoteric interpretations of the scriptures, now wishes to devote himself to the contemplation of God in solitude. After having discussed their respective philosophical positions, they realize that Hayy's philosophical religion and Asal's allegorical interpretation of traditional religion are the same. Hayy returns to the inhabited island where people follow the traditional religion, with its literalism and avoidance of allegory. He tries to teach them his philosophical religion but without much success, and he finally realizes that not everyone is intellectually capable of grasping it. In fact the majority of the people of the inhabited island are no better than animals.

Ibn Tufayl was clearly defending the autonomy of philosophy, with Hayy representing pure philosophy and Asal philosophical theology. Though ostensibly defending the harmony of religion and philosophy, Ibn Tufayl shows that religious and philosophical truths are not really on the same level. For Hayy (and Ibn Tufayl), only philosophical truth arrived at by pure reason is worth having and reserved for the privileged few. Religious truth is for the unreflecting masses, who should restrict their activities to obeying the religious prescriptions and following the tradition. The ordinary Muslim is not likely to be flattered.

AVERROES (1126–1198)

Abu al-Walid Muhammad b. Ahmad ibn Rushd or Averroes came from a family of jurists, and he himself was trained in the legal sciences, later serving as a judge in Seville and Cordoba. He also studied medicine and philosophy and is considered one of the greatest commentators on Aristotle. His philosophical views are the subject of furious debate among the specialists, and the nonspecialist has to tread with care. It is on the very subject that concerns us, the relation between philosophy and religion, that the most diverse opinions exist on Ibn Rushd's real position.

According to Ernest Renan, Averroes was a supreme rationalist who was opposed to all religious dogmas, and his theological writings were smokescreens to hide his true views from the intolerant orthodox doctors of law. Most scholars in the twentieth century have rejected this view and believe that Ibn Rushd was a sincere Muslim, convinced that philosophy and revelation were both true. Nor do the modern scholars accept the idea that Ibn Rushd propounded the theory of "double truth," one for the uneducated masses and one for the cultured few. On the contrary, there exists a religious truth that is true for all men irrespective of education or status or understanding. In fact, Ibn Rushd attacks the theologians and their lucubrations, preferring the literal meaning of the Koran that seems to him wiser. The theologians are only likely to confuse people.

According to Ibn Rushd, the sharia commands the study of philosophy but only for those capable of understanding and using Aristotle's demonstrative method.

The Koran contains passages that are in need of interpretation, but this should only be attempted by those with a solid grounding in scholarship. Other parts of the Koran and other texts which form a part of the sharia are to be taken literally, to interpret them would amount to unbelief and heretical innovations.

It is difficult to know what Ibn Rushd's views on the resurrection of the dead are, because he seems to have changed his mind or, at least, refined his theory. Scholars also seem to be divided in their opinions. For de Boer,[541] Ibn Rushd believed in the "perishable nature of all that is individual, by which theory individual immortality is also taken away." Whereas George Hourani[542] believes that according to Ibn Rushd, "our physical bodies are dissolved at death, but we may receive new celestial ones in a resurrection, and these would hold our reconstituted individual souls." While Marmura[543] holds that in his technical writings (e.g., commentaries on Aristotle), Ibn Rushd's theory left no room for the soul's individual immortality, in his other writings, Ibn Rushd "affirms a doctrine of individual immortality, whether this is confined to the soul or involves bodily resurrection." In yet another work, Ibn Rushd affirms a doctrine of bodily resurrection. For Fakhry,[544] Ibn Rushd's theory entails that "the only form of survival possible is intellectual, i.e., that of the material or 'possible' intellect, once it is reunited with the active intellect," Hourani, Marmura, and de Boer seem to agree that Ibn Rushd's theory was not likely to please the orthodox clergy; Mamura even goes back to a Renan-like hypothesis in claiming that Ibn Rushd was perhaps protecting himself against charges of unbelief in presenting different arguments to different audiences.

On another important issue—the position of women in Islam—Averroes's opinion must have driven the orthodox wild. According to Averroes, much of the poverty and distress of the times arises from the fact that women are kept like "domestic animals or house plants for purposes of gratification, of a very questionable character besides, instead of being allowed to take part in the production of material and intellectual wealth, and in the preservation of the same."[545]

Averroes had a profound influence on the Latin philosophers and scientists of the thirteenth century. A school of Averroists arose at the University of Padua where Averroes's work on Aristotle was responsible for the development of the inductive, empirical sciences. And yet, Averroes had no influence at all on the development of Islamic philosophy. After his death, he was practically forgotten in the Islamic world. Philosophy itself went into a decline within Islam, which was now to be dominated by Ash'arism, with its attendant petrifying dogma. In the words of Arberry,

> As for Islam, the sweet reason of Averroes' patient voice would be silenced by the thunder of Ibn Taimiya's uncompromising denunciation. By the time the illustrious Ibn Khaldun (d. 1406) came to draw up his catalogue of the sacred and profane sciences, philosophy had fallen so far from grace as to be relegated to a string of contemptuous paragraphs following the discussion of magic, talismans and alchemy, and to share with astrology the signal honor of his summary refutation."[546]

There was a rather misguided attempt by the Islamic renaissance movement, the Nahda, at the beginning of the century to take Averroes on board as an out-and-out rationalist who advocated a secular state. The movement was much influenced by Renan's interpretation of Averroes, an interpretation that over-emphasized Averroes's rationality and belittled his religious and juridical work.

Greek Science and Islamic Civilization

Here in the domain of science, we come at last to the true greatness of Islamic civilization, its true universal nature. A brief glance at the words of Arabic origin that have entered European languages will reveal the extent of the influence of Islamic civilization on European science: alkali; zircon; alembic; sherbet; camphor; borax; elixir; talc; the stars Aldebaran, Altair, and Betelgeuse; nadir; zenith; azure; zero; cipher; algebra; algorism; lute; rebeck; artichoke; coffee; jasmine; saffron; and taraxacum. But of course Islamic science was founded on the works of the ancient Greeks, and the Muslims are important as the preservers and transmitters of Greek (and Hindu) learning that may well have been lost otherwise. Although the Islamic scientists did not often improve substantially on the works of the Greeks, they did make original contributions to trigonometry; indeed they are seen as the inventors of plane and spherical trigonometry; which did not exist among the Greeks. Original work was also done in optics by al-Haitham (Alhazen) (d. 1039) and al-Farisi (d. 1320). Islamic work on alchemy, magic, and astrology also played an important part in the development of European science—the idea of power over nature stimulated research and experimentation. Much work was also done in medicine, algebra, arithmetic, geometry, mechanics, and astronomy.

As Ibn Khaldun reminds us, Arabs did not play a great part in the original development of Islamic science: "It is strange that most of the learned among the Muslims who have excelled in the religious or intellectual sciences are non-Arabs with rare exceptions; and even those savants who claimed Arabian descent spoke a foreign language, grew up in foreign lands, and studied under foreign masters." As Martin Plessner says, emphasizing the internationality and inter-religiousnesss of Islamic science, most of the credit must go to Persians, Christians, and Jews:

> Islamic science did not remain exclusively in the hands of Muslims, even after its "Arabization." Christians and Jews continued to make so active a contribution that the Fons vitae of Ibn Gabirol (Avicebron) could pass for the work of a Muslim until the nineteenth century when S. Munk identified the author as Jewish. The medical works of Isaac Israeli and Maimonides are in no way different from the works of Islamic authors; the same is true of the scientific writings of the Christian bishop Barhebraeus. The very fact that the books of Islamic authors could be translated into Hebrew and Latin without significant

changes demonstrates the "interreligiousness" no less than the internationality of Islamic science.[547]

Plessner goes on to make two important points that are the main thrust of my arguments on Islamic science:

Science was perhaps the one cultural area that was least accessible to "Islamization." Moreover, the continued and undiminished hostility of official orthodoxy against the ancient sciences remained as characteristic of Islam as it was of Christianity until deep into the Middle Ages, and of orthodox Jewry to the very threshold of our present time. Knowledge not founded on revelation and tradition was deemed not only to be irrelevant but to be the first step on the path to heresy.[548]

There is a persistent myth that Islam encouraged science. Adherents of this view quote the Koran and hadith to prove their point: "Say, shall those who have knowledge and those have it not be deemed equal?" (Koran 39.12); "Seek knowledge, in China if necessary"; "The search after knowledge is obligatory for every Muslim." This is nonsense, because the knowledge advocated in the preceding quotes is religious knowledge. Orthodoxy has always been suspicious of "knowledge for its own sake," and unfettered intellectual inquiry is deemed dangerous to the faith.

The Muslims made a distinction between the native or Islamic sciences and foreign sciences. Islamic science consisted of religion and language (Koranic exegesis, the science of hadith, jurisprudence, scholastic theology; grammar, lexicography, rhetoric, and literature). The foreign sciences or "the sciences of the ancients" were defined as those common to all peoples and religious communities, as opposed to such sciences whose development was peculiar to Islam. As Grunebaum says, the foreign sciences are primarily the propaedeutic, physical, and metaphysical sciences of the Greeks: the various branches of mathematics, philosophy, natural history (zoology, botany, etc.), medicine, astronomy, music, magic, and alchemy.

But as Grunebaum says, the study of these foreign sciences was always looked upon with suspicion and even animosity, which increased in the later Middle Ages. A part of the hostility can be attributed to the fact that the ancient authorities were non-Muslim and foreign. All foreign sciences endangered the faith.[549]

The sciences were also seen as praiseworthy, blameworthy, or neutral. All sciences are blameworthy that are useless for acting rightly toward God. The Prophet is reputed to have prayed to God to protect him from useless knowledge. Useful knowledge was that which was necessary or helpful for the practice of religion. Eventually the ancient sciences were to lose out in this perpetual battle between the theological and the philosophical-scientific approach, since they were not required for the realization of the kind of life that God had ordained. Thus, despite the contributions of the Muslim scholars and scientists, these sciences had no root in the fundamental needs and aspirations of Islamic civilization. Islam considered the main task and aim of man to be to serve God, to which end the native sciences, history, and geography, were, of course essential. Any effort beyond that, e.g., the natural sciences, is not essential to the central cultural task and thesefore can be discarded.

Both Grunebaum and Renan make the same point that Islamic science developed for a while despite Islam. Grunebaum puts the matter thus: "Those accomplishments of Islamic mathematical and medical science which continue to compel our admiration were developed in areas and in periods where the elites were willing to go beyond and possibly against the basic strains of orthodox thought and feeling."[550]

Renan makes a similar point:

> Science and philosophy flourished on Musalman soil during the first half of the middle ages; but it was not by reason of Islam, it was in spite of Islam. Not a Musalman philosopher or scholar escaped persecution. During the period just specified persecution is less powerful than the instinct of free enquiry, and the rationalist tradition is kept alive, then intolerance and fanaticism win the day. It is true that the Christian Church also cast great difficulties in the way of science in the middle ages; but she did not strangle it outright, as did the Musalman theology. To give Islam the credit of Averroes and so many other illustrious thinkers, who passed half their life in prison, in forced hiding, in disgrace, whose books were burned and whose writings almost suppressed by theological authority, is as if one were to ascribe to the Inquisition the discoveries of Galileo, and a whole scientific development which it was not able to prevent.[551]

Not only did orthodoxy stifle the research of the scientists but it was also obvious "that their researches had nothing to give to their community which this community could accept as an essential enrichment of their lives." For us, looking from the outside, this loss of scientific endeavor is an impoverishment of Islamic civilization, but for the Muslims there was no loss since this science did not serve the Muslim aim of serving God. The idea of knowledge for its own sake was meaningless in the Muslim context; Sarton in his history of science gives the example of Muslim zoology: "One can find in many Arabic and Persian writings speculations on the order of nature as far as the distribution of the three kingdoms is concerned. The Muslims, with but few exceptions, were hardly interested in the scientific aspects of these matters, but rather in their theological implications; they were not thinking so much of evolution from the human or naturalistic point of view as of creation from the divine one."[552]

As an example of the persecution of the scientists that Renan alluded to previously, we might cite the case of Ibn al-Haitham (Alhazen), whose works were branded as heretical and then forgotten in the Muslim East.

> A disciple of Maimonides, the Jewish philosopher, relates that he was in Baghdad on business, when the library of a certain philosopher (who died in 1214) was burned there. The preacher, who conducted the execution of the sentence, threw

into the flames, with his own hands, an astronomical work of Ibn al-Haitham, after he had pointed to a delineation therein given of the sphere of the earth, as an unhappy symbol of impious Atheism.[553]

12

Sufism or Islamic Mysticism

As one of the greatest scholars of Sufism, R. A. Nicholson, said, the earliest Sufis were ascetics and quietists rather than true mystics. These early Sufis were inspired by Christian ideals, seeking salvation by shunning the meretricious delights of this world. Eventually, asceticism was seen as only the first stage of a long journey whose ultimate aim was a deep and intimate knowledge of God. Light, Knowledge, and Love were the main ideas of this new Sufism. "Ultimately they rest upon a pantheistic faith which deposed the One transcendent God of Islam and worshipped in His stead One Real Being who dwells and works everywhere, and whose throne is not less, but more, in the human heart than in the heaven of heavens."[554]

Sufis were undoubtedly influenced by certain passages in the Koran, but the historical development of Sufism owes as much or more to the influence of Christianity, Neoplatonism, Gnosticism, and Buddhism (the Sufis learned the use of the rosary from Buddhist monks, among other more substantial matters).

For us, in this chapter, what is interesting is the way that later Sufis "made a complete break with the formal system of Islamic law, asserting that the shackles of the law do not bind those who have attained knowledge." This was true of individuals as much as whole orders of dervishes. Many Sufis were good Muslims, but some were only nominally Muslim, while a third group were "Muslim after a fashion." One of the most important figures in the history of Sufism, Abu Said (d. 1049), had nothing but contempt for Islam and all positive religion, forbidding his disciples to go on pilgrimage to Mecca, and so on. Bayazid (d. ca. 1581) also set little value on the observance of the precepts of the sharia.

The Bektashi order seems to have come into existence around about the beginning of the sixteenth century. Heavily influenced by Christian and Gnostic ideas, the Bektashis rejected as worthless all external ceremonies of Islam and all other religions.

There was even a group of dervishes, collectively known as the malamatiya,

276

who committed the most outrageous acts possible to draw upon themselves deliberately the contempt of the populace. This in turn enabled them to show their own contempt for the contempt that others had of them.

The great achievement of the Sufis was their insistence that true religion had nothing to do with the doctrinal and legal system of orthodoxy, which only restricted man's religious horizon. In the mystic's vision there were no heavenly rewards and hellish punishments, the written word of God was abrogated by a direct and intimate revelation. Instead of being ruled by fear, the mystic is more concerned with the love and knowledge of God, detachment from the self, and "the divine service is regarded as a service of hearts," rather than the observance of external rules that had to be obeyed blindly.

The more Sufism moved toward pantheism the more it produced

> a series of works, which, under pretense of orthodoxy and devoutness, in reality substituted for the personal God and the future life of Islam notions that were irreconcilable with either and were supported by an interpretation of the Quran so far-fetched as to be ludicrous and irreverent. The most famous of these are the poem of Ibn al-Farid [1161–1235] . . . and the treatise of Ibn Arabi [1155–1240] . . , "Gems of Maxims." Both these works at different times brought their owners into danger, and were the cause of riots (see Ibn Iyas, *History of Egypt*, . . . where the latter book is described as the work of a worse unbeliever than Jew, Christian, or Idolater). Of the comments on the Quran which this work contains it is sufficient to cite that on the story of the Golden Calf; according to Ibn Arabi . . . . Moses found fault with his brother for not approving of the worship of the Calf, since Aaron should have known that nothing but God could ever be worshipped, and therefore the Calf was (like everything else) God.[555]

Sufi philosophy had the consequence of erasing the boundaries between the different creeds—Islam is no better than idolatry, or as one student of Ibn Arabi put it, "The Koran is polytheism pure and simple." Ibn Arabi himself wrote that his heart was a temple for idols, a Kaaba for pilgrims, the tables of the Torah and the Koran; love alone was his religion.

"I am neither Christian, nor Jew, nor Muslim," sings another mystic. The Sufis did not lay much store by the different creeds and their particulars. As Abu Said wrote, "Until mosque and madrasa are quite effaced, the work of the dervishes will not be accomplished; until belief and unbelief are quite alike, no man will be a true Muslim." And, to quote Nicholson,

> Hafiz sings more in the spirit of the freethinker, perhaps than of the mystic
>
> > "Love is where the glory falls
> > of thy face—on convent walls
> > Or on tavern floors, the same
> > Unextinguishable flame

> Where the turbaned anchorite
> Chanteth Allah day and night
> Church bells ring the call to prayer
> And the Cross of Christ is there."556

Several famous Sufis were, in the words of Goldziher, "subjected to cruel inquisition." The early Sufis aroused considerable suspicion in the authorities and the orthodox as can be seen from the history of the Sufi Dhu 'l Nun (d. 860). This Sufi had many disciples, and such influence over the people that he was denounced as a zindiq by the envious. The caliph Mutawakkil had him put into prison but later released him seeing his moral qualities.

Perhaps the most famous mystic put to death for what were considered blasphemous utterances was al-Hallaj557 (executed 922). He spent many years in prison before being flogged, mutilated, exposed on a gibbet, and finally decapitated and burned, all because he advocated personal piety rather than dry legalism and because he tried to bring "dogma into harmony with Greek philosophy on a basis of mystic experience." Twelve years later, al-Shalmaghani was also put to death on charges of blasphemy.

Al-Suhrawardi (executed 1191) was at first patronized by the viceroy at Aleppo, but his mysticism aroused much suspicion among the orthodox who eventually demanded his execution. The viceroy dared not oppose the "true believers," and so had Suhrawardi executed.

Badr al-Din, the eminent jurist, was "converted" to Sufism after his meeting with a Sufi, Shaikh Husain Akhtali. He got involved with an underground communist movement, was arrested, tried, and hanged as a traitor in 1416. He had openly developed his heretical ideas based on the views of the mystic Ibn al-Arabi.

Is Islam Tolerant of Heresy?

Early Islam developed the idea of *bida*—innovation—and according to a famous hadith, every innovation is heresy, every heresy is error, and every error leads to hell. Innovation was the opposite of sunna. Some early theologians went so far as to demand the death penalty for anyone introducing an innovation. Fortunately, this attitude did not last when the need to introduce new practices arose, henceforth, a distinction was drawn between good and bad bida (innovation). In the words of al-Shafi'i: "An innovation which contradicts the Koran, a sunna, . . . or ijma is a heretical bida, if however, something new is introduced which is not evil in itself and does not contradict the above-mentioned authorities of religious life, then it is a praiseworthy, unobjectionable innovation." This convenient device enabled Muslims to accept as good bida things that in theory were absolutely contrary to Islam. Goldziher has emphasized a very important point:

There is no parallel between dogma in Islam and dogma in the religious system of any Christian church. In Islam there are no councils and synods that, after vigorous debate, fix the formulas that henceforth must be regarded as sound belief. There is no ecclesiastic office that provides a standard of orthodoxy. There is no exclusively authorized exegesis of the sacred texts, upon which the doctrines of a church, and the manner of their inculcation, might be based. The consensus is the highest authority in all questions of religious theory and practice, but it is a vague authority, and its judgment can scarcely be precisely determined. Its very concept is variously defined. In theological questions it is especially difficult to reach unanimity about what is to be accepted without dispute, as the verdict of consensus. Where one party sees consensus, another may be far from seeing anything of the sort.[558]

Despite Goldziher's insights in the above passage, it gives a misleading picture of an Islam of doctrinal free-for-all where anything goes—you can believe and think what you like. If this were the case, what would justify us in calling it Islam at all? Contrary to the idea of a fluid, slippery Islam, Schacht poses before us the notion of, for instance, Islamic law that became "increasingly rigid and set in its final mold." True, there was, as always, enormous discrepancy between theory and practice, but Islamic law did succeed in imposing itself on the practice, especially on the law of family.

There may not have been a single church body to fix the dogma of the faithful, but in reality throughout Islamic history certain doctrines were definitely adopted in certain areas of the Islamic world. For instance, about 1048–1049, the doctrines of the school of Malik were adopted in the Maghrib. "The triumph of these doctrines caused the abandonment of all efforts to seek an allegorical interpretation for those verses of the Koran for which there was no satisfactory literal interpretation. Had not Malik b. Anas for instance said 'we know that Allah is seated on his throne, but not how this word is to be understood.' To believe it is a duty; asking questions about it is heresy"! In other words a certain doctrine was adopted and put into practice and represented the orthodoxy—there was no question of a doctrinal free-for-all or liberalism.

A little later, in 1130 the Almohad state was founded in North Africa and Spain and was based on definite principles derived from the authoritarian teachings of Ibn Tumart. There was no need for a church body to establish the dogma; the rulers of the new state did that.

Many apologists of Islam who wish to argue for the thesis that Islam was very tolerant of dissent and heresy quote the works of Ibn Taymiyya and al-Ghazali who are supposed to have stretched "the limits of Islam to the utmost." The minimum belief that was required to be counted as a Muslim was the unity of God and the prophethood of Muhammad. But even this minimum is not as liberal as it sounds and was enough to exclude the dualists (the real zindiqs), the Sufis who did not have much regard for prophets, and the freethinkers (al-Razi, Ibn Rawandi) who found all prophets charlatans. Furthermore, as we saw earlier, al-Ghazali, far from being tolerant, banished from Islam those who believed in the eternity of the world and who denied the resurrection of the body, considering them unbelievers, and even asked for their execution. By al-Ghazali's criteria, some of the greatest philosophers and poets in Islam were fit for the gallows. And, as always, the unbeliever is never somehow considered when any final assessment of Islam's tolerance is discussed. Infidelity is the greatest of all sins, more serious than murder, and carries with it the death penalty. Finally, what evidence is there that the works of al-Ghazali or Ibn Taymiyya had any influence on practice? These same apologists, quite rightly, point out the discrepancy between theory and practice, and yet are quite happy to quote the views of the two theologians without ascertaining whether their theories were ever applied in practice. In fact, we know that in the Islamic West the writings of al-Ghazali were burned as they were considered dangerous and contrary to the true faith.

Was Islam, nonetheless, tolerant in practice? The short answer is *no*.

The preceding passage from Goldziher also gives the impression that Islam was free of persecution of heretics. I hope this chapter will have disabused readers of this myth. Even the great Goldziher has to admit that "the spirit of tolerance prevailed only in the early period. . . . The evil spirit of intolerance first appeared on both sides . . . as a result of the cultivation of scholastic dogmatic theology." It was left to Sufism to reject confessional distinctions and spread the balm of tolerance.

Since the distinction between religion and politics was blurred, especially under the Abbasids, every dangerous doctrine had its religious and political aspect. The political authorities did persecute what they saw as subversive sects, holding them responsible for civil instability.

The Abbasids ruthlessly persecuted the Shiites, many of whom were imprisoned, hanged, or poisoned. But the Umayyads were not entirely without their witch hunts—witness the burning, in 737, of Bayan al-Tamimi the Shiite along with al-Mughira b. Sa'd and some of his followers who regarded him as divine. Nor must we forget the ruthless and cruel elimination of the Kharijites under the governor of Iraq, al-Hajjaj, in the early years of Umayyad rule.

We have already mentioned the two inquisitions under the Abbasids. They ended with the accession to power of Caliph Mutawakkil, who reversed the situation by declaring the Mu'tazilite doctrines to be heretical and by returning to the traditional faith. Severe measures were taken against those seen as heretics. In the words of Nicholson, "henceforth there was little room in Islam for independent thought. The populace regarded philosophy and natural science as a species of infidelity. Authors of works on these subjects ran a serious risk unless they disguised their true opinions and brought the results of their investigations into apparent conformity with the text of the Koran."[559]

The situation undoubtedly varied from country to country, ruler to ruler, period to period. In general, the Umayyads are seen as more tolerant than the Abbasids precisely because they did not yet define themselves as Muslims. This tolerance often had odd consequences: "It is characteristic of the anti-Islamic spirit which appears so strongly in the Umayyads that their chosen laureate and champion should have been a Christian who was in truth a lineal descendant of the pagan bards."[560] Al-Akhtal who is considered one of the three greatest poets of the Umayyad period was a Christian who was liable to turn up at court unannounced coming into the presence of the caliph reeking of wine and wearing a gold cross. Even more than that al-Akhtal had written some mischievous verses against Islam. This tolerance was proof for Henri Lammens that the Umayyads were more Arabs than Muslims.[561]

This example brings out one important point, namely, as long as one had royal patronage, protection, and talent, then one could get away with blasphemy, heresy, and even unbelief. For instance, the Persian family of the Barmakids were advisers to several Abbasid caliphs even though they were often accused of unbelief, or at least of secretly harboring anti-Islamic sentiments. When the royal favor was withdrawn, this influential family fell from grace.

An indication that heresy was not tolerated under Islam is the fact that anyone wanting to eliminate a rival often had recourse to accusing that person of heresy. For example, Abu Ubaid made a great name for himself at the Abbasid court and was rapidly promoted. Jealous officials resentful of his success accused Abu Ubaid's son of heresy. His son was summoned before the caliph and asked to read from the Koran placed in front him. Being practically illiterate, he stumbled through some lines. This was taken to be proof that he was a freethinker and he was therefore executed. The fear of being labeled a heretic was all-pervasive. A famous story relates the first time the philosopher Averroes was presented to the Almohad ruler Abu Yaqub Yusuf. The latter asked Averroes how philosophers viewed heaven: was it an eternal substance or did it have a beginning. Averroes was so terrified by this dangerous question that he could not speak. Yusuf put him at ease and Averroes began to show the extent of his learning. Had there not been a climate of fear, it is unlikely Averroes would have behaved in this manner.

We might also mention the constant persecution of the Ismailis. Abbas, the lord of the city of al-Rai, is said to have exterminated over 100,000 Ismailis. Another heretical sect was the Khubmesihis, who taught that Jesus was superior to Muhammad and seem to have been centered in Istanbul in the seventeenth century. Adherence to this sect was liable to lead to imprisonment and execution. The sect was said to be inspired by the heretic Kabid who held similar views and was executed in 1527.

. Thus we had the spectacle of periodic persecution of various groups (Kharijite, Shiite, Ismailis, etc.) considered either doctrinally suspect or politically subversive; individuals (philosophers, poets, theologians, scientists, rationalists, dualists, freethinkers, and mystics) were imprisoned, tortured, crucified, mutilated, and hanged; their writings burned (e.g., the writings of Averroes, Ibn Hazm, al-Ghazali, al-Haitham, and al-Kindi). Significantly, none of the heretical works of Ibn Rawandi, Ibn Warraq, Ibn al-Muqaffa, and al-Razi has survived. Other individuals are forced to flee from one ruler to another more tolerant ruler (e.g., al-Amidi). Some were exiled or banished (Averroes). Many were forced to disguise their true views and opinions by difficult or ambiguous language. Those who managed to get away with blasphemy were those protected by the powerful and influential.

13

Al-Ma'arri

Abu 'L-ala Ahmad b. Abdallah al-Ma'arri (973–1057),[562] sometimes known as the Eastern Lucretius, is the third of the great zindiqs of Islam. No true Muslim feels comfortable in his poetic presence because of his skepticism toward positive religion in general and Islam in particular.

Born in Syria not far from Aleppo, al-Ma'arri was struck at an early age with smallpox, which was eventually to lead to his total blindness. He studied in Aleppo, Antioch, and other Syrian towns before returning to his native town of Maara. When he was beginning to make a name for himself as a poet, al-Ma'arri was attracted by the famous center of Baghdad. He set out for Baghdad in 1008, but only stayed eighteen months. Returning home, he lived in semi-retirement for the next fifty years until his death. However such was his fame that eager disciples flocked to Maara to listen to his lectures on poetry and grammar.

His poetry was deeply affected by a pervasive pessimism. He constantly speaks of death as something very desirable and regards procreation as a sin. At times, at least, he denies the resurrection:

1

We laugh, but inept is our laughter;
We should weep and weep sore,
Who are shattered like glass, and thereafter
Re-molded no more.

He is said to have wanted this verse inscribed over his grave:

2

This wrong was by my father done
To me, but ne'er by me to one.

282

In other words, it would have been better not to have been born:

3

> Better for Adam and all who issued forth from his loins
> That he and they, yet unborn, created never had been!
> For whilst his body was dust and rotten bones in the earth
> Ah, did he feel what his children saw and suffered of woe.

As for religion, all men unquestioningly accept the creed of their fathers out of habit, incapable of distinguishing the true from the false:

4

> Sometimes you may find a man skillful in his trade, perfect in sagacity and in the use of arguments, but when he comes to religion he is found obstinate, so does he follow the old groove. Piety is implanted in human nature; it is deemed a sure refuge. To the growing child that which falls from his elders' lips is a lesson that abides with him all his life. Monks in their cloisters and devotees in the mosques accept their creed just as a story is handed down from him who tells it, without distinguishing between a true interpreter and a false. If one of these had found his kin among the Magians, or among the Sabians, he would have declared himself a Magian, or among the Sabians he would have become nearly or quite like them.

For al-Ma'arri, religion is a "fable invented by the ancients," worthless except for those who exploit the credulous masses:

5

> So, too, the creeds of man: the one prevails
> Until the other comes; and this one fails
> When that one triumphs; ay, the lonesome world
> Will always want the latest fairy-tales.

At other times he refers to religions as "noxious weeds":

6

> Among the crumbling ruins of the creeds
> The Scout upon his camel played his reeds
> And called out to his people—"Let us hence!
> The pasture here is full of noxious weeds.

He clearly puts Islam on the same level as all other creeds, and does not believe a word of any of them:

7

Hanifs [= Muslims] are stumbling, Christians all astray
Jews wildered, Magians far on error's way.
We mortals are composed of two great schools
Enlightened knaves or else religious fools.

8

What is religion? A maid kept close that no eye may view her;
The price of her wedding-gifts and dowry baffles the wooer.
Of all the goodly doctrine that I from the pulpit heard
My heart has never accepted so much as a single word.

9

The holy fights by Moslem heroes fought,
The saintly works by Christian hermits wrought
And those of Jewry or of Sabian creed—
Their valour reaches not the Indian's deed
Whom zeal and awe religiously inspire
To cast his body on the flaming pyre.
Yet is man's death a long, long sleep of lead
And all his life a waking. O'er our dead
The prayers are chanted, hopeless farewells ta'en;
And there we lie, never to stir again.
Shall I so fear in mother earth to rest?
How soft a cradle is thy mother's breast!
When once the viewless spirit from me is gone,
By rains unfreshed let my bones rot on!

Here, 9, in excerpt, al-Ma'arri, while admiring the Indian more than the Muslim,
and the Indian custom of cremation, still insists that death is not such a terrible
thing, it is only a falling asleep. In his collection of poems known as the *Luzumiyyat*,
al-Ma'arri clearly prefers this practice of cremation to the Muslim one of burial.
On Judgment Day, according to Muslim belief, two angels, Munker and Nakir,
open the graves of the dead and cross-examine them on their faith in a cruel
fashion. Those found wanting are pushed back into the grave where they await
hell. No wonder al-Ma'arri prefers cremation. Of course, Muslims should find
the very idea of cremation totally abhorrent:

10

And like the dead of Ind I do not fear
To go to thee in flames; the most austere
Angel of fire a softer tooth and tongue
Hath he than dreadful Munker and Nakir.

Margoliouth has compiled the following sentiments from al-Ma'arri's poems:[563]

11

Do not suppose the statements of the Prophets to be true; they are all fabrications. Men lived comfortably till they came and spoiled life. The "sacred books" are only such a set of idle tales as any age could have and indeed did actually produce. What inconsistency that God should forbid the taking of life, and Himself send two angels to take each man's! And as for the promise of a second life—the soul could well have dispensed with both existences.

Further thoughts on prophets reveal that al-Ma'arri did not consider them any better than the lying clergy:

12

The Prophets, too, among us come to teach,
Are one with those who from the pulpit preach;
They pray, and slay, and pass away, and yet
Our ills are as the pebbles on the beach.

Islam does not have a monopoly on truth:

13

Mohammed or Messiah! Hear thou me,
The truth entire nor here nor there can be;
How should our God who made the sun and the moon
Give all his light to One, I cannot see.

As for the ulama, the Muslim "clergy" or divines, al-Ma'arri has nothing but contempt for them:

14

I take God to witness that the souls of men are without
intelligence, like the souls of moths.
They said, "A divine!" but the divine is an untruthful
disputatious person, and words are wounds.

15

For his own sordid ends
The pulpit he ascends
And though he disbelieves in resurrection,
Makes all his hearers quail
Whilst he unfolds a tale
Of Last Day scenes that stun the recollection.

16

They recite their sacred books, although the fact informs me
that these are a fiction from first to last.
O Reason, thou (alone) speakest the truth.
Then perish the fools who forged the religious traditions or interpreted them!

Al-Ma'arri was a supreme rationalist who everywhere asserts "the rights of reason against the claims of custom, tradition and authority."

17

Oh, cleave ye to Reason's path that rightly ye may be led
Let none set his hopes except upon the Preserver!
And quench not the Almighty's beams, for lo, He hath given to all
A lamp of intelligence for use and enjoying.
I see humankind are lost in ignorance: even those
Of ripe age at random guess, like boys playing mora [a child's guessing game].

18

Traditions come from the past, of high import if they be True;
ay, but weak is the chain of those who warrant their truth.
Consult thy reason and let perdition take others all:
Of all the conference Reason best will counsel and guide.

A little doubt is better than total credulity.

19

By fearing whom I trust I find my way
To truth; by trusting wholly I betray
The trust of wisdom; better far is doubt
Which brings the false into the light of day.

(The thoughts in quatrain 19 can be compared to Tennyson's
    "There is more truth in honest doubt,
    Believe me, than in all the creeds.")

Al-Ma'arri attacks many of the dogmas of Islam, particularly the Pilgrimage, which he calls "a heathen's journey." "Al-Ma'arri . . . regards Islam, and positive religion generally, as a human institution. As such, it is false and rotten to the core. Its founders sought to procure wealth and power for themselves, its dignitaries pursue worldly ends, its defenders rely on spurious documents which they ascribe to divinely inspired apostles, and its adherents accept mechanically whatever they are told to believe."[564]

20

O fools, awake! The rites ye sacred hold
Are but a cheat contrived by men of old
Who lusted after wealth and gained their lust
And died in baseness—and their law is dust.

21

Praise God and pray
Walk seventy times, not seven, the Temple round
And impious remain!
Devout is he alone who, when he may
Feast his desires, is found
With courage to abstain

22

Fortune is (so strangely) allotted, that rocks are visited
(by pilgrims) and touched with hands and lips,
Like the Holy Rock (at Jerusalem) or the two Angles of Quraysh,
howbeit all of them are stones that once were kicked.

Al-Ma'arri is referring to the two corners of the Kaaba in Mecca in which are set the Black Stone and the stone that is supposed to mark the sepulcher of Ishmael.

23

Tis strange that Kurash and his people wash
Their faces in the staling of the kine;
And that the Christians say, Almighty God
Was tortured, mocked, and crucified in fine:
And that the Jews should picture Him as one
Who loves the odor of a roasting chine;
And stranger still that Muslims travel far
To kiss a black stone said to be divine:
Almighty God! will all the human race
Stray blindly from the Truth's most sacred shrine?

24

They have not based their religion on any logical ground, whereby they might decide between Shi'ites and Sunnis. In the opinion of some whom I do not mention (with praise), the Black Stone is only a remnant of idols and (sacrificial) altarstones.

Here in verse 24 al-Ma'arri is attributing an opinion to a critic, thereby protecting himself from charges of heresy, but we know from excerpts 22 and 23 that he deems most of the rites of the Pilgrimage including the kissing of the Black Stone to be superstitious nonsense.

Religions have only resulted in bigotry and bloodshed, with sect fighting sect, and fanatics forcing their beliefs onto people at the point of a sword. All religions are contrary to reason and sanity:

25

If a man of sound judgment appeals to his intelligence,
he will hold cheap the various creeds and despise them.
Do thou take thereof so much as Reason delivered (to thee),
and let not ignorance plunge thee in their stagnant pool!

26

Had they been left alone with Reason, they would not have accepted a spoken
lie; but the whips were raised (to strike them).
Traditions were brought to them, and they were bidden say,
"We have been told the truth"; and if they refused, the sword was drenched
(in their blood).
They were terrified by scabbards full of calamities, and tempted by great bowls
brimming over with food for largesse.

27

Falsehood hath so corrupted all the world,
Ne'er deal as true friends they whom sects divide;
But were not hate Man's natural element,
Churches and mosques had risen side by side.

Space forbids us from giving further examples of his merciless attacks on every kind of superstition—astrology, augury, belief in omens; the custom of exclaiming "God be praised" when anyone sneezes; myths such as the patriarchs lived to be hundreds of years old, holy men walked on water or performed miracles, etc.

Al-Ma'arri further offended Muslim sensibilities by composing "a somewhat frivolous parody of the sacred volume," i.e., the Koran, and "in the author's judgment its inferiority was simply due to the fact that it was not yet polished by the tongues of four centuries of readers." As if this were not enough, al-Ma'arri compounded his errors in the eyes of the orthodox by his work, the *Epistle of Forgiveness*. Nicholson, who was the first to translate it into English at the beginning of the century, sums up its contents admirably:

Here the Paradise of the Faithful [Muslims] becomes a glorified salon tenanted by various heathen poets who have been forgiven—hence the title—and received among the Blest. This idea is carried out with much ingenuity and in a spirit of audacious burlesque that reminds us of Lucian. The poets are presented in a series of imaginary conversations with a certain Shaykh Ali b. Mansur, to whom the work is addressed, reciting and explaining their verses, quarreling with one another, and generally behaving as literary Bohemians.[565]

Another remarkable feature of al-Ma'arri's thought was the belief that no living creature should be injured or harmed in any way. He adopted vegetarianism in his thirtieth year and held in abhorrence all killing of animals, whether for food or sport. Von Kremer has suggested that al-Ma'arri was influenced by the Jains of India in his attitude to the sanctity of all living things. In his poetry, al-Ma'arri firmly advocates abstinence from meat, fish, milk, eggs, and honey on the ground that it is an injustice to the animals concerned. Animals are capable of feeling pain, and it is immoral to inflict unnecessary harm on our fellow creatures. Even more remarkably, al-Ma'arri protests against the use of animal skins for clothing, suggests wooden shoes, and reproaches court ladies for wearing furs. Von Kremer has justly said that al-Ma'arri was centuries ahead of his time.

During his lifetime al-Ma'arri was charged with heresy, but he was not prosecuted, nor suffered any punishment for reasons that Von Kremer and Nicholson have carefully analyzed. Al-Ma'arri himself tells us that it is often wise to dissimulate, and thus we find many orthodox passages in his poetry that were meant to throw the sniffers of heresy off the scent. At heart, he seems to have been a thorough skeptic who managed to ridicule practically every dogma of Islam. Viva al-Ma'arri!

14

Women and Islam[566]

Richard Burton[567] in his "Terminal Essay" defending Islam against Western criticism argued that "the legal status of womankind in al-Islam is exceptionally high" and that the "Moslem wife has greatly the advantage over her christian sisterhood." He also goes on to claim that Islam is sex-positive: "Moslems study the art and mystery of satisfying the physical woman." His evidence for the claim was the abundance of pornographic literature with titles like the *Book of Carnal Copulation* and the *Initiation into the Modes of Coition and Its Instrumentation.* Burton must have been aware that these works were written by men for men, though the significance of this fact seems to escape him. One of the books cited by Burton— *The Book of Exposition in the Art of Coition*—begins "Alhamdolilillah Laud to the lord who adorned the virginal bosom with breasts and who made the thighs of women anvils for the spear handles of men." In other words women were created by God for man's pleasure—as his sex object, in modern parlance.

In fact, a much more famous work, Shaykh Nefzawi's *The Perfumed Garden,*[568] a sixteenth-century treatise that Burton himself was to translate from the French, is very revealing of Islamic attitudes toward women and their sexuality. Women's sexuality is never denied but seen as a source of danger: Do you know that women's religion is in their vaginas? asks the Shaykh. They are insatiable as far as their vulvas are concerned, and so long as their lust is satisfied they do not care whether it be a buffoon, a negro, a valet, or even a despised man. It is Satan who makes the juices flow from their vaginas. The Shaykh quotes Abu Nuwas with approval:

> Women are demons and were born as such
> No one can trust them as is known to all
> If they love a man it is only out of caprice
> And he to whom they are most cruel loves them most
> Beings full of treachery and trickery, I aver
> That man that loves you truly is a lost man

He who believes me not can prove my word
By letting woman's love get hold of him for years
If in your own generous mood you have given them
Your all and everything for years and years,
They will say afterwards, "I swear by God! my eyes
Have never seen a thing he gave me!"
After you have impoverished yourself for their sake
Their cry from day to day will be for ever "Give":
"Give man, get up and buy and borrow"
If they cannot profit by you they'll turn against you
They will tell lies about you and calumniate you
They do not recoil to use a slave in the master's absence
If once their passions are aroused and they play tricks
Assuredly if once their vulva is in rut
They only think of getting in some member in erection
Preserve us, God! from women's trickery
And of old women in particular. So be it.

Here we have a complete inventory of a woman's faults as seen by Muslim men—deceit, guile, ingratitude, greed, insatiable lust, in short, a gateway to hell. In contrast to his dithyramb on the position of women in Islam in the "Terminal Essay," in his Introduction to his translation of the *Perfumed Garden* a year later, Burton finally concedes "the contempt which the Mussulman in reality feels for woman."

Bullough, Bousquet, and Bouhdiba also regard Islam as a sex-positive religion in contrast to Christianity, which "made something unclean out of sexuality," to use Nietzsche's phrase. But in the last page and a half of his survey Bullough suddenly feels obliged to qualify his remarks by admitting that Islam "at the same time relegated women to the status of inferior beings." Though he still thinks Lane-Poole's judgment, that "the fatal blot in Islam is the degradation of women," is "exaggerated."

Similarly, Bousquet compares Islam to Christianity: "Islam is clearly and openly favorable to the pleasures of the flesh as such, without any secondary consideration. Christianity is clearly hostile to them." But he also has to admit, "the greatly inferior position imposed on the woman by Islamic law, in particular from the sexual point of view."[569]

Only Bouhdiba, while rejoicing in Islam's superiority on matters sexual, seems unable to find any evidence, at least in the Koran, of any misogyny and glides blithely on with his sexual, Islamic fantasies of the "infinite orgasm" and "the perpetual erection."

To see Islam as sex-positive is to insult all Muslim women, for sex is seen entirely from the male point of view; a woman's sexuality, as we shall see, is either denied or, as in *The Perfumed Garden*, seen as something unholy, something to be feared, repressed, a work of the devil. But still as Slimane Zeghidour put it, sexuality occupies as fundamental a place in Islamic doctrine as it does in psychoanalytical theory. I hope to show that in its obsession with cleanliness,

Islam reveals a disgust with the sexual act and the sexual parts that is pathological and always the same contempt for women.

According to the *Dictionary of Islam*,[570] "although the condition of women under Muslim law is most unsatisfactory, it must be admitted that Muhammad effected a vast and marked improvement in the condition of the female population of Arabia." Bousquet concurs; the reforms effected in favor of women make Muhammad seem "a champion of feminism" in that particular historical context. Two reforms often quoted are the prohibition against burying female children alive and the establishment of rights of inheritance of women ("whereas," adds Burton, "in England a 'Married Woman's Property Act' was completed only in 1882 after many centuries of the grossest abuse").

But as Ahmed al-Ali shows in *Organisations Sociales chez les Bedouins*, the practice of burying unwanted female children probably had a religious origin and was extremely rare. Muslim writers have simply exaggerated its frequency to highlight the supposed superiority of Islam. As far as inheritance is concerned, a woman has half the share of a man and as we shall see later, she by no means, pace Burton, has complete power over the disposal of her own property. Muhammad, in this as in so many other matters, simply did not go far enough; Muhammad's ideas of women were like those of his contemporaries—women were charming, capricious playthings, liable to lead one astray.

According to the scholar Schacht, women under Islam were in many ways worse off: "The Quran in a particular situation had encouraged polygamy and this from being an exception, now became one of the essential features of the Islamic law of marriage. It led to a definite deterioration in the position of married women in society, compared with that which they had enjoyed in Pre-Islamic Arabia and this was only emphasized by the fact that many perfectly respectable sexual relationships of Pre-Islamic Arabia had been outlawed by Islam."[571]

Bedouin women working alongside their husbands enjoyed considerable personal freedom and independence. Leading a nonsedentary life, tending cattle, she was neither cloistered nor veiled, but active; her contributions to the community much appreciated and respected. Segregation was totally impractical. If ill-treated by their husbands many simply ran away to a neighboring tribe. Despite Islam—rather than thanks to Islam—even in the nineteenth century, "Amongst the Bedouins their armies are led by a maiden of good family, who, mounted amid the fore ranks on a camel shames the timid and excites the brave by satirical or encomiastic recitations."[572]

The tenth-century Arab Historian, al-Tabari's account of Hind bint Otba, the wife of Abu Sufyan, the head of one of the aristocratic families of Mecca, gives a vivid picture of the independence of aristocratic women before Islam. Women swore allegiance as much as men, took part in negotiations with the new military chief of the city—that is, Muhammad himself—and were often frankly hostile to the new religion. When Muhammad arrived at Mecca in A.D. 630 with 10,000 men, a rather overawed Abu Sufyan finally led out a deputation to make a formal submission and swear allegiance. The women led by Hind gave theirs only very reluctantly. Hind reproached Muhammad for having imposed obligations on women that he had not imposed on men. When the Prophet enjoined them never to kill their children, Hind retorted that this was rather fine coming from a military leader who had spilled so much blood at the battle of Badr when seventy men had been killed and many prisoners later executed on Muhammad's own orders.

Modern reformist Muslim intellectuals—male or female—when confronted by the apparent backwardness of the position of women (a situation which has remained stagnant for centuries), have tended to invent a mythological golden age at the dawn of Islam when women putatively enjoyed equal rights. For example, even Nawal el Saadawi,[573] the Egyptian feminist who has done more than anyone else to speak positively of Muslim women's right to express their sexuality, writes of "the regression of the Arab woman in Islamic philosophy and culture in contrast to her situation at the time of Muhammad or in the Spirit (or essence) of Islam." Similarly the Algerian Rachid Mimouni[574] says, "It is clear that it is not the religion of Allah (which is at fault) but its interpretation. . . . Fundamentalism is an imposture. It discredits the message of Mohammad." The thought is that it is not Islam that is to blame for the degrading of women. Of course to talk of "the essence of Islam" is simply to perpetuate the malignant influence of religious authority and to perpetuate a myth. These same Muslim thinkers, when faced by the textual evidence of the inherent misogyny of Islam, are confused and anguished. Refusing to look reality in the face, they feel obliged to interpret these sacred texts, to apologize, to minimize their manifest hostility to women—in short, to exonerate Islam. Others try to argue that these traditions were perpetuated by dubious Muslims whose motives were suspect.

Yet to do battle with the orthodox, the fanatics, and the mullas in the interpretation of these texts is to do battle on their (the fanatics') terms, on their ground. Every text that you produce they will adduce a dozen others contradicting yours. The reformists cannot win on these terms—whatever mental gymnastics the reformists perform, they cannot escape the fact that Islam is deeply antifeminist. *Islam is the fundamental cause of the repression of Muslim women and remains the major obstacle to the evolution of their position.*[575] Islam has always considered women as creatures inferior in every way: physically, intellectually, and morally. This negative vision is divinely sanctioned in the Koran, corroborated by the hadiths and perpetuated by the commentaries of the theologians, the custodians of Muslim dogma and ignorance.

Far better for these intellectuals to abandon the religious argument, to reject these sacred texts, and have recourse to *reason* alone. They should turn instead to human rights. The Universal Declaration of Human Rights (adopted on December 10, 1948, by the General Assembly of the United Nations in Paris and ratified by most Muslim countries) at no point has recourse to a religious argument. These rights are based on natural rights, which any adult human being capable of choice has. They are rights that human beings have simply because they are human beings. Human reason or rationality is the ultimate arbiter of rights—human rights, the rights of women.

Unfortunately, in practice, in Muslim countries one cannot simply leave the theologians with their narrow, bigoted world view to themselves. One cannot ignore the ulama, those learned doctors of Muslim law who by their fatwas or decisions in questions touching private or public matters of importance regulate the life of the Muslim community. They still exercise considerable powers of approving or forbidding certain actions. Why the continuing influence of the mullas?

The Koran remains for all Muslims, not just "fundamentalists," the uncreated word of God Himself. It is valid for all times and places; its ideas are absolutely true and beyond all criticism. To question it is to question the very word of God, and hence blasphemous. A Muslim's duty is to believe it and obey its divine commands.

Several other factors contribute to the continuing influence of the ulama. Any religion that requires total obedience without thought is not likely to produce people capable of *critical thought,* people capable of free and independent thought. Such a situation is favorable to the development of a powerful "clergy" and is clearly responsible for the intellectual, cultural, and economic stagnation of several centuries. Illiteracy remains high in Muslim countries. Historically, as there never was any separation of state and religion, any criticism of one was seen as a criticism of the other. Inevitably, when many Muslim countries won independence after the Second World War, Islam was unfortunately linked with nationalism, which meant that any criticism of Islam was seen as a betrayal of the newly independent country—an unpatriotic act, an encouragement to colonialism and imperialism. No Muslim country has developed a stable democracy; Muslims are being subjected to every kind of repression possible. Under these conditions healthy criticism of society is not possible, because critical thought and liberty go together.

The above factors explain why Islam in general and the position of women in particular are never criticized, discussed, or subjected to deep scientific or skeptical analysis. All innovations are discouraged in Islam—every problem is seen as a religious problem rather than a social or economic one.

Adam and Eve[576]

Islam took the legend of Adam and Eve from the Old Testament and adapted it in its own fashion. The creation of mankind from one person is mentioned in the following suras:

4.1. O Mankind! Be careful of your duty to your Lord who created you from a single soul and from it created its mate and from them twain hath spread abroad a multiple of men and women

39.6. He created you from one being, then from that (being) He made its mate.

7.189. He it is who did create you from a single soul and therefrom did make his mate that he might take rest in her.

From these slender sources Muslim theologians have concluded that man was the original creation—womankind was created secondarily for the pleasure and repose of man. The legend was further developed to reinforce the supposed inferiority of women. Finally, the legend was given a sacred character so that to criticize it was to criticize the very words of God, which were immutable and absolute. Here is how Muhammad describes women in general: "Be friendly to women for womankind was created from a rib, but the bent part of the rib, high up, if you try to straighten it you will break it; if you do nothing, she will continue to be bent."

The story of Adam and Eve is further elaborated in:

2.35-36. And We said: O Adam! Dwell thou and thy wife in the Garden, and eat ye freely (of the fruits) thereof where ye will; but come not nigh this tree lest ye become wrongdoers.

But Satan caused them to deflect therefrom and expelled them from the (happy) state in which they were; and We said: Fall down, one of you a foe unto the other! There shall be for you on earth a habitation and provision for a time.

7.19-20. And (unto man): O Adam! Dwell thou and thy wife in the Garden and eat from whence ye will, but come not nigh this tree lest ye become wrongdoers.

Then Satan whispered to them that he might manifest unto them that which was hidden from of their shame and he said: Your Lord forbade you from this tree only lest ye should become angels or become of the immortals.

20.120-121. But the Devil whispered to him saying: O Adam! Shall I show thee the tree of immortality and power that wasteth not away?

Then they twain ate thereof, so that their shame became apparent unto them, and they began to hide by heaping on themselves some of the leaves of the Garden. And Adam disobeyed his Lord, so went astray.

God punishes Adam and Eve for disobeying his orders. But there is nothing in these verses to show that it was Eve (as in the Old Testament) who led Adam astray. And yet Muslim exegetists and jurists have created the myth of Eve the temptress that has since become an integral part of Muslim tradition. Muhammad himself is reputed to have said: "If it had not been for Eve, no woman would have been unfaithful to her husband."

The Islamic tradition also attributes guile and deceit to women and draws its support from the following text in the Koran:

12.22-34. [Joseph has been installed in the house of the man who bought him.] Now the woman in whose house he was solicited him, and closed the doors on them. "Come," she said, "take me!" "God be my refuge," he said. "Surely my lord has given me a goodly lodging. Surely the evildoers do not prosper." For she desired him; and he would have taken her but that he saw the proof of his Lord. So was it, that We might turn away from him evil and abomination;

he was one of Our devoted servants. They raced to the door; and she tore his shirt from behind. They encountered her master by the door. She said, "What is the recompense of him who purposes evil against thy folk, but that he should be imprisoned or a painful chastisement?" Said he, "It was she that solicited me"; and a witness of her folk bore witness, "If his shirt has been torn from before then she has spoken truly, and he is one of the liars; but if his shirt has been torn from behind, then she has lied, and he is one of the truthful." When he saw his shirt was torn from behind he said, "This is of your women's guile; surely your guile is great. Joseph, turn away from this and thou woman, ask forgiveness of thy crime; surely thou art one of the sinners." Certain women that were in the city said, "The Governor's wife has been soliciting her page; he smote her heart with love; we see her in manifest error." When she heard their sly whispers, she sent to them, and made ready for them a repast, then she gave to each one of them a knife. "Come forth, attend to them," she said. And when they saw him, they so admired him that they cut their hands, saying, "God save us! This is no mortal; he is no other but a noble angel." "So now you see," she said. "This is he you blamed me for. Yes, I solicited him, but he abstained. Yet if he will not do what I command him, he shall be imprisoned, and be one of the humbled." He said, "My Lord, prison is dearer to me than that they call me to; yet if Thou turnest not from me their guile, then I shall yearn toward them, and so become one of the ignorant." So his Lord answered him, and He turned away from him their guile; surely He is the All-hearing, and the All-knowing.

Modern Muslim commentators interpret these verses to show that guile, deceit, and treachery are intrinsic to a woman's nature. Not only is she unwilling to change, she is by nature incapable of changing—she has no choice.[577]

In attacking the female deities of the polytheists, the Koran takes the opportunity to malign the female sex further.

4.117. They invoke in His stead only females; they pray to none else than Satan, a rebel.

43.15–19. And they allot to Him a portion of his bondmen! Lo! man is verily a mere ingrate.

Or chooseth He daughters of all that He hath created, and honoureth He you with sons?

And if one of them hath tidings of that which he likeneth to the Beneficent One (i.e., tidings of the birth of a girl-child), his countenance becometh black and he is full of inward rage.

(Liken they then to Allah) that which is bred up in outward show, and in dispute cannot make itself plain?

And they make the angels, who are the slaves of the Beneficent, females. Did they witness their creation? Their testimony will be recorded and they will be questioned.

52.39. Or hath He daughters whereas ye have sons?

37.149-50. Now ask them (O Muhammad): Hath thy Lord daughters whereas they have sons?

Or created We the angels females while they were present?

53.21-22. Are yours the males and His the females
That indeed were an unfair division!

53.27. Lo! it is those who disbelieve in the Hereafter who name the angels with the names of females.

If Mr. Bouhdiba is not convinced by these, here are some more verses from the Koran that seem to us of a misogynist tendency:

2.178 O ye who believe! Retaliation is prescribed for you in the matter of the murdered; the freeman for the freeman, and the slave for the slave, and the female for the female.

2.228. Women who are divorced shall wait, keeping themselves apart, three (monthly) courses. And it is not lawful for them that they should conceal that which Allah hath created in their wombs if they are believers in Allah and the Last Day. And their husbands would do better to take them back in that case if they desire a reconciliation. And they (women) have rights similar to those (of men) over them in kindness, and men are a degree above them. Allah is Mighty, Wise.

2.282 But if he who oweth the debt is of low understanding, or weak or unable himself to dictate, then let the guardian of his interests dictate in (terms of) equity. And call to witness, from among your men, two witnesses. And if two men be not (at hand) then a man and two women, of such as ye approve as witnesses, so that if the one erreth (through forgetfulness) the other will remember.

4.3. And if ye fear that ye will not deal fairly by the orphans, marry of the women, who seem good to you, two or three or four; and if ye fear that ye cannot do justice (to so many) then one (only) or the (captives) that your right hand possesses. Thus it is more likely that ye will not do injustice.

4.11. Allah chargeth you concerning (the provision for) your children: to the male the equivalent of the portion of two females.

4.34. Men are in charge of women, because Allah hath made the one of them to excel the other, and because they spend of their property (for the support of women). So good women are the obedient, guarding in secret that which Allah hath guarded. As for those from whom ye fear rebellion, admonish them and banish them to beds apart; and scourge (beat) them. Then if they obey you, seek not a way against them Lo! Allah is ever High Exalted, Great.

4.43. O ye who believe! Draw not near unto prayer when ye are drunken, till ye know that which ye utter, nor when ye are polluted, save when journeying on the road, till ye have bathed. And if ye be ill, or on a journey, or one of you cometh from the closet, or ye have touched women, and ye find not water, then go to high clean soil and rub your faces and your hands. Lo! Allah is Benign, Forgiving.

5.6. And if ye are sick on a journey, or one of you cometh from the closet, or ye have contact with women and ye find not water, then go to clean high ground and rub your faces and your hands with some of it.

33.32–33. O ye wives of the Prophet! Ye are not like any other women. If ye keep your duty (to Allah), then be not soft of speech lest he in whose heart is a disease aspire to you, but utter customary speech.

And stay in your houses. Bedizen not yourselves with the bedizenment of the time of ignorance. Be regular in prayer, and pay the poor due, and obey Allah and His Messenger.

33.53. And when ye ask of them (the wives of the Prophet) anything ask it of them from behind a curtain. That is purer for your hearts and for their hearts.

33.59. O Prophet! Tell thy wives and thy daughters and the women of the believers to draw their cloaks close round when they go abroad. That will be better, that so they may be recognized and not annoyed.

Equally, in numerous hadiths on which are based the Islamic laws we learn of the woman's role—to stay at home, to be at the beck and call of man, to obey him (which is a religious duty), and to assure man a tranquil existence. Here are some examples of these traditions:

—If it had been given me to order someone to prostrate themselves in front of someone other than God, I would surely have ordered women to prostrate themselves in front of their husbands. . . . A woman cannot fulfill her duties toward God without first having accomplished those that she owes her husband.

—The woman who dies and with whom the husband is satisfied will go to paradise.

—A wife should never refuse herself to her husband even if it is on the saddle of a camel.

—Hellfire appeared to me in a dream and I noticed that it was above all peopled with women who had been ungrateful. "Was it toward God that they were ungrateful?" They had not shown any gratitude toward their husbands for all they had received from them. Even when all your life you have showered a woman with your largesse she will still find something petty to reproach you with one day, saying, "You have never done anything for me."

—If anything presages a bad omen it is: a house, a woman, a horse.

—Never will a people know success if they confide their affairs to a woman.

Islamic culture and civilization is profoundly antifeminist, as the following sayings from various caliphs, ministers, philosophers, and theologians through the ages reveal:

Omar the second caliph (581–644) said: "Prevent the women from learning to write! say no to their capricious ways."

On another occasion he said, "Adopt positions opposite those of women. There is great merit in such opposition." And again, "Impose nudity on women because clothes are one reason for leaving the house, to attend marriages and to appear in public for ceremonies and parties. When a woman goes out frequently she risks meeting another man and finding him attractive even if he is less attractive than her husband; for she is attracted and distracted by anything she does not possess".

The antifeminist sayings of Ali (600–661), the Prophet's cousin and the fourth caliph, are famous:[578]

"The entire woman is an evil and what is worse is that it is a necessary evil!"

"You should never ask a woman her advice because her advice is worthless. Hide them so that they cannot see other men! . . . Do not spend too much time in their company for they will lead you to your downfall!"

"Men, never ever obey your women. Never let them advise you on any matter concerning your daily life. If you let them advise you they will squander all your possessions and disobey all your orders and desires. When alone they forget religion and think only of themselves; and as soon as it concerns their carnal desires they are without pity or virtue. It is easy to get pleasure from them but they give you big headaches too. Even the most virtuous among them is of easy virtue. And the most corrupt are whores! Old age does not spare them of their vices. They have three qualities worthy of an unbeliever: they complain of being oppressed when in fact it is they who oppress; they take solemn oaths and at the same time lie; they make a show of refusing the advances of men when in fact they long for them ardently. Let us implore God's help to escape their sorcery."

And finally to a man teaching a woman to write: "Do not add evil to unhappiness."

It will be appropriate to end this introduction with two quotes from the famous and much revered philosopher al-Ghazali (1058–1111), whom Professor

Montgomery Watt describes as the greatest Muslim after Muhammad. In his "The Revival Of The Religious Sciences," Ghazali defines the woman's role:[579]

> She should stay at home and get on with her spinning, she should not go out often, she must not be well-informed, nor must she be communicative with her neighbours and only visit them when absolutely necessary; she should take care of her husband and respect him in his presence and his absence and seek to satisfy him in everything; she must not cheat on him nor extort money from him; she must not leave her house without his permission and if given his permission she must leave surreptitiously. She should put on old clothes and take deserted streets and alleys, avoid markets, and make sure that a stranger does not hear her voice or recognize her; she must not speak to a friend of her husband even in need. . . . Her sole worry should be her virtue, her home as well as her prayers and her fast. If a friend of her husband calls when the latter is absent she must not open the door nor reply to him in order to safeguard her and her husband's honour. She should accept what her husband gives her as sufficient sexual needs at any moment. . . . She should be clean and ready to satisfy her husband's sexual needs at any moment.

The great theologian then warns all men to be careful of women for their "guile is immense and their mischief is noxious; they are immoral and mean spirited." "It is a fact that all the trials, misfortunes and woes which befall men come from women," moaned al-Ghazali.

In his *Book of Counsel for Kings,* al-Ghazali sums up all that a woman has to suffer and endure because of Eve's misbehavior in the Garden of Eden:

> As for the distinctive characteristics with which God on high has punished women, (the matter is as follows): "When Eve ate fruit which He had forbidden to her from the tree in Paradise, the Lord, be He praised, punished women with eighteen things: (1) menstruation; (2) childbirth; (3) separation from mother and father and marriage to a stranger; (4) pregnancy; (5) not having control over her own person; (6) a lesser share in inheritance; (7) her liability to be divorced and inability to divorce; (8) its being lawful for men to have four wives, but for a woman to have only one husband; (9) the fact that she must stay secluded in the house; (10) the fact that she must keep her head covered inside the house; (11) the fact that two women's testimony has to be set against the testimony of one man; (12) the fact that she must not go out of the house unless accompanied by a near relative; (13) the fact that men take part in Friday and feast day prayers and funerals while women do not; (14) disqualification for rulership and judgeship; (15) the fact that merit has one thousand components, only one of which is attributable to women, while 999 are attributable to men; (16) the fact that if women are profligate they will be given [only] half as much tornment as the rest of the community at the Resurrection Day; [This does not seem like a punishment! An error of translation?] (17) the fact that if their husbands die they must observe a waiting period of four months and ten days before remarrying; 18) the fact that if their husbands divorce them

they must observe a waiting period of three months or three menstrual periods before remarrying.[580]

Such are some of the sayings from the putative golden age of Islamic feminism. It was claimed that it was the abandonment of the original teachings of Islam that had led to the present decadence and backwardness of Muslim societies. But there never was an Islamic utopia. To talk of a golden age is only to confirm and perpetuate the influence of the clergy, the mullas, and their hateful creed that denies humanity to half the inhabitants of this globe, and further retards all serious attempts to liberate Muslim women.

I shall now examine in detail all the different ways Islam has devised to subjugate all Muslim women.

An Inferior Being

Muhammad is reported to have told his men to treat kindly those two weaklings "women and slaves." In general Islam treats women as intellectually, morally, and physically inferior. First comes man, then comes the hermaphrodite (who in Islam has a distinct legal status), and last the woman. Conservative Muslim thinkers have even revived discredited anthropological theories purporting to show that the cranial capacity of women is far smaller than that of a man. "Women have less reason and faith" goes one famous hadith. A woman is seen as being in a state of impurity during her menstruation, but this impurity is not limited to her period of menstruation. It is reported that Muhammad had never touched a woman who did not belong to him. When the women who gave him their allegiance asked to shake him by the hand, he replied, "I never touch the hand of women." Further hadiths on this subject:[581]

—Better for a man to be splashed by a pig than for him to brush against the elbow of a woman not permitted him.

—Better to bury an iron needle in the head of one of you than to touch a woman not permitted him.

—He who touches the palm of a woman not legally his will have red-hot embers put in the palm of his hand on Judgment Day.

—Three things can interrupt prayers if they pass in front of someone praying: a black dog, a woman, and an ass.

Liberal Muslims may wish to dismiss these hadiths as inauthentic but what will they say to the Koran which also says: "Draw not near unto prayer when ye are drunken, till ye know that which ye utter, nor when ye are polluted, save when journeying on the road, till ye have bathed. And if ye be ill, or on a journey, or one of you cometh from the closet, or ye have touched a woman, and ye find not water, then go to high clean soil and rub your faces and your hands" (sura 4.43; see also sura 5.6).

The theologians ultimately lean on the Koran to prove their point that women are inferior to men and in doing so, of course cut short any argument, for no one argues against the word of God. Thus they find divine sanction for their absurd pseudoscientific views. Here are the relevant verses:

> 3.36. And when she had given birth to it, she said, "O my Lord! Verily I have brought forth a female,"—God knew what she had brought forth; a male is not as a female—and I have named her Mary, and I take refuge with thee for her and for her offspring, from Satan the stoned."

> 43.18. What! make they a being (i.e., a woman) to be the offspring of God who is brought up among trinkets, and is ever contentious without reason.

> 4.122. And whose word is more sure than God's?

Women are by nature inferior and can be compared to a bottle whose crack is irreparable. Muhammad used to say: "Handle the bottles (women) with care."

Inequality in Matters of Sexuality

Bullough, Burton, Bousquet, and Bouhdiba insist that Islam is a sex positive religion, thereby underlining their own male-centered vision. For in Islam, a woman's sexuality or her sexual needs are not taken into account. For Muslim jurists, marriage is one of two legitimate ways that a man can have relations with a woman (the other being concubinage with a slave woman). As one Muslim jurist put it, marriage for a Muslim male is "the contract by which he acquires the reproductive organ of a woman, with the express purpose of enjoying it."[582] The converse, of course, is not the case; the reproductive organ of the husband is not exclusively reserved for one woman. The Koran permits men an unlimited number of women (sura 4.3).

"Happy now the believers, humble in their prayers, shunning vain conversation, paying the poor-due, and who restrain their appetites except with their wives or the slaves whom their right hands possess: for in that case they shall be free from blame." (suras 23.1, 5, 6).

The Koran knows man is incapable of impartiality—"You will not be able to deal equally between your wives, however much you wish to do so"(sura 4.129)— and yet allows polygamy (which would be more fairly called polygyny, since of course women are not permitted more than one husband). As G. H. Bousquet in his classic *L'Ethique Sexuelle de l'Islam* continually emphasizes, the Muslim conception of marriage has nothing in common with the Christian one. There is in Islam a complete absence of the idea of association, partnership, or companionship between the married couple. The Arabic word for "marriage" is "nikah" which is also the word for "coition," and in contemporary French slang "niquer" means "to fuck." Bousquet's conclusion on the subject of Muslim marriages could be summarized thus: The Muslim marriage is essentially an act by which a woman, often without being consulted, must put herself sexually at the disposition of her husband, if need be next to three other wives and an unlimited number of concubines. She must be ready to be turned out as soon as she ceases to please and never expect a conjugal partnership to arise.[583]

Muslim jurists have insisted that the justice demanded of husbands toward their many wives is in the nature of expenses or gifts for each of the wives and not that of love or sexual relations. The Prophet, of course, has special privileges divinely sanctioned by the Koran: He can have more than four wives without being obliged to share his nights equally between them:

> O Prophet! We allow thee thy wives whom thou hast dowered, and the slaves whom thy right hand possesseth out of the booty which God hath granted thee, and the daughters of thy uncle, thy paternal and maternal aunts who fled with thee to Medina, and any believing woman who hath given herself up to the Prophet, if the Prophet desired to wed her—a Privilege for thee above the rest of the Faithful. We well know what we have settled for them, in regard to their wives and to the slaves; . . . that there may be no fault on thy part. . . . Thou mayst decline for the present whom thou wilt of them, and thou mayest take to thy bed her whom thou wilt, and whomsoever thou shalt long for of those thou shalt have before neglected, and this shall not be a crime in thee. (p. 33.49–51)

As Aisha, the prophet's wife once remarked to Him, "God comes to your aid rather conveniently when it is a question of your desires." The Prophet enjoyed the embraces of nine wives and, according to al-Ghazali, Muhammad was able to perform his conjugal duties to all his nine wives in one morning. What is clear is that women are seen as objects: to be acquired and gotten rid of according to the man's whim and fancy. If one wife does not suffice, advises al-Ghazali, take some more (up to four). If still you have not found peace, change them. What could be simpler!

A wife cannot legitimately ask her husband to satisfy her sexually—she can only demand that she be fed, clothed, and housed. Sexually, the husband is the master of the enjoyment of his wife. The converse is not true. The husband's refusal to make love to his wife is simply considered as a free renunciation of his legitimately acquired sexual rights.

Muslim jurists are unanimous in saying that if the husband is incapable of sexual intercourse with his wife because of the ablation of his penis, the wife can ask for and obtain divorce immediately. However if his incapacity is due to other causes—impotence, for example—divorce is not granted straightaway. The husband is given one lunar year to consummate the marriage.

Of course, it is legally essential that the wife be a virgin when she asks for a divorce. Once the marriage has been consummated the woman's sexual rights seem to vanish. According to the Shafi'ites, the woman can ask for divorce only in the case of the ablation of her husband's penis—no other case is admitted. According to the Malekites and Hanefites, once the marriage has been consummated the woman has no rights whatsoever in this field; the husband is only obliged to have sexual intercourse with her once. Islam protects the rights of men and men only. The famous story of the debate over sodomy illustrates further the Muslim attitude toward sex. It appears there were certain men in Muhammad's entourage who "enjoyed their women from front and from behind." Some women asked Muhammad's opinion. Muhammad received the appropriate revelation which is recorded in the Koran sura 2.223: "Your women are as your field—go unto them as you will." The ambiguity of the phrase has been a source of conflict ever since. Nobody ever thought of consulting the women themselves; they were excluded from the debate. Muslim theologians concluded that a man could take his wife when he wanted and how he wanted, from the front or from the back, as long as he ejaculated in the woman's vagina. In other words, man can choose the time and mode of the cultivation of his field as long as he sows the seed in a place from which he will reap the best harvest.

Sodomy was considered a grave sin though there seems to be disagreement on whether it was punishable by death or not. Muhammad also said less ambiguously: "The woman should never refuse her husband even on the saddle of a horse" (or, according to another version, "on the top of a burning oven"). On another occasion the Prophet cursed the woman who always says "later" or pretends to have her period to escape her marital duties. Yet another hadith recounts: Two prayers that never reach the heavens are that of the escaping slave and that of the reluctant woman who frustrates her husband at night.

The wife who refuses her husband is considered insubordinate and the husband has the right to punish her physically, something which is again divinely sanctioned in the Koran (see sura 4.34 quoted earlier).

She can also lose her right to maintenance and protection. For example, under Egyptian law (Article 67, Code du Statut Personnel): "A woman loses her right to maintenance if she refuses to give her self to her husband without a legitimate reason."

We have seen how by marriage the husband acquires the "reproductive organ" ("al bud") of his wife and that the converse is not the case. In fact, the woman has no rights over her own "bud," her own sexual organ. As Mohammad Qotb, a well-known Muslim writer put it,[584]

> The guardian does not have the right to invite people to steal something which does not belong to him. Similarly the girl who is only simply the guardian of her honor (her bud) does not have the right to make use of it (her sexual organ) nor can she invite anyone to violate it. For it is not simply a case of her own honor but also a case of her parent's honor, the honor of her family, of society and of all humanity.

Here we might say a few words about circumcision. Nowhere is there a greater divergence between theory and practice as in the case of circumcision, and, for once, Muslim practice is far more demanding than Islamic law. For the majority of Muslims, membership in Islam necessarily implies circumcision. In Java "to circumcise" means "to receive someone in the bosom of Islam." It is, if you like, the Muslim equivalent of Christian baptism. For Christians the Muslim is by definition circumcised—the Turk of Aleppo in Shakespeare's *Othello* is the "circumcised dog." And yet in Islamic law it is simply a recommendation, not an obligation. It is not at all alluded to in the Koran. It is nonetheless held to be founded upon the customs of the Prophet. However, the early Muslims do not seem to have taken it too seriously: Omar the pious caliph once said that Muhammad was sent to the World to Islamize it, not to circumcise it.

In modern Muslim society circumcision is a universal custom followed by even the most liberated, Westernized families. The circumcision of a child is a great occasion for a family and is celebrated with much pomp and ceremony, that is surpassed only by marriage festivities. Is circumcision necessary or is it a barbaric tradition left over from pre-Islamic times? Here is how Bouhdiba characterizes the whole operation:[585]

> As to the mutilated child the only resource left to him is to shout his pain and cry out at the castrating violence done to his body. This bruise to his flesh, these men and women who are torturing him, this gleaming razor, the screeches of the nosey old women, the sacrificial cock, . . . and all those men and women who come to congratulate the patient's "happy accession to Islam"—that is what a circumcision amounts to for a child. . . . Add to this the painful wound which is slow to heal (sometimes long and terrible weeks), sometimes accidents leading to serious complications: infections, hemorrhages, severance of the penis, arteries of the penis cut, . . . Nothing can justify the practice of circumcision especially in view of the enormous physical and psychological damage it can inflict. It is not without reason that some talk of barbaric and traumatizing operations.

This leads us to female circumcision. According to the nineteenth century *Dictionary of Islam* and Burton, it was widespread in Arabia, where "clitoris cutter" was a legitimate profession practiced by old women, and perhaps most other Islamic countries. Bousquet thinks it was rare in North Africa. Bouhdiba writing in 1978 is of the opinion that it was rare in Morocco, Tunisia, Algeria, Turkey, and Iran but practiced everywhere else. According to the Minority Rights Group's Report "Female Genital Mutilation: Proposals for Change," published in 1992, the practice is still followed widely across Western, Saharan, and Eastern Africa, as well as in Yemen and Oman, by Muslims, Christians, Jews, and animists. "Tens of millions of girls are affected every year." Unlike the public nature of the boy's circumcision, female excision is practiced discreetly, and does not have the symbolic significance either—defloration of a virgin on the night of her wedding constitutes far more than the excision, the equivalent of a boy's circumcision.

Again, female excision is not mentioned in the Koran and learned doctors of theology, when they deign to address the matter, spend very little time on it, simply recommending it as a pious act. What exactly does the operation involve? According to the omniscient Burton,[586] "in the babe [the clitoris] protrudes beyond the labiae and snipping off the head forms female circumcision." "Excision," continues Burton,

> is universal amongst the negroids of the Upper Nile, the Somal and other adjacent tribes. The operator, an old woman, takes up the instrument, a knife or razor blade fixed into a wooden handle, and with three sweeps cuts off the labia and the head of the clitoris. The parts are then sewn up with a packneedle and a thread of sheepskin; and in Dar-For a tin tube is inserted for the passage of urine. Before marriage the bridegroom trains himself for a month on beef, honey and milk; and if he can open his bride with the natural weapon he is a sworder to whom no woman in the tribe can deny herself. If he fails, he tries penetration with his fingers and by way of last resort whips out his whittle and cuts the parts open. The sufferings of the first few nights must be severe.

In modern times little seems to have changed; here is how the *Economist* describes the situation in 1992: "The procedure varies from mildly painful to gruesome, and can involve the removal of the clitoris and other organs with knives, broken glass, and razors—but rarely anesthetic. It can lead to severe problems with menstruation, intercourse and childbirth, psychological disturbances and even death." In this gruesome act of "disbudding" of the female are embodied all the Muslim males' fears of female sexuality. Female circumcision is "the proper complement of male circumcision, evening the sensitiveness of the genitories by reducing it equally in both sexes: an uncircumcised woman has the venereal orgasm much sooner and oftener than a circumcised man and frequent coitus would injure her health," Burton assures us. With the subsequent reduction in the sensitiveness of the sexual parts of the woman, the man has to multiply his efforts to satisfy her; and if the woman's clitoris has been entirely removed this may well prove impossible. This latter fact has been the source of much psychosexual neuroses among the Arab male. "Anatomy is destiny," says Freud, in which case a mutilated anatomy is a mutilated destiny. I shall return to the subject of female circumcision in my chapter on "Assimilation & Multiculturalism" where I shall discuss attempts to eradicate this barbaric custom.

"When the faithful cohabits with his wife, the angels surround them from the earth to the heavens, sensual pleasure and desire have the beauty of mountains. Each time you make love, you are making an offering," said Muhammad addressing a gathering of true believers. The Koran endorses this view: sura 5.89. "Do not deprive yourselves of pleasures deemed legitimate by God;" sura 24.32. "And marry those among you who are single." On another occasion, Muhammad said, "I married many times and those who do not follow my example are not with me. Those of you who is capable of setting up house should marry." Muhammad also forbade one of his followers to take up a vow of chastity. And of course, Muhammad himself had a particularly active sex life, which for many Christian historians was but licentious self-indulgence.

Thus Islam is favorable to the pleasures of the flesh—especially for men— pleasures that are present in paradise. But what precisely is there about the Islamic heaven that so many find delicious and others like Karl Popper find intolerable? Paradise is full of the sexual orgasms—of men. Beautiful nymphets have been especially created by God to reward the faithful (Muslim) male inhabitants of heaven:

78.31-33. "But for the God-fearing is a blissful abode, enclosed gardens and vineyards; and damsels with swelling breasts for companions; and a full cup."

55.54-58. "On couches with linings of brocade shall they recline, and the fruit of the two gardens shall be within easy reach: . . . Therein shall be the damsels with retiring glances, whom nor man nor djinn hath touched before them: . . . Like jacynths and pearls: . . ."

45.70-74. "In these gardens will be chaste and beautiful virgins. . . . nymphs, cloistered in their tents. . . . which neither man nor demon will have touched before them."

46.10-22. "They shall recline on jeweled couches face to face, and there shall wait on them immortal youths with bowls and ewers and a cup of purest wine (that will neither pain their heads nor take away their reason); with fruits of their own choice and flesh of fowls that they relish. And theirs shall be the dark-eyed houris, chaste as hidden pearls: a guerdon for their deeds."

56.35-38. "We created the houris and made them virgins, loving companions, for those on the right hand."

52.19-20. "Eat and drink in peace as a reward for what you have accomplished, resting on elbows on beds lined up in rows. We shall give them as wives wide-eyed houris."

37.48-49. "Near them shall be blushing virgins with large, beautiful eyes who will be like hidden pearls."

44.51-55. "The pious will be in a peaceful abode among, gardens and fountains; clothed in satin and brocade, face to face. We shall marry them to wide-eyed houris. In utter tranquility, they will demand all kinds of fruit."

38.49-53. "The pious will have a beautiful place to come back to; the gardens of Eden with their gates wide open where reclining on beds they will ask for abundant fruit and exquisite drinks, all the while next to them will be blushing virgins as companions. This what has been promised you on Judgment Day."

2.25. "In these gardens, they will have wives of purity and live for ever."

It was not for nothing that Muhammad said, "There will be no bachelors in Paradise." In these utterly childish and sensual fantasies, the woman once again has been created to serve man—there are no fantasies of dark-eyed gigolos serving reclining, sensual women. The Koranic paradise was further elaborated with much glee by Muslim commentators. As Suyuti,[587] for example, wrote: "Each time we sleep with a houri we find her virgin. Besides, the penis of the Elected never softens. The erection is eternal. The sensation that you feel each time you make love is utterly delicious and out of this world and were you to experience it in this world you would faint. Each elected will marry seventy houris, besides the women he married on earth, and all will have appetising vaginas."

Thus we need to qualify the statement that "Islam is sex-positive." We have already qualified it in one way—it is sex positive only from the male point of view: the entire ethico-juridical system elaborated by the ulamas is conceived in the interest of the male. We need to qualify it in two more ways. Islam may be sex-positive but not without restrictions whose transgression is punishable by death. We shall look at this aspect later in the chapter. Finally, in its attitudes toward purity and impurity we find a totally negative phobia; and it is to this we shall now turn.

"If ye are polluted than purify yourselves," says the Koran 5.9. Minor impurity resulting from, for example, touching one's penis is effaced by an ablution. Major impurity entails the washing of the whole body, and as the Prophet said, "He who leaves but one hair unwashed on his body will be punished in hell accordingly." Major impurity results from sexual contact; any emission of sperm (male or female— Muslims believed that women also discharged a fluid at the moment of orgasm); sexual intercourse; anal intercourse; bestiality; menstruation; puerperium (after childbirth); nocturnal emissions. No moral idea is involved, the simple fact of intercourse renders you impure—whether the intercourse was permissible or not in Islamic law is irrelevant. For example, theologians pose the question: Is the fast of someone who has intercourse in the middle of the afternoon with a young boy or a foreign woman valid? Reply: if there has been no orgasm then the fast is still valid. The question of sin does not arise. Nor is there a question of hygiene. Minor impurity means that the polluted person cannot pray, perform the ritual circumambulation of the Kaaba, or touch the Koran. A person guilty of major impurity, in addition to the above prohibitions, cannot recite the Koran or penetrate the mosque. All the natural bodily functions seem to be a source of one kind of impurity or other. Islamic law is full of absurd details that can only be described as obsessional and probably neuroses inducing. As Bouhdiba put it,[588] Muslim society has produced men and women made sick by cleanliness; a whole society with an anal complex. This association of sex with pollution can only be described as negative, though of course we are aware that these laws concerning purity play an important part in integrating the individual in the society to which he belongs.

We have already seen how a woman during menstruation is considered impure and is forbidden to fast, pray, go round the Kaaba, to read or even touch the Koran, to enter a mosque, or to have sexual relations with her husband. This is not in consideration of the delicate condition of the woman, as some modern apologists would have us believe—she is not dispensed of these things but is actually actively forbidden them because of her impurity.

The Koran time and again enjoins women to be pious and above all to be obedient—to God and to their husbands: surah 4.34. Virtuous women are obedient. Women are expected to be submissive, submissive to God, to a religion enunciated, elaborated, and interpreted by men. Women are totally excluded from any religious deliberations: sura 16.43. "And before you We sent only men to whom We revealed the Revelation. If you do not know that, question the People of the Book."

Modern Muslim apologists have made exaggerated claims about the role played by the wives of the Prophet in the propagation of the religion. In reality this role was either very limited or nonexistent. The Koran simply asks the wives of the Prophet to stay at home. Visitors to Muhammad's house were forbidden to talk directly to his wives. Surah 33.32–33. "O Wives of the Prophet do not be too seductive of speech lest the evil-hearted should desire you. Keep to accustomed speech. Stay in your homes. Do not try to imitate the ostentatious clothes of the women of the former times of ignorance. Get on with your prayers; give alms and obey God and his Apostle."

> 33.53. O Believers do not enter the Prophet's houses until leave is given you for a meal. Do not enter before the appropriate moment. When you are invited, enter! As soon as you have taken the meal retire, without seeking familiar talk. For this offends the Prophet and he is ashamed of you. But God is not ashamed of the truth. When you ask for something from His wives ask them from behind a curtain! That is more decent for your hearts and for theirs. It is not right for you to offend God's Apostle; nor to marry His widows after Him. That would be an enormous sin in God's eyes.

When and how could these wives teach under such daunting conditions? There is certainly no mention of it in the Koran, which limits itself to ordering them to obey God and His Apostle, to act decorously and to threaten them if they do not obey.

33.30–31. "O Wives of the Prophet! Those of you who commit a proven sin shall be doubly punished. That is easy enough for God. But those of you who obey God and His Apostle and do good works shall be doubly rewarded; for them We have made a generous provision.

It is safe to say that women have played no role in the development of Muslim dogma.

The inequality between men and women[589] in matters of giving testimony or evidence; or being a witness is enshrined in the Koran: sura 2.282 (quoted above).

How do Muslim apologists justify the above text? Muslim men and women writers point to the putative psychological differences that exist between men and women. The Koran (and hence God) in its sublime wisdom knew that women are sensitive, emotional, sentimental, easily moved, and influenced by their biological rhythm, lacking judgment. But above all they have a shaky memory. In other words, women are psychologically inferior. Such are the dubious arguments used by Muslim intellectuals—male and, astonishingly enough, female intellectuals like Ahmad Jamal, Ms. Zahya Kaddoura, Ms. Ghada al-Kharsa, and Ms. Madiha Khamis. As Ghassan Ascha points out, the absurdity of their arguments are obvious.

By taking the testimony of two beings whose reasoning faculties are faulty we do not obtain the testimony of one complete person with a perfectly functioning rational faculty—such is Islamic arithmetic! By this logic, if the testimony of two women is worth that of one man, then the testimony of four women must be worth that of two men, in which case we can dispense with the testimony of the men. But no! In Islam the rule is not to accept the testimony of women alone in matters to which men theoretically have access. It is said that the Prophet did not accept the testimony of women in matters of marriage, divorce, and hudud. Hudud are the punishments set down by Muhammad in the Koran and the hadith for (1) adultery—stoning to death; (2) fornication—a hundred stripes; (3) false accusation of adultery against a married person—eighty stripes (4) apostasy—death; (5) drinking wine—eighty stripes; (6) theft—the cutting off of the right hand; (7) simple robbery on the highway—the loss of hands and feet; robbery with murder—death, either by the sword or by crucifixion.

On adultery the Koran 24.4 says: "Those that defame honourable women and cannot produce four witnesses shall be given eighty lashes." Of course, Muslim jurists will only accept four male witnesses. These witnesses must declare that they have "seen the parties in the very act of carnal conjunction." Once an accusation of fornication and adultery has been made, the accuser himself or herself risks punishment if he or she does not furnish the necessary legal proofs. Witnesses are in the same situation. If a man were to break into a woman's dormitory and rape half a dozen women, he would risk nothing since there would be no male witnesses. Indeed the victim of a rape would hesitate before going in front of the law, since she would risk being condemned herself and have little chance of obtaining justice. "If the woman's words were sufficient in such cases," explains Judge Zharoor ul Haq of Pakistan, "then no man would be safe." This iniquitious situation is truly revolting and yet for Muslim law it is a way of avoiding social scandal concerning the all-important sexual taboo. Women found guilty of fornication were literally immured, at first; as the Koran 4.15 says: "Shut them up within their houses till death release them, or God make some way for them." However this was later canceled and lapidation substituted for adultery and one hundred lashes for fornication. When a man is to be stoned to death, he is taken to some barren place, where he is stoned first by the witnesses, then the judge, and then the public. When a woman is stoned, a hole to receive her is dug as deep as her waist—the Prophet himself seems to have ordered such procedure. It is lawful for a man to kill his wife and her lover if he catches them in the very act.

In the case where a man suspects his wife of adultery or denies the legitimacy of the offspring, his testimony is worth that of four men. Sura 24.6: "If a man accuses his wife but has no witnesses except himself, he shall swear four times by God that his charge is true, calling down upon himself the curse of God if he is lying. But if his wife swears four times by God that his charge is false and calls down His curse upon herself if it be true, she shall receive no punishment." Appearances to the contrary, this is not an example of Koranic justice or equality between the sexes. The woman indeed escapes being stoned to death but she remains rejected and loses her right to the dowry and her right to maintenance, *whatever the outcome of the trial.* A woman does not have the right to charge her husband in a similar manner. Finally, for a Muslim marriage to be valid there must be a multiplicity of witnesses. For Muslim jurists, two men form a multiplicity but not two or three or a thousand women.

In questions of heritage, the Koran tells us that male children should inherit twice the portion of female children:

> 4.11–12. A male shall inherit twice as much as a female. If there be more than two girls, they shall have two-thirds of the inheritance, but if there be one only, she shall inherit the half. Parents shall inherit a sixth each, if the deceased have a child; but if he leave no child and his parents be his heirs, his mother shall have a third. If he have brothers, his mother shall have a sixth after payment of any legacy he may have bequeathed or any debt he may have owed.

To justify this inequality, Muslim authors lean heavily on the fact that a woman receives a dowry and has the right to maintenance from her husband. It is also true that according to Muslim law the mother is not at all obliged to provide for her children, and if she does spend money on her children, it is, to quote Bousquet, "recoverable by her from her husband if he is returned to a better fortune as in the case of any other charitable person. Therefore there is no point in the husband and wife sharing in the taking charge of the household; this weighs upon the husband alone. There is no longer any financial interest between them."[590]

This latter point referred to by Bousquet simply emphasizes the negative aspects of a Muslim marriage—that is to say, the total absence of any idea of "association" between "couples" as in Christianity. As to dowry, it is, of course, simply a reconfirmation of the man's claims over the woman in matters of sex and divorce. Furthermore, in reality the woman does not get to use the dowry for herself. The custom is either to use the dowry to furnish the house of the newly married couple or for the wife to offer it to her father. According to the Malekites, the woman can be obliged by law to use the dowry to furnish the house. Muslim law also gives the guardian the right to cancel a marriage—even that of a woman of legal age—if he thinks the dowry is not sufficient. Thus the dowry, instead of being a sign of her independence, turns out once more to be a symbol of her servitude.

The woman has the right to maintenance but this simply emphasizes her total dependence on her husband, with all its attendant sense of insecurity. According to Muslim jurists, the husband is not obliged under Islamic law to pay for her medical expenses in case of illness. Financial independence of the woman would of course be the first step in the liberation of Muslim women and thus it is not surprising that it is seen as a threat to male dominance. Muslim women are now obliged to take equal responsibility for looking after their parents. Article 158 of Syrian law states "The child—male or female—having the necessary means is obliged to take responsibility for his or her poor parents." The birth of a girl is still seen as a catastrophe in Islamic societies. The system of inheritance just adds to her misery and her dependence on the man. If she is an only child she receives only half the legacy of her father; the other half goes to the male members of the father's family. If there are two or more daughters, they inherit two-thirds. This pushes fathers and mothers to prefer male children to female so that they can leave the entirety of their effects or possessions to their own descendants. "Yet when a new-born girl is announced to one of them his countenance darkens and he is filled with gloom"; (sura 43.15). The situation is even worse when a woman loses her husband—she only receives a quarter of the legacy. If the deceased leaves more than one wife, all the wives are still obliged to share among themselves a quarter or one-eighth of the legacy.

The right to bloody vengeance[591] is acknowledged by Islam. Sura 2.178 states, "Believers, retaliation is decreed for you in blood shed: a free man for a freeman, a slave for a slave; and a female for a female." It is clear from this text that a free man and woman do not have the same legal status. Muslim jurists have decided, that in cases of manslaughter, the pecuniary compensation (in Arabic, "diya") in the case of a woman is half that of a man. For the Malekites, the diya for a woman or a male Jew or Christian is equivalent to half of that of a Muslim male—whether it concerns manslaughter or premeditated murder. Muslim jurists have also decided that anyone who causes the loss of a fetus must pay the diya; the diya for a male Muslim fetus is double that of a female fetus.

Men's authority over women and the obedience women owed to the men are divinely sanctioned in the Koran (suras 4.34 and 2.228 mentioned earlier).

Muslim jurists[592] are unanimous in their view that men are superior to women in virtue of their reasoning abilities, their knowledge, and their supervisory powers. And since it is the man who assumes financial responsibility for the family, it is argued, it is natural that he should have total power over the woman. These same jurists, of course, totally neglect changing social conditions where a woman may contribute her salary to the upkeep of her family—power over women remains a divine command and "natural" or "in the nature of things." Muslim thinkers continue to confine Muslim women to the house—to leave the house is against the will of God and against the principles of Islam. Confined to their houses, women are then reproached for not having any experience of the outside world! Catch 22 or simply Islamic logic? Here is an example of this wonderful logic:

> [By leaving the house a woman] runs the risk of meeting dangers which are contrary to the spiritual qualities of womanhood which she incarnates and with which she fulfils the noblest virtues in life. To leave the house is to go against the will of God and is condemned by Islam. Her household chores are limited

and thus her experience which she acquires [is also limited]; whereas the man's tasks outside the house, embrace a wider horizon; his experience and his relationships are greater and more varied.

The rights of women are referred to in sura 2.228, quoted earlier. The pre-eminence of men, however, is never forgotten. Women have the right to maintenance ("nafaqa," in Arabic), that is, food, shelter, and clothing. And that, according to Ms. Khamis is largely sufficient—what more could a woman reasonably ask? The duties as opposed to the rights of a woman are another matter. Some jurists seem to think that a Muslim woman should occupy herself with household chores, quoting a famous hadith that recounts that the Prophet ordered his daughter Fatima to confine herself to the house and her household chores and her husband Ali to all his duties outside the house. Other jurists hold the view that her task is not to occupy herself with the house, "Her sole duty is to stay at home to satisfy the sexual appetite of her husband." Al-Ghazali, in the "Proof of Islam," sums up the traditional view:

> [a man marries] in order to have an untroubled mind as far as house work is concerned: kitchen, cleaning, bedding. A man, supposing he is able to do without sex, is not capable of living alone at home. If he were to take on himself the task of doing all the housework, he would no longer be able to dedicate himself to intellectual work or knowledge. The virtuous wife by making herself useful at home is her husband's helpmate . . . and at same time satisfies his sexual desires.[593]

Above all the virtuous woman is obedient and her obedience is firmly linked to her obedience to God. According to a hadith, the woman who accomplishes her five prayers, fasts, guards her chastity, and obeys her husband, will go to paradise. The Muslim jurists further assure obedient women that their rewards "will be the same as those Muslims who fight for the defense and propagation of the Islamic faith." Traditions enjoining wives to be obedient are numerous:

—The woman who dies and with whom the husband is satisfied will go to paradise.

—If it had been given me to order someone to prostrate themselves in front of someone other than God, I would surely have ordered women to prostrate themselves in front of their husbands. . . . A woman cannot fulfill her duties toward God without first having accomplished those that she owes her husband.

—The virtuous woman is the one who engenders joy every time her husband looks at her; and who obeys him as soon as he orders her and who preserves her chastity and his belongings in his absence.

The wife can refuse to do her housework—that is her right—but in doing so she is being disobedient to her husband and consequently to God. As Simone de Beauvoir[594] so perceptively remarks,

Man enjoys the great advantage of having a God endorse the codes he writes and since man exercises a sovereign authority over woman, it is especially fortunate that this authority has been vested in him by the Supreme Being. For the Jews, Mohammedans, and Christians, among others, man is master by divine right; *the fear of God, therefore, will repress any impulse towards revolt in the downtrodden female.* One can bank on her credulity. Woman takes an attitude of respect and faith toward the masculine universe.

If she refuses to obey her husband, he can file a complaint with a magistrate who invariably finds her in the wrong and orders her to obey. If she refuses to submit to the judgment of the magistrates, the Penal Code of Egypt and Libya, Article 212, stipulates[595] that "the judgments can be implemented in a coercive manner if the situation demands it. The houses can be besieged by the forces of order if the need arises following the instructions of the judge." This law is based on the Islamic ban on a woman leaving her house. Islam has given man the means to chastise his wife if she remains disobedient (see sura 4.34 discussed above). She, of course, has no right to admonish her husband; men are warned not to listen to them: "Unhappiness to the slave of a woman," says a hadith. Another says, "Take up positions opposing women; there is much merit in such opposition." Yet another says, "As soon as man begins to obey every whim of a capricious woman, God throws him in hell." According to theologians,[596] the husband has the right to administer corporal punishment to his wife if she

1. refuses to make herself beautiful for him;
2. refuses to meet his sexual demands;
3. leaves the house without permission or without any legitimate reason recognized by law; or
4. neglects her religious duties.

A Hadith attributes the following saying to the Prophet: "Hang up your whip where your wife can see it." There are a number of other hadiths that contradict this one. In those, Muhammad explicitly forbids men to beat their wives—in which case the Prophet himself is contradicting what the Koran, enshrining divine law, permits.

What recourse does a woman have against a difficult husband? The Koran talks vaguely of a mutual "agreement" (sura 4.128). For modern theologians, even though it is the husband who is violent, demanding, or difficult, it is still the wife who has to adapt herself, to bend, and accommodate her husband's whims.

The Veil[597]

The Arabic word "hijab" is sometimes translated as *veil*, but it can signify anything that prevents something from being seen—a screen, a curtain, or even a wall—and the hymen. The root of the verb "hajaba" means "to hide." By extension, hijab is used to mean something that separates, demarcates a limit, establishes a barrier. Finally, hijab has the sense of a moral interdiction. The Koran also uses two other words, "djilbah" and "khibar." The former is likewise translated as "veil," but also as "outer garment" and even "cloak." "Khibar" is similarly translated as "veil," but also as "shawl." In this philological aside, we may also mention the names of other garments that are used to cover Muslim woman in part or entirely throughout the Islamic world. In Morocco, Algeria, and Tunisia we find haik, safsari, akhnif, and adjar. In Egypt, Israel, Syria, Iraq, and among the Bedouins, we find abaya, tarna, izar, milhafa, khabara, chambar, niqab, litham, and bourqou; in Iran, bourda, tchador, pitcha, and rouband; in Turkey, yatchmek, yalek, harmaniya, and entari; in India and Pakistan, burka.

In the struggle for the liberation of the Muslim woman the veil has become a symbol of her servitude. Thus in 1923 the President of the Egyptian Feminist Union, Ms. Houda Cha'araoui, and her colleagues defiantly threw their veils into the sea. Similarly in 1927 there was a campaign of "de-hijabization" in communist Turkestan. Not less than 87,000 Uzbek women publicly repudiated their "black cowls", though not before 300 of their sisters had been killed by the male heads of the Muslim families for betraying Islam. In 1928, at the independence celebrations, the Shah of Afghanistan ordered his wife to "unveil" herself in public. Following the public scandal, the shah was obliged to backtrack and cancel his projects for the emancipation of women. He himself was obliged to abdicate. In 1936 Reza Shah of Iran forbade the tchador by a special decree. Obviously the people were not ready to break with tradition and so after mass protests in 1941 he also had to retreat and abrogate the law.

The hijab was imposed by the Koran (see suras 33.53, 33.59, and 33.32–33) and also:

> 24.30–31. Enjoin believing women to turn their eyes away from temptation and to preserve their chastity; to cover their adornments—except such as are normally displayed;—to draw their veils over their bosoms and not to reveal their finery except to their husbands.

The veil and the injunction to Muslim women to stay at home came with Islam; for it is clear, as I have already indicated, that Bedouin women enjoyed considerable freedom, accompanied their husbands on long marches and made themselves indispensable in the camps. But all this was to change as Islam became more and more an urban phenomenon and as it came into contact with other more developed civilizations whose customs the Muslims adopted. The veil was adopted by the Arabs from the Persians, and the woman's obligation to stay closed in at home was a tradition copied from the Byzantines, who in turn had adopted an ancient Greek custom. Of course, Muslim theologians have a totally different explanation of the origin of the hijab. According to them it was imposed on women by God to please one person, i.e., Omar ibn al-Khallab. They refer to a tradition that recounts that Omar one day said to the Prophet: "The pious and the profligate have easy access to your house and see your wives. Why don't you order the mothers of all believers to cover themselves?" And Muhammad received the revelations quoted earlier. According to another version, attributed to Aisha, Omar accidentally touched her hand and excused himself by saying that had he the power no one would steal a glance at her. Yet another rendition is recounted by historian al-Tabari. The real function of the hijab is to cover up the *awra* which we have no right to see. By "awra" is meant "the shameful parts of the body and those parts we hide out of dignity and pride. As for women, they are entirely *awra*."[598] According to Muslim jurists, awra for men consists of those parts between the navel and the knees-and they are concealed in all cases except for exposure to his wives and concubines. No one seems to agree on women's awra. According to Hanafites, the woman can uncover her face and hands, only so long as this does not lead to or provoke temptation, seduction, or discord. For the other three Sunnite sects a woman can only uncover her face and hands in cases of emergency—the need for medical attention, for example. The liberal attitude of the Hanafites is only apparent and not real[599]—in reality, a woman has only to be smiling and pretty for the ulamas to strictly reimpose the veil. Even old women are advised to remain covered. Koran 24.60 says, "It shall be no offence for old spinsters who have no hope of marriage to discard, their cloaks without revealing their adornments. Better if they do not discard them." Those wishing to keep women's faces and hands uncovered rely on the following hadith recounted by Aisha, the Prophet's wife: "Asma, the daughter of Abu Bakr [and the sister of Aisha] was one day in front of the Prophet without a veil. The Prophet said to her—'Asma, a grown woman should only show this.' " And He showed her face and her hands.

Meanwhile various Muslim experts contradict each other on this point. Some insist that even a woman's heels should be well-hidden, citing an appropriate hadith to back up their arguments. Not only is it a symbol of women's servitude but also a symbol of the woman's total lack of trust in the father, the brother, or the husband; and at the same time the male possessiveness: for the brother, and the father she is the merchandise that must not be shop soiled; and for the husband she is an object to be used at home and then carefully wrapped and put away, lest another covet her. The question of hijab continues to play an important role in modem debate and is of more than academic importance. A *New York Times* reporter described the situation in April 1992 in Iran:

> The most visible battle for women's rights is still fought through their ward-robes. In the 13-year revolution, perhaps no other issue has been debated with such fury as the rules for what constitutes "good hejab" or head covering. "Re-search proved female hair had a kind of radiance" that might tempt men, Iran's first president under the revolution, Abol-Hassan Banisadr, said in the early days of the Islamic republic. In the years that followed, women were insulted, arrested, fined and even lashed for bad hejab. . . . After the all-encompassing

chador, held in place with one's hand or one's teeth, the second most acceptable garment is the rappoush [a loose, long garment] worn with a scarf.

Do women have the right to leave their houses?[600] Hijab also applies to the "hiding" of women behind the walls of her house. The Koran is clear on this point in sura 33.33, ordering the wives of the Prophet to stay in their homes. For reformists this only applies to the wives of the Prophet; for conservatives it applies to all Muslim women. Ghawji, a conservative, has systematically set out under what conditions a woman can leave her house, giving copious quotes from the Koran and the hadiths.

1. She may leave only in case of a real need.
2. The exit must be authorized by her husband or legal guardian.
3. She must be well-covered, including her face, to avoid tempting any men who might be around; she must move with her head bowed down looking neither left nor right. (Koran 24.31).
4. She must not put on perfume. The Prophet has said: "Any woman who puts on perfume and passes in front of men is a fornicator."
5. She must not walk in the middle of the road among men. The Prophet on noticing the confusion on leaving a mosque, said: "You women do not have the right to walk amongst men—stick to the sides."
6. She must walk in a chaste and modest manner (sura, 24.31).
7. When talking to a stranger, her voice must remain normal (sura 33.32).
8. If inside a shop or an office, she must avoid being left alone behind a closed door with a man. The Prophet has said: "There can never be a tete-a-tete between a man and a woman without the devil interfering and doing his worst.
9. She must never shake the hand of a man.
10. Even at a female friend's house, she must not discard any clothes covering her in case there is a man hiding in the house. The Prophet has said: "Any woman who takes off her cloak in other than her own house or the house of her husband is rending apart the envelope that protects her in front of God."
11. The wife must not go beyond a thirty-kilometer limit without being accompanied by her husband or a relative.
12. A woman must never attempt to imitate a man.

Jurists have elaborated in precise detail what a woman who does leave the house should wear. She can wear anything she likes as long as it conforms to the following conditions:

1. Her dress must cover the entire body except the face and hands.
2. The dress must not be too fine or elaborate.
3. It must be of thick material and not transparent.

4. It must not cling to her body tightly; it should be loose.
5. It must not be perfumed.
6. It must not resemble any kind of man's wear.
7. It must not resemble the clothes of unbelievers.
8. It must not be "luxurious" or glamorous or of too great a value.

These jurists cite hadiths forbidding women to put on perfume, to wear a wig, to put on make up, or otherwise to interfere with nature. These same authors who condemn make-up for interfering with divine creation see no contradiction in demanding the excision of the clitoris, which is seen as a pious act to be encouraged. According to a famous hadith, if you "Leave the woman without clothes, they will remain at home."

Thanks to the courageous efforts of certain reformists, women at last did win the right to education. Unable to stem the tide of the feminist movement, and faced with a fait accompli, the conservatives now claimed Islam had never denied women this right, and that it was the duty of every Muslim to educate himself or herself. The University of al-Azhar, a bastion of male privilege, opened its doors to women in 1961. These claims on behalf of Islam are of course false.[601] Traditions discouraging or prohibiting the education of women are numerous: "Prevent them from writing;" "Do not add an evil to unhappiness" are the norm. Indeed if Islam had sincerely approved of educating women, why was it that women had remained illiterate and ignorant for so many centuries? If she is to stay at home, if she is forbidden to talk to strange men, how will she acquire her learning? If her family gives her permission to learn, what will she be allowed to study? Essentially, most modern Muslim thinkers propose religious education for women, with a few courses on sewing, knitting, and looking after the house. These thinkers base their arguments on the hadith where the Prophet said, "Do not teach women writing; teach them spinning and the sura 'The Night' (al-Nur)." The message is clear—she must not overstep her domestic domain. She was created by God to be a wife and mother; hence, any venture into pure chemistry, astronomy, or geometry is against her nature, her needs, and the needs of her family.

It should be apparent by now[602] that by going to work Muslim women would automatically upset a great many Islamic laws governing women and the family. In Islam only men work, earn money, spend it, and are responsible for their wives' maintenance—all of which give men legitimate, divinely sanctioned authority over their wives. Some apparently reformist thinkers insist that every Muslim woman has the right to work. But on closer examination, we see that by "work," these thinkers mean something very limited: teachers of girls, nurses looking after only women, doctors for women. According to the learned doctors, she can do any kind of job except (1) those which are incompatible with her faith—such as cleaning drains, fishing in lakes or rivers; (2) those that are incompatible with her feminine nature—ticket inspector, police officer, dancer; (3) those which she is incapable of handling physically, for example, factory work; (4) those that demand the use of a horse or a bicycle; (5) and, of course, those that require the use of reason—she cannot be a judge or imam. Other thinkers forbid women the job of actress, air hostess, or saleswoman. The arguments most frequently used to limit women's work are (1) a woman's nature; she was made by nature to stay at home, look after her husband's sexual demands, and raise children; (2) her limited reasoning powers; and (3) her psychological weakness because of menstruation, pregnancy, and childbirth.

These thinkers are afraid that as soon as a woman leaves her husband's house, she will fall into sin. They reduce all contact between men and women to sex. So that work that might be seen as a confirmation of woman's being, a fulfilment of her person, of her human dignity, of her personal freedom, is in the eyes of the Muslim thinkers nothing but a degradation of her dignity and honor.

Despite all the obstacles put in front of them, Muslim women have managed to leave their households, have acquired educations, have started to work, and forge careers for themselves; thus, they have laid claims to their rights as consonant with their new position in society. For example, in 1952 Egyptian feminists assembled their forces and claimed the right to vote and the right to become members of Parliament. The ulamas of the University of al-Azhar rallied their forces and in June 1952 promulgated a fatwa liberally sprinkled with quotes from the Koran and the hadiths that demonstrated that Islam condemned any attempt by women to aspire to any post as a member of Parliament. The learned doctors further pointed out that[603] (1) women did not possess enough intellectual force; (2) women, because of their femininity, are exposed to dangers that could lead them to abandon reason and propriety; (3) according to Abu Bakr, when the Prophet heard that the Persians had made the daughter of Chosroes their queen he exclaimed: "Never will a people who trust their affairs to a woman succeed"; (4) failure inevitably follows on the appointment of a woman to a public post; (5) Islamic law accords to a woman's testimony only half the weight of a man's; (6) according to the Koran "men decide for women in view of the fact that God has given preference to the former over the latter; (7) God obliges men to be present at the mosque on Fridays and to conduct the holy war but not women; and (8) public posts were attributed by Islamic law only to men fulfilling certain conditions.

For all these reasons the learned doctors decided that Islamic law forbade women to assume any posts of public responsibility and in particular the post of member of Parliament. Happily, despite the efforts of the ulamas, Egyptian women got the vote in 1956. In Syria, women got the vote in 1949, again despite the obstacles put in their path by the ulamas.

Islam explicitly forbids certain professions to women: head of state, head of the armed forces, imam, and judge.

The system of guardianship in Islam[604] further limits the rights of women. According to the Malekites, Shafi'ites, and Hanbalites, even a woman of legal age cannot conclude her own marriage contract on her own. Her legal guardian alone has this right. According to the Hanafites, a woman can conclude her own marriage but with the agreement of her guardian. Of course, the guardian must be male and Muslim. If a woman is a virgin, irrespective of age, her guardian can force her to marry someone of his choice, according to the Malekites, Shafi'ites, and Hanbalites. Even the theoretical right to choose her husband accorded her by the Hanfites turns out to be illusory. Theoretically, on reaching puberty a woman can no longer be forced to marry against her will; but since a majority of girls are forced to marry before they reach puberty, the right to choose remains a fiction. Even assuming she reaches puberty, under the Hanfites she simply has the right to say "Yes" or "No" to the person picked by her guardian. There is no question of her going out and choosing her own husband. It is the legal guardian who will choose for her, and characteristically when making his inquiries, the desirable qualities of the husband will be described in a few lines whereas the desirable qualities of the wife will be explained in a text twelve times longer.

In any case, when and how could a Muslim woman possibly go out and meet her Prince Charming in view of all the constraints imposed on her by Islam that we have described in this chapter—forbidden to leave the house, forbidden to talk to men? Child marriages continue to be practiced, and the fact that the Prophet himself married Aisha when she was only nine and he was fifty-three encourages Muslim society to continue with this iniquitous custom. As Bousquet, writing in the 1950s, noticed, in North Africa generally and in Algeria particularly, even after a century of French rule, consummation of marriages with young girls continues, often resulting in serious accidents, and sometimes death.

In all cases a Muslim woman is not permitted to marry a non-Muslim. All Muslim males can at any moment separate themselves from their wives, can repudiate their wives without formality, without explanations, and without compensation. It is enough for the husband to pronounce the phrase "You are divorced" and it is done. The divorce is revocable for up to a period of three months. If the husband pronounces "You are divorced" three times, then the divorce is definitive. In the latter case the divorced wife cannot return to her husband until she has been married, "enjoyed," and divorced by another husband. Divorce depends entirely on the will and caprice of the husband—he may divorce his wife without any misbehavior on her part, or without assigning any cause. The mother has the right to keep custody of the children, but as soon as she decides to remarry, she automatically loses her right to her children from the previous marriage. In the case where the husband has the custody of children, if he remarries he does not lose this right to keep his children. Thus the woman is faced with the choice of remarrying and losing custody of her children or keeping her children and not marrying. This of course leads to total insecurity for the women. Divorce is very frequent in Arab countries; instead of keeping four wives at the same time—which is rather expensive—a man simply changes his wife several times as recommended by the great al-Ghazali. If a woman asks a man for a divorce, he may agree if he is paid or compensated in some way. In such a case she is not entitled to the repayment of her dowry. The Koran sanctions such a dissolution: 2.229. "If ye fear that they cannot observe the ordinances of God, then no blame shall attach to either of you for what the wife shall herself give for her redemption."

An annulment of a marriage means a woman loses the right to the dowry and must give back what she has already received. Divorced women do have the right to remarry but "must wait keeping themselves from men, three menstrual courses" (2.228).

Finally, I shall end with a revised list of what a woman has to suffer under Islam because of her misdemeanors in the Garden of Eden. She is forbidden to (1) be a head of state; (2) be a judge; (3) be an imam; (4) be a guardian; (5) leave her house without permission of her guardian or husband; (6) have a tete-a-tete with a strange man; (7) shake a man's hand; (8) put on makeup or perfume outside the house; (9) uncover her face for fear of "temptation"; (10) travel alone; (11) inherit the same amount as a man—she must make do with half; (12) bear witness in cases of hudud (see page 310) and accept that her testimony is worth only half that of a man; (13) perform the religious rituals when menstruating; (14) choose where she will live before she is ugly or old; (15) marry without permission from her guardian; (16) marry a non-Muslim; and (17) divorce her spouse.

The measure of a society's degree of civilization is the position it accords to women, in which case Islam fares very badly indeed. In the words of the great John Stuart Mill, "I am convinced that social arrangements which subordinate one sex to the other by law are bad in themselves and form one of the principal obstacles which oppose human progress; I am convinced that they should give place to a perfect equality."

Case Histories: The Women of Pakistan

To be a woman in Pakistan is a terrible thing."
> Pakistani woman, suspended from her job in
> a hotel in 1990 for shaking hands with a man.[605]

I tell you, this country is being sodomized by religion.
> Pakistani businessman, ex-air force officer.[606]

Let these women be warned. We will tear them to pieces. We will give them such terrible punishments that no one in future will dare to raise a voice against Islam.
> Pakistani mulla (priest) addressing the
> dissenting women of Rawalpindi.[607]

Today, in Pakistan, respect for women no longer exists, and crimes against them have increased dramatically. They claim to have "Islamized" us. How can you Islamize people who are already Muslim? Ever since Zia gave power to the mullahs, it seems as though every man feels he can get hold of any female and tear her apart.

Ms Farkander Iqbal, Deputy Police
Superintendent, Lahore, Pakistan.[608]

One of the ironies of the creation of Pakistan in 1947 as a homeland for the Muslims of India, is that its founder, Muhammad Ali Jinnah, was not at all religious. In fact, in today's Islamic Republic of Pakistan, Jinnah would very probably be flogged in public: during his years in England, Jinnah had developed a decidedly un-Islamic taste for whiskey, and even pork. It is also now clear that Jinnah envisaged a basically secular state; he said in one of his last major speeches:

> You are free; you are free to go to your temples, you are free to go to your mosques or to any other place of worship in this State of Pakistan. . . . You may belong to any religion or caste or creed—*that has nothing to do with the business of the state* [my emphasis]. . . . We are starting with this fundamental principle that we are citizens and equal citizens of one state. . . . Now, I think we should keep in front of us our ideal and you will find that in course of time Hindus would cease to be Hindus and Muslims would cease to be Muslims, not in the religious sense, *because that is the personal faith of each individual* [my emphasis], but in the political sense as citizens of the State.[609]

When asked by a journalist in July 1947 if Pakistan would be a religious state, Jinnah replied, "You are asking a question that is absurd. I do not know what a theocratic state means." Why, in that case, had Pakistan been deemed necessary? M. J. Akbar has argued convincingly that Pakistan was not demanded by the Muslim masses of India; it was created by an alliance of the clergy (mullas) and powerful landlords. "While the landlords and capitalists allowed the clergy to make Pakistan a religious state, the clergy allowed the landlords guaranteed property rights and the capitalists unbridled control over the economy. Theocracy and landlordism/capitalism are the two pillars of Pakistan and BanglaDesh."[610]

After Jinnah's untimely death in 1948, the Prime Minister Liaquat Ali Khan prepared a constitution that was also essentially secular. This was not at all acceptable to the mullas, who began foaming at the mouth at the very mention of democracy. Under pressure from them, the democratic constitution was withdrawn. Then in 1951, Liaquat Ali Khan was assassinated by an unknown gunman, who many believe was paid by the mullas.

In 1971, after years of military rule, Zulfikar Ali Bhutto took over as martial law administrator and, in 1972, as prime minister. Though Bhutto was also essentially secular minded, he was no democrat. He also made overtures to the mullas; banned gambling and alcohol, despite his own well-known taste for whiskey; and declared that the Ahmadi sect was non-Muslim. In 1977, General Zia al-Haq took over in a military coup declaring that the process of Islamization was not going fast enough. The mullas had finally got someone who was prepared to listen to them.

Zia imposed martial law, total press censorship, and began creating a theocratic state, believing that Pakistan ought to have "the spirit of Islam." He banned women from athletic contests and even enforced the Muslim fast during the month of Ramadan at gunpoint. He openly admitted that there was a contradiction between Islam and democracy. Zia introduced Islamic laws that discriminated against women. The most notorious of these laws were the Zina and Hudud Ordinances that called for the Islamic punishments of the amputation of hands for stealing and stoning to death for married people found guilty of illicit sex. The term "zina" included adultery, fornication, and rape, and even prostitution. Fornication was punished with a maximum of a hundred lashes administered in public and ten years' imprisonment.

In practice, these laws protect rapists, for a woman who has been raped often finds herself charged with adultery or fornication. To prove zina, four Muslim adult males of good repute must be present to testify that sexual penetration has taken place. Furthermore, in keeping with good Islamic practice, these laws value the testimony of men over women. The combined effect of these laws is that it is impossible for a woman to bring a successful charge of rape against a man; instead, she herself, the victim, finds herself charged with illicit sexual intercourse, while the rapist goes free. If the rape results in a pregnancy, this is automatically taken as an admission that adultery or fornication has taken place with the woman's consent rather than that rape has occurred.

Here are some sample cases.[611]

In a town in the northern province of Punjab, a woman and her two daughters were stripped naked, beaten, and gang-raped in public, but the police declined to pursue the case.

A thirteen-year-old girl was kidnapped and raped by a "family friend." When her father brought a case against the rapist, it was the girl who was put in prison charged with "zina," illegal sexual intercourse. The father managed to secure the child's release by bribing the police. The traumatized child was then severely beaten for disgracing the family honor.

A fifty-year-old widow, Ahmedi Begum,[612] decided to let some rooms in her house in the city of Lahore to two young veiled women. As she was about to show them the rooms, the police burst into the courtyard of the house and arrested the two girls and Ahmedi Begum's nephew who had simply been standing there. Later that afternoon, Ahmedi Begum went to the police station with her son-in-law to inquire about her nephew and the two girls. The police told Ahmedi they were arresting her too. They confiscated her jewelry and pushed her into another room. While she was waiting, the police officers shoved the two girls, naked and bleeding, into the room and then proceeded to rape them again in front of the widow. When Ahmedi covered her eyes, the police forced her to watch by pulling her arms to her sides. After suffering various sexual humiliations, Ahmedi herself was stripped and raped by one officer after another. They dragged her outside where she was again beaten. One of the officers forced a policeman's truncheon, covered with chili paste, into her rectum, rupturing it. Ahmedi screamed in horrible agony and fainted, only to wake up in prison, charged with zina. Her case was taken up by a human rights lawyer. She was released on bail after three months in prison, but was not acquitted until three years later. In the meantime, her son-in-law divorced her daughter because of his shame.

Was this an isolated case? Unfortunately no. The Human Rights Commission of Pakistan said in its annual report that one woman is raped every three hours in Pakistan and one in two rape victims is a juvenile. According to Women's Action Forum, a woman's rights organization, 72 percent of all women in police custody in Pakistan are physically and sexually abused. Furthermore, 75 percent of all women in jail are there under charges of zina. Many of these women remain in jail awaiting trial for years.

In other words, the charge of zina is casually applied by any man who wants to get rid of his wife, who is immediately arrested, and kept waiting in prison, sometimes for years. Before the introduction of these laws the total number of women in prison was 70; the present number is more than 3000. Most of these women have been charged under the Zina or Hudud Ordinances.[613]

Safia Bibi, a virtually blind sixteen-year-old domestic, was raped by her land-lord and his son. As a result, she became pregnant and later gave birth to an illegitimate child. Though her father brought a case against the men, they were acquitted since there were not the requisite number of male witnesses. However, Safia's pregnancy was proof of fornication and she was accordingly sentenced to three years' imprisonment, fifteen lashes, and a fine of a thousand rupees. The judge smugly stated that he had given a light sentence in view of her age and near blindness. Happily, public pressure resulted in the revocation of the sentence. Since Zia's Islamization program got under way, the number of attacks on women has increased. In every way the lot of women has worsened under the Islamic laws. With the passage of the sharia bill in 1991, the position was further degraded, if that is possible. As one prominent feminist put it, "The shariah bill is a means to control women and marginalize them instead of bringing in a just order. It is a law that facilitates aggression against women but ignores the corruption in the country and it disregards violence against women."[614]

The Western press naively believed that the election of Benazir Bhutto as Pakistan's prime minister in November 1988 would revolutionize women's role not just in Pakistan, but in the entire Islamic world. Under Islamic law of course, women cannot be head of an Islamic state, and Pakistan had become an Islamic republic under the new constitution of 1956. Thus, Benazir Bhutto had defied the mullas and won. But her government lasted a bare twenty months, during which period Nawaz Sharif, who was the prime minister briefly in the early 1990s, is said to have encouraged the mullas in their opposition to having a woman as the head of an Islamic state. Benazir Bhutto's government was dismissed on charges of corruption, and her husband imprisoned in 1990.

The lot of the Muslim woman was harsh before Benazir's election, and nothing has changed. She has pandered to the religious lobby, the mullas, the very people who insist that a woman cannot hold power in an Islamic state, and has repeatedly postponed any positive action on the position of women. As one woman opposition member of the National Assembly put it in 1990, "Benazir Bhutto has not demonstrated a commitment to anything other than her own desire to wield power."[615] Benazir Bhutto has shown herself to be far less radical than the Western media had hoped for. She agreed to an arranged marriage with a man she had known for seven days, and she constantly wears the traditional headscarf. At this year's Cairo Conference on Population (September 1994), she again went out of her way to take the side of the Muslim conservatives. "We thought we elected a Cory [Aquino], but it looks like we got Imelda instead," said one disappointed member of the National Assembly.[616]

The statistics concerning the women of Pakistan show the same grim picture. Pakistan is one of only four countries in the world where female life expectancy (51 years) is lower than the male (52); the average female life expectancy for all poor countries is 61. A large number of Pakistani women die in pregnancy or childbirth, six for every 1000 live births. Despite the fact that contraception has never been banned by orthodox Islam, under Zia the Islamic Ideology Council of Pakistan declared family planning to be un-Islamic. Various mullas condemned family planning as a Western conspiracy to emasculate Islam. As a result, the average fertility rate per woman in Pakistan is 6.9. Pakistan is also among the world's bottom ten countries for female attendance at primary schools. Some people put female literacy in the rural areas as low as 2 percent (*Economist*, March 5, 1994). As the *Economist* put it, "Some of the blame for all this lies with the attempt of the late President Zia ul Haq to create an Islamic republic. . . . Zia turned the clock back. A 1984 law of his, for instance, gives a woman's legal evidence half the weight of a man's." (*Economist*, Jan. 13, 1990).

Indeed a large part of the blame lies with the attitudes inculcated by Islam, which has always seen woman as inferior to man. The birth of a baby girl is the occasion for mourning. Hundreds of baby girls are abandoned every year in the gutters and dust bins and on the pavements. An organization working in Karachi to save these children has calculated that more than five hundred children are abandoned a year in Karachi alone, and that 99 percent of them are girls.[617]

At the time of a wedding, the family of the bride provides the dowry. Many families are under social pressure to provide a large dowry, which is a crushing burden for many of them. There tends to be a prenuptial agreement between the families regarding the size of the dowry. Yet, despite this agreement, many young newly married women are subjected to further pressure—even beatings—to ask their parents to provide more. When this is not forthcoming, the young woman is burned to death. In 1991 alone there were more than two thousand dowry deaths. Many deaths go unreported, since the family wants to avoid scandal at all costs. Few such cases are investigated by the police, and most of them are passed off as "kitchen accidents."

Two young sisters were taken to a hospital,[618] where the doctor diagnosed an infection of the bones caused by a lack of sunlight. The girls' father had forbidden them to leave their home. This forced seclusion sometimes takes a bizarre and tragic form, as in the case of those Muslim girls known as the Brides of the Koran, who are compelled by their families to marry the Koran. In large feudal, land-owning families, especially in the province of Sind, women are allowed to marry only within the family—in many cases only to first cousins—to ensure that the family property stays in the family. A marriage outside the family would entail a break up of the property when the woman inherited her proper share of the family estate. When the family runs out of eligible male cousins, the young woman is forced to marry the Koran in a ceremony exactly like a real wedding except that the bridegroom is lacking. The bride is sumptuously dressed, guests are invited, food, and festivities follow. At the ceremony itself, the bride is instructed to place her hand on the Koran, and she is wedded to the holy book. The rest of her life is spent in total seclusion from the outside world. She is not allowed to see a man—in some cases, not even on television. These brides are expected to devote their time to studying the Koran or doing craft work. Such desolate emptiness takes its toll, and many of the brides of the Koran become mentally ill. As one out of an estimated 3,000 brides of the Koran in the Sind put it, "I wish I had been born when the Arabs buried their daughters alive. Even that would have been better than this torture."

Little did Jinnah realize how literally true his words were when he said in a 1944 speech:[619] "No nation can rise to the height of glory unless your women are side by side with you. We are victims of evil customs. It is a crime against humanity that our women are shut up within the four walls of the houses as prisoners."

Despite the secular vision of its founder, Jinnah, Pakistan has drifted toward a theocratic state. Pakistani politicians have been totally cowardly in giving in to the demands of the mullas. Fear of fundamentalists has only encouraged the fundamentalists even more. It is difficult for the largely secularized West to realize what power these people can sometimes wield over the masses, encouraging them to carry out the most vile acts imaginable, all in the name of God. For instance, a mob in Karachi, hysterically manipulated by a mulla, stoned to death an abandoned infant on the presumption that it was illegitimate and thus could not be tolerated. Another mob cut off a man's hand because the mulla leading them alleged that the man was a thief; no proof, no trial, just the mulla's word. Benazir Bhutto has moved more and more toward appeasing the religious right. It would be just as well to remind her of her own words uttered in 1992 when she was not in power:

Does [Pakistan] want to be a democracy in which human rights are respected and where an enlightened vision of Islam prevails? Or will it be content to make do with an authoritarian government dominated by fundamentalists? And which authority should legislate—parliament or the federal court dispensing the sharia (Islamic law)? In the absence of answers to these questions, the situation is confused today, and confusion spawns anarchy. (*Le Monde*, March 4, 1992)

But we do not need to leave with a completely pessimistic picture. Pakistani women have shown themselves to be very courageous, and more and more are fighting for their rights with the help of equally brave organizations such as Women's Action Forum (WAF) and War Against Rape. WAF was formed in 1981 as women came onto the streets to protest against the Hudood Ordinances, and to demonstrate their solidarity with a couple who had recently been sentenced to death by stoning for fornication. In 1983, women organized the first demonstrations against martial law.

15

Taboos: Wine, Pigs, and Homosexuality

Of Whiskey and Wine

Khushwant Singh, the Indian man of letters and surely one of the most underrated Indian novelists writing in English, wrote of his visit to Pakistan:

> Prohibition is as much of a farce in the Islamic Republic of Pakistan as it was in Morarji Desai's India. A drinking man can find liquor in the mirages of the Sahara desert. In Pakistan it does not run like the river Ravi in spate, but it does trickle in tumbler fulls in most well-to-do Pakistani homes. You may have whiskey served in metal tumblers or in a tea-pot and have to sip from a China cup. It costs more than twice as much as in India but also goes down twice as well because it tastes of sin.[620]

Later Singh watched a debate on television between three mullas and the Pakistan Minister of Information. The next evening, Singh found himself sitting next to the same minister of information at a formal dinner. The minister read a speech welcoming Singh and the rest of the Indian delegation. In reply, Singh got up and told the minister that the next time he met the mullas, he should recite them the following verses:

> Mulla, if your prayer has power
> Let me see you shake the mosque!
> If not, take a couple of pegs of liquor
> And see how the mosque shakes on its own.

"There was," continued Singh, "a roar of applause in which the minister joined. Then he whispered in my ear: 'If these fellows [i.e., the mullas] had their way, they would make our girls' hockey teams play in burqas.' " (The burqa is a stifling, tentlike garment that totally covers a woman from head to toe, with only a small embroidered grill opening at eye-level to allow her to peer through at the outside world.)

Hanif Kureishi, a British writer whose father was of Pakistani origin, went to several parties in Karachi, Pakistan. At one attended by people of power—landowners, diplomats, businessmen, and politicians—Kureishi found that

> they were drinking heavily. Every liberal in England knows you can be lashed for drinking in Pakistan. But as far as I could tell, none of this English-speaking international bourgeoisie would be lashed for anything. They all had their favorite trusted bootleggers. . . . I once walked into a host's bathroom to see the bath full of floating whisky bottles being soaked to remove the labels, a servant sitting on a stool serenely poking at them with a stick.[621]

Charles Glass writing in the *Times Literary Supplement* (22 April 1994), recounts this story of hypocrisy in Saudi Arabia:

> Possession of alcohol was illegal, but I was offered wine and, in the houses of royal princes, cabinet ministers, and ambassadors, whisky (the favoured drink was Johnny Walker Black Label). I learned that a prince with whom I had shared a whisky in the evening would in the morning sentence a man to prison for drinking.

There is no country in the entire Islamic world where there is no alcoholic drink available, and where some Muslim is not transgressing the Islamic prohibition against wine and spirits. While the rich and sophisticated drink their smuggled bottles of whiskey or gin, the poor produce their own wine or alcoholic drink from dates, palms, and sugar cane. I can vouch from personal experience that even during the holy month of Ramadan in 1990, both the brothels and the wine shops were open in Algeria.

The prophet Muhammad in one verse of the Koran (sura 16.69) praises wine as one of the signs of God's grace to mankind. However, as the early companions of the Prophet often got drunk, Muhammad was obliged to show some disapproval (suras 2.216; 4.46), until finally in sura 5.92 He actually forbade it outright: "O true believers! Surely wine and maysir and stone pillars and divining arrows, are an abomination of the work of Satan; therefore avoid them, that ye may prosper." According to Islamic law, drinking wine is punishable by eighty lashes, though according to some traditions repeated drinking of wine is punishable by death.

As remarked in an earlier chapter, Arabs of the time of Muhammad found it difficult to embrace Islam because of its prohibition of wine and restriction of sexual intercourse. For the Arabs, these were the two delicious things, "al-atyaban." Pre-Islamic poetry[622] is full of references to the joys of drinking wine in taverns and wine shops. Even with the advent of Islam, the praise of wine remained an integral part of Arabic poetry for centuries—in fact, no other literature can boast such a rich collection of wine poems, known as "khamriyya" in Arabic. Once again, as with the development of Islamic science and philosophy, Islamic literature flourished despite Islam, rather than thanks to it.

At the court of the caliphs where royal patronage was enough to shield the revelers from the prescribed eighty lashes, wine flowed freely at parties. But ordinary Arabs also refused to give up wine despite the risk of imprisonment. We might quote Abu Mihjan, who was imprisoned and later exiled by the Caliph Umar in the early days of Islam for continuing the praise of wine:

> Give me, o friend, some wine to drink; though I am
>   well aware of what God has revealed about wine.
> Give me pure wine to make my sin bigger because only
>   when it is drunk unmixed is the sin complete
>
> Though wine has become rare and though we have been
> deprived of it and though Islam and the threat of
> punishment have divorced us from it:
> Nevertheless I do drink it in the early morning hours
> in deep draughts, I drink it unmixed and from time to
> time I become gay and drink it mixed with water.
> At my head stands a singing girl and while
>   she sings she flirts;
> Sometimes she sings loudly, sometimes
> softly, humming like flies in the garden.

Abu Mihjan could not even face the thought of being without wine after he was dead, and so he composed the following verse:

> When I die bury me by the side of a vine so that my
> bones may feed on its juices after death.
> Do not bury me in the plains because I am afraid that then
> I cannot enjoy wine when I am dead.[623]

This tradition of wine songs continued under the Umayyads who were totally unable to silence them. The wider significance of this defiance has been subtly analyzed by Goldziher[624], who wrote: "The Umayyad rule was ill-equipped to silence wine songs, as it expresses the spirit of opposition to the piety of Medina, which was contrary to the old Arab way of life. Thus the tradition of glorifying wine was not interrupted in Arabic poetry and rarely is a voice raised against its enjoyment. *So we find the phenomenon of a people's poetry being for centuries a living protest against its religion*" (my emphasis).

Khamriyya or wine poems thus became a means of protest and rebellion defying not only Koranic precepts, but the entire culture that attempted to shackle with arbitrary restrictions the independent spirit of the poets, who detested any kind of asceticism.

In the first Muslim century we have poets like Ibn Sayhan, al-Ukayshir, and Ibn Kharidja singing of the pleasures of love, music, and wine. Al-Ahwas went as far as possible in his defiance of religion and of the political regime of the time—a defiance that landed him in the pillory.

In the second century, we have the illustrious Walid b. Yazid who was surrounded by a large group of poets singing the praises of wine and the hedonistic life. We also have the group of poets whom Bencheikh[625] calls the "Libertines of Kufa:"

> It is here, and at its best, that Bacchism appears as the expression of a rebellion, that the attitudes of the poet take on subversive overtones. The rebellion is spectacularly directed against religious precepts; it is not an accident that most of the poets of this group fall under the accusation of zandaka, and several of them paid with their life for their desire to reject a constraining socio-cultural system.

We have already met many of these poets in our chapter on heresy. Other names include Bakr b. Kharidja, who spent most of his time in taverns, and Ziyad al-Harithi, who indulged in orgies of drinking with his friend Muti b. Iyas.

Here we might mention another habitué of taverns, the black slave Abu Dulama,[626] the court jester under the early Abbasids, but also the poet who used low expressions and displayed "all sorts of filth with cynical joy," in brief, a kind of Arabic Eddie Murphy. He also took the court jester's liberty of attacking Islam and Islamic laws with much insolence.

Numerous other wine poets lived a generally dissolute life, going from one drinking bout to another, but finding enough time to write some Bacchic verse. Wine also played an important part in the writings of the mystics, where it was one of the symbols of ecstasy.

Abu Nuwas (762–ca. 814) was the greatest wine poet—and probably the greatest poet—in the Arabic language. He appears in countless comic episodes in the *Thousand and One Nights*, where he is often in the company of Harun al-Rashid. Many specialists would rate him the greatest poet in the Arabic language. He was born in Ahwaz in 747. We know little of his parents, but Abu Nuwas always considered himself more Persian than Arabian. He spent his youth in Basra and Kufa, studying philology and poetry. He eventually made his way to the court of Harun al-Rashid in Baghdad. Nicholson[627] describes him as "A man of the most abandoned character, which he took no pains to conceal, Abu Nuwas, by his flagrant immorality, drunkeness, and blasphemy, excited the Caliph's anger to such a pitch that he often threatened the culprit with death, and actually imprisoned him on several occasions."

Abu Nuwas was capable of writing in many different styles but the inspirational fount of his poetry was wine and love. When he was not singing the praises of beautiful boys, he was composing incomparable wine songs, which rarely exceeded fourteen lines. For example:

> Ho! a cup, and fill it up, and tell me it is wine,
> For I will never drink in shade if I can drink in shine!
> Curst and poor is every hour that sober I must go,
> But rich am I whene'er well drunk I stagger to and fro.
> Speak, for shame, the loved one's name, let vain disguise
> alone:
> No good there is in pleasure o'er which a veil is thrown.[628]

At least Abu Nuwas cannot be accused of hypocrisy. He also advocates excess, suggesting that, in the end, one will be forgiven by the merciful God:

> Accumulate as many sins thou canst:
> The Lord is ready to relax His ire.
> When the day comes, forgiveness thou wilt find
> Before a mighty King and gracious Sire,
> And gnaw thy fingers, all that joy regretting
> Which thou didst leave thro' terror of Hell-fire!

The greatest poet after Nuwas was Ibn al-Mu'tazz (executed in 908) who was also celebrated for his wine songs and descriptions of drinking customs.

As we began, we can end with Pakistan and Khushwant Singh. Faiz Ahmed Faiz (1911–1984) is often considered Pakistan's national poet. He carried on the tradition of wine songs in Islamic literature. Singh describes his visits to Faiz in this manner: "When I went to his room in the morning, he was drinking [usually Scotch]. I had my breakfast and left. . . . When I returned at noon, he was drinking. I had my lunch and retired for a siesta. Later in the evening I joined him for a couple of drinks and had my dinner. He continued drinking. [This continued] till the early hours of the morning."

Faiz was a communist, at least during one period of his life, but, in Singh's words, "his daily consumption of premium brand of Scotch and imported cigarettes would have fed a worker's family for a month."[629]

Faiz wrote:

> There will be no more war.
> Bring the wine and the glasses
>   champagne and goblets
> Bloodletting is a thing of the past: so is
> weeping.[630]

Pigs and Pork

In 1968, when he was in Karachi, Pakistan, Salman Rushdie persuaded Karachi television to produce Edward Albee's *The Zoo Story*. Rushdie takes up the story:

The character I played had a long monologue in which he described his landlady's dog's repeated attacks on him. In an attempt to befriend the dog, he bought it half a dozen hamburgers. The dog refused the hamburgers and attacked him again. "I was offended," I was supposed to say. "It was six perfectly good hamburgers with not enough pork in them to make it disgusting." "Pork," a TV executive told me solemnly, "is a four-letter word." He had said the same thing about "sex," and "homosexual," but this time I argued back. The text I pleaded, was saying the right thing about pork. Pork, in Albee's view, made hamburgers so disgusting that even dogs refused them. This was superb anti-pork propaganda. It must stay. "You don't see," the executive told me, . . . "the word pork may not be spoken on Pakistan television." And that was that.[631]

George Orwell's *Animal Farm* is banned from Islamic countries since the main characters are pigs, even though they are shown to be ultimately ruthless and tyrannical.

From time to time, in some Muslim countries, religious police raid toy shops to sniff out mugs in the form of the Muppet character Miss Piggy—if any are found, they are smashed publicly.

"You know," remarks writer Paul Theroux, "you have travelled through the looking-glass when you are in a country where Miss Piggy is seen as the very embodiment of evil."

The Islamic aversion to even literary pigs is depriving Muslims of such delights of English literature as P. G. Wodehouse's stories of Lord Emsworth and his prize sow, the Empress of Blandings. Though, perhaps, the Muslims are well rid of Winnie the Pooh and his friend Piglet.

The absolute disgust and revulsion engendered in the Muslim mind at the thought of eating this "most loathsome beast" is nothing short of fanatical and worthy of psychoanalytical consideration. John Stuart Mill[632] clearly saw the significance and special nature of this hatred:

Nothing in the creed or practice of Christians does more to envenom the hatred of Mahomedans [Muslims] against them than the fact of their eating pork. There are few acts which Christians and Europeans regard with more unaffected disgust than Mussulmans regard this particular mode of satisfying hunger. It is, in the first place, an offence against their religion; but this circumstance by no means explains either the degree or the kind of their repugnance; for wine also is forbidden by their religion, and to partake of it is by all Mussulmans accounted wrong, but not disgusting. Their aversion to the flesh of the "unclean beast" is, on the contrary, of that peculiar character, resembling an instinctive antipathy, which the idea of uncleaness, when once it thoroughly sinks into the feelings, seems always to excite even in those whose personal habits are anything but scrupulously clean, and of which the sentiment of religious impurity, so intense in the Hindoos, is a remarkable example.

The Koran expressly forbids pork:

Sura 5.3. You are forbidden carrion, blood, and the flesh of swine; also any flesh dedicated to any other than God.

Sura 6.145. Say: I do not find, in what is revealed to me, aught forbidden to him who eats thereof except it be carrion, or blood outpoured, or the flesh of swine—that is an abomination—or an ungodly thing that has been hallowed to other than God. (See also 2.173; 16.115.)

In sura 6.145, the reason given for the prohibition is that pork is an "abomination." At least, Yusuf Ali, Arberry, and Sale translate the Arabic word "rijas" as abomination, and John Penrice's famous dictionary and glossary of the Koran also gives "abomination" as the correct translation; yet Dawood and Rodwell translate it as "unclean." We shall return to this point shortly.

The attitudes and remarks about food restrictions and the eventual adoption of certain prohibitions in the Koran can be understood only if we see them as attempts at Muslim self-definition, especially vis-à-vis Judaism. The Koranic precepts developed in a milieu "in which each religious community was distinguished by its own regulations concerning food."[633] Thus at suras 2.168, 5.87, 6.118, and 7.32, the Koran castigates those who would impose arbitrary dietary laws rather than be grateful to God's bounty. These verses are clearly aimed at Christian ascetics and those pagans who had recently converted to Judaism and had adopted noachic precepts concerning food regulations. Later, "it became important to define Islam as against Judaism."

Muhammad was not a systematic thinker, and it is futile to look for a coherent set of principles in the Koran. Muhammad dealt with a number of problems as they arose, and we can trace the historical background of many of the rules and regulations prescribed in the Koran. Thus we find conflicting or even contradictory tendencies in the Koran and early Islamic dietary laws concerning food; these have been named the restrictive and the liberal tendencies by Cook.[634]

For instance, let us look at the liberal tendency, probably derived from Christian polemic against the Jews. The enormous number of Jewish prohibitions led Muhammad to criticize those who imposed excessive restrictions on themselves, for God does not wish to weigh down the faithful with too many useless and arbitrary rules concerning food (sura 2.286). The Jewish prohibitions are even seen as divine punishment for the sins of the Jews (suras 4.158, 16.119). Similarly the insistence on the lawfulness of fish arose from opposition to Samaritan and Judeo-Christian practice.

The restrictive tendency was probably derived from the Jews. The Koran and all Muslim law schools, of course, prohibit pig. Rodinson points out that this prohibition was found among the Judaizing pagans and was also a feature of the dietary laws of certain Judeo-Christians. It was probably through this route that this prohibition was adopted in Arabia.

If asked why he does not eat pork, the average Muslim will reply, "It is forbidden in the Koran." That is sufficient for him, no further explanation is deemed necessary. More often, with middle-class, educated Muslims, the chances are the reply will be "because the pig is a dirty animal, and in hot countries is prone to disease." The more sophisticated may even go on to name the diseases that are to be found in pigs or are transmitted by them to humans, such as trichinosis.

These hygienic reasons for the prohibition of pork are older than one would imagine, but nonetheless false. For example, Maimonides (1135–1204) said: "All the food which the Torah has forbidden us to eat have some bad and damaging effect on the body. . . . The principal reason why the Law forbids swine's flesh is to be found in the circumstances that its habits and its food are very dirty and loathsome."[635]

Pigs were not known, or hardly known to the pre-Islamic Arabs.[636] Pliny in his *Natural History* noted the absence of pork in Arabia. We know from Sozomenus (fifth century A.D.) that certain pagan Arabs abstained from pork and observed other Jewish ceremonies. If that is the case, why would Muhammad prohibit an animal that was not likely to be found in Arabia, let alone eaten? This prohibition makes more sense if we see it as something adopted later as the Arabs came into contact with the Samaritans and Jews in Palestine and began forging their own religious identity.

The Koran describes swine's flesh as an abomination, and not as "unclean." The Muslims took over the prohibition from the Jews and Samaritans. This only pushes the question one step farther back. Why did the latter groups prohibit it? Modern social anthropologists are reluctant to assign origins to belief and behavior, but as far as I know, no modern anthropologist accepts the view that pigs were forbidden because of hygienic reasons, though certain historians, theologians, and archaeologists do. Let us look at the reasons why the hygienic explanations are not acceptable.

Trichinosis[637] is a disease caused by a small parasite nematode worm, *Trichinella spiralis,* which is passed onto man in undercooked, infected meat—almost always pork. It is only rarely a serious disease, but complications can arise. Symptoms include fever, muscle pain, sore eyes, and malaise. No one, needless to say, in the biblical Middle East knew anything of *T. spiralis,* or of the relationship of the parasite to pigs or humans. Only in 1835 was the parasite first found in human muscles, but, at that time, it was still considered harmless. Not until 1859, twenty-four years later, was it realized that the parasite could be transmitted to man through eating pork and recognized that these parasites could cause disease. Moreover, symptoms are not always easy to detect. In the United States there are said to be 350,000 new infections a year, and yet only 4.5 percent show any symptoms.

Many people point to the heat in the Middle East as the prime cause of parasites being present in pork.

But trichinosis is a disease of *cold and temperate regions,* thus it is more common in Europe and America than the Near or Middle East.

Cattle, sheep, and goats are also responsible for transmitting certain diseases to humans. Undulant fever is contracted from handling infected cattle or from milk; Malta fever is passed onto man from goats; anthrax, a very serious disease, is transmitted to man by sheep and cattle and can lead to symptoms like fever and result in pus and scabs.

What of the putative dirty habits of the pigs? Pigs are not particularly worse than chickens and goats who also eat dung. Water buffaloes wallow in filthy, muddy water. Amongst the Northwestern Melanesians described by Malinowski, dogs were considered much dirtier than pigs.[638]

In any case, if their habits engendered such disgust, why were they domesticated? We know that they were domesticated in Southwest Asia sometime between 9,000 B.C. and 6,000 B.C., and formed an important element of the Sumerian diet. Herodotus tells us there were swineherds who belonged to a separate class in Egypt. But if there were swineherds, then there must have been a demand for pig meat. If the Jews were aware of the diseases caused by eating undercooked pork, why was this knowledge not available to other groups that did eat pork? In fact, Hippocrates claimed that eating pig flesh gave strength.

Christianity spread the use of pork, but the earliest Christian converts were Jews. Had hygienic considerations been the real reason for the prohibition of pork, then surely they would have continued to be valid, and Christians would have adopted the prohibition.

That terms such as "disgusting" and "dirty" are hopelessly subjective can be seen from the fact that later Muslim law schools permitted certain animals to be eaten that would disgust the average European. For example,[639] three of the four main Sunni schools and the jurist Ibn Hazm permit eating the lizard. Surely there is no more revolting a creature than the hyena, which lurks around dead meat, stinking carcasses, and rotting bodies; yet the Shafi'ites, Ibn Hazm, and the normally intolerant Hanbalis allow it to be eaten. The Malikis, Shafi'ites, and Ibn Hazm also permit the hedgehog as food. All the schools, without exception, allow the camel and locust for Muslim consumption.

What then is the real reason for the taboo on eating pork? According to Robertson Smith,[640] the ancient Semites had a ritual attitude to swine, its flesh being forbidden for ordinary food, though it could be eaten on special occasions. Among the Syrians swine's flesh was taboo, "but it was an open question whether this was because the animal was holy or because it was unclean." Ideas of sanctity and noncleanliness were not yet distinguished. According to Frazer,[641] the Jews also had an ambiguous attitude to swine—did they worship or abominate them? Frazer suggests that the Jews revered swine, and we know that

> some of the Jews used to meet secretly in gardens to eat the flesh of swine
> and mice as a religious rite. Doubtless this was a very ancient ceremony, dating
> from a time when both the pig and the mouse were venerated as divine, and

when their flesh was partaken of sacramentally on rare and solemn occasions as the body and blood of gods. And in general it may perhaps be said that all so-called unclean animals were originally sacred; the reason for not eating them was that they were divine.

A similar situation prevailed in Egypt.

These explanations, though adequate for that which concerns pigs, are inadequate to explain all the details of the dietary laws in the Old Testament, with their various systems of classification. Nor do Frazer and Robertson Smith explain why certain animals acquire the status of divine.

All modern explanations of the dietary laws in the Old Testament take their starting point from the discussions found in Mary Douglas's *Purity and Danger* (1966) and *Implicit Meanings* (1975).

Essentially, Douglas sees "food taboos" in terms of category relationships, of boundaries, and hence of anomalies and ambiguities that do not fit the boundaries. According to Douglas,[642] animals were expected to have those essential physical features proper to their respective habitats, with the means of locomotion as the crucial feature." Thus, cattle were expected to go on four (cloven) hooves, birds primarily to fly (rather than to walk), and fish to have fins. Rodents were prohibited because of their indeterminate movement." The Biblical classification "rejects creatures which are anomalous, whether in living between two spheres, or having defining features of another sphere, or lacking defining features." "Holiness requires that individuals shall conform to the class to which they belong . . . that different classes of things shall not be confused."

"Cloven-hoofed, cud-chewing ungulates are the model of the proper kind of food for a pastoralist": thus the pig, which *is* cloven-hoofed but is *not* a ruminant, is therefore excluded, and nothing is said about its putative dirty habits in the Old Testament. "As the pig does not yield milk, hide, nor wool, there is no other reason for keeping it except for its flesh. And if the Israelites did not keep pigs they would not be familiar with its habits."

Edwin Firmage[643] finds Douglas's thesis wanting in many respects. I can only give a very sketchy account of his criticisms and his own proposals for the solution. The means of locomotion is not the unifying principle behind the perception of uncleanness (why cloven hooves and not simple hooves?). "Why does anomaly ipso facto make these things unclean and inedible?"

Instead Firmage provides his own answers:

The driving force . . . was surely the notion that Israel had been called to be a holy people. It was the priest's special concern to see to it that the conditions for holiness were observed, first of all in the sanctuary but also among the people at large. He was to teach the people what constituted ritual uncleanness, and how it was to be eliminated. The priests took the notion of Israel's calling a step further, however, when they created the dietary law. . . . It goes beyond the more limited notion of personal purity, in that it distinguishes not any person who is pure from one who is not, but Israelites as against other nations. When, therefore, the priests realized that the Israelite diet too should come under the requirements of the injunctions of holiness, they had in the sacrificial animals ready made models of cleanness by which they could judge the purity of items in the Israelite diet. . . . These same commonly sacrificed species also provided the bulk of the ordinary man's diet of meat. However, while man's diet included those animals regularly given to the deity, man nevertheless enjoyed a greater variety of meats than the deity. The question for the priest was, then: which of these other meats were consistent with the paradigm of "proper" meats defined by the sacrificial species? The handful of species fit for God's altar-table, universally accepted as such from the beginning, provided the required definition of cleanness for the rest of the animal world. The priests drew an analogy between the Israelite diet and that of YHWH, whose staples (the sacrificial species) became the measure of fitness for all other animals in the ordinary Israelite's diet.

When it came to applying this standard of comparison, only those animals which superficially resembled the sacrificial model were allowed.

But the priest had to give some general guidelines for the layman, and he accordingly picked out those features that he believed could easily be applied in deciding difficult or borderline cases. "The present criteria themselves are therefore not exactly the raison d'être of most of the dietary prohibitions. They are, however, indicative of the more general and fundamental criterion of dissimilarity with the temple paradigm. It is this which is the mainspring of the dietary law."

The weakness of Firmage's argument lies in the idea of "the handful of species fit for God's altar-table, universally accepted as such from the beginning." In other words, the Israelites had some prior notion of what was fit to be sacrificed. It is surely inadequate to tell us that certain species were accepted from the beginning as fit for God's altar table. That is the very problem that is worrying us—what criteria did they use to arrive at those "handful of species?" The Israelites took the sacrificial species as their paradigm, but how did they choose this paradigm in the first place?

We might briefly look at the solutions proposed by Marvin Harris[644] and Simoons. Harris gives an ecological explanation for the abomination of the pig. Pigs were orginally kept for their meat—as a source of animal protein. In the forest habitat, the pig lived on roots, tubers, and fruits. Once this forest disappeared the pig had to be raised on grain, and therefore competed for man's own food resources. Thus the pig became too expensive to serve as a source of meat. The prohibition against eating pork was a means of ensuring that farmers did not yield to the temptation to raise pigs, which would have been disastrous for the community. This theory, while ingenious, raises further questions. If pigs were raised on what Firmage calls marginal food, then surely they would not have posed such a serious threat to the community's resources. There is also the question of the amount of deforestation occurring in forested areas. De Planhol,[645] the greatest authority on geography and Islam, has shown that it was the *prohibition* of pork that led to deforestation. The prohibition "led to the grazing of sheep and goats in the wooded mountains, and certainly accelerated deforestation, which was catastrophic in these arid and semi-arid countries." De Planhol gives the example of Albania: when we pass through the countryside from the Muslim to the Christian sections, the amount of woodland immediately becomes much greater.

Pigs can still be a useful animal after deforestation.

According to Simoons[646] the prejudice against pigs and pork developed among pastoral peoples living in arid and semi-arid regions. Pigs were unsuited to the pastoral way of life, but were widely diffused among agricultural peoples. There was a conflict between two peoples and two ways of life. The pig symbolized the way of life of one group, while contempt for the pig was a symbol of the other group. There is obviously something in this, but many would not find it acceptable because it does not explain all the other dietary laws.

Many scholars, however, come back to the notion of group loyalty and allegiance. For instance, Edmund Leach says:[647]

> In nearly all societies food is one of the tags by which members of the different social classes are differentiated. We eat this; they eat that. What we eat is "good," "prestigious," "clean"; what they eat is "bad," "defiling," "dirty." Where populations of mixed religion live side by side in one locality one way of marking out the boundaries of social class/caste/religion is by having different rules about food taboos. This is very markedly the case in India where one can encounter every possible combination of prohibition in castes which are living side by side.

For our purposes, the above account is enough to explain why Muhammad chose certain prohibitions—as a means of marking out the boundaries from other religions, and as a means of acquiring Muslim identity. The prohibition of pork thus has nothing to do with the dirty habits of the pig or the diseases it can transmit to man; pigs and their habits were hardly known to the Arabs.

Having emphasized the nearly universal loathing in Islam for pork, I shall now give examples[648] of exceptions to the rule. It seems that both Avicenna and Haly Abbas (al-Majusi) favored eating pork for its medicinal qualities. De Planhol cites the example of the Ghomara Riffian heretics of the Middle Ages who permitted the flesh of female pigs to be eaten. Berbers of Iherrushen and Ikhuanen in North Gzennaya, Morocco, raised pigs until recent times. People tend to be secretive about it in Morocco, though according to Westermarck, its inhabitants used to eat the liver of the wild boar to gain strength. In China, Muslims will eat pork but simply call it "mutton." The Druse are also said to partake of the flesh of swine.

IN PRAISE OF PIGS

The modern, relatively hairless pigs that we know today derive from *Sus scrofa vittatus,* which has been bred in China since Neolithic times, but which reached

Europe only in the eighteenth century. Charles Lamb sang the praises of the pig in the nineteenth century, and here is how a modern philosopher describes the virtues of the pig:

> Surely the pig was created expressly for the table. . . . The pig also looks like food: a round, plump offering on sticks, ready at any moment to lose its individuality and slide down the metaphysical ladder from thing to stuff. Furthermore, he tastes good, and can be made to taste better, the more you work on him. He is the source of charcuterie, the highest of all culinary art-forms, which surpasses in boldness and finesse anything that the Jews or Muslims, for all their ingenuity, have been able to achieve from their abstinence. . . . I cannot think, therefore, that God's purpose was rightly perceived by the author of Leviticus, and am even inclined to the view that, when it comes to the pig, there is something ungrateful, even blasphemous, in refusing to eat him.[649]

Homosexuality

The greater tolerance for homosexuality in the Islamic world has been recognized for a long time. From the nineteenth century onward, many Westerners have been going to Muslim North Africa to look for the homosexual adventure that their own society condemned.

At the beginning of Compton Mackenzie's novel of homosexuality, *Thin Ice,* published in 1956, the narrator and his friend Henry Fortescue go to Morocco where Henry is erotically aroused by their porter, Ali. Henry goes up country in pursuit of Ali, while the British vice-consul reassures the narrator that there was no danger, that conditions in the interior were not as bad as they were painted. Then the vice-consul adds: "Curious. It passed through my mind yesterday that your friend was that way inclined. Well, nobody in the Moslem world between Tangier and the Khyber Pass is going to criticize his tastes."[650]

Starting at the latter end of the Islamic world, let us look at the situation in the Khyber Pass. The emperor Babur[651] (1483–1530), was to pass through the Khyber Pass and eventually make his home in India. In his autobiography, Babur tells us with much delicacy how he fell in love with a boy:

> In those leisurely days I discovered in myself a strange inclination, nay! as the verse says, "I maddened and afflicted myself" for a boy in the camp-bazaar, his very name, Baburi, fitting in. . . . From time to time Baburi used to come to my presence but out of modesty and bashfulness, I could never look straight at him; how then could I make conversation and recital? In my joy and agitation I could not thank him (for coming); how was it possible for me to reproach him with going away? What power had I to command the duty service to myself? One day, during that time of desire and passion when I was going with companions along a lane and suddenly met him face to face, I got into such a state of confusion that I almost went right off. To look straight at him or put words

together was impossible. . . . In that frothing up of desire and passion, and under that stress of youthful folly, I used to wander, barehead, bare-foot, through street and lane, orchard and vineyard.

Sir Richard Burton was to confirm Islamic tolerance for homosexuality, particularly at the Khyber Pass end:

The cities of Afghanistan and Sind are thoroughly saturated with Persian vice [i.e., homosexuality], and the people sing

> The worth of cunt the Afghan knows
> Kabul prefers the other "chose!"

The Afghans are commercial travelers on a large scale and each caravan is accompanied by a number of boys and lads almost in woman's attire with khol'd eyes and rouged cheeks, long tresses and henna'd fingers and toes . . . they are called Kuch-i-safari or traveling wives.[652]

Burton gives further examples of the "vice," ranging from Persia to Morocco, but as his "Terminal Essay," in which they appear, is now famous, I will not quote from it further. Instead I will give one last example of the prevalence of and tolerance toward homosexuality from the work of the ethnographer Cline, writing in 1936, about his field work in Western Egypt at the oasis of Siwah: "All normal Siwan men and boys practice sodomy. . . . Among themselves the natives are not ashamed of this; they talk about it as openly as they talk about the love of women, and many, if not most of their fights arise from homosexual competition."[653] Even marriages between men and boys were celebrated with great festivities and reveling; brideprices for boys were as much as fifteen times that paid for a girl.

Though some scholars find the Koranic attitude, at worst, mildly negative or even ambiguous, I think it is clear from the following references that it was fairly condemnatory: sura 4.16: "If two men among you commit indecency, punish them both."

Suras 7.80, 81: "And Lot said to his people: Do you commit indecent acts that no nation has ever committed before? You lust after men in preference to women. You really are a degenerate people."

Sura 26.165: "Will you fornicate with males and abandon your wives, whom God has created for you? Surely you are a people transgressing all limits."

Sura 27.55: "And tell of Lot. He said to his people: Do you commit indecency though knowing its shameful character, lusting after men instead of women."

We know from the punishment meted out to the people of Lot ("who were utterly destroyed," sura 26.166) that sodomy was not to be tolerated. However, the ambiguity creeps in in the passages of the Koran describing the delights of paradise: sura 52.24. "And there shall wait on them [the Muslim faithful] young boys of their own, as fair as virgin pearls."

Sura 56.17. "And there shall wait on them immortal youths with bowls and ewers and a cup of purest wine."

Sura 76.19. "They shall be attended by boys graced with eternal youth, who will seem like scattered pearls to the beholders."

Are these boys available for sexual dalliance, or are they there only to serve?

If the Koran remains ambiguous on this point, the hadith or traditions are, by contrast, quite clearly and harshly against the practice of sodomy. The Prophet found sodomites abhorrent and asked for their execution—for both the active and passive agent.

The various schools differ as to the punishment of the homosexual. Ibn Hanbal and his disciples insisted on death by stoning, while the other schools demanded whipping, usually a hundred lashes. But it seems unlikely that these punishments were ever applied, since tolerance seems to have been the order of the day from the beginning.

We have enough historical and philological evidence[654] to show that homosexuality was known in pre-Islamic Arabia. Our evidence is richer for the seventh century. The early caliphs punished homosexuals rather severely—by stoning, burning, and throwing them off a minaret, etc. During the Abbasid period there seems to have been many caliphs who were homosexual: al-Amin (ruled 809); al-Mutasim (833); the Aghlabid Ibrahim (875); at Cordoba, Abd al-Rahman (912); and the great Saladin (Salah al-Din, 1169), famous for his jihad against the Crusaders. As for Muslim Spain in the eleventh century, Henri Peres tells us: "Sodomy is practised in all the courts of the Muluk al-Tawaif. It is sufficient to point out here the love of al-Mutamid for Ibn Ammar and for his page Saif; of al-Mutawakkil for an ephebe; of Rafi al-Dawla, son of Mutaskim, for his minion whose name we do not know; of al-Mutamin of saragossa for one of his Christian pages."

Homosexuality was common in all parts of society, from schools to religious brotherhoods. The hammams or Turkish saunas, decorated most un-Islamically with erotic mosaics, paintings, or statues, were a meeting point for many homosexuals. Male prostitution was also common in most large towns; often young boys offered themselves for a price to travelers in hostels.

Our greatest evidence for the prevalence and tolerance of homosexuality, of course, comes from the poets. Some of the greatest poets in the Arabic language have glorified homosexual love, often in the most overt and frank language imaginable. Here, once again, the name of Abu Nuwas stands out. Here is a poem attributed to him in the *Perfumed Garden*:[655]

> O the joy of sodomy! So now be sodomites, you Arabs.
> Turn not away from it—therein is wondrous pleasure.
> Take some coy lad with kiss-curls twisting on his
> temple and ride him as he stands like some gazelle
> standing to her mate.

—A lad whom all can see girt with sword and belt
not like your whore who has to go veiled.

Make for smooth-faced boys and do your very best to
mount them, for women are the mounts of devils!

There are several such poems attributed to Abu Nuwas in the *Perfumed Garden and the Thousand and One Nights,* with accompanying scandalous stories of homosexual adventures.

Though I have concentrated on male homosexuality, there is also evidence to suggest that lesbianism existed to the same extent, and was no less tolerated. *The Perfumed Garden* has a chapter on lesbians where this verse extolling the virtues of tribadism is quoted:

A girl who is slender, not clumsy and flabby, will show
    you how to rub and grind.
So quickly come and lose no time in savoring true delight.
And then you'll know that all I say about the joy that
Lesbians feel is right.
How wretched and unhappy the vagina that a penis splits!
It loses all the ecstasy that another girl can give and
entails, to boot, the infamy and shame
that fall on girls who lie with men.[656]

Whatever the sociological, psychological, or biological reason for the prevalence of homosexuality in Muslim society, there is no doubt that it was tolerated to an extent unimaginable in the Christian West.

16

Final Assessment of Muhammad

Muhammad was undoubtedly one of the great men of history in the sense that had he not existed the whole history of mankind might have been different. But, in the words of Popper,[657] "if our civilisation is to survive, we must break with the habit of deference to great men. Great men make great mistakes." Though Islamic dogma has portrayed him as sinless, Muhammad never claimed perfection or infallibility for himself. As Tor Andrae said, this is one of his most likable characteristics; he was always aware of his own shortcomings and was capable of self-criticism.

Muhammad was a man of great charm. More than one source speaks of his irresistible smile and the great charisma that was able to inspire loyalty and affection in his men. He was also a military leader of genius, and a statesman with tremendous powers of persuasion and diplomacy. What exactly were his achievements? Montgomery Watt, one of the few Western scholars who has unqualified admiration bordering on worship for Muhammad, sums up his achievements in this manner:[658] "In the first place he had what might be termed the gifts of a seer. He was aware of the deep religious roots of the social tensions and malaise at Mecca, and he produced a set of ideas which, by placing the squabbles of Mecca in a wider frame, made it possible to resolve them to some degree."

Let us stop there and see what Watt's claims amount to. We have already referred to the theories of Bousquet and Crone that refute the notion that Mecca was at the time undergoing some spiritual crisis. Here I will quote Margoliouth[659] who also anticipated Watt's arguments nearly fifty years earlier, only to refute them himself. Margoliouth pointed out that the pre-Islamic Arabs beliefs were more than sufficient for their spiritual needs, and there is no evidence of a social malaise:

But that the fetishism of the Arabs was otherwise insufficient for their religious needs is an assertion which does not admit of proof. A god is an imaginary being who can do good or harm; and everything goes to show that the Arabs who had not seen the great world were firmly convinced that their gods or goddesses could do both. . . . So far as the religious sentiment required gratification, there is no evidence to show that paganism failed to gratify it. We gather from the inscriptions of the pagan Arabs that a wealth of affection and gratitude was bestowed upon their gods and patrons.

Professor Watt continues:[660] "The ideas he proclaimed eventually gave him a position of leadership, with an authority not based on tribal status but on 'religion.' Because of his position and the nature of his authority, clans and tribes which were rivals in secular matters could all accept him as leader. This in turn created a community whose members were all at peace with one another."

Here, for once, I feel that Watt is not doing full justice to Muhammad's real achievement and, moreover, confusing theory and practice. As Goldziher[661] said, "Muhammad was the first man of their kind who said to the people of Mecca and the unbridled masters of the Arabian desert that forgiveness was no weakness but a virtue and that to forgive injustice done to oneself was not contrary to the norms of true 'muruwwa' [virtue] but was the highest muruwwa— was walking in Allah's road."

Only by insisting on forgiveness was Muhammad able to persuade the tribes and clans to accept the idea that from now on Islam, rather than tribal affiliation, was to be the unifying principle of society. For up to then, the tribes had been divided by centuries of blood feuds, revenge killings, retaliation, and animosity. Muhammad taught the equality of all believers before Allah. Unfortunately, theory is one thing and practice another. First, Muhammad himself did not practice what he preached. Far too often, in his behavior toward the Jews, the Meccans, and his rivals, Muhammad gave vent to his cruel tendencies, with no sign of forgiveness. Bukhari[662] gives this instance of Muhammad's cruelty:

> Some of the people of the tribe of Ukl came to the Prophet and embraced Islam; but the air of Medina did not agree with them, and they wanted to leave the place. And the Prophet ordered them to go where the camels given in alms were assembled, and to drink their milk which they did, and recovered from their sickness. But after this they became apostates, and renounced Islam, and stole the camels. Then the Prophet sent some people after them, and they were seized and brought back to Medina. Then the Prophet ordered their hands and their feet to be cut off as punishment for theft, and their eyes to be pulled out. But the Prophet did not stop the bleeding, and they died.

William Muir[663] sums up some of the other atrocities recounted—it must be borne in mind, by impeccable Muslim authorities such as Ibn Ishaq and Al-Tabari:

Magnanimity or moderation are nowhere discernible as features in the conduct of Muhammad toward such of his enemies as failed to tender a timely allegiance. Over the bodies of the Quraish who fell at Badr he exulted with savage satisfaction; and several prisoners, accused of no crime but of scepticism and political opposition were deliberately executed at his command. The Prince of Khaibar, after being subjected to inhuman torture for the purpose of discovering the treasures of his tribe was, with his cousin, put to death on the pretext of having treacherously concealed them, and his wife was led away captive to the tent of the conqueror. Sentence of exile was enforced by Muhammad with rigorous severity on two whole Jewish tribes at al-Madinah; and of a third, likewise his neighbors, the women and children were sold into distant captivity, while the men, amounting to several hundreds,were butchered in cold blood before his eyes.

Finally, Watt paints an absurdly rosy picture of tribal harmony under Muhammad's leadership. The preceding example of Muhammad's cruelty will do equally as an illustration of the fact that not all tribes accepted his leadership. Again, Goldziher has shown how intertribal rivalry continued long after Islam had condemned it. As I have already discussed Arab versus Arab rivalry, I will not dwell on it here. Muhammad certainly did not leave a united nation at his death. This is borne out by the wars of succession; the second, third, and fourth caliphs all were assassinated. The assassination of Uthman in 656 led to much chaos and bloody anarchy, and for this reason was known as "al-Bab al-Maftuh," "the door opened [to civil warfare]."

As Margoliouth said: "The Prophet undoubtedly wished to make Muslim life as sacrosanct within the Muslim world as in the old tribal system the tribesman's life had been within the tribe; but in this he failed, since his first followers eventually waged civil war with each other, and in the history of Islam the victims of massacres by Muslim Sultans have frequently been Muslim communities, and, indeed, families claiming descent from the Prophet himself."[664]

Watt[665] continues: "To prevent their warlike energies from disrupting the community the conception of the jihad or Holy War directed these energies outwards against non-Muslims."

Watt is not alone in admiring the Arab expansion and the rise of the subsequent Islamic empire. Imperialism is not much in fashion now, but hardly anyone bothers to criticize the Islamic variety that resulted in such death and destruction, described in a previous chapter. How Watt can consider the holy war, whose express purpose is to exterminate paganism, kill unbelievers, and conquer by military means other people's land and possessions, as a great moral achievement to be admired is a mystery to me.

Muhammad's Sincerity

A vast amount of useless ink has been spilled on the question of Muhammad's sincerity. Was he a knowing fraud or did he sincerely believe that all the "revelations" that constitute the Koran were direct communications from God? Even if we allow Muhammad total sincerity, I do not see how it can possibly matter to our moral judgment of his character. One can sincerely hold beliefs that are false. More important, one can sincerely hold beliefs that are immoral or not worthy of respect. Certain racists sincerely believe that Jews should be exterminated. How does their sincerity affect our moral condemnation of their beliefs? It seems that "sincerity" plays a similar role to the "insanity plea" made in modern courtrooms, by lawyers wishing to exonerate their villainous clients. On this question, the least that Muhammad can get away with is self-deception, something that even Watt[666] recognizes: "It should be clear that, even if true, the alleged fact that the revelations fitted in with Muhammad's desires and pandered to his selfish pleasure would not prove him insincere; it would merely show him to be capable of self-deception." In other words, if he was sincere, then he was also incredibly self-deluded, if not sincere, then he was an impostor. Apologists who have argued that Muhammad was an astute politician, a realist, a brilliant statesman, a great judge of character, a wise lawgiver and superb diplomat, perfectly sober, and not given to epileptic fits, cannot now suddenly plead that Muhammad was also capable of extraordinary self-deception. Thus the conclusion forces itself upon us that in later life, he consciously fabricated "revelations," often for his own convenience, to sort out his domestic problems. At the same time, one can unhesitatingly agree with so many scholars that at Mecca, Muhammad was totally honest and sincere in his conviction that he had conversed with the deity. But it cannot under any circumstances be denied that at Medina, his conduct and the nature of his revelations changed. Muir[667] admirably sums up this period of Muhammad's life:

> Messages from heaven were freely brought down to justify political conduct, in precisely the same manner as to inculcate religious precept. Battles were fought, executions ordered, and territories annexed, under cover of the Almighty's sanction. Nay, even personal indulgences were not only excused but encouraged by the divine approval or command. A special license was produced, allowing the Prophet many wives; the affair with Mary the Coptic bondmaid was justified in a separate sura; and the passion for the wife of his own adopted son and bosom friend was the subject of an inspired message in which the Prophet's scruples were rebuked by God, a divorce permitted, and marriage with the object of his unhallowed desires enjoined. If we say that such "revelations" were believed by Mahomet sincerely to bear the divine sanction, it can only be in a modified and peculiar sense. He surely must be held responsible for that belief; and, in arriving at it, have done violence to his judgement and better principles of his nature.

The casual way that Muhammad produced revelations in his later phase is illustrated by this anecdote. Umar, later the second caliph, once went to the Prophet and remonstrated with him for saying prayers for his enemy, Abdallah Ibn Ubbay. While Umar wondered if he had gone too far in criticizing the Prophet, the latter produced a revelation, "Do not pray over any of them who dies at any time, neither should you stand upon his grave."

To Umar the coincidence did not apparently suggest the remotest suspicion; to us the revelation appears to have been nothing more than a formal adoption of a suggestion of Umar, which the Prophet supposed to represent public opinion. On another occasion when Umar (or another) bethought him of having the Call to Prayer, so as to avoid imitation of Jews and Christians, he communicated the suggestion to the Prophet, he found that he had been just anticipated by the Angel Gabriel. On three other occasions he claimed to have coincided with Allah; having made a suggestion to the Prophet, he was presently told that a revelation had come down embodying his idea in his own words. The occurrence flattered his vanity, but suggested no suspicion of imposture. Other followers were perhaps less simple, but were aware of the danger of ridiculing the Koran. Quarrels occasionally arose between Moslems owing to the fact that the Koran had been repeated to them in different forms, and each naturally claimed that his version only was correct: the Prophet, never at a loss, asserted that the Koran had been revealed in no fewer than seven texts.[668]

"One of the most interesting and harmful delusions to which men and nations can be subjected is that of imagining themselves special instruments of the Divine Will," wrote Russell.[669] Unfortunately, both Muhammad and the Muslims suffered from this delusion. Only Muslims were guaranteed salvation—indeed, salvation outside Islam was unthinkable. God had chosen them to spread the Message to mankind.

Moral Reforms

Muhammad has to his credit the abolition of the ancient custom of burying female infants alive. But whether he also ameliorated the general conditions of women is difficult to assess because of our lack of knowledge of pre-Islamic practices. Nonetheless, some scholars have asserted that women under Islam were definitely worse off than before. Perron in his classic *Femmes Arabes Avant et Depuis L'Islamisme* tells us that the position of women since Islam has seriously deteriorated, and they have lost their former intellectual and moral position:[670]

Certain prerogatives that Islam abolished formed a part of the natural rights of women, and which had formerly given her greater powers of action and freedom. The Arab pagan woman former times had liberty of her person, a choice in the place of her marriage; she looked or waited for a husband whom she found at her pleasure, out of intellectual sympathy as well as other affinities.

However it would be churlish not to mention that some scholars, such as Bousquet, believe that Muhammad did his best to improve the conditions of women but did not go far enough; As Lane Poole put it, "Muhammad might have done better." Certainly, in the matter of property, the woman, under Islam is the equal of the man. In every other way, she is man's inferior.

But equally, Bousquet points out the disastrous example set by Muhammad in his marriage to Aisha, when she was only nine years old. This custom of child marriages has persisted to modern times and can lead to tragic consequences. But Muslims are reluctant to criticize a habit established by the Prophet.

Muhammad also introduced another institution that led to serious evil, namely, the institution of compensation for oaths.

> At sura xvi.93 there is a commandment to keep oaths, but in sura v.91 this rule is modified by the introduction of the principle of compensation, whereby the violation of an oath may be atoned by some other performance; and in sura lxvi this new principle is confirmed and applied to a case wherein the Prophet himself is concerned. . . . It has had the decidedly serious result that there appears to be no mode known to Mohammedan law whereby an oath can be made legally binding; for not only does the Koran expressly state that the performance of certain charitable acts will serve as a substitute for specific performance, but the Prophet is credited with the maxim according to which if a man having taken an oath to do something discovers some preferable course, he is to take that preferable course and make compensation.[671]

Otherwise, Muhammad's life is full of contradictions, showing that he was often ready to compromise his principles for political gain or power, as when he agreed to erase his title "Apostle of God" from a document, because it stood in the way of the ratification of a treaty. He rails against idolatry, yet incorporates all the idolatrous practices of pagan Arabs into the ceremonies of the pilgrimage—such as the kissing of the Black Stone. He abolishes the arrow game as superstition, and yet he seems to have kept the superstitions of his ancestors—he attached great importance to omens, especially those connected with names. He firmly believed in the evil-eye and the possibility of averting it by means of charms. Parents are held in high honor in the early suras, but when the younger generation was joining Muhammad against the wishes of their parents, such filial devotion toward their unbelieving parents was thought undesirable; therefore, suddenly youths were forbidden to pray for their parents. Muhammad's encouragement of the shedding of kindred blood also had a disastrous influence on his followers. While on the whole the Koran does preach moderation in many things, it does become more and more intolerant as it proceeds. The assassination of Muhammad's enemies was, unfortunately, quoted as precedents in the traditions and used even in modern times by the apologists of Khomeini wishing to defend his call for the murder of Rushdie. In the words of Margoliouth,[672] "the experiences of the Prophet's life, the constant bloodshed which marked his career at Medina, seem to have impressed his followers with a profound belief in the value of bloodshed as opening the gates of Paradise." It is difficult to realize the extent to which so many Muslim governors, caliphs, and viziers, such as Hajjaj or Mahmud of Ghazni, referred to the example of Muhammad to justify their killings, looting, and destruction—"kill, kill the unbelievers, wherever you find them." As Margoliouth said, "we cannot fail to find the source of this most painful feature of Islam (the shedding of blood) throughout its history in the Prophet's massacres of his opponents, and in the theory of the Koran that copious bloodshed is the characteristic of a true prophet at a certain stage of his career." Western freethinkers, such as Russell, find Jesus Christ less admirable than Socrates or the Buddha. What do they reproach him with? Among other things, for having cursed a fig-tree, causing it to wither and die, while apologists of Islam, Western and Muslim, are trying to excuse the murders perpetrated by Muhammad. I certainly cannot put Muhammad on the same moral plane as Socrates, the Buddha, Confucius, or, for that matter, Jesus Christ.

Perhaps the worst legacy of Muhammad was his insistence that the Koran was the literal word of God, and true once and for all, thereby closing the possibility of new intellectual ideas and freedom of thought that are the only way the Islamic world is going to progress into the twenty-first century.

17

Islam in the West

In Europe, the riots, demonstrations, and book burnings carried out by fanatical Muslims subsequent to the Rushdie affair woke Europeans up to the consequences of the presence, in their midst, of several million people who did not espouse secular values, who even explicitly set out to defy those values. Since 1989, France and Great Britain have taken different positions on the Muslim spokesmen's increasingly shrill demand for greater freedom in following their own customs, sometimes in defiance of the secular laws of the two countries. Muslims were urged to murder a British citizen. Scandalously, the British police did not take a single step to arrest the people concerned, those who had publicly incited Muslims to murder Rushdie. During the same period in France, the then-prime minister, Michel Rocard, clearly and firmly told the Muslims that anyone advocating murder would be arrested immediately. The British police showed themselves unresolved and feeble when Dr. Siddiqui of the Muslim Institute, in London, urged a crowd of Muslims at a public meeting not to obey British laws if they went against the sharia, the Islamic law. In France, on the other hand, a Turkish imam who had claimed that the sharia had precedence over French laws was deported within forty-eight hours! Nowhere are the different approaches more apparent than in the case of genital mutilation, sometimes known as female circumcision. In an article in the British daily, the *Independent* 7 July 1992, we read that: "Local authorities and social workers have turned a 'blind eye' to the genital mutilation of young girls among African and other Third World communities in Britain for fear of being labeled racist," even though genital mutilation was made illegal in 1985. The article goes on to say, "Social and health service staff are also 'nervous' about preventing or reporting mutilation as they feel it conflicts with anti-racist policies. 'There continues to be confusion as to what is legitimate in culture, which should be respected, and what is human rights abuse.' " More than ten thousand girls are said to be at risk. The year before in France in March 1991, three Malians were in court. One, Armata Keita, was charged with voluntary assault resulting

351

in the mutilation of a child under 15; the other two, Sory and Semit Coulibaly, the parents of the children excised, were accused of abetting the crime. In a report in *Le Monde,* later reprinted in English in the *Guardian Weekly* 24 March 1991, Catherine Sviloff, a lawyer representing the Enfance et Partage association, is quoted as saying that she did not doubt the honorable intentions of those who practiced excision: "But just because one understands a 'respectable' motive doesn't mean the act is necessarily justifiable. That would be the same thing as authorizing excision." The report continues, "Sviloff therefore took the view that there was 'room for repression' and that failure to condemn would be tantamount to 'condoning' the act. Monique Antoine, representing the Planning Familial association, also stressed that an overcomprehensive attitude could result in 'inverted racism.'"

The prosecutor went on to remark: "Excision is unacceptable. To pardon such acts today is to condemn many children living on French soil and refuse them the protection of the law." Armata Keita was sentenced to a five-year prison term and the Coulibalys were given a five-year suspended sentence and two years' probation. The two cases raise very fundamental issues about cultural relativism, multiculturalism, equality before the law, and the dangers of fragmenting French and British society into religious and cultural ghettos, each with its own laws. What kind of society do we want to live in and create? Are we going to revert to a destructive tribalism, or remain united with allegiance to a common core of values? The rest of this chapter will look at some of these issues. It is heavily indebted to Mervyn Hiskett's *Some to Mecca Turn To Pray, Islamic Values and the Modern World* (London, 1993), a work, that, I believe, should be read by every politician in the West, or indeed by anyone concerned with preserving secular values. Hiskett's book serves the same purpose in the British context as Arthur Schlesinger's *The Disuniting of America, Reflections on a Multicultural Society* (New York, 1992), that is, emphasizing the dangers of "fragmentation, resegregation, and tribalization."

Muslims in Britain and What They Want

Britain is said to have approximately one-and-a-half million Muslims, a majority from the Indian subcontinent. Most, if not all, are there of their own free will, seeking to better their economic situation. In the last fifteen years, many Muslims have made it clear that they have no intention of being assimilated into the host society; instead, it is up to the host society to change, to accord them separate rights, and separate privileges. Some of their most articulate spokesmen have spelled out what they hope to achieve. Dr Zaki Badawi,[673] former Director of the Islamic Cultural Centre, London, wrote: "A proseletyzing religion cannot stand still. It can either expand or contract. Islam endeavors to expand in Britain. Islam is a universal religion. It aims at bringing its message to all corners of the earth. It hopes that one day the whole of humanity will be one Muslim community, the Umma."

An imam, a prayer leader of Muslims, in Bradford, England, rejected all Gods other than Allah and dismissed the Christian doctrine of the Trinity as "an extreme and absurd example of the false divination of humans." As for Britain, "it is a sick and divided nation," and only the imposition of Islam can heal it. For him, "The implementation of Islam as a complete code of life cannot be limited to the home and to personal relationships. It is to be sought and achieved in society as a whole." The government must be brought into line with what is appropriate for an Islamic, not a secular state. Every Muslim must "extend the sphere of Islamic influence in the world." We notice the double standards inherent in all such Muslim demands. While the Muslims feel free to insult Christianity, they themselves go into paroxysms of rage and violence at the slightest hint of criticism of Islam, which must be "accepted uncritically as divine revelation by non-Muslims as well as by Muslims, and that this must be reflected in the structure and conduct of the state, and of society." A report on Muslim attitudes to education in Britain, prepared by the Islamic Academy, Cambridge, and the Islamic Cultural Centre, London, makes it clear that Muslims are not happy about the secular approach to education. Muslims want to keep their basic, Islamic values, which are threatened by the values of the host community, even if it means disobeying the laws of Britain. As Hiskett justly observes:

> At no point in this joint statement do the scholarly authors address the possibility that the only real way to avoid lifestyles that are "destructive of basic [Islamic] values" is not to have migrated into them in the first instance; but rather to have remained within those vast areas of the Islamic umma where the lifestyles remain consonant with these values. Muslim spokesmen, when faced with such a rejoinder, will argue that many of them—the second and third generations—have been born in the United Kingdom and that it is therefore unreasonable to propose this solution. On the contrary, the proper conclusion, so it would seem from their public statements, is that the receiving society must now change to accommodate them and not the other way round. This is surely the crux of the argument that has increasingly vexed public opinion in Britain since these Muslim immigrants have become sufficiently articulate to engage public attention.[674]

IMPLICATIONS OF MUSLIM DEMANDS

The implications of the Muslim demands on the wider British are enormous. Unless great vigilance is exercised, we are all likely to find British society greatly impoverished morally, and all the gains, social and moral, may well be squandered in an orgy of multicultural liberalism. Take the issue of ritual slaughter of animals. In Britain, slaughterhouses are tightly controlled by humane slaughter legislation, that is, laws whose aim is to reduce the unnecessary suffering of animals. And yet, in the words of Peter Singer[675] in his classic *Animal Liberation,* slaughter according to a religious ritual need not comply with the provision that the animal be stunned before being killed. Orthodox Jewish and Moslem [Muslim] dietary laws forbid the consumption of meat from an animal who is not "healthy and moving" when killed. Stunning, which is thought to cause injury prior to cutting the throat, is therefore unacceptable. The idea behind these requirements may have been to prohibit the eating of flesh from an animal who had been found sick or dead; as interpreted by the religiously orthodox today, however, the law also rules out making the animal unconscious a few seconds before it is killed. The killing is supposed to be carried out with a single cut with a sharp knife, aimed at the jugular veins and the carotid arteries. At the time this method of slaughter was laid down in Jewish law it was probably more humane than any alternative; now, however, it is less humane, under the best circumstances, than, for example, the use of the captive-bolt pistol to render an animal instantly insensible.

As Singer points out, it is absurd to think that those who attack ritual slaughter are "racists"; one does not have to be anti-Muslim to oppose what is done to animals in the name of religion.

It is time for adherents of both these religions to consider again whether the current interpretations of laws relating to slaughter are really in keeping with the spirit of religious teaching on compassion. Meanwhile, those who do not wish to eat meat slaughtered contrary to the current teachings of their religion have a simple alternative: not to eat meat at all. In making this suggestion, I am not asking more of religious believers than I ask of myself; it is only that the reasons for them to do it are stronger because of the additional suffering involved in producing the meat they eat.

The British legislation concerning slaughter was passed for ethical reasons, in other words, any method of slaughter other than that recommended by these laws was considered immoral. And in giving in to Muslim and Jewish demands for their own methods of butchering we in effect condone behavior that we have previously judged immoral. We sanction immorality because of our respect for the religion of others. Cruelty to animals is all right as long as it is religious cruelty!

Similar double standards seem to exist in our attitude to Muslim women in the West. After the Rushdie affair, several organizations were set up by Muslim women who felt threatened by fundamentalists, for example, Women Against Fundamentalism. Hannana Siddiqui, a founding member, says: "Women are being forced into arranged marriages, homelessness and denial of education. The multiculturalists fail to intervene and support these women. For them it is all part of a culture and religion which must be tolerated. And the anti-racists allow this to continue because they see the fight against racism as the central struggle."[676]

Multiculturalists are incapable of critical thought, and in a deep sense are more racist than the racists they claim to fight. Instead of fighting injustice wherever it occurs, they turn a blind eye if it is black-on-black violence or Muslim-on-Muslim barbarity. Many young Muslim girls running away from home, some to escape arranged marriages, are hunted down by professional bounty hunters and returned to their families, sometimes with tragic results: The murder of the girl concerned, or her suicide, or her severe punishment from all the male members of the family. The police and even social workers turn a blind-eye in the name of multiculturalism, and hence the need for women's organizations such as Women Against Fundamentalism. It is tragic that these British women do not feel protected by the British laws, and in a sense they are not, if the police continue to turn a blind eye.

Undoubtedly the most articulate advocate of a theocratic Islamic world order is Dr. Kalim Siddiqui, director of the Muslim Institute, London. He was one of the founding members of the so-called Muslim Parliament of Great Britain, whose aim was to "define, defend and promote the Muslim interest in Britain." Dr. Siddiqui has written an enormous number of books and articles on Islam and its mission in the West, and the world. Constantly recurring themes are the coming Islamic global dominion, the greatness of the Ayatollah Khomeini; the need for an armed struggle; the need to eliminate all political, economic, social, cultural, and philosophical influences of the Western civilization that have penetrated the world of Islam; all the transcendent authority belongs to Allah; and the indivisible unity of religion and politics.

Scattered throughout his writings is his hatred for democracy, science, philosophy, nationalism, and free will. He has nothing but contempt for the "compromisers who have been trying to prove that Islam is compatible with their secular ambitions and western preferences"[677] and who tried to reestablish Iran as a liberal and democratic nation-state with a few cosmetic "Islamic features." Such people "must realize that their [Western] education has equipped them to serve the political, social, economic, cultural, administrative and militarily systems that we must destroy." Muslims must accordingly, "attack those intellectuals who are infatuated with the west and the east, and recover your 'true identity.' . . . with a population of almost one billion and with infinite sources of wealth, you can defeat all the powers."

As Hiskett points out:

As is so often the case when considering Islam, one has to concede the power of certain of its ideas. But when it comes to having these ideas advocated within our own shores, and as alternatives to our own institutions, one must then ask oneself: Which does one prefer? Western secular, pluralist institutions, imperfect as these are? Or the Islamic theocratic alternative? And if one decides in favor of one's own institutions, warts and all, one then has to ask again: How far may the advocacy of Islamic alternatives go, before this becomes downright subversive? And at that point, what should then be done about it? Finally, do liberal, democratic politicians have the political and moral guts to do what is needed? Or will they simply give way, bit by bit and point by point, to insistent and sustained pressure from the Muslim "Parliament" and other Muslim special-interest lobbies like it?[678]

MULTICULTURALISM

One would have thought that education ought to have played an important part in the assimilation of the children of immigrants into mainstream British culture. But something has gone drastically wrong. Assimilation is no longer in vogue. Multiculturalism and bilingualism have been the fashion since the 1970s at least. The notion that one could produce a good little Englishman or Englishwoman out of raw immigrants is now condemned as chauvinism, racism, cultural imperialism, or cultural genocide.

But multiculturalism is based on some fundamental misconceptions. There is the erroneous and sentimental belief that all cultures, deep down, have the same values; or if these values are different, they are all equally worthy of respect. Multiculturalism, being the child of relativism, is incapable of criticizing cultures, of making cross-cultural judgements. The truth is that not all cultures have the same values, and not all values are worthy of respect. There is nothing sacrosanct about customs or cultural traditions—they can change under criticism. After all, the secularist values of the West are not much more than two hundred years old. Respect for other cultures, for values other than our own is a hallmark of a civilized attitude. But if these other values are destructive of our own cherished values, are we not justified in fighting them—by intellectual means, that is, by reason, argument, criticism, and legal means, by making sure the laws and constitution of the country are respected by all? It becomes a duty to defend those values that we would live by. Hiskett makes the point that "while religious beliefs are tolerated, religious practices and institutions may not necessarily be accorded the same freedom if they conflict with the law or constitution of the wider state." This, unfortunately, is unacceptable to many Muslims, as we saw earlier. While, in a democracy, a Muslim has absolute freedom of personal religion, it is another matter altogether if he goes on to demand the death penalty of those of whom he does not approve; if he tries to

demand his own literary censorship across the public domain; constrain his daughter, born and educated as a British citizen, with all the rights that carries, into a distasteful marriage; slaughter his beasts in a manner the non-Muslim majority considers inhumane (the Muslims are not alone in this); require that the school curriculum omit the theory of evolution from the biology lesson because his sons and daughters attend that school; insist that the academic year be disrupted to accommodate his movable annual festivals and so on.[679]

THE BETRAYAL BY THE POLITICIANS

As Hiskett put it, " In Britain, at any rate, a further requirement toward controlling the extent to which the leaven of Islam spreads, to the detriment of the democratic, secularist mainstream, is greater political will and public awareness. One spur to Islamic forwardness is the short-term expediency of non-Muslim politicians trawling for Muslim votes."[680] Hiskett goes on to quote a letter from a prospective Labor parliamentary candidate, published in the British daily newspaper *The Daily Telegraph* of December 31, 1990:

As a nation we have extended to fundamentalist Islam a tolerance which as you rightly state (editorial, Dec 28), we would never extend to any other religious group and which is contrary to all the principles on which our freedom is based. The question must be: why have we done this? Blame can be laid squarely at the doors of both the Government and the parliamentary Labour Party and leadership; the former perhaps mostly for reasons of trade, the latter for electoral advantage.

I will leave it to Conservatives to deal with the motives of their party leadership; as one who was a Labour candidate in the last general election, I express my shame and regret at the way the Labour party has behaved in putting votes before democratic principles.

In numerous constituencies it is believed that fundamentalist Islam can manipulate the outcome of an election.

A decision must have been made that freedom of speech take second place to electoral success; that not to antagonize certain fundamentalist Moslems is more important than the life of Salman Rushdie.

The leadership has therefore kept quiet and, in doing so, has prostituted for votes the most basic principles of life and liberty.

In the event of Labour coming to power, it has put itself in danger of creating the equivalent of the Jewish vote in the United States.

Now we, in this country, are in grave danger of seeing the Labour party serving the whim of what is, though numerically a tiny section of the electorate, one that is strategically positioned and ruthless enough to utilize its influence solely to its own advantage.

I never thought I would work for more than 20 years for the principles of the Labour movement before witnessing its leadership and parliamentary party abandoning some of them so shamelessly in order to achieve ephemeral electoral success.

Michael Knowles.

The Conservative government, for reasons of trade, has equally betrayed democratic principles. In order to protect its economic interests in Saudi Arabia—in the form of arms sales worth millions of pounds by British firms—successive British governments have failed to criticize the undemocratic practices of Saudi Arabia and have even censored BBC television programs that were critical of Saudi Arabia. The various British governments have also tolerated humiliating conditions for British Christians working in Saudi Arabia who are forced to practice their religion in hiding, in sharp contrast to the freedom of worship allowed Muslims in Britain, to the extent of permitting the construction of a mosque, financed by Saudi Arabia, in the heart of London without respect for the surrounding architectural tradition.

France has also compromised with fundamentalist Iran in the interest of trade, by refusing to prosecute Iranian assassins, or by refusing to hand them over to a third country where these men were wanted for questioning in connection with certain murders of Iranian dissidents.

One can understand the reluctance of Western governments to criticize Muslim states, for reasons of realpolitik, but surely the West should be more positive in defending its democratic principles, threatened by its own Muslim minorities within its own borders.

THE BETRAYAL BY THE EDUCATORS

How can schools possibly succeed in integrating the children of immigrants when teachers are spending large parts of their time in class pointing out ethnic, racial, and religious differences among the students, and encouraging the same children and their parents in persisting in attitudes that "contradict the most basic requirements of integration"? There is no absolute separation of state and religion in Great Britain, and the law requires schools to have an act of collective worship. Under the philosophy of multiculturalism, this has resulted in the introduction of Islam and Islamic propaganda into the classroom. I believe that only the disestablishment of the Church of England and the introduction of a strictly laic educational system will lead to integration.

> The laical, or state schools should thereupon maintain an attitude of courteous agnosticism to all religions (not the mealy-mouthed 'celebratory approach' of the multiculturalists); but should partake of none. Not only should there no longer be a requirement of collective worship; religious education of any kind— Christian, Islamic and, most importantly, multiculturalist— should be removed from the curriculum of non-denominational [i.e., nonreligious] state schools and from the National Curriculum. However, British and European history should be taught to all pupils in all state schools; and this should include a comprehensive and strictly historical account of the development of Judaeo-Christian culture, and the Celtic–Anglo-Saxon Christian heritage. It should be taught with the deliberate intention to help the children identify with this culture in its modern, largely post-Christian expression.
>
> Laical state schools should, under no circumstances, make any concessions to Islam, or to any other religion, concerning what they teach. Thus these schools will continue to teach art, music and drama. It must be made clear to all parents, of whatever religious persuasions, that such subjects are part of the school curriculum and exceptions cannot be made.[681]

The Betrayal by the Intellectuals

I began the book with the betrayal of the intellectuals, and I shall end with it.

Here I shall concentrate on the undermining of confidence in Western secular values by certain Western intellectuals. Self-denigration is said to be a peculiarly English vice; but, it is in fact far more prevalent throughout the Western world than one would imagine. In an article that first appeared in the *New York Times,* later reprinted in *The International Herald Tribune,* 15 February 1994, the philosopher Richard Rorty asked "Why Can't America's Left Be Patriotic?" America's left is unpatriotic:

> In the name of "the politics of difference," it refuses to rejoice in the country it inhabits. It repudiates the idea of a national identity, and the emotion of national pride.
>
> This repudiation is the difference between traditional American pluralism and the new movement called "multiculturalism."
>
> Pluralism is the attempt to make America what the philosopher John Rawls calls "a social union of social unions," a community of communities, a nation with far more room for difference than most.
>
> Multiculturalism is turning into the attempt to keep these communities at odds with one another.

A shared national identity is an essential part of citizenship. We can take pride in our country, and still respect cultural differences. A nation "cannot reform itself unless it has an identity, rejoices in it, reflects upon it and tries to live up to it." We might feel ashamed of our country, but the emotion of shame is only appropriate insofar as we identify with our country, feel that it is our country. At any rate, I am convinced that despite all the shortcomings of Western liberal democracy, it is far more preferable to the authoritarian, mind-numbing certitudes of Islamic theocracy. Karl Popper defends democracy and also laments the propensity of Western intellectuals to self-hatred:

> Democracies have serious drawbacks. They certainly are not better than they ought to be. But corruption can occur under any kind of government. And I think that every serious student of history will agree, upon consideration, that our Western democracies are not only the most prosperous societies in history— that is important, but not so very important—but the freest, the most tolerant, and the least repressive large societies of which we have historical knowledge. . . . One must fight those who make so many young people unhappy by telling them that we live in a terrible world, in a kind of capitalist hell. The truth is that we live in a wonderful world, in a beautiful world, and in an astonishingly free and open society. Of course it is fashionable, it is expected, and it is almost demanded from a Western intellectual to say the opposite.[682]

On the world stage, too, we need to have far more confidence in our values. Judith Miller, writing in *Foreign Affairs,* makes the same point:

> Ultimately, the triumph of militant Islam in the Middle East may say as much about the West as about the Arabs and the failure of their existing systems. Islamists, by and large, have come to power when no one is willing to oppose them at home and abroad. In any world order, Americans should not be ashamed to say that they favor pluralism, tolerance and diversity, and that they reject the notion that God is on anyone's side. . . . Islamic militancy presents the West with a paradox. While liberals speak of the need for diversity with equality, Islamists see this as a sign of weakness. Liberalism tends not to teach its proponents to fight effectively. What is needed, rather, is almost a contradiction in terms: a liberal militancy, or a militant liberalism that is unapologetic and unabashed.[633]

The West needs to be serious about democracy, and should eschew policies that compromise principles for short-term gains at home and abroad. The rise of fascism and racism in the West is proof that not everyone in the West is enamored of democracy. Therefore, the final battle will not necessarily be between Islam and the West, but between those who value freedom and those who do not.

Glossary

ABD. Slave. Common in names, e.g., Abdullah—slave of God.

ABU. Father of. Common in names, e.g., Abu Hamid.

AKL. Reason; intelligence.

AMIR., EMIR. A ruler, a commander, a chief, a nobleman.

BIDA. An innovation in Muslim belief or practice; the converse of sunna, the alleged practice of the Prophet.

DAR AL-HARB. The abode of war, i.e., territory not under Muslim sovereignty, against which warfare for the propagation of Islam is licit. The converse of Dar al-Islam, the abode of Islam.

DHIMMI. A member of one of the protected religions, i.e., the non-Muslim religions tolerated by the Muslim state in accordance with the sharia, on payment of certain taxes and on acceptance of an inferior social status.

FAQIH. A doctor of the sharia; a canon lawyer of Islam.

FATIHA. The opening chapter of the Koran.

FATWA. The formal opinion of a canon lawyer (mufti)

HADD., (plural) HUDUD. Punishment the limits of which have been defined in the Koran and the Hadith.

HADITH. A tradition of the sayings or practice of the Prophet. One of the main sources of Islamic law.

HAJJ. The pilgrimage to Mecca.

HIJRA. The Prophet's flight to Medina from Mecca, in A.D. 622 on September 20. The Muslim era begins at the beginning of the Arab year in which the Hijra took place.

HALAKHAH. The legal side of Judaism (as distinct from *haggadah*, the nonlegal material).

IBN. Son of. Corresponds to Hebrew *ben*.

IJMA. Consensus of the Islamic community. One of the foundations of law and practice.

IMAM. Leader in prayer; leader of the whole community of Islam.

ISNAD. The chain of transmitters of a tradition.

JIHAD. The duty of Muslims to fight all unbelievers.

JINN. Intelligent creatures of air and fire.

JIZYA. The poll-tax paid by dhimmis.

KHALIFA. Caliph. The successor of the Prophet, and thus head of all Muslims, combining in himself both the temporal and religious powers.

KAABA. The cubelike building in the center of the mosque at Mecca that contains the Black Stone, a meteorite considered holy and dating from pre-Islamic times.

KAFIR. An infidel, i.e., a non-Muslim.

KHARAJ. Land tax paid by dhimmis.

KIYAS (QIYAS). Method of reasoning by analogy.

MADRASA. A school for Muslim learning.

MAGHRIB. Arabic-speaking countries of North Africa, west of Egypt.

MATN. The subject matter of a tradition.

MIDRASH. A Jewish term referring to an exegesis, especially of scripture, where the exegetical material is attached to the text of scripture. The earliest collections of Midrashim come from the second century A.D., but much of their contents is older.

MISHKATU'L MASABIH. A well-known book of Sunni tradtion, much used by Sunni Muslims in India, . . . It was orginally compiled by the Imam Husain al-Baghawi, the celebrated commentator, who died 1117 or 1122, . . . It was revised in 1336 by Waliyu-ddin.

MISHNAH. A method and form of Jewish scriptural exegesis in which the exegetical material was collected on its own. The Mishnah of Rabbi Judah ha-Nasi (ca. 135–ca. 220) was very influential.

MUEZZIN. The caller of the azan or "summons to prayer." When the mosque has a minaret, he calls from the top of it, but in smaller places of worship, from the side of the mosque, the first muezzin was Bilal, son of a black slave girl.

MUFTI. The officer who expounds the law. He assists the qadi (qazi) or judge and supplies him with fatwas, or decisions. He must be learned in the Koran and Hadith, and in the Muslim works of law.

MULLA (MULLAH). A member of the ulama.

QADI (KADI). A judge in a court administering the sharia.

QIYAS. Analogy, especially in jurisprudence.

RAMADAN. The ninth month of the Muslim calendar, during which Muslims fast between sunrise and sunset.

RASUL. Someone sent; an apostle.

SAHIH. Authentic, genuine.

SALAAM. Arabic "Al-Salam" = Peace. The ordinary salutations of the Muslim is "al-Salamu alaikum" i.e. "the peace be on you." And the usual reply is "Wa alaikum al-salam" i.e., "And on you also be the peace."

SHARIA. Islamic law consisting of the teachings of the Koran, the sunna of the Prophet which is incorporated in the recognized traditions; the consensus of the scholars of the orthodox community; the method of reasoning by analogy (Kiyas or Qiyas).

SHAYKH (SHEIKH). Old man, leader of a tribe; a title of respect.

SHIA. The supporters of Ali's claims to the caliphate. Evolved into the principal minority religious group of Muslims. Includes Twelver Shia and the Ismailis.

SHIRK. The unforgivable sin of associating anyone or anything with Allah.

SUNNA. Properly, a custom or practice, and later narrowed down to the practice of the Prophet or a tradition recording the same.

SUNNI. A member of the majority group of Muslims, usually called orthodox.

TALMUD. The Jewish compilations that embody the Mishnah, or oral teaching of the Jews, and the Gemara, or the collection of discussions on the Mishnah. The two main forms of the Talmud, the Palestinian (or Jerusalem) and the Babylonian were completed by the middle of the fifth century and the year 500, respectively.

ULAMA. A scholar, especially in religious subjects; the whole Muslim ecclesiastical class.

ZINA. Adultery, fornication.

ZINDIQ. Dualist, heretic.

Abbreviations of
Journals and Encyclopedias

CHI.   *Cambridge History of Islam*
DOI.   *Dictionary of Islam*
EB.   *Encyclopaedia Britannica,* eleventh edition
EI1.   *Encyclopaedia of Islam,* first edition
EI2.   *Encyclopaedia of Islam,* new edition
EJ.   *Encyclopaedia Judaica,* new English edition
EP.   *Encyclopaedia of Philosophy*
ER.   *Encyclopaedia of Religion*
ERE.   *Encyclopaedia of Religion and Ethics*
EU.   *Encyclopedia of Unbelief*
FA.   *Foreign Affairs*
FI.   *Free Inquiry*
JE.   *Jewish Encyclopaedia*
JRAS.   *Journal of the Royal Asiatic Society*
JSAI.   *Jerusalem Studies in Arabic and Islam*
MW.   *Muslim World*
NH.   *New Humanist*
OCD.   *Oxford Classical Dictionary*
RSO.   *Rivista degli Studi Orientali*

Notes

1. Mill (1), p. 83.
2. Mill (1), p. 79.
3. Hayek (1), p. 122.
4. DOI, p. 458.
5. Ettinghausen, pp. 12–13.
6. Watt (3), p. 38.
7. Nicholson (2), p. 291.
8. Ibn Kammuna, intro., p. 8.
9. Ibid., pp. 145ff.
10. Ibid., p. 3, note 5.
11. Ali Dashti, p. 10
12. Ibid., p. 48.
13. Ibid., p. 50.
14. Ibid., p. 56.
15. Amir Taheri, p. 290
16. Pipes, p. 74
17. Ibid., p. 75.
18. Ibid., p. 75.
19. Ibid., p. 75.
20. Donohue and Esposito, p. 114.
21. Pipes, pp. 75–76.
22. Ibid., pp. 79–80
23. Amir Taheri, p. 212.
24. Barbulesco and Cardinal, pp. 203–14.
25. Pipes, p. 71.
26. Halliday, p. 17. The term "closet hooligan" is also due to Halliday.
27. Gibbon, Vol. 5, pp. 240ff.
28. Hume (3), p. 450 (Of the Standard of Taste).
29. Hobbes, p. 136.
30. Dante, *Inferno*, canto xxviii, line 31.

31. Dante, p. 331, Note 31.
32. Gershwin, p. 149. Gershwin noted that "Happily, in all the years that the song has been around, I have received only one letter remarking on its possible irreverence."
33. Amir Taheri, pp. 226–27.
34. DOI article Jihad, pp. 243f.
35. Halliday, p. 19.
36. Macdonogh (ed.), pp. 55–56.
37. NYRB, p. 31, xxxix, No. 9, May 14, 1992.
38. Barrauld.
39. Morey.
40. Flew in NH, July 1993, No. 2, Vol 109.
41. Nicholson (2), p. 143.
42. Nicholson (3), p. 5.
43. Quoted in Lewis (5), p. 194, note 1.
44. Intro to Bat Ye'or (1).
45. Rodinson (2), p. 59.
46. Wansbrough (1), p. ix, Preface.
47. Rippin, p. ix, Preface.
48. Freeman, pp. 113–14.
49. Russell (1), p. 58.
50. Robinson, pp. 117–18.
51. Dawkins (2).
52. OCD art. Tacitus, p. 1034.
53. Montaigne, p. 113.
54. In Bayle art. Mahomet and Nestorius.
55. Bat Ye'or (2), p. 425.
56. Ibid., p. 96.
57. Holt in Lewis and Holt, p. 300.
58. Jeffery (2), p. 32.
59. Quoted in Holt, p. 302.
60. Bousquet (4), note 2, p. 110.
61. Edwards in EU, p. 715.
62. Ibid., p. 715.
63. Lewis (4), p. 95.
64. Ibid., p. 95.
65. Bat Ye'or (2), p. 427.
66. Ibid., p. 429.
67. Watt (2), p. 17.
68. Oxford Companion to Literature, p. 171.
69. Carlyle, p. 297.
70. Ibid., pp. 288–301.
71. Ibid., p. 307.
72. Ibid., p. 306.
73. Ibid., p. 299.
74. Ibid., p. 332.
75. Ibid., p. 343.
76. Ibid., p. 344.

77. Daniel, p. 306.
78. Ibid., p. 307.
79. Watt (4), p. x, Intro.
80. Lewis in intro to Goldziher (2), p. xi.
81. Watt (1), p. 2.
82. Watt (7), pp. 625–27.
83. Watt (10), p. 116.
84. Watt (2), p. 183.
85. Benda pp. 76–77.
86. Russell (5), p. 107.
87. Popper (1), Vol. II, pp. 369–88.
88. Thompson, pp. 326–27.
89. Daniel, p. 305.
90. Pipes, p. 164.
91. Quoted in MW, Vol. I, No. 2, April 1911.
92. Ibid.
93. Pipes, p. 165.
94. Ibid., p. 166.
95. Russell (1), p. 58.
96. Crone (3), pp. 6–7.
97. Russell (4), p. 165.
98. Koestler, p. 125.
99. Ibid., p. 127.
100. Conquest, pp, 678–79.
101. Eribon, pp. 305–306.
102. Macey, p. 110.
103. Lewis (4), p. 194, note 1.
104. Stillman, p. 16.
105. Watt (8), p. 15.
106. Lewis (4), p. 186.
107. Easterman, pp. 92–93.
108. Goldziher (2), pp. 4–5.
109. Quoted by Anatole France in "The Unrisen Dawn," London, 1929, pp. 110–11.
110. Renan (1), p. 352.
111. Zwemer (1), p. 24.
112. Quoted by Jeffery (1), p. 1.
113. Quoted by Dashti, p. 94.
114. Quoted by Dashti, p. 1.
115. Quoted by Zwemer (3), p. 150.
116. Zwemer (3), p. 148.
117. Ibid., p. 150.
118. Ibid., p. 157.
119. Noldeke (1) in ERE VOL I, p. 659.
120. Noldeke (1) in ERE VOL I, p. 665.
121. Margoliouth (3) in MW vol. 20, p. 241.
122. Muir (1), p. xci.
123. Zwemer (3), p. 158.

124. Noldeke (1) in ERE Vol I, p. 660.
125. Zwemer (3), p. 159.
126. Ibid., p. 160.
127. Ibid., p. 159.
128. Ibid., p. 161.
129. Juynboll art. Pilgrimage in ERE.
130. Quoted by Bousquet in afterword to Hurgronje (3), p. 287.
131. Noldeke (1) in ERE, Vol, I, p. 664.
132. Zwemer (4) in MW, Vol, 8, p. 359.
133. Widengren art. Iranian Religions in EB, p. 867.
134. Hinnels in Numen 16:161–85, 1969.
135. Article "Zoroastrianism," in JE, pp. 695–97.
136. Goldziher (3), pp. 163–86.
137. Jeffery (1), p. 14.
138. Torrey, p. 106.
139. Tisdall, p. 78.
140. Tisdall, p. 80.
141. Stutley, p. 16.
142. Dowson, p. 20.
143. Jeffery (1), p. 120.
144. Quoted by Zwemer (3), pp. 126–27.
145. Macdonald in EI1 article "Djinn."
146. Zwemer (1), p. 17.
147. Torrey, p. 60.
148. Torrey, p. 105.
149. Quoted by Obermann, p. 94.
150. Torrey, p. 108.
151. Tisdall, p. 23.
152. Torrey, p. 109ff.
153. Wensinck art. AL Khadir in EI1.
154. Obermann, p. 100.
155. Jeffery (1), p. 141.
156. Bell, p. 136.
157. Torrey, pp. 46–47.
158. Hurgronje (2), p. 16.
159. Burton, John. The Collection of the Quran, Cambridge, 1977, p. 225.
160. Hurgronje (2), p. 23.
161. Humphreys, p. 82.
162. Hurgronje (2), p. 24.
163. Ibid., p. 25.
164. Smirnov, p. 48.
165. Ibid., pp. 48–49.
166. Humphreys, p. 83.
167. Ibid., p. 83.
168. Goldziher (1), p. 19. Vol 2.
169. Ibid., p. 43. Vol 2.
170. Ibid., p. 44.

171. Ibid., p. 108.
172. Ibid., p. 169.
173. Ibid., p. 236.
174. Humphreys, p. 83.
175. Schacht (3), pp. 4–5.
176. Ibid., pp. 149–63.
177. Crone (3), p. 7.
178. Humphreys, p. 84.
179. Cook (1), p. 68.
180. Adams article "Quran" in ER.
181. Wansbrough (1), p. 20.
182. Ibid., p. 79.
183. Ibid., p. 51.
184. Ibid., p. 97.
185. Ibid., p. 44.
186. Jeffery (2), p. 342.
187. Wansbrough (1), p. 56.
188. Humphreys, pp. 84–85.
189. Cook (1), p. 65.
190. Ibid., p. 74.
191. Ibid., pp. 75–76.
192. Ibid., pp. 76–82.
193. Humphreys, p. 85.
194. Cook and Crone, p. 9.
195. Ibid., p. 8.
196. Ibid., pp. 14ff.
197. Ibid., p. 18.
198. Ibid., p. 21.
199. Cook (1), p. 86.
200. Crone (2), p. 215.
201. Ibid., p. 230.
202. Jeffery (2) in MW Vol. XVI, No 4. Oct 1926.
203. Reade, p. 428.
204. Muir (1), p. 503–506.
205. Caetani Annali dell' Islam, trans in MW vol vi.
206. Jeffery (2), p. 335.
207. Buhl in MW Vol 1, 1911, pp. 356–64.
208. Quoted by Jeffery (2), p. 336.
209. Margoliouth (2), pp. 88–89, pp. 104–106.
210. Humphreys, pp. 92–98.
211. Quoted by Humphreys, p. 97.
212. Quoted in Rodinson (1), pp. 157–58.
213. Muir (1), p. 240.
214. Ibid., pp. 307–308.
215. Tor Andrae, p. 218.
216. Stillman, p. 16.
217. Jahanbegloo, p. 107.

218. Hogbin in Firth, p. 256.
219. Muir (1), p. 241, note 1.
220. Rodinson (1), p. 213.
221. Jahanbegloo, p. 37.
222. Runciman (1), p. 348.
223. Quoted in Stillman, p. 147.
224. Rodinson (1), pp. 207–208.
225. Muir (1), p. 414.
226. Watt (9), pp. 114–15.
227. Margoliouth (5) art. Mohammed in ERE VIII p. 878.
228. Huxley (1) Preface, p. ix.
229. Rodinson (1), pp. 217–18.
230. Guillaume, p. 74.
231. Quoted by Zwemer (3), p. 25.
232. Ali Dashti, p. 148f.
233. Goldziher (2), p. 173.
234. Ali Dashti, p. 150.
235. Bell/Watt, p. 66.
236. Adams art. Quran in ER.
237. Jeffery (4), in MW Vol. 25, p. 11.
238. Adams art. Quran in ER.
239. Guillaume, p. 189.
240. Quoted in Morey, p. 121.
241. Noldeke in EB 11th Edn Vol. 15, pp. 898–906.
242. Ali Dashti, pp. 49–50.
243. Bell/Watt, p. 93.
244. Quoted in Rippin, p. 26.
245. Bell/Watt, pp. 94–95.
246. Ali Dashti, p. 98.
247. DOI art. Quran, p. 520.
248. Margoliouth (2), p. 139.
249. Ali Dashti, p. 155.
250. Gore Vidal in New Statesman Society, June 26, 1992, p. 12.
251. Art. Polytheism in ER.
252. Hume (1), p. 56.
253. DOI art. Genii, p. 134.
254. Goldziher (1), vol. 2, p. 259.
255. Bell/ Watt, p. 122.
256. Hume (2), pp. 192–193, Part 5.
257. Ibid., p. 203, Part 7.
258. Lewis (4), p. 175.
259. Schopenhauer Vol 2, pp. 356–59.
260. Hume (1) p. 59.
261. Crone (2) pp. 234–45.
262. Margoliouth (2), p. 149.
263. Macdonald art. Kadar in EI1.
264. Wensinck (1), pp. 51–52.

265. Mill (2), pp. 113–14.
266. Bousquet (1), p. 9.
267. Mackie (2), p. 256.
268. Mackie (1), p. 230.
269. Russell (3), p. 19.
270. Flew (2), p. 277.
271. Gibb, p. 38.
272. Mackie (2), p. 256.
273. Quoted in DOI, p. 147.
274. Paine, p. 270.
275. Paine, p. 52.
276. Mackie (1), p. 232.
277. Voltaire, p. 17.
278. Rodinson (4), p. 49.
279. Watt (9), p. 136.
280. Ibid., p. 135.
281. Spinoza, p. 124.
282. Fox, p. 176.
283. Thompson, p. 328.
284. Fox, p. 218.
285. Margulis/Schwartz, pp. 224–39.
286. Ingersoll, p. 149.
287. Fox, p. 218.
288. Howell Smith, p. 75.
289. Watt (9), pp. 134–35.
290. Kauffmann, pp. 110–16.
291. Birx, p. 417–18.
292. Darwin, Introduction.
293. Ruse, p. 47.
294. Darwin, Introduction.
295. Huxley (2), pp. 52–62.
296. Young, p. 402.
297. Nietzsche, p. 628.
298. Dawkins (1), pp. 141, 249.
299. Hawking, pp. 122, 143–49.
300. Einstein, p. 39.
301. Atkins, p. vii, Preface.
302. Feuerbach, p. 195–96.
303. Hume (4), p. 114–15.
304. Hospers, p. 454.
305. Quoted by Feuerbach, p. 304.
306. Hoffmann (ed), pp. 233–52.
307. Wells (1) in EU art. "Jesus, Historicity of."
308. Hoffmann, p. 179.
309. Quoted in Hoffmann and Larue (ed), pp. 135–36.
310. Hoffmann and Larue, pp. 21–22.
311. Ibid., p. 199.

312. Ibid., p. 13.
313. Wells (3), p. 657.
314. Wells (4), p. 44–46.
315. Hoffmann and Larue, p. 15.
316. Ibid., p. 16.
317. Stein, p. 178.
318. Hoffmann, p. 177.
319. Ibid., p. 184.
320. Wells (1), p. 364.
321. Ibid., p. 365.
322. Wells (2).
323. Schacht (3), p. 156.
324. Hoffmann and Larue, p. 15.
325. Ibid., p. 48.
326. Momigliano (ed), p. 161.
327. Flew (1), p. 107.
328. Nietzsche, p. 618.
329. Ibid., p. 484.
330. Ibid., p. 535.
331. Ibid., p. 612.
332. Russell (3), p. 72.
333. Dawkins (2).
334. Nietzsche, p. 618.
335. Russell (3), p. 25.
336. Gibb, p. 27.
337. DOI, p. 285.
338. Russell (3), p. 24.
339. Quine, p. 209.
340. Russell (3), p. 24.
341. Robinson, p. 117.
342. Russell (3), pp. 156–57.
343. Russell (4), pp. 5, 29, 114.
344. Quoted in MW Vol. 28, p. 6.
345. Hurgronje (1), p. 264.
346. Ibid., p. 261.
347. Lewis, preface to Kepel The Prophet and Pharaoh, London 1985, pp. 10–11.
348. Schacht (1), p. 69.
349. Ibid., pp. 70–71.
350. Ibid., p. 75.
351. Ibid., p. 201.
352. Ibid., p. 79.
353. Schacht (2), p. 397.
354. Schacht (1), p. 205.
355. Goldziher (2), pp. 63–64.
356. Schacht (2), p. 399.
357. Nietzsche, pp. 596–97.
358. Gibb, p. 67.

359. Hurgronje (1), p. 277.
360. Quoted in FA, Summer 1993.
361. Found as appendix to Melden.
362. Mayer, p. 177.
363. See, in general, Gaudeul.
364. Huntington in FA, Vol. 72, No. 3, 1993.
365. Locke, pp. 19–22.
366. Kant, pp. 7–8.
367. Paine, p. 51.
368. Quoted in Alley, p. 56.
369. Ibid., p. 71.
370. In Oxford Companion to the Supreme Court, New York, 1992, pp. 262–63.
371. Bouquet, p. 269.
372. Kennedy, p. 144.
373. Schacht (1), pp. 126–27.
374. Ibid., pp. 130–32.
375. Hayek (1), pp, 152–53.
376. Quoted by Mayer, pp. 60–61.
377. Ibid., pp. 62–63.
378. Melden. p. 3.
379. Lewis (3), pp. 89–98.
380. Schacht (1), p. 125.
381. Arnold article "Khalifa," in EI1.
382. Mayer, p. 35.
383. Ibid., p. 21.
384. Ibid., p. 91.
385. Ibid., p. 160.
386. Ibid., p. 187.
387. Ibid., p. 47.
388. Ibid., p. 49.
389. Ibid., p. 58.
390. Ibid., p. 58.
391. Ibid., p. 62.
392. Ibid., p. 73.
393. Ibid., p. 98.
394. Ibid., p. 112.
395. Bousquet (3).
396. Kramer, p. 38.
397. Hurgronje (1), p. 60.
398. Pryce-Jones, p. 376.
399. Popper (1) Vol. 2, p. 283.
400. Wolpert, p. 178.
401. Creswell, p. 1.
402. Ettinghausen and Grabar, p. 25.
403. Creswell, p. 111.
404. Ettinghausen, p. 67.
405. Schacht (4), p. 546.

406. Quoted in Arberry (1), pp. 34–35.
407. Hayek (2), p. 410.
408. Zakariya.
409. Cook (1), p. 86.
410. Cook and Crone, p. viii Preface.
411. Humphreys, pp. 280–81.
412. Goldziher (1) Vol 1, p. 12.
413. Ibid., p. 15.
414. Ibid., p. 43.
415. Ibid., p. 34.
416. Lewis (6), p. 101.
417. Goldziher (1), p. 98.
418. Quoted by Goldziher (1), p. 79.
419. Lewis (6), pp. 37–38.
420. Cambridge History of Islam, p. 40.
421. Lewis (6), p. 42.
422. Bosworth (2), p. 6.
423. DOI, p. 680.
424. Lewis (6), p. 36.
425. Brunschvig art. Abd in EI2.
426. Goldziher (1) Vol 1, p. 139.
427. Ibid., p. 140.
428. Ibid., p. 146.
429. Ibid., p. 155.
430. Article "Khurrammi" in EI2.
431. Lewis (4), p. 172.
432. Thomas, H. An Unfinished History of the World, London, 1981, p. 602.
433. Chaudhuri, N. Thy Hand, Great Anarch, Delhi, 1987, p. 774.
434. Tarkunde, V. M., Radical Humanism, Delhi, 1983, p. 11.
435. Kedourie, p. 322, in B. Lewis (ed), The World of Islam, London, 1976.
436. Makiya, p. 235.
437. Quoted in Lewis (4), p. 117.
438. DOI art. Jihad, p. 243.
439. Runciman (2), p. 145.
440. Schumpeter.
441. Wensinck in EI1, art.Amr b.al-As.
442. See Bat Ye'or (2), pp. 317–18.
443. Bosworth (1), p. 43.
444. Chachnamah, p. 155.
445. Alberuni, p. 22.
446. Smith, p. 207.
447. Ibid., pp. 258–59.
448. Ibid., p. 349.
449. Ibid., p. 417.
450. Gascoigne, p. 227.
451. Conze, p. 117.
452. Humphreys, C., p. 95.

453. Harle, p. 199.
454. Smith, pp. 235–36.
455. Rowland, p. 196.
456. Intro. to Bat Ye'or (1).
457. Stillman, p. 24.
458. Ibid., p. 28.
459. Ibid., p. 38.
460. Ibid., p. 62.
461. Ibid., p. 63.
462. Ibid., p. 76.
463. Bat Ye'or (1), p. 61.
464. Bat Ye'or (2), p. 95.
465. Lewis (5), pp. 4–9.
466. Lewis (4), p. 179.
467. Lewis (5), p. 8.
468. Ibid., p. 52.
469. Ibid., p. 183.
470. Wistrich, p. 196.
471. Bat Ye'or (1), p. 57.
472. Quoted in Tritton, p. 38.
473. Ibid., p. 45.
474. Ibid., p. 54.
475. Runciman (1), p. 321. vol. 3.
476. Grousset, pp. 486–546.
477. Choksy, in MW, Vol. 80, 1990, pp. 213–33.
478. Article "Madjus," in EI1.
479. Ibid.
480. Fletcher, pp. 171–72.
481. Lewis (6), p. 101.
482. Fletcher, p. 173.
483. Lewis (5), p. 168.
484. Wistrich, p. 222.
485. Bat Ye'or (1), p. 99.
486. Tritton, p. 232.
487. Bosworth (1), p. 49.
488. Bat Ye'or (1), p. 67.
489. Goldziher (1), Vol 1, pp. 43–44.
490. Goldziher (1), Vol 2, p. 65.
491. Ibid., p. 62.
492. Art. "Kharidjites," in EI1.
493. Art. "Kadar," in EI1.
494. Goldziher (2), p. 82.
495. Ibid., p. 87.
496. Art. Mutazilites in EI1.
497. Watt (1), p. 73.
498. Goldziher (2), p. 91.
499. Ibid., p. 91.

500. Arberry (1), p. 24.
501. Koran (1) Sale, p. 53.
502. Goldziher (2), p. 102.
503. Gibb, p. 80.
504. Gabrieli, p. 34.
505. Goldziher (2), p. 106.
506. Nicholson (2), p. 284.
507. Art. Mani in EP.
508. Art. Manes in Concise Oxford Dictionary of the Christian Church. Oxford, 1980.
509. Quoted in Nicholson (2), pp. 372–73.
510. Gabrieli, pp. 23–38.
511. Vadja, p. 184.
512. Ibid., pp. 173–229.
513. Goldziher (1), Vol. 2, pp. 363–64.
514. Art. Bashshar b. Burd in EI2.
515. Nicholson (2), p. 374.
516. Quoted by Margoliouth (6).
517. Nicholson (2), p. 291.
518. Ibid., p. 298.
519. Margoliouth (6).
520. Art. al-Mutanabbi in EI1.
521. Margoliouth (6).
522. Nyberg, pp. 131–35.
523. Gabrieli, p. 34.
524. Art. Ibn al-Rawandi in EI2.
525. Quoted by Nicholson (4).
526. Rosenthal, pp. 13–14.
527. Arnaldez (2) in EI2.
528. Arberry (1), p. 42.
529. Walzer, p. 209.
530. Ibid., p. 18.
531. Arberry (1), p. 56.
532. Arnaldez (2) in EI2.
533. Alberuni, p. 627.
534. Walzer, p. 15.
535. al-Razi, pp. 20–21.
536. Cambridge History of Islam, Vol 2B, p. 803.
537. In Introduction to al-Razi, p. 10.
538. Quoted in Intro to al-Razi, p. 7.
539. Article al-Razi in EI1; Gabrieli.
540. CHI Vol 2B, p. 801.
541. De Boer, p. 196.
542. Art. Ibn Rushd in ER.
543. Art Falsafa in ER.
544. Fakhry, p. 324.
545. De Boer, p. 198.
546. Arberry (1), p. 69.

547. Plessner, p. 427.
548. Ibid., pp. 427–28.
549. Von Grunebaum (3), p. 15.
550. Ibid., p. 114.
551. Renan (2).
552. Quoted in Von Grunebaum (3), p. 123.
553. De Boer, p. 153.
554. Nicholson (3), p. 8.
555. Margoliouth (6).
556. Nicholson (3), p. 88.
557. Art. al-Halladj in EI1.
558. Goldziher (2), pp. 162–63.
559. Nicholson (2), p. 284.
560. Ibid., p. 241.
561. Art. al-Akhtal in EI1.
562. The whole of this chapter is based on the works of Nicholson esp Nicholson (1). Most of the translations are by Nicholson and appear in Nicholson (1).
563. Margoliouth (6).
564. Nicholson (1), p. 173.
565. Nicholson (2), p. 318–19.
566. The influence of Ascha should be apparent on every single page of this chapter, even though I rarely quote him directly.
567. Burton vol x, p. 195.
568. Shaykh Nefzawi (1), pp. 203–204.
569. Bousquet (1), p. 49.
570. Art. "Women," in DOI.
571. Schacht (4) in CHI, p. 545.
572. Art. Women in DOI.
573. Quoted in Ascha, p. 13.
574. Mimouni, p. 156.
575. Ascha, p. 11.
576. Ibid., pp. 23f.
577. Ibid., pp. 29f.
578. Ibid., pp. 38f.
579. Ibid., p. 41.
580. Quoted in Tannahill, pp. 233–34.
581. Ascha, pp. 49f.
582. Bousquet (1), p. 118.
583. Ibid., p. 156.
584. Ascha, p. 58.
585. Bouhdiba, pp. 217–18.
586. Burton, p. 279, vol v.
587. Quoted in Bouhdiba, pp. 95–96.
588. Bouhdiba, pp. 59–74.
589. Ascha, pp. 63f.
590. Bousquet (1), p. 120.
591. Ascha, pp. 76f.

592. Ibid., p. 89.
593. Ibid., pp. 95–96.
594. De Beauvoir, p. 632.
595. Ascha, pp. 100–101.
596. Ibid., p. 108.
597. Ibid., pp. 123f.
598. Zeghidour, p. 34.
599. Ascha, p. 126.
600. Ibid., pp. 132f.
601. Ibid., p. 146.
602. Ibid., pp. 161f.
603. Ibid., p. 174.
604. Ibid., pp. 185f.
605. Quoted by Schork.
606. Quoted by Kureishi, p. 18.
607. Ibid., p. 22.
608. Quoted by Goodwin, p. 72.
609. Quoted in Wolpert Stanley, *Jinnah of Pakistan,* Oxford, 1984, pp. 339–40.
610. Akbar, p. 31.
611. Schork.
612. Goodwin, pp. 49–50.
613. Schork.
614. Goodwin, p. 61.
615. Schork.
616. Ibid.
617. Goodwin, p. 64.
618. Schork.
619. Ahmed R. (ed), *Sayings of Quaid-i-Azam (Jinnah),* Karachi, 1986, p. 98.
620. Singh (2), p. 122.
621. Kureishi, p. 16.
622. Art. "Khamriyya," in EI2.
623. Goldziher (1), Vol. 1, pp. 32–33.
624. Ibid., p. 35.
625. Art. Khamriyya in EI2.
626. Art. Abu Dulama in EI1.
627. Nicholson (2), p. 293.
628. Ibid., p. 295.
629. Singh (1), pp. 76–77.
630. Faiz, p. 123.
631. Rushdie, p. 38.
632. Mill (1), p. 141.
633. Art. "Ghidha," in EI2.
634. Cook (2), pp. 242f.
635. Quoted in EJ, Vol. 6, p. 43.
636. Art. "Ghidha," in EI2.
637. See Simoons in general for the whole of this section.
638. Malinowski, *The Sexual Life of Savages in North Western Melanesia,* London, 1982, p. 400.

639. Cook (2).
640. Robertson Smith, The Religion of the Semites, p. 153.
641. Frazer, The Golden Bough, p. 472.
642. Douglas (1), pp. 54–55.
643. Firmage, pp. 177–208.
644. Discussed in Firmage, p. 194.
645. Art. "The Geographical Setting," in CHI.
646. Simoons.
647. Personal communication.
648. Quoted in Simoons.
649. Scruton R. "The higher meaning of food," Times Literary Supplement, Sept. 30, 1994.
650. Mackenzie, p. 38.
651. Babur, p. 120.
652. Burton, p. 236, vol x.
653. Quoted in Leach, p. 210.
654. Art. "Liwat," in EI2.
655. Shaykh Nefzawi (2), pp. 37–39.
656. Ibid., p. 24.
657. Popper (1), Vol. I, Preface.
658. Art. Muhammad in CHI, Vol. 1A, p. 55.
659. Margoliouth (2), pp. 24–25.
660. Art. Muhammad in CHI, Vol. 1A, p. 55.
661. Goldziher (1), Vol 1, p. 25.
662. Quoted in DOI, pp. 63–64.
663. Muir (1), pp. 497–98.
664. Margoliouth (5), p. 877.
665. CHI Vol 1A, p. 55.
666. Watt (5), p. 325.
667. Muir (2), p. 660.
668. Margoliouth (2), p. 218–19.
669. Russell (1), p. 161.
670. Perron, p. 105.
671. Margoliouth (1), pp. 48–49.
672. Ibid., pp. 56–60.
673. Hiskett, p. 235.
674. Ibid., pp. 238–39.
675. Singer, pp. 153–56.
676. Quoted in New Statesman and Society, May 1, 1992, p. 19.
677. Hiskett, p. 269.
678. Ibid., p. 273.
679. Ibid., p. 328.
680. Ibid., p, 331.
681. Ibid., p. 312.
682. Popper (2).
683. Miller in FA, Spring 1993, Vol. 72, No. 1, pp. 43–56.

Selected Bibliography

Abdallah, Anouar et al. *Pour Rushdie. Cent intellectuels arabes et musulmans pour la liberté d'expression.* Paris, 1993.

Adams, C. E. "Quran: The Text and Its History." In ER, pp. 157–76.

Akbar, M. J. *India: The Siege Within.* London, 1985.

Alberuni. *India.* Translated by Sachau. London, 1914.

Alley, R. S., ed. *James Madison on Religious* Liberty. Amherst, N.Y., 1985.

Al-Ma'arri. *The Luzumiyat of Abu'L-Ala.* Translated by Ameen Rihani. New York, 1920.

Andrae, Tor. *Mohammed, the Man and His Faith.* Translated by T. Menzel. New York, 1955.

Arberry, A. J. [1] *Reason and Revelation.* London, 1957.

————. [2] *Sufism: An Account of the Mystics of Islam.* London, 1957.

————, ed. [3] *Religion in the Middle East: Three Religions in Concord and Conflict.* Cambridge, 1969.

Arnaldez, R. [1] *Ibn Rusd.* In EI2, pp. 909–20.

————. [2] *Falsafa* In EI2, pp. 769–75.

Ar-Razi. *The Spiritual Physick.* Translated by A. J. Arberry. London, 1950.

Ascha, Ghassan. *Du Status inférieur de la femme en Islam.* Paris, 1989.

Atkins, P. *Creation Revisited.* Oxford, 1992.

Babur. *Memoirs* (Babur-Nama). Translated by A. Beveridge. Delhi, 1979.

Barbulesco, Luc, and Philippe Cardinal. *L'Islam en questions.* Paris, 1986.

Barreau, Jean-Claude. *De l'Islam en général et du monde moderne en particulier.* Paris, 1991.

Bat Ye'or. [1] *The Dhimmi: Jews and Christians under Islam.* London, 1985.

————. [2] *Les Chrétientés d'Orient entre Jihad et Dhimmitude, VII-XX siècle.* Paris, 1991.

————. [3] *Juifs et chrétiens sous l'Islam.* Paris, 1994.

Bayle, Pierre. *Dictionnaire historique et critique,* 5th ed. Amsterdam, 1740, translated by J. P. Bernard, T. Birch, and J. Lockman as *A General Dictionary, Historical and Critical.* 10 vols. London, pp. 1734–41.

Bell, R. *The Origin of Islam in Its Christian Environment.* London, 1926.

Bell, R., and W. M. Watt. *Introduction to the Quran.* Edinburgh, 1977.

Benda, Julien. *The Betrayal of the Intellectuals.* Boston, 1955.

Birx, H. Art. "Evolution and Unbelief." In EU, vol 1.

Blachere, R. *Introduction au Coran.* Paris, 1991.

Bosworth, C. E. [1] "The Concept of Dhimma in Early Islam." In Benjamin Brande and B. Lewis, eds., *Christians and Jews in the Ottoman Empire.* 2 vols. New York, 1982.

————. [2] *The Islamic Dynasties.* Edinburgh, 1980.

Bouhdiba, Abdelwahab. *La Sexualité en Islam.* Paris, 1975.

Bouquet, A. C. *Comparative Religion.* London, 1954.

Bousquet, G. H. [1] *L'Éthique sexuelle de l'Islam.* Paris, 1966.

————. [2] "Voltaire et Islam." In *Studia Islamica* 38 (1968).

————. [3] "Une explication marxiste de l'Islam." In *Hesperis,* 1 (1954).

————. [4] "Loi musulmane et droit européen." In *Revue psychologique des peuples* 3 (1950).

Boyce, Mary. *Zoroastrians: Their Religious Beliefs and Practices.* London, 1984.

Brunschvig, R. "Abd." In EI2, pp. 25–40.

al-Bukhari. *al Jami al-Sahih.* Translated by G. H. Bousquet. Paris, 1964.

Bullough Vern L. *Sexual Variance in Society and History.* Chicago, 1976.

Burton, Richard. *The Book of the Thousand Nights and a Night.* 17 vols. London, n.d.

Carlyle, T. *Sartor Resartus: On Heroes and Hero Worship.* London, 1973.

Chachnamah. *An Ancient History of Sind.* Translated from Persian by Mirza Kalichbeg Fredunbeg. Karachi, 1900.

Choksy, Jamsheed. "Conflict, Coexistence and Cooperation: Muslims and Zoroastrians in Eastern Iran during the Medieval Period." In MW, vol. 80, 1990.

Conquest, Robert. *The Great Terror.* London, 1968.

Conze, E. *Buddhism: Its Essence and Development.* New York, 1975.

Cook, M. [1] *Muhammad.* Oxford, 1983.

————. [2] "Early Islamic Dietary Law." In JSAI 7, 1964, p. 242.

Cresswell, K. A. C. *Early Muslim Architecture.* London, 1958.

Crone, P. [1] *Slaves on Horses.* Cambridge, 1980.

————. [2] *Meccan Trade and the Rise of Islam.* Oxford, 1987.

————. [3] *Roman, Provincial and Islamic Law?* Cambridge, 1987.

Crone, P., and Hinds, M. *God's Caliph.* Cambridge, 1986.

Crone, P., and Cook, M. *Hagarism: The Making of the Muslim World.* Cambridge, 1977.

Dante. *The Divine Comedy.* Translated by M. Musa. London, 1988.

Darwin, C. *The Origin of Species.* London, 1872

Dashti, Ali. *Twenty-Three Years: A Study of the Prophetic Career of Mohammed.* London, 1985.

Dawkins, Richard. [1] *The Blind Watchmaker.* London, 1988.

————. [2] "A Deplorable Affair." In *New Humanist,* vol. 104, London, May 1989.

De Beauvoir, Simone. *The Second Sex.* London, 1988.

De Boer, T. J. *The History of Philosophy in Islam.* London, 1933.

Douglas, Mary. [1] *Purity and Danger.* London, 1966.

————. [2] *Implicit Meanings.* London, 1975.

Donohue, J. J., and Esposito, J. L. *Islam in Transition.* Oxford. 1965.

Dowson. *Hindu Mythology and Religion.* Calcutta, 1991.

Easterman, D. *New Jerusalems.* London, 1992.

Einstein, A. *Ideas and Opinions.* Delhi, 1989.

Eribon, Didier. *Michel Foucault.* Paris, 1989.

Ettinghausen, Richard. *Arab Painting.* Geneva, 1977.

Ettinghausen, Richard, and Grabar Oleg. *The Art and Architecture of Islam 650–1250.* London, 1991.

Faiz Ahmed Faiz. *The True Subject.* Translated by Naomi Lazard. Lahore, 1988.

Fakhry, M. J. *A History of Islamic Philosophy.* London, 1983.

Firmage, E. "The Biblical Dietary Laws and the Concept of Holiness." In *Studies in the Pentateuch* (1990), edited by J. A. Emerton.

Feuerbach, Ludwig. *The Essence of Christianity.* Amherst, N.Y., 1989.

Firth, R., ed. *Man and Culture.* London, 1980.

Flew, Antony. [1] *God, Freedom and Immortality.* Amherst, N.Y., 1984.

———. [2] "The Terrors of Islam." In P. Kurtz and T. Madigan, eds., *Defending the Enlightenment.* Amherst, N.Y., 1987.

Fox, R. L. *The Unauthorised Version.* London, 1991.

Frazer, J. G. *The Golden Bough.* London, 1959.

Freeman, D. *Margaret Mead and Samoa.* London, 1984.

Gabrieli, F. "La Zandaqa au 1ᵉʳ siècle Abbaside." In C. Cahen et al., *L'Élaboration de l'Islam.* Paris, 1961.

Gascoigne, Bamber. *The Great Moghuls.* London, 1976.

Gaudeul, Jean-Marie. *Appelés par le Christ. Ils viennent de l'Islam.* Paris, 1991.

Geiger, Abraham. *Judaism and Islam.* Translated by F. M. Young. New York, 1970.

Gershwin, Ira. *Lyrics.* London, 1977.

Gibb, H. A. R. *Islam.* Oxford, 1953.

Gibbon, E. *Decline and Fall of the Roman Empire.* 6 vols. London, 1941.

Goldziher, Ignaz. [1] *Muslim Studies.* 2 vols. Translated by C. R. Barber and S. M. Stern. London, 1967–71

———. [2] *Introduction to Islamic Theology and Law.* Translated by Andras and Ruth Hamori. Princeton, 1981.

———. [3] "Parsism and Islam." In *Revue de l'histoire des religions,* vol. 43 (1901), 1–29.

Goodwin, Jan. *Price of Honor.* Boston, 1994.

Grousset, R. *L'Empire des Steppes.* Paris, 1941.

Guillaume, Alfred. *Islam.* London, 1954.

Halliday, Fred. "The Fundamental Lesson of the Fatwa." In *New Statesman and Society,* 12 February 1993.

Harle, J. C. *The Art and Architecture of the Indian Subcontinent.* London, 1986.

Hawking, S. *A Brief History of Time.* London, 1988.

Hayek, F. A. [1] *The Road to Serfdom.* London, 1944.

———. [2] *The Constitution of Liberty.* London, 1960.

Hiskett, Mervyn. *Some to Mecca Turn to Pray.* St. Albans, 1993.

Hoffmann, R. Joseph. *The Origins of Christianity.* Amherst, N.Y., 1985.

Hoffmann, R. Joseph. and G. A. Larue, eds. *Jesus in History and Myth.* Amherst, N.Y., 1986.

Holt, P. M. "The treatment of Arab History by Prideaux, Ockley and Sale." In Holt and Lewis, eds., pp. 291–302.

Hospers, John. *An Introduction to Philosophical Analysis.* London, 1973.

Howell Smith, A. D. *In Search of the Real Bible.* London, 1943.

Hughes, T. P. *A Dictionary of Islam.* London, 1935.

Hume, David. [1] *The Natural History of Religion.* Oxford, 1976.

———. [2] *Dialogues Concerning Natural Religion.* Oxford, 1976.

———. [3] *Enquiries Concerning the Human Understanding and Concerning the Principle of Morals.* Oxford, 1966.

———. [4] *Essential Works of David Hume.* New York, 1965

Humphreys, Christmas. *A Popular Dictionary of Buddhism.* London, 1984.
Humphreys, R. S. *Islamic History, A Framework for Inquiry.* Princeton, 1991.
Huntington, S. "The Clash of Civilisations." In FA, Summer 1993, vol 72, no. 3.
Hurgronje Snouck, C. [1] *Selected Works,* G. H. Bousquet and J. Schacht, eds. Leiden, 1957.
———. [2] *Mohammedanism.* New York, 1916.
———. [3] "La Légende qoranique d'Abraham et la politique religieuse du prophète Mohammad." In *Revue Africaine,* vol. 95 [1951], 273–88, translated by Bousquet.
Huxley, T. H. [1] *Science and Hebrew Tradition.* London, 1895.
———. [2] *Man's Place in Nature and Other Essays.* London, 1914.
Ibn Kammuna. *Examination of the Three Faiths.* Translated by Moshe Perlmann. Berkeley and Los Angeles, 1971.
Ingersoll, R. *Some Mistakes of Moses.* Amherst, N.Y., 1986.
Jahanbegloo, R. *Conversations with Isaiah Berlin.* London, 1991.
Jeffery, Arthur. [1] *The Foreign Vocabulary of the Koran.* Baroda, 1938.
———. [2] "The Quest of the Historical Mohammed." In MW, vol. 16, no. 4, October 1926.
———. [3] "Eclecticism in Islam." In MW 12.
———. [4] "Progress in the Study of the Quran Text." In MW, vol. 25.
Jynboll, T. W. "Pilgrimage." In ERE, vol. 8, pp. 10–12.
Kanan Makiya. *Cruelty and Silence.* New York, 1993.
Kant, Immanuel. *On History.* Translated by Beck, Anchor, Fackenheim. New York, 1963.
Kaufmann, W. J., III. *Universe.* New York, 1985.
Kennedy, J. M. *The Religions and Philosophies of the East.* London, n.d. (ca. 1910)
Koestler, A. *The Yogi and The Commissar.* New York, 1946.
Koran. [1] Translated by Arberry. London, 1964.
———. [2] Translated by Dawood. London, 1956.
———. [3] Translated by Palmer. London, 1949.
———. [4] Translated by Pickthall. London, 1948.
———. [5] Translated by Rodwell. London, 1921.
———. [6] Translated by Sale. London, 1896.
———. [7] Translated by Yusuf Ali. Lahore, 1934.
Kramer, M. "Islam vs. Democracy." In *Commentary,* January 1993, pp. 35–42.
Kraus, P, and S. Pines. "Ar Razi." In EII, vol. 3, pp. 1134–36.
Kureishi, Hanif. *My Beautiful Laundrette and the Rainbow Sign.* London, 1986.
Lane, Edward William. *The Manners and Customs of the Modem Egyptians.* London, 1968.
Leach, Edmund. *Social Anthropology.* London, 1982.
Levy, R. *The Social Structure of Islam.* 2 vols. Cambridge, 1957.
Lewis, Bernard. [1] *Islam in History.* Chicago, 1993.
———. [2] "Islam and Liberal Democracy." In *Atlantic Monthly,* February 1993.
———. [3] *Islam and the West.* New York, 1993.
———. [4] *Race and Slavery in the Middle East.* New York, 1990.
———. [5] *The Jews of Islam.* Princeton, 1984.
———. [6] *The Arabs in History.* New York, 1966.
Lewis, Bernard, and P. M. Holt, eds. *Historians of the Middle East.* London, 1962.
Locke, J. *A Letter Concerning Toleration.* Amherst, N.Y., 1990.
MacDonogh, Steve, ed. *The Rushdie Letters.* Lincoln, 1993.
Macdonald, D. B. "Djinn." In EI2, pp. 546–48.

Macey, D. *Lives of Michel Foucault.* London, 1990.

Mackenzie, Compton. *Thin Ice.* London, 1956.

Mackie, J. L. [1] *Ethics.* London, 1977.

———. [2] *The Miracle of Theism.* Oxford, 1982.

Margoliouth, D. S. [1] *The Early Development of Mohammedanism.* London, 1914.

———. [2] *Mohammed and the Rise of Islam.* London, 1905.

———. [3] "Ideas and Ideals of Modern Islam." In MW, vol. 20.

———. [4] "Mahomet." In EB 11th ed., vol. 17.

———. [5] "Muhammad." In ERE, vol. 8.

———. [6] "Atheism (Muhammadan)." In ERE.

Margulis, Lynn, and K. V. Schwartz. *Five Kingdoms.* San Francisco, 1982.

Marmura, M. E. "Falsafah." In ER, pp. 267–76.

Mayer, A. E. *Islam and Human Rights.* Boulder, 1991.

Melden, A. I. *Human Rights.* Belmont, 1970.

Mernissi, Fatima. *Le Harem politique.* Paris, 1987.

Mill, J. S. *Utilitarianism. Liberty. Representative Government.* London, 1960.

———. *Three Essays on Religion.* London, 1874.

Miller, J. "The Challenge of Radical Islam." In FA, vol. 72, no. 2, Spring 1993.

Mimouni, Rachid. *De la barbarie en général et de l'intégrisme en particulier.* Paris, 1992.

Momigliano, A., ed. *The Conflict between Paganism and Christianity in the 4th Century.* Oxford, 1970.

Morey, Robert. *The Islamic Invasion.* Eugene, 1992.

Muir, Sir W. *The Life of Muhammad.* Edinburgh, 1923.

Naipaul, V. S. *Among the Believers.* London, 1983.

Nefzawi, Shaykh. [1] *The Glory of the Perfumed Garden.* London, 1978.

———. [2] *The Perfumed Garden.* London, 1963.

Nicholson, R. A. [1] *Studies in Islamic Poetry.* Cambridge, 1921.

———. [2] *Literary History of the Arabs.* Cambridge, 1930.

———. [3] *The Mystics of Islam.* London, 1963.

———. [4] "The Risalatul Ghufran." In JRAS 1900; 1902.

Nietzsche. *The Portable Nietzsche.* Ed. W. Kaufmann. New York, 1974.

Noldeke, T. [1] "Arabs (Ancient)." In ERE, pp. 659–72.

———. [2] "Koran." In EB, 11th ed., vol. 15, pp. 898–906.

Nyberg H. S. *Deux réprouvés: Amr Ibn Ubaid et Ibn Ar Rawandi dans classicisme et déclin culturel (symposium de Bordeaux).* Paris, 1957.

Obermann, Julian. "Islamic Origins: A Study In Background and Foundation." In *The Arab Heritage.* Nabih Faris, ed. Princeton, 1944.

Paine, Thomas. *The Age of Reason.* Secaucus, 1974.

Penrice, John. *A Dictionary and Glossary of the Koran.* Delhi, 1990.

Peres, Henri. *La Poésie andalouse en arabe classique.* Paris, 1953.

Pipes, Daniel. *The Rushdie Affair. The Novel, The Ayatollah, and the West.* New York, 1990.

Plessner, Martin. "The Natural Sciences and Medicine." In *The Legacy of Islam,* Schacht and Bosworth, eds., pp. 425–60.

Popper, K. R. [1] *The Open Society and its Enemies.* 2 vols. London, 1969.

———. [2] "The Importance of Critical Discussion." In *Free Inquiry,* vol. 2, no. 1. Amherst, N.Y., 1981/1982.

Pryce-Jones, David. *The Closed Circle.* London, 1990.

Quine, W. V. O. *Quiddities. An Intermittently Philosophical Dictionary.* Cambridge, 1987.

Reade, W. *The Martyrdom* of Man. London, 1948.

Rippin, A. *Muslims: Their Religious Beliefs and Practices.* Vol. 1. London, 1991.

Renan, Ernest. [1] *Histoire et parole, oeuvres diverses.* Paris, 1984.

———. [2] *Islamisme et la science.* Lecture given at the Sorbonne, 29 March 1883. Basel, Bernheim, 1883.

Robertson, J. M. *A Short History of Freethought.* London, 1906.

Robinson, Richard. *An Atheist's Values.* Oxford, 1964.

Rodinson, Maxime. [1] *Muhammad.* New York, 1980.

———. [2] "The Western Image and Western Studies of Islam." In *The Legacy of Islam,* Joseph Schach and C. E. Bosworth, eds. Oxford, 1974.

———. [3] "Ghidha." In EI2.

———. [4] *Les Arabes.* Paris, 1991.

Rosenthal, F. R. *The Classical Heritage of Islam.* London, 1975.

Runciman, S. [1] *A History of the Crusades.* Cambridge, 1951–1954.

———. [2] *The Fall of Constantinople,* 1453. Cambridge, 1990.

Rushdie, Salman. *Imaginary Homelands.* London, 1991.

Russell, Bertrand. [1] *Unpopular Essays.* New York, 1950.

———. [2] *Fact and Fiction.* London, 1961.

———. [3] *Why I Am Not a Christian.* London, 1979.

———. [4] *Theory and Practice of Bolshevism.* London, 1921.

———. [5] *In Praise of Idleness.* London, 1935.

Shacht, Joseph. [1] *An Introduction to Islamic Law.* Oxford, 1964.

———. [2] "Islamic Religious Law." In *The Legacy of Islam,* Schacht and Bosworth, eds. Oxford, 1974.

———. [3] "Law and Justice." In *The Cambridge History of Islam.* 4 vols. Cambridge, 1970.

———. [4] *The Origins of Muhammadan Jurisprudence.* Oxford, 1950.

Shacht, Joseph, and C. E. Bosworth. *The Legacy of Islam.* Oxford, 1974.

Schopenhauer, Arthur. *Parerga and Paralipomena.* 2 vols. Translated by E. F. J. Payne. Oxford, 1974.

Schork, Kurt. "Pakistan's Women in Despair." In *Guardian Weekly,* September 23, 1990.

Schumpeter, Joseph. "L'Impérialisme arabe." In *Revue Africaine* 2 (May-June 1950).

Simoons, F. J. Eat *Not This Flesh.* Madison, 1961.

Singer, Peter. *Animal Liberation.* London, 1976.

Singh, Khushwant. [1] *More Malicious Gossip.* Delhi, 1991.

———. [2] *Sex, Scotch and Scholarship.* Delhi, 1992.

Smith, V. A. *The Oxford History of India.* Delhi, 1985.

Smirnov, N. A. *Russia and Islam.* London, 1954.

Snouck Hurgronje, C. [1] *Selected Works.* G. H. Bousquet and J. Schacht, eds. Leiden, 1957

———. [2] *Mohammedanism.* New York, 1916.

———. [3] "La Légende qoranique d'Abraham et la politique religieuse du prophète Mohammad." In *Revue Africaine,* vol. 5 [1951], 273–88, translated by G. H. Bousquet.

Spinoza, B. *A Theologico-Political Treatise.* Translated by Elwes. New York, 1951

Stein, Gordon. *An Anthology of Atheism and Rationalism.* Amherst, N.Y., 1980.

Stillman, N. A. *The Jews of Arab Lands.* Philadelphia, 1979.

Stephen Humphreys, R. *Islamic History: A Framework for Inquiry.* Princeton, 1991.

Stutley, M. J. *A Dictionary of Hinduism.* London, 1977.

Taheri, Amir. *Holy Terror.* London, 1987.

Thompson, T. L. *The Historicity of the Patriarchal Narratives.* London, 1974.
Tisdall, William. *Original Sources of Islam.* Edinburgh, 1901.
Torrey, C. C. *The Jewish Foundation of Islam.* New York, 1933.
Tritton, A. S. *The Caliphs and their Non-Muslim Subjects.* London, 1970.
Vadja, Georges. "Les Zindiqs en pays d'Islam au début de la période Abbaside." In RSO, vol. 17 (1938), pp. 173–229.
Vatikiotis, P. J. *Islam and the State.* London, 1987.
Voltaire. *Dictionnaire philosophique.* Translated by Besterman. London, 1971.
Von Grunebaum, G. E. [1] *Classical Islam.* Chicago, 1970.
———. [2] *Medieval Islam.* Chicago, 1953.
———. [3] *Islam, Essays in the Nature and Growth of a Cultural Tradition.* Chicago, 1955.
Walzer, R. *Greek into Arabic.* Oxford, 1962.
Wansbrough, J. [1] *Quranic Studies.* Oxford, 1977.
———. [2] *The Sectarian Milieu.* Oxford, 1978.
Watt, W. Montgomery. [1] *Free Will and Predestination in Early Islam.* London, 1948.
———. [2] *Introduction to the Quran.* Edinburgh, 1977.
———. [3] *Islamic Philosophy and Theology.* Edinburgh, 1979.
———. [4] *Muhammad at Mecca.* Oxford, 1953.
———. [5] *Muhammad at Medina.* Oxford, 1956.
———. [6] "Muhammad." In *Cambridge History of Islam.* Cambridge, 1970
———. [7] "Religion and Anti-Religion." In *Religion in the Middle East: Three Religions in Conflict and Concord.*
———. [8] *The Faith and Practice of al-Ghazali.* London, 1967.
———. [9] *Muslim-Christian Encounters.* London, 1991.
———. [10] *Islamic Revelation in the Modern World.* Edinburgh, 1969.
Welch, A. T. "Al-Kuran." In EI2, p. 400f.
Wells, G. A. [1] Art. "Jesus, Historicity of." In KU, vol. 1.
———. [2] Art. in FI, vol 3., no. 4, Fall 1983.
———. [3] Art. "Strauss." In KU, vol. 2.
———. [4] Art. "Bauer." In KU, vol. 1.
Wensinck, A. J. [1] *The Muslim Creed.* Cambridge, 1932.
———. [2] Art. "Al-Khadir." In EI1.
Werblowsky, Z. Art. "Polytheism." In ER.
Wolpert, Lewis. *The Unnatural Nature of Science.* London, 1992.
Young, J. Z. *An Introduction to the Study of Man.* Oxford, 1974.
Zakariya, Fouad. *Laïcité ou islamisme.* Paris, 1989.
Zeghidour, Slimane. *La Voile et la rannière.* Paris, 1990.
Zwemer, S. [1] *Islam: A Challenge to Faith.* New York, 1908.
———. [2] *The Moslem Doctrines of God.* New York, 1905.
———. [3] *The Influence of Animism on Islam.* London, 1920.
———. [4] "Animistic Elements in Moslem Prayer." In MW, vol. 8.

Index